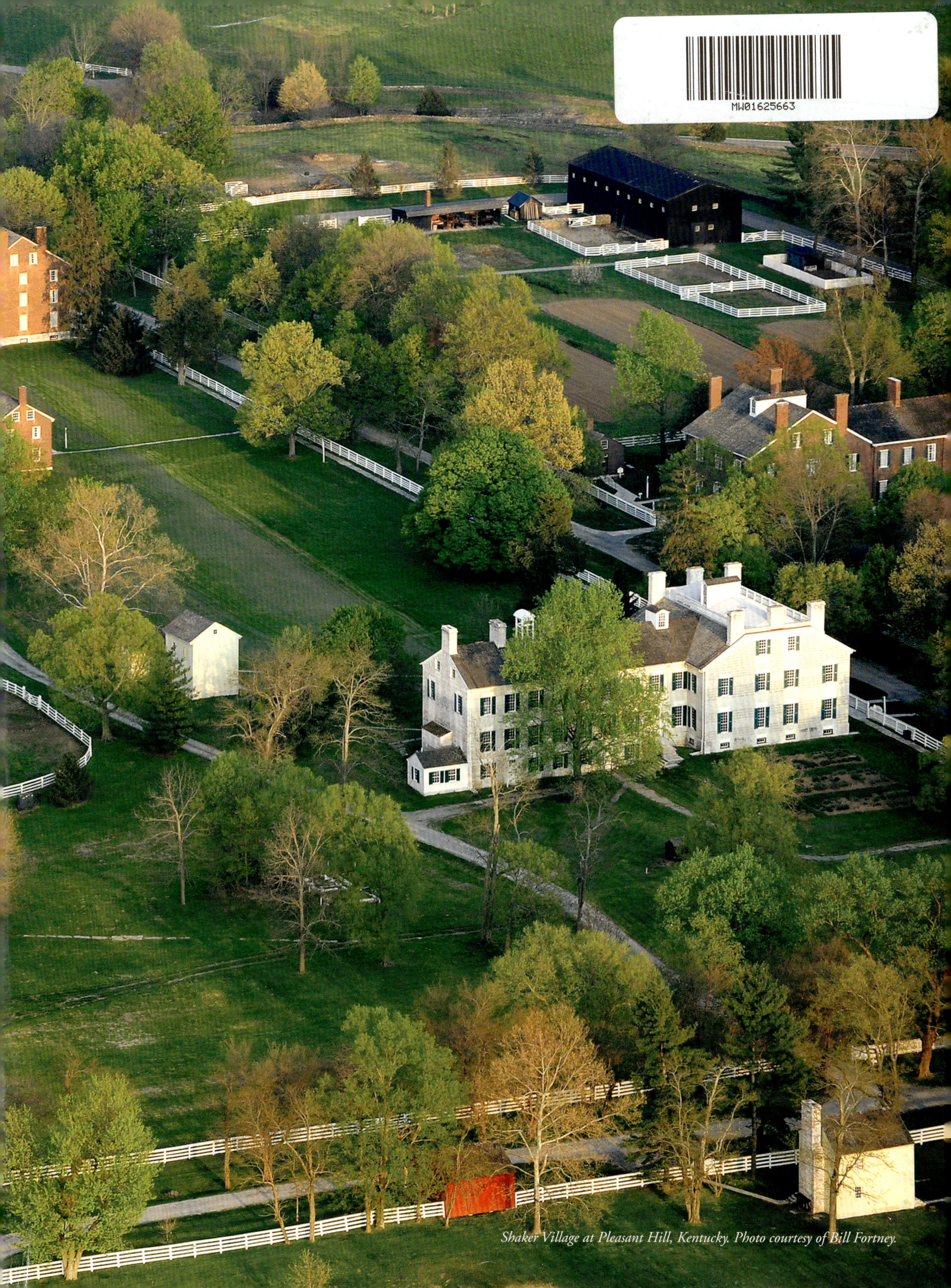

Shaker Village at Pleasant Hill, Kentucky. Photo courtesy of Bill Fortney.

SHAKER VILLAGE OF PLEASANT HILL

50th Anniversary of the Restoration

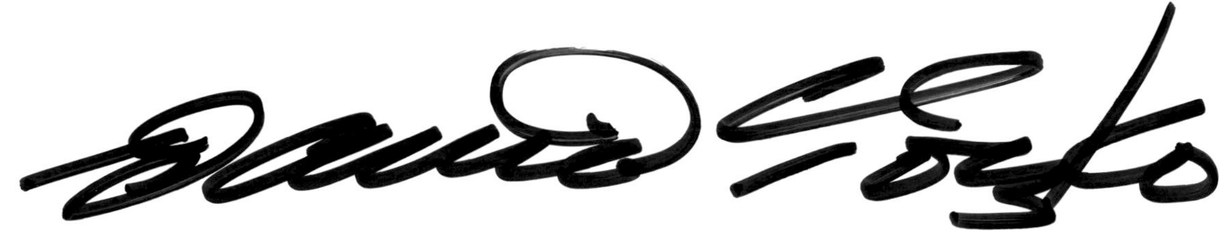

Photographs and Text by
David Toczko

Foreword by
Ashley Judd

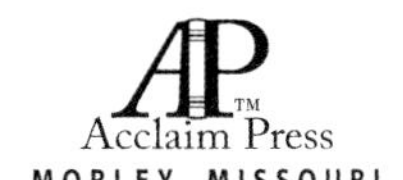

Acclaim Press
MORLEY, MISSOURI

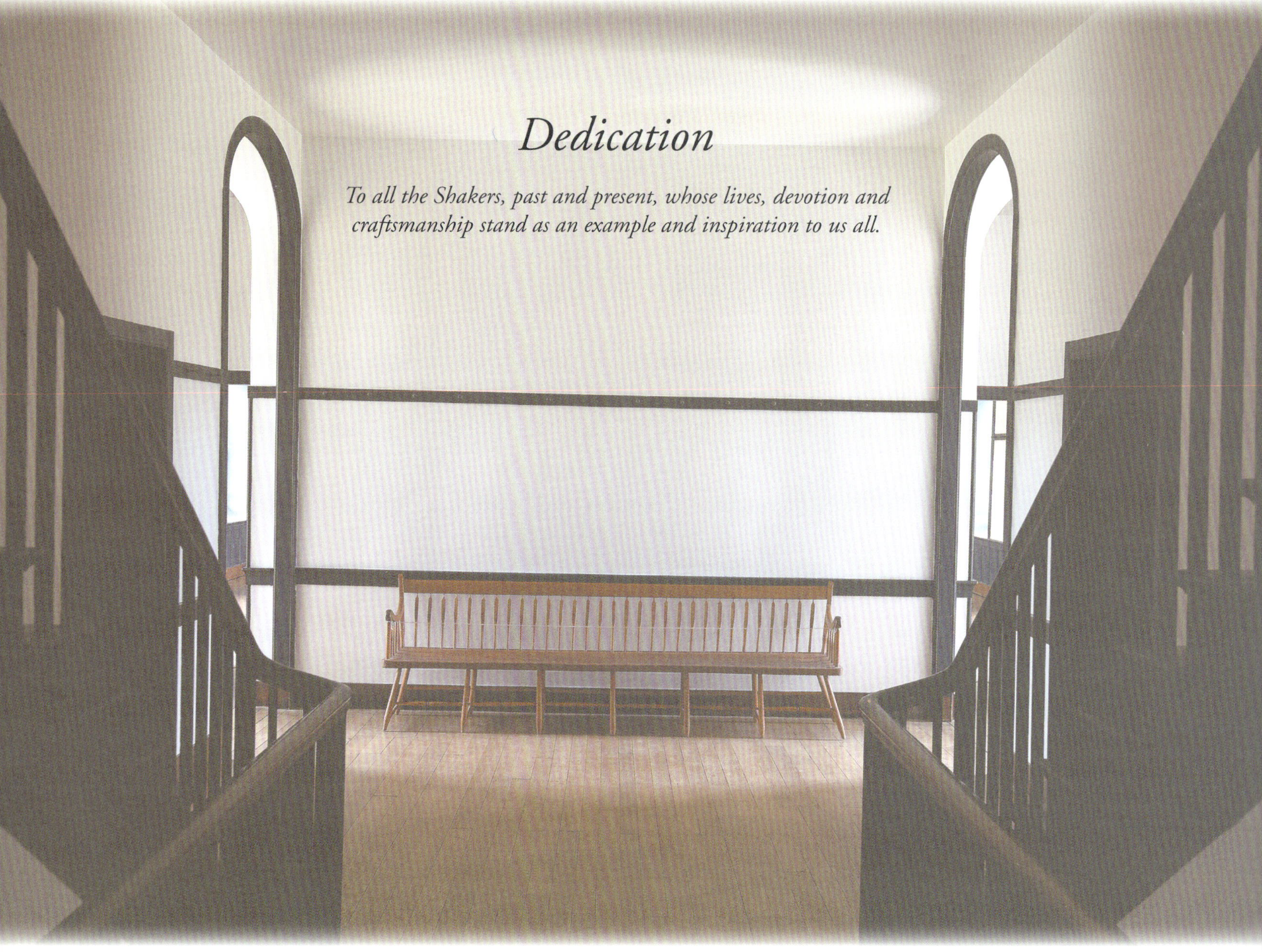

Dedication

To all the Shakers, past and present, whose lives, devotion and craftsmanship stand as an example and inspiration to us all.

AP™
Acclaim Press
— Your Next Great Book —
P.O. Box 238
Morley, Missouri 63767
(573) 472-9800
www.acclaimpress.com

Designer: Shelley Davidson
Cover Design: M. Frene Melton

Library of Congress Cataloging-in-Publication Data

Toczko, David.
Shaker Village of Pleasant Hill : 50th Anniversary of the Restoration / photographs and Text by David Toczko.
p. cm.
Includes index.
ISBN-13: 978-1-935001-60-7 (alk. paper)
ISBN-10: 1-935001-60-4 (alk. paper)
1. Architectural photography--Kentucky--Pleasant Hill. 2. Shaker architecture--Kentucky--Pleasant Hill--Pictorial works. 3. Historic buildings--Kentucky--Pleasant Hill--Pictorial works. 4. Pleasant Hill (Ky.)--Buildings, structures, etc.--Pictorial works. I. Title.

TR650.T63 2010
770.9769'485--dc22

2010035737

First Printing 2010
Printed in China
0 9 8 7 6 5 4 3 2 1

Contents

Acknowledgements

While the work presented here is mine, it could not have been possible without the support, advice and encouragement of friends, family and loved ones. To all of you, my deepest thanks.

I also wish to thank the administration and staff of Shaker Village of Pleasant Hill. Throughout the time spent there photographing, they graciously afforded me both the opportunity and the access required to gather the images. A special thanks to Madge Adams, Larrie Currie, Jennifer Broadwater, Lorrin Ingerson and Donna Phillips. Georgana Riddell, Chief Interpreter at Pleasant Hill, was of invaluable help with the captions for this book. Her deep love and vast knowledge of the Village made that part of the project not only easier, but truly a learning experience for me.

A special thank you to Ashley Judd whose foreword puts into words what I hope my images convey. Ashley's unheralded devotion to and support of Shaker Village stand as examples of what a special place this is and how lucky we are that it was saved for future generations to enjoy.

Foreword

It is my hope that the stunning photographs in this book will help carry the message of Shaker Village, reminding those who already know about this sublime place and the sustained peace it shelters to return to its hallowed ground for nurturing, and introducing those born into a frantic, hyper-connected world to the timeless values of stillness, singleness of purpose, and presence.

My Mamaw and Papaw loved Shaker Village, and thus I, their devoted grandchild, was taught to cherish and esteem its ineffable quiet, great loveliness, and inimitable history. We enjoyed the Village on many levels. It was an endlessly interesting place where we could explore history, and the old-timey way in which an admirably devout, talented, and practical people lived, worked, and worshiped, and how for them, each of these acts were in fact indistinguishable. It was a place where we could pick up special crafts, reflections of the native artistry that inheres in so many "simple" people, taking home pieces of art that reflected our values as people of a particular place, reminding us of our own rural background. It was a place where we experienced the hushed awe of great natural beauty in a setting so heart achingly perfect, being there in and of itself felt worshipful of the Divine, whose Hand could not be doubted. It was a place where we could dine, enjoying wonderful meals on special occasions, such as birthdays and, well, the sheer specialness of simply being together. Our visits, meandering and sweet, always involved taking pictures under certain trees. I have these snapshots. They are treasures. Dario and I always have our picture made in these precise spots, our "Mamaw and Papaw" pictures, a ritual and homage that is deeply poignant.

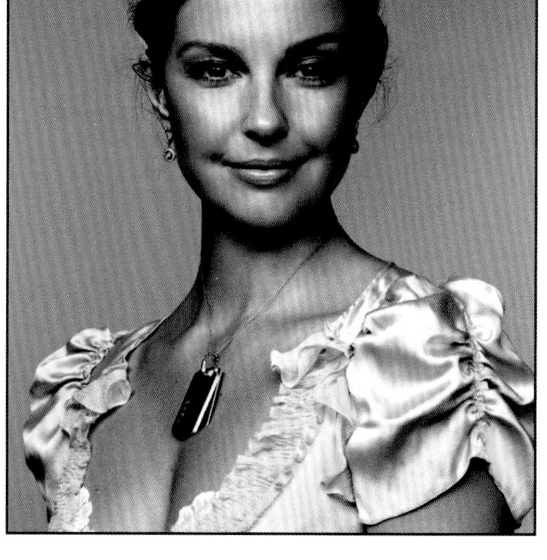

So much of the world in which we live is a lurid delusion comprised of cunningly effective deceptions, created and maintained by profit maximizing firms. We are indoctrinated to believe that our life's meaning and our happiness comes from things, products, external achievements. We have become human doings, instead of human beings. Social media and the extraordinary connectivity available any time, anywhere, comes at great costs to the robustness of our souls, the stillness of our spirits, the peace of our minds. Advances in brain imaging literally show the changing neuroanatomy of young people's brains, the deleterious effects of unregulated use of TV, Internet, video games, the normalization of violence, abuse, and trauma, especially sexual. Of the many consequences of such habits and content, there is a commensurate loss of human interaction and connection to the essential rhythms of the earth and sky. Visits to Shaker Village, and places like it, are the antidote to the venom of modern life.

These photographs are not idealized versions of reality. They are not photoshopped, retouched, or computer generated. Anyone who visits Shaker Village can see, at the level at which their eyes, hearts, and souls allow them, the profound beauty of Center Family Dwelling, the stunning red barn (known as the Corn Cribb), the fields of native grasses and wildflowers, Fulling Mill Falls, the 3,000 acres in autumn, the dogwood in spring. Come. See for yourself, what you can see, and feel how differently... how much better... you feel. Return, and see what more you can take in, experience, feel, and appreciate. Store within you the reserve of sanctuary, and draw upon it in the business of your daily life.

I believe modern life contributes significantly to mania, to a frantic energy perhaps best summarized by one word: more. Shaker Village, by contrast, by preserving a way of life in which less is revered and preserved, allows for the possibility of what the mania aspires to be, yet never can: ecstasy. Shaker Village nurtures an organic sense of belonging, a relieving sense of well being, and a peace that transcends all external circumstances.

Shaker Village is a rarity in our rapidly de-greening world. 6,000 acres of woods are clear-cut every day in America alone; that is 4 aces a minute.[1] As Kentuckians, we must preserve this oasis, perpetuating its message of spirituality through simplicity in a protected natural setting, honoring the way of life and the vision of a people who loved God in their daily lives in a way our modern world would do well to imitate.

Join me in visiting and supporting Shaker Village. I'll see you under the dogwood tree for our very own family picture, the family of Kentuckians and Americans who grasp the enormous treasure of Shaker Village, and are committed to benefiting from and preserving its legacy.

~ Ashley Judd
Board Member

[1] USDA Forest Service: http://www.fs.fed.us/projects/four-threats/

Introduction

Two hundred years ago, a small group of devotees stood on a hilltop in the rolling Bluegrass section of Kentucky and envisioned heaven on earth, later to be known as Pleasant Hill. This dream turned reality grew to over 500 adult members and 300 structures at its pinnacle in the 19th century. After the Shakers were gone, the buildings and property passed into private hands and changed ownership many times over the next 37 years. Some buildings disappeared, and others fell into varying states of decay and disuse. New buildings, primarily farm buildings, were constructed amid the Shaker-built structures. Because of excellent Shaker craftsmanship, the large structures of the community remained intact.

The buildings took on new functions. The Trustees' Office was operated as a restaurant. The Meeting House became the Shakertown Baptist Church and for a time, served as an auto repair shop. The Carpenter's Shop served as a general store and the Farm Deacon's Shop was a gas station. Many of the smaller workshops were converted to tenant houses with Victorian porches disguising the Shaker lines. Goodwill Industries leased the Centre Family Dwelling for storage and a caretaker lived in the rear portion of the building.

Fifty years ago, in 1961, another small group of visionaries led by Earl D. Wallace stood on that same hill and saw not only the grandeur, historical and cultural value that had been, but what may be once again. Thus was born Shaker Village of Pleasant Hill and the acquisition, restoration and preservation of the community began. Mr. Wallace was elected Chairman of the Board of Trustees, a position he held until his death in 1990. James Lowry Cogar, the first curator of Colonial Williamsburg, returned to Kentucky in 1962 to become the first President of Shaker Village. Mr. Cogar was responsible for the innovative plan for adaptive use of historic buildings and excellence in restoration standards. He insisted upon the purchase of 2,250 acres of original Shaker land to act as a buffer against commercial encroachment.

In 1964, Mr. Cogar hired James C. Thomas who had worked with the restoration of Louisville's Locust Grove, the last home of General George Rogers Clark. A year after Mr. Cogar's retirement in 1974, James Thomas became the second President of Shaker Village, and served in that capacity until his retirement in May 2005.

When restoration began in 1966, it became apparent that no government agency or trust would provide long term support and Pleasant Hill must be self-sufficient. Admission income would not be enough to ensure the project's long term survival. The Board of Trustees understood the need to create a unique environment where visitors would be immersed in the Shaker experience. Dining, overnight lodging and craft sales would fulfill that vision and assure success. Work began to bring Pleasant Hill back to its nineteenth-century appearance. All utilities were buried, walks repaired or replaced and original paint colors discovered and duplicated. In 1965, U.S. Highway 68 was re-routed to bypass the village and, in 1968, the main village road was restored to its original appearance. The same year, a few exhibition buildings, lodging accommodations, the dining room and first crafts sales shop opened to the public. In 1986, Shaker Village acquired the West Lot, an adjoining property of 480 acres and three original Shaker buildings. Restoration of this area was completed in 1992. While only 34 of the original Shaker structures remain, this still represents the largest restored Shaker community in existence.

Taken over a four year period during every season and nearly every time of day, the following photos are organized as a pictorial walking tour of the Village beginning at the western edge of the property and moving eastward. Much of the information for the text in this book was obtained from Shaker Village of Pleasant Hill and its very knowledgeable interpreters. The archival photos, as part of the Public Domain, were obtained from the Library of Congress.

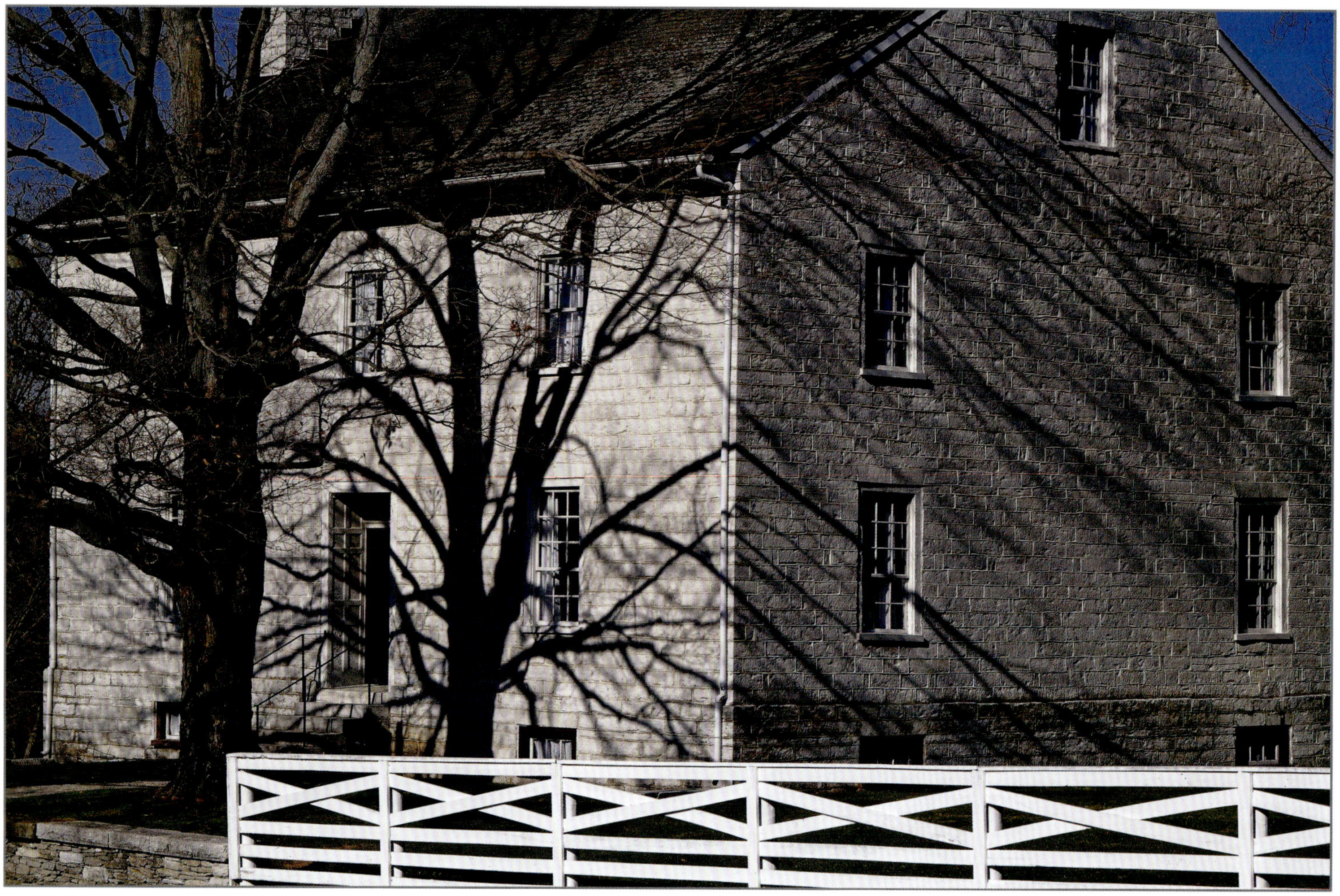

Dwelling at the West Lot which was one of two locations known as Gathering Orders for prospective members. These members lived the life of a Shaker, but remained apart from the general community until fully accepting the faith and signing the Covenant. The property was re-acquired in 1986 and restoration completed in 1992.

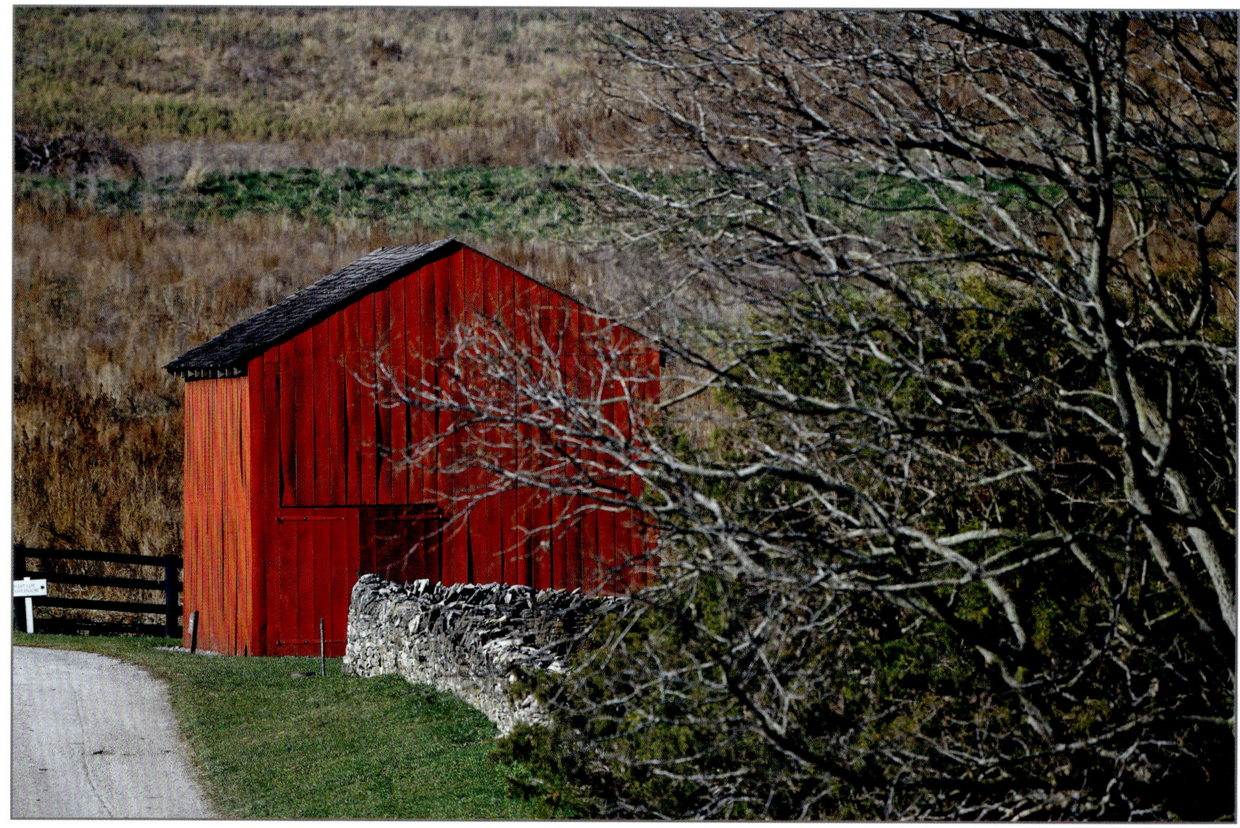

Outbuilding at the West Lot. Many such single-purpose structures surrounded each main dwelling and supported their agrarian life.

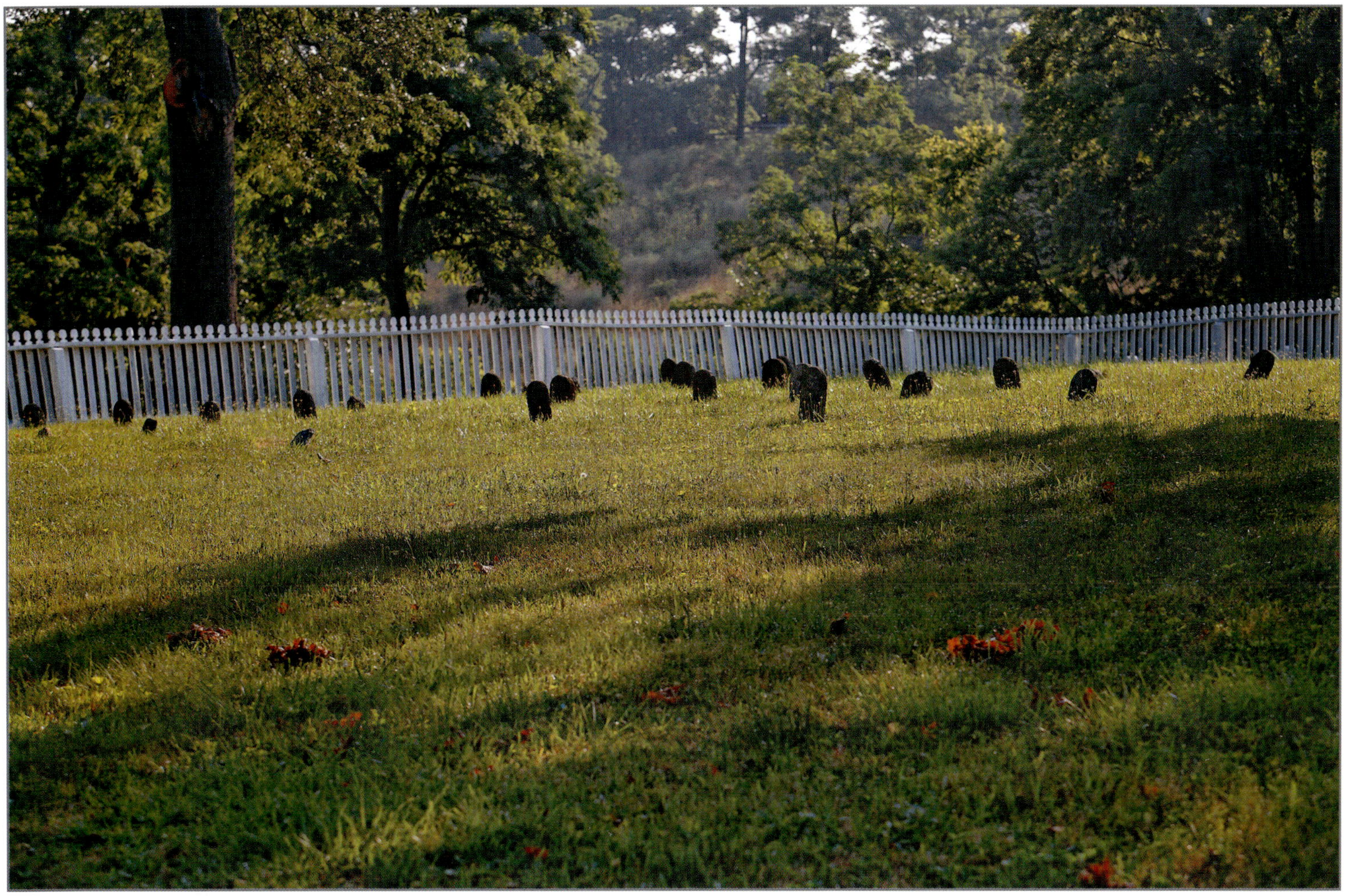

The 1811 Shaker Cemetery. Shakers interred there were not separated by male and female, but rather buried in order of death. Not all Shaker communities erected individual headstones, but Pleasant Hill is an example of one community that did with the majority of the headstones simply bearing the initials of the individual. Only two non-Shakers are buried there, one being a paroled confederate soldier from Georgia, William Henry Outlaw, who fell ill on the march home and died while under the Shakers' care at Pleasant Hill.

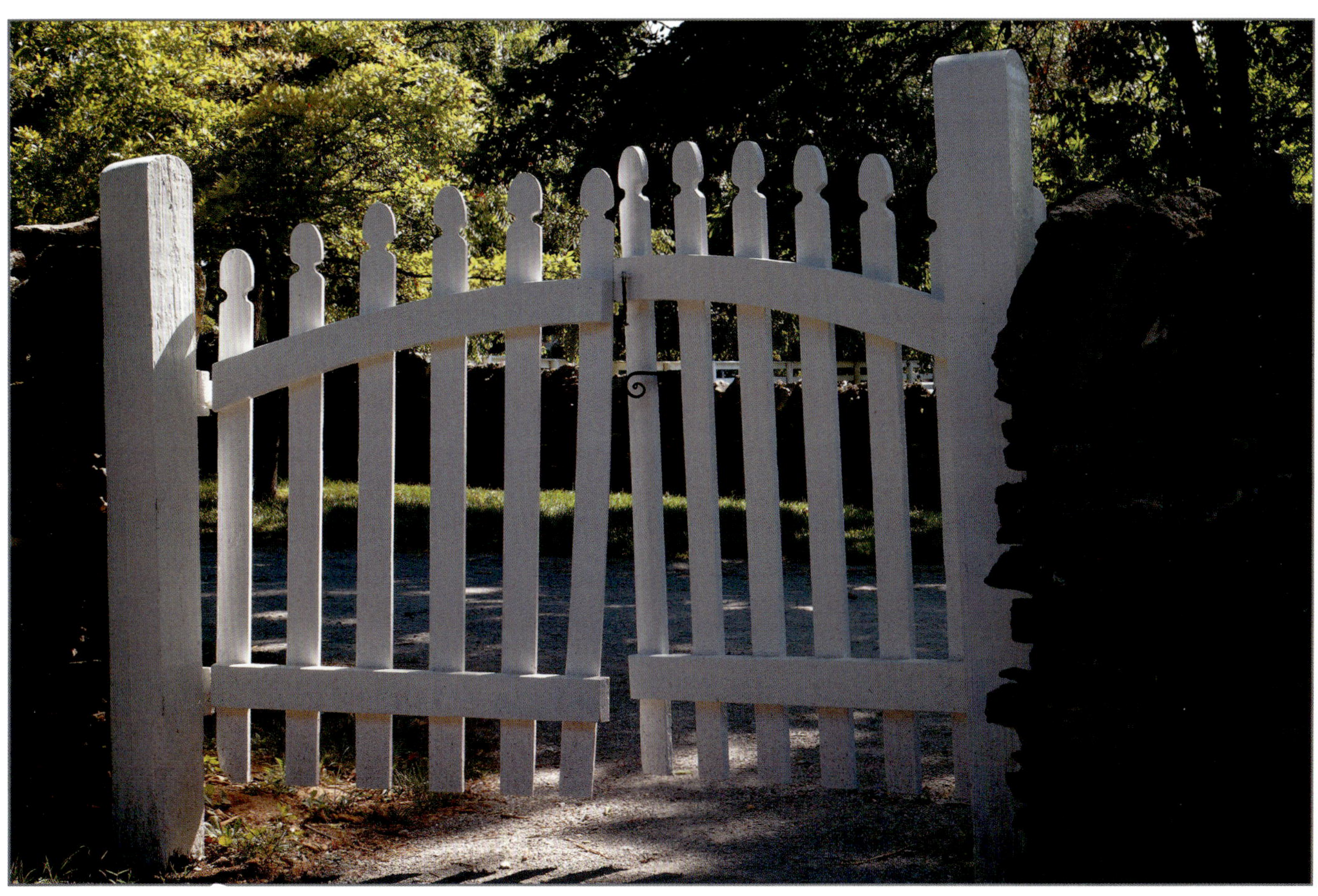

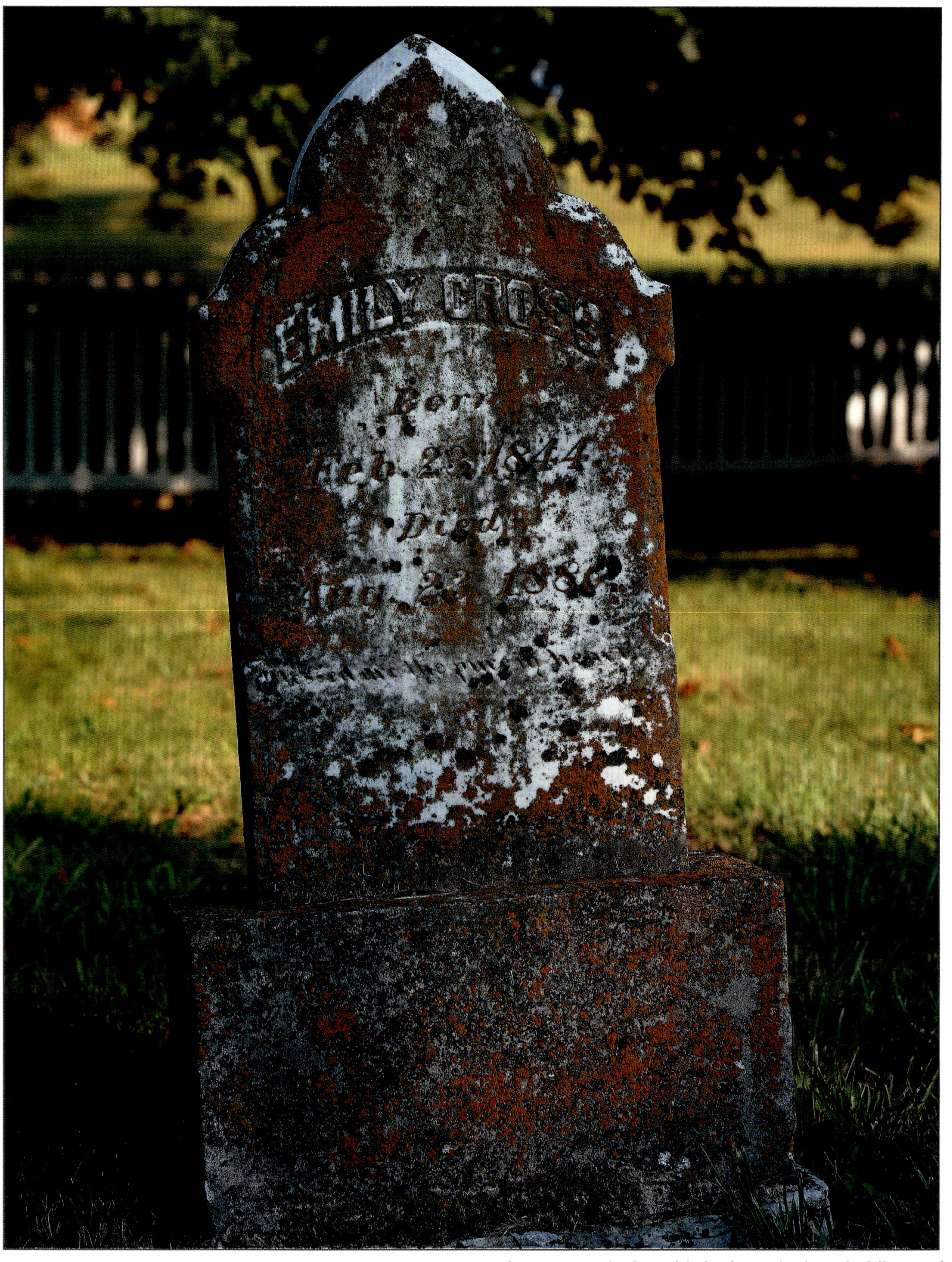

Above: An example of one of the headstones that bears the full name of a Shaker, Emily Cross 1844 to 1880.

Opposite: The 1837 Turnpike viewed from the graveyard looking eastward towards the Village.

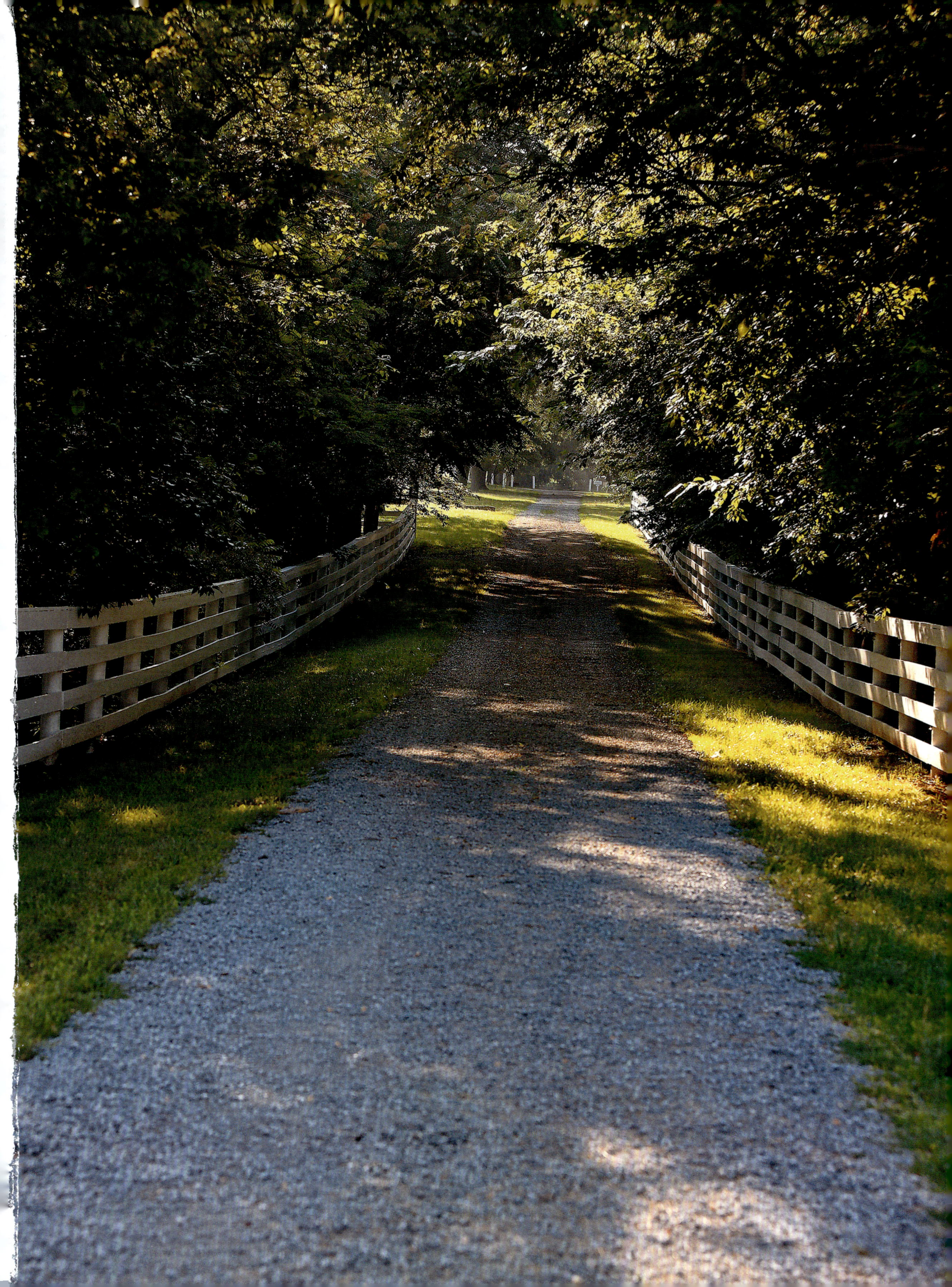

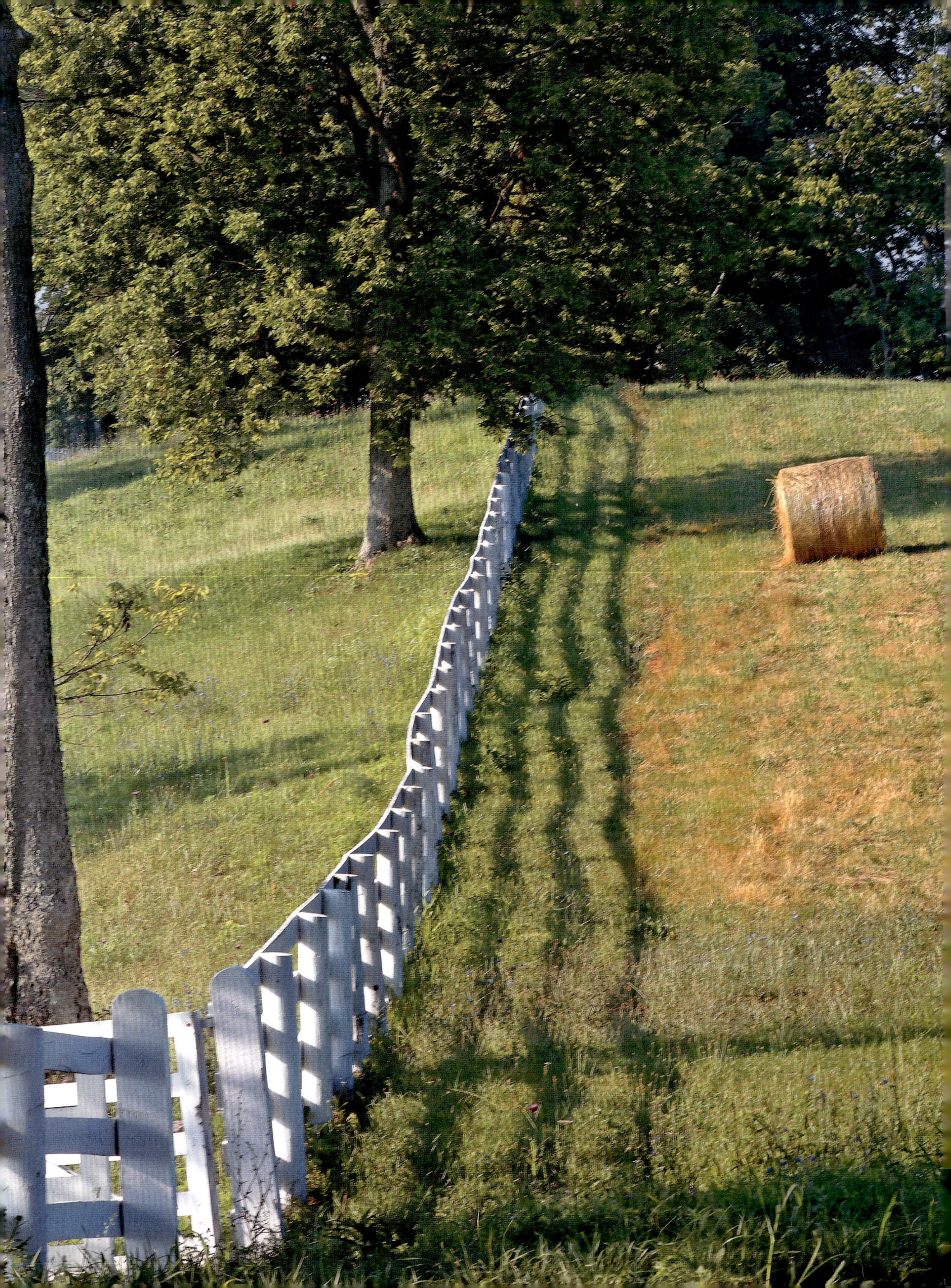

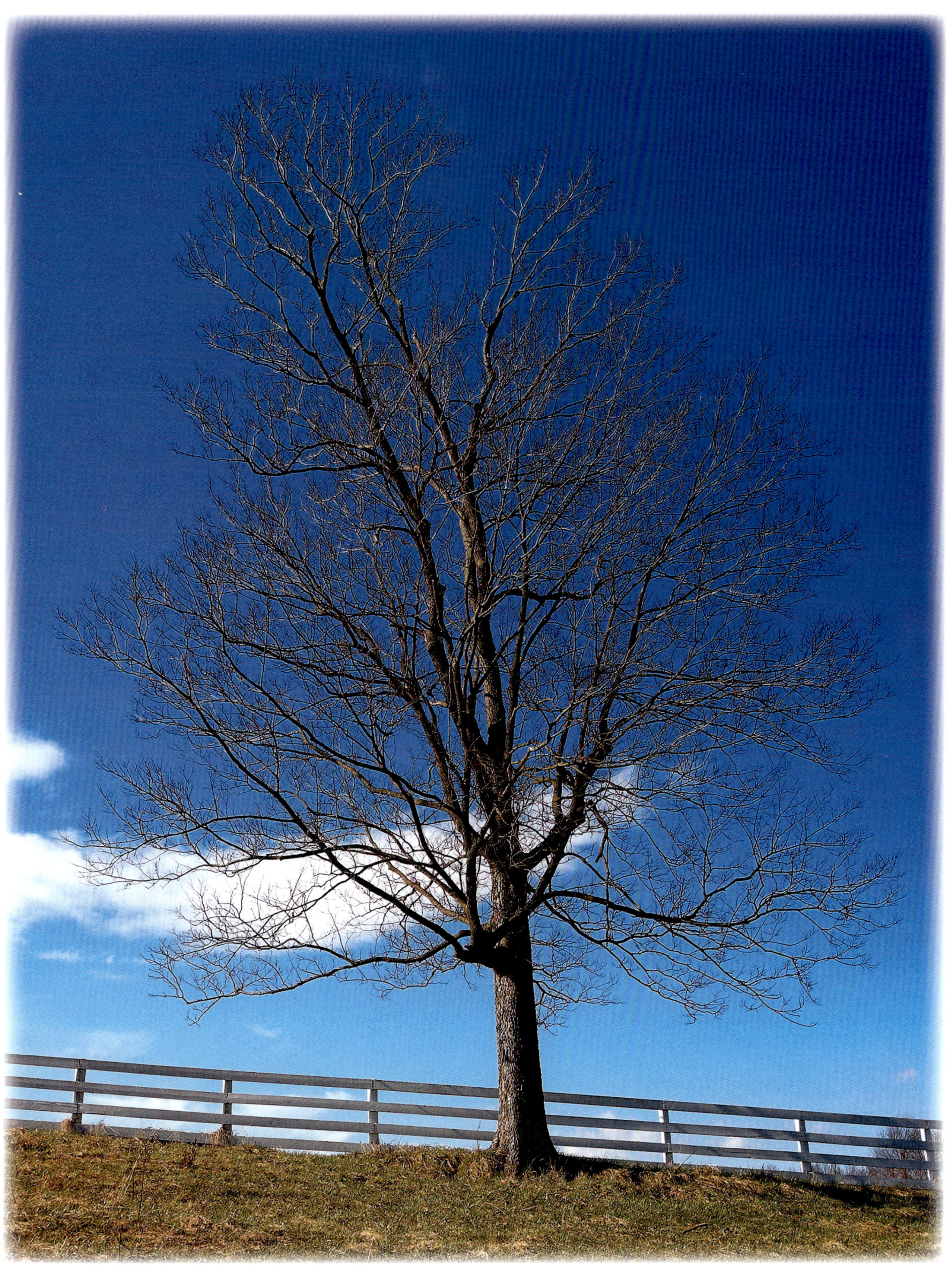

Pleasant Hill currently owns 3,000 of the original 5,000 acres of rolling Kentucky countryside that made up the community.

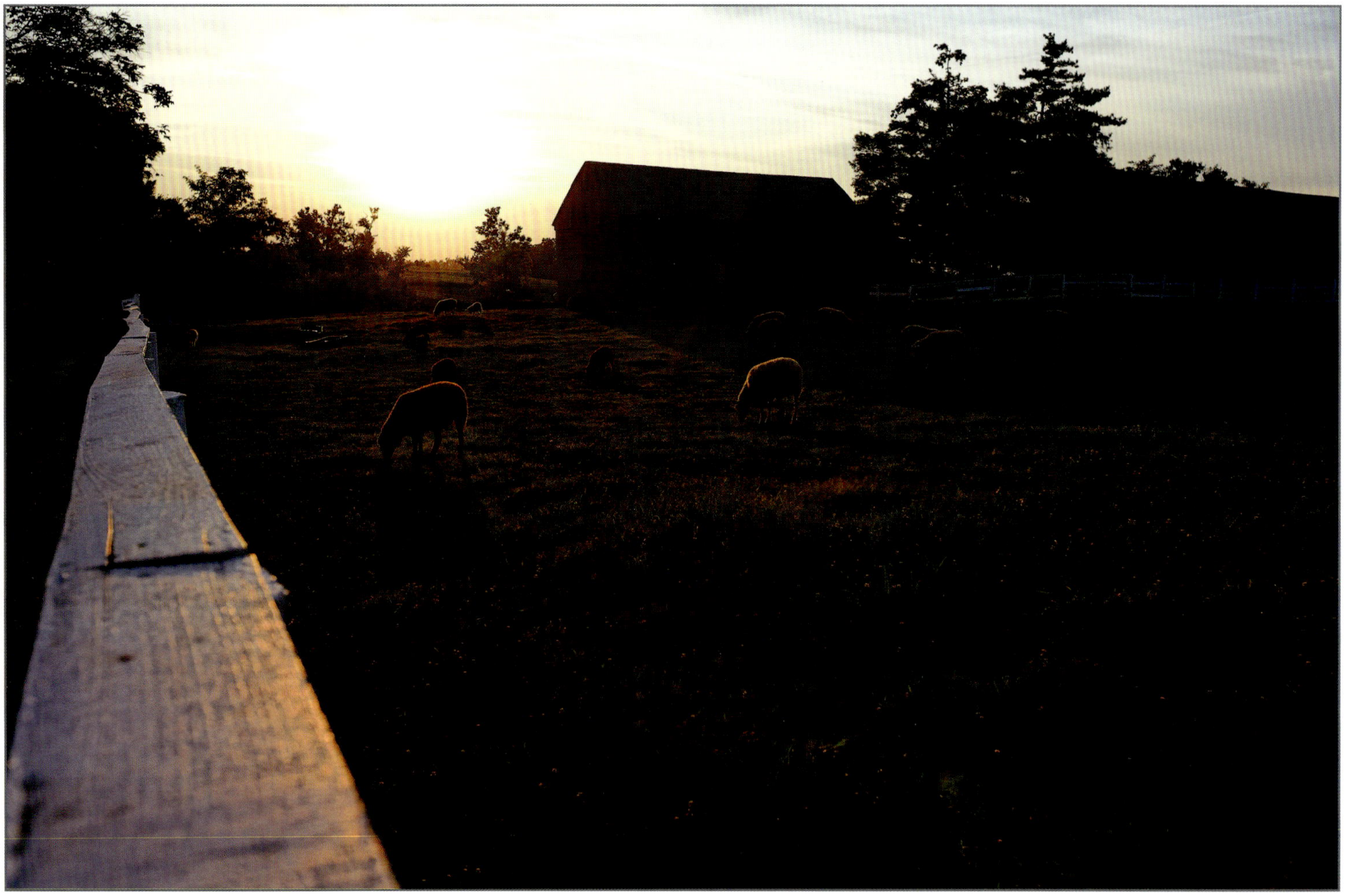

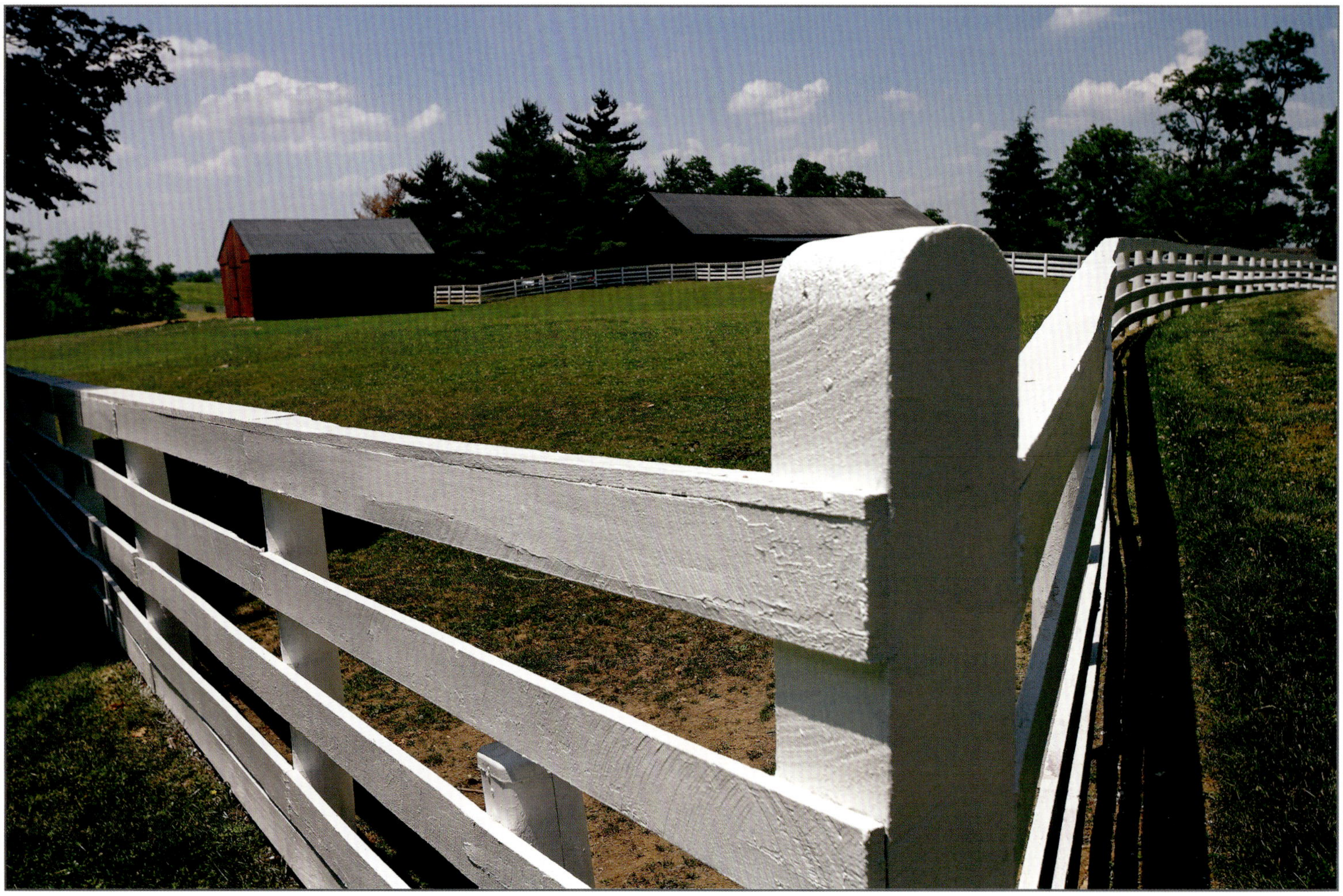

Support buildings for the West Family Dwelling showing the only remaining corn crib on the property.

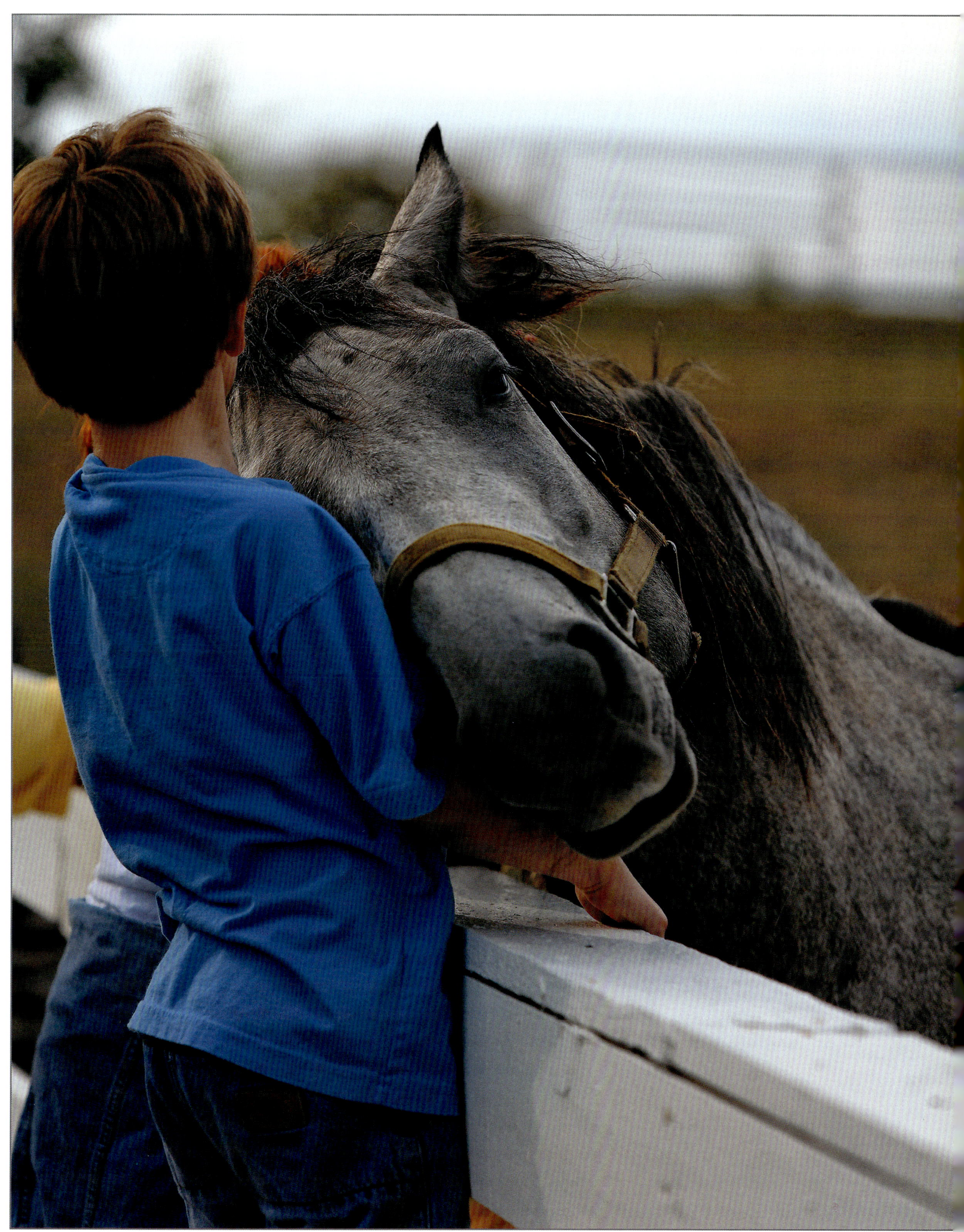

"Nell", one of a pair of Morgan-Percheron mix draft horses residing at Pleasant Hill.

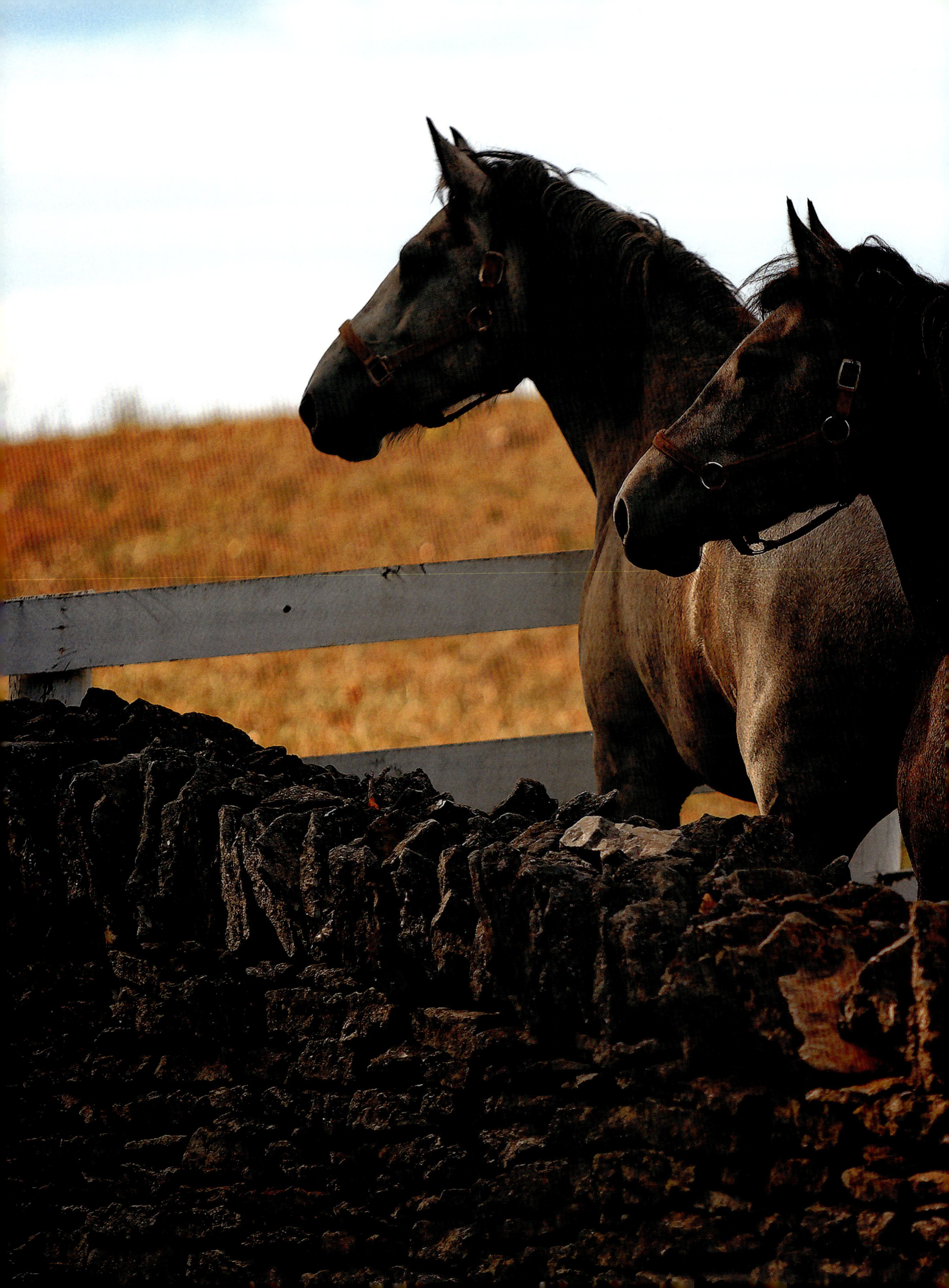

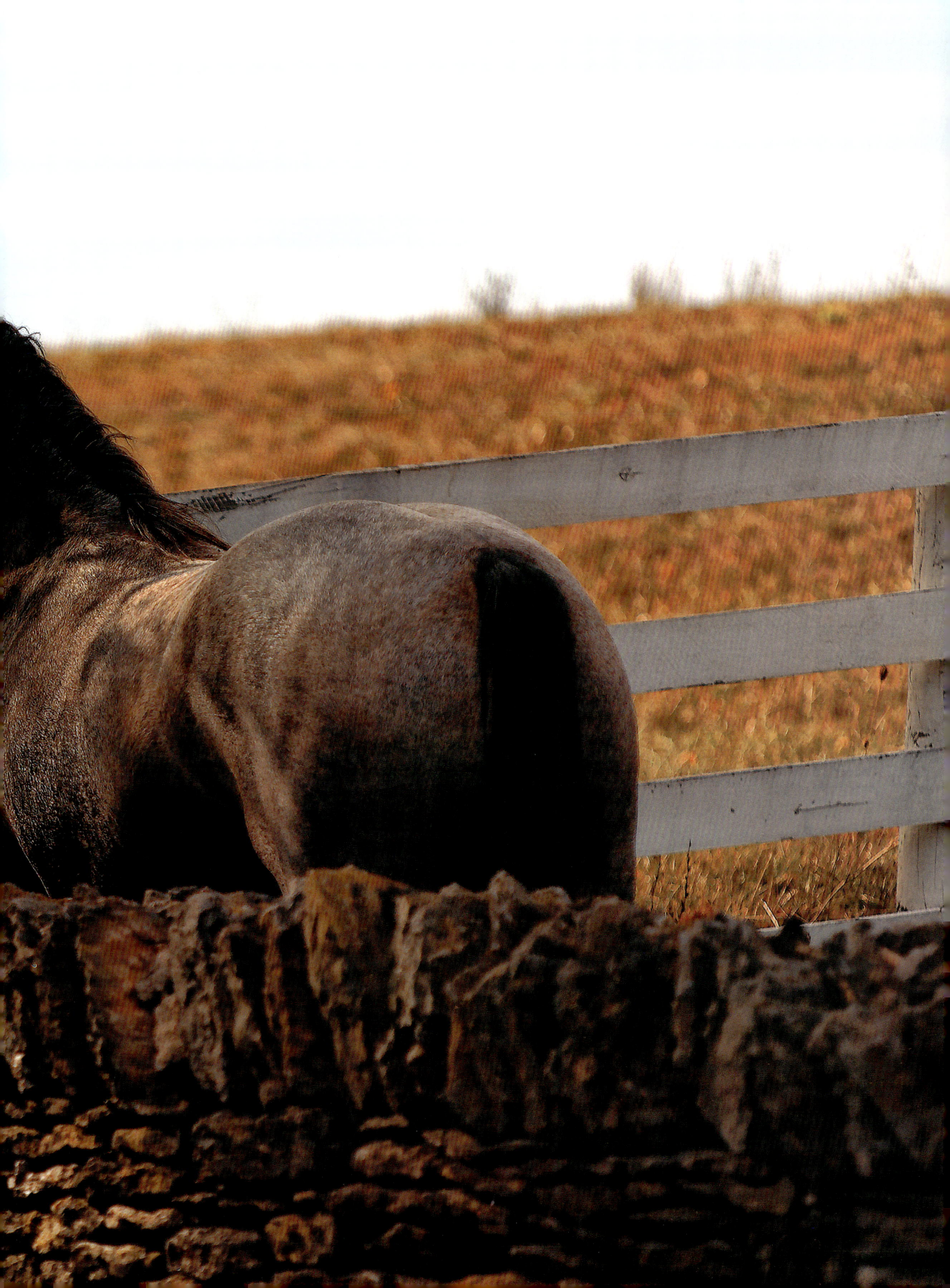

Previous spread: "Nell" and "Heather". The Percheron was the Shaker's draft horse of choice.

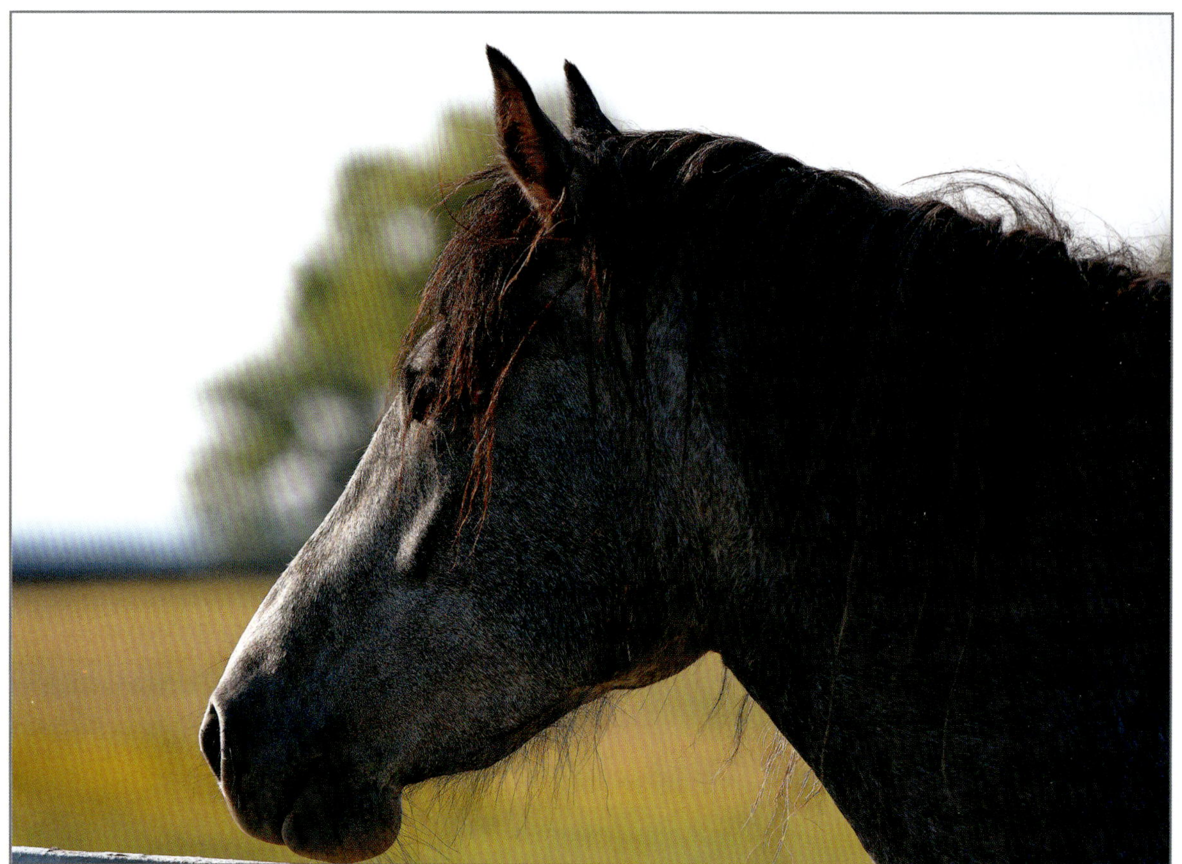

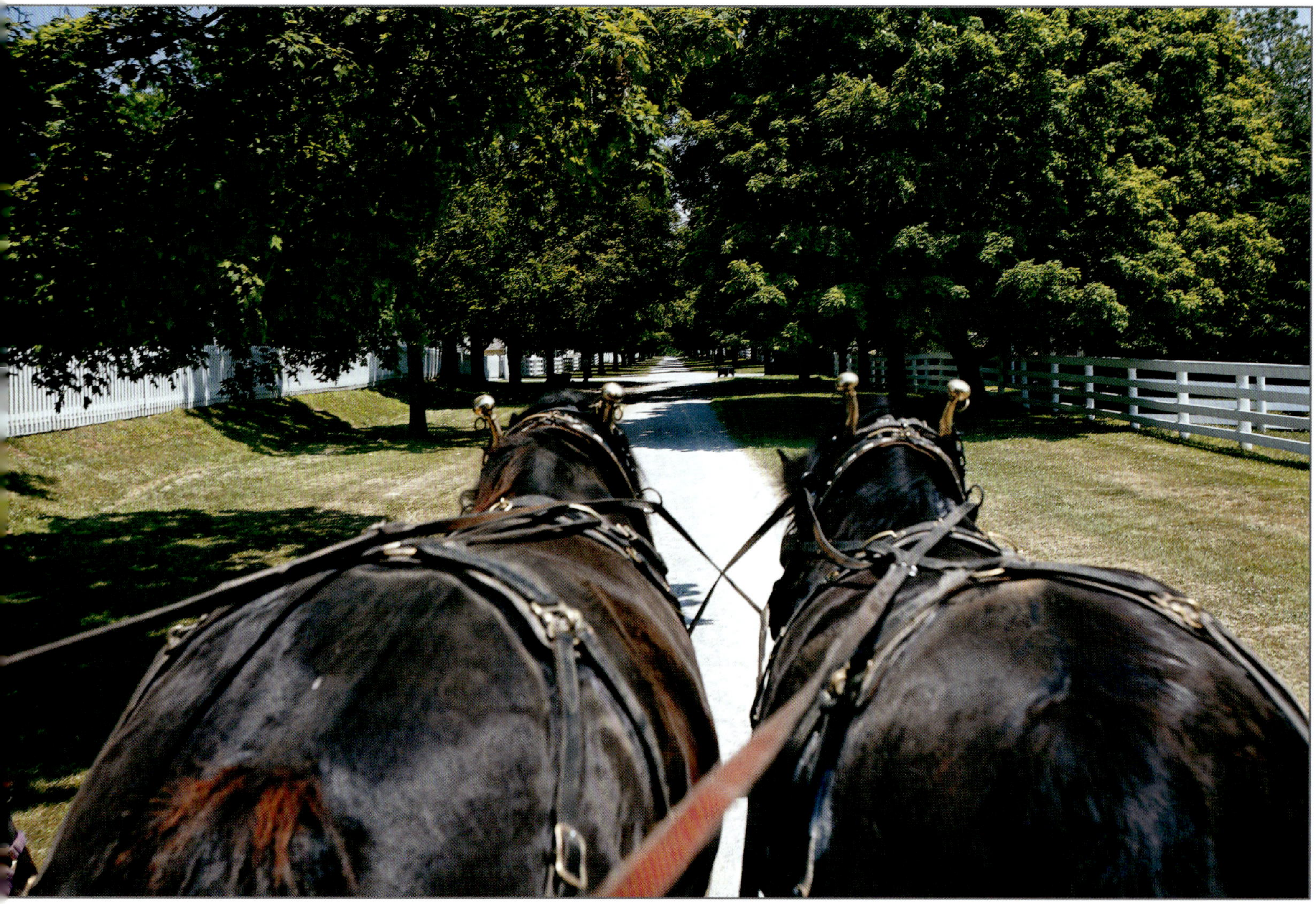

Part of the mission of Pleasant Hill is to help maintain the breeds of animals commonly found in use at the Village during the period the Shakers flourished.

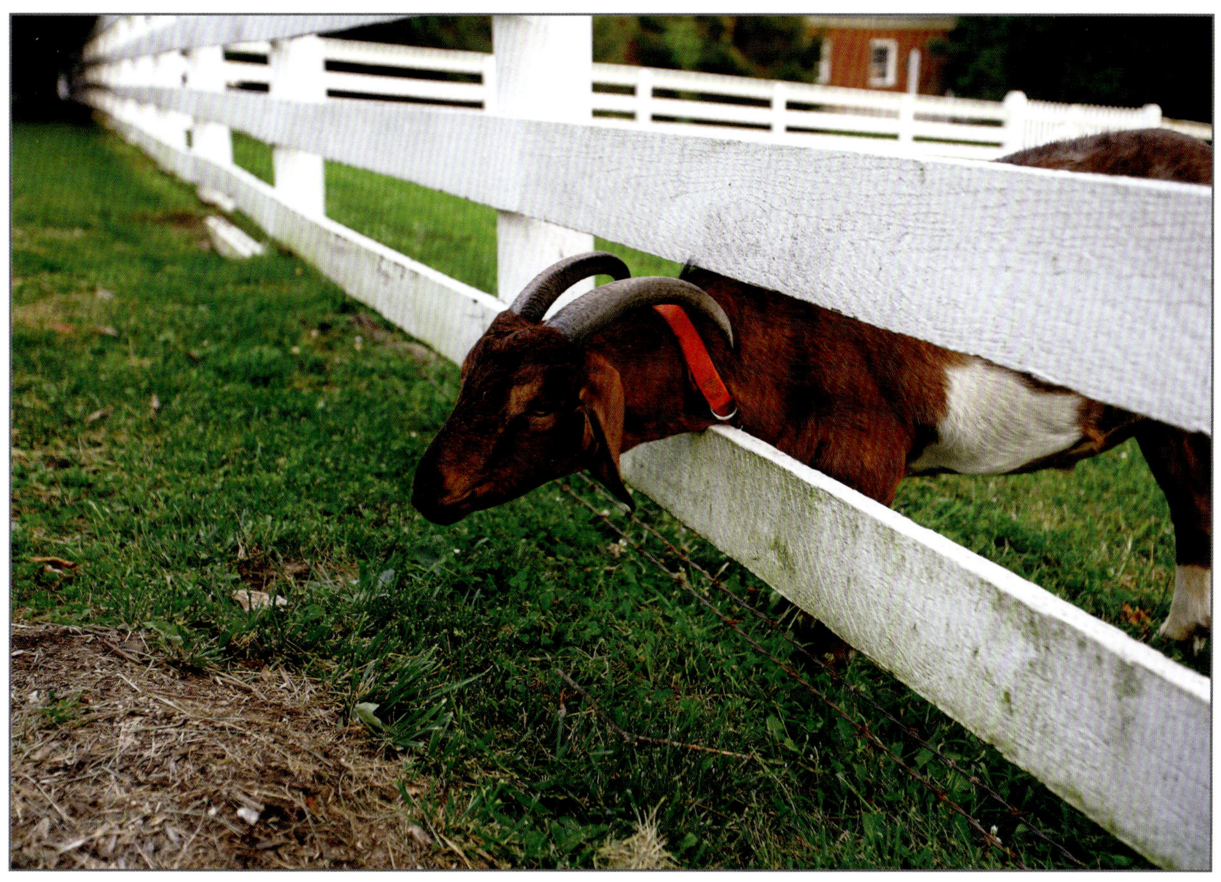

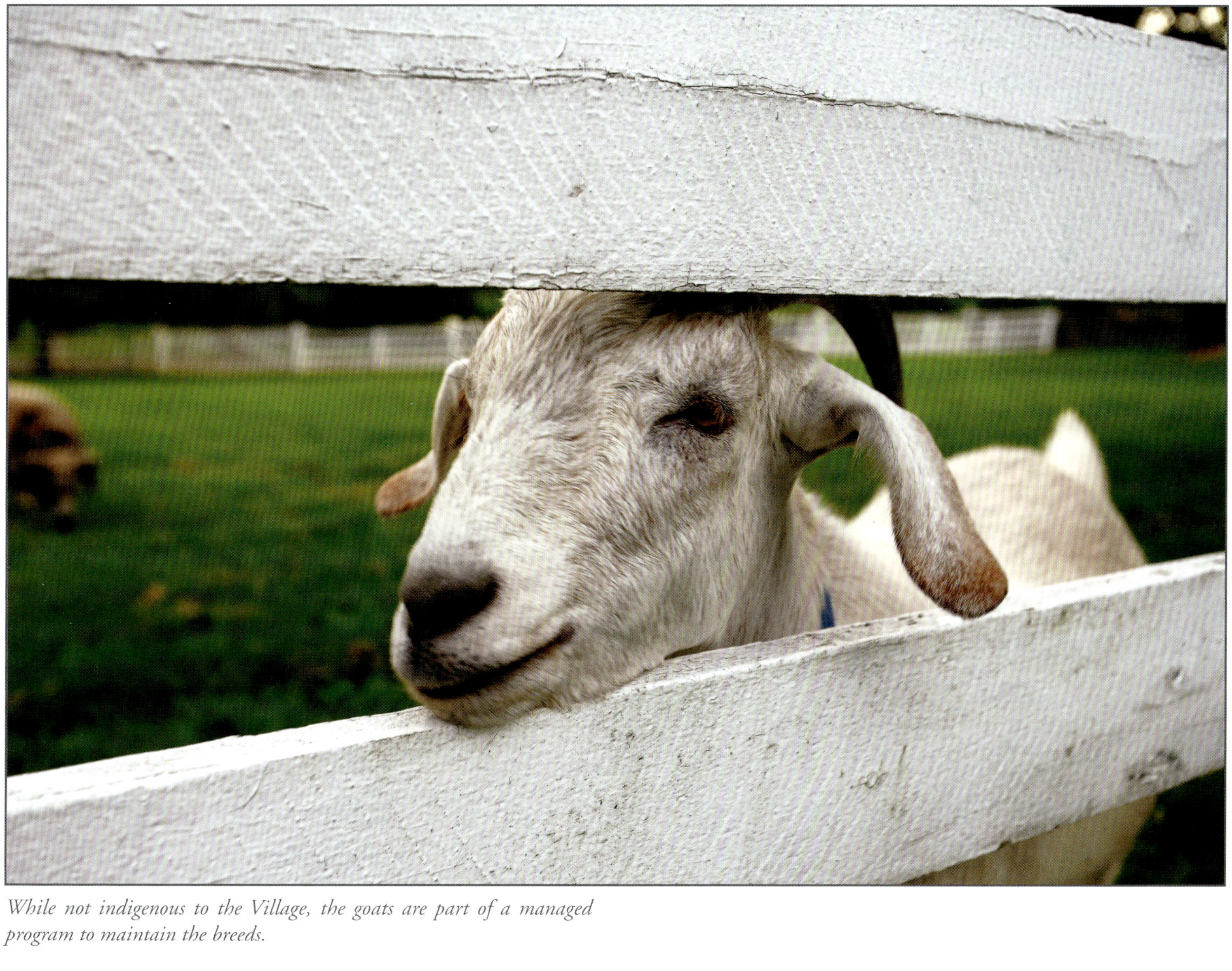

While not indigenous to the Village, the goats are part of a managed program to maintain the breeds.

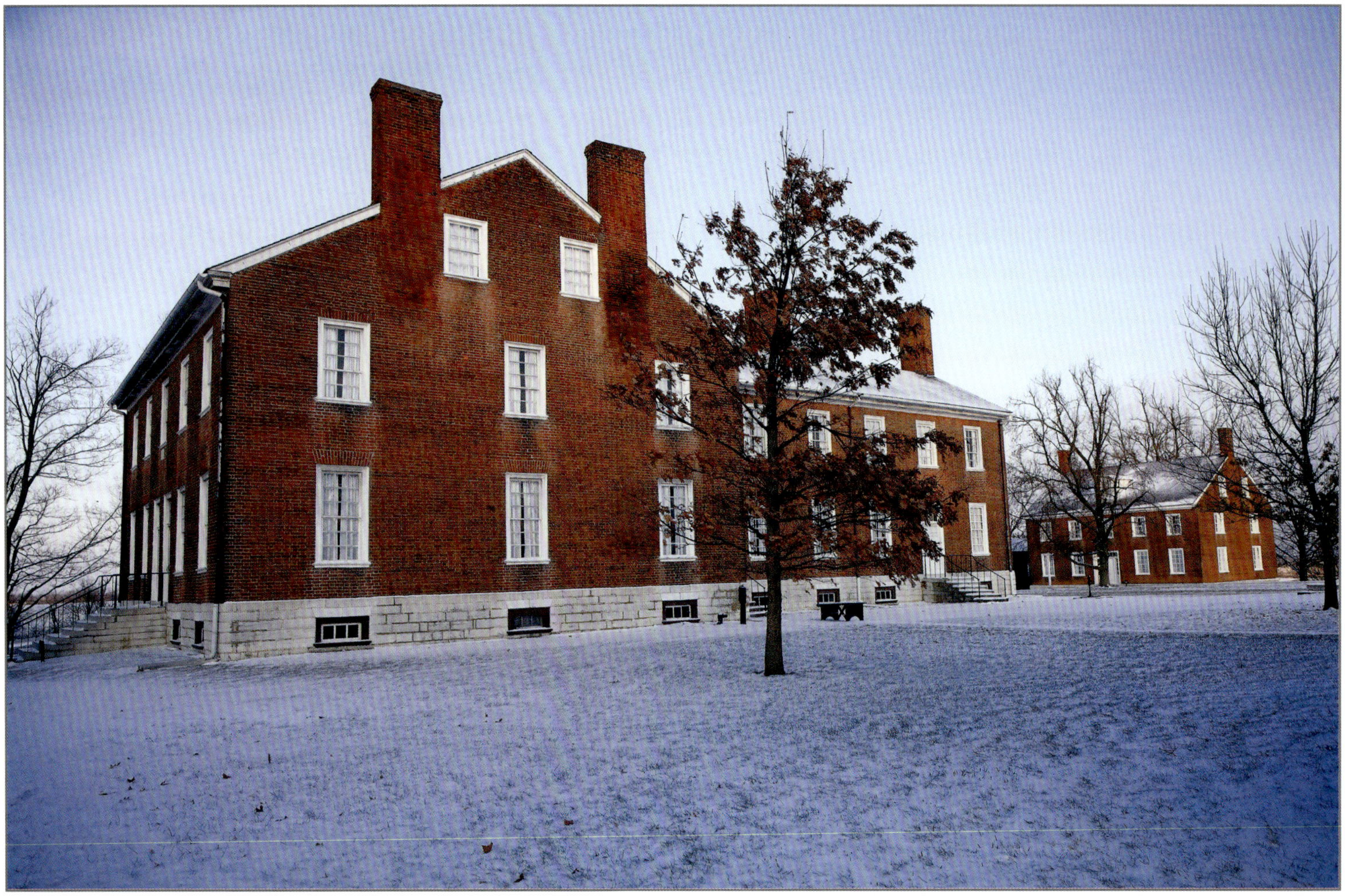

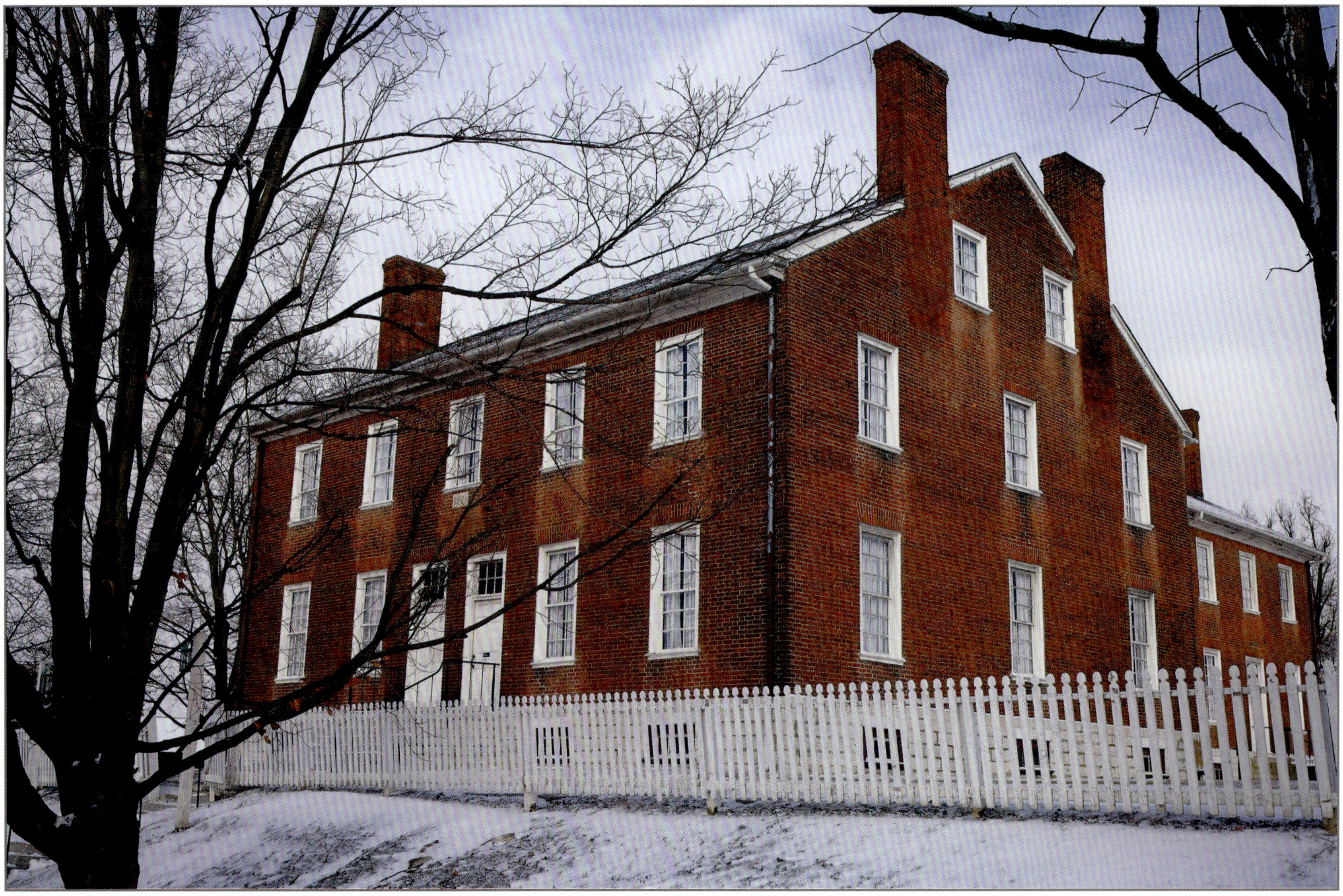

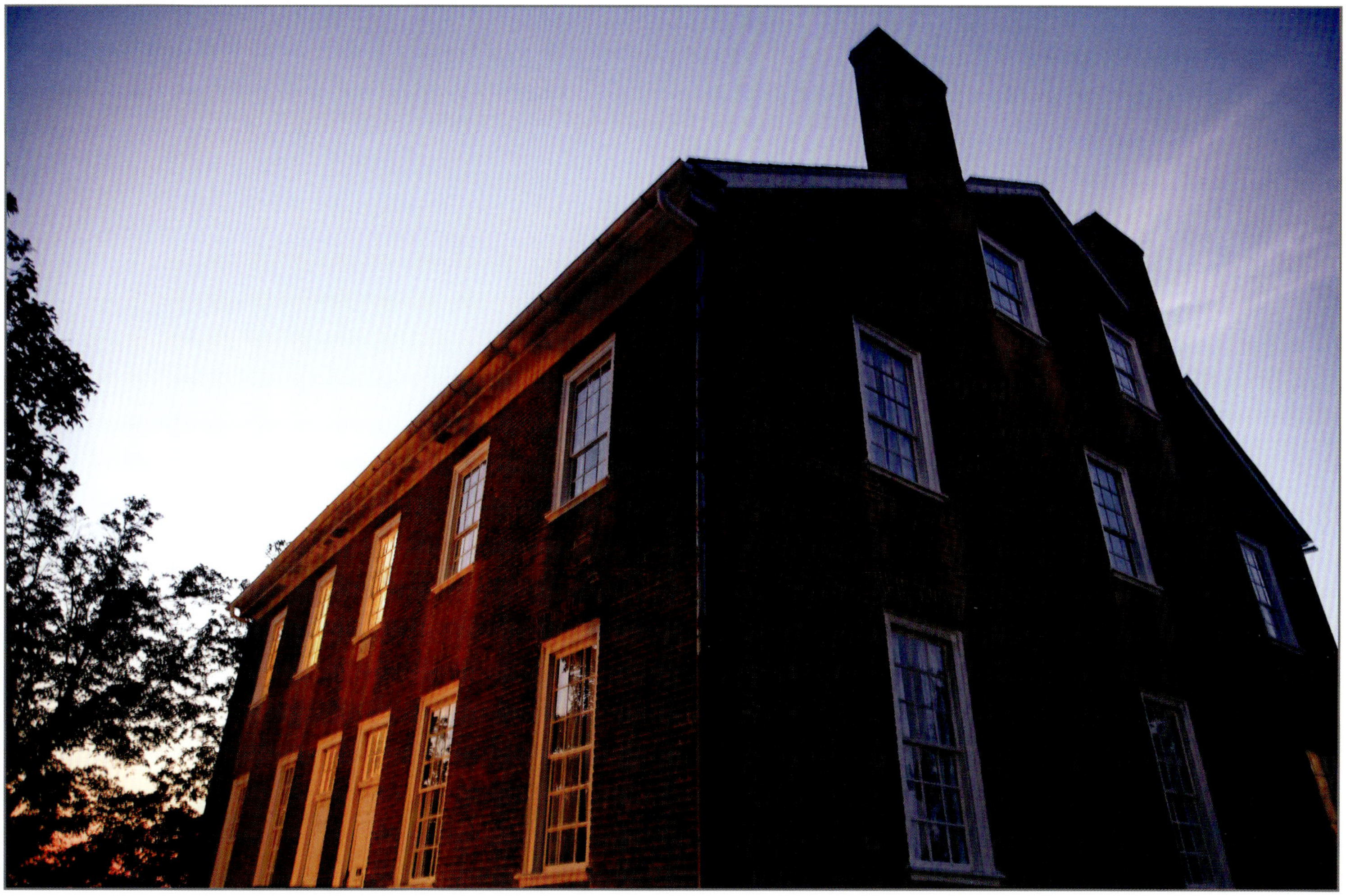

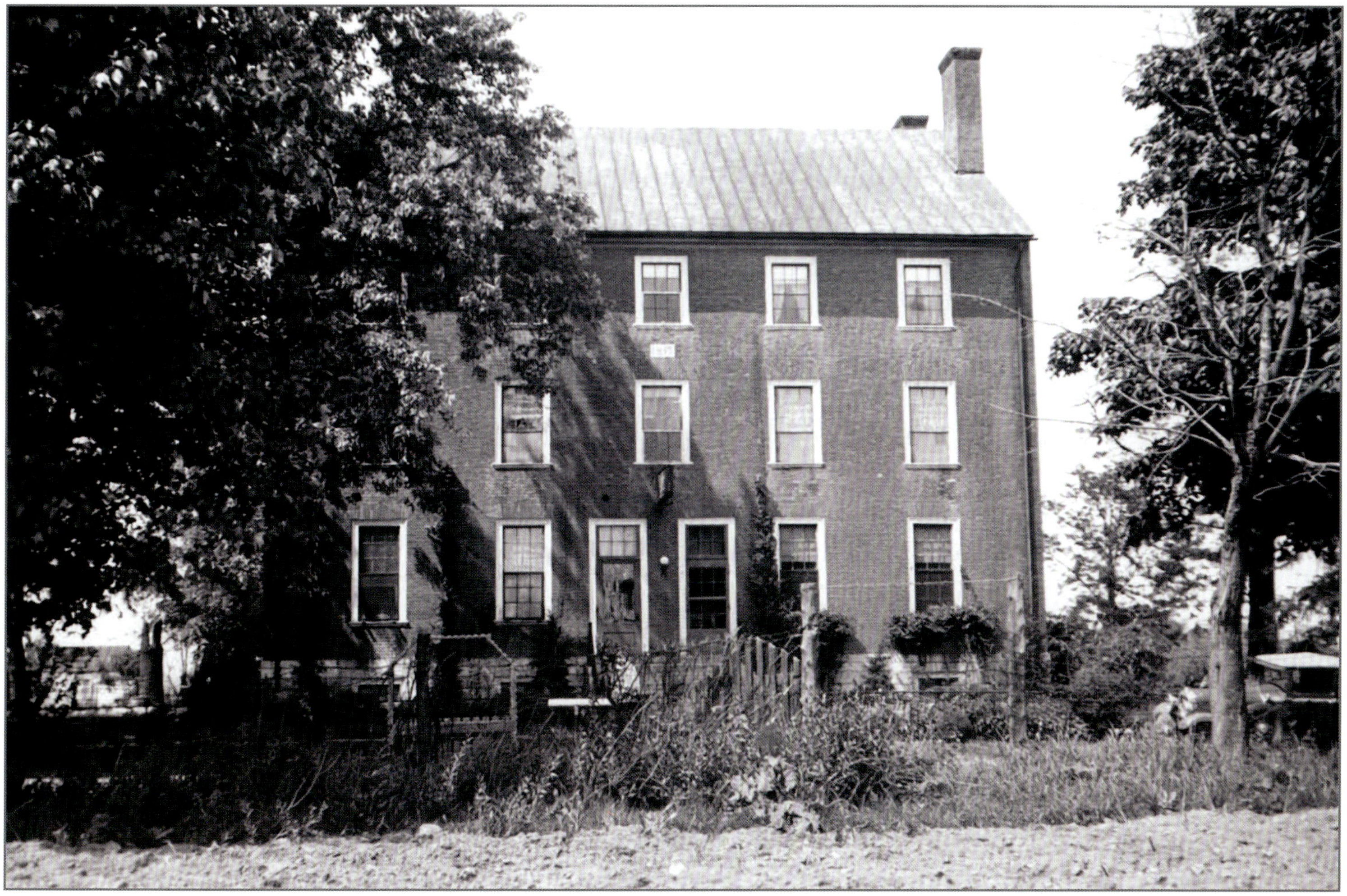

The West Family Dwelling was reserved for the aged members of the community as well as physically and/or mentally challenged members along with their care-givers.

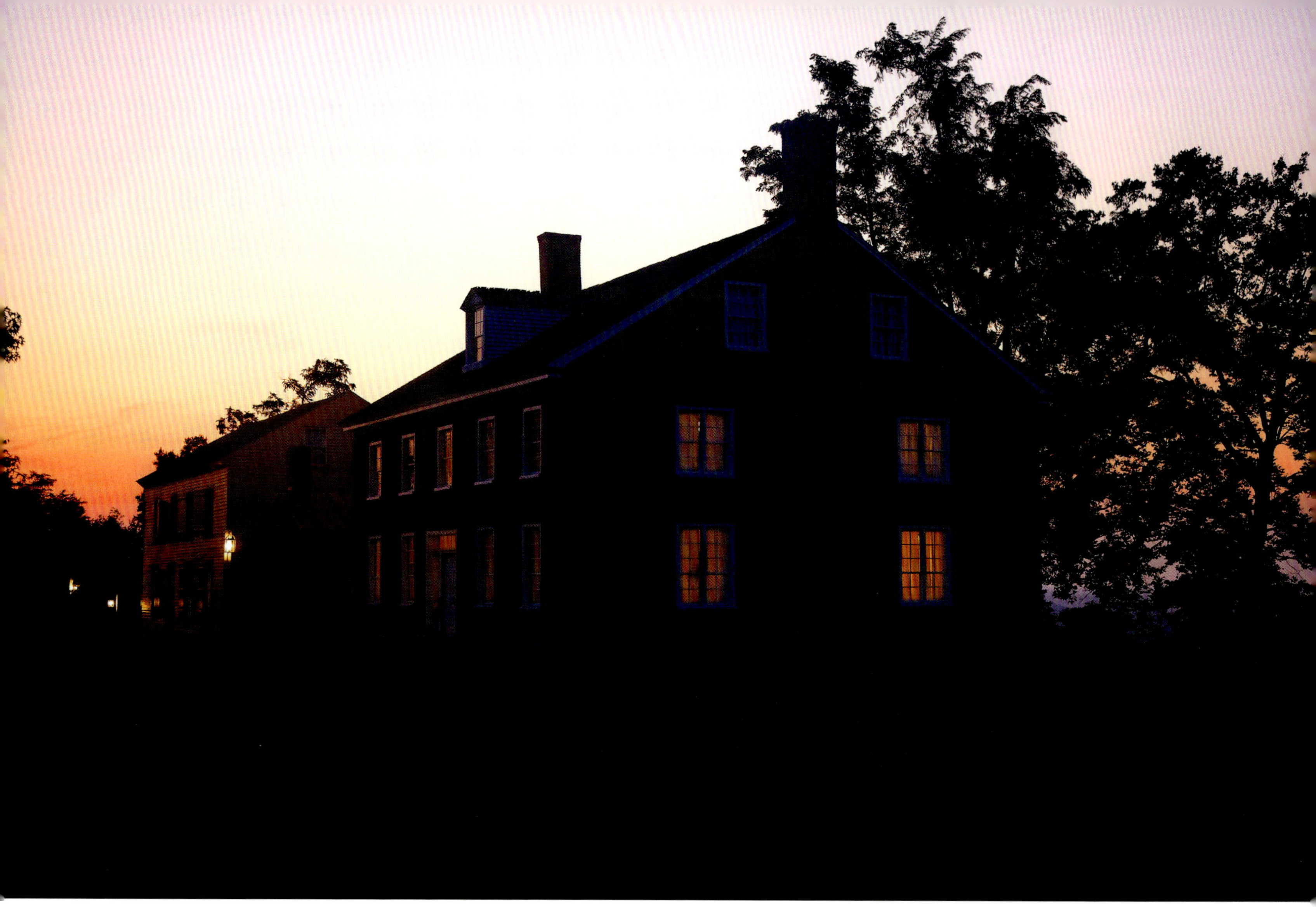

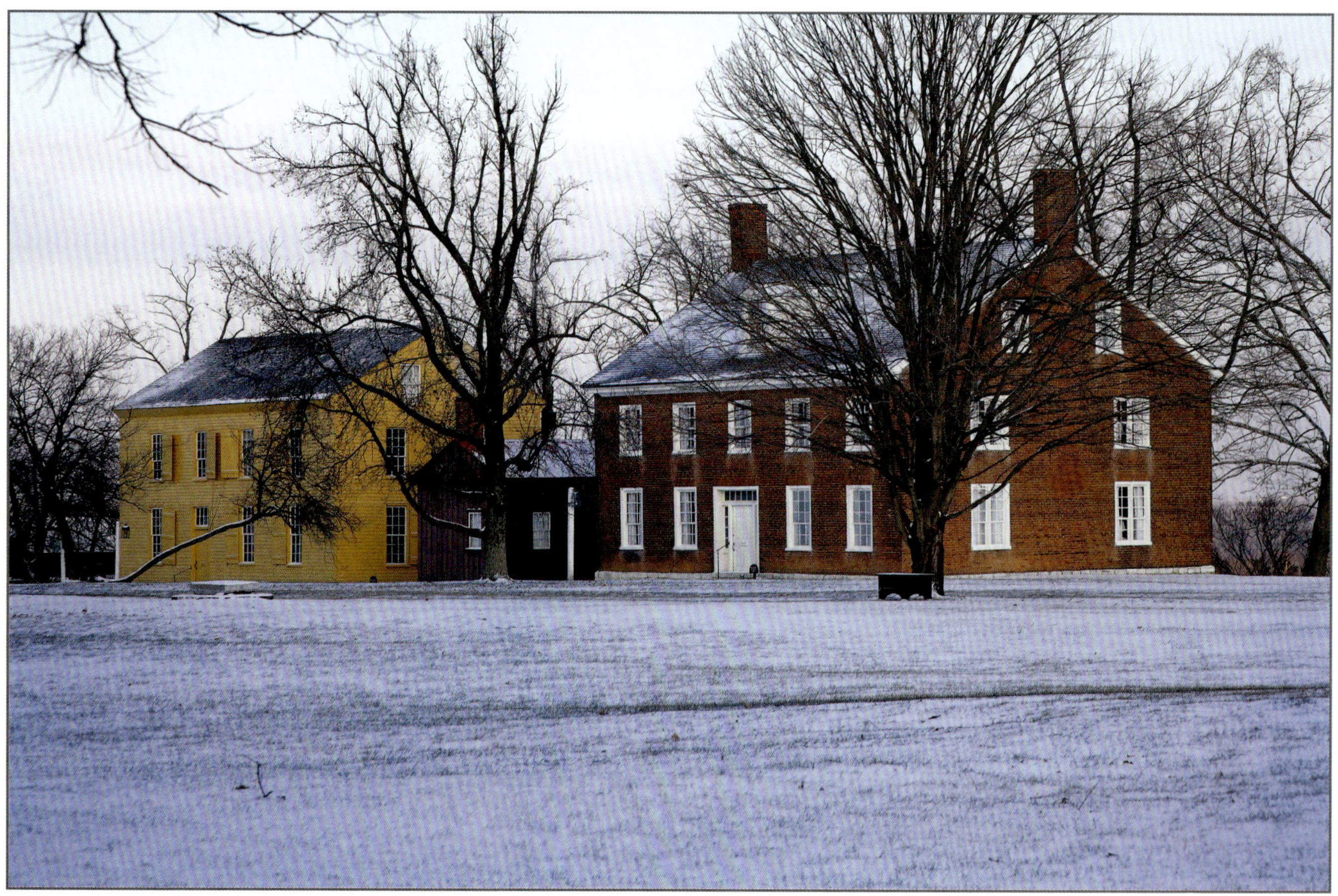

The Sisters' Shop and Wash House are two examples of the support buildings for the West Family.

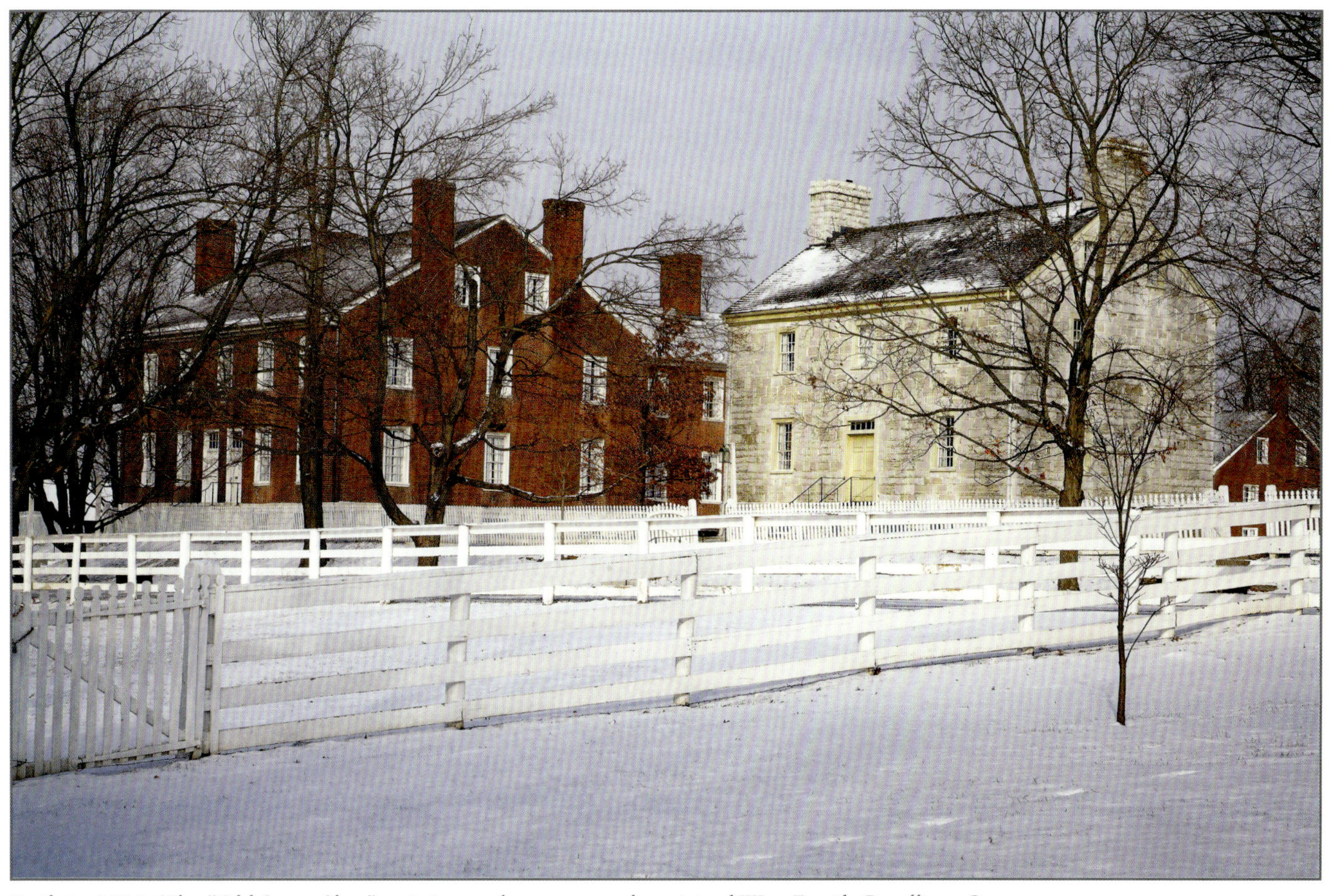

Built in 1811, The "Old Stone Shop" as it is now known, was the original West Family Dwelling. Once the larger brick structure was erected, it became the offices of William Pennebaker the community's doctor, and his brother Frank, the community's dentist.

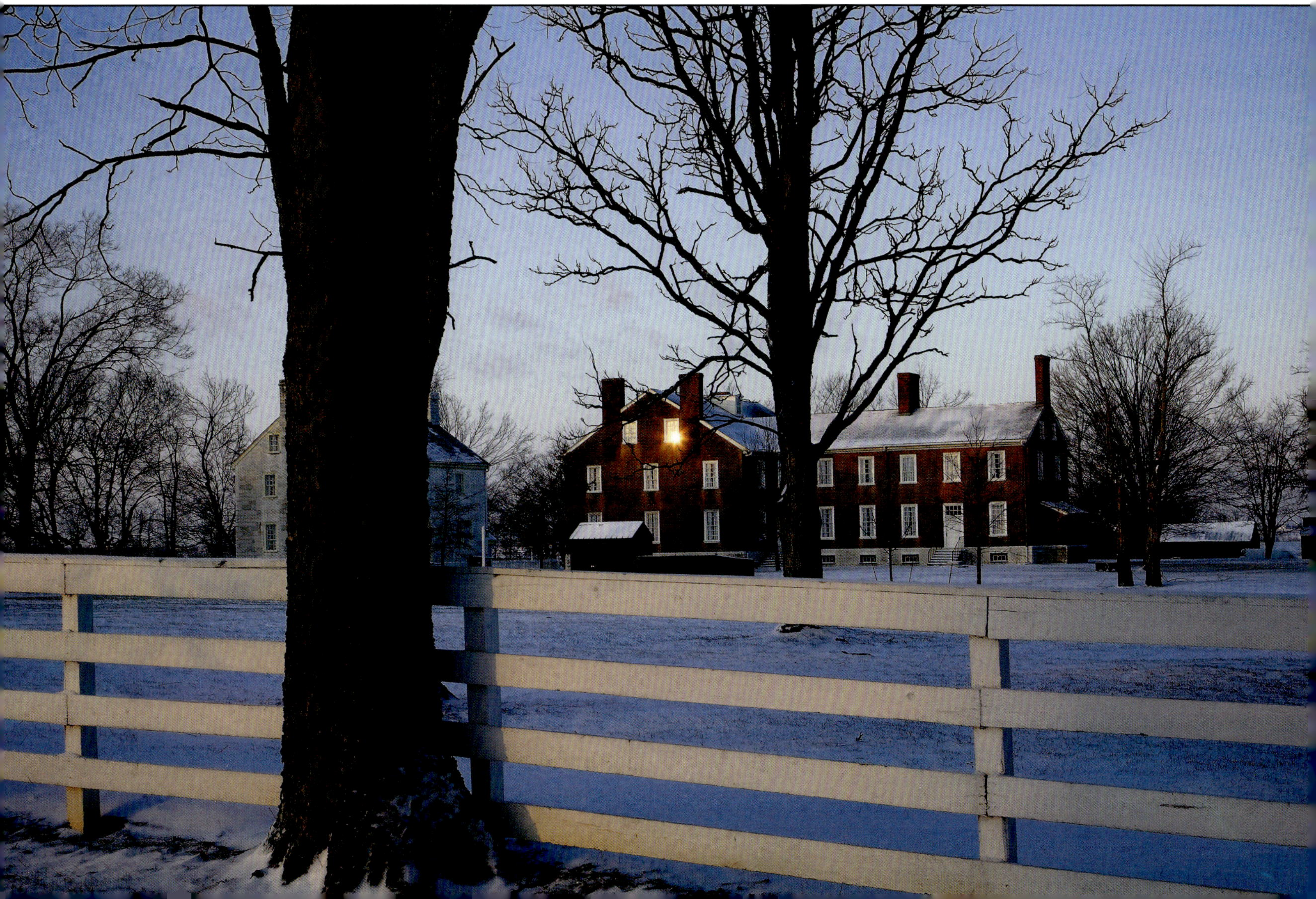

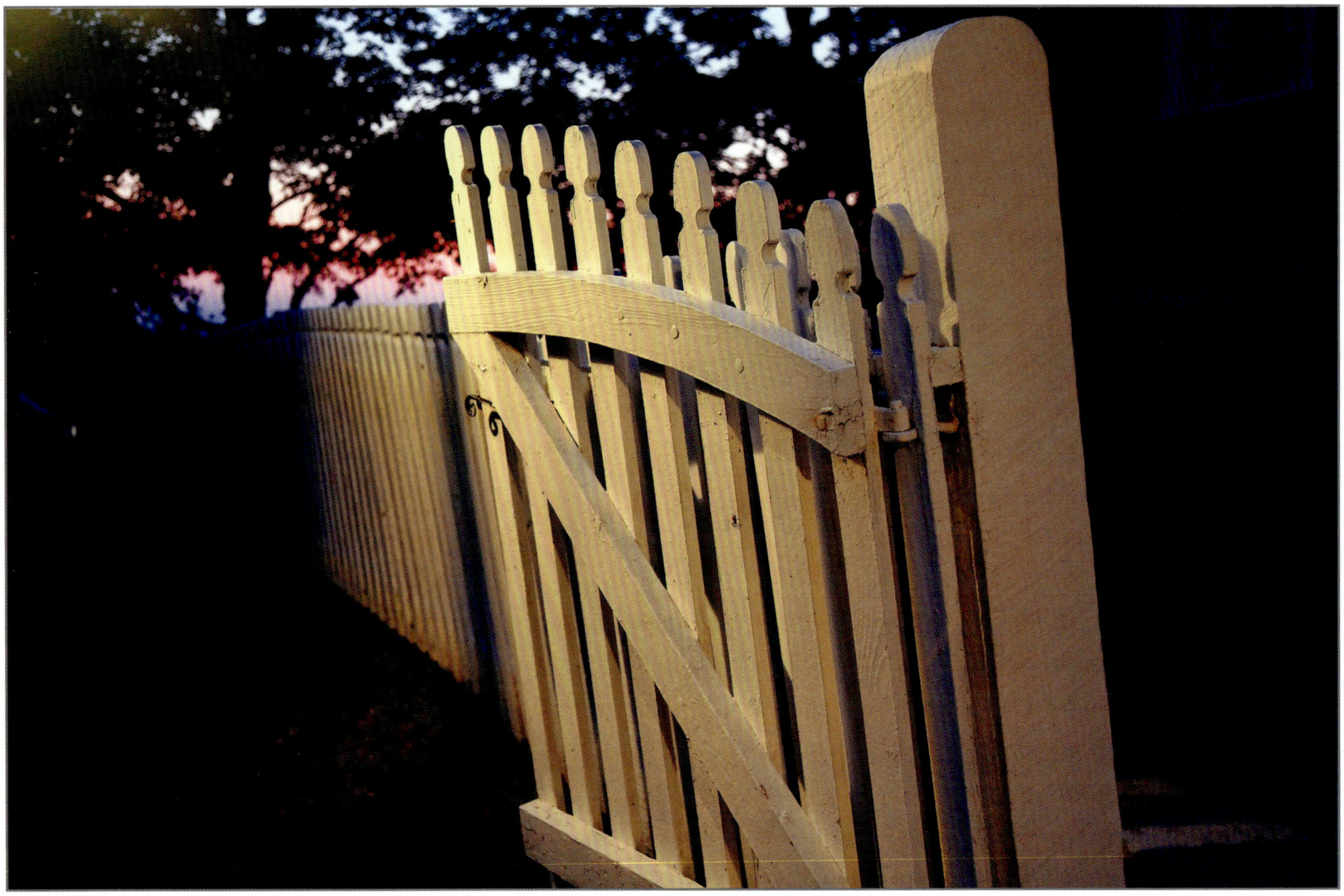

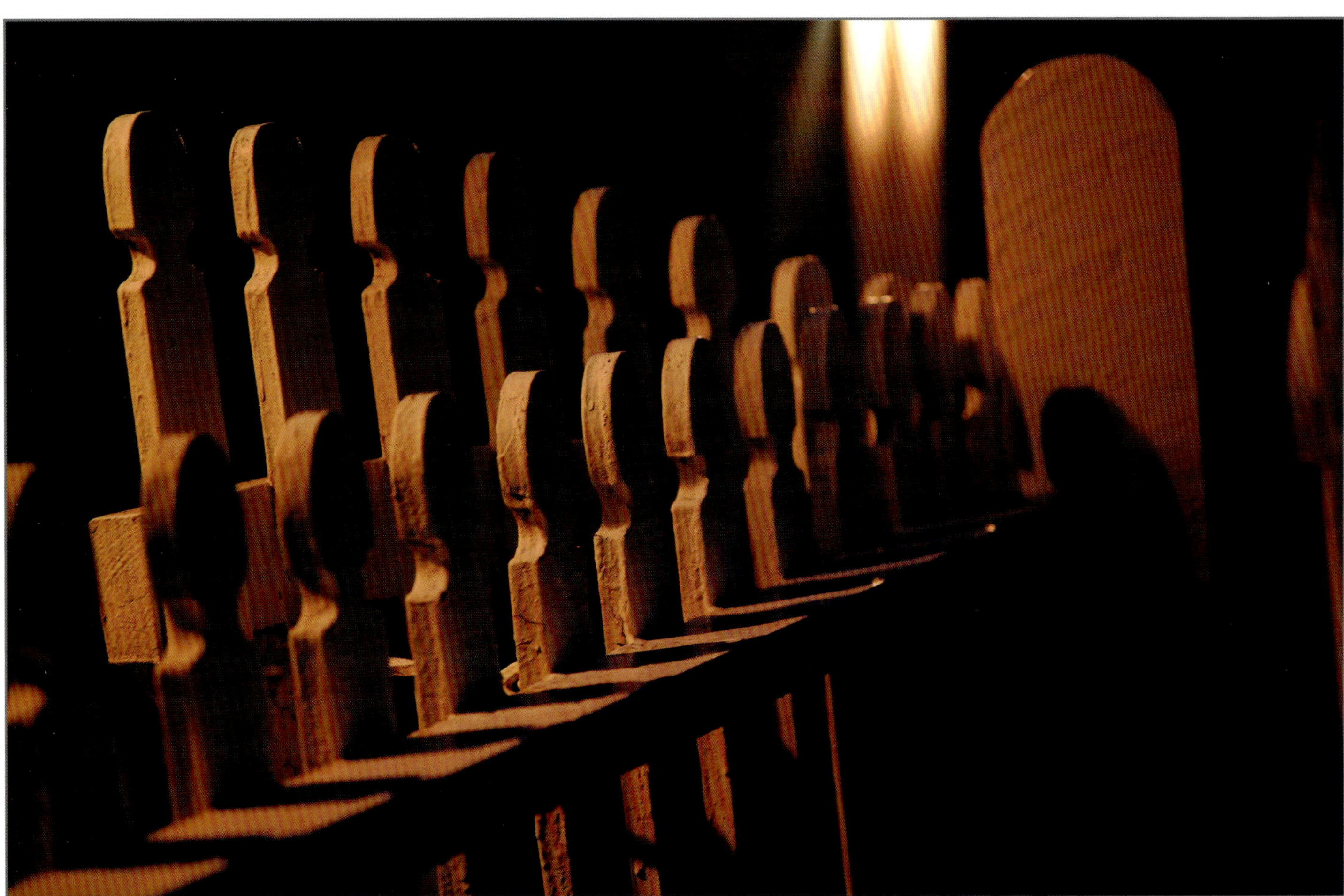

Examples of the decorative fencing in front of the main structures of the Village. Fencing transitions to plain board fencing in front of support structures and fields.

Opposite: A view from the third floor of the West Family Dwelling. The third floors of most dwellings were reserved for out of season garment storage.

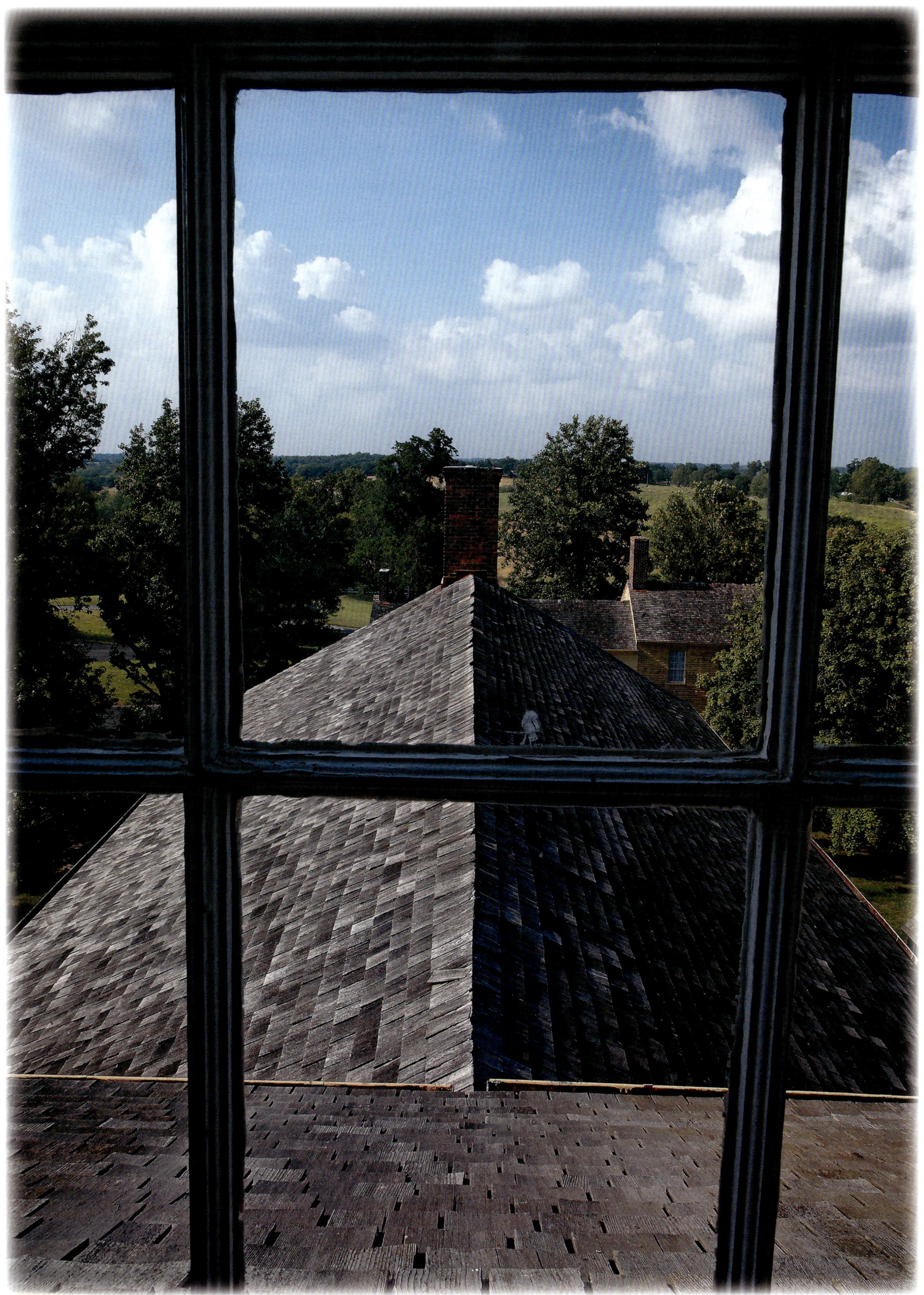

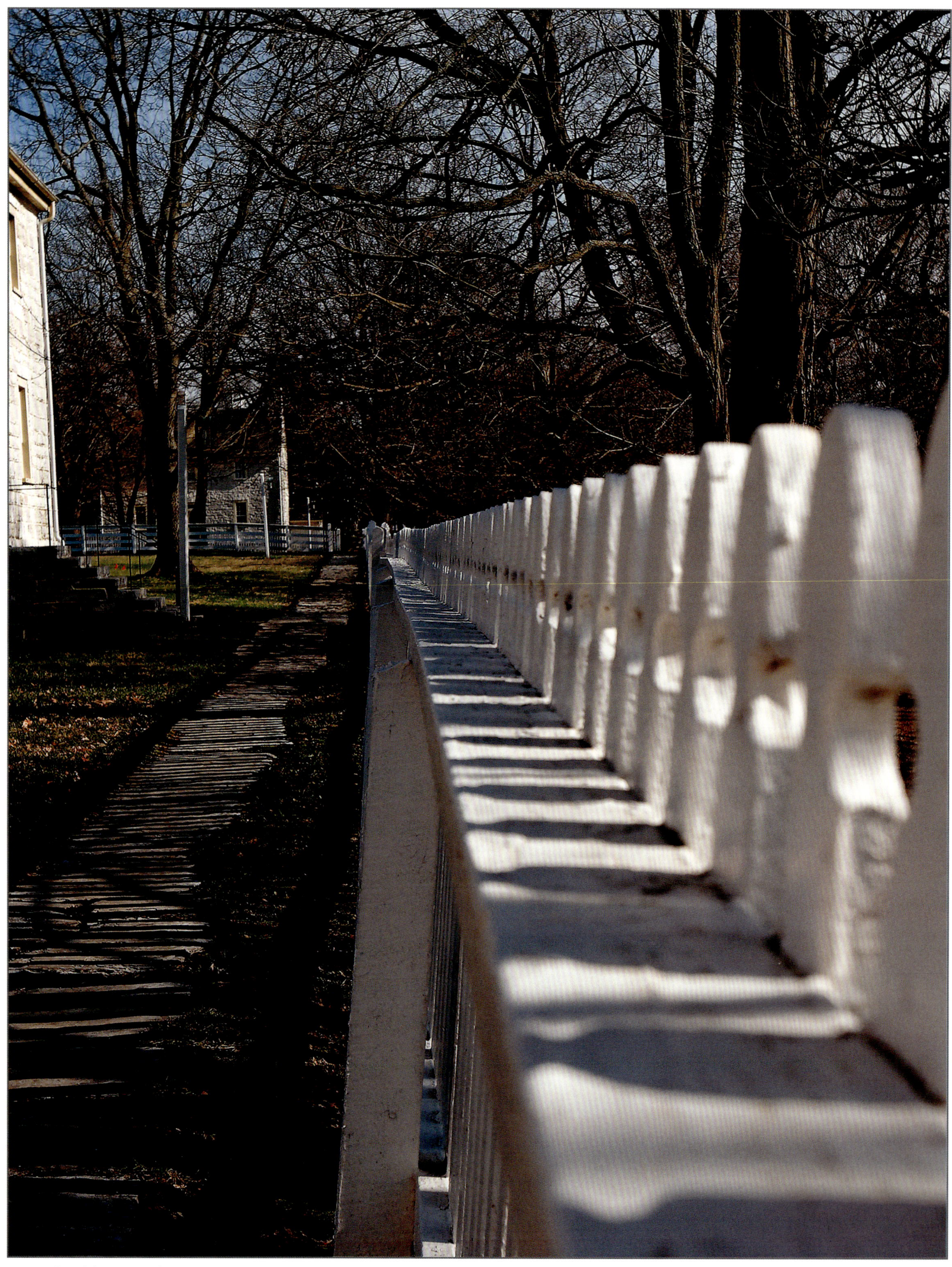

Examples of decorative fencing and limestone sidewalks along the fronts of main structures.

Opposite: A view of the fireplace in the "Winter Kitchen" located in the basement of the West Family Dwelling.

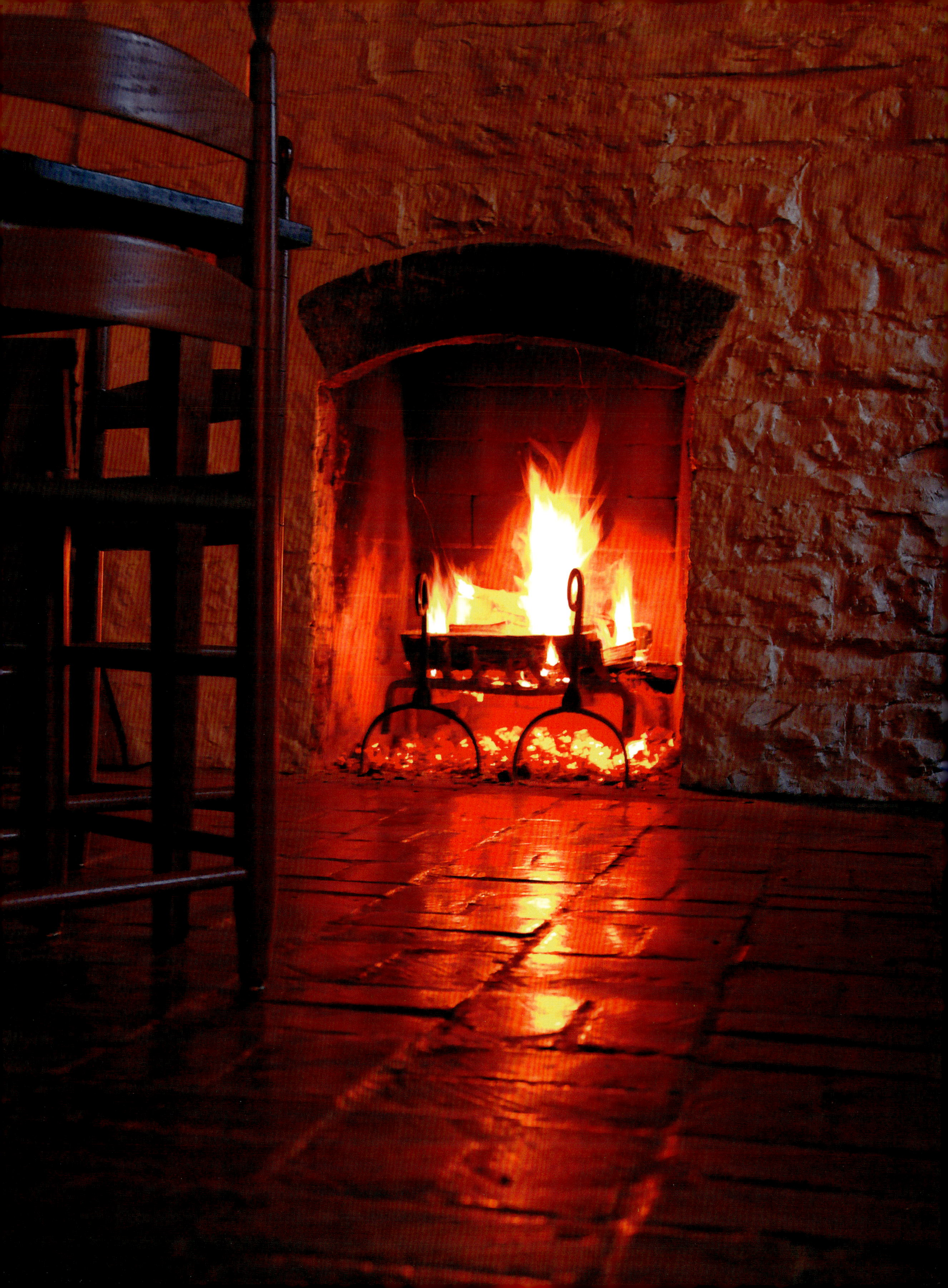

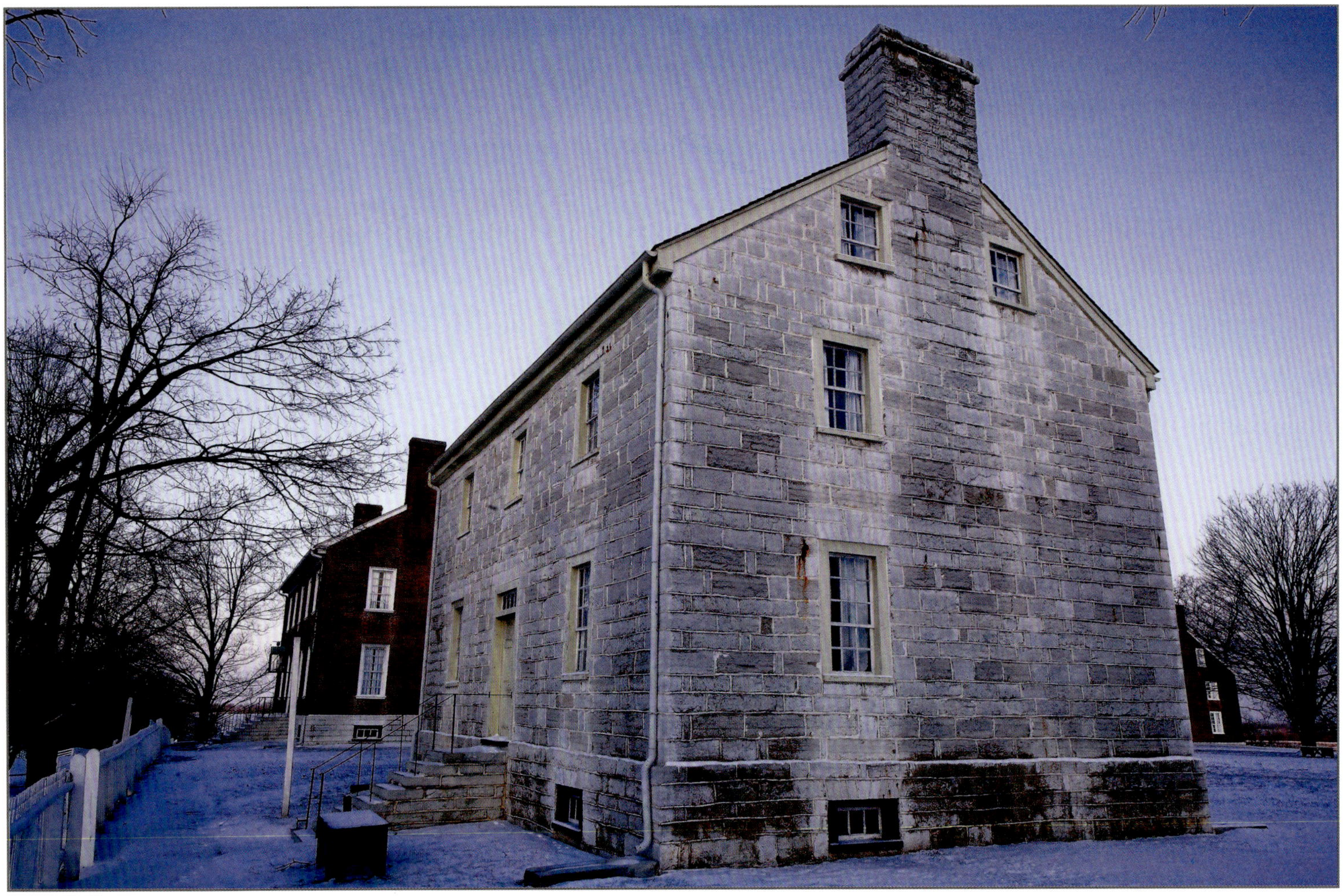

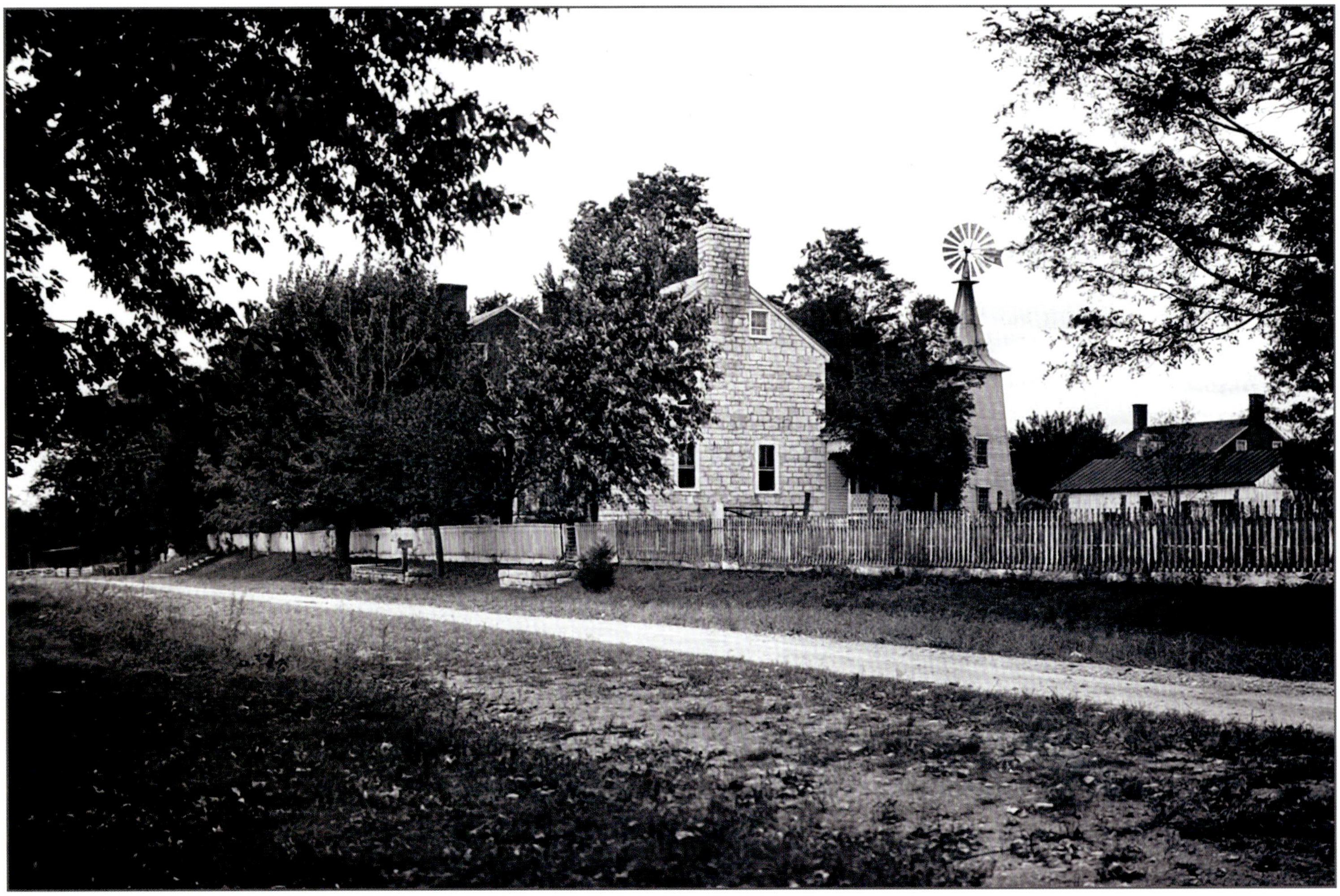

The original West Family Dwelling.

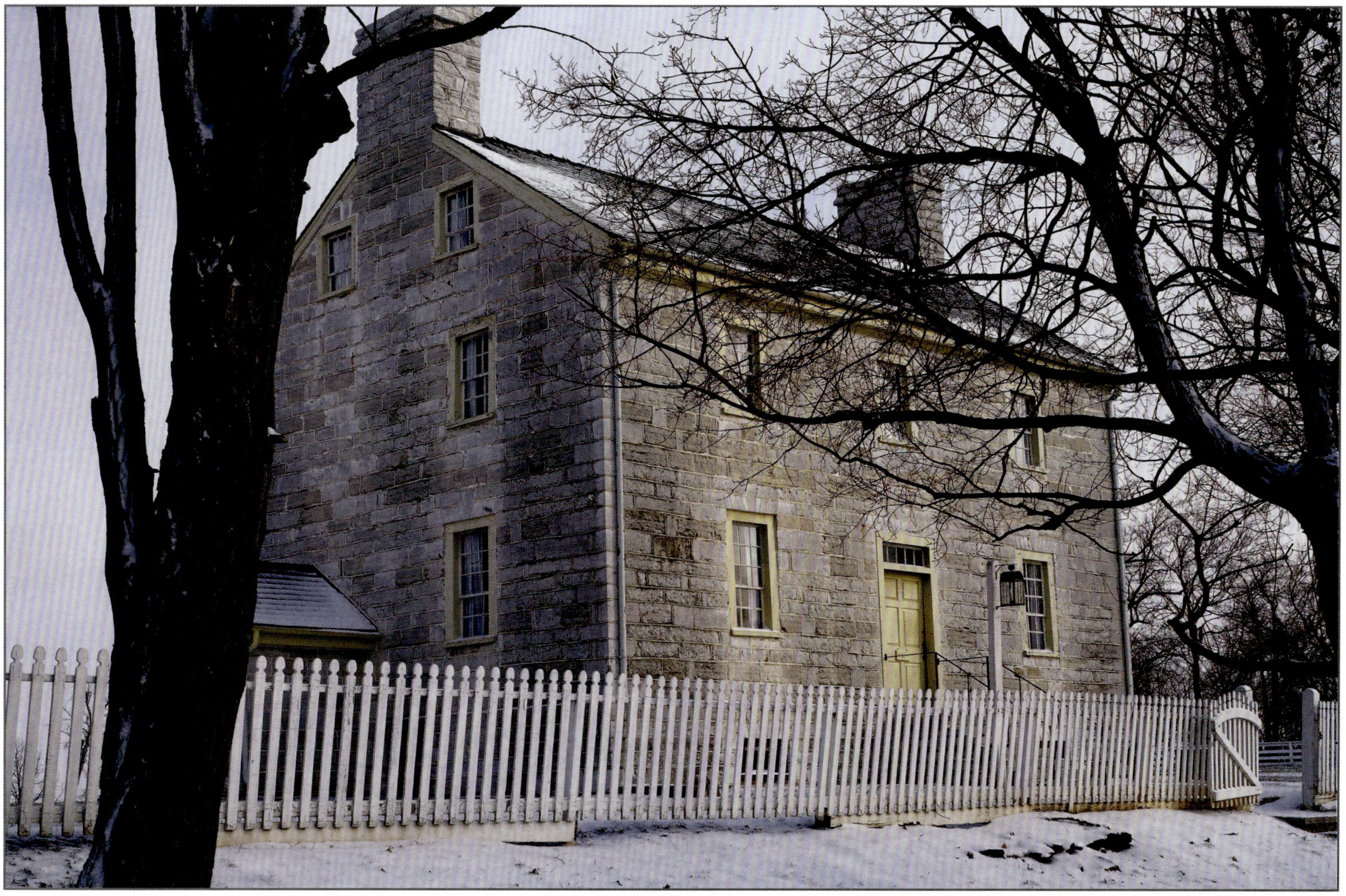

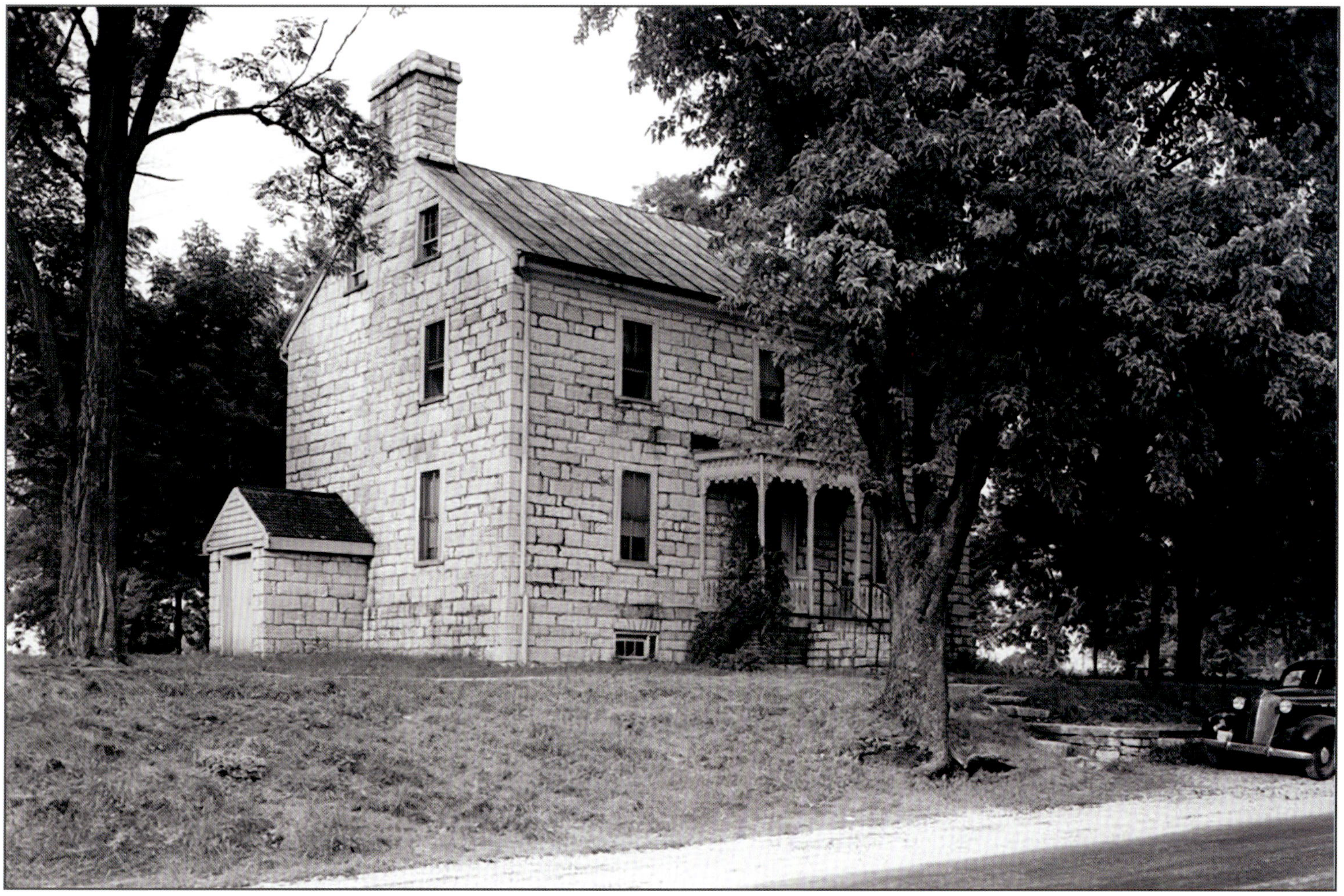

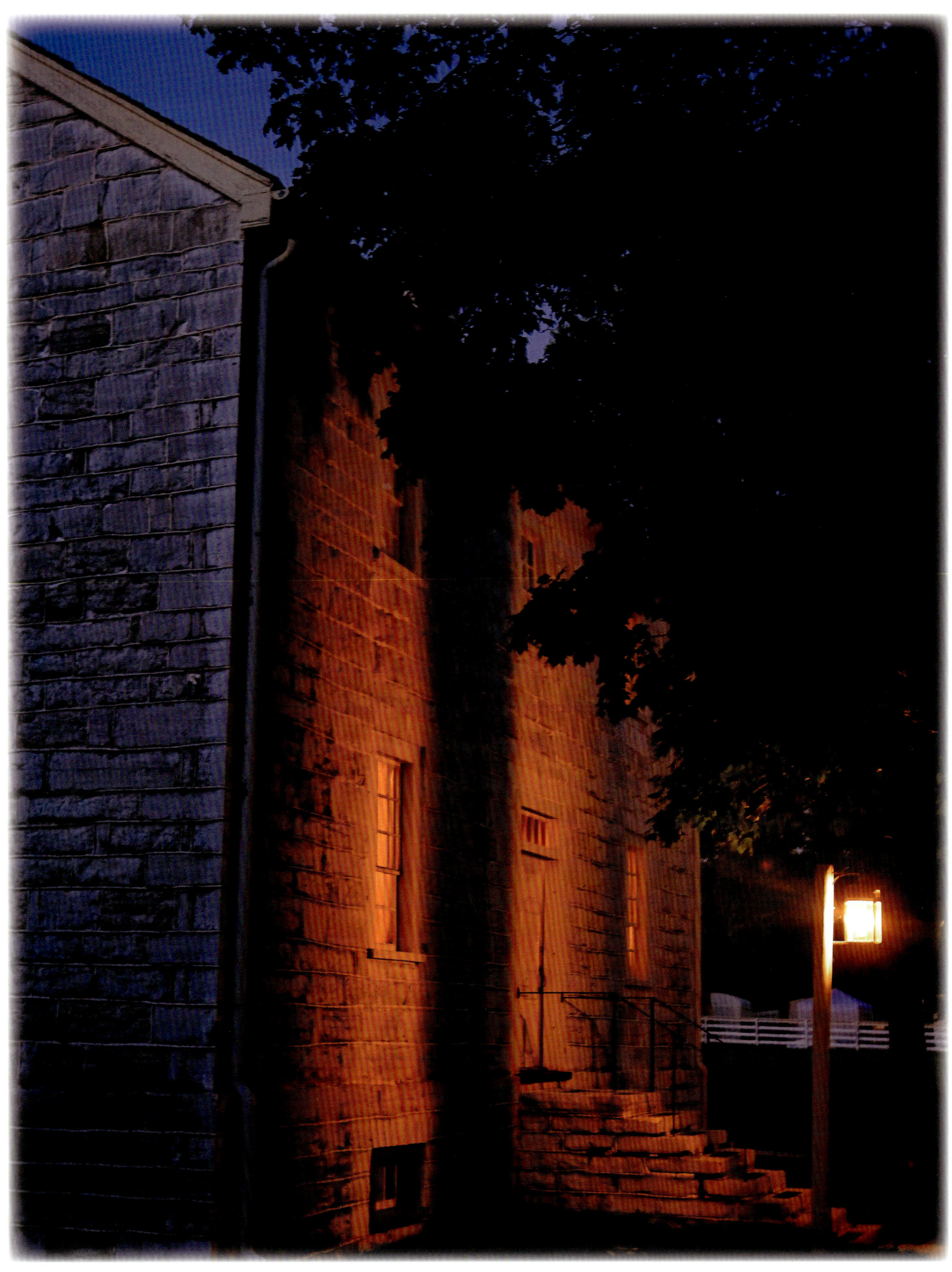

Dusk accentuates the detail in the limestone blocks and mortar of the "Old Stone Shop".

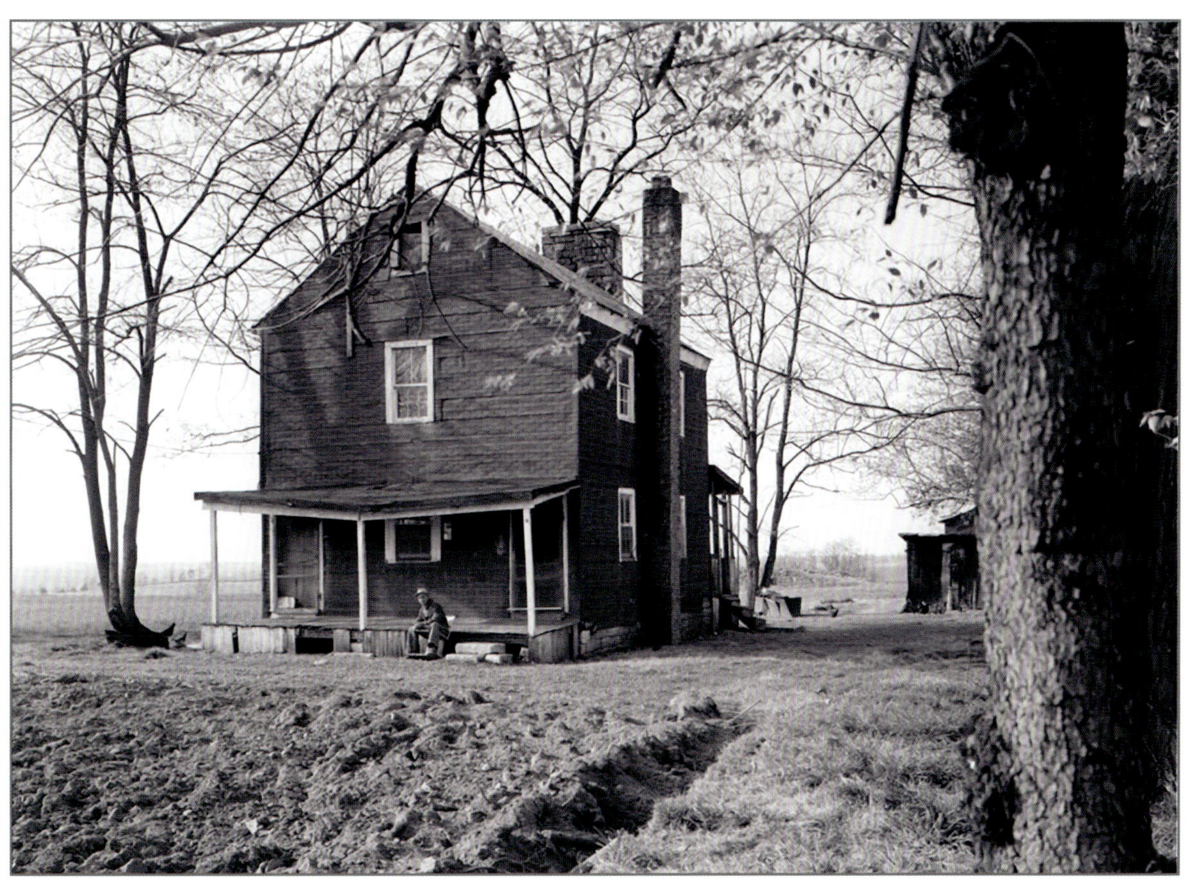

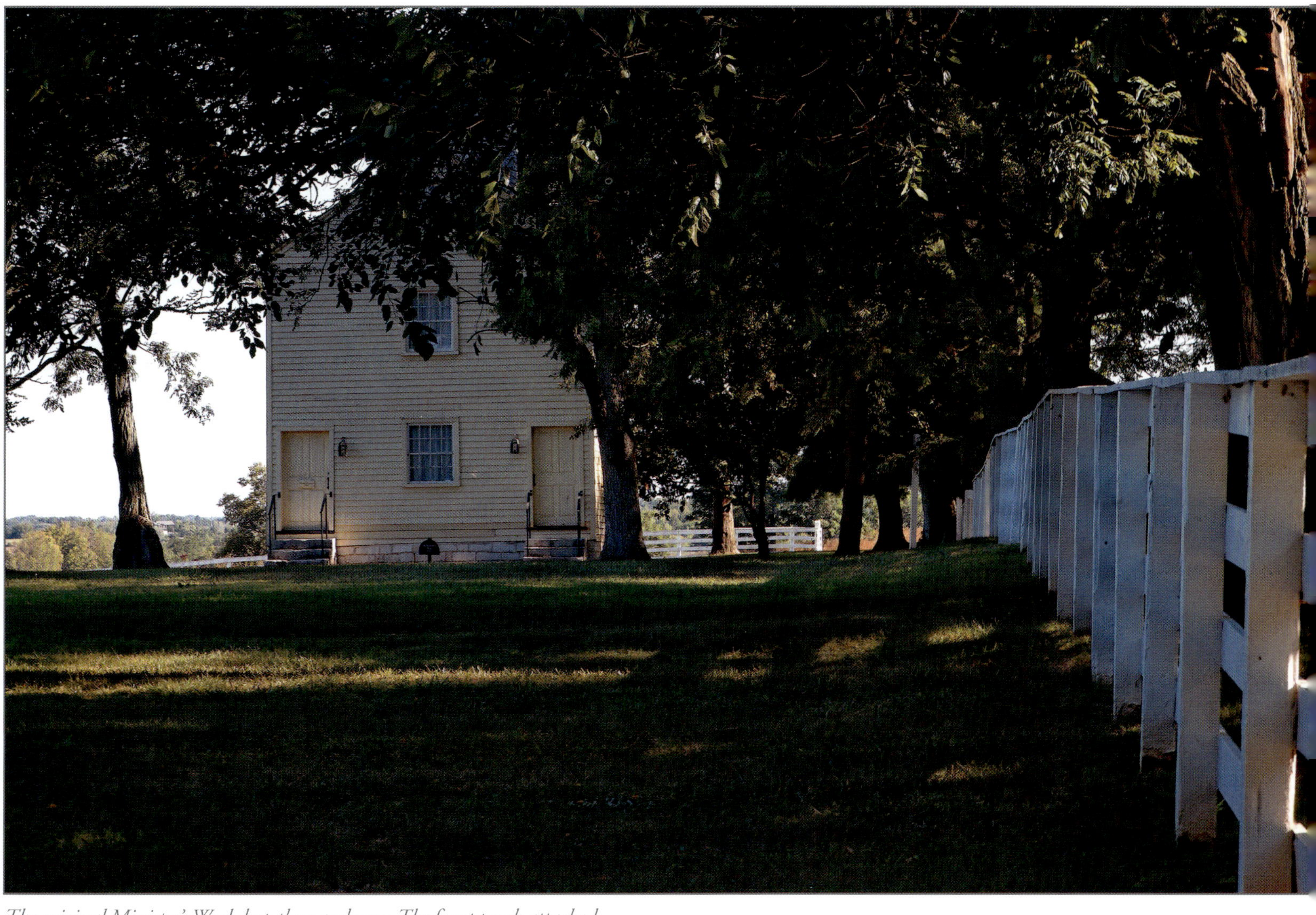

The original Ministry's Workshop then and now. The front porch attached in the archive photo was not restored as it was determined it was an addition made after 1850, the date to which the Village was restored.

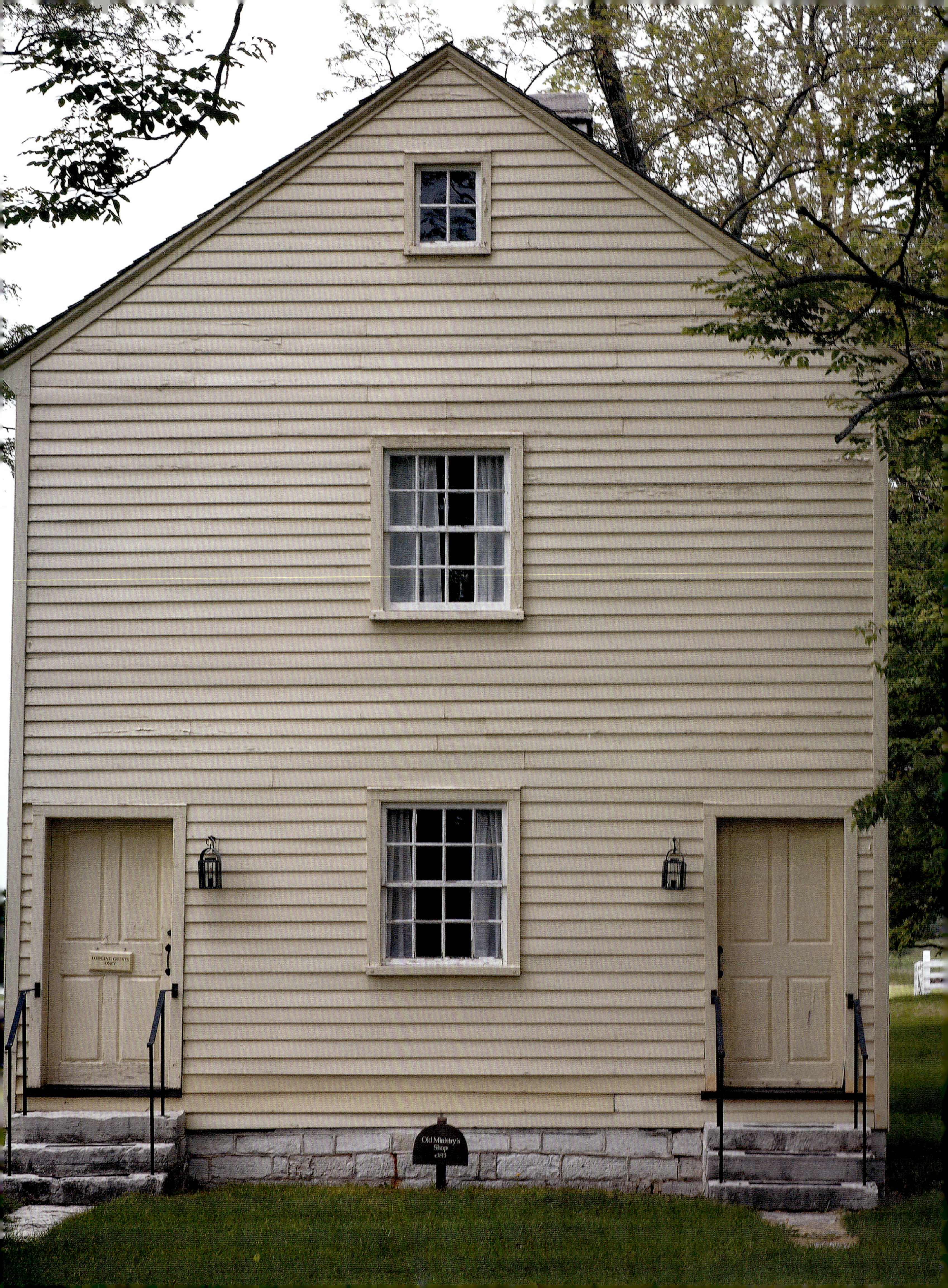
Old Ministry's
Shop
c1813

Opposite and right: Now overnight lodging for guests, the original Ministry's Workshop is one of the few remaining structures oriented on the North/South axis. As the community grew, it was later oriented East/West to take better advantage of the property as well as the sun and prevailing winds.

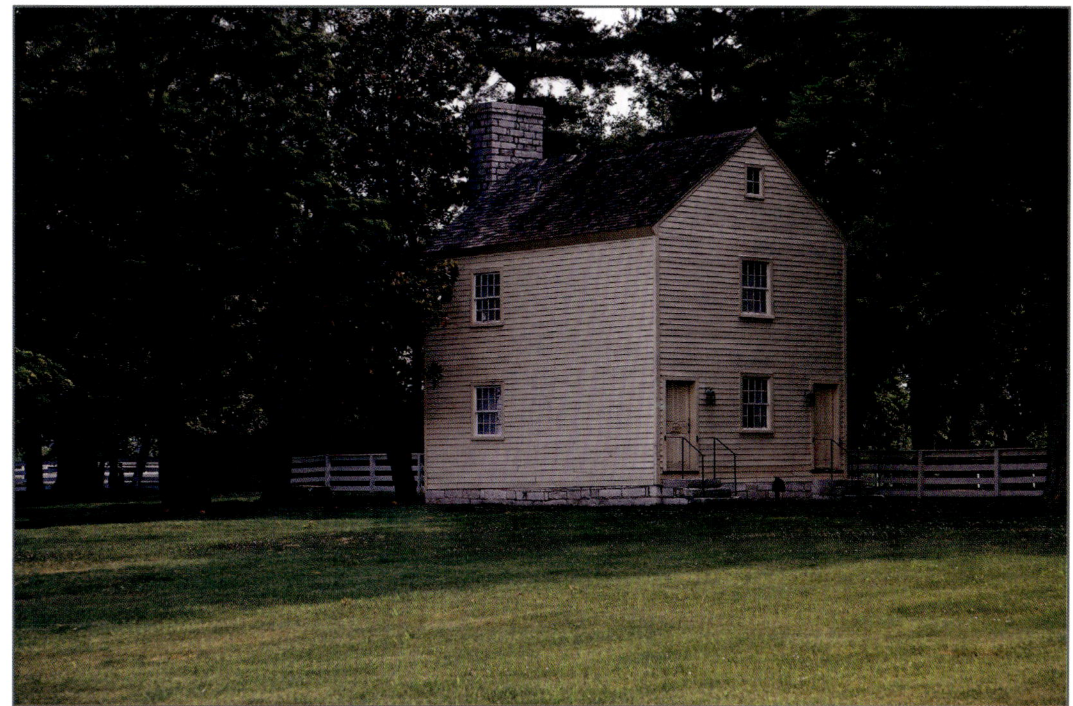

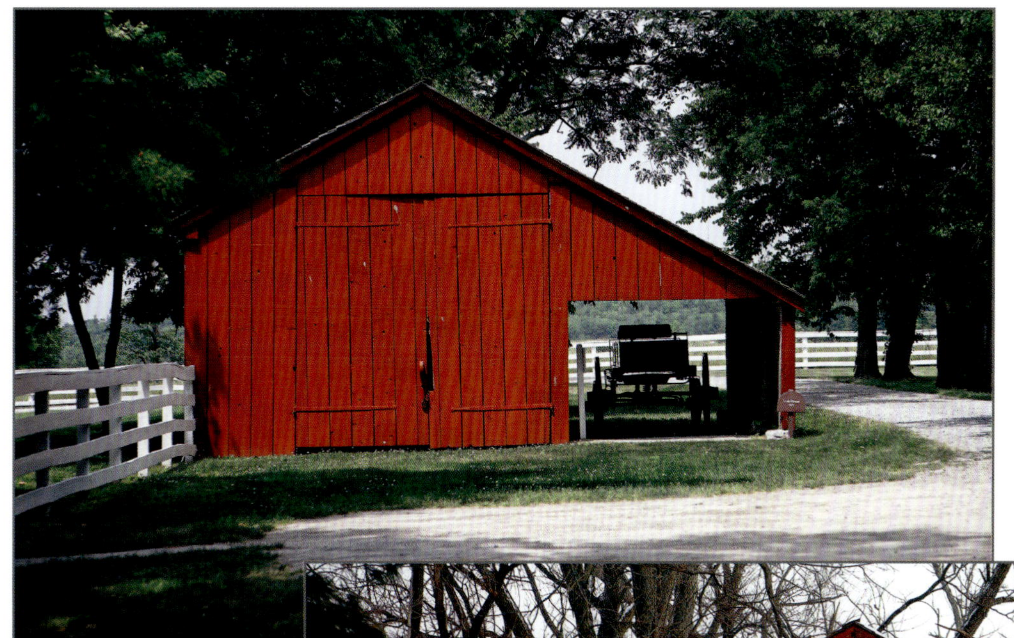

The Scale House in various seasons of the year. Many of their products were sold by weight so the Scale House played an important role in their commercial activities. Production yields of their crops were meticulously recorded in the journals using this scale.

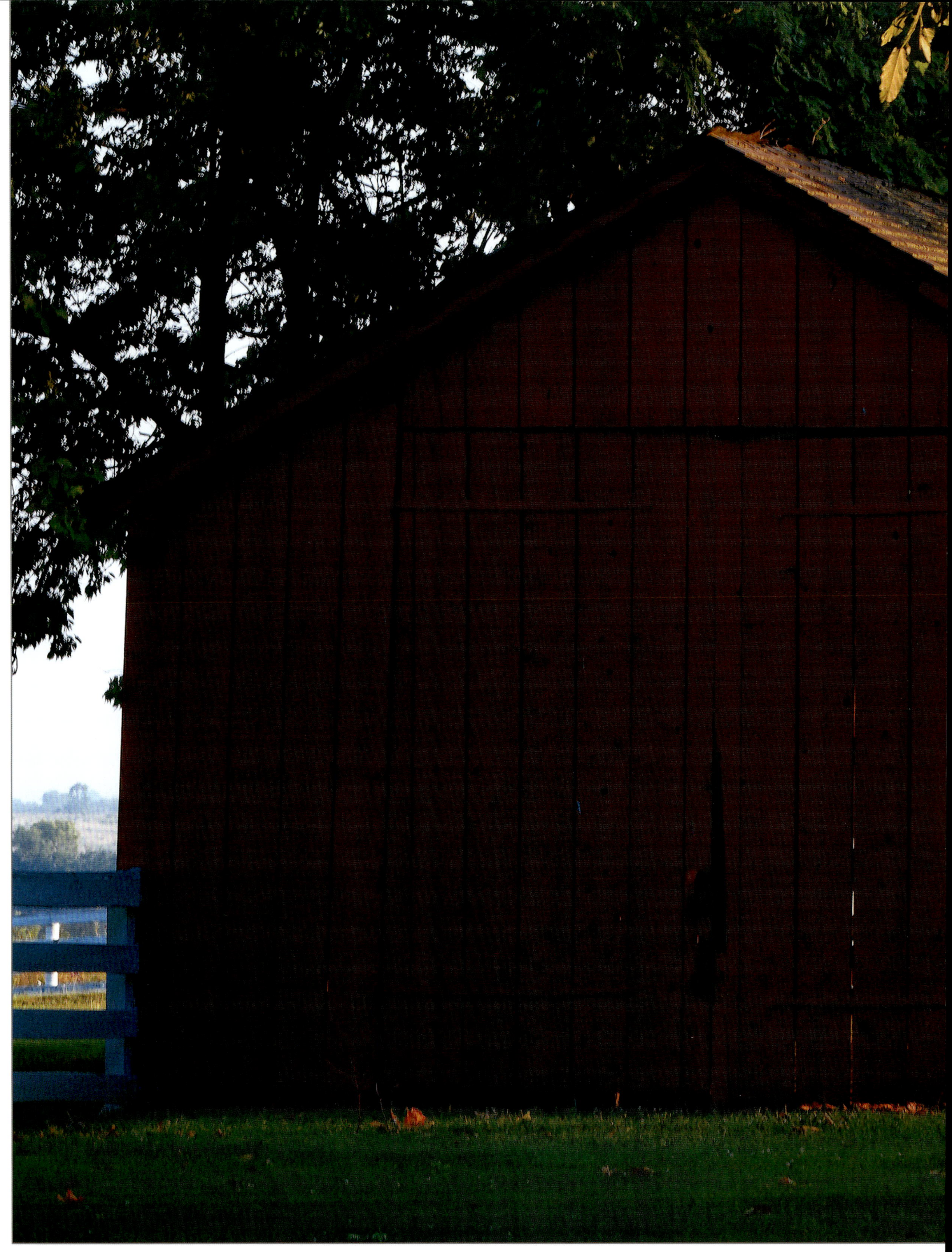

The dump wagon pictured, while not an original Shaker invention, was modified by William Pennebaker who holds several patents for those improvements.

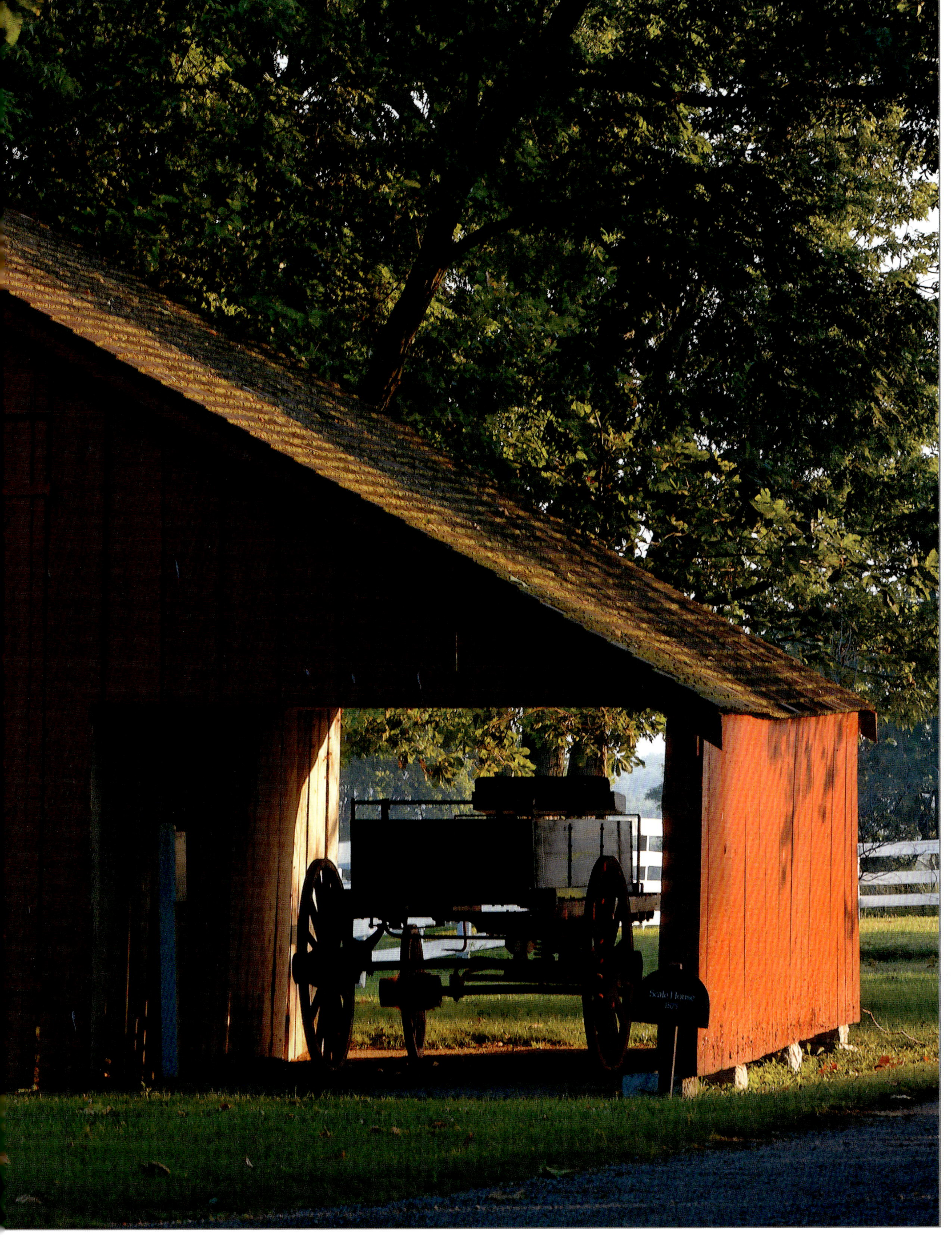
Scale House

The Farm Deacon's Building served several purposes between the time of the Shakers and the Village's restoration.

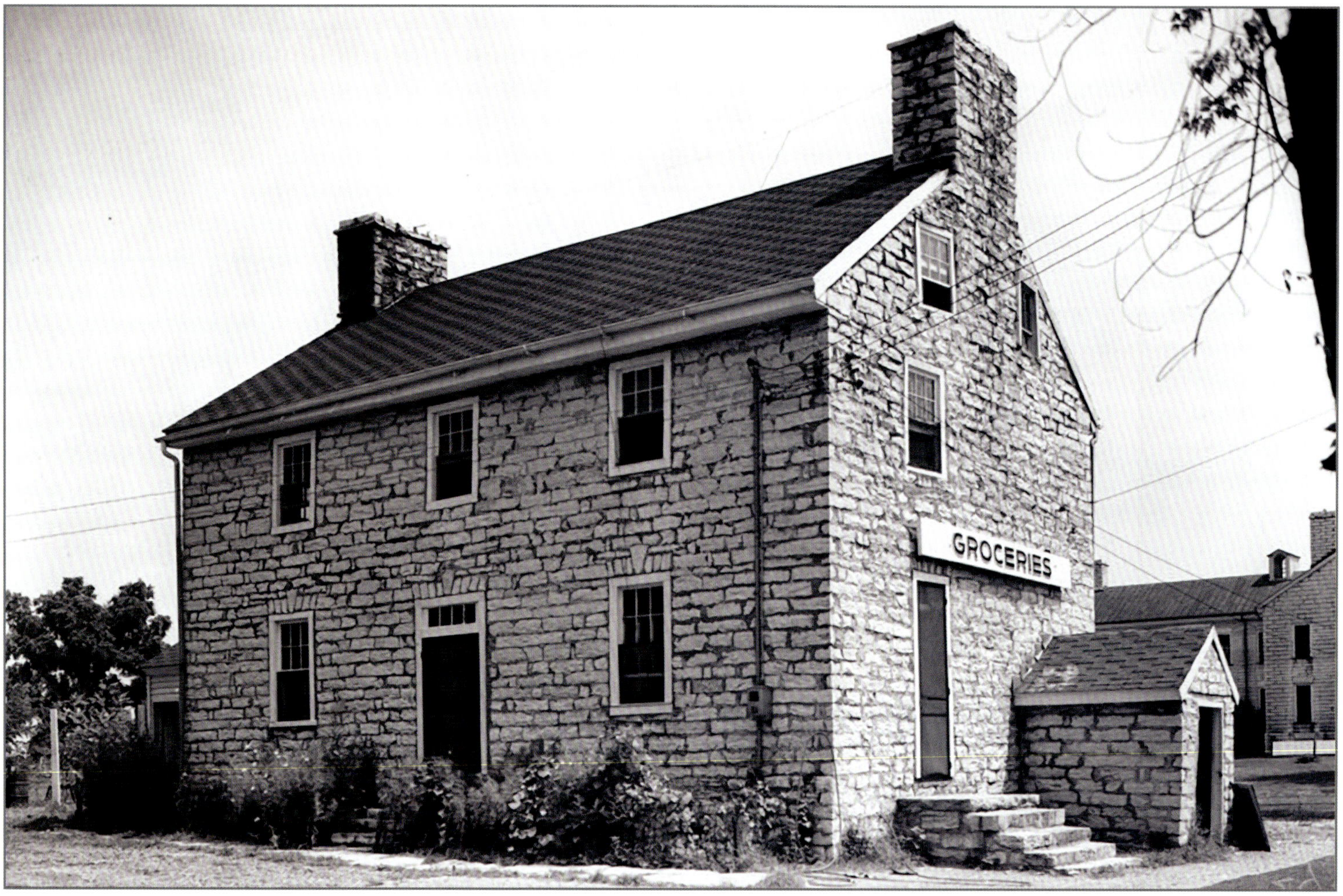

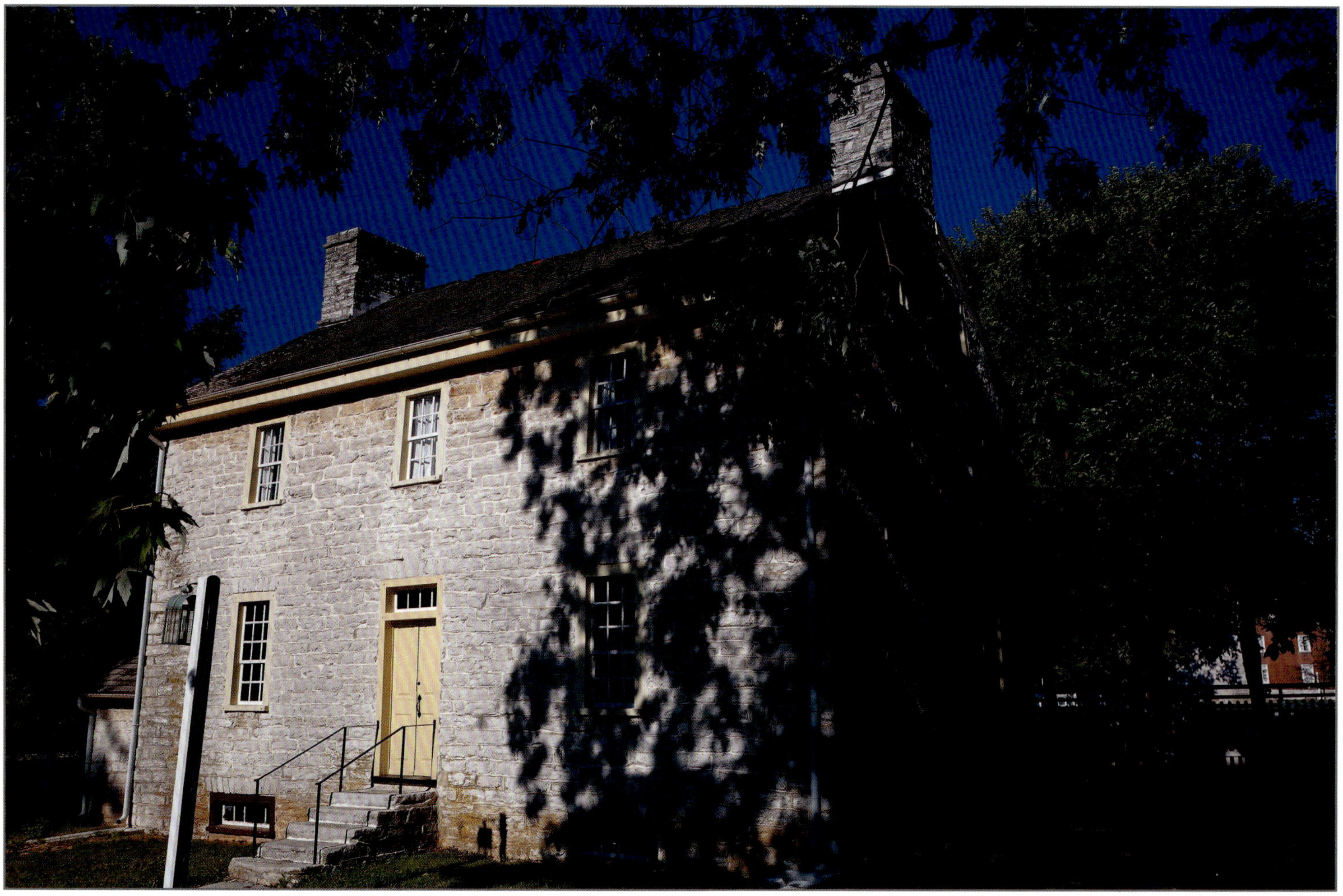

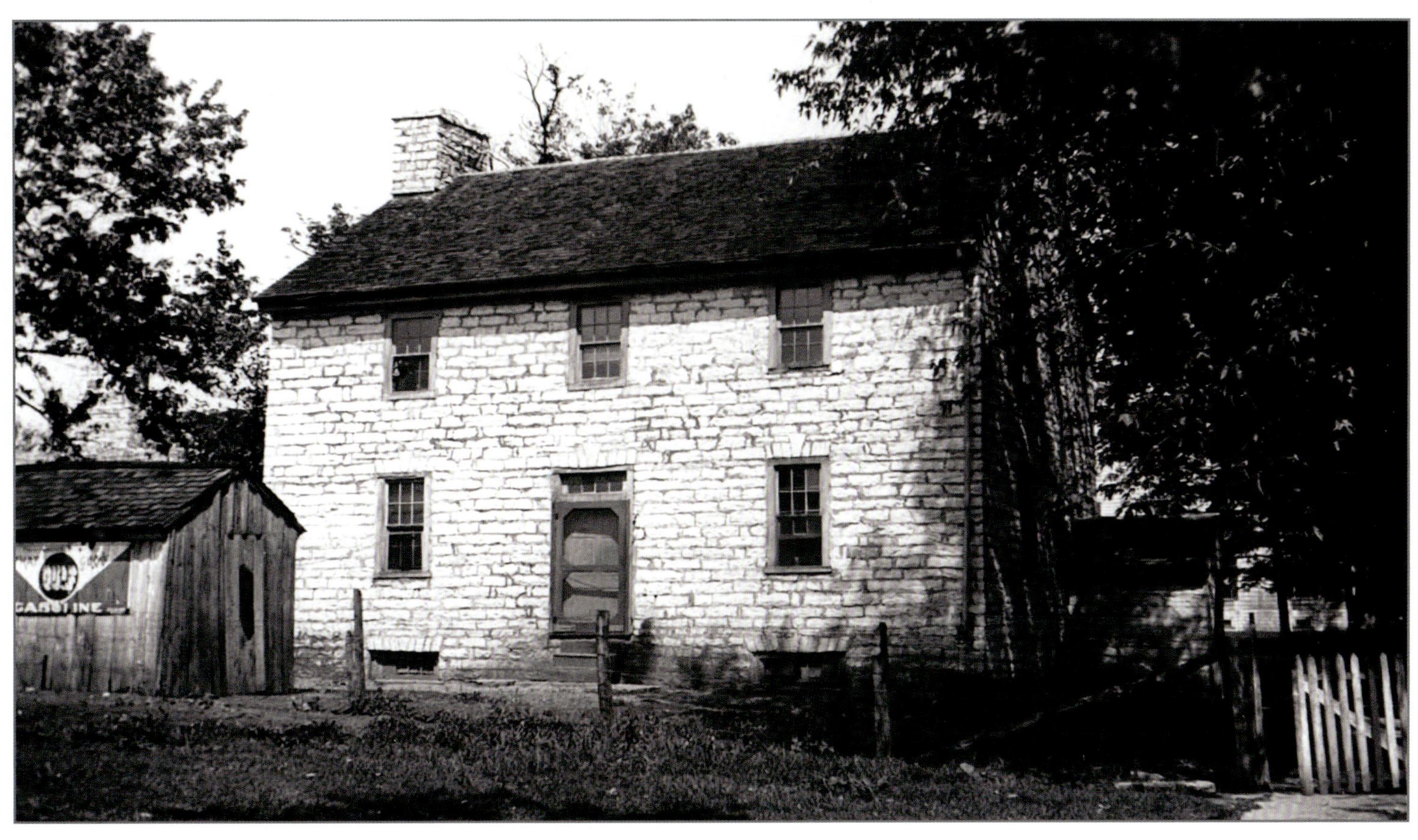

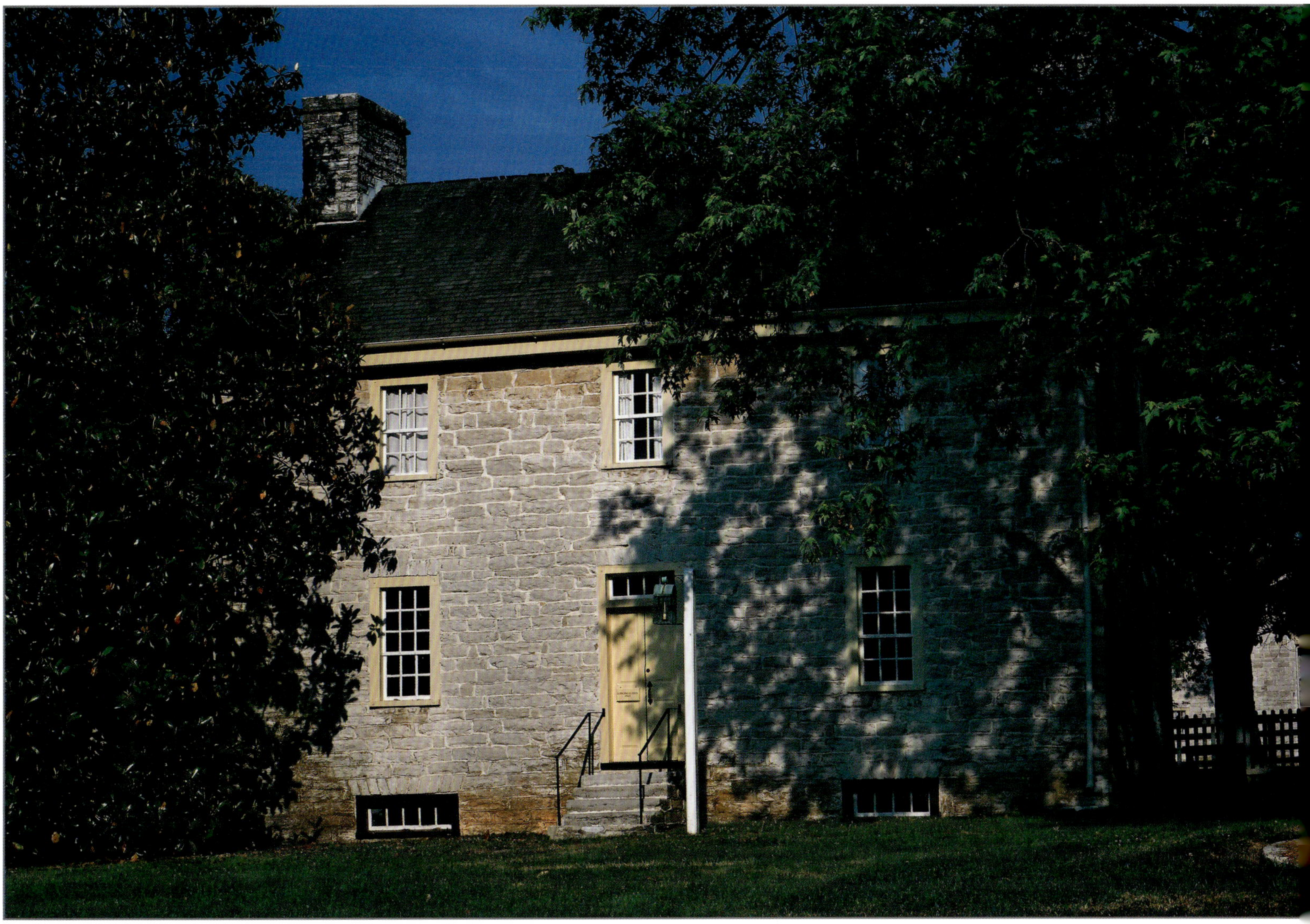

The 1809 Farm Deacon's Building, the first permanent Shaker structure constructed at Pleasant Hill, was the original Centre Family Dwelling

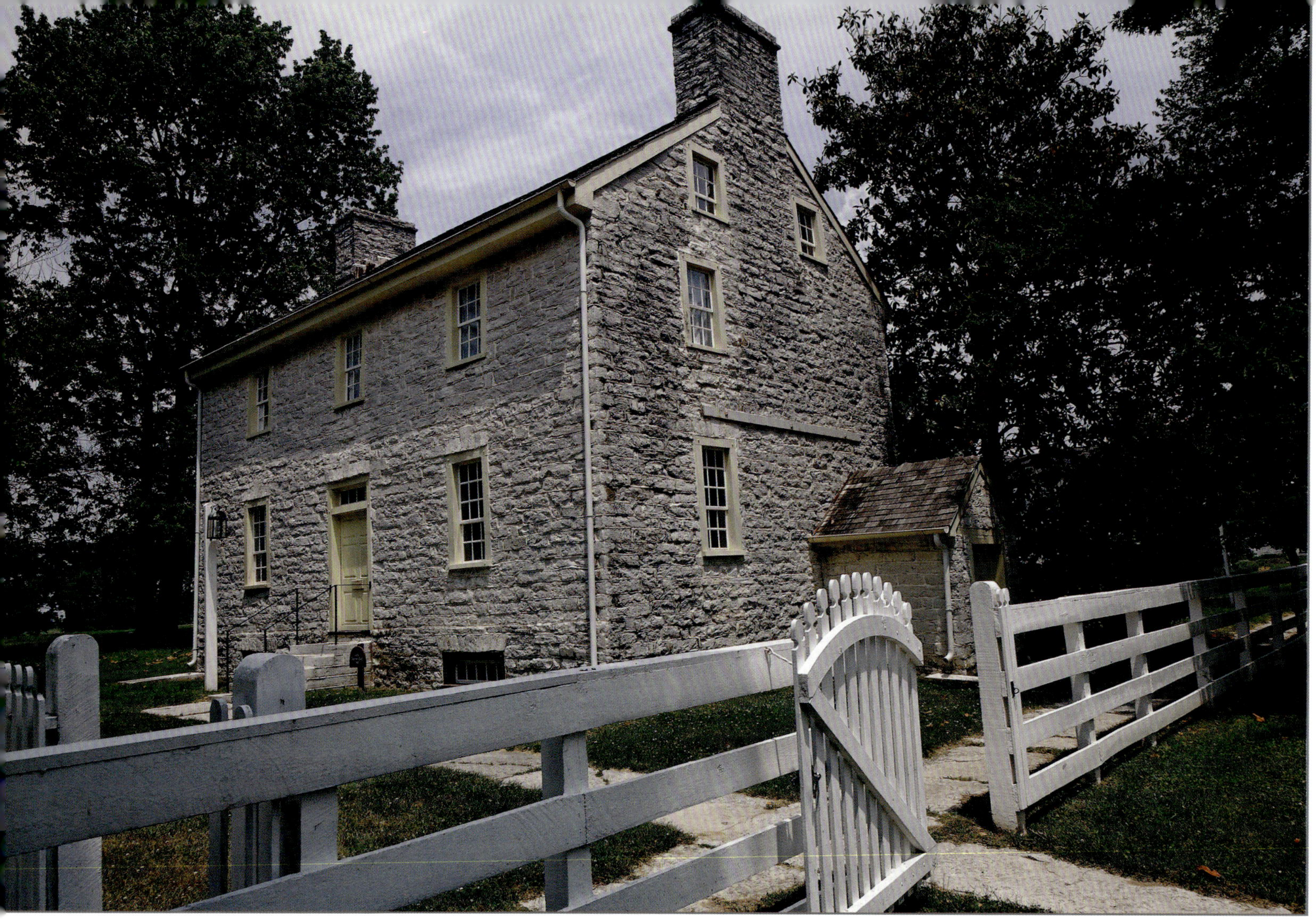

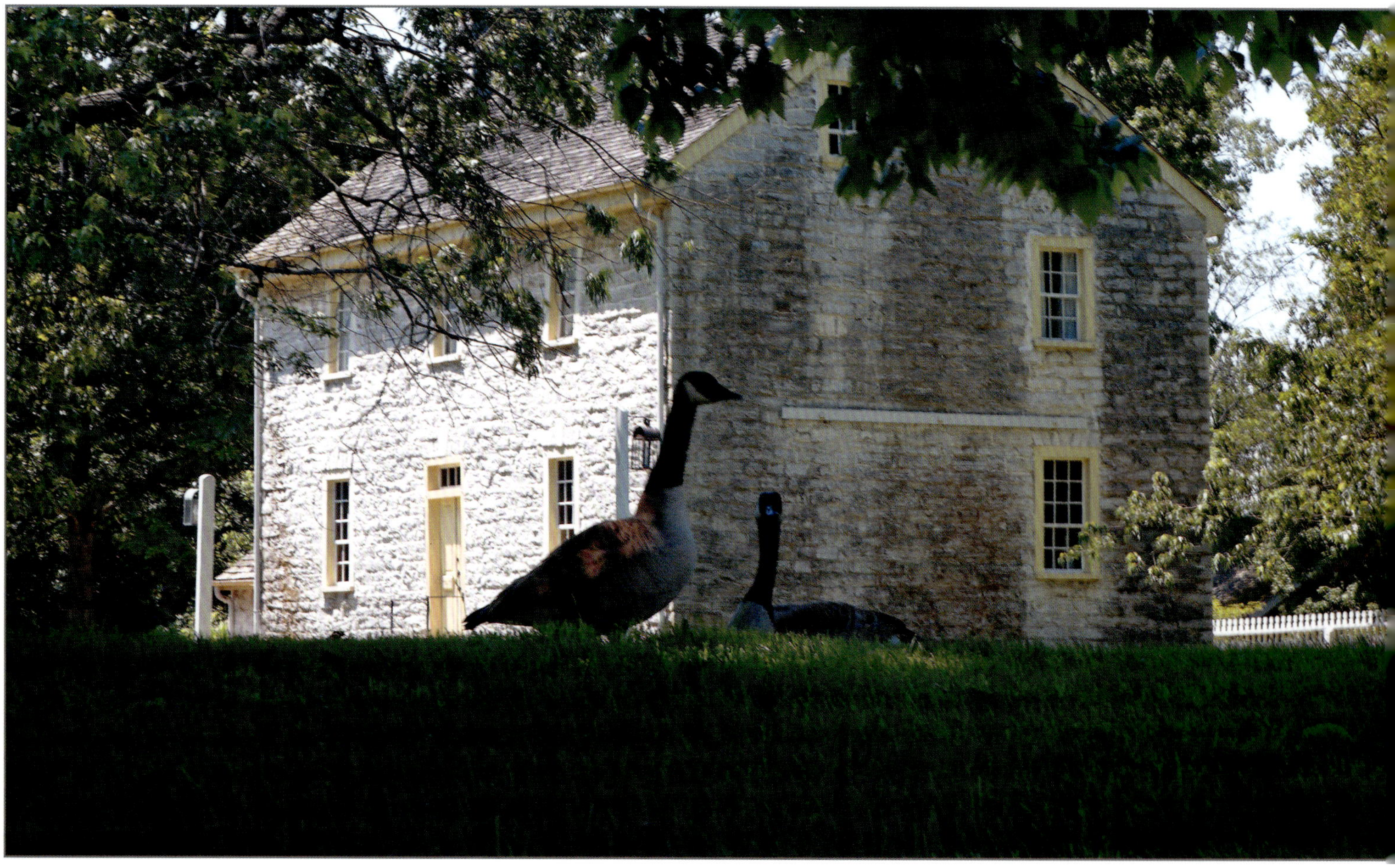

Micajah Burnett, master designer of Pleasant Hill, help frame the Farm Deacon's Building as a 17 year-old. Many years later he took up residency in the building until his death at the age of 87.

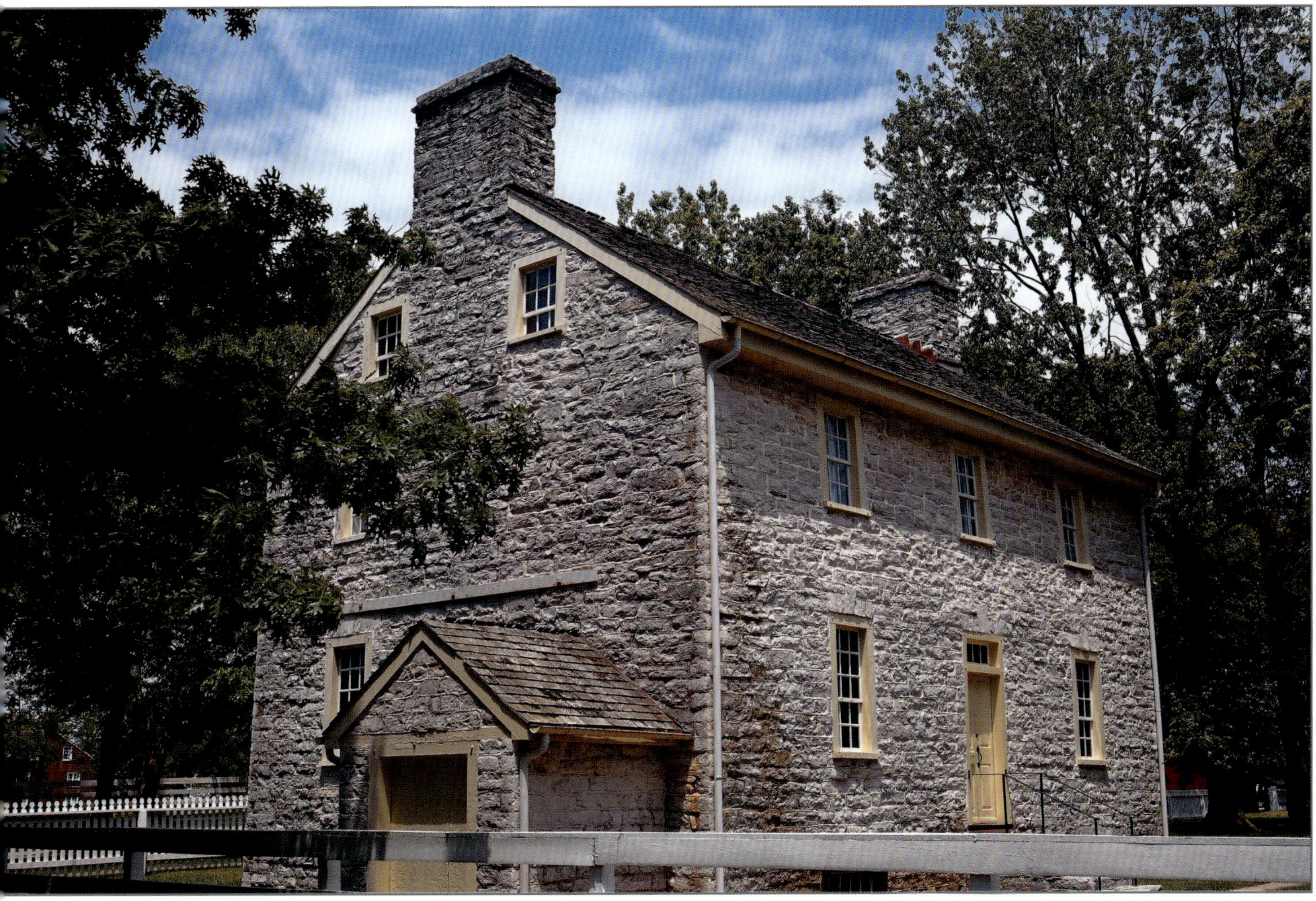

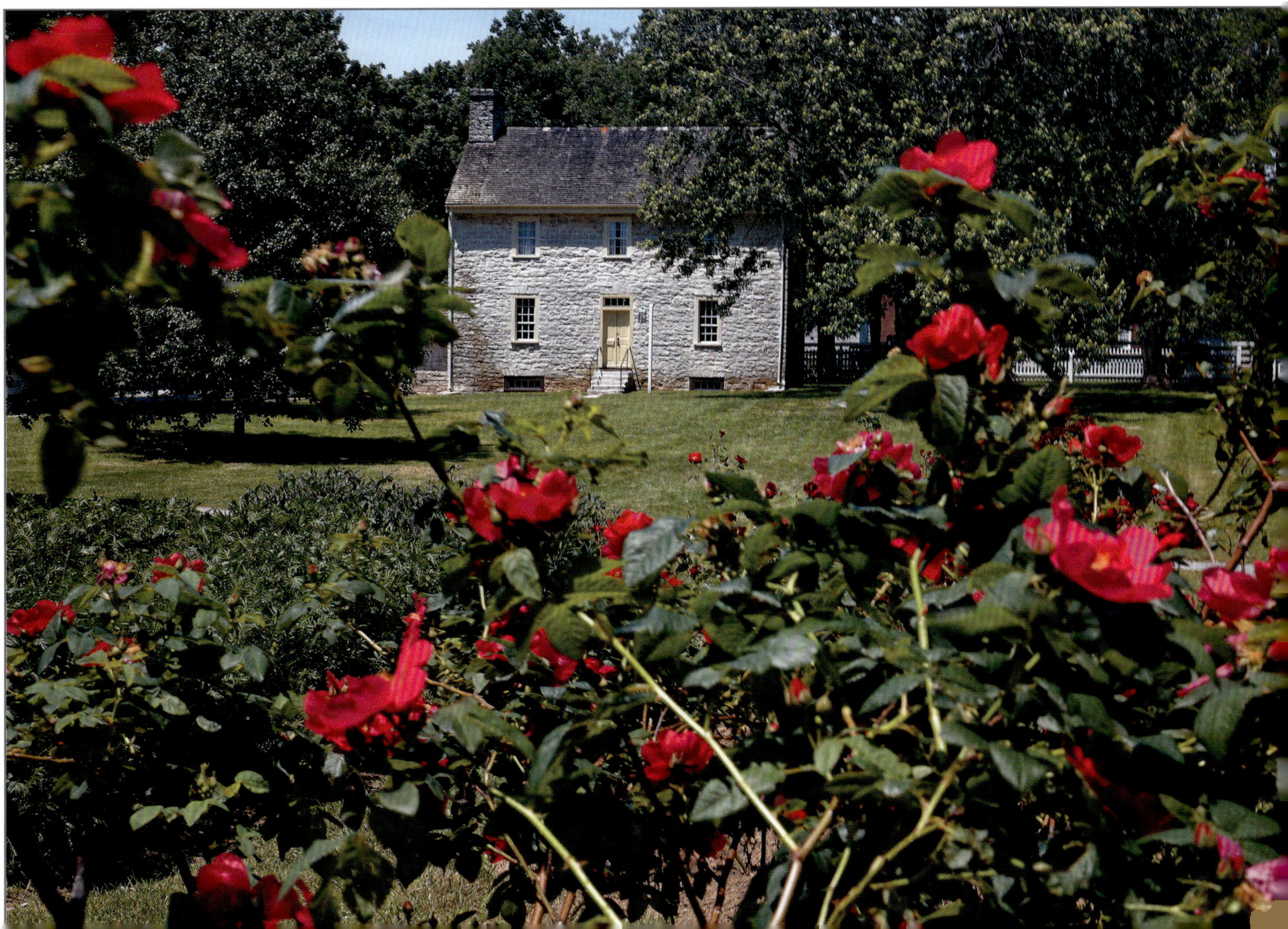

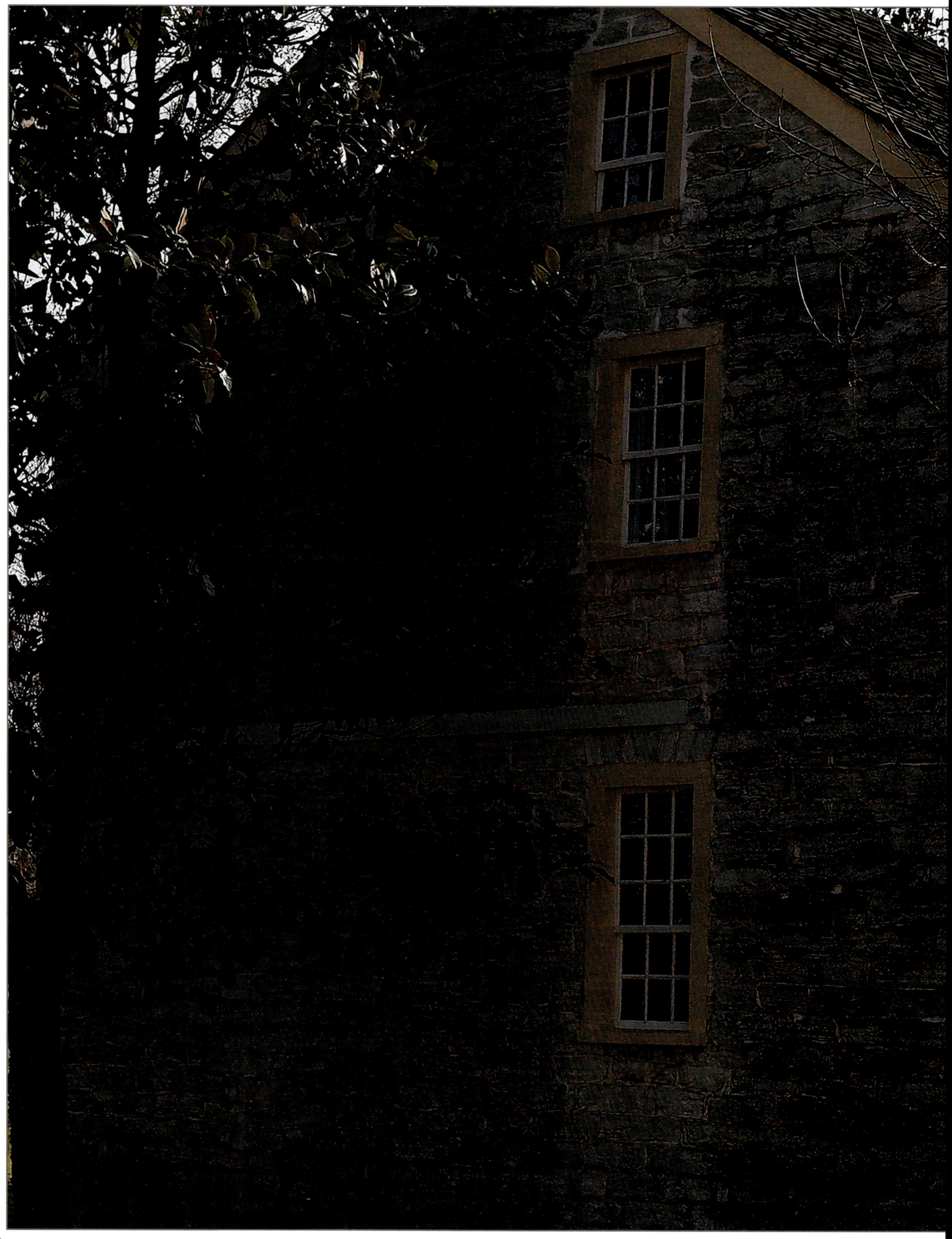

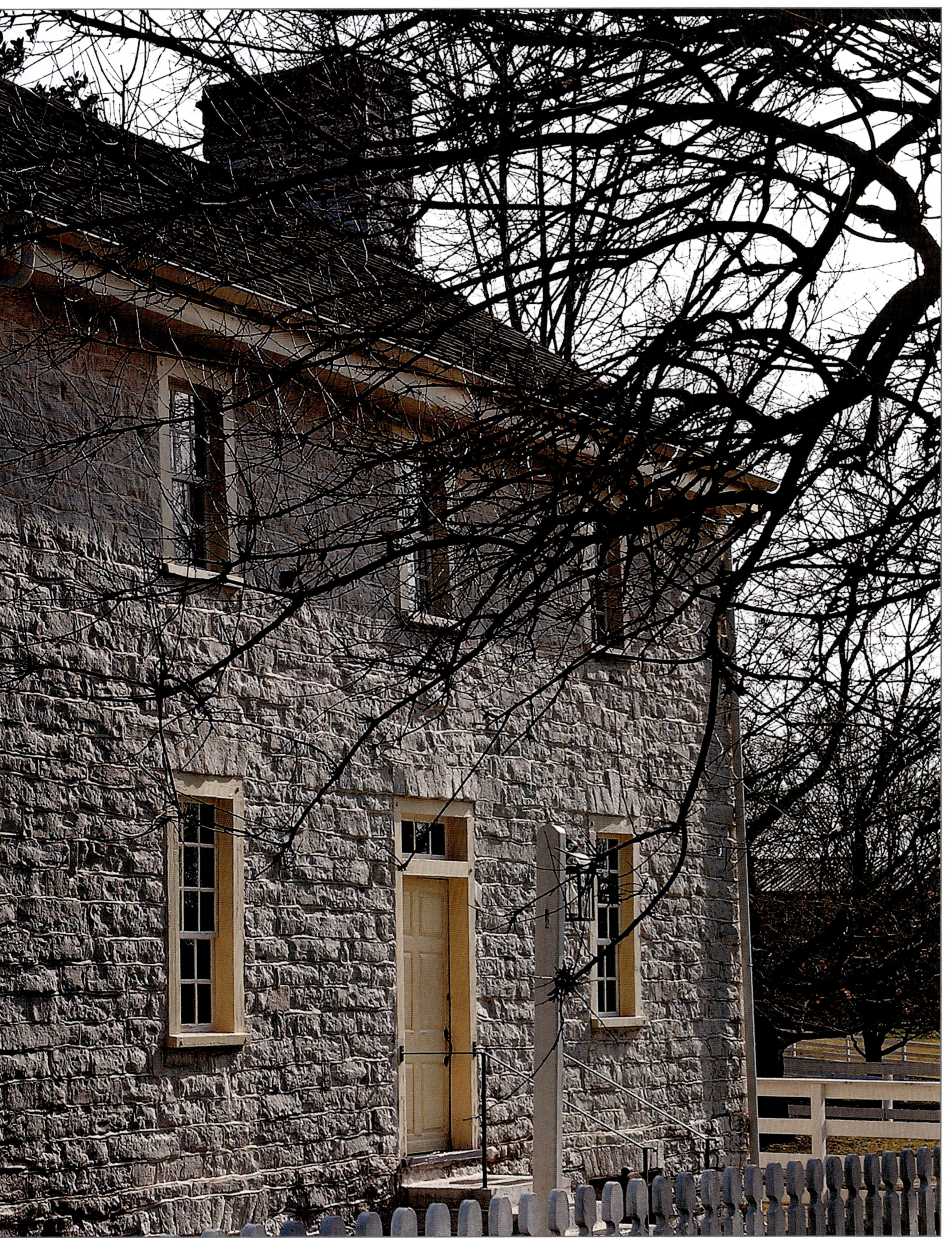

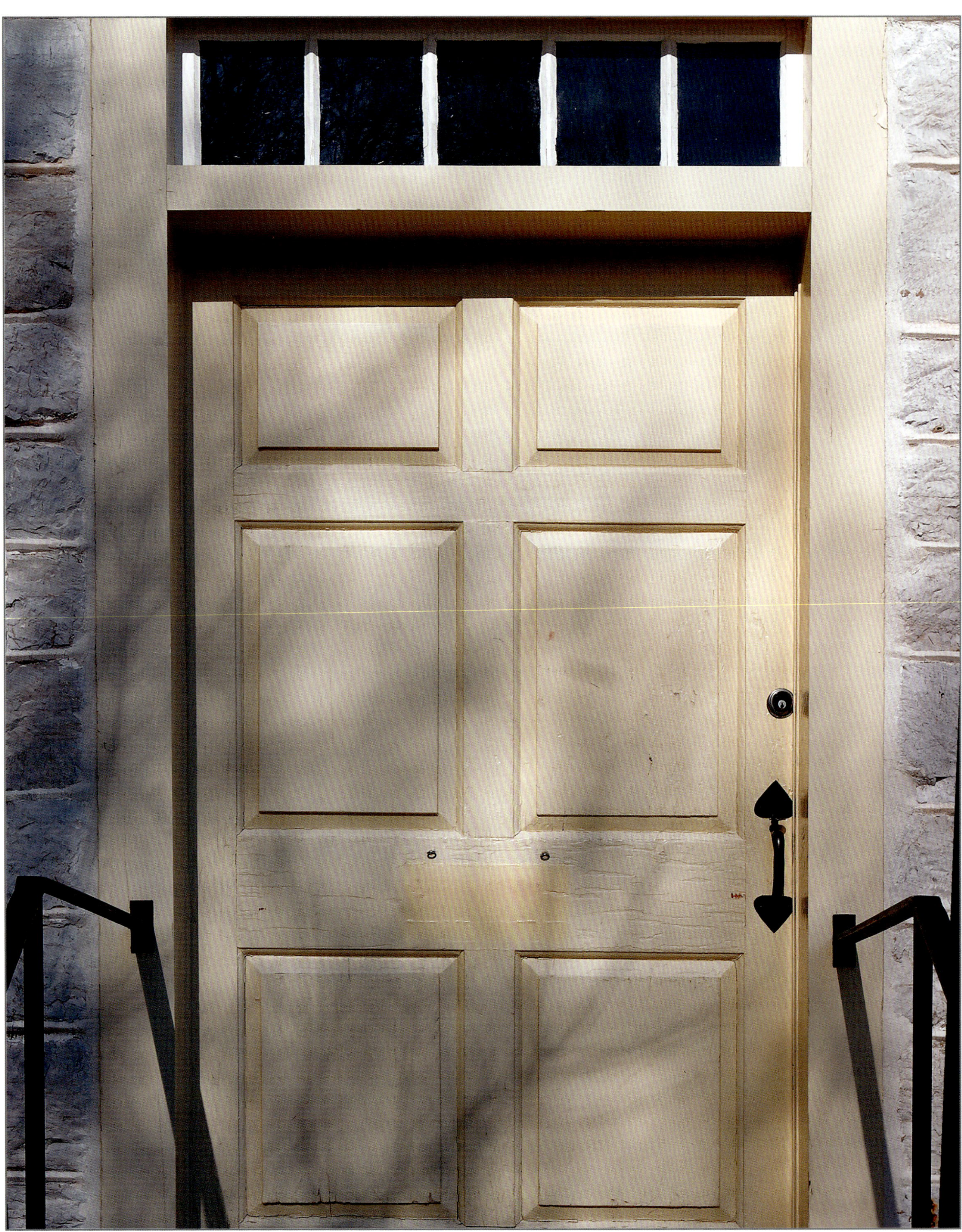

Previous spread: The tones and textures of this building make it one of the most interesting and beautiful in the Village. The Shakers felt it had been constructed "rather hastily" and were not satisfied with its appearance. Their mastery of the skills of quarrying and laying the limestone blocks grew over the years culminating with the 1824 Centre Family Dwelling which now stands as the focal point of the Village.

Above: While the Farm Deacon's Building does not have the classic twin doors, the front door was used by the men while the back door, leading to the detached kitchen, was used by the women.

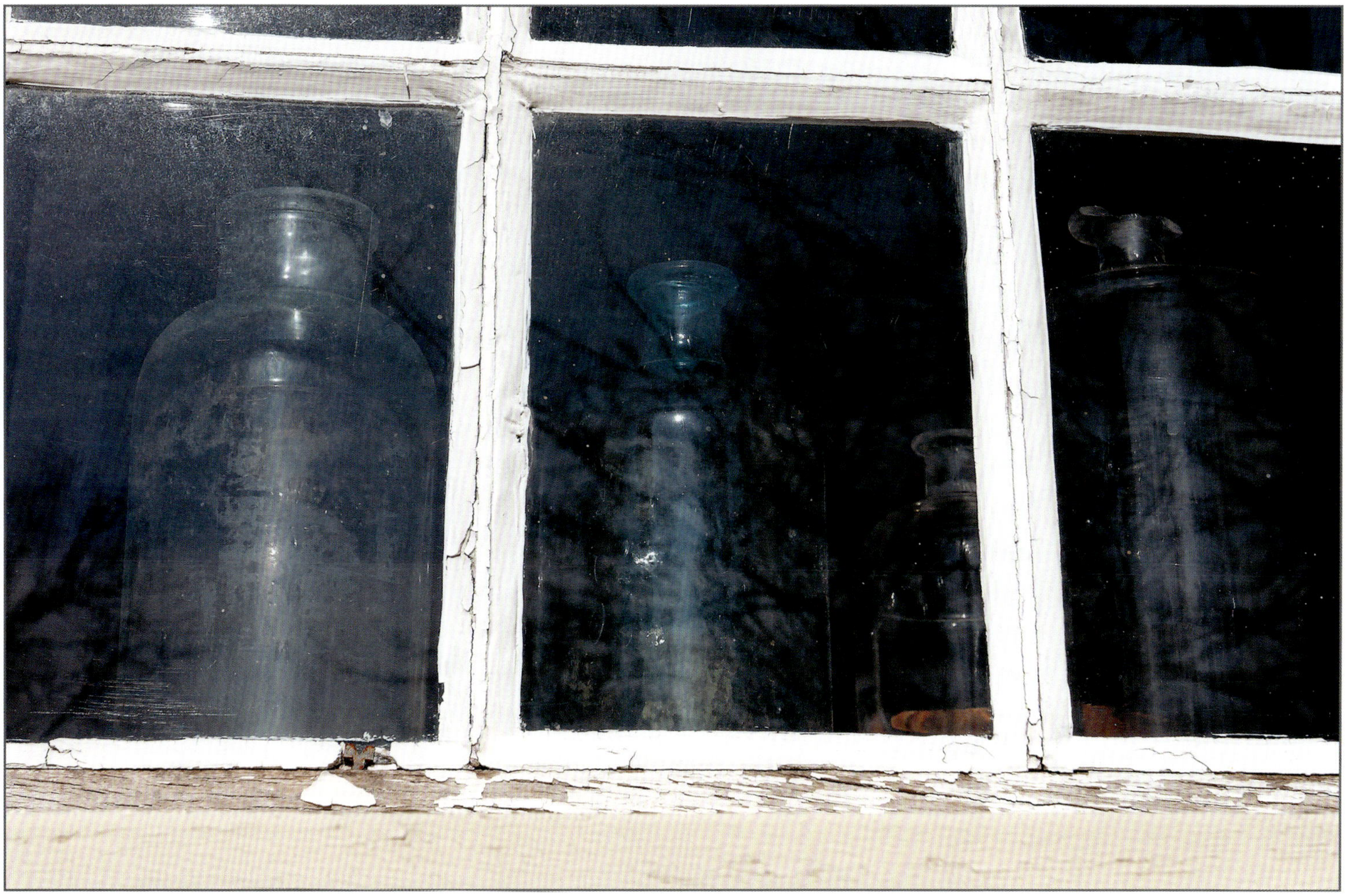

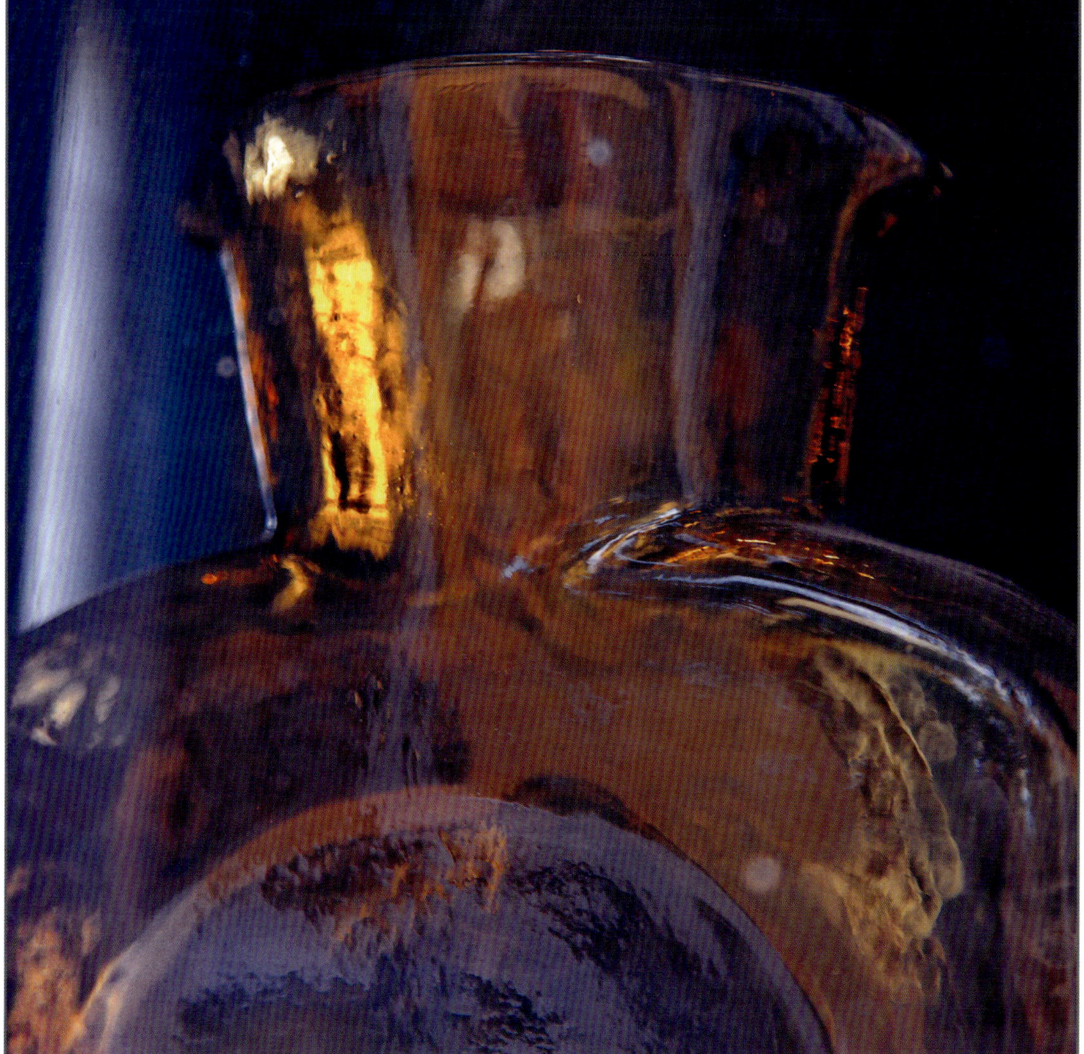

Many of the herbs and spices grown in the gardens were used for medicinal purposes and stored in glass jars.

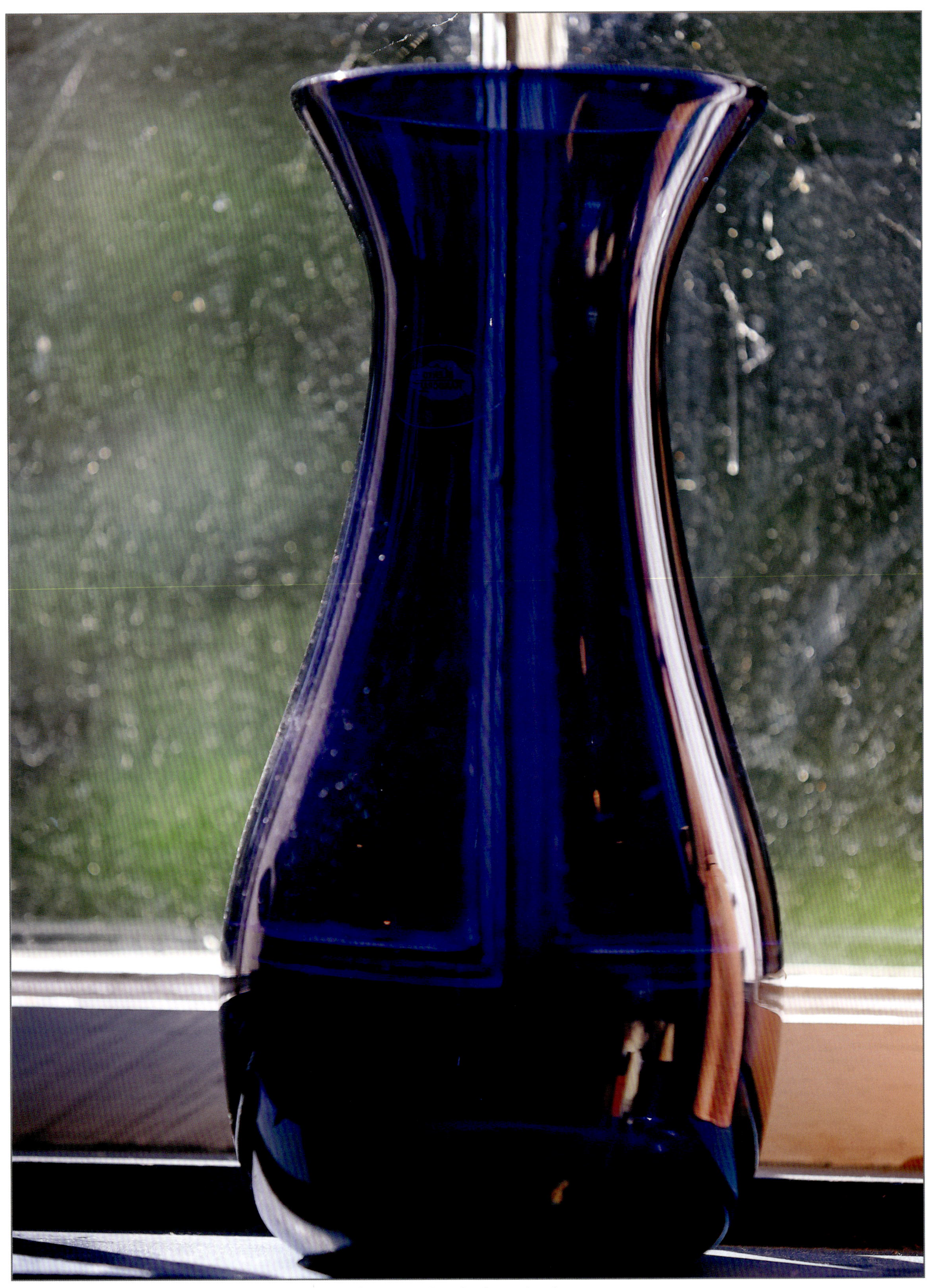

Indigo, one of the Shaker's favorite colors was used in applications such as dye for wool and paint.

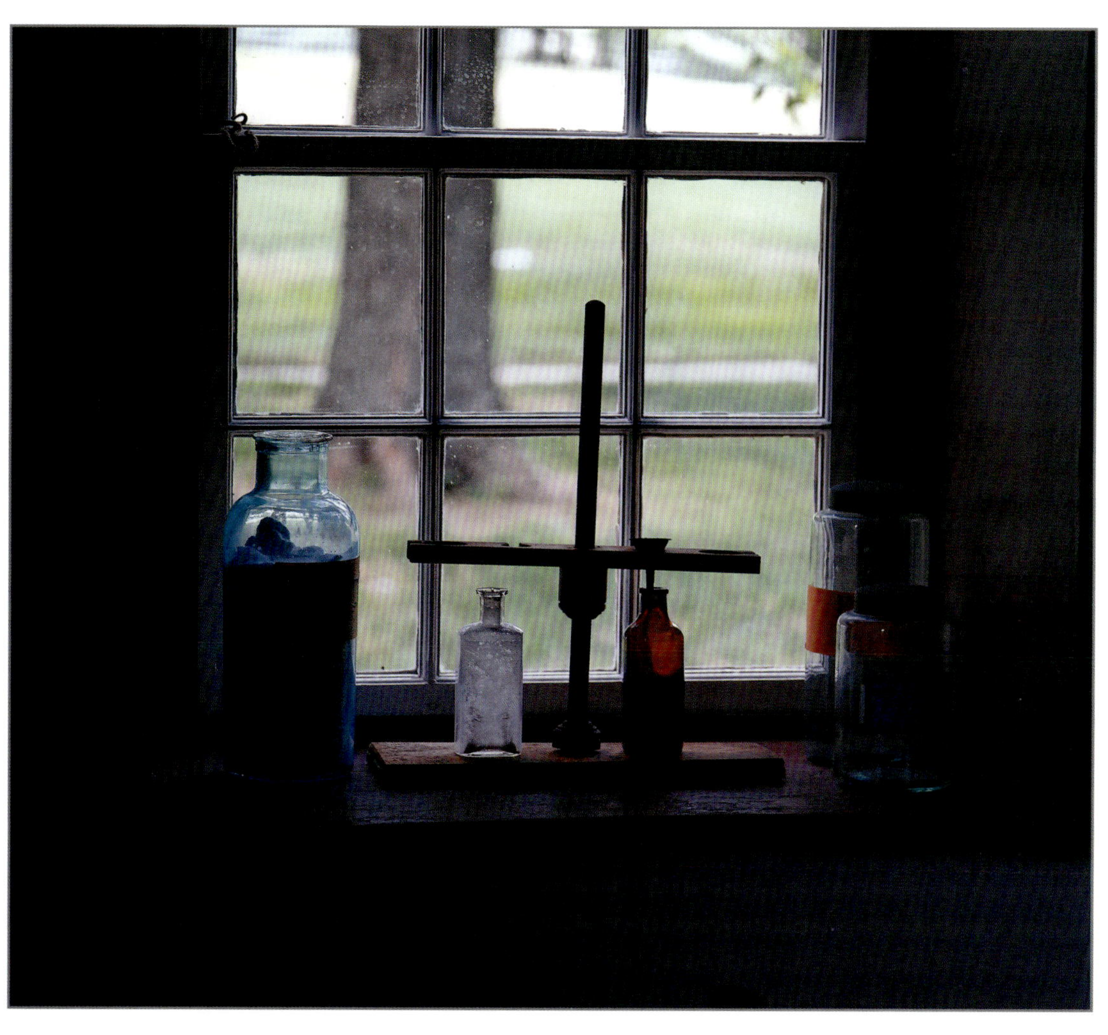

The Shakers were known as the first pharmacists and hold several patents for their medicinal remedies. The "Outside World" sought out the Shaker's remedies as life expectancy for a Shaker was nearly double that of the general population and felt their remedies were at least part of the reason why.

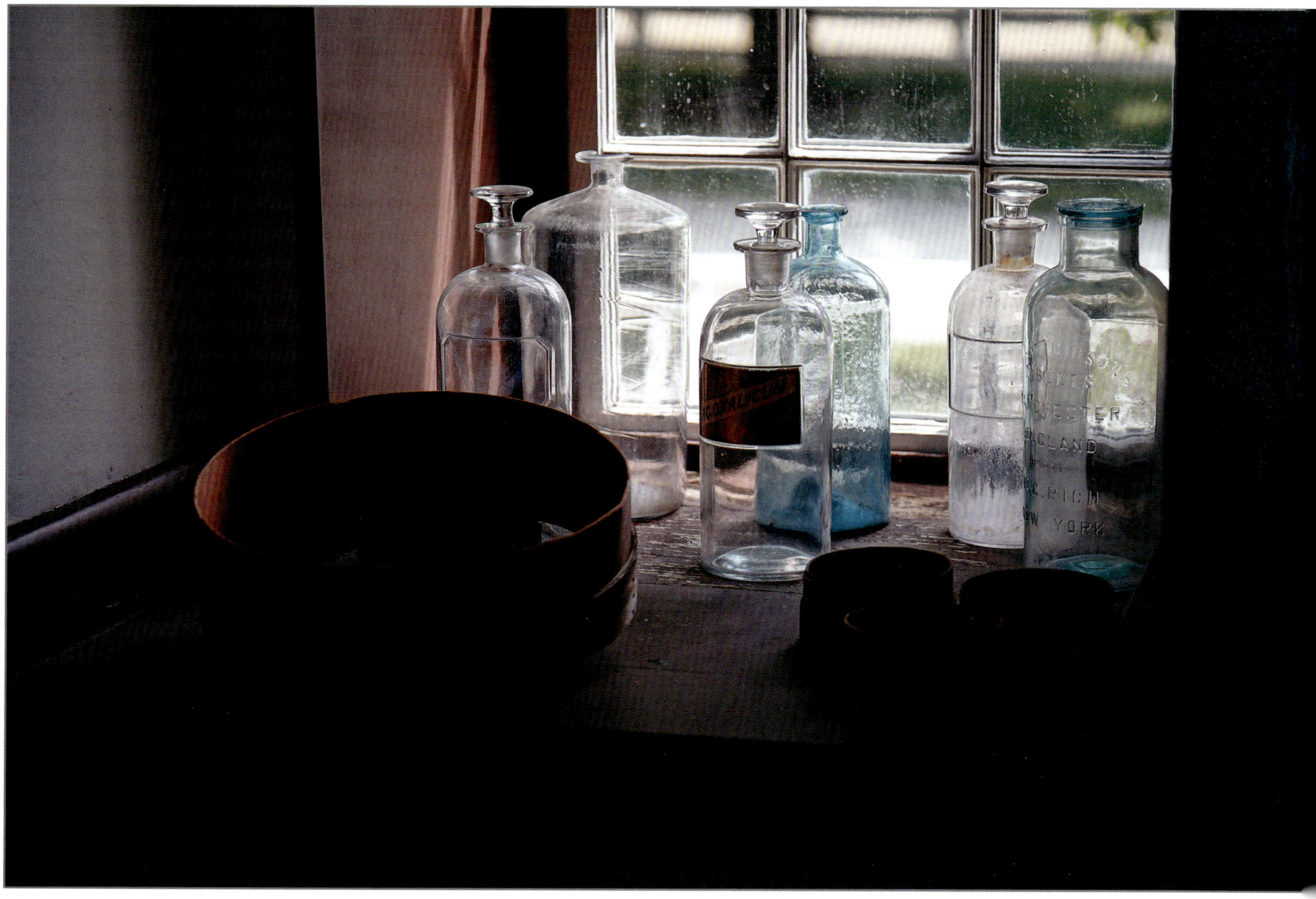

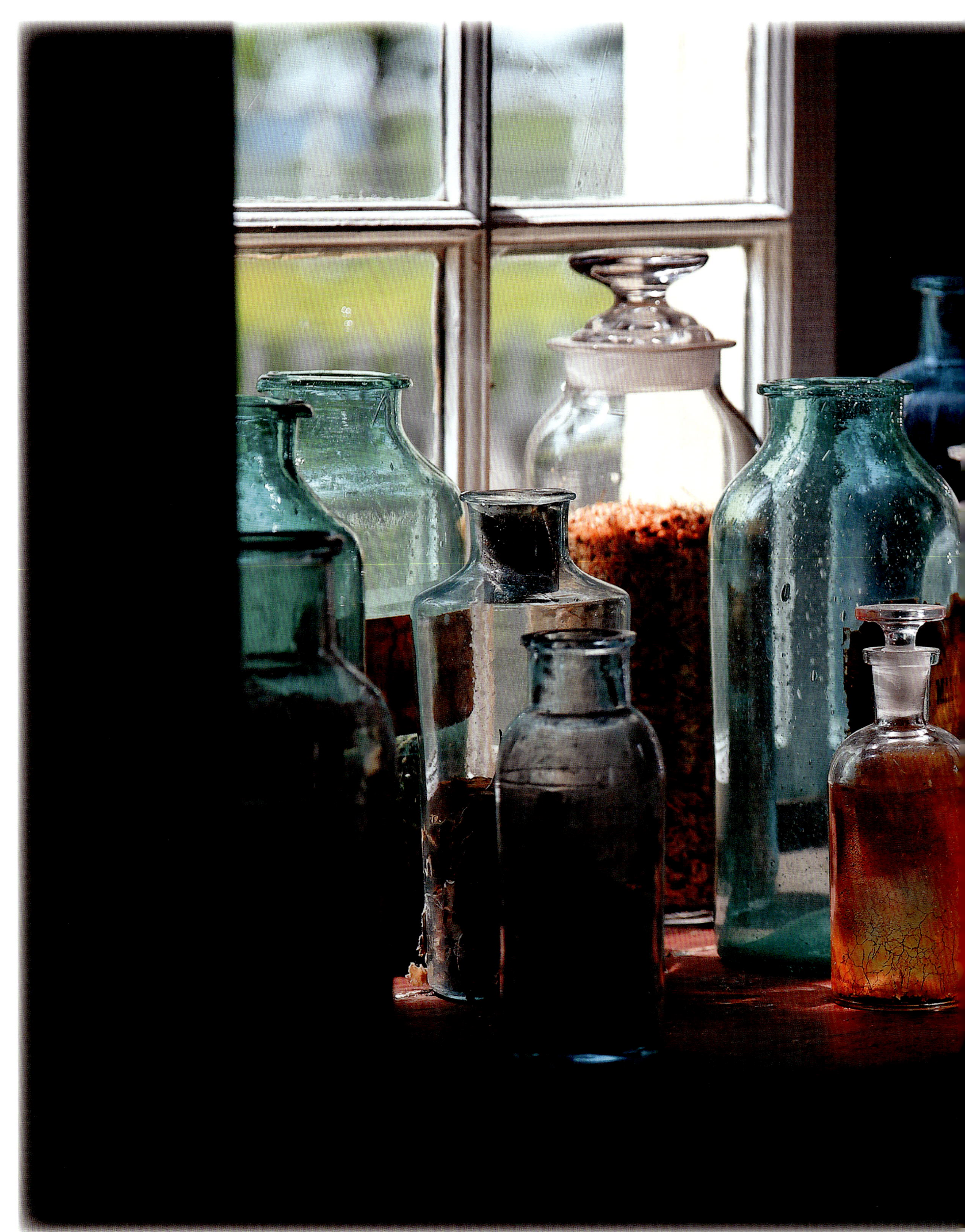

Many of these jars are Shaker originals and, upon closer examination, the original labels can still be seen.

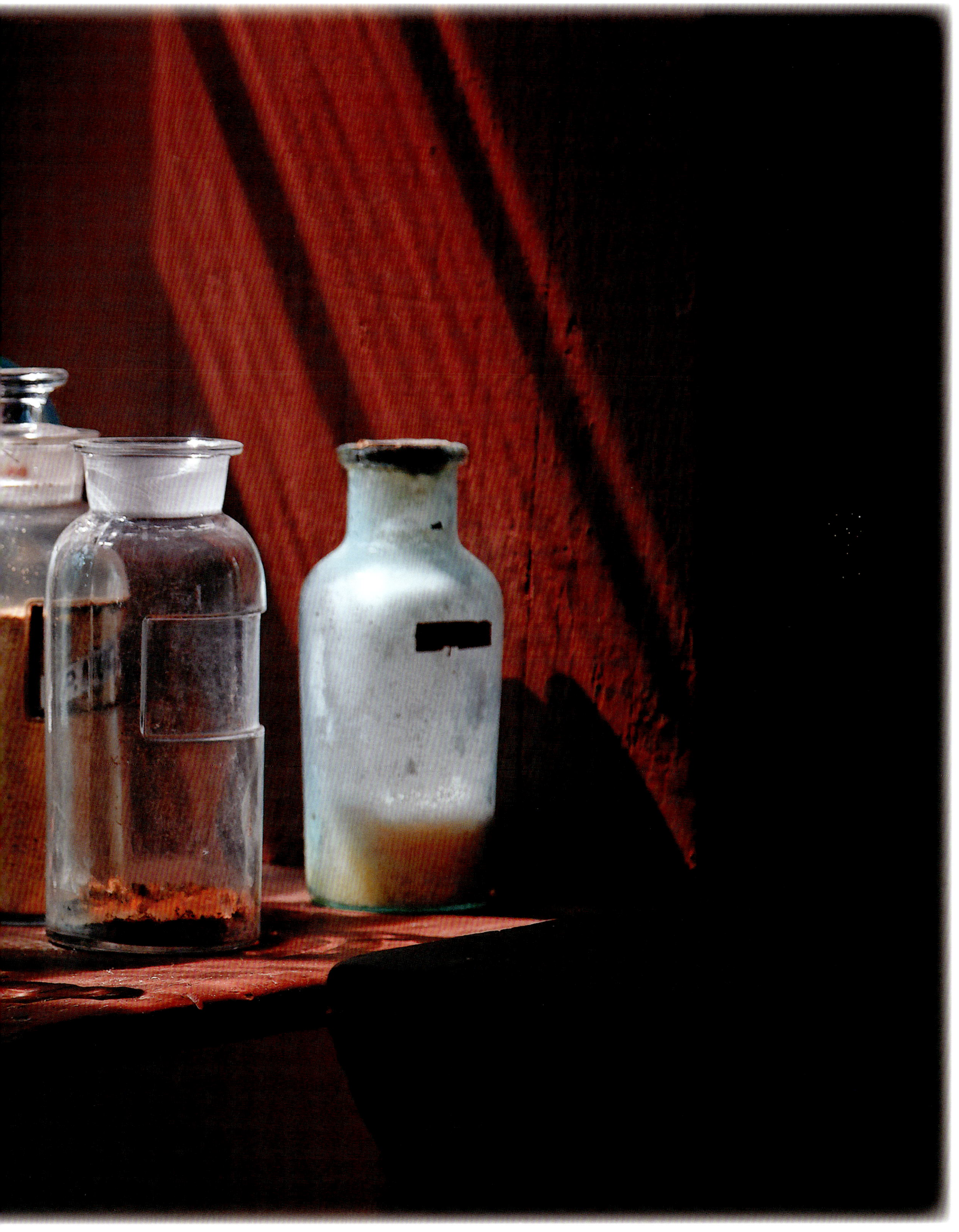

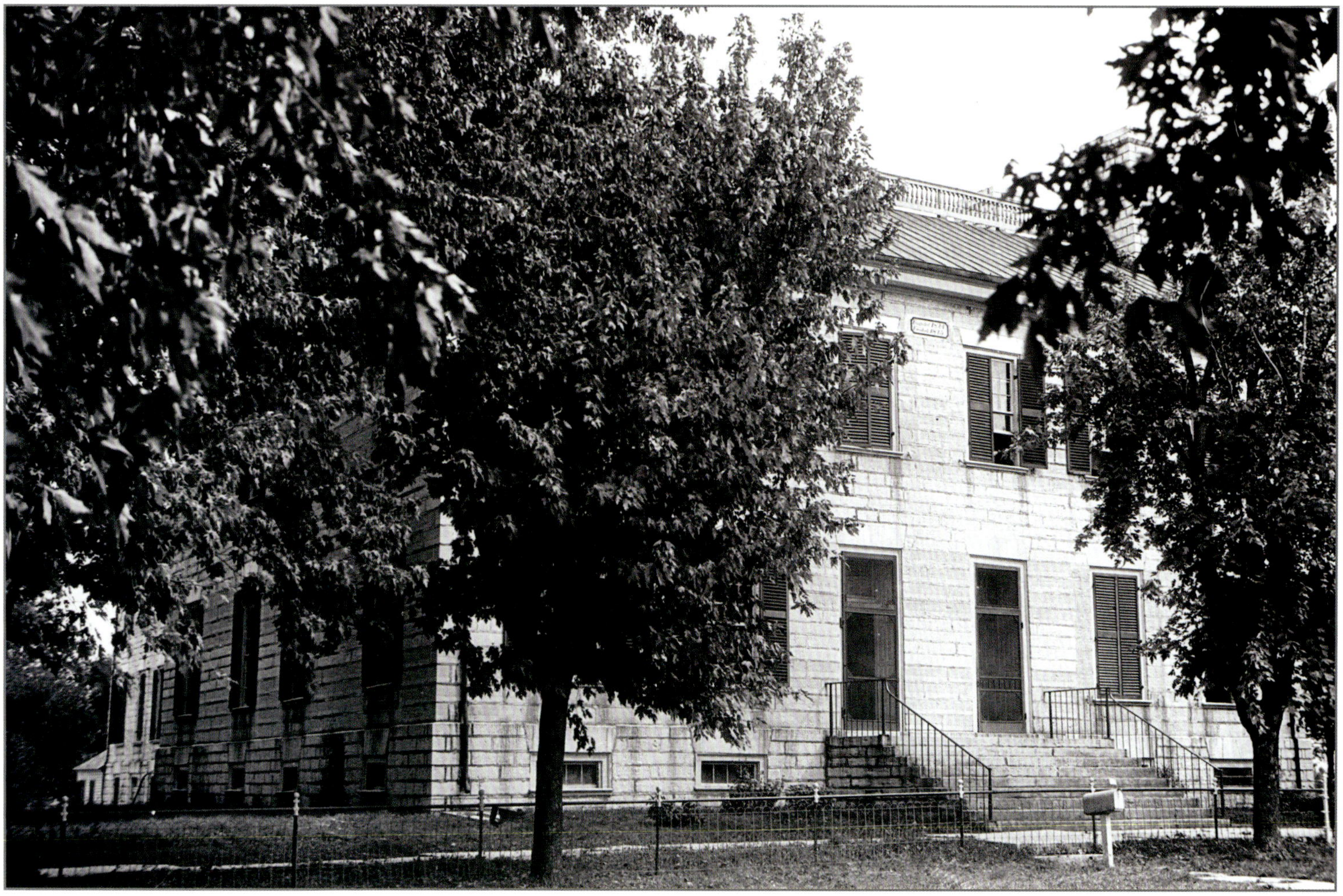

While the Keystone indicates a completion date of 1825, the Centre Family Dwelling structure was not actually completed until 1834 with the residents taking occupancy in September of that year. Several setbacks to the community as well as higher priority projects delayed its completion. When completed, the Centre Family Dwelling was the largest stone structure in the state of Kentucky second only to the old state capitol building in Frankfort.

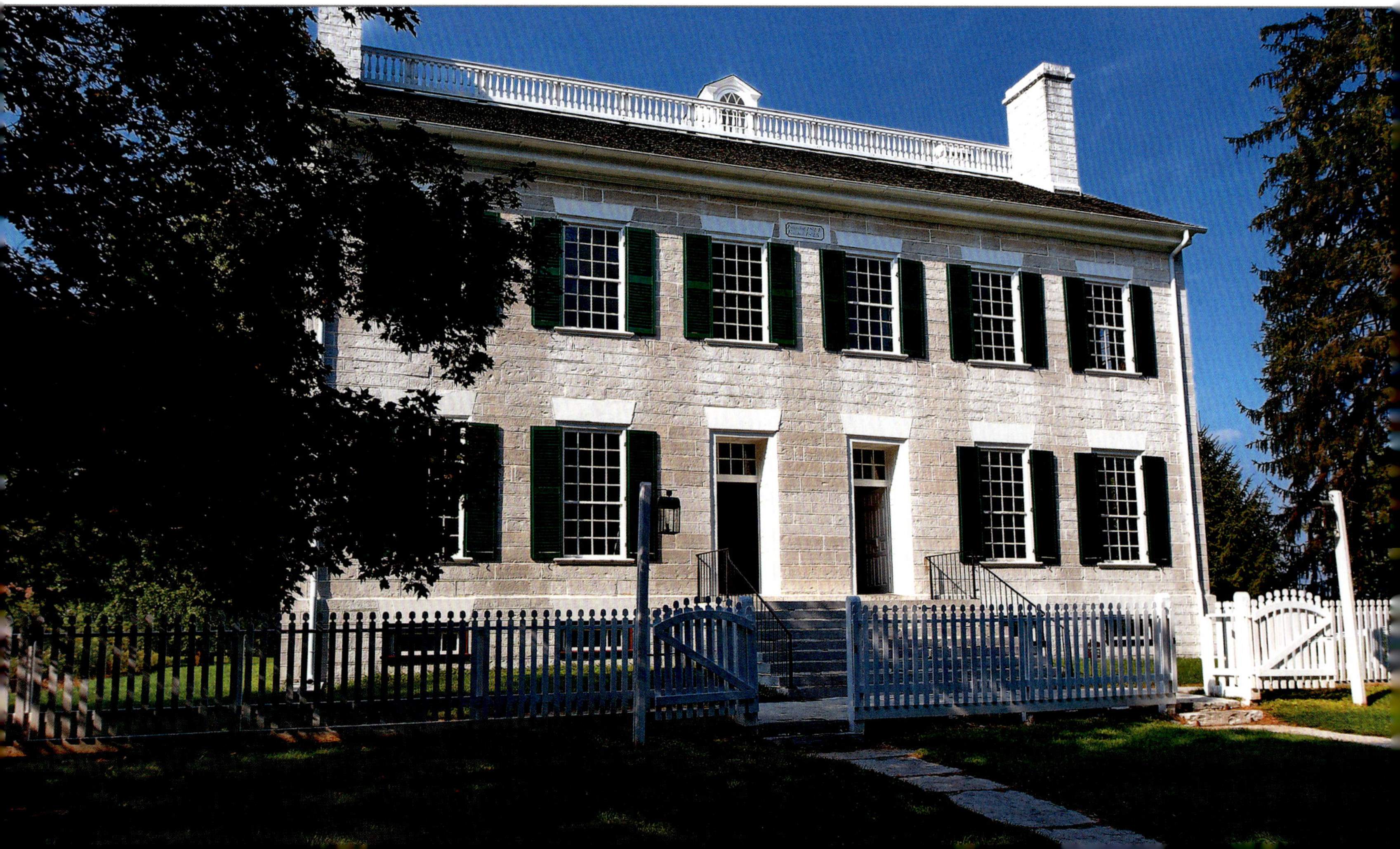

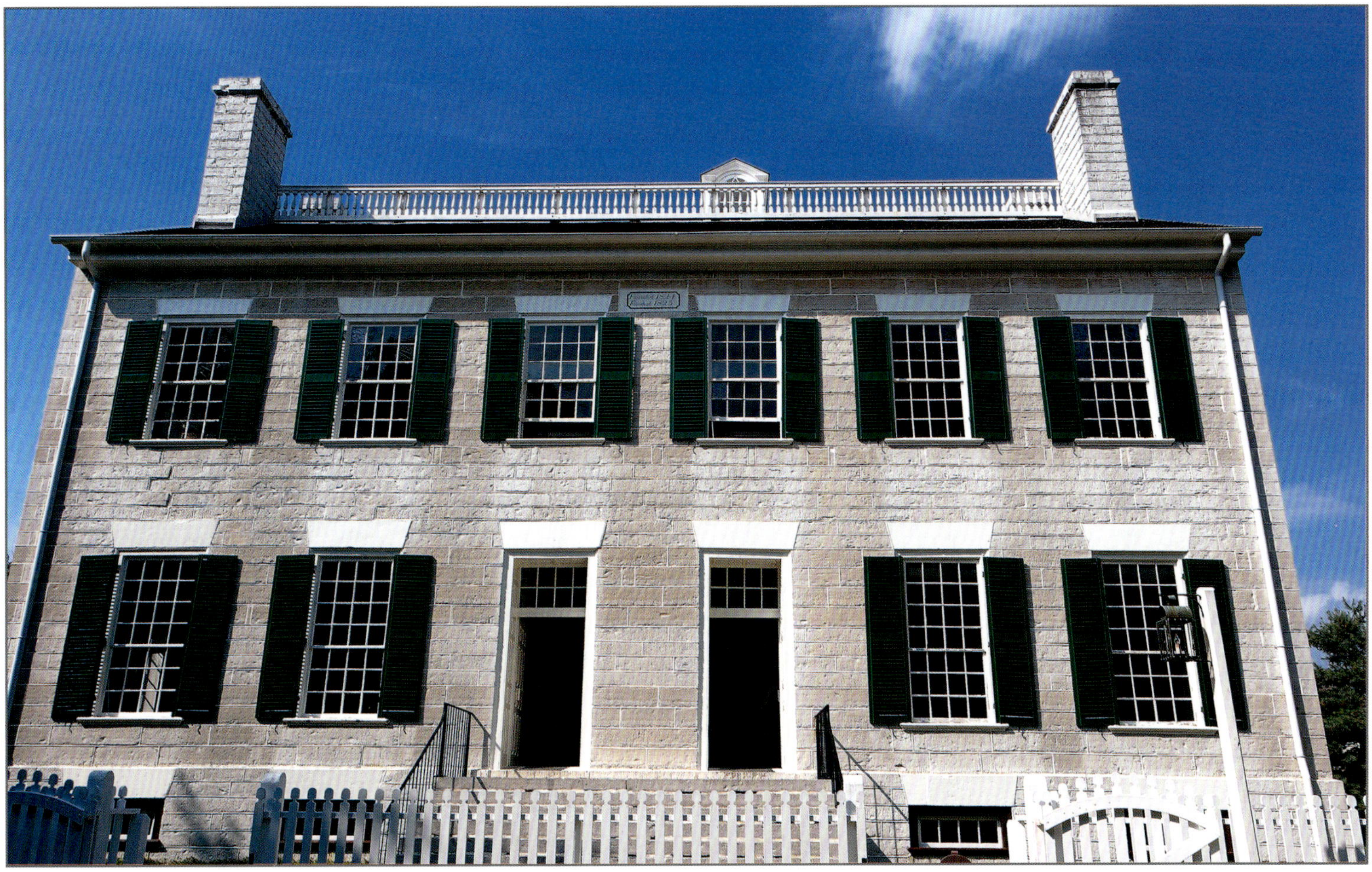

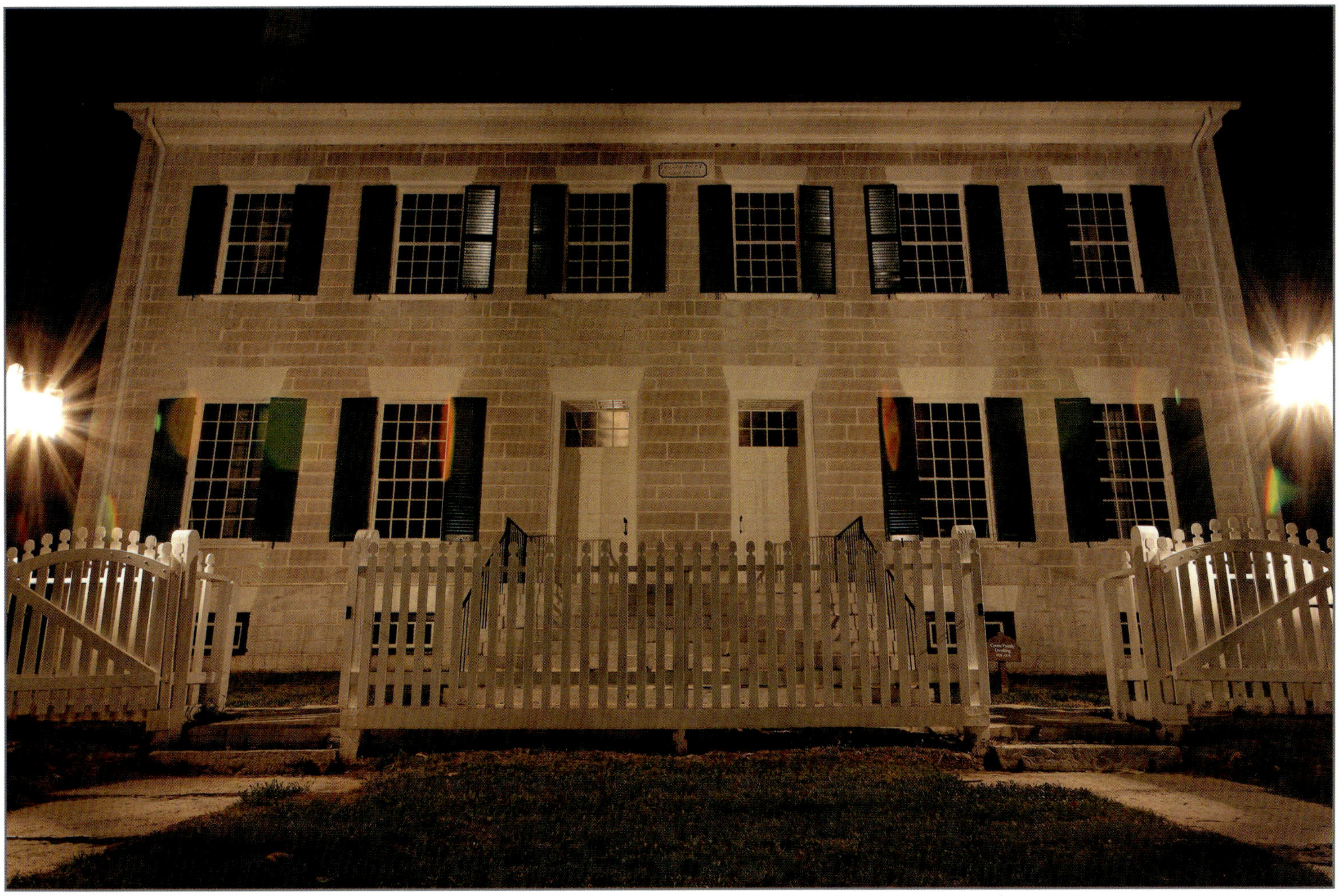

The Centre Family Dwelling consists of four levels, forty rooms and 24,960 square feet. There are 14 bedrooms which typically slept anywhere from three to eight members with men residing on the east side and women on the west.

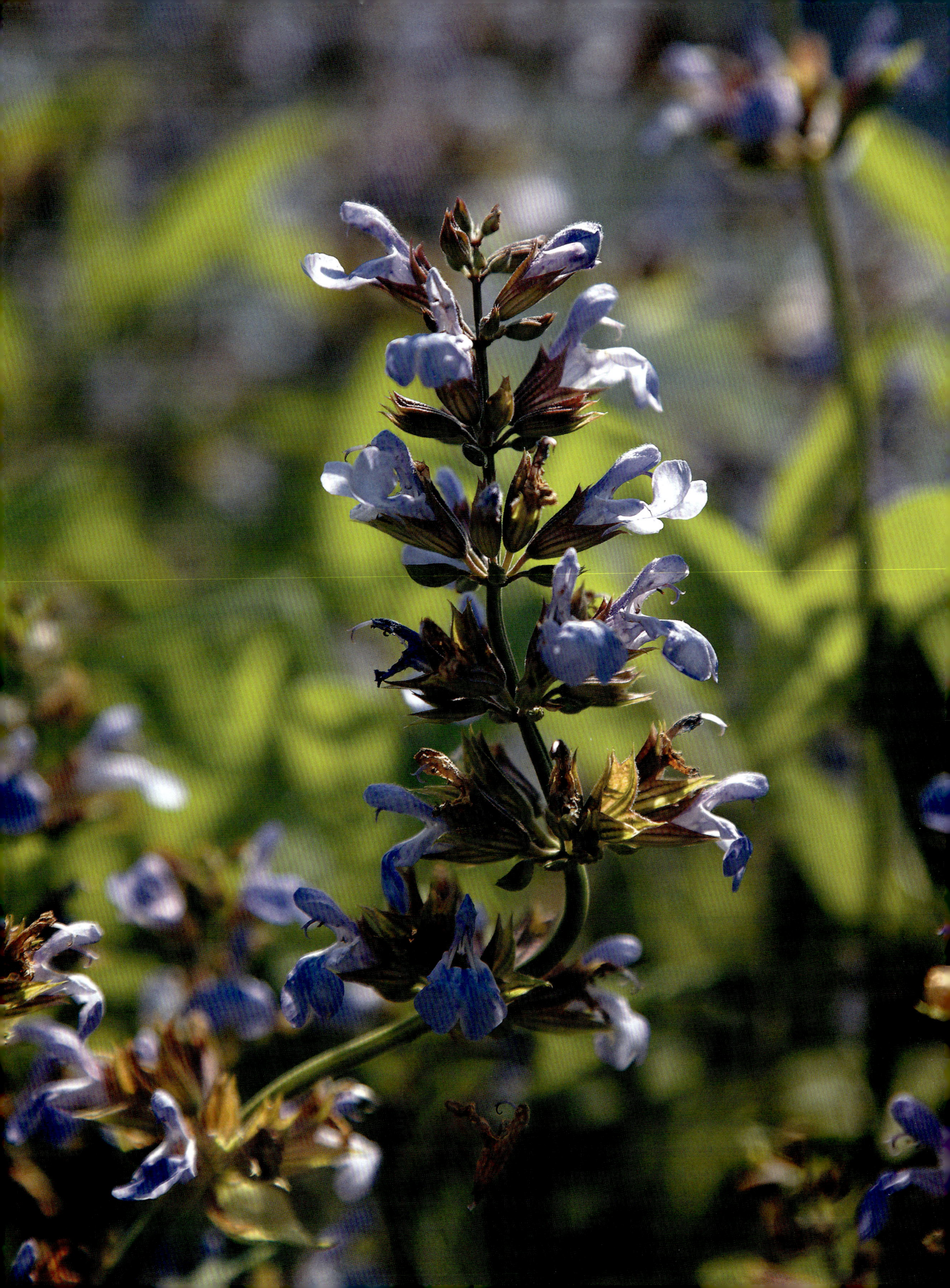

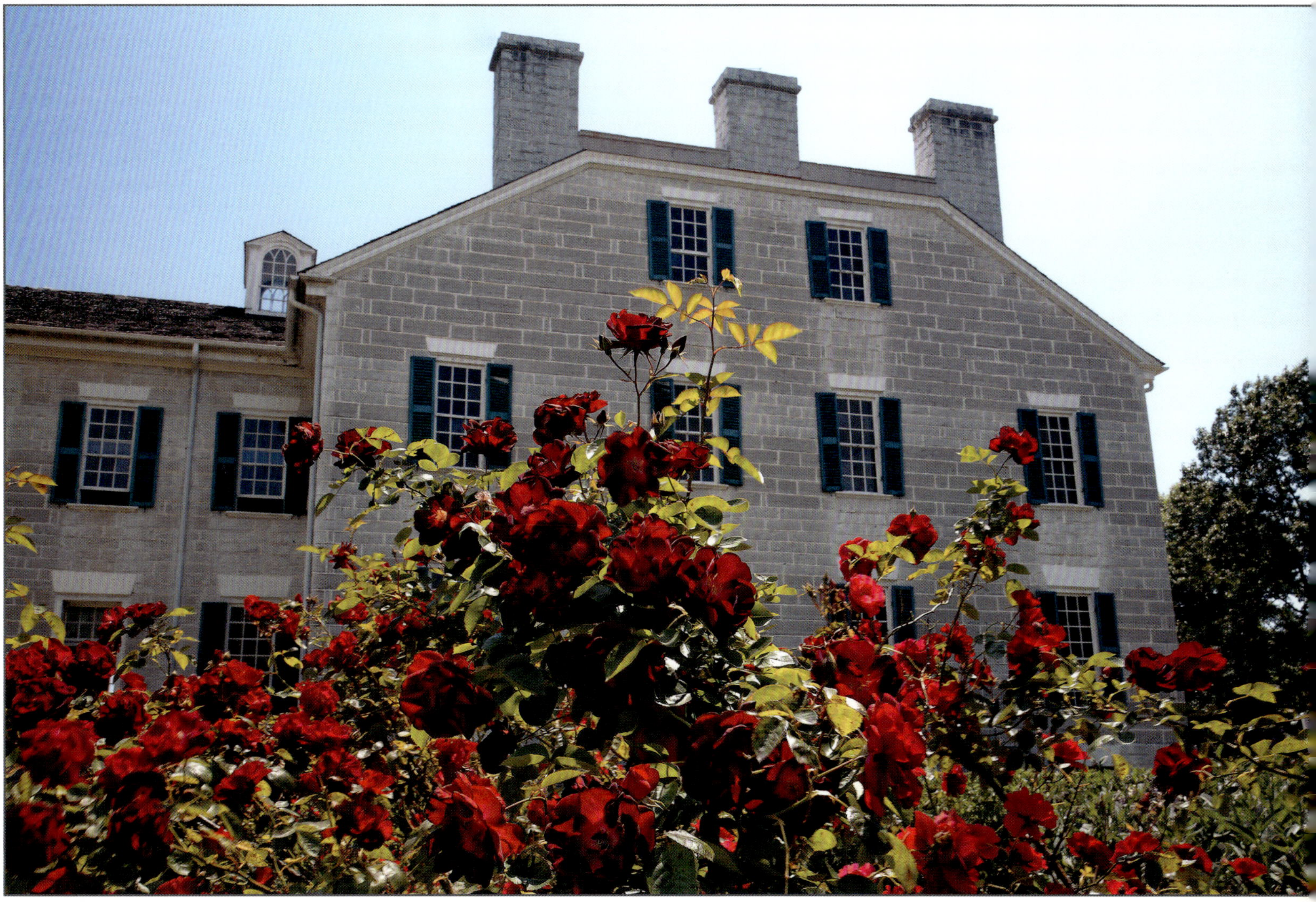

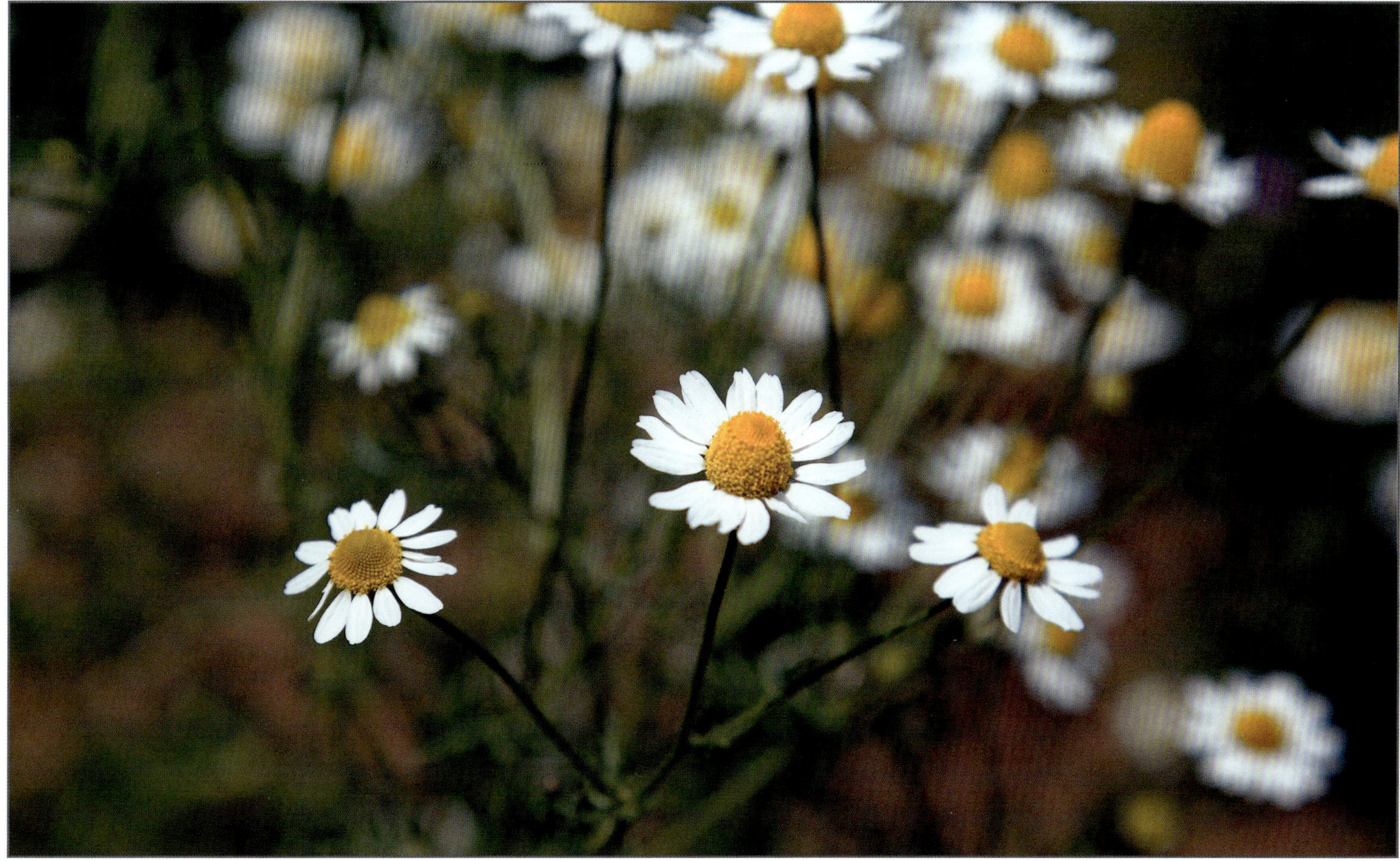

Herbs and flowers grown in the gardens of today would have been typical to the gardens grown by the Shakers in the 1850's.

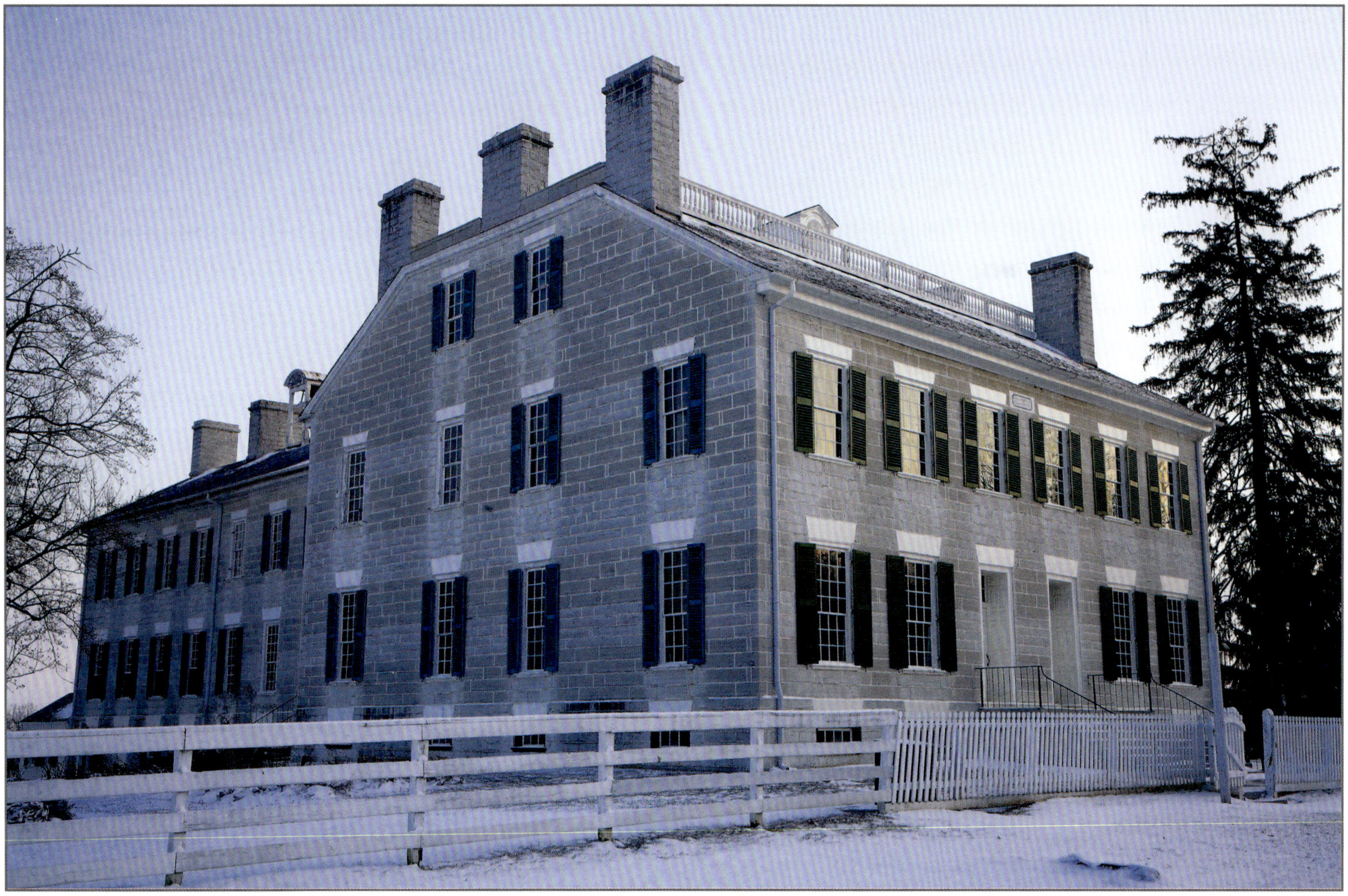

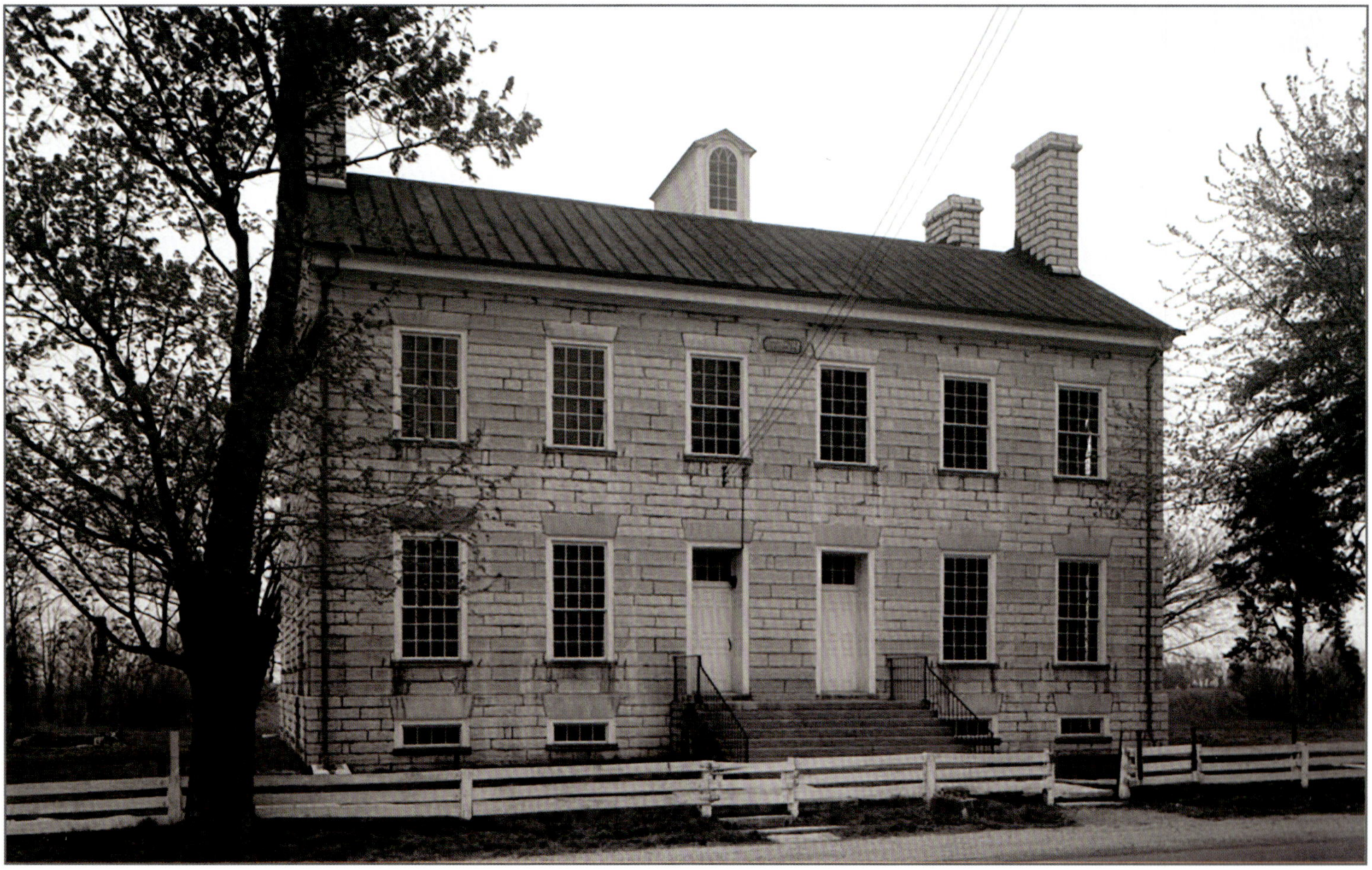

When restoration began, the Centre Family Dwelling was found to be in generally good condition. This is attributed to the structure being built of solid limestone with the exterior walls constructed two-and-a-half to three feet thick and interior, load-bearing walls eighteen to twenty inches thick.

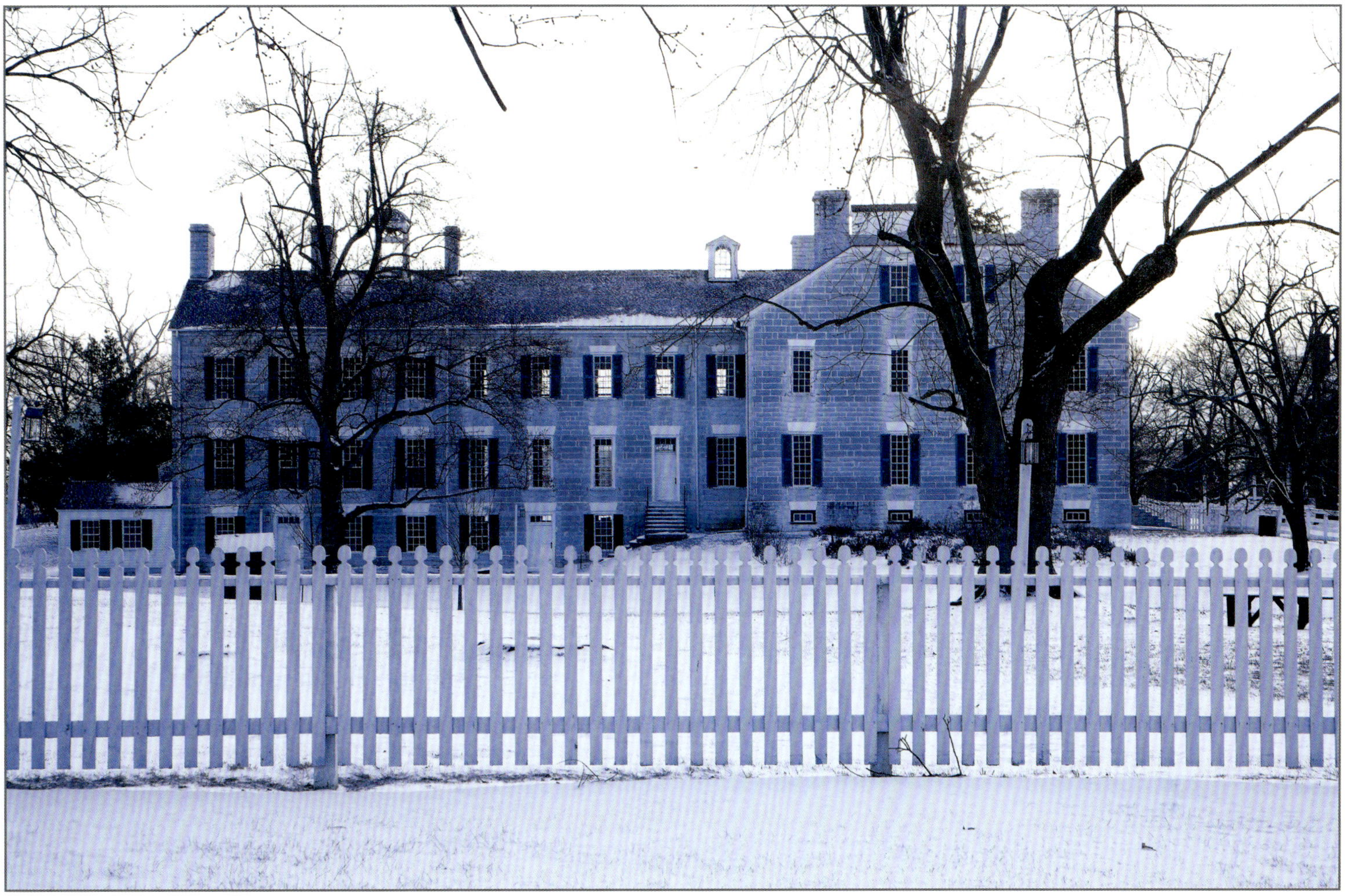

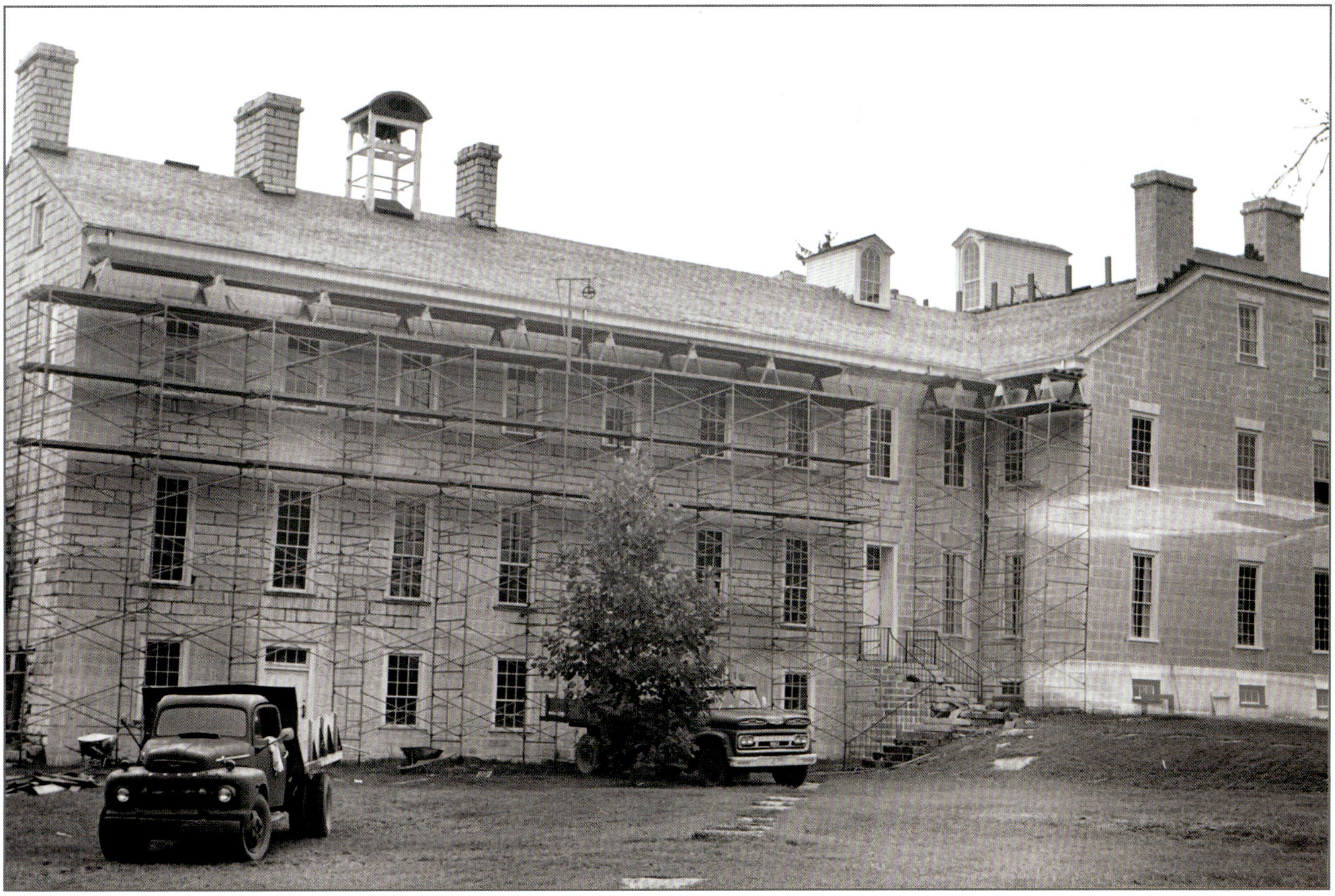

The Centre Family Dwelling during restoration in the early 1960's. The major work performed was re-pointing the mortar joints on the exterior of the building.

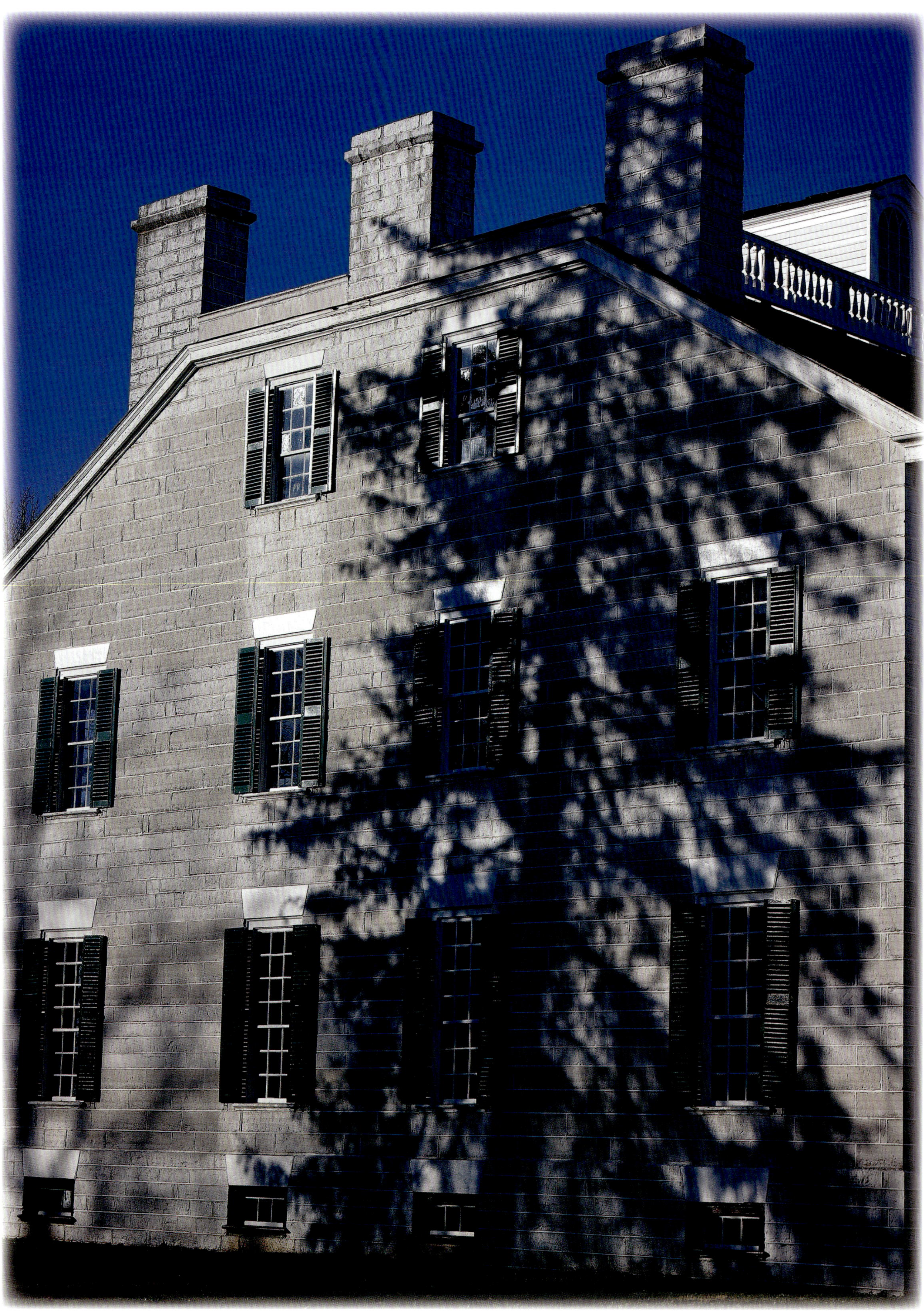

Views of the Centre Family Dwelling from the east side.

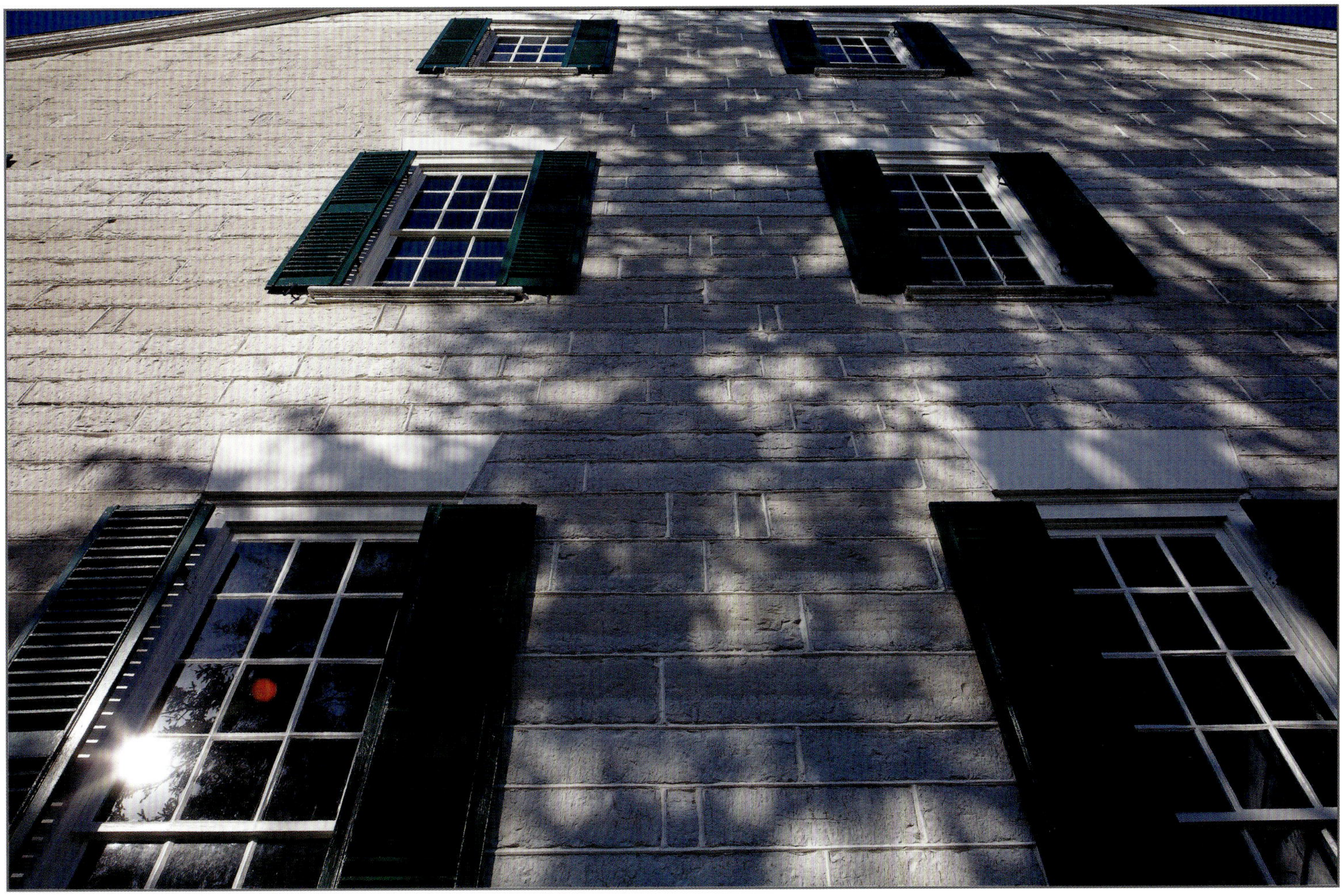

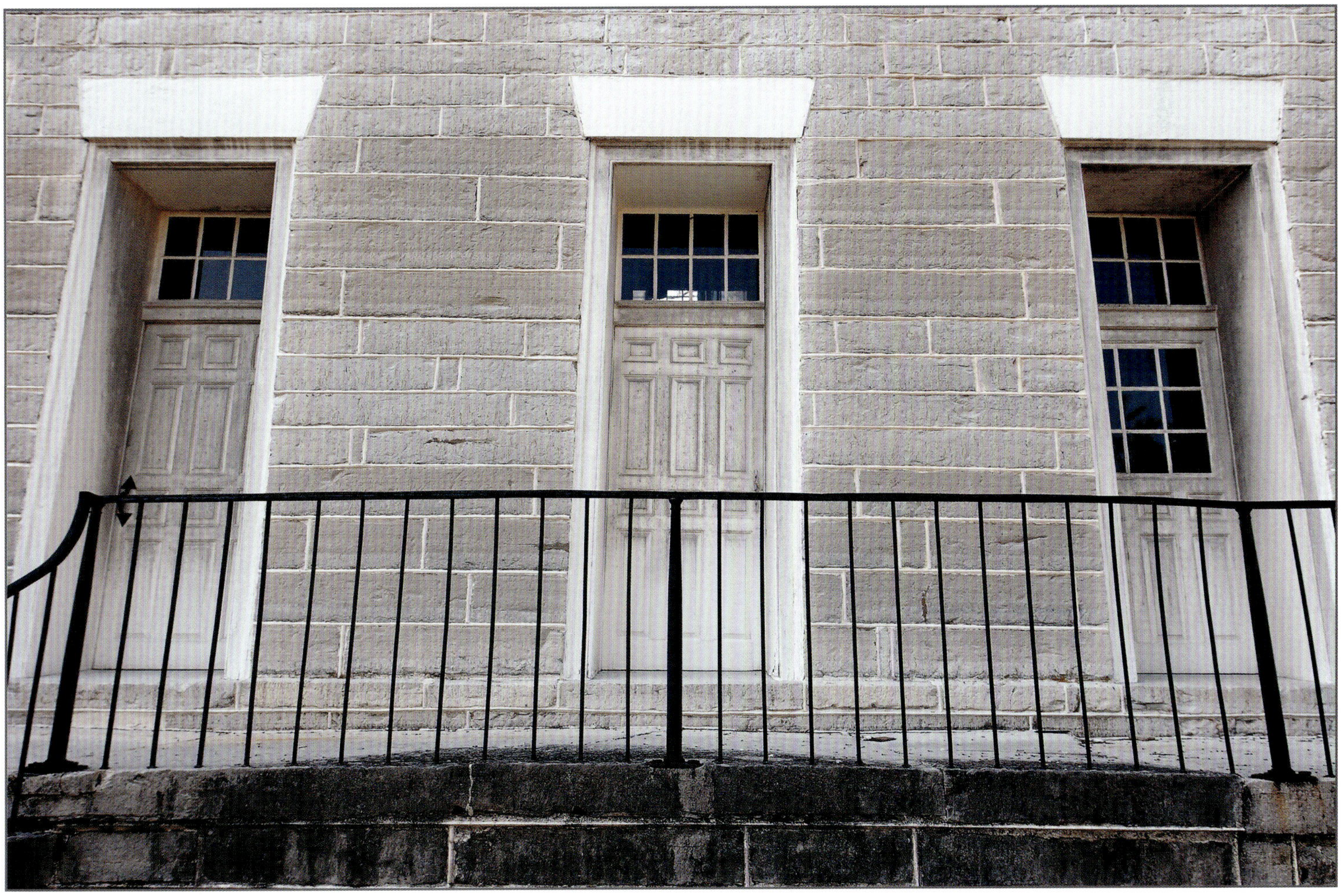

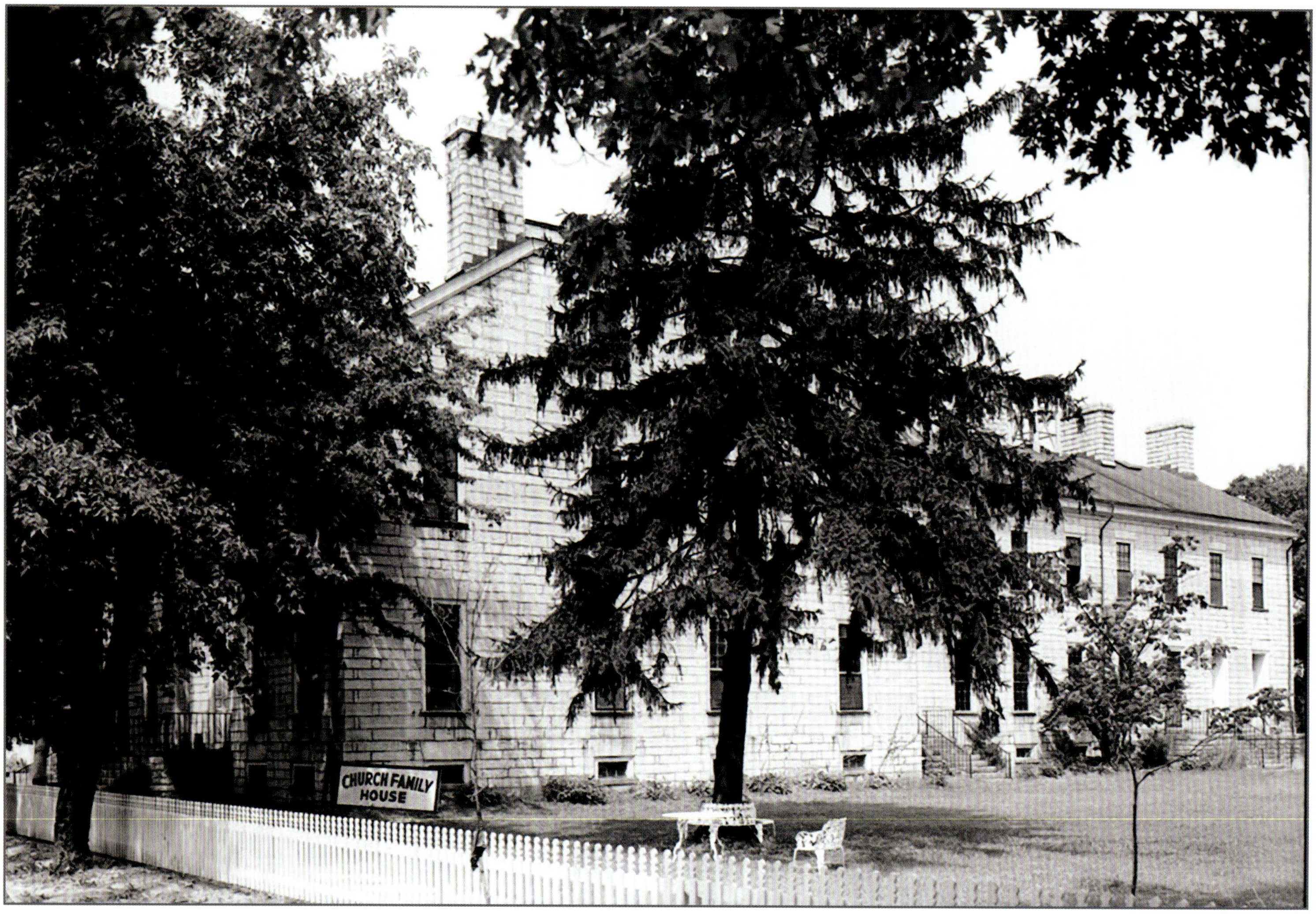

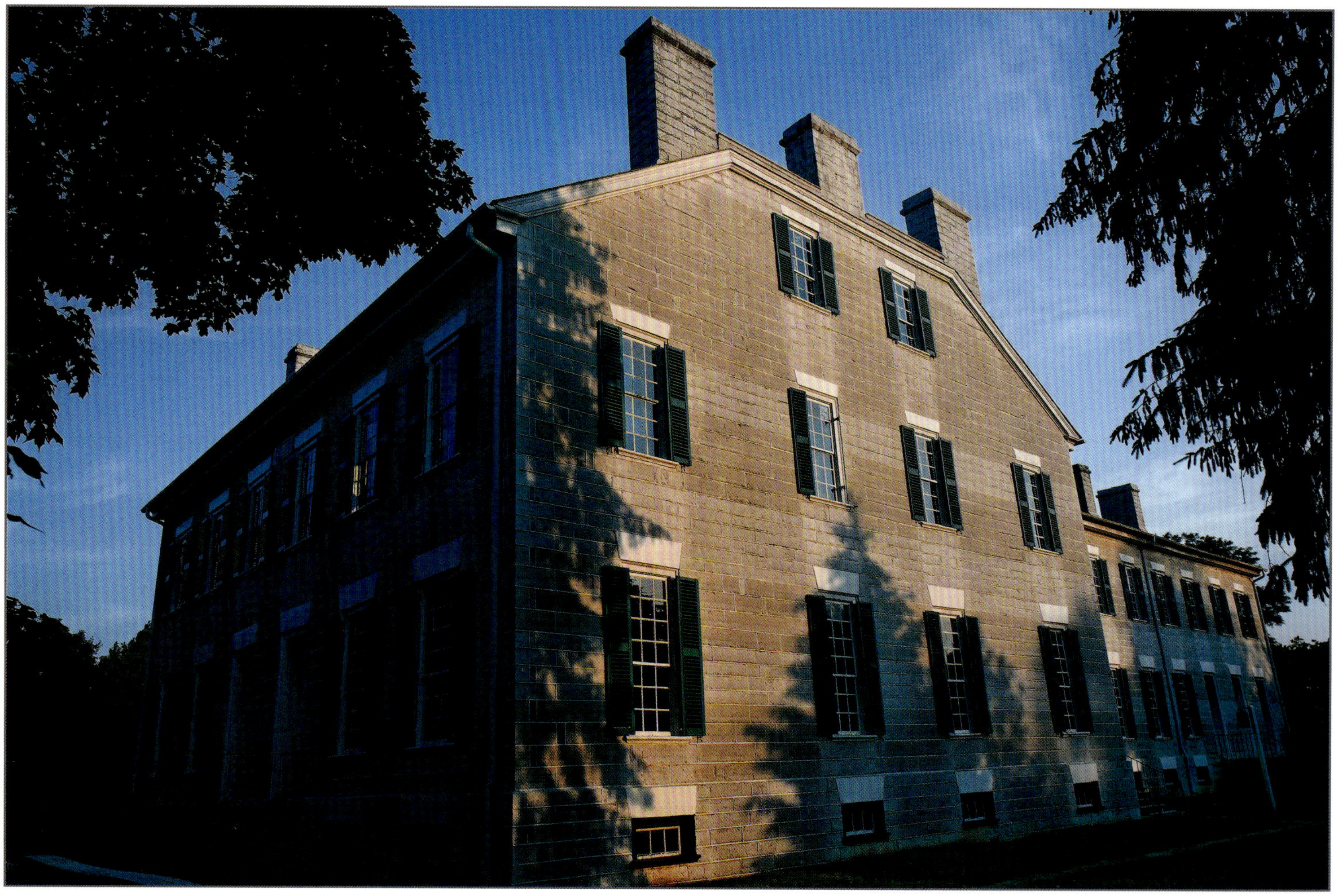

Views of the Centre Family Dwelling from the east side.

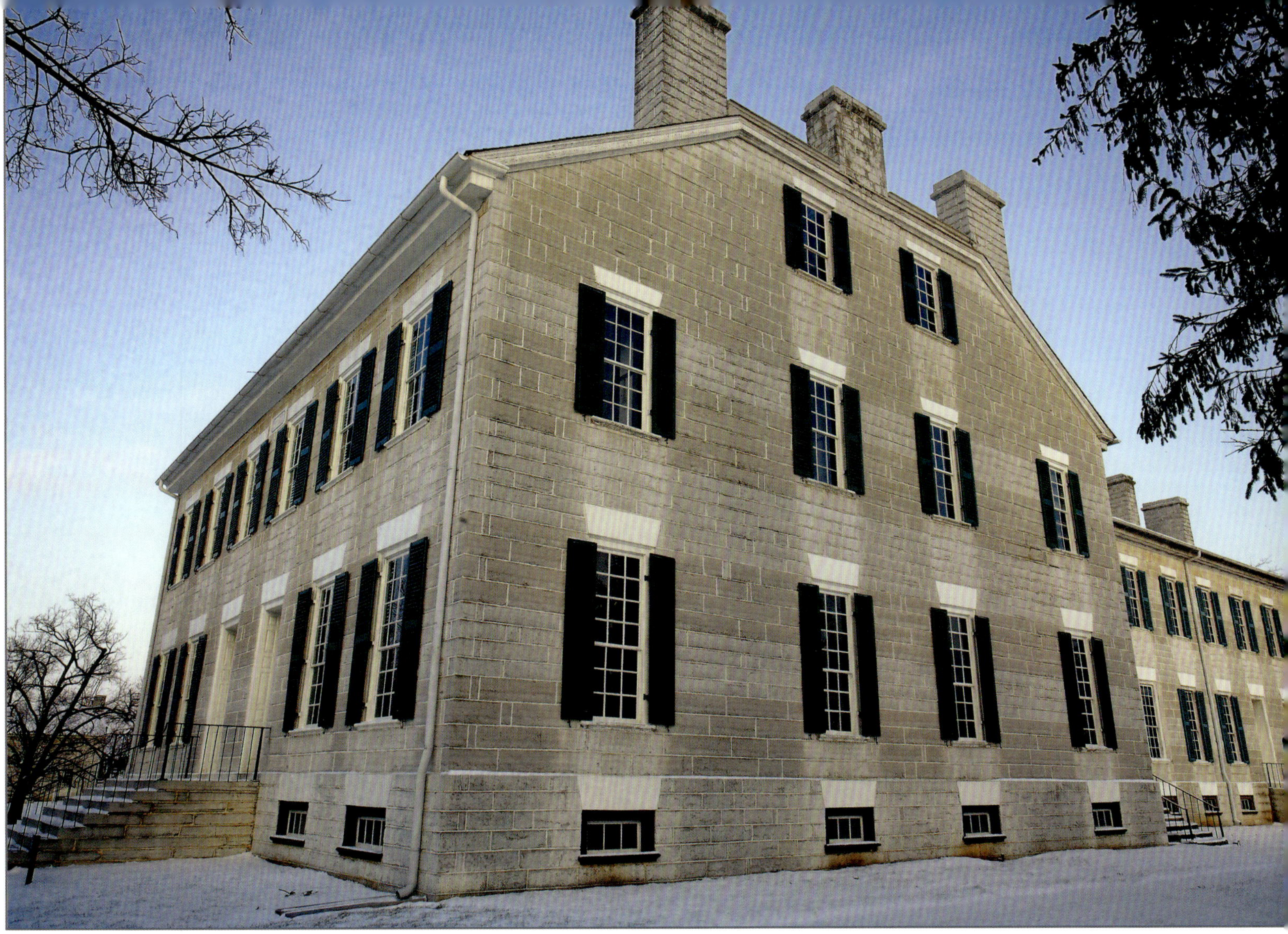

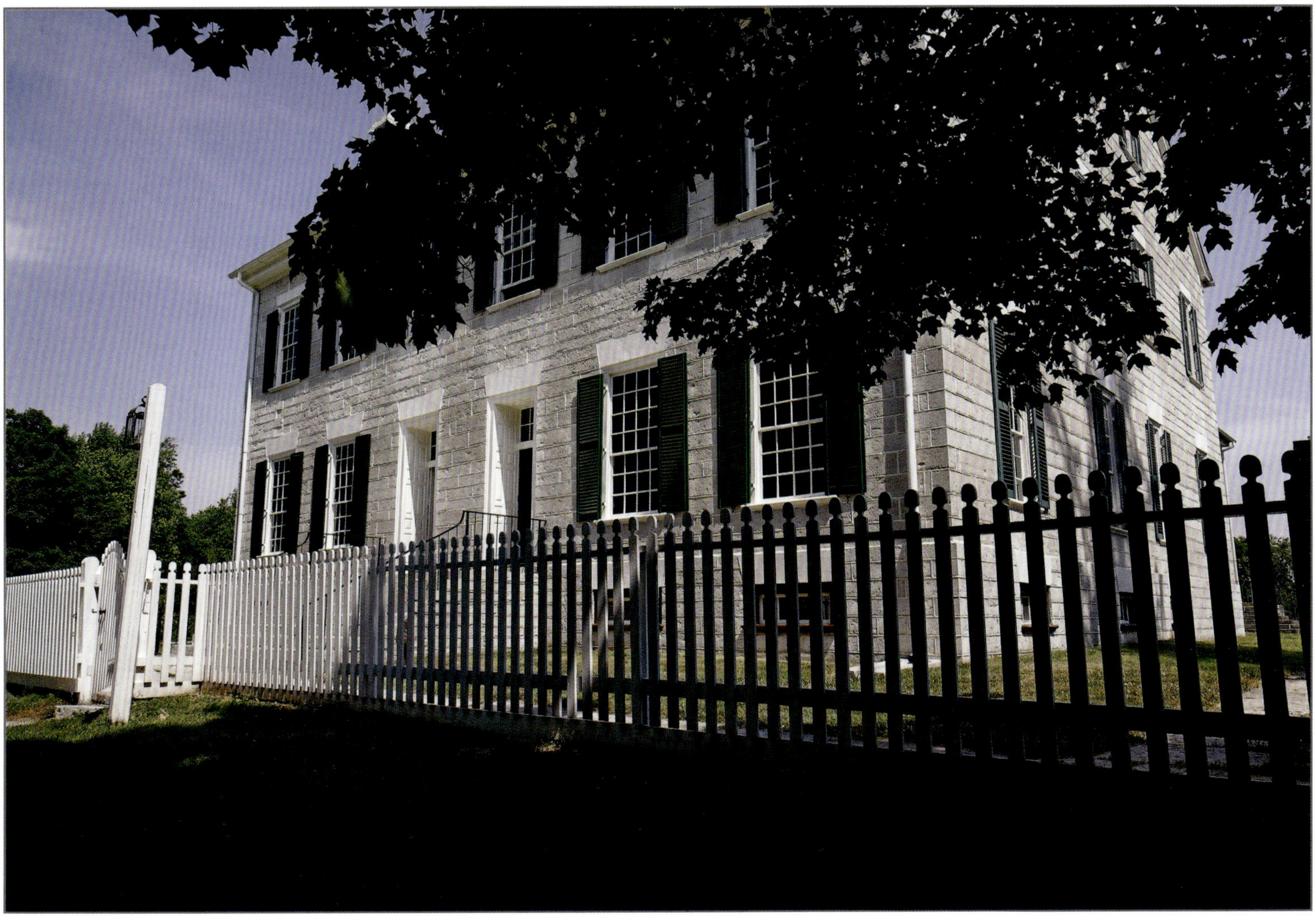

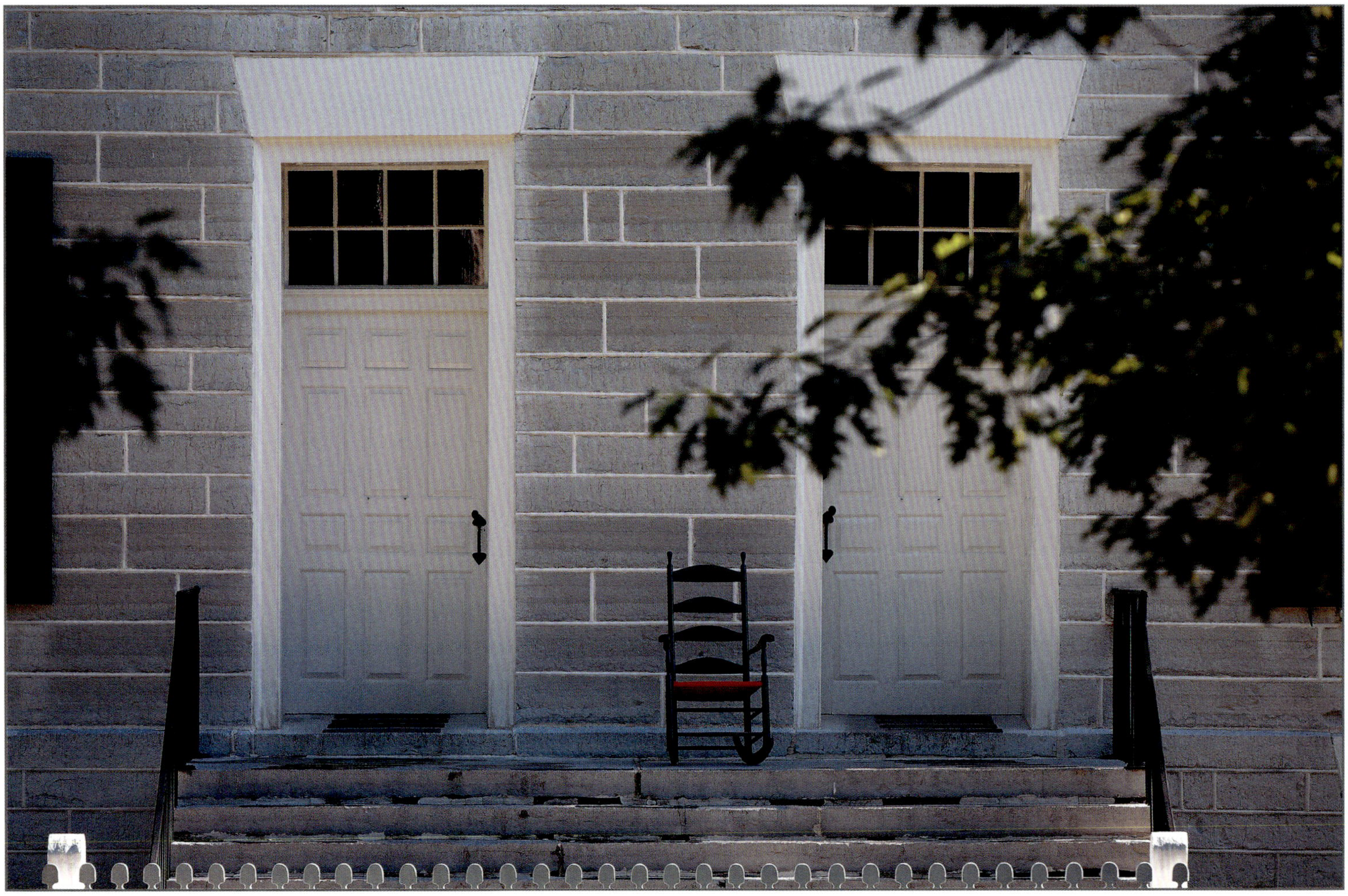

Above: The classic twin front doors of the Centre Family Dwelling. While men and women used separate doors and lived on separate sides, there was no hard and fast rule as to which side of the building was to be used by whom. It was more a matter of convenience and practicality based on where their job functions were located in relation to the building. In the case of the Centre Family Dwelling, the men entered and resided on the east side and the women on the west. This seems to be more prevalent at Pleasant Hill than other communities. South Union, for example, has only one main door on its Centre Family, but has separate steps for the men and women.

Right: Period dressed interpreters provide a wealth of historical information about the Shakers, their way of life and context of that time in history. Information given is often times a result of them reading and studying the journals kept by the Shakers themselves.

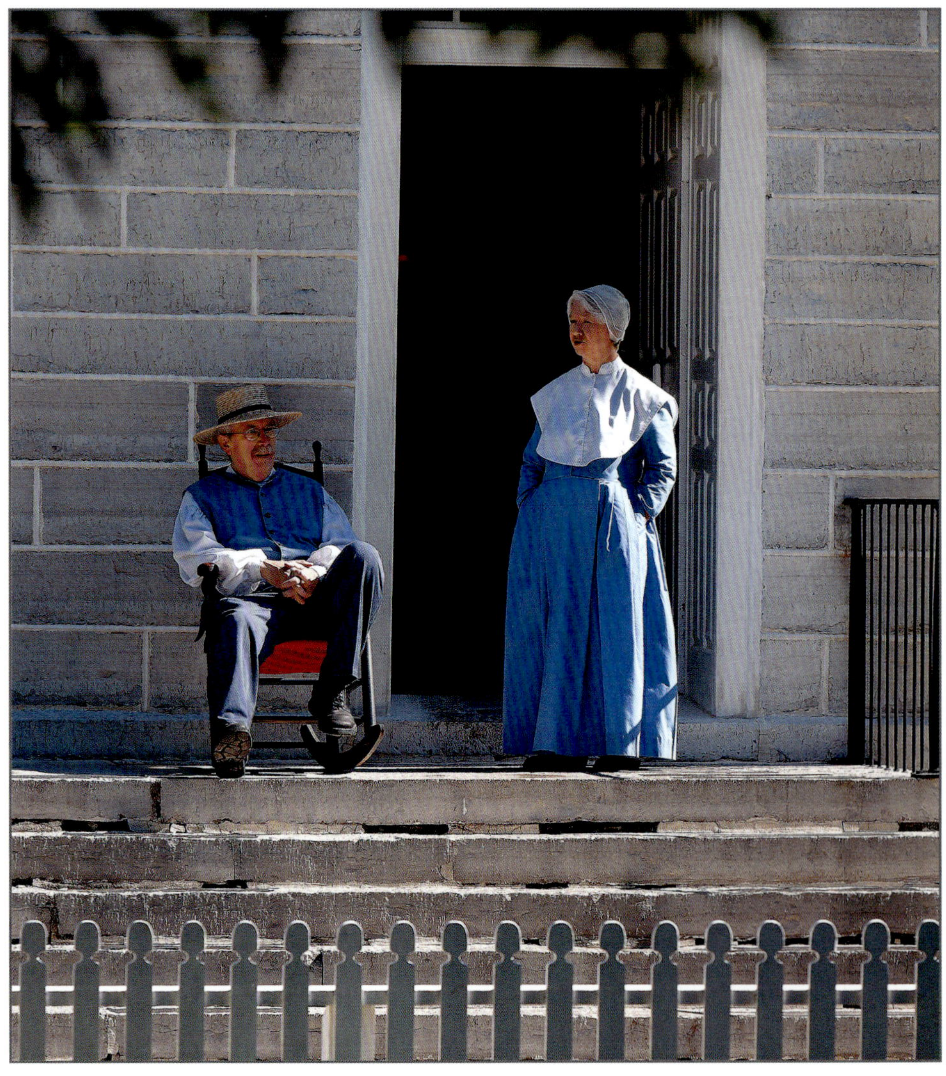

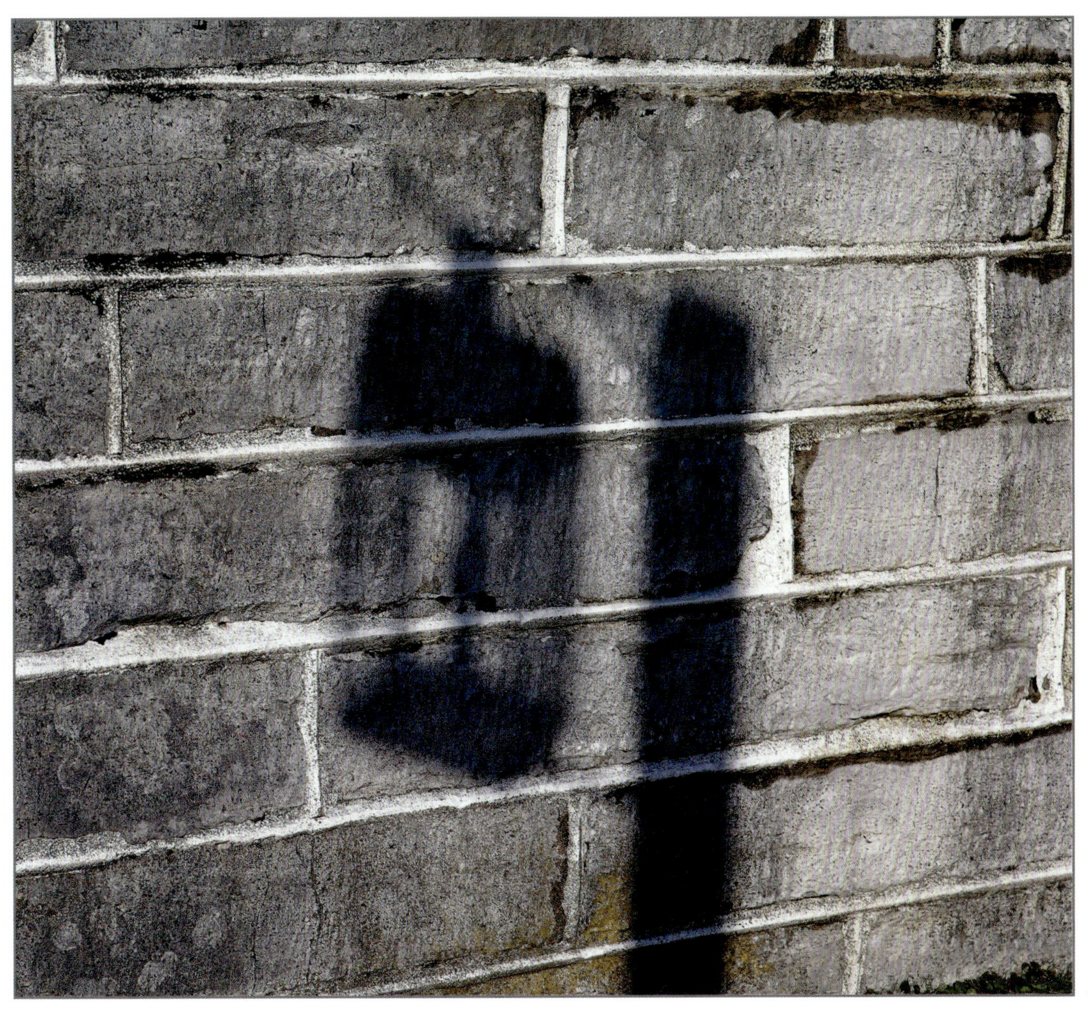

The sun casts a shadow of a lamp post against the limestone block exterior of the Centre Family Dwelling. The Shaker's mastery of quarrying and laying the limestone can easily be seen when compared to the first stone structure now known as the Farm Deacon's Building.

Below: Another example of the decorative fencing near the Centre Family Dwelling.

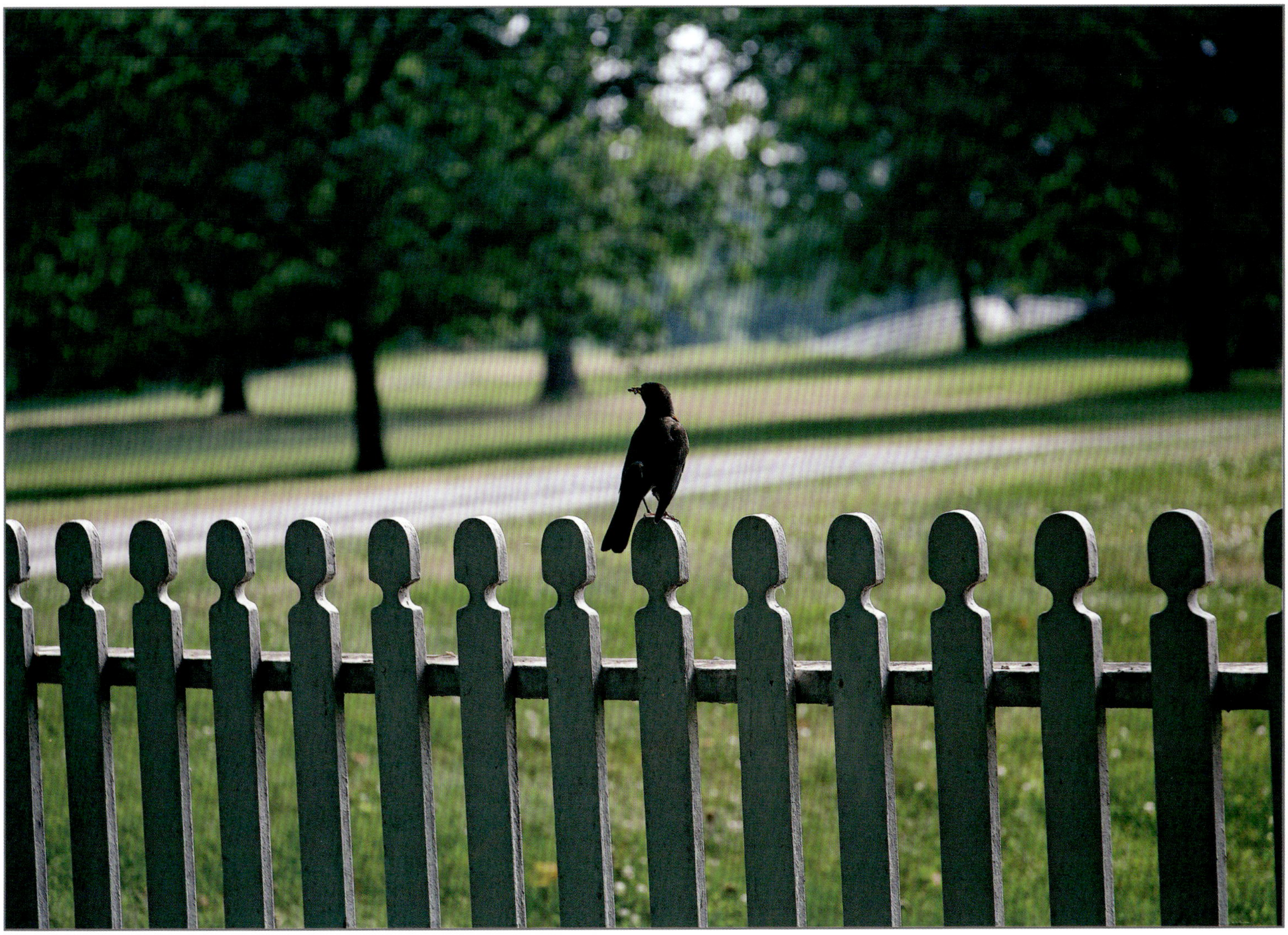

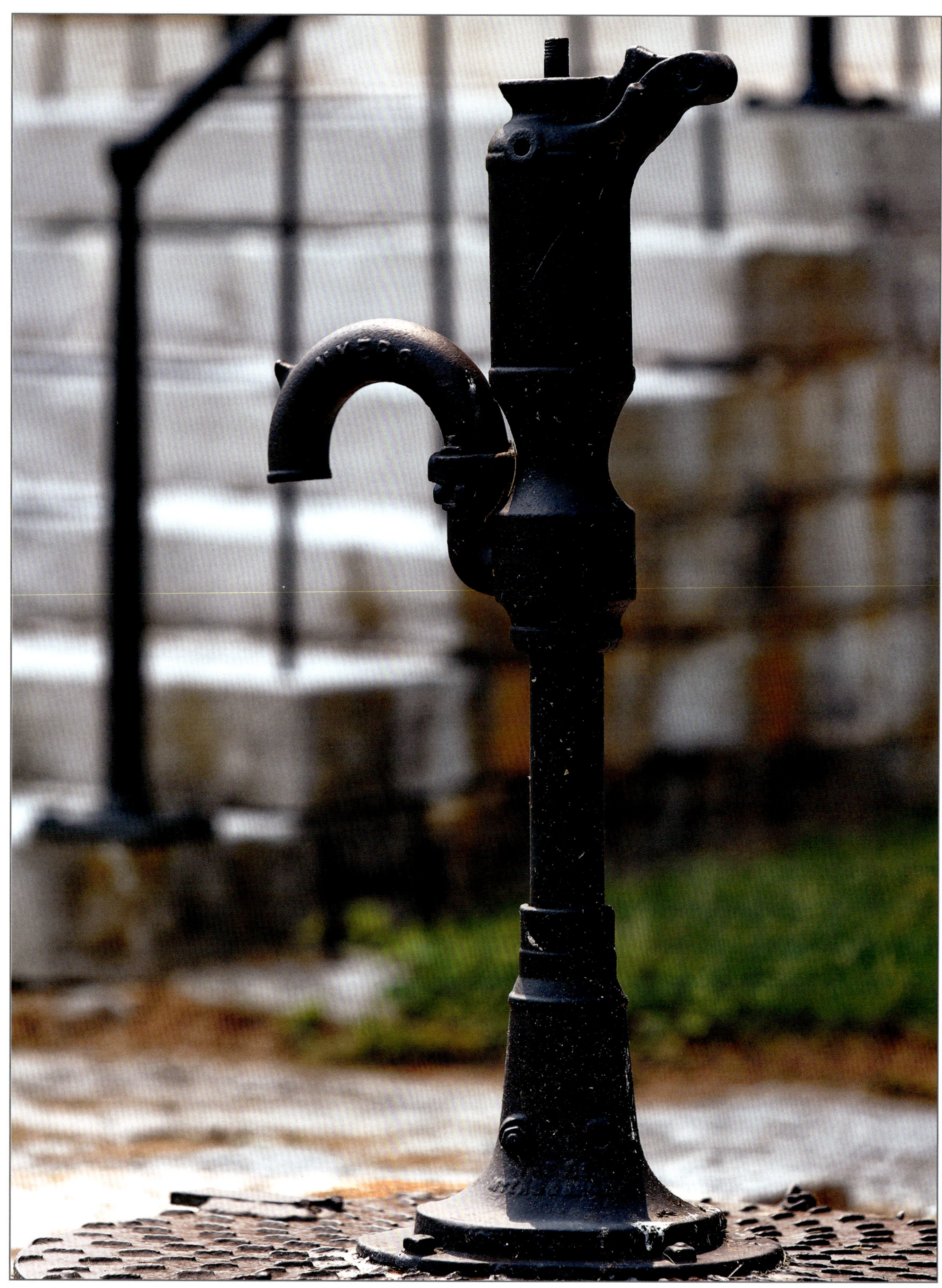

Before the addition of running water, much of the water was gathered by use of cisterns.

As the sun moves across the sky, the architectural details of the building create interesting shadows and patterns. Every visit to Pleasant Hill is a unique experience depending on the season of year and the time of day.

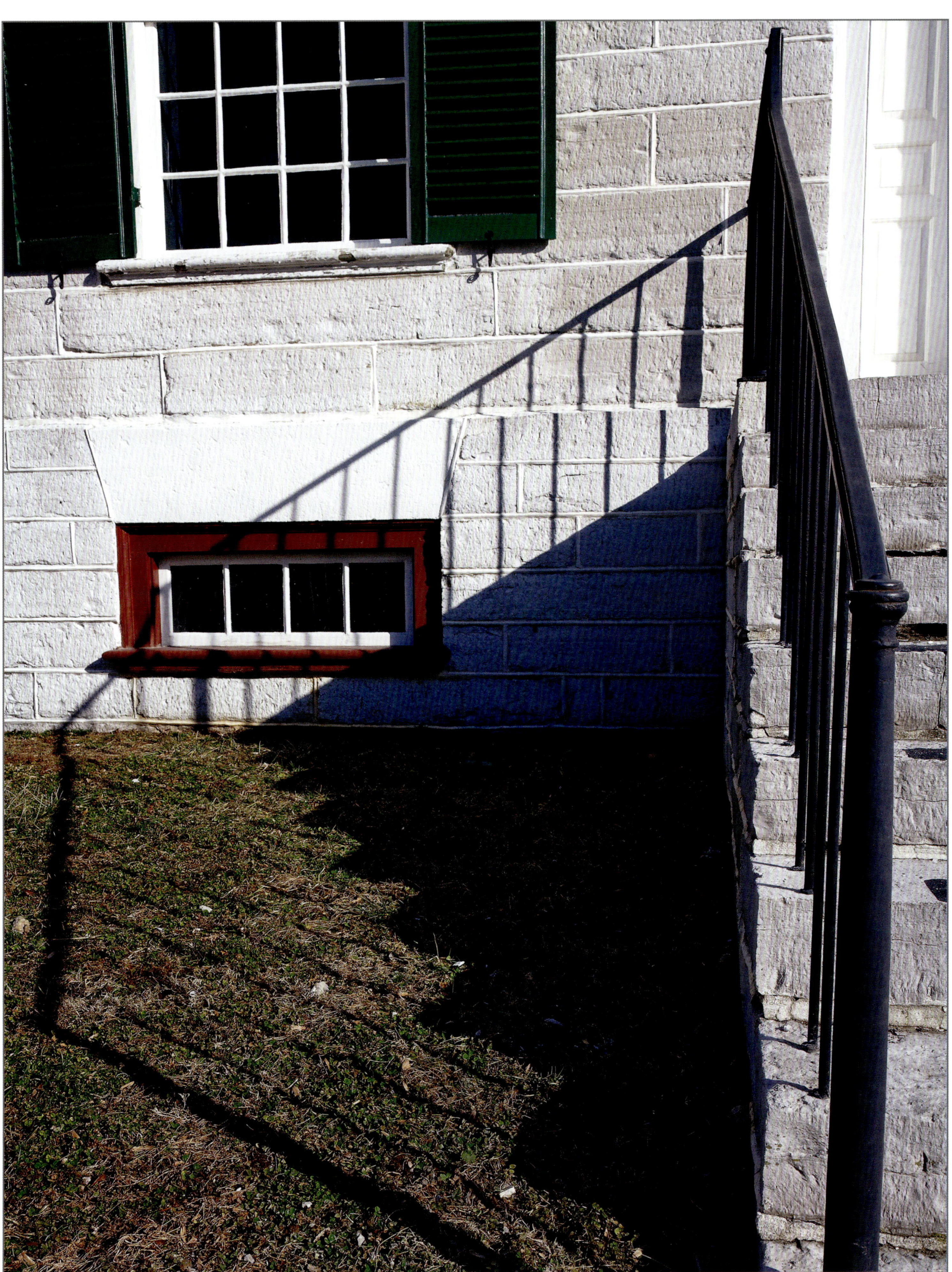

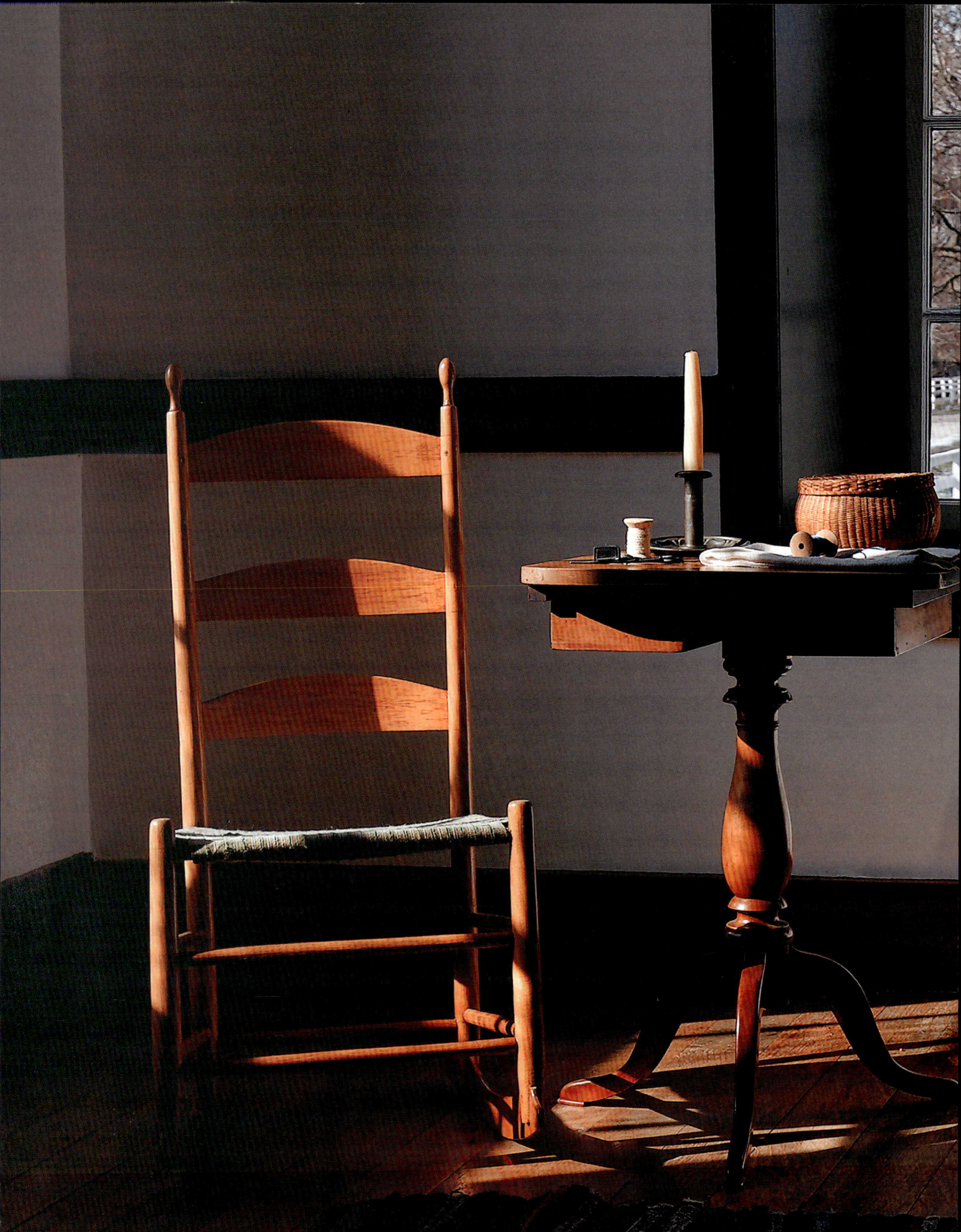

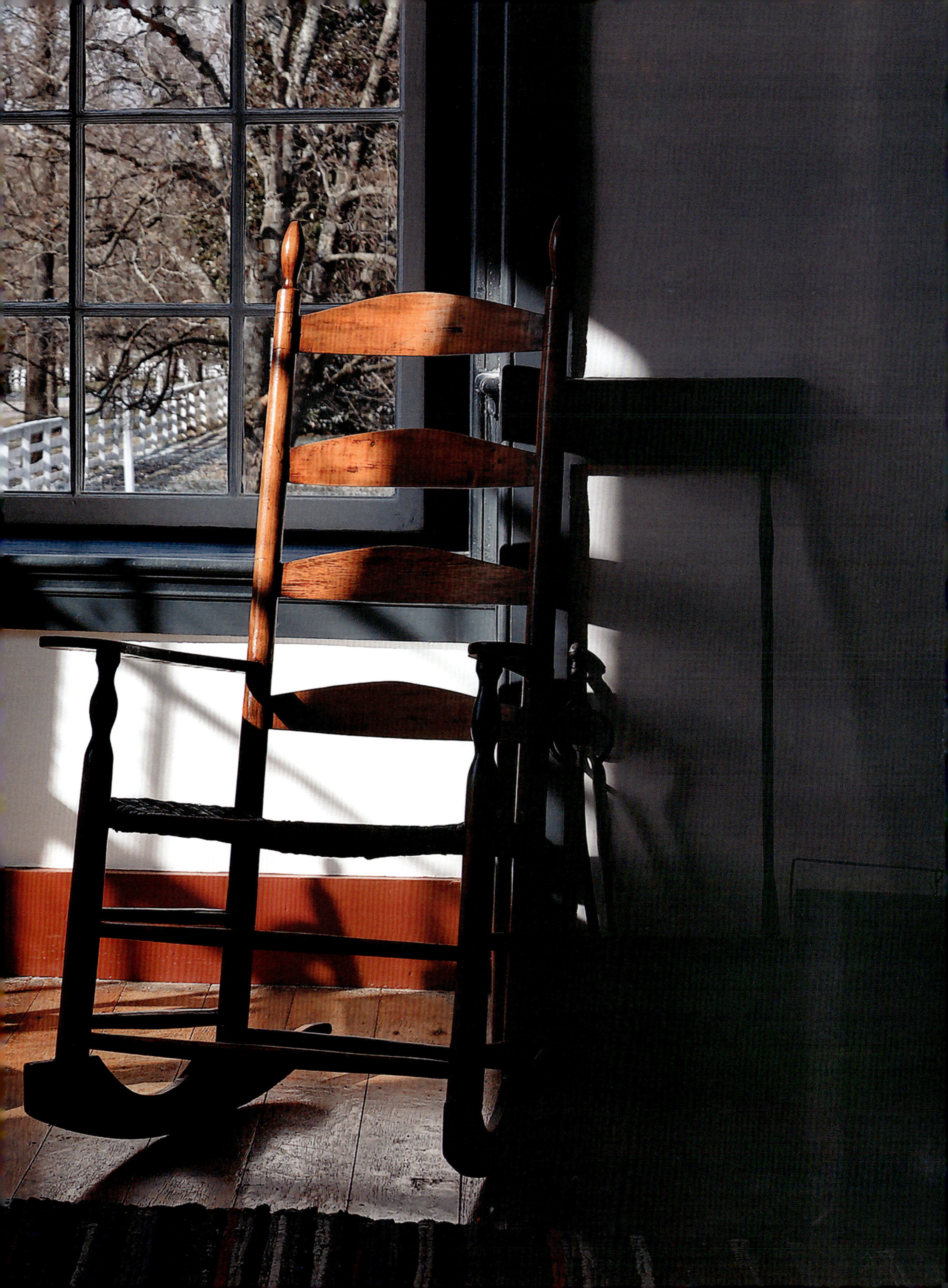

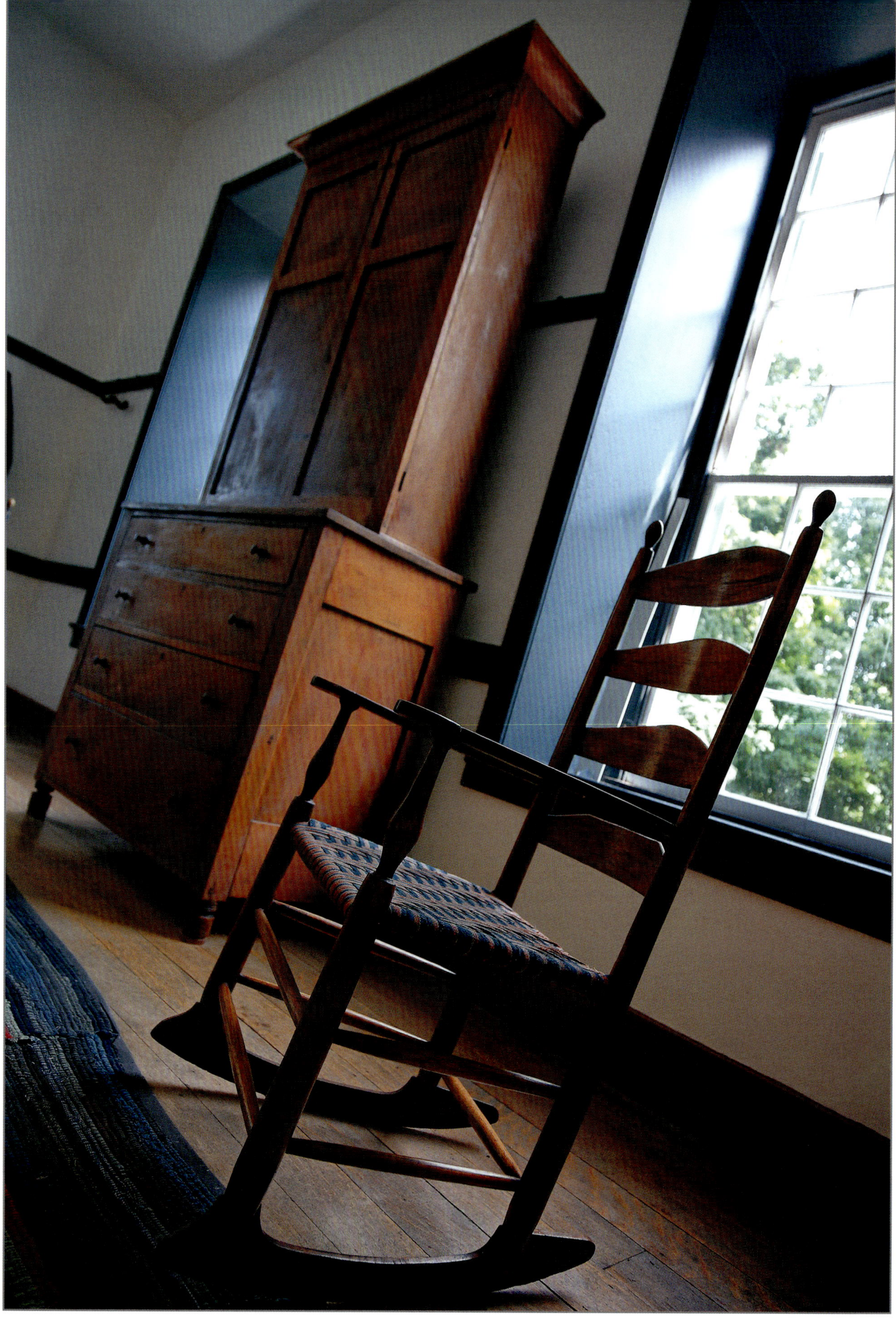

Previous spread: While life was simple and utilitarian, this room on the Sisters' side of the Centre Family Dwelling shows how comfortable and inviting the Shaker style of furniture can be. Again, the building was oriented to take advantage of natural lighting thus conserving resources such as candles. This also reduced the heat generated in the buildings and reduced the chances of fire. There were some areas, closets for example, where candles were forbidden to be used due to the high chance of fires. The majority of the plaster and flooring, as well as the paint, is original to the building. The red paint was made using brick dust for its strength and durability and thus its use on the baseboards.

Above: Rooms on the Brothers' side of the Centre Family Dwelling further illustrate the use of natural light and ventilation. Again, three to eight members would reside in a room depending on the community's population. Children did not occupy the main dwellings, but rather resided separately with their care givers in what were referred to as "Children's Orders".

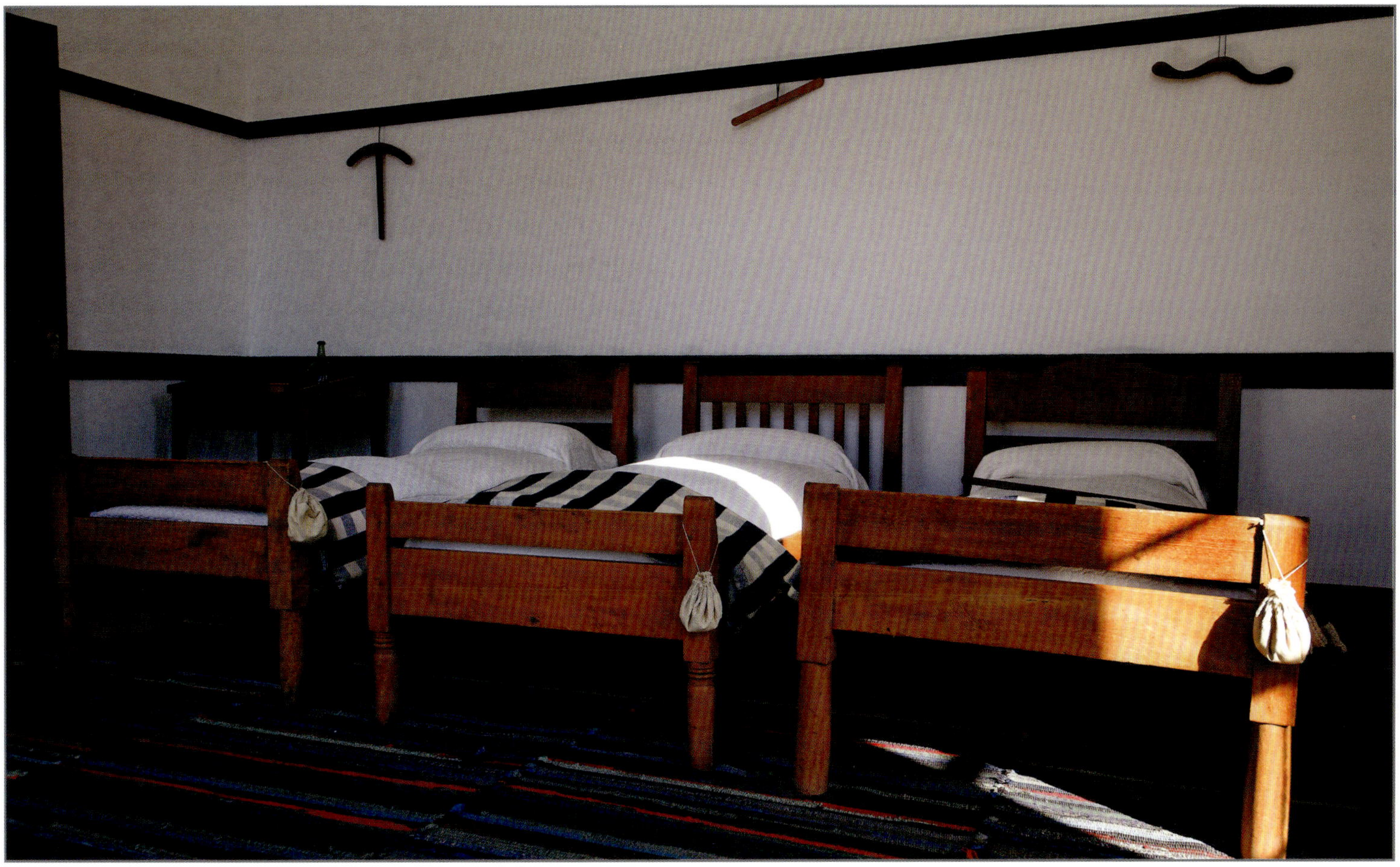

The small bags hanging from the beds contain insect repelling herbs such as southernwood, wormwood, yarrow and lavender.

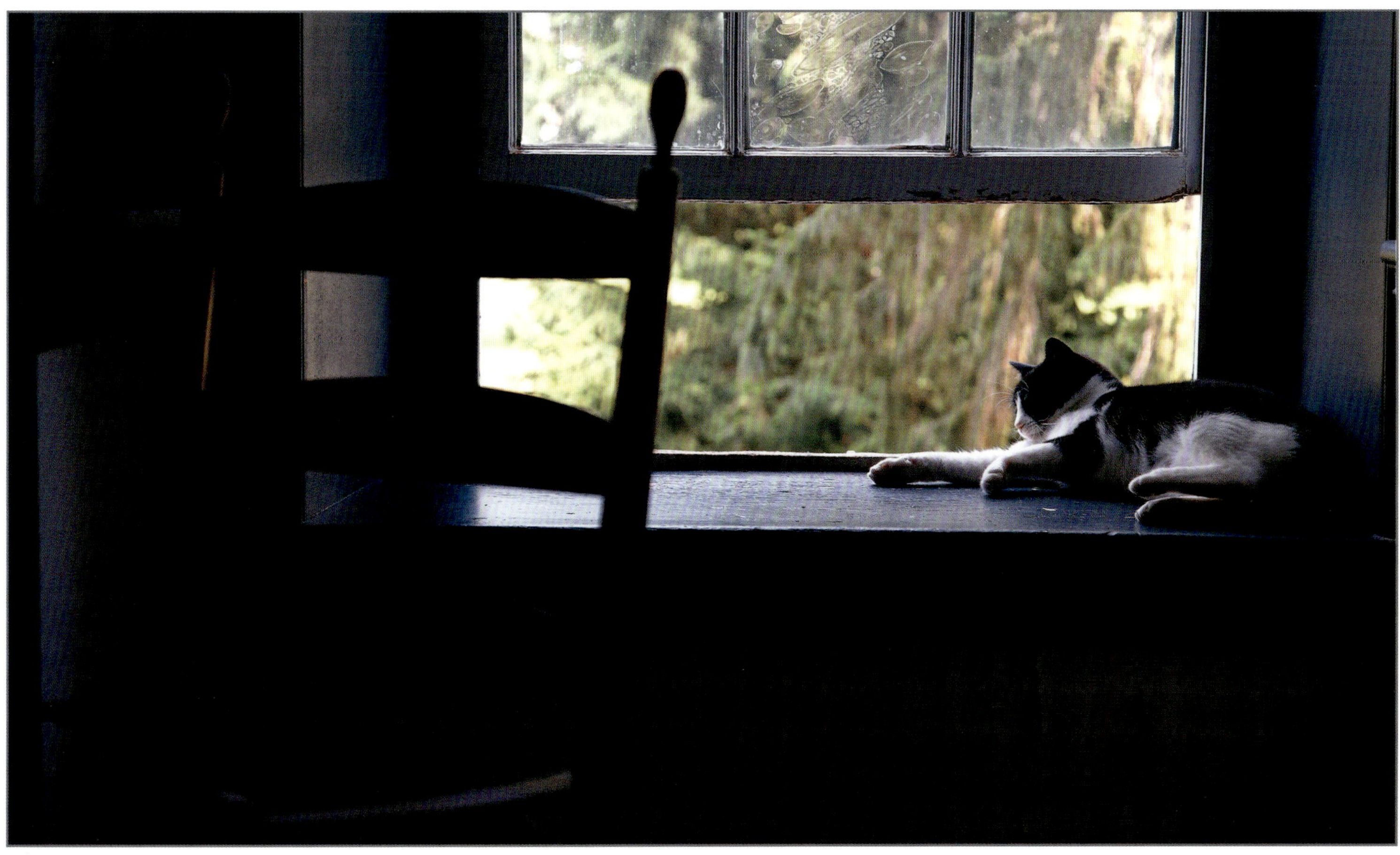

Another example of natural light and ventilation featuring "Gabby", the Village's unofficial mascot. In the early years Shakers did not keep pets. Millennial Law stated members were not to give animals Christian names. This view may have evolved over the years as later photos exist of Sisters holding cats in their laps.

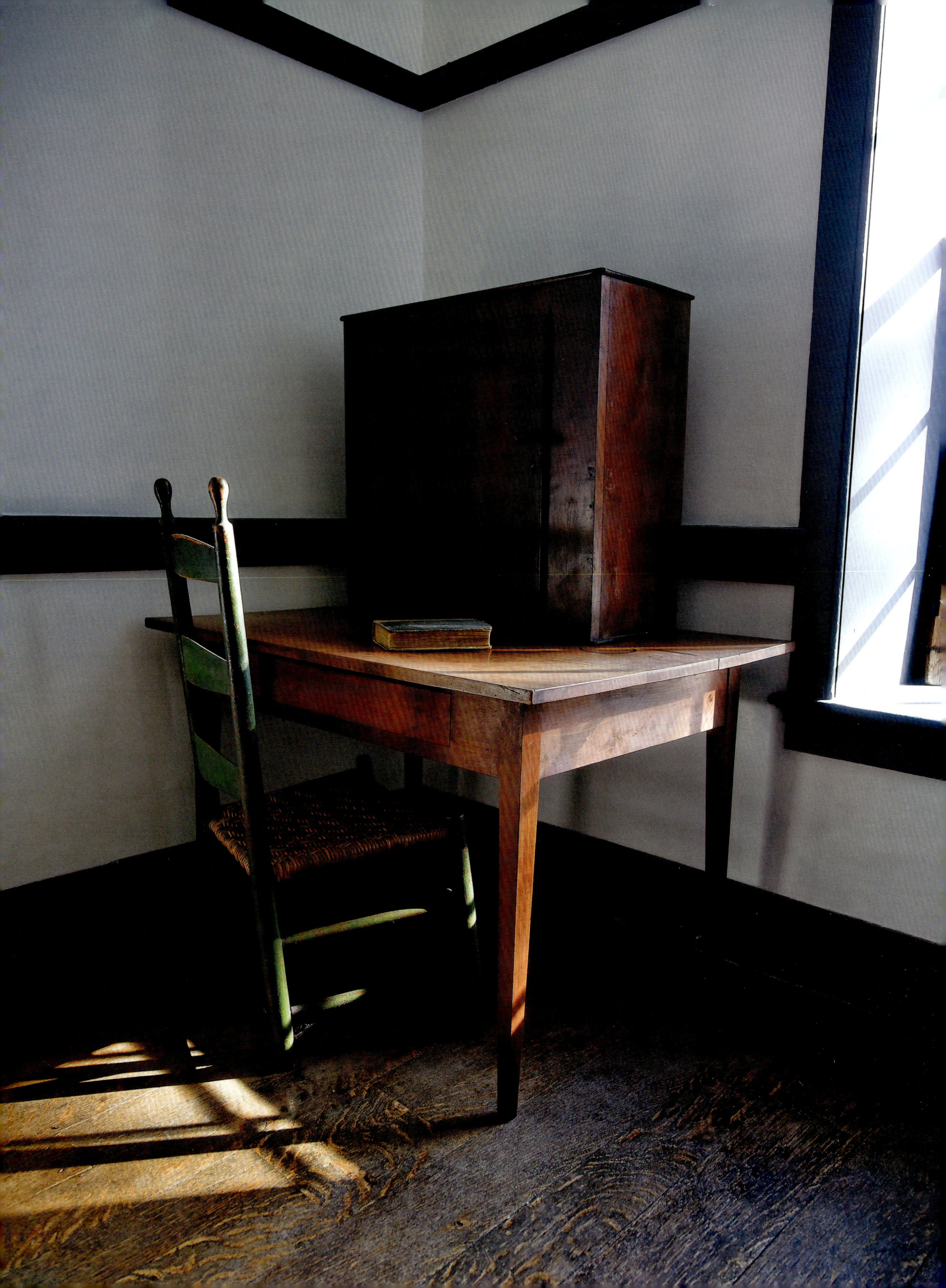

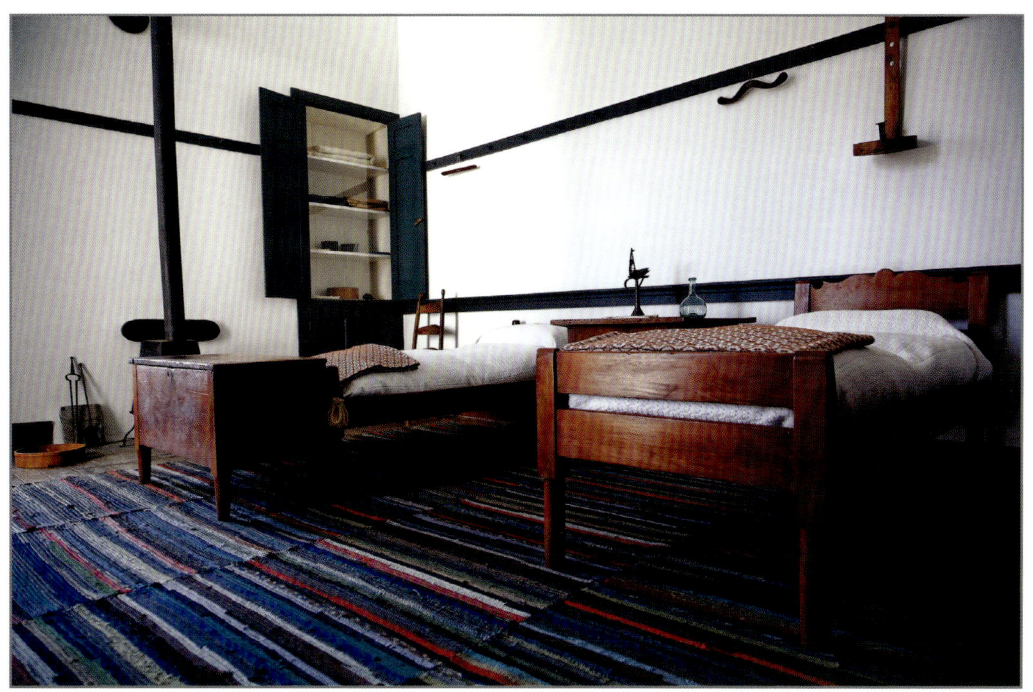

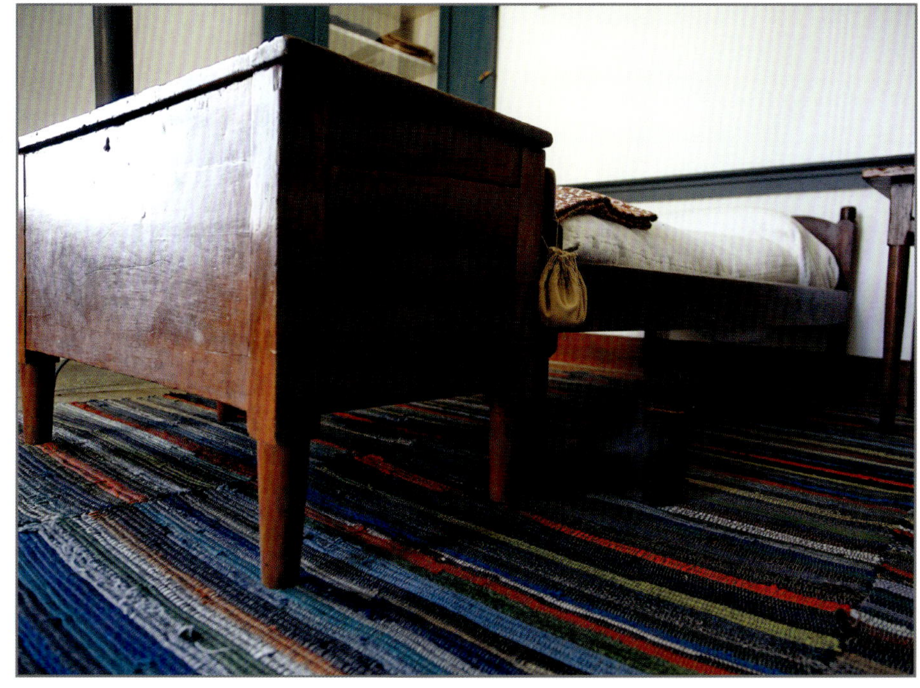

Further examples of the simple, yet functional style of the Shakers. The chest on the desk would have been used to store small, personal effects such as shaving gear and the like. The bible on the desk is a King James Version which was in plentiful supply about the Village. If an adult member who was illiterate joined the community, they were taught to read so they could study the Bible. The shoes viewable in the photos would have been made by members of the community. Several times a year a survey was taken of who needed shoes and what type and then they were made-to-order. The shoes were designed not to have a specific left or right foot orientation. Legend has it this was so the wearer did not have to fumble in the dark trying to figure out which shoe goes on which foot.

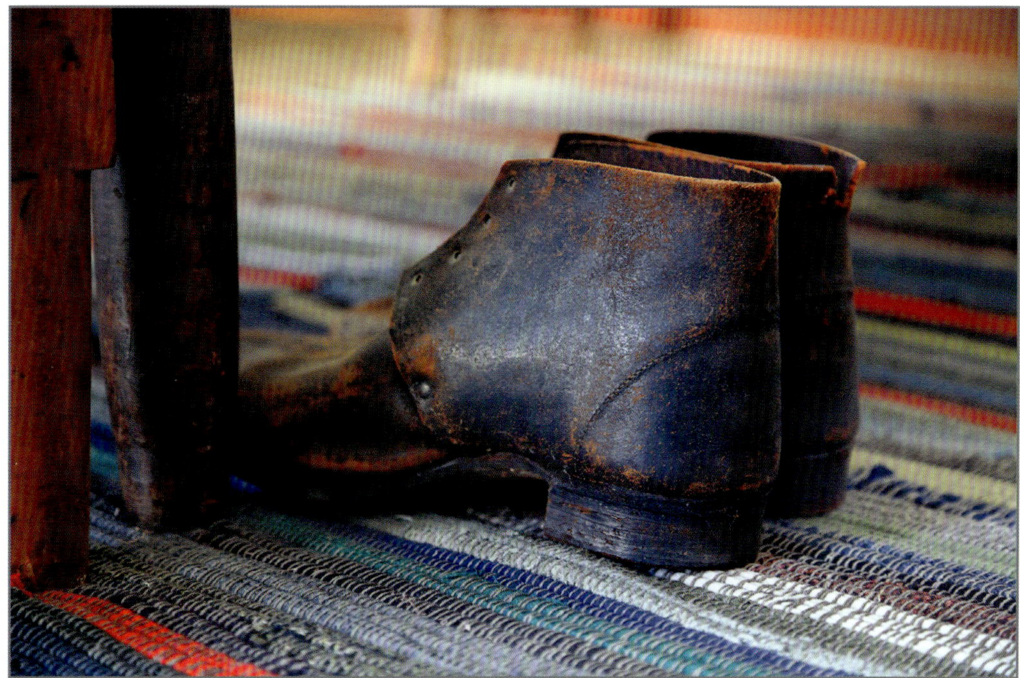

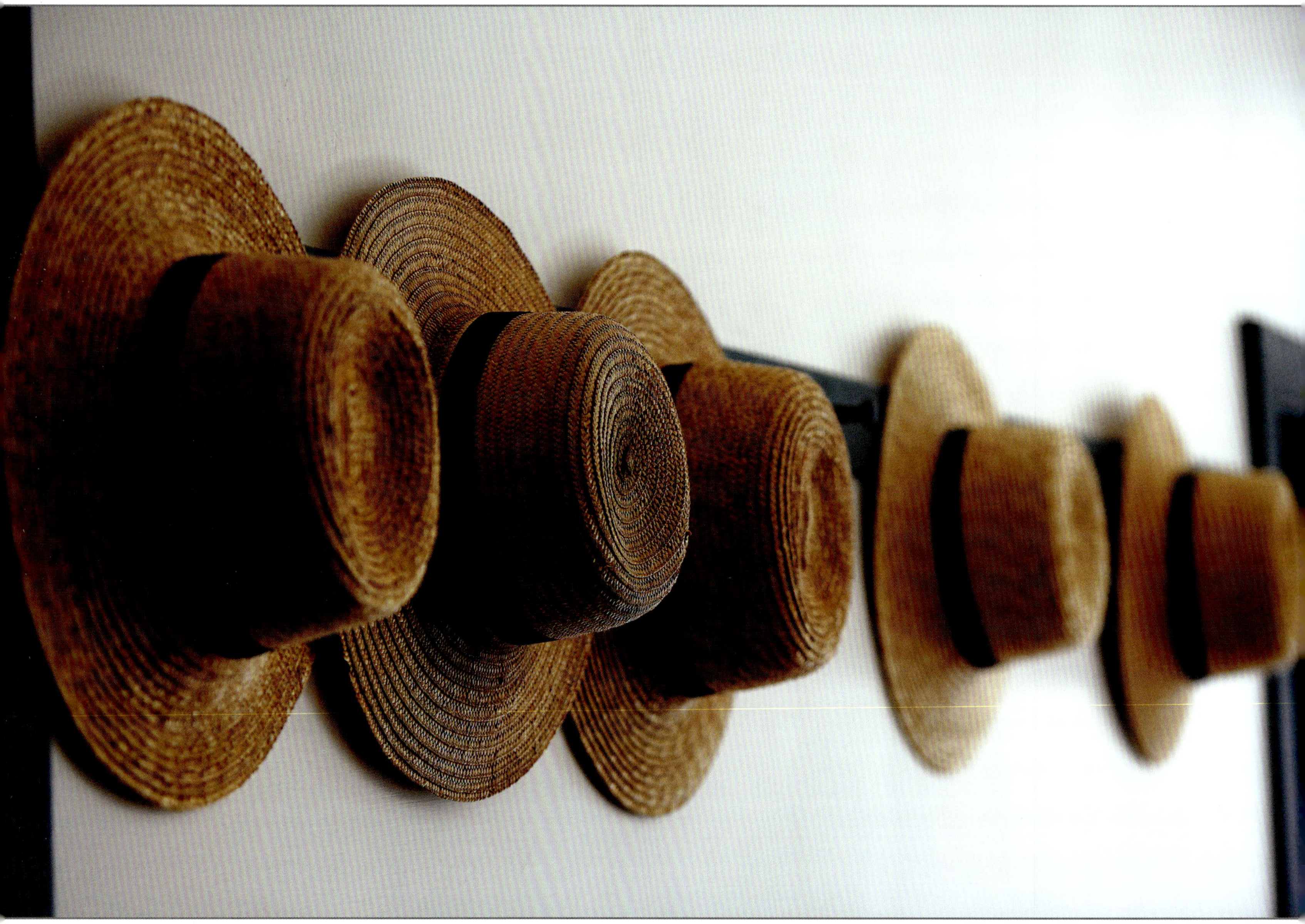

Straw hats were worn during the summer months while felt hats were worn in the winter. One of the first skills young boys would be taught was how to make hats. If they over produced, the surplus would be offered for sale to the general public. This also illustrates a use for the more than three hundred wooden pegs in the Centre Family Dwelling alone. While hat making was not a huge commercial endeavor, the women did make palmetto bonnets for sale, importing the palmetto from Cuba, drying it and making bonnets for the outside world.

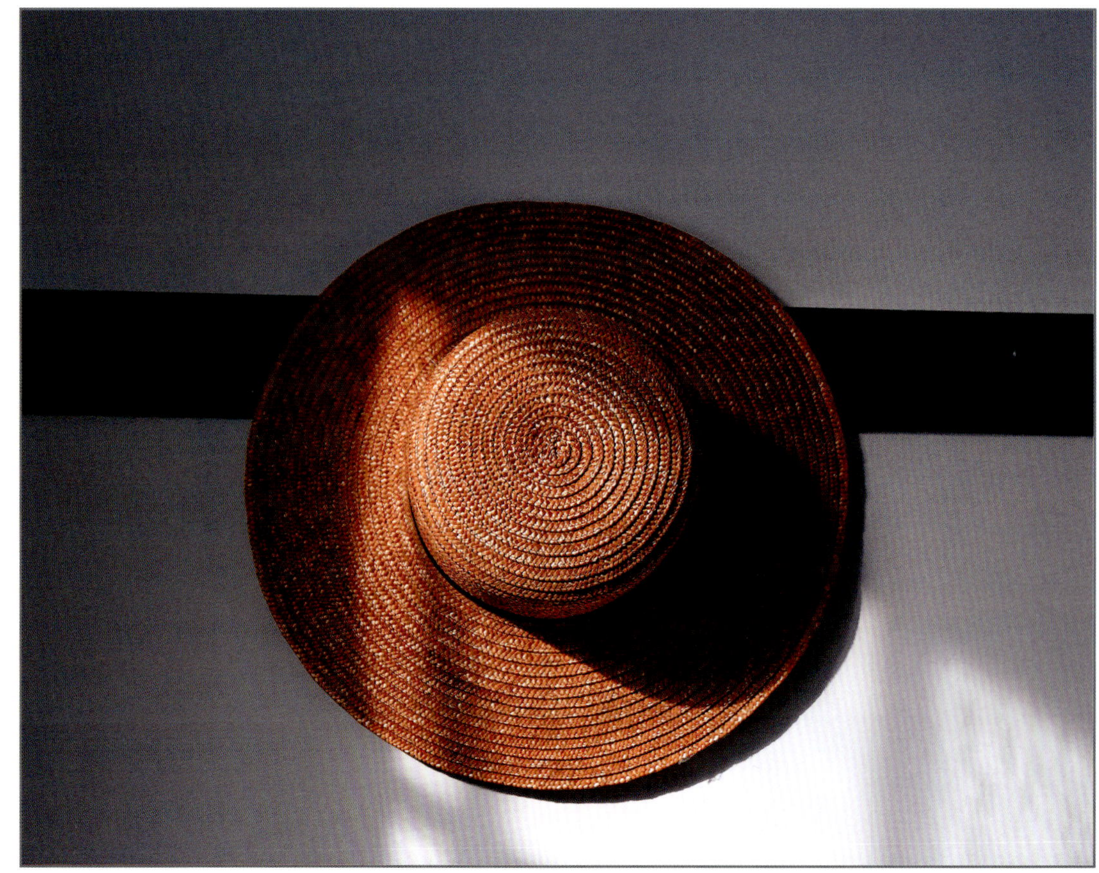

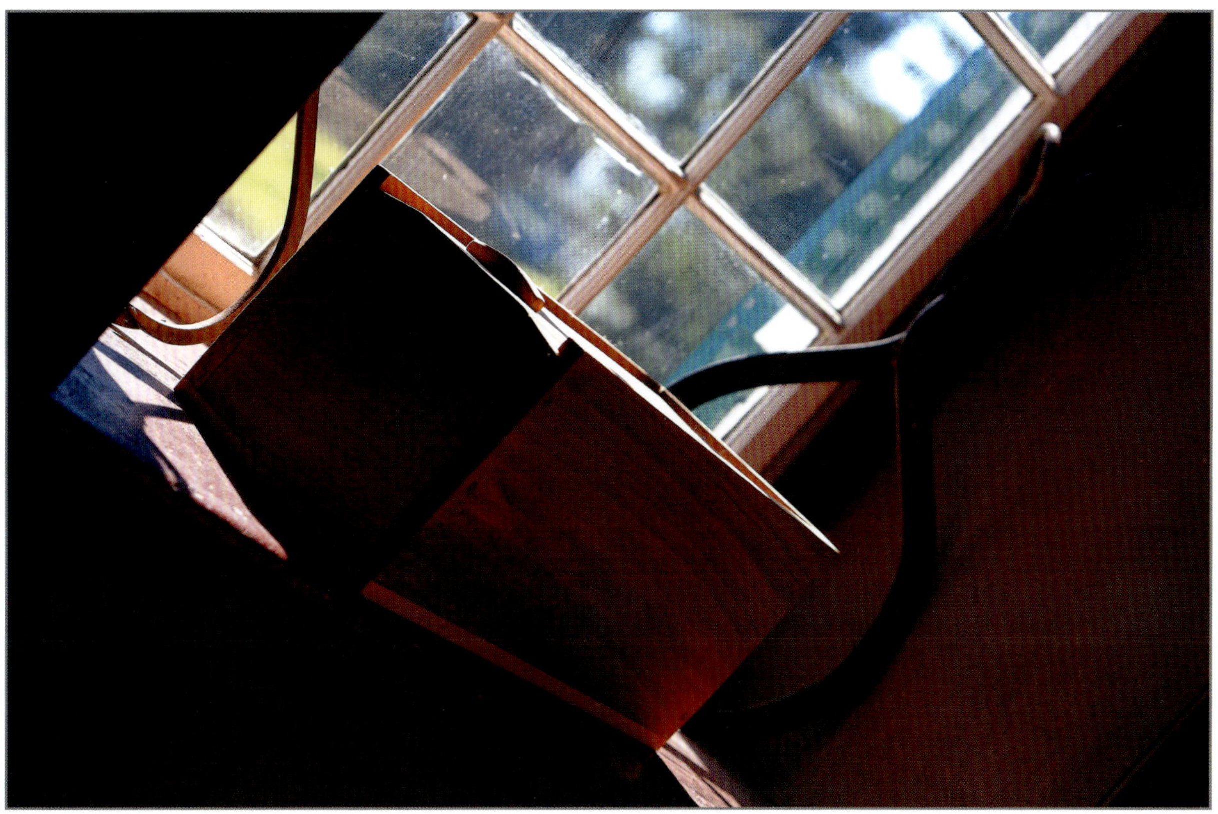

A reproduction bread box sits in the kitchen window of the Centre Family Dwelling.

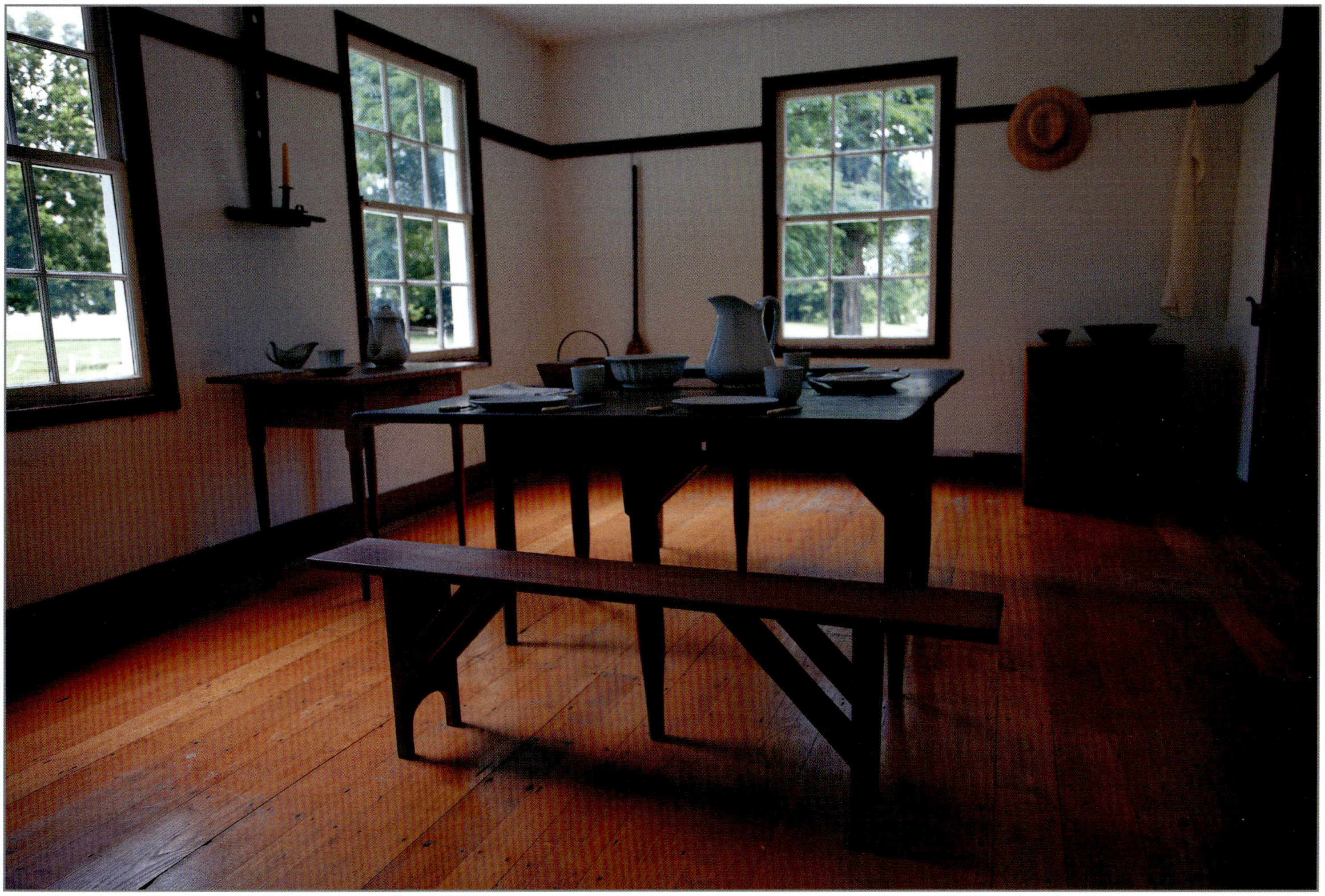

The Ministry's Dining Room located at the back of the Centre Family Dwelling was added to the original building by knocking out the back wall of one of the bee hive ovens in the kitchen. Members of the Ministry lived, worked and ate separately from the general population. This was done so they could remain impartial and unbiased in their decision making. In 1847, the Millennial Laws were revised stating the Ministry should not work, live or eat "under the same roof" as the general population. The Pleasant Hill Shakers once again showed their ingenuity by adding on this separate dining room so that technically they were not "under the same roof", but still in close proximity to the kitchen.

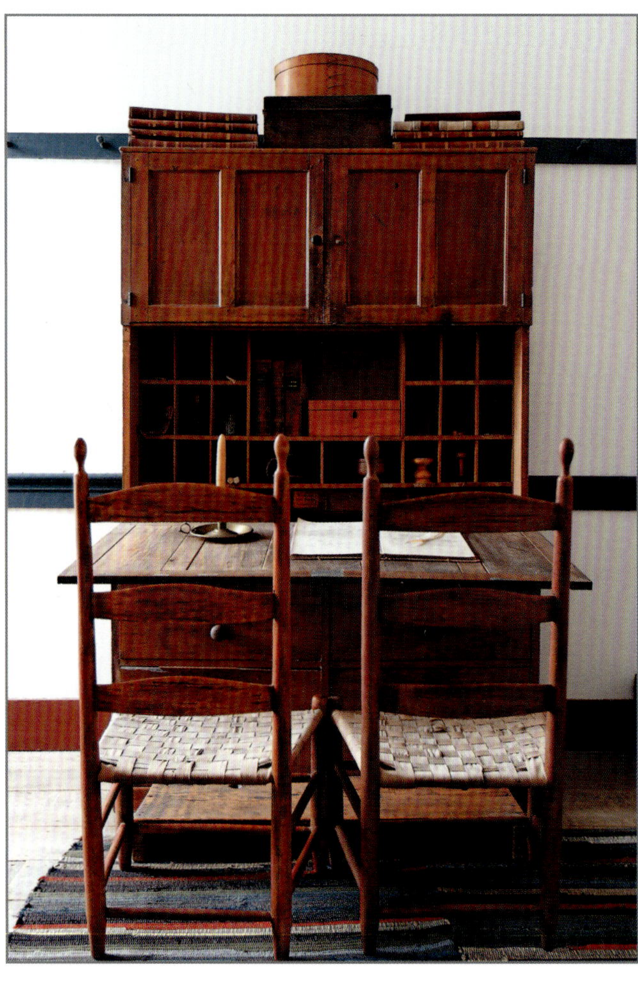

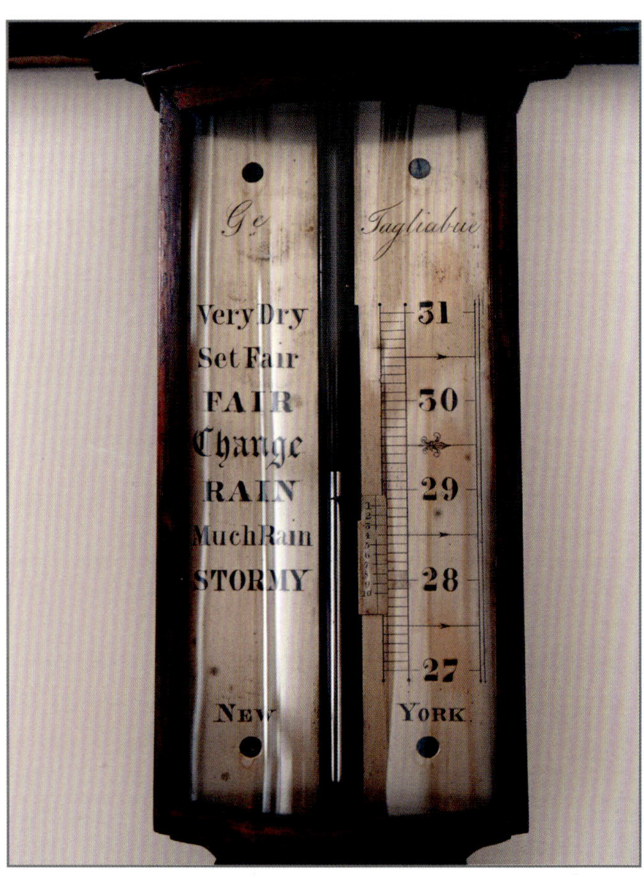

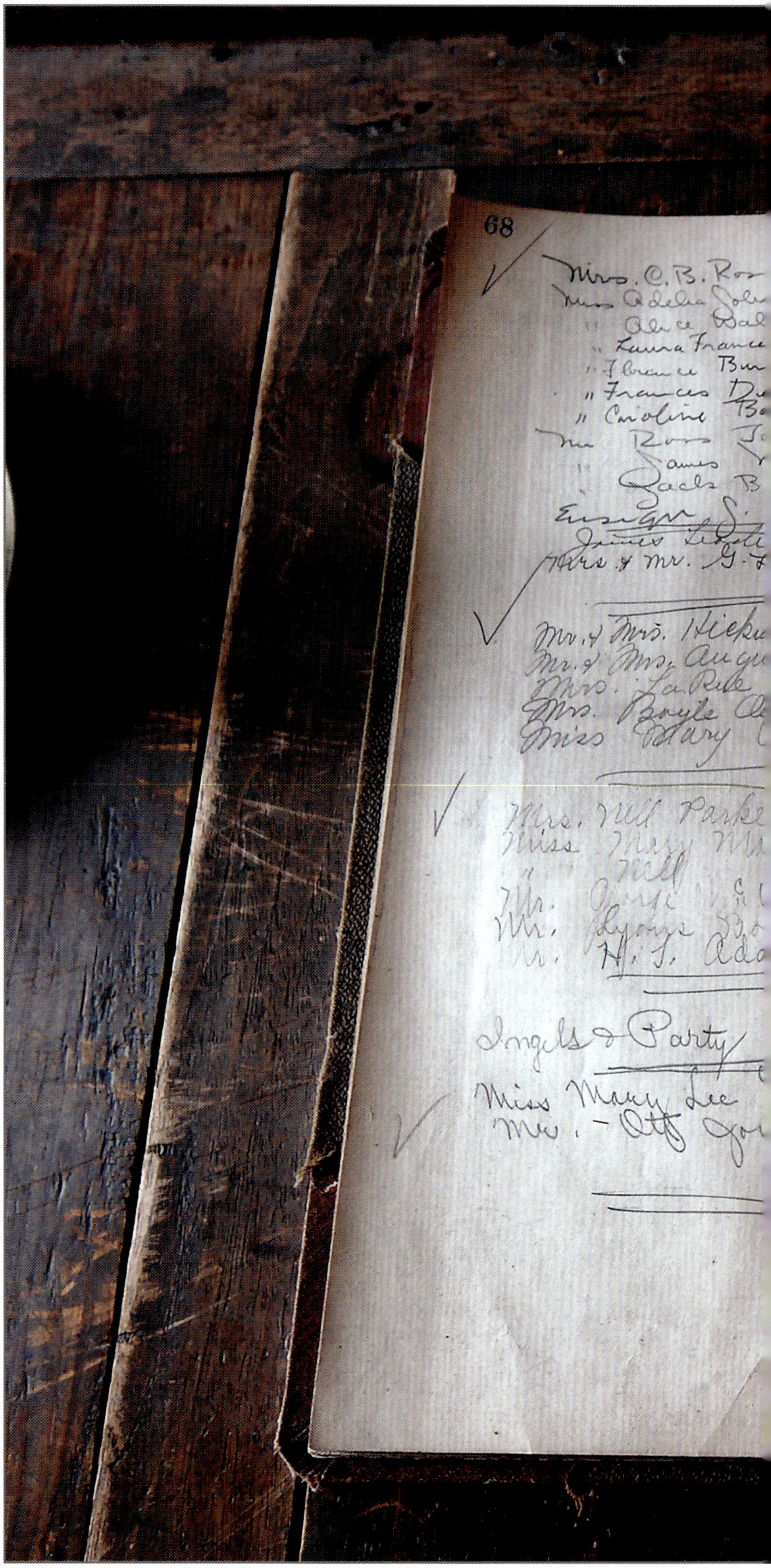

The barometer illustrates their agrarian lifestyle and how dependent the Shakers were on the land and weather. The Shakers kept meticulous records, a duty that fell to the Trustees of the community. Entries were made three times each day noting the weather conditions. In addition to the community's records, many of the literate members kept personal journals which have provided important insights into Shaker life at that time as well as the construction of the buildings. This proved very helpful when restoration efforts began as no blueprints of the structures were available.

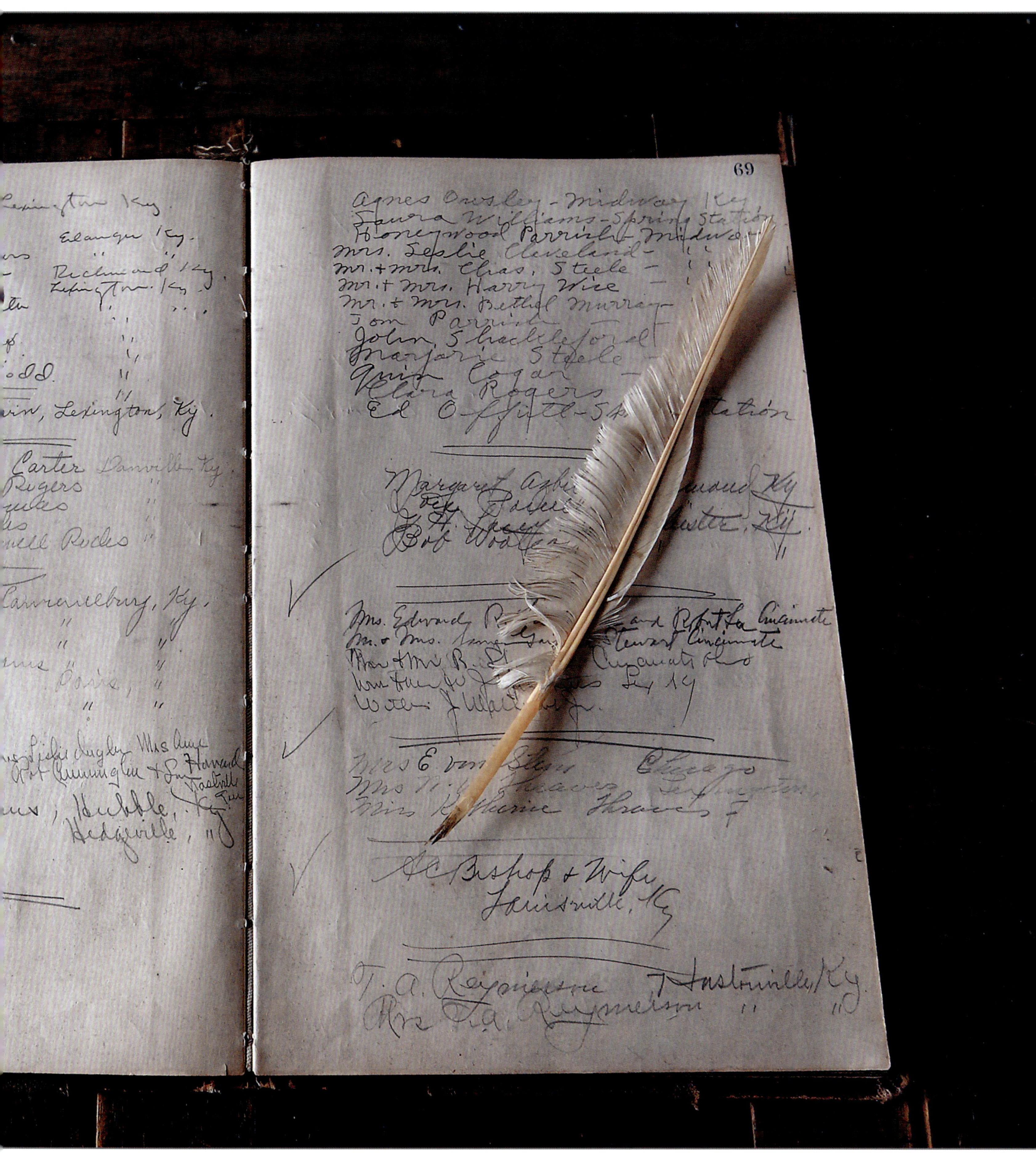

The record book pictured here is a guest registry from the time the East Family Dwelling was operated as an inn.

Baskets were made onsite to support daily living more so than as a commercial venture. Again, any surplus would have been offered for sale to the general population. Interestingly, this was a job reserved for men who performed other woodworking tasks.

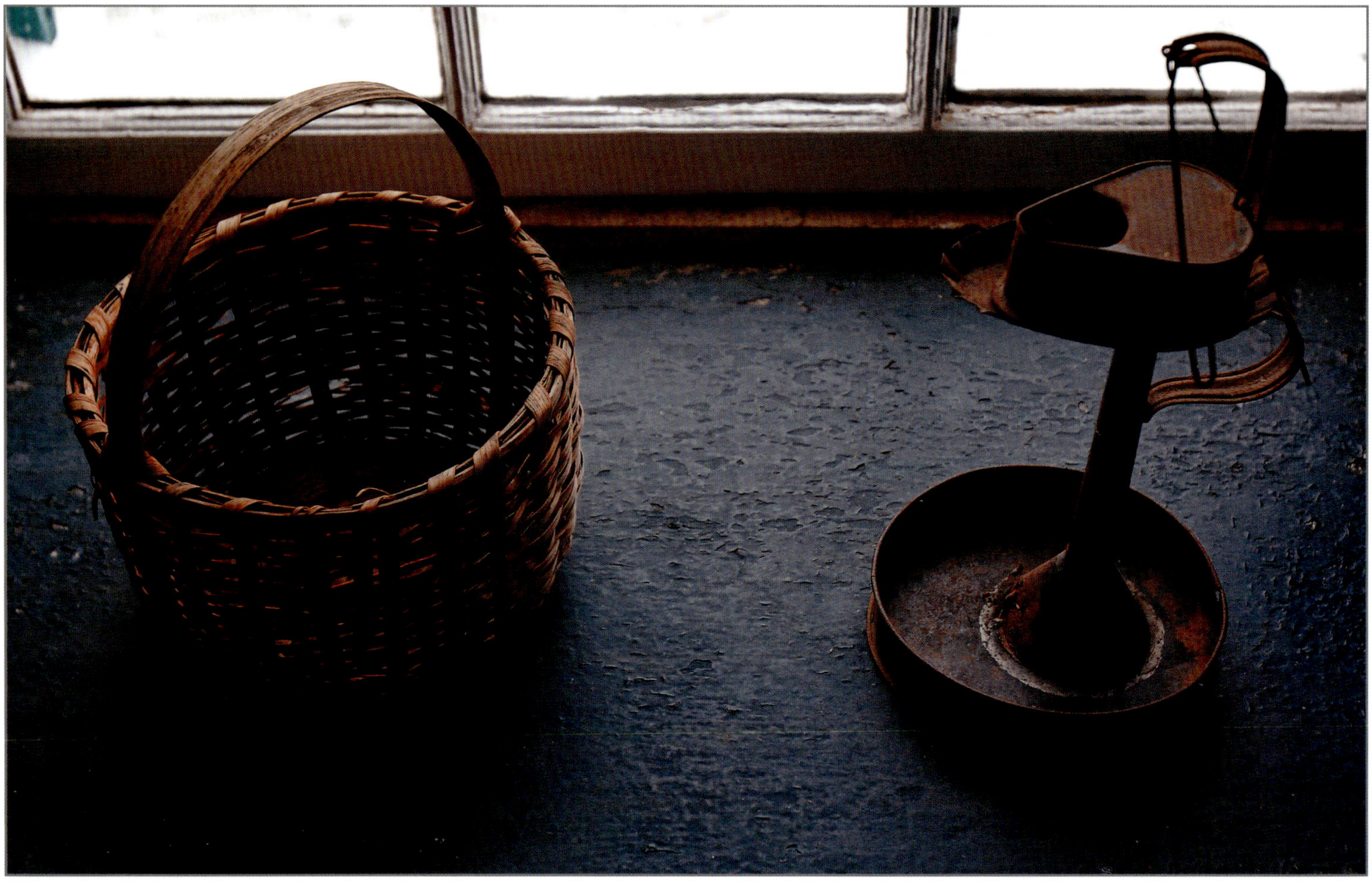

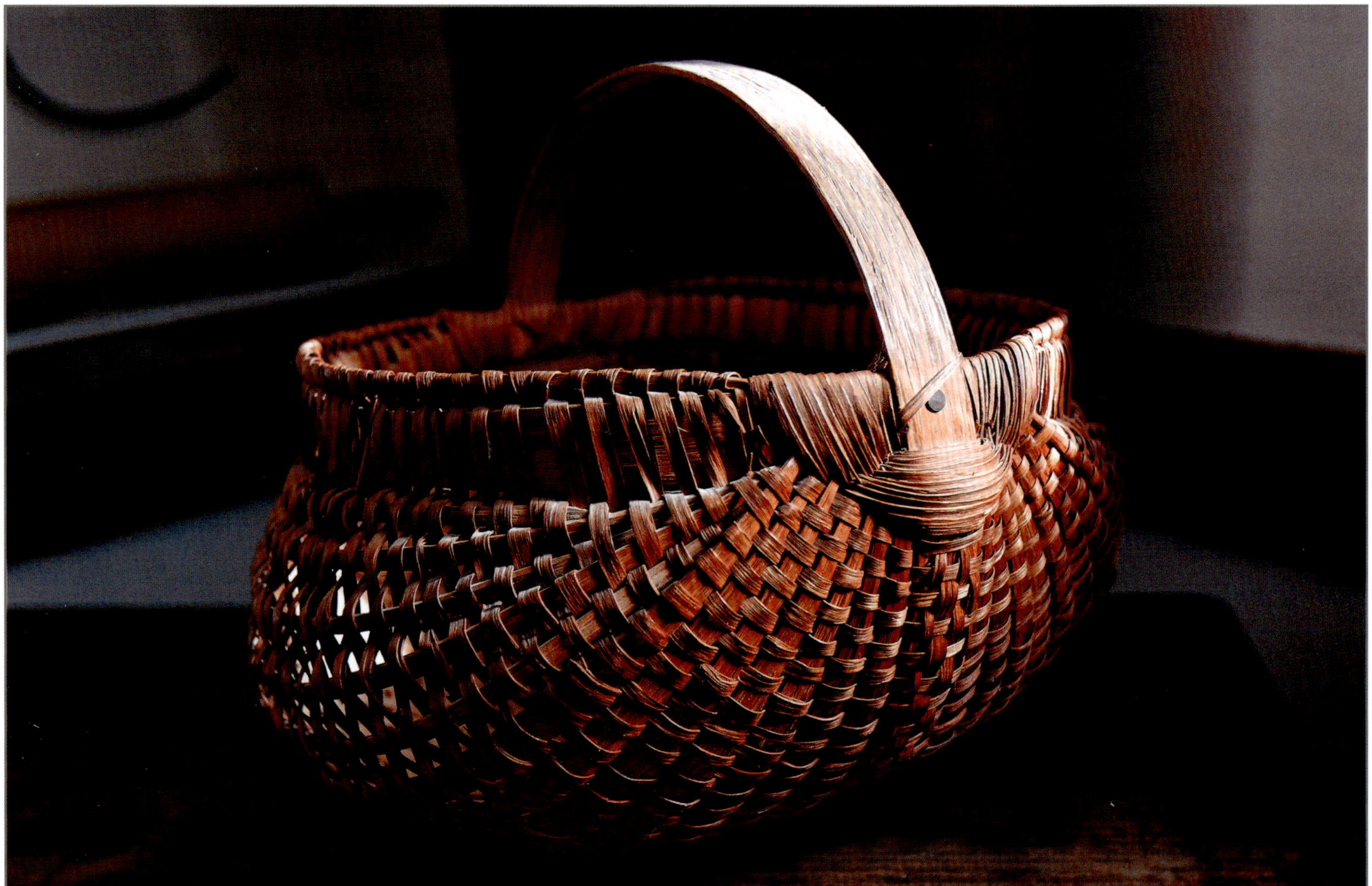

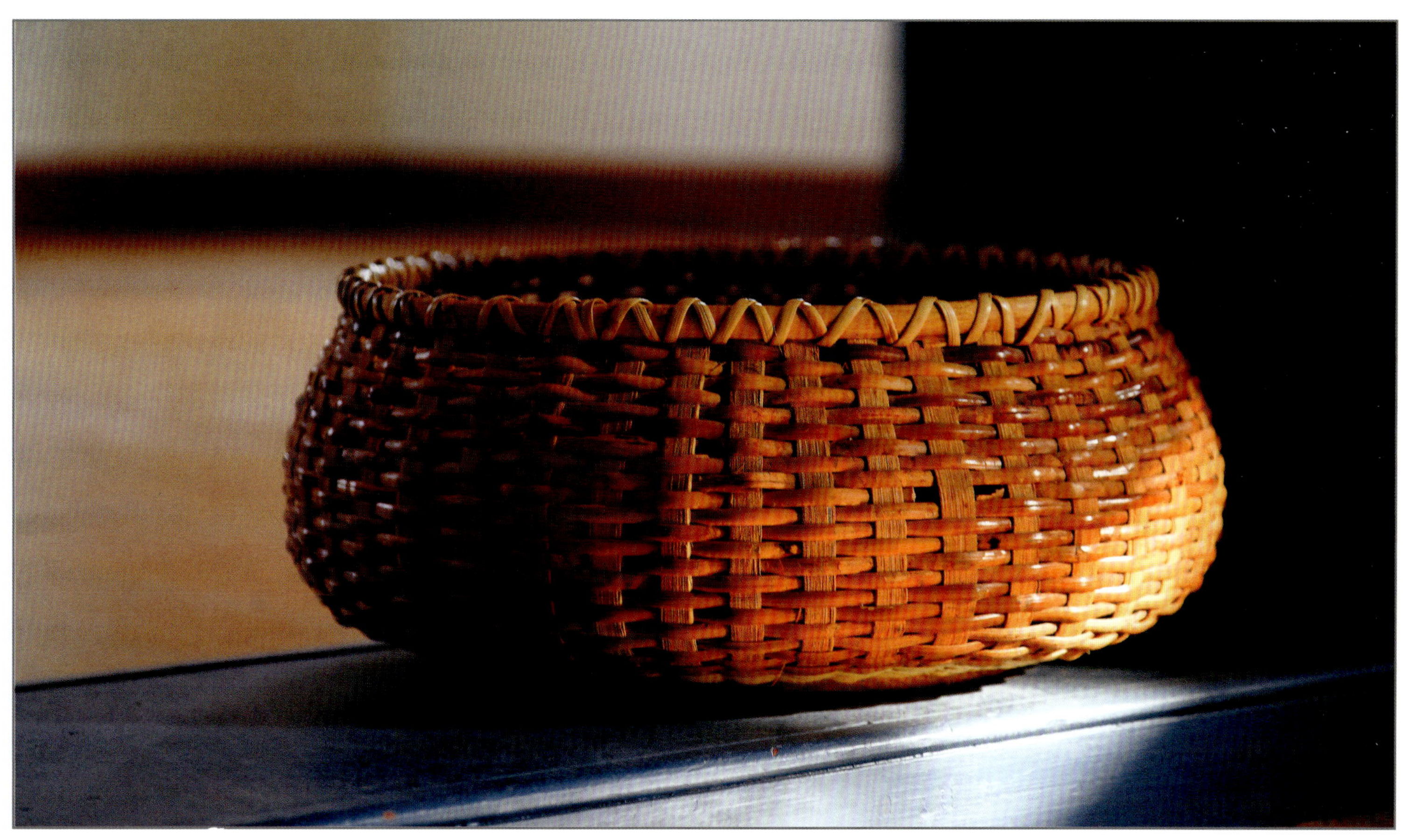

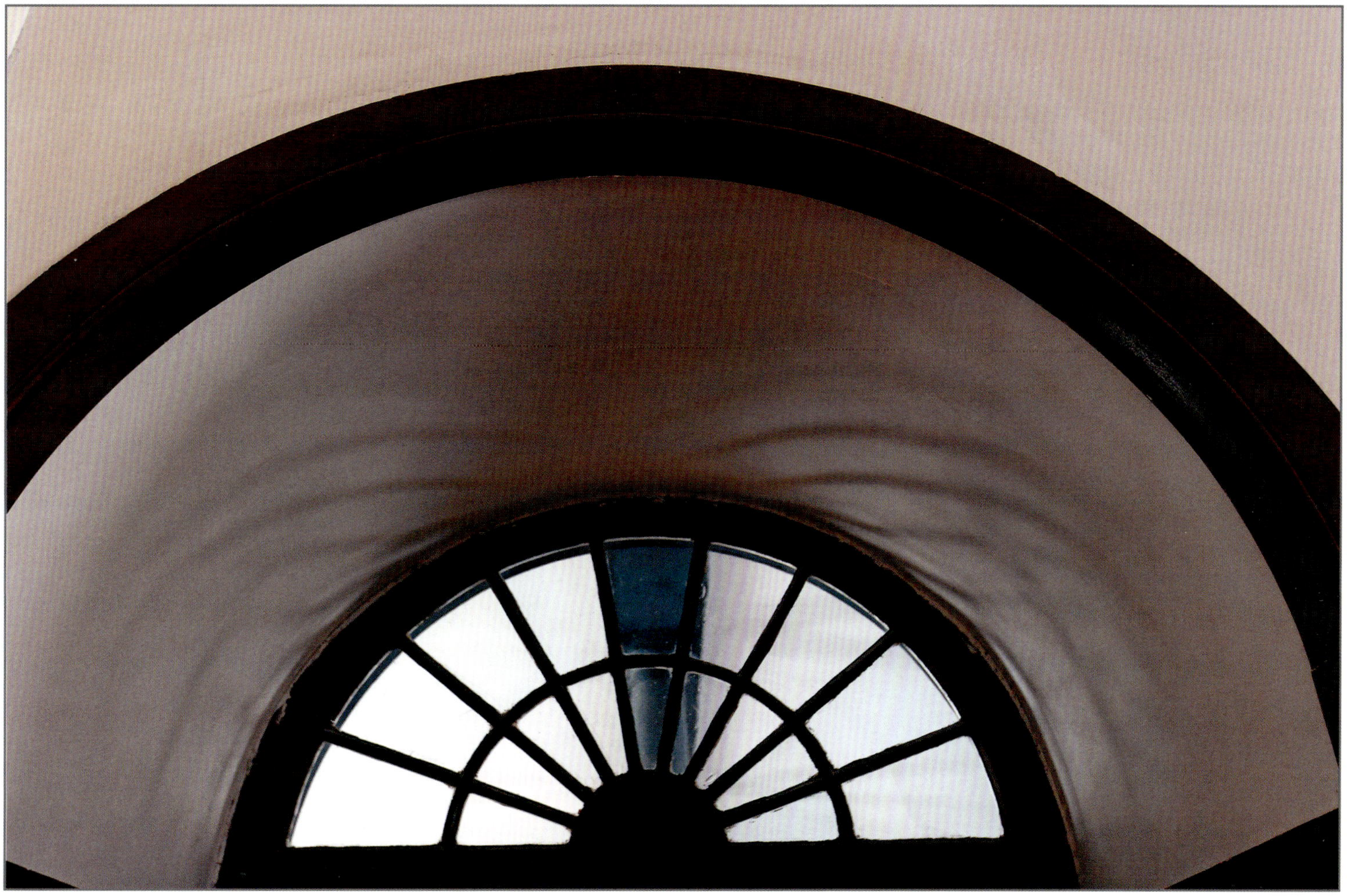

The transom light door leading from the Centre Family dining room to the kitchen is another example of the use of natural light and ventilation. Some members took exception to the transoms, feeling they were too ornate. While beautiful in its simplicity, it also shows the utilization of the strength of the arch as well as the classic and efficient use of the space. Journals indicate the sentiment of the Shakers at the time was if it was necessary to make something, make it functional but do not hesitate to make it beautiful.

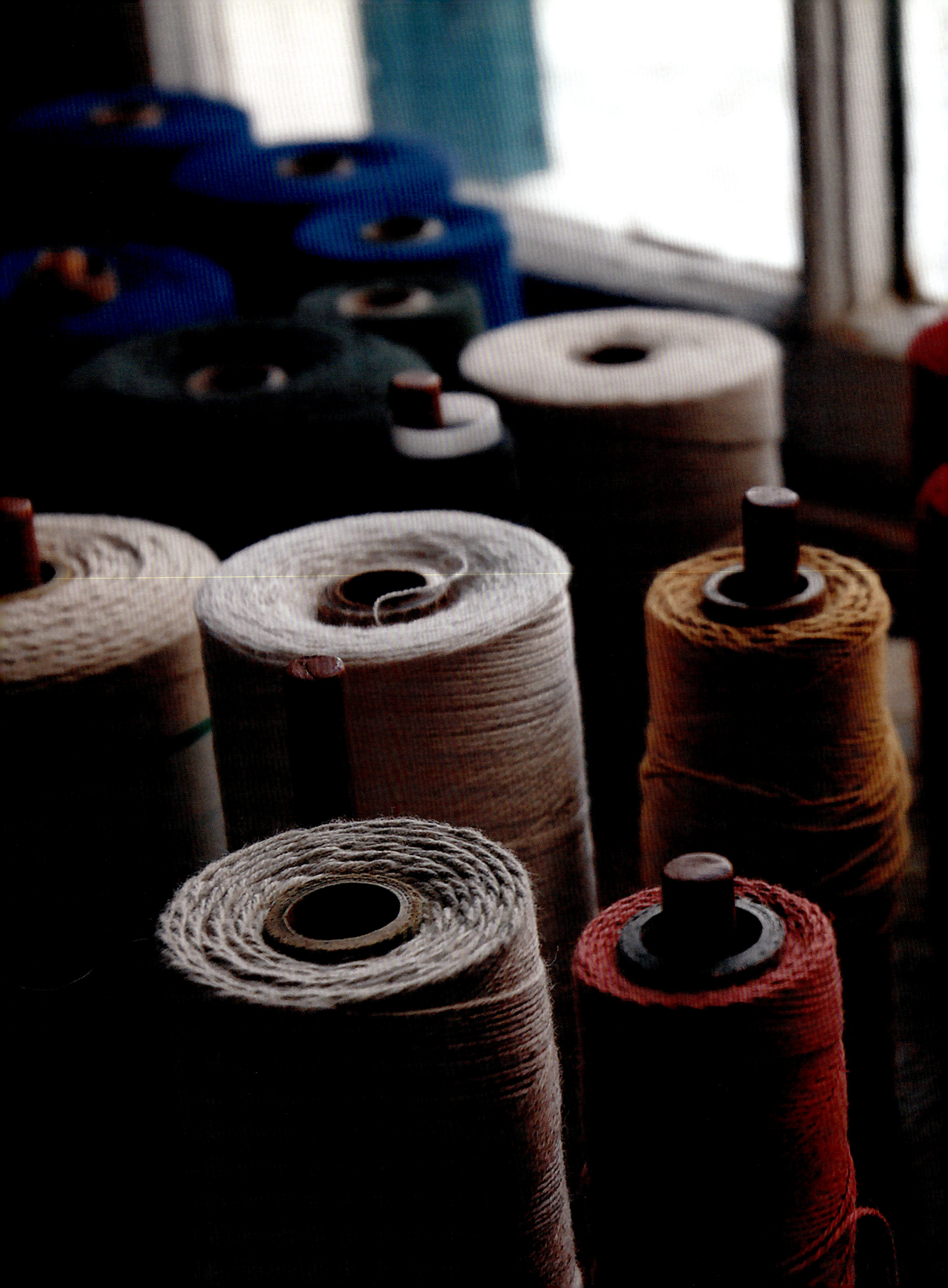

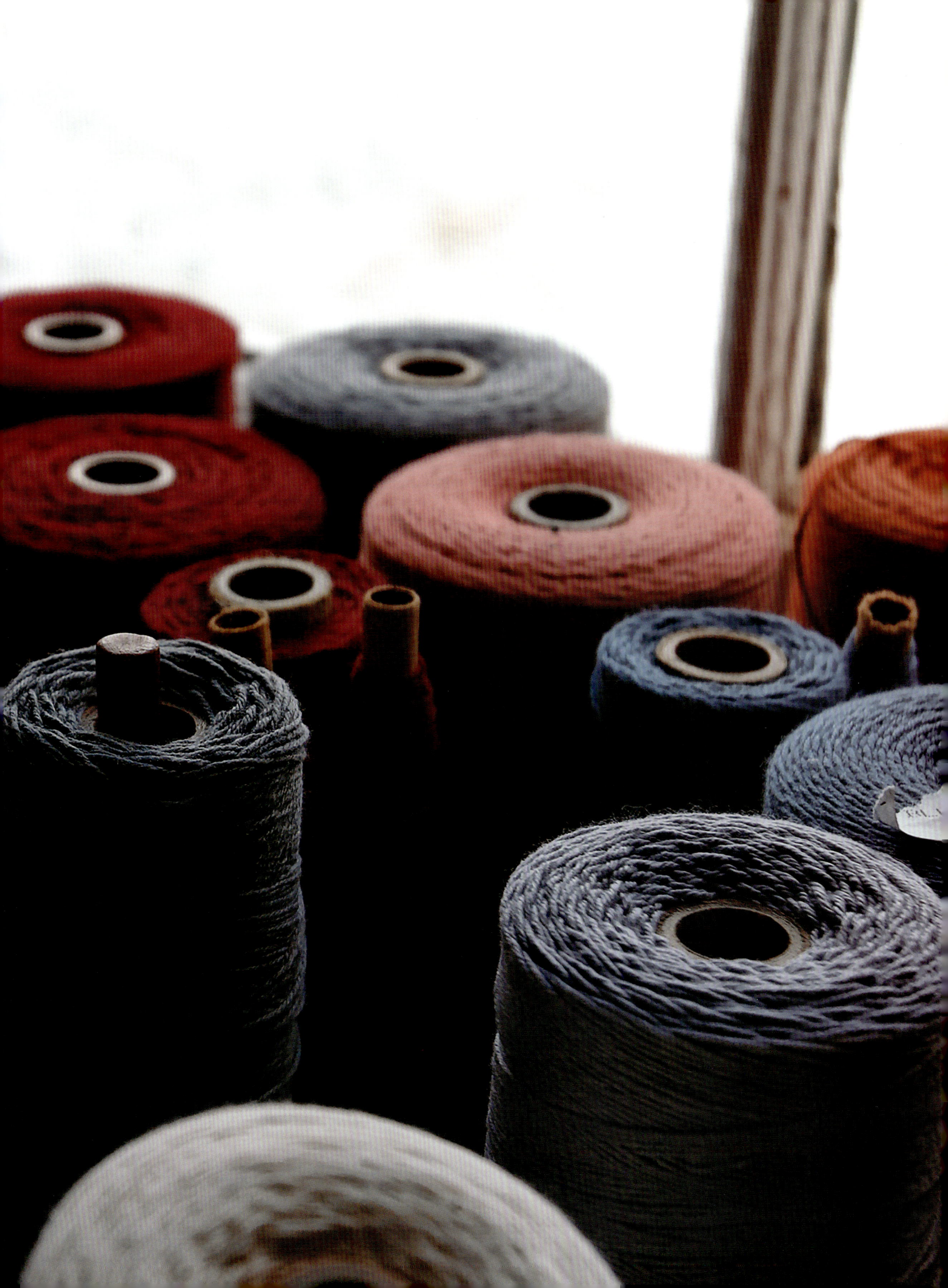

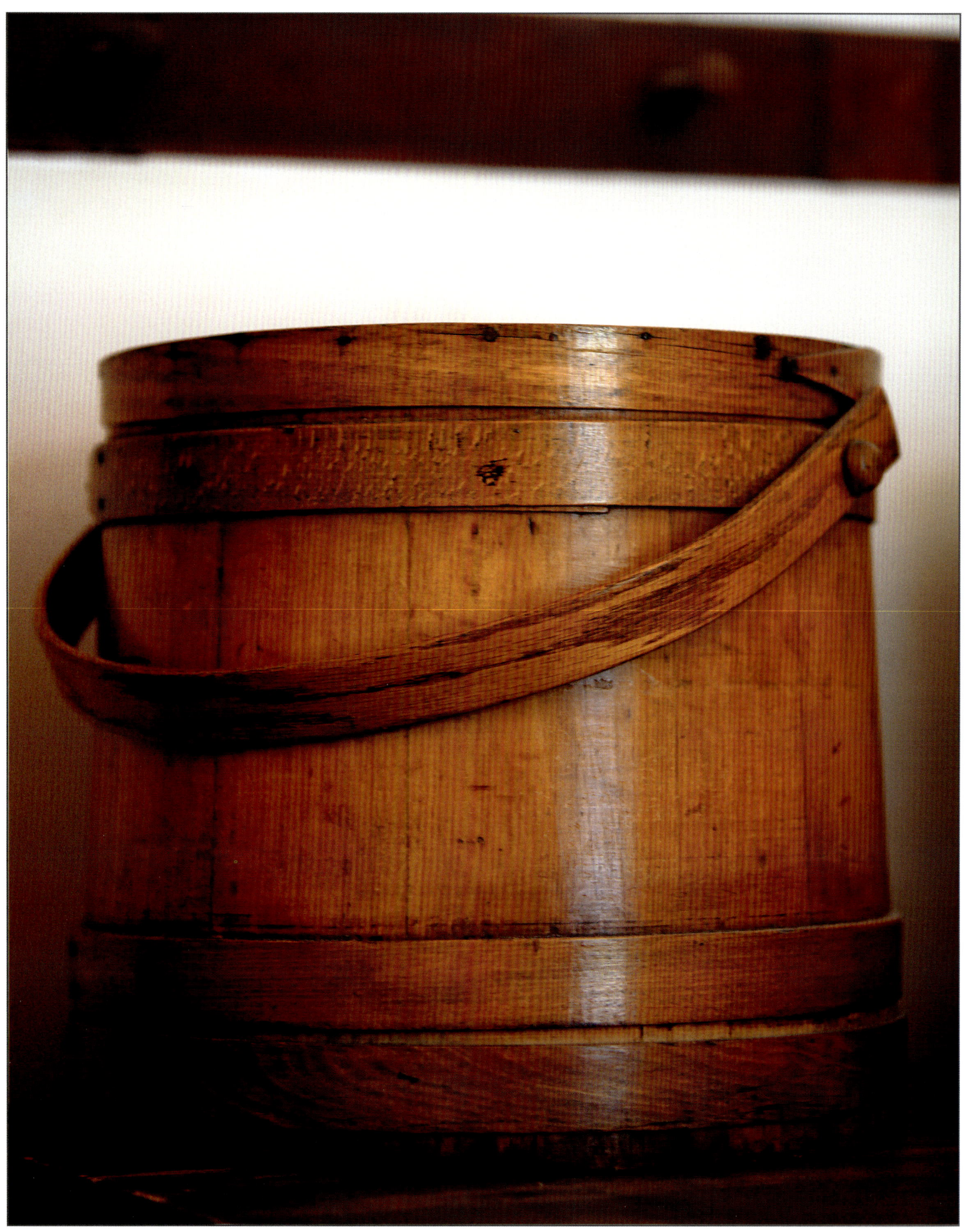

Previous spread: Shakers embraced colors that could be made with a natural dye source and were not constrained to drab colors. These would have been obtained onsite as well as purchased from outside sources. Typically in the 19th century the wool would have been sheared from sheep onsite then spun and weaved into articles of clothing and other items as needed.

Above: A firkin, a small wooden keg, would have been just one of the many items manufactured in the Cooper's Shop. Often times these containers were used as a modern day lunch pail.

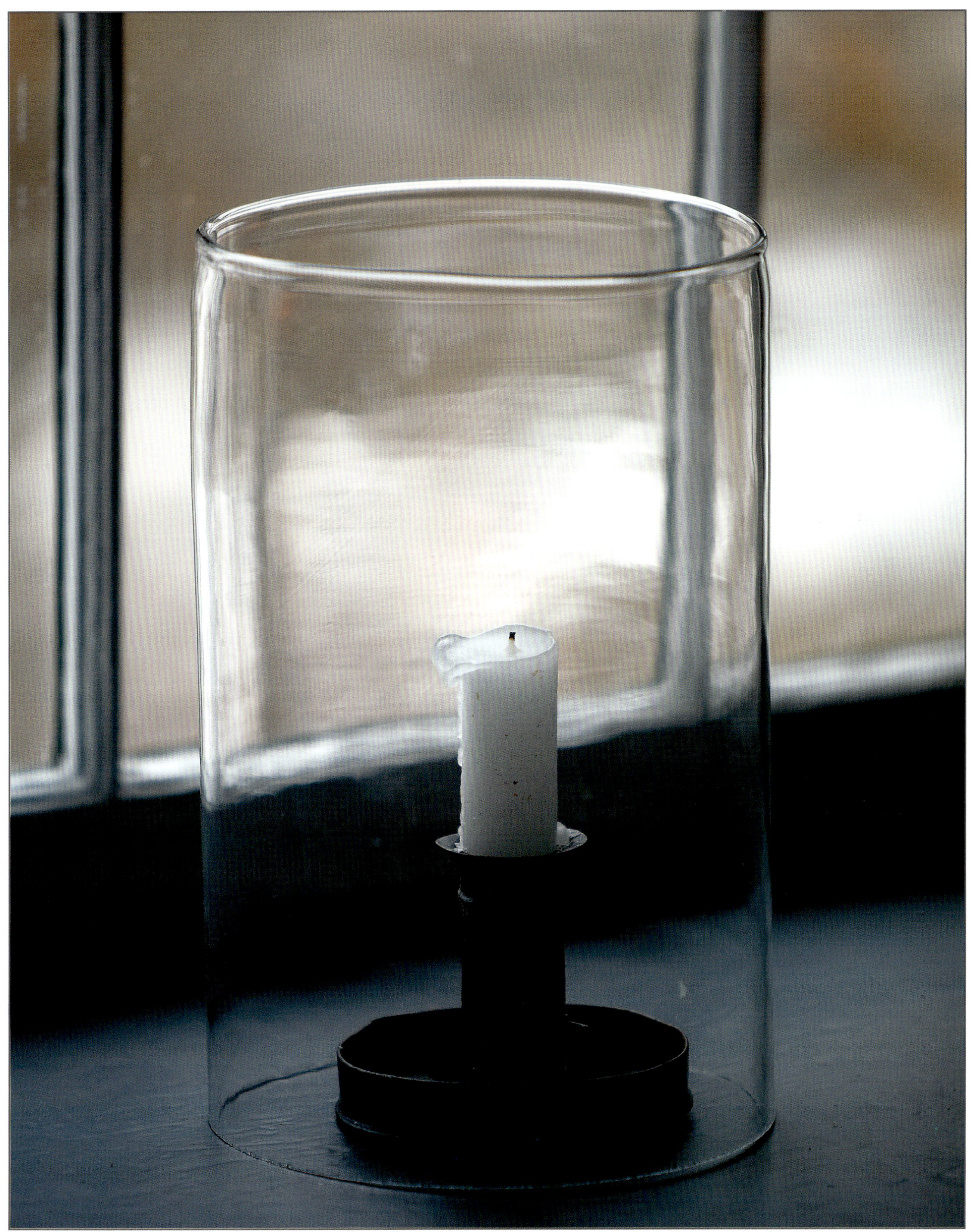

Candles provided the primary source of light for the Shakers. Beeswax candles were preferred for their long burning and low smoke. Bees were raised on the property for their honey and beeswax. 800 to 1,000 pounds of honey were harvested a year and with over 900 fruit trees on the property, the bees played an important role in pollination.

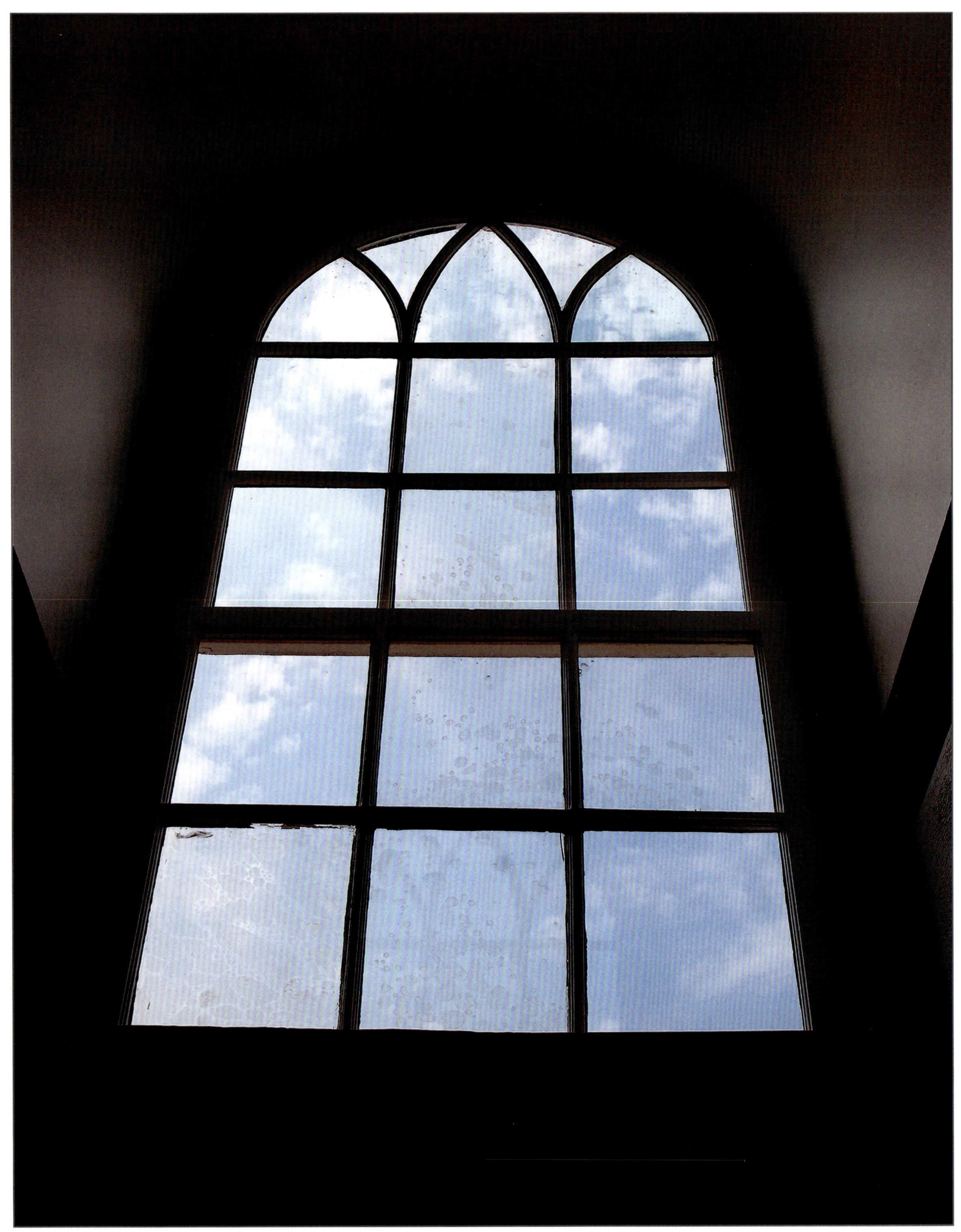

Glass for the windows was not produced at the village, but rather purchased from the outside world. Given the number of windows in the Centre Family Dwelling alone, it illustrates the Shakers were becoming affluent. They felt they were creating Heaven on earth and that their structures should reflect that fact. The name Shaker becomes identified with quality at this time. When the outside world bought Shaker products, they knew they would get quality products and be dealt with on Christian terms.

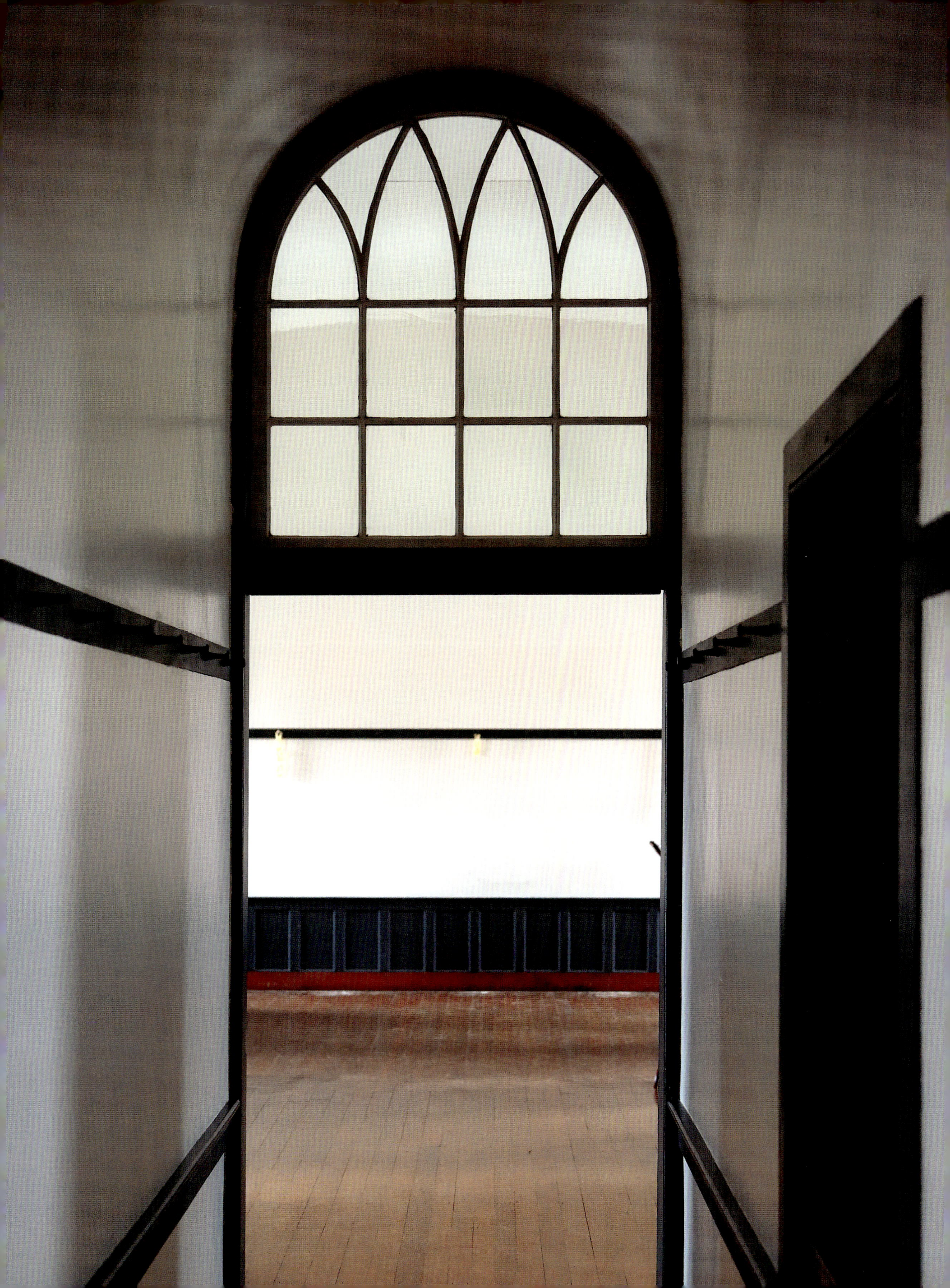

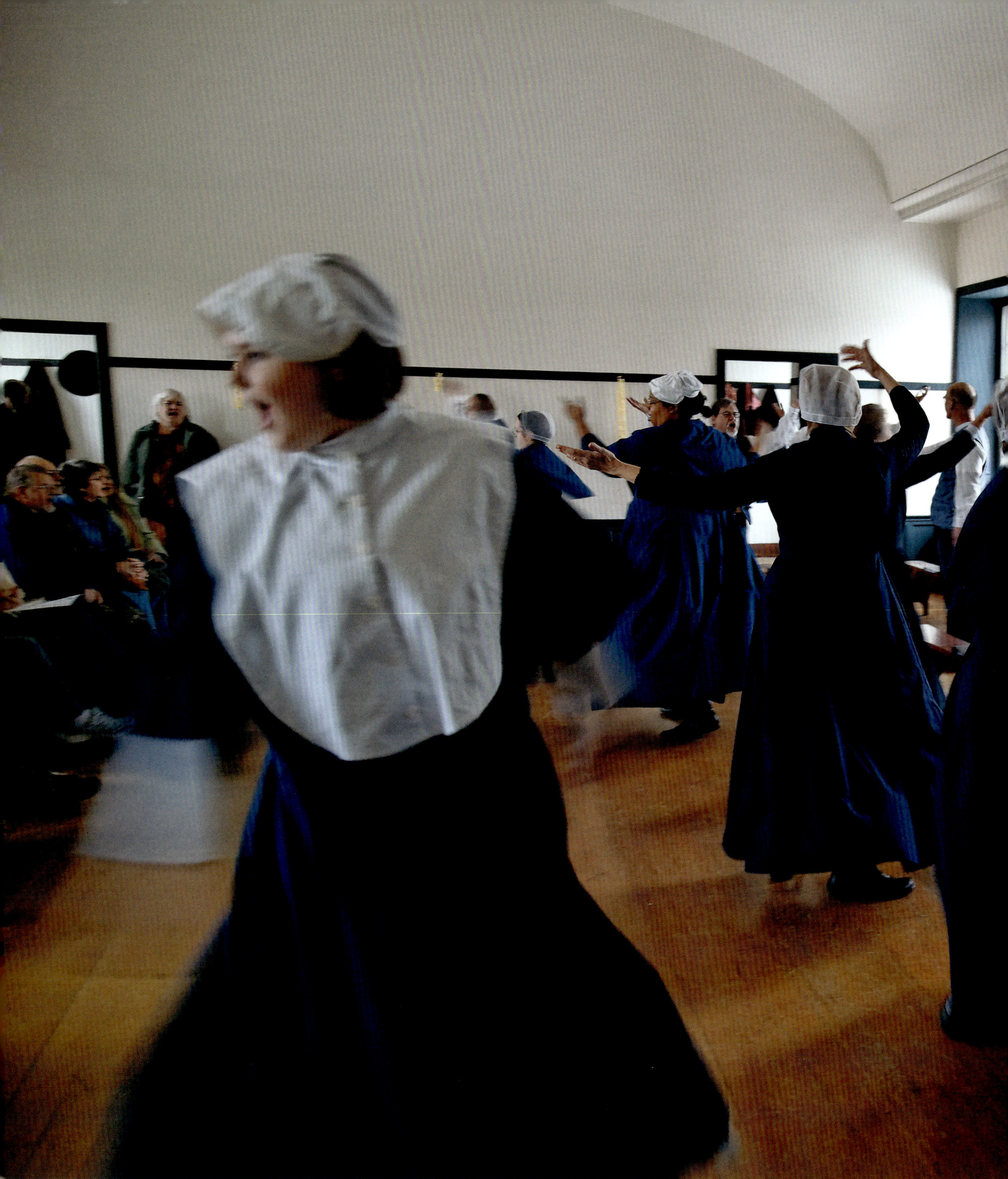

With acoustics nearly as good as those of the Meeting House, the Meeting Room of the Centre Family Dwelling was a place where Family members would come together on a daily basis for fellowship and worship. The area was also used to practice the dances used in Sunday worship with men and women alternating days to practice. If sickness befell one family or the community, each family had a meeting room in their dwelling where they could still worship and not endanger the entire community. This was done on numerous occasions and noted in the journals.

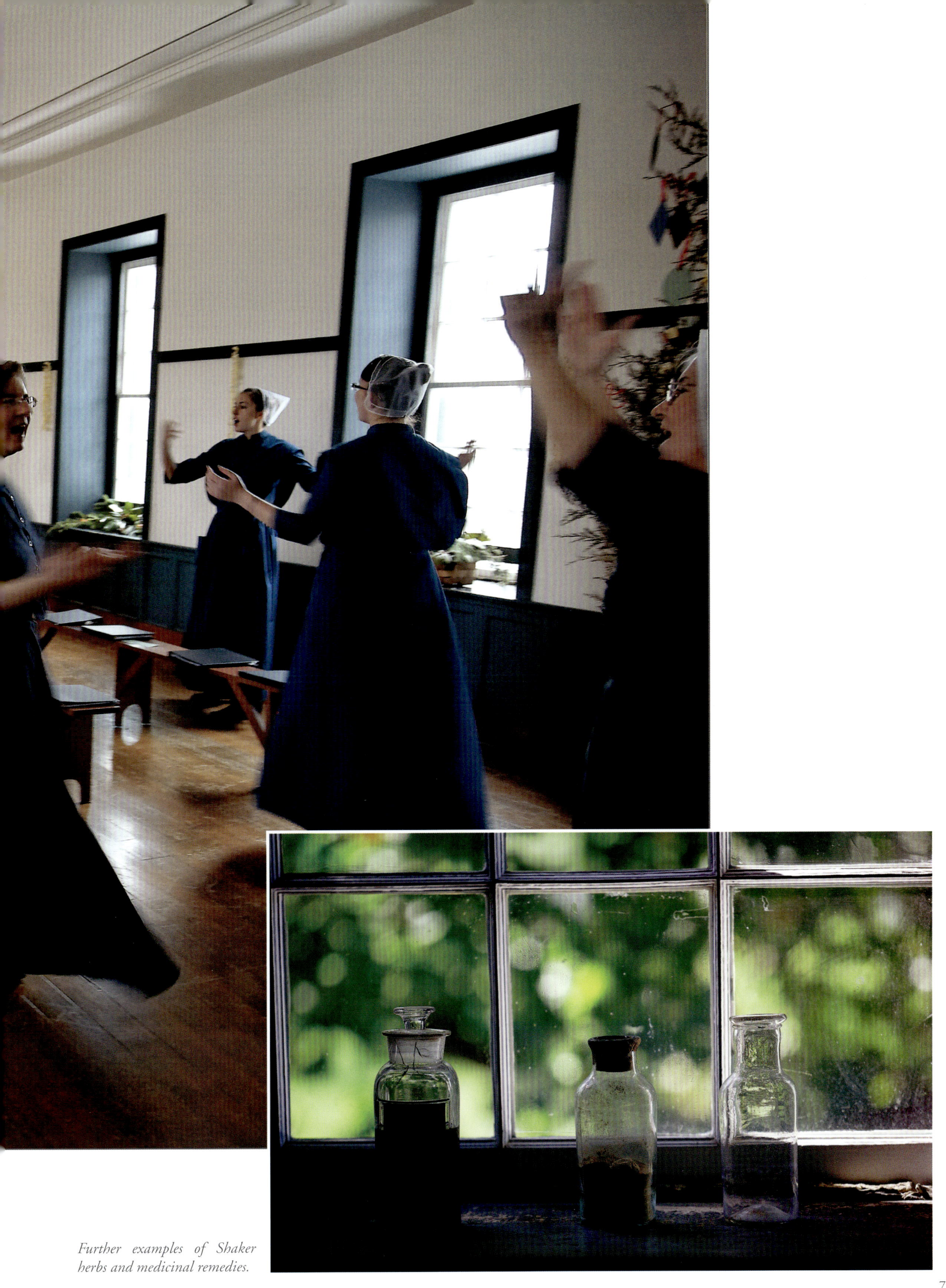

Further examples of Shaker herbs and medicinal remedies.

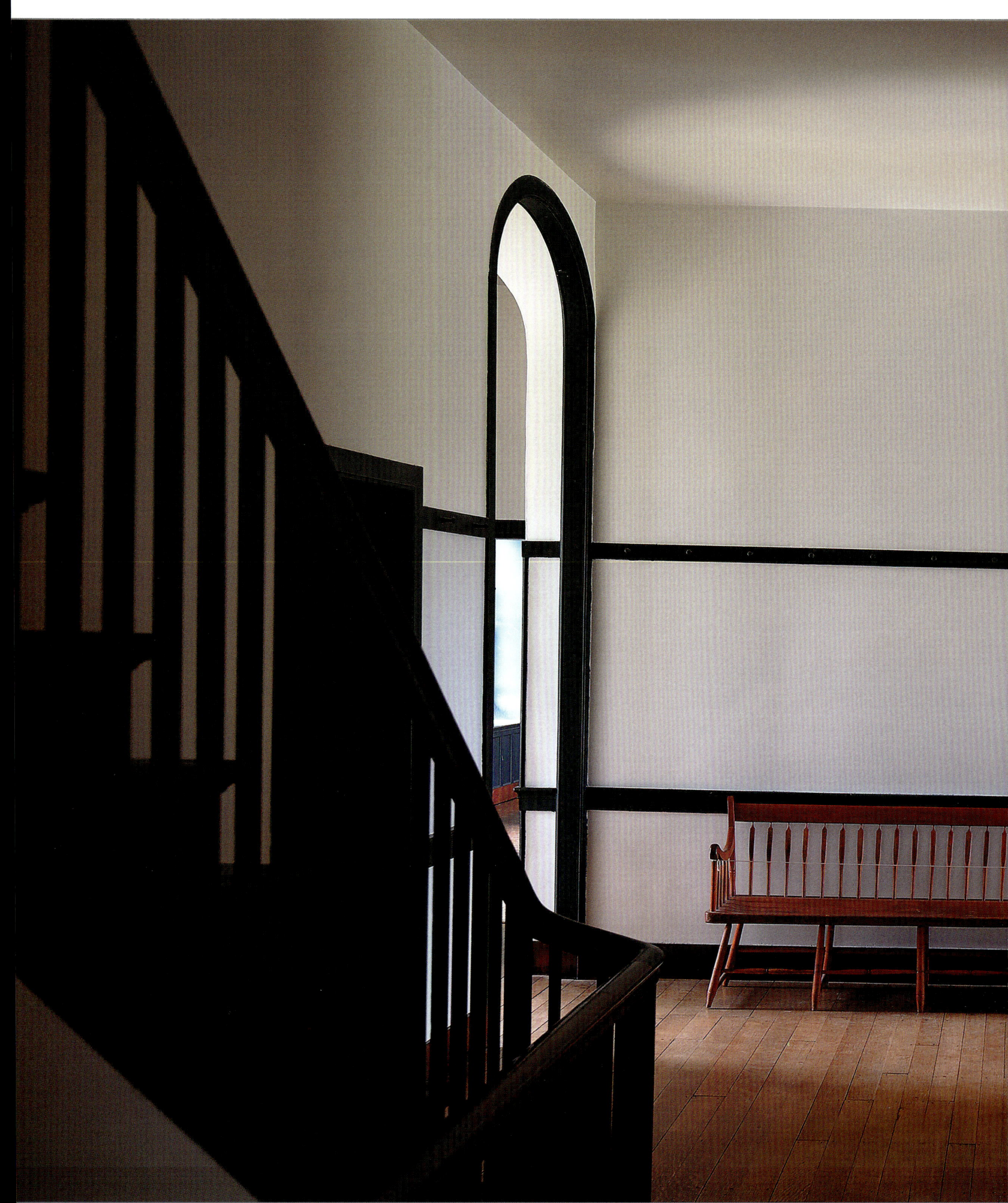

The "Circle of Light" in the Centre Family Dwelling is probably the best example of natural light and the architectural designs used to take advantage of it.

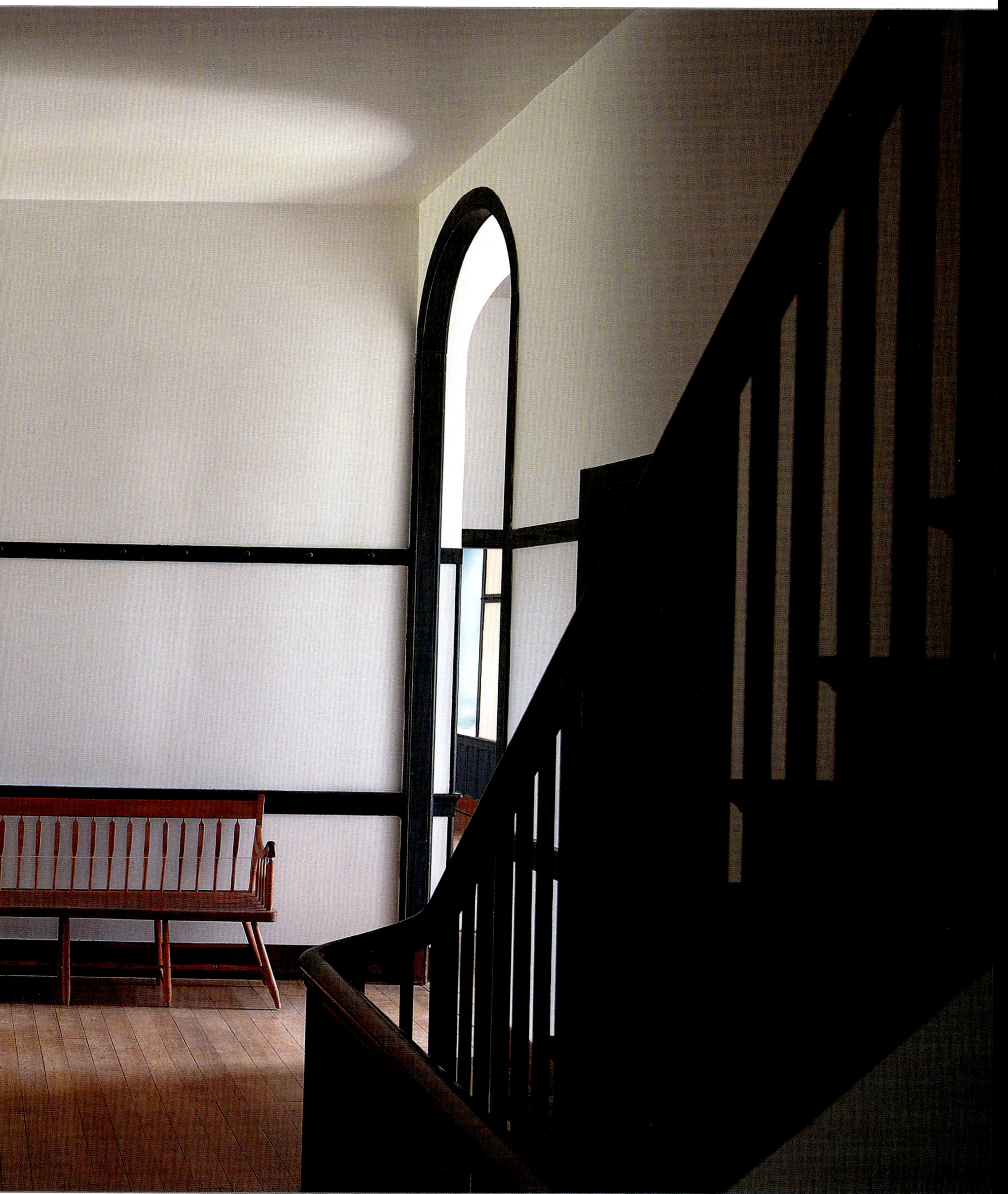

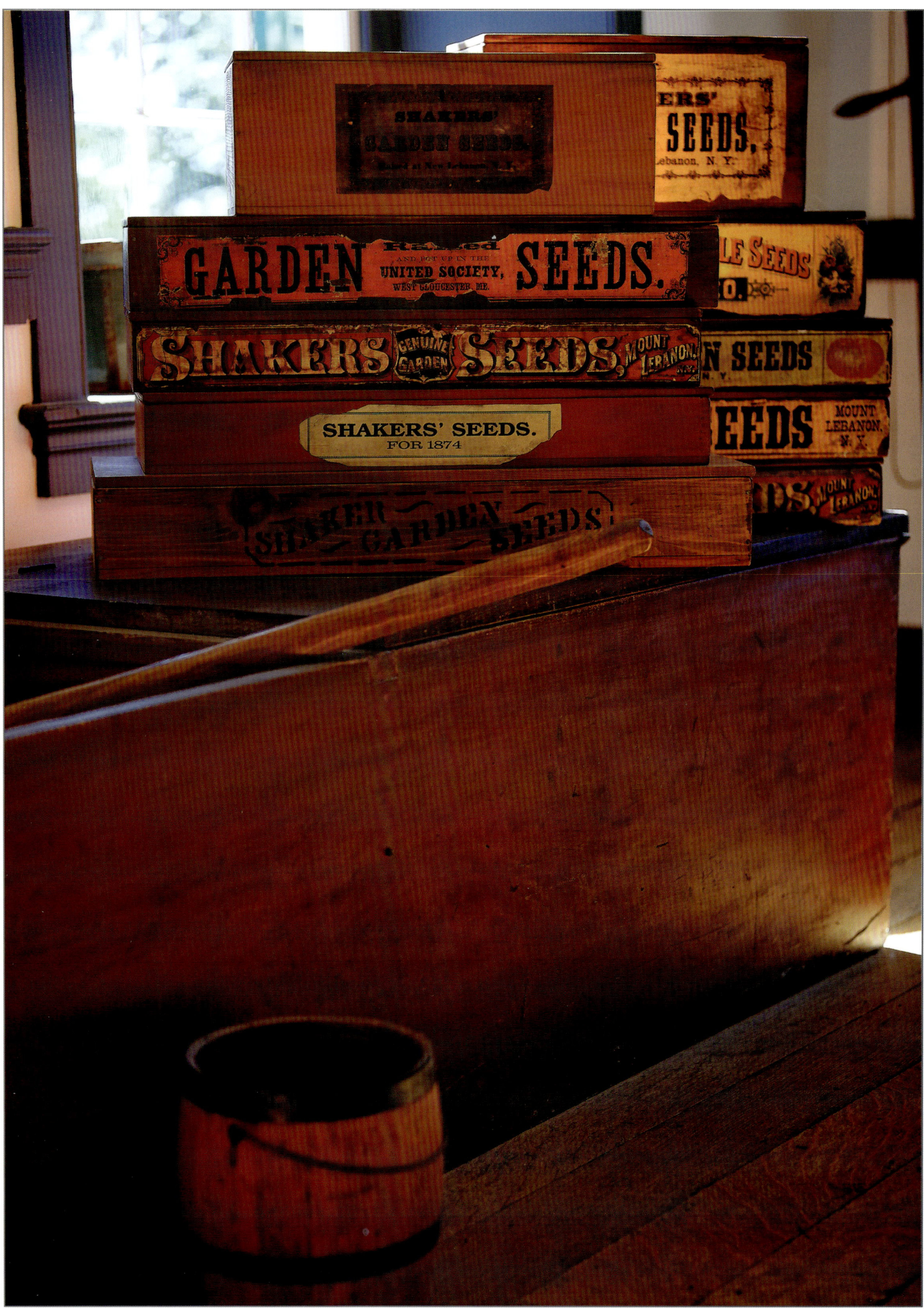
SHAKERS'
GARDEN SEEDS.
SEEDS,
Lebanon, N. Y.
GARDEN
Raised
AND PUT UP IN THE
UNITED SOCIETY,
WEST GLOUCESTER, ME.
SEEDS.
SHAKERS
GENUINE GARDEN
SEEDS,
MOUNT LEBANON, N.Y.
SHAKERS' SEEDS.
FOR 1874
SHAKER GARDEN SEEDS
MOUNT LEBANON, N.Y.

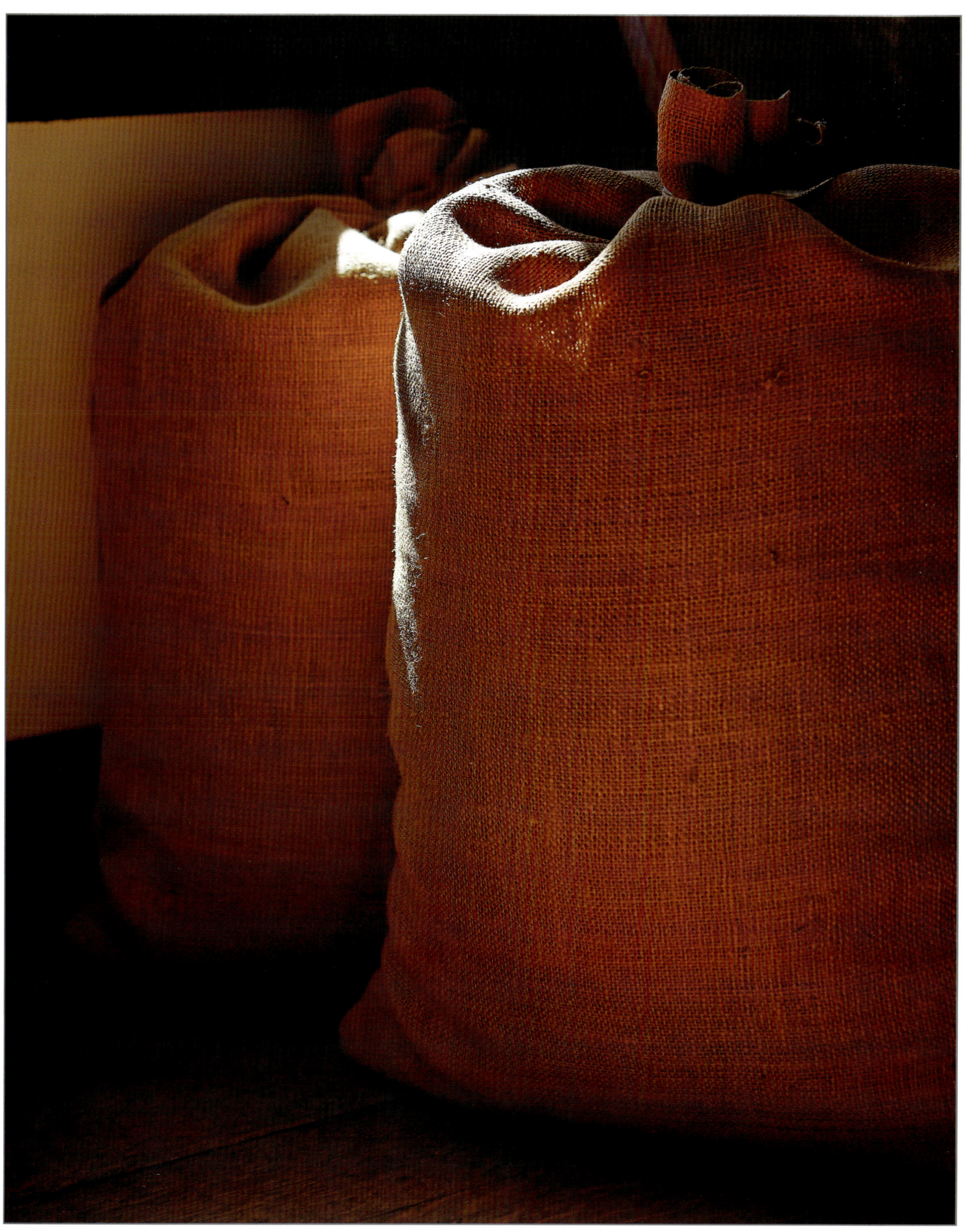

The seed business was one of the biggest business ventures for the Shakers for more than fifty years. Each Shaker seed packet came with an unconditional 100% germination guarantee. One of the Shaker's innovations was the use of seed packets for marketing and selling their products. In 1847, they purchased a printing press to produce their own packaging rather than rely on an outside source. They never changed the appearance of their seed packets. At the end of their business venture in the 1870's, when they collected unsold merchandise from outside retailers, they noted in the journals how other seed manufacturers had not only adopted the seed packet idea, but how fancy and colorful they were. One entry laments this was how the world was changing where the general population was more interested in fancy packaging as opposed to quality.

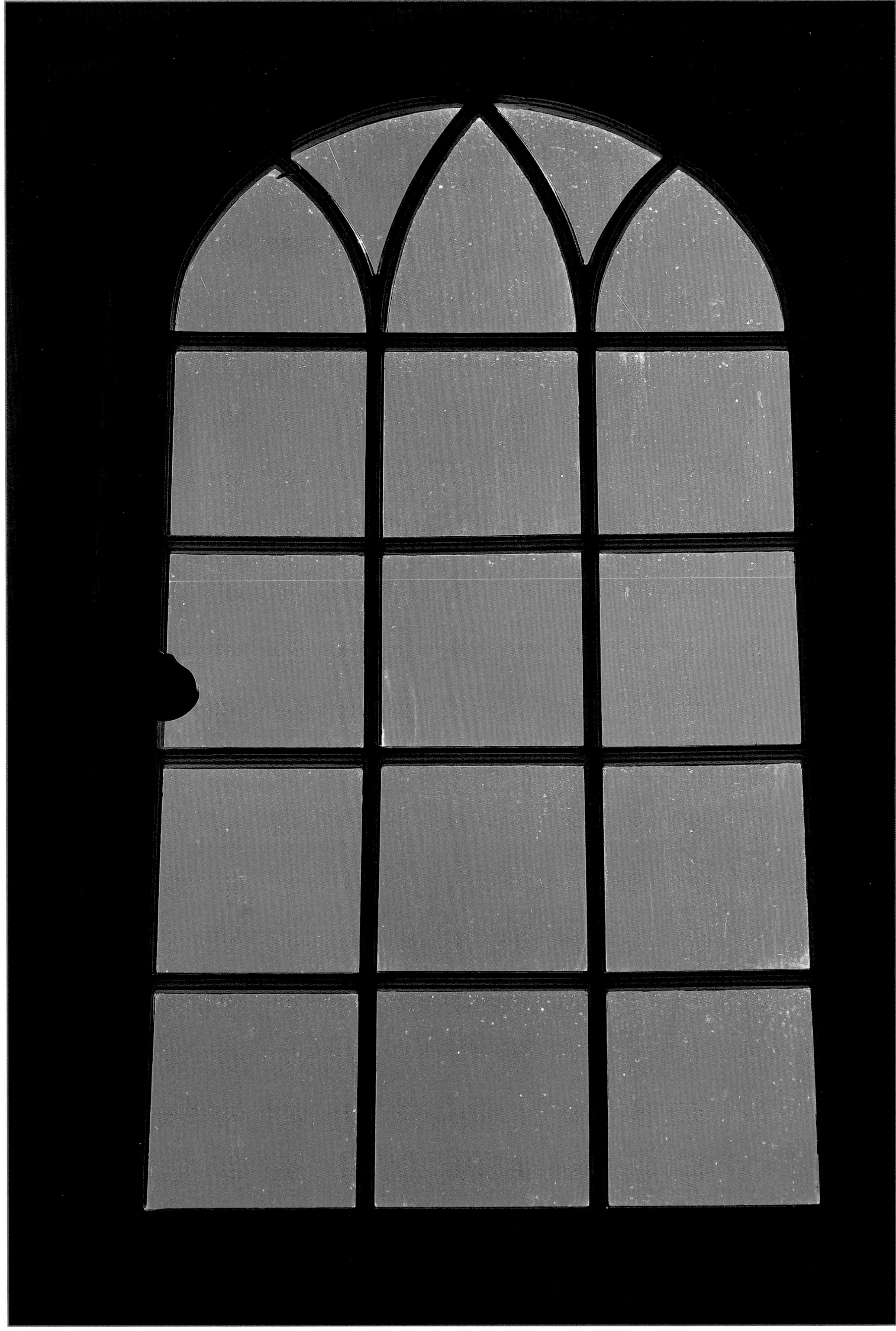

Opposite: An example of the fine glass work throughout the Centre Family Dwelling. This door provides access to the roof and is commonly referred to as the "Stairway to Heaven". Access to the roof was critical in those days as roof fires were of major concern for all the structures. Heating and cooking were done by fireplaces and roof shingles were made of wood at the time… a dangerous combination.

Below: The horseshoe dresser and chest storage unit located on the third floor of the Centre Family Dwelling. The top floor of dwellings was generally reserved for out of season clothing storage. This also illustrates other design features throughout the structure for light and ventilation. This has been referred to as the Shaker air-conditioning. When this unit is opened in the summer, it creates a natural draft up the stairs to draw the heat from below and create a breeze.

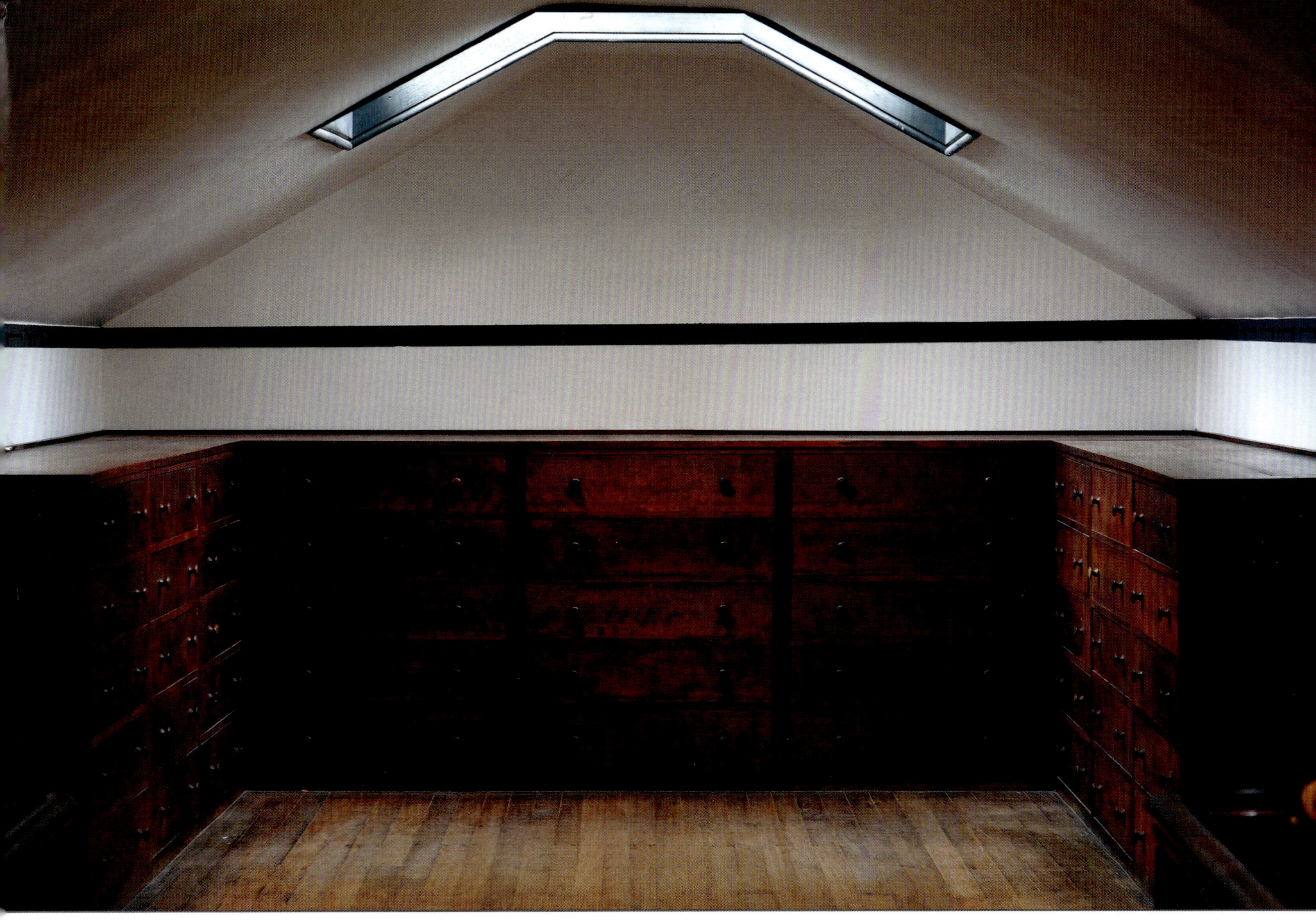

Costumed interpreters relate the lives of the Shakers through their reading and studying of the journals.

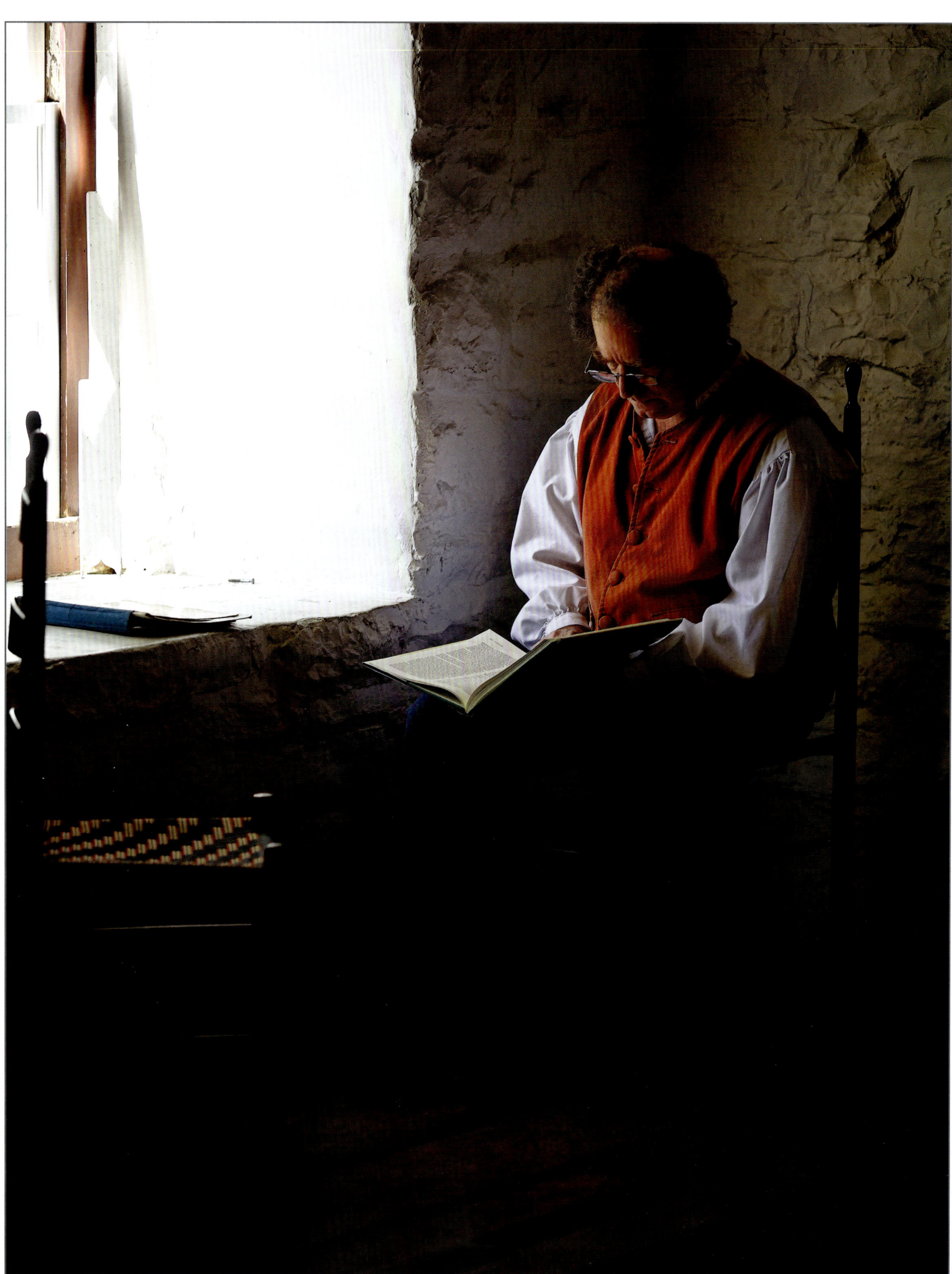

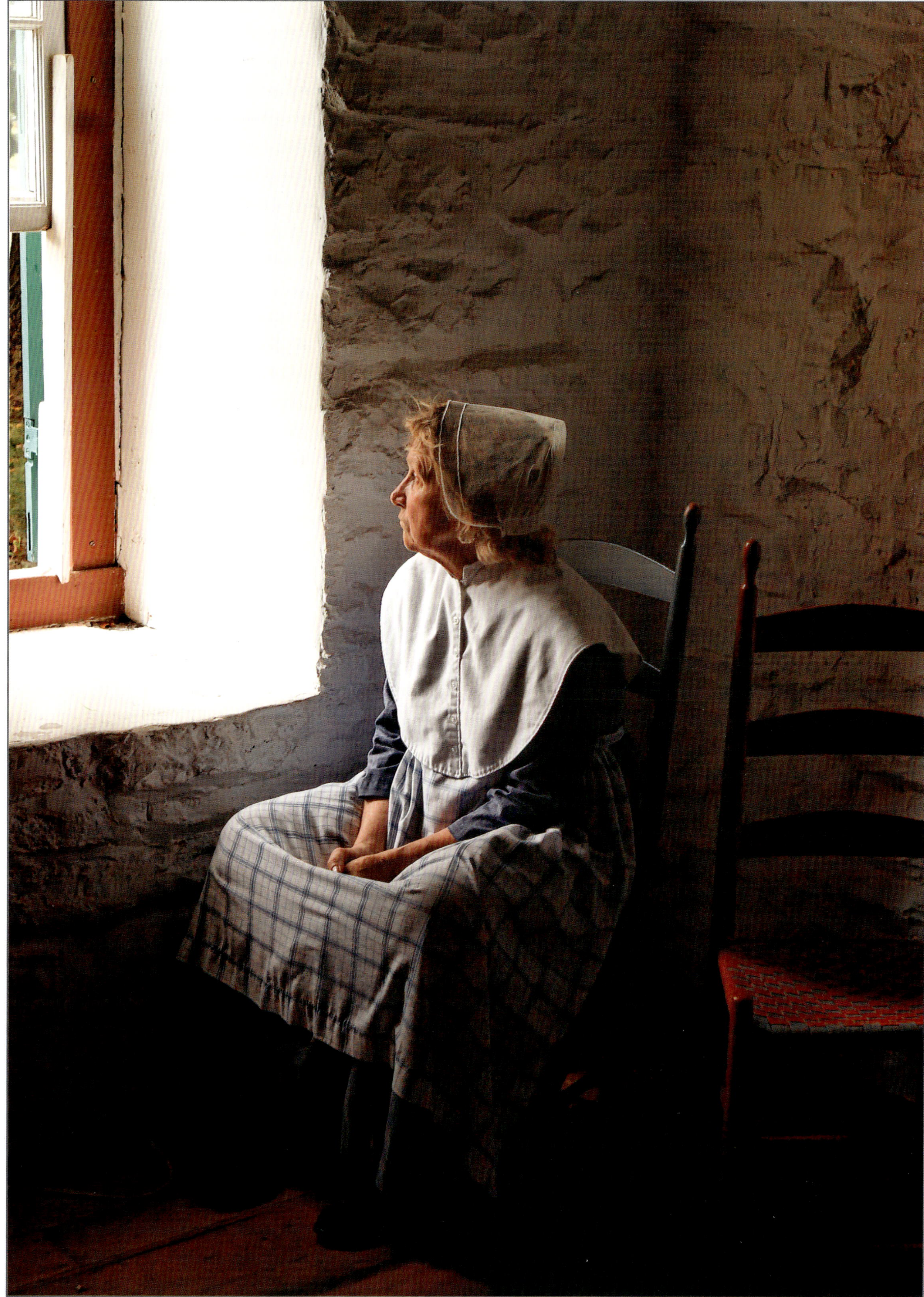

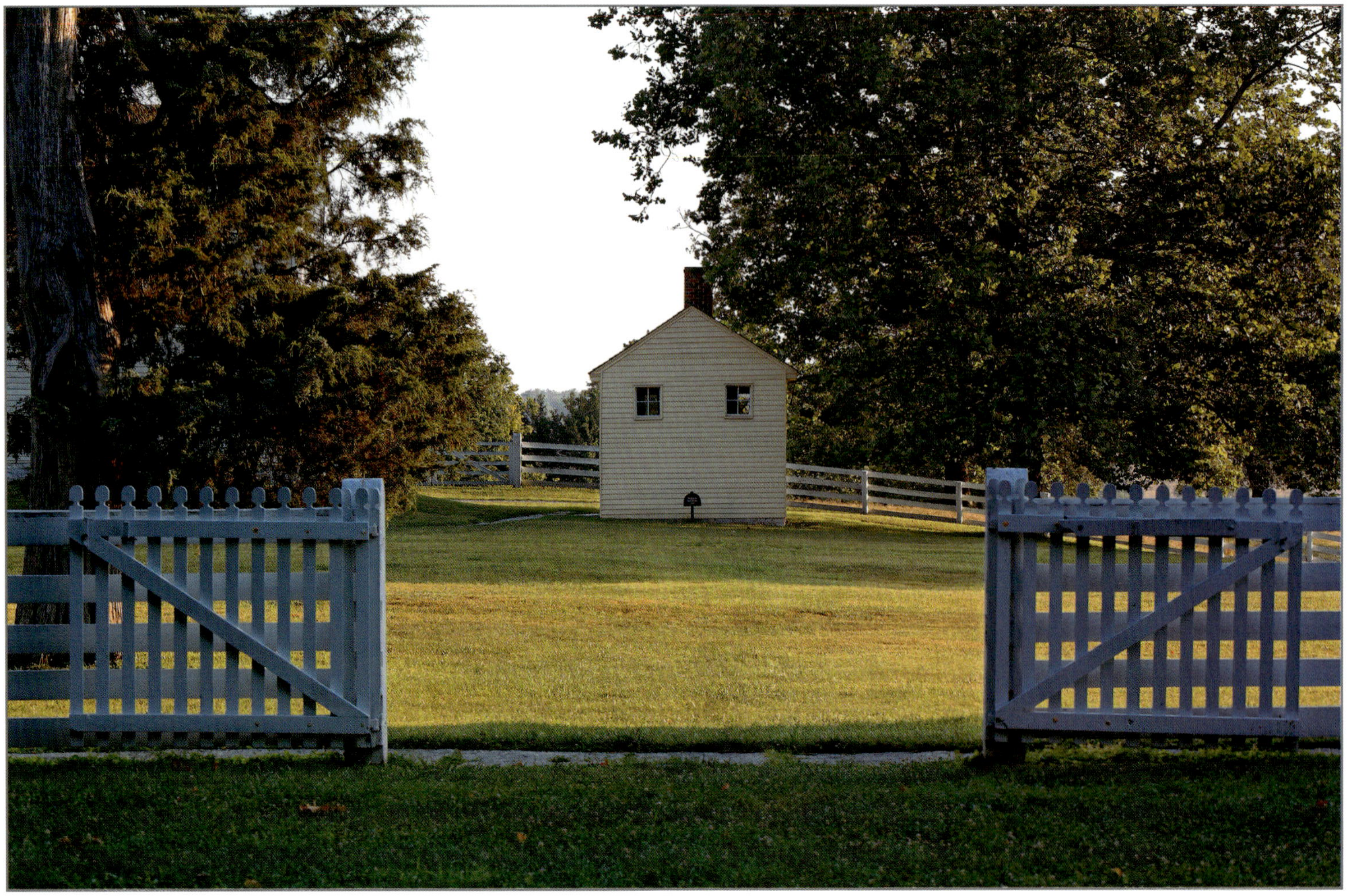

The Shakers had the first successful central gravity flow system in the region. In the early 1830's, a reliable spring-fed water source was discovered on the property. Underground pipes were laid and a water house constructed. Water was pumped to the water house by means of a horse on a treadmill. It was noted in the journals this could be accomplished "without undo stress to the animal". Running water was first supplied to the Centre Family Dwelling. Later, the stone pillars were raised and underground pipe laid so that water could also be provided to the East Family Dwelling. Over a twenty year period, underground pipe was laid to every main structure on the property.

The object sticking out from the roof is a float which indicates the water level in the tank. This would have been visible from the spring allowing the men to know when the tank needed to be filled and when to stop pumping to a full tank.

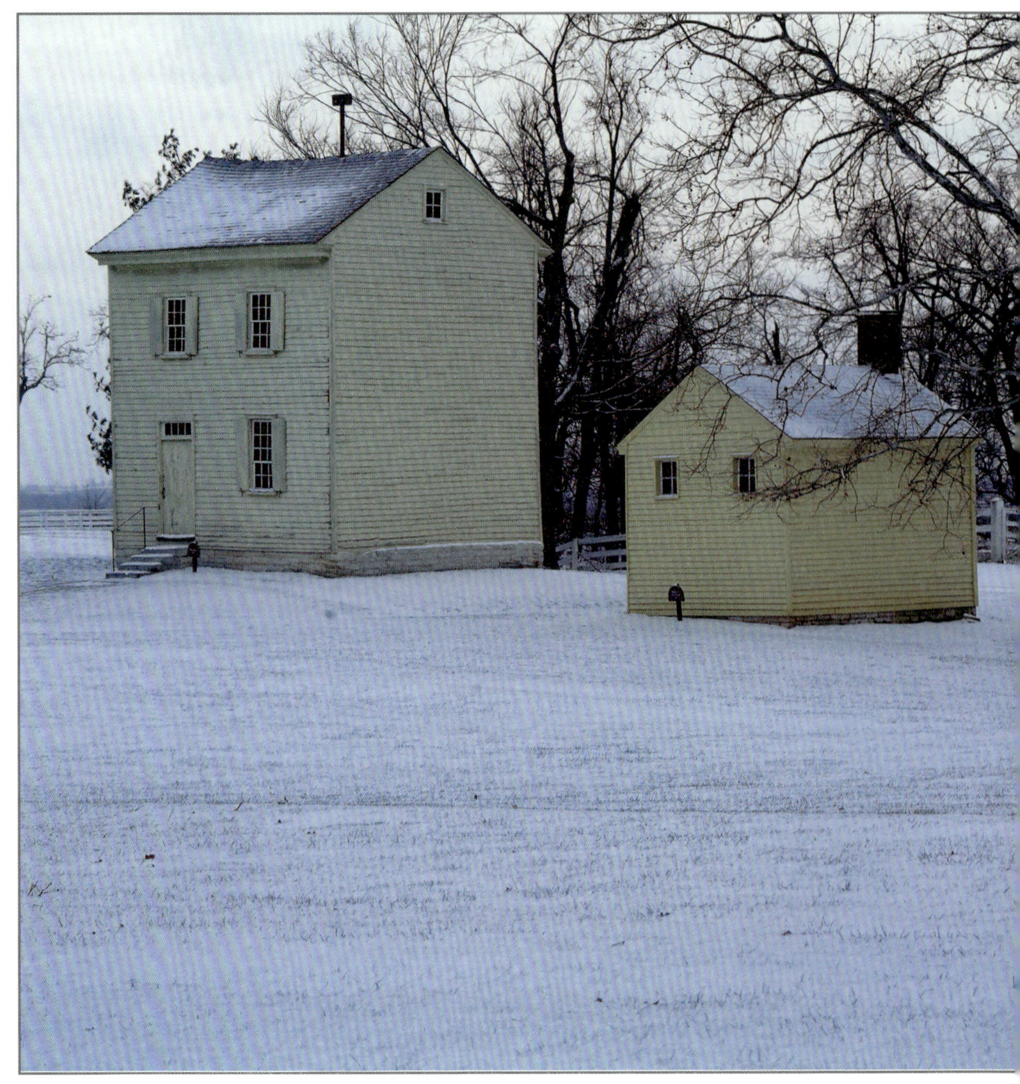

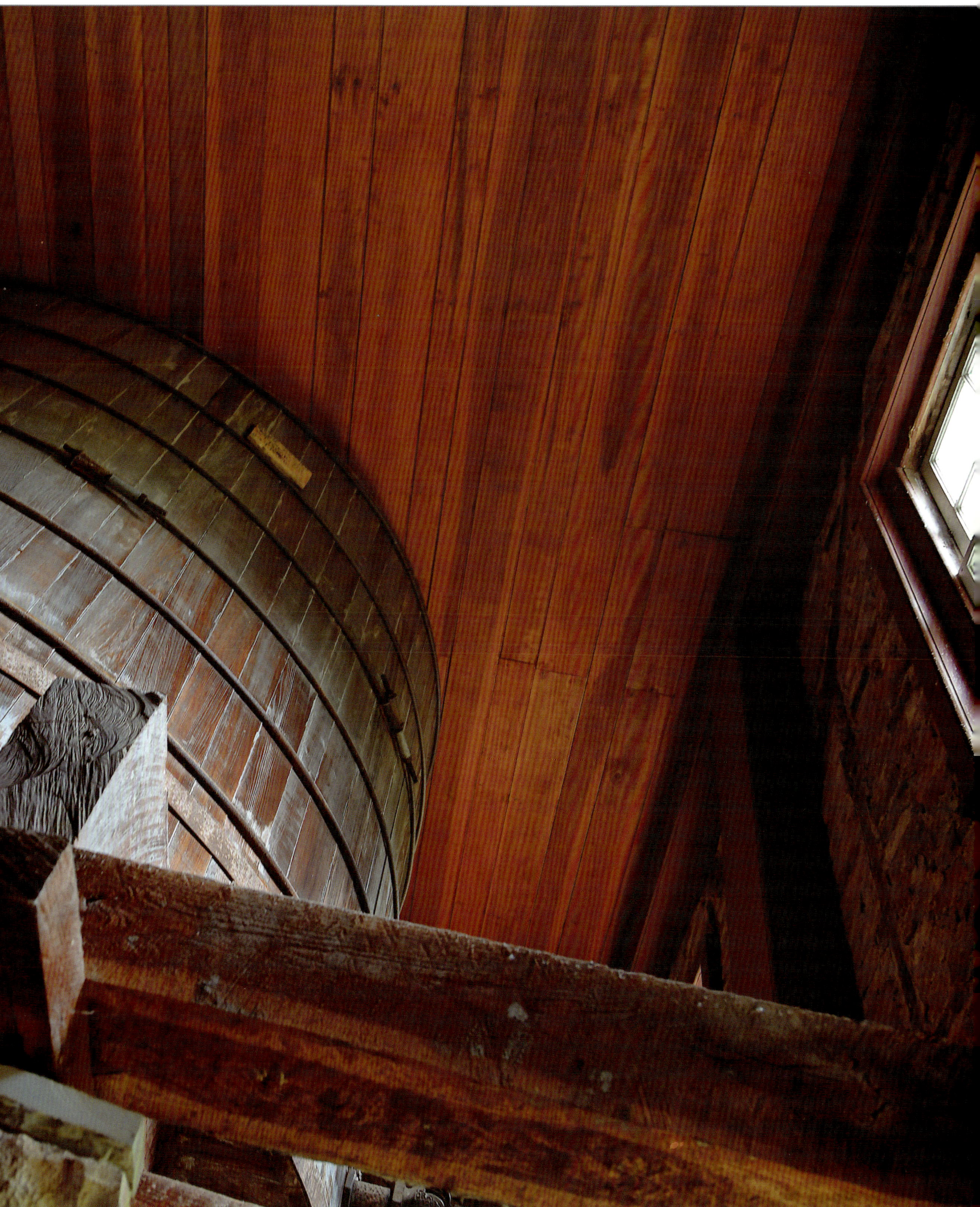

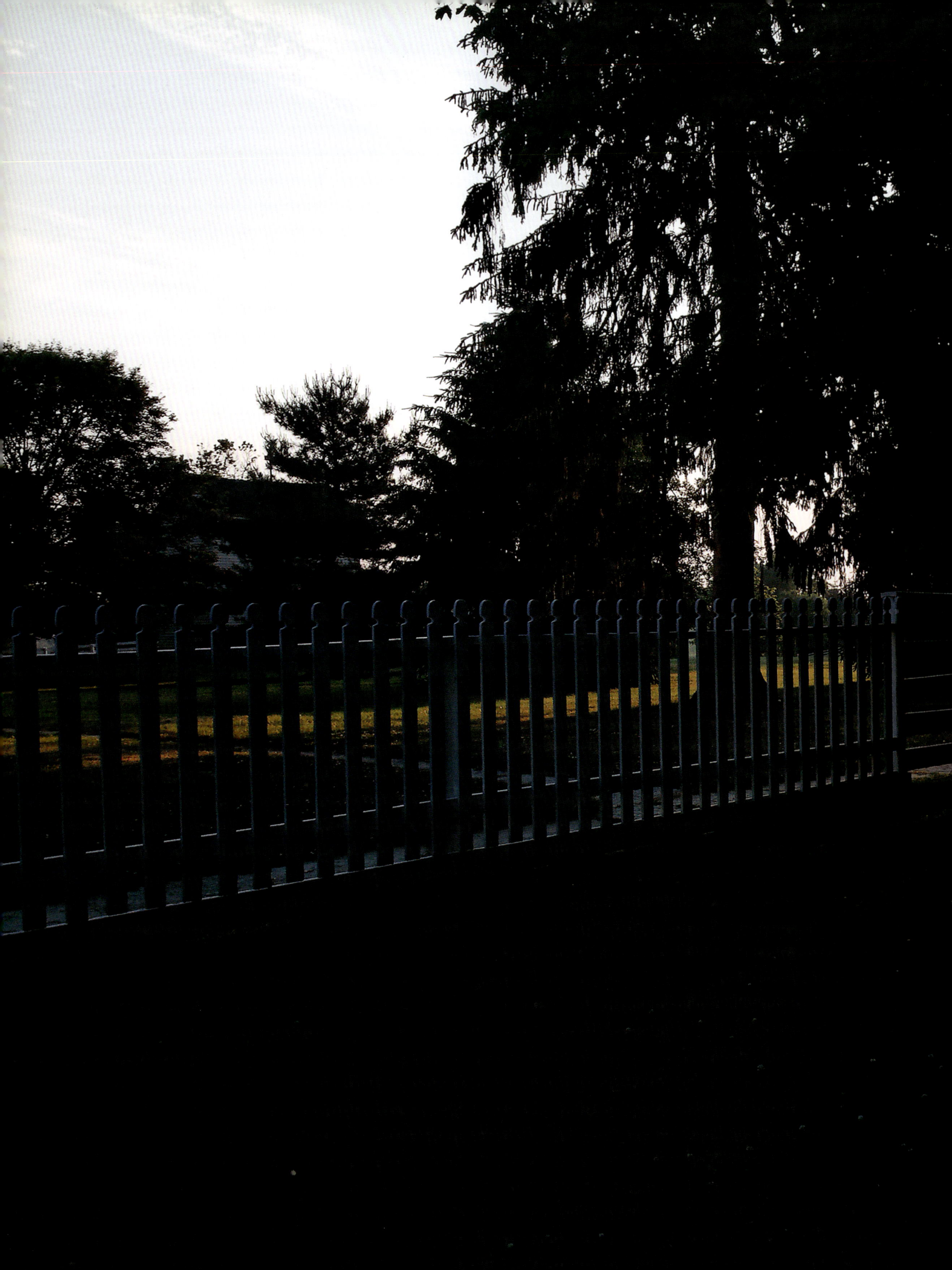

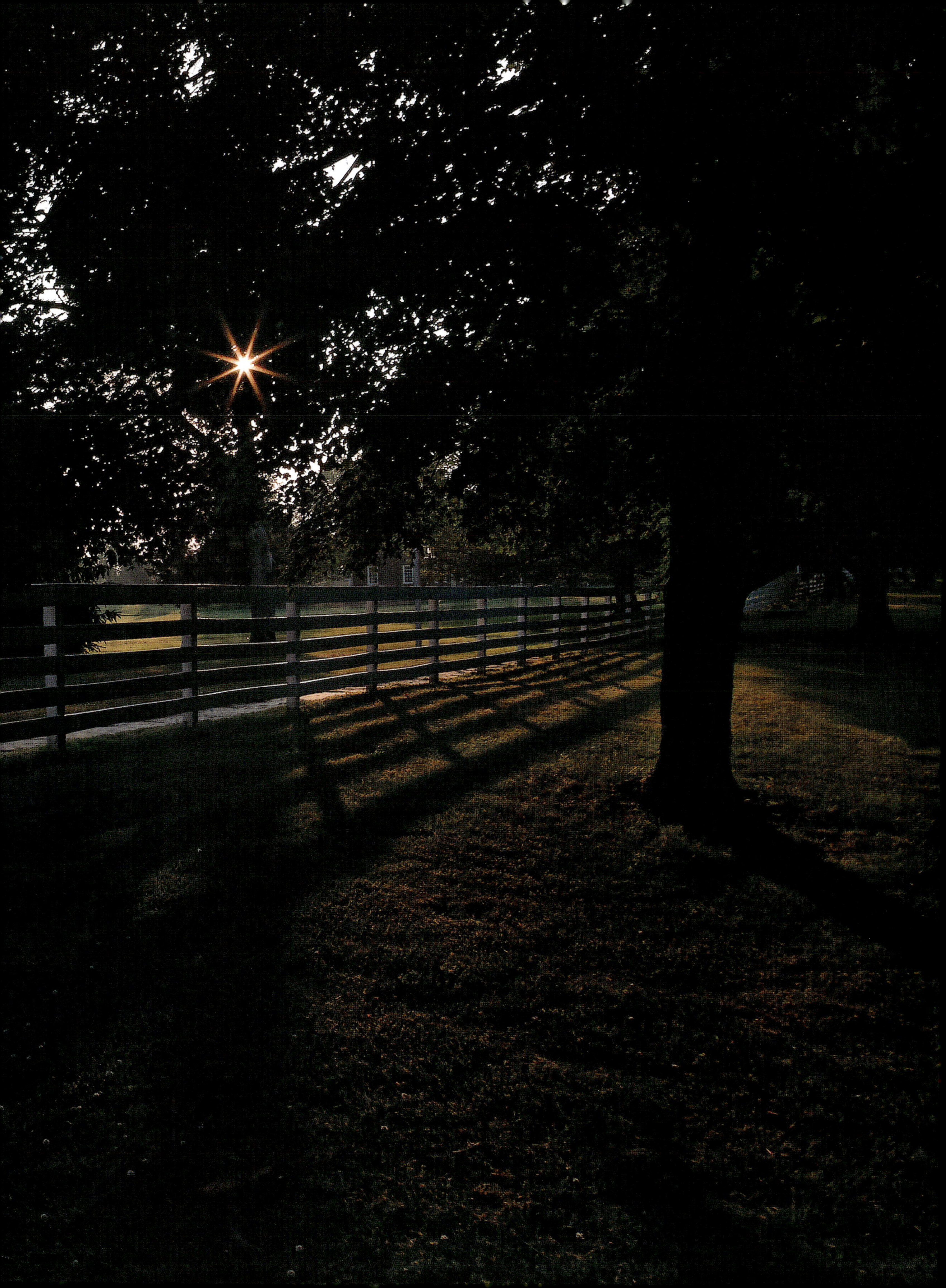

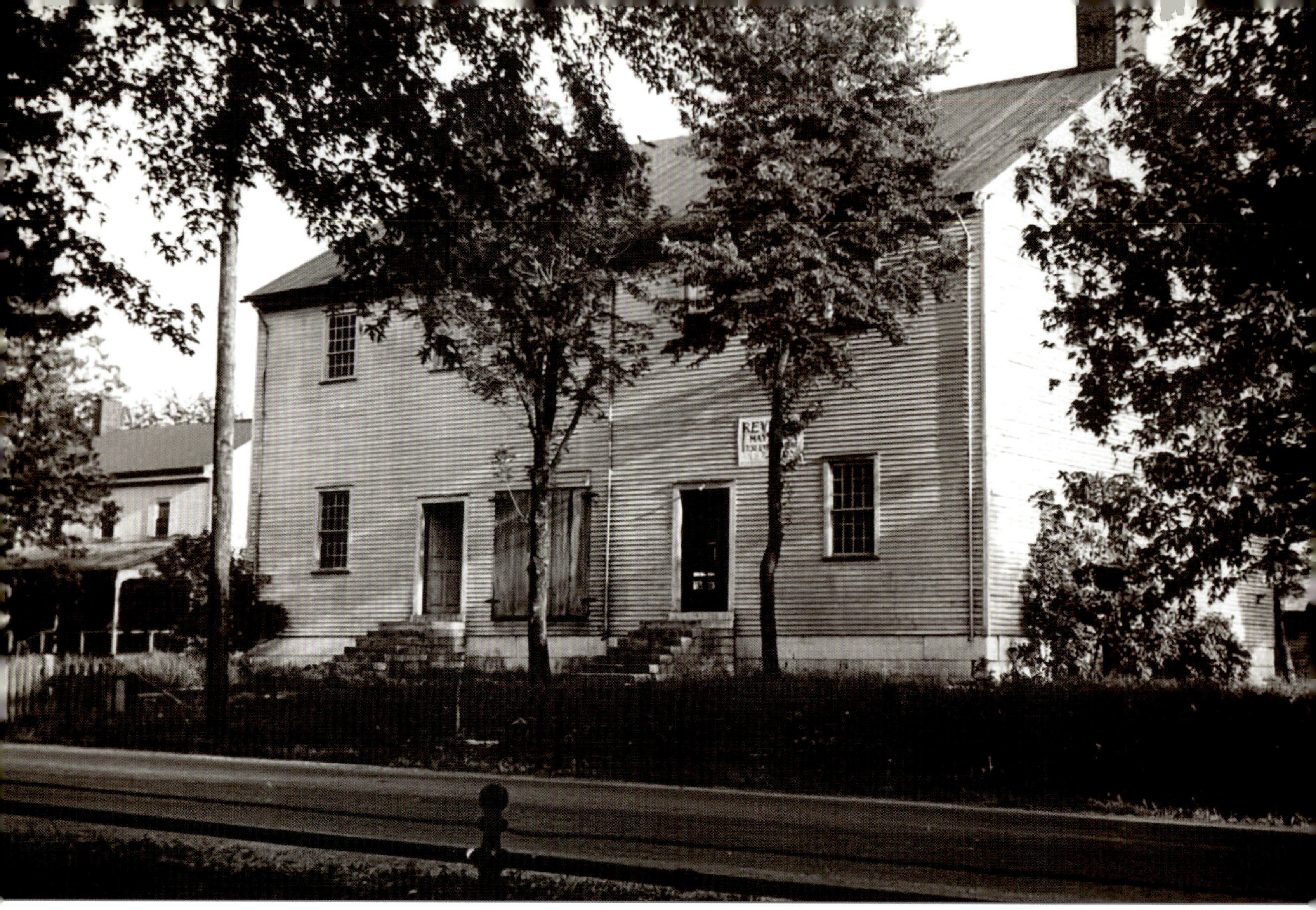

The 1820 Meeting House shown prior to restoration when it was used as an auto repair shop. The center windows were removed and a sliding door added. Cars were driven into the building and onto the main floor of the Meeting House where work was performed. Oil stains from the cars are still visible on the original ash hardwood floors today. This attests to the strength of the engineering of the building and its open span floor.

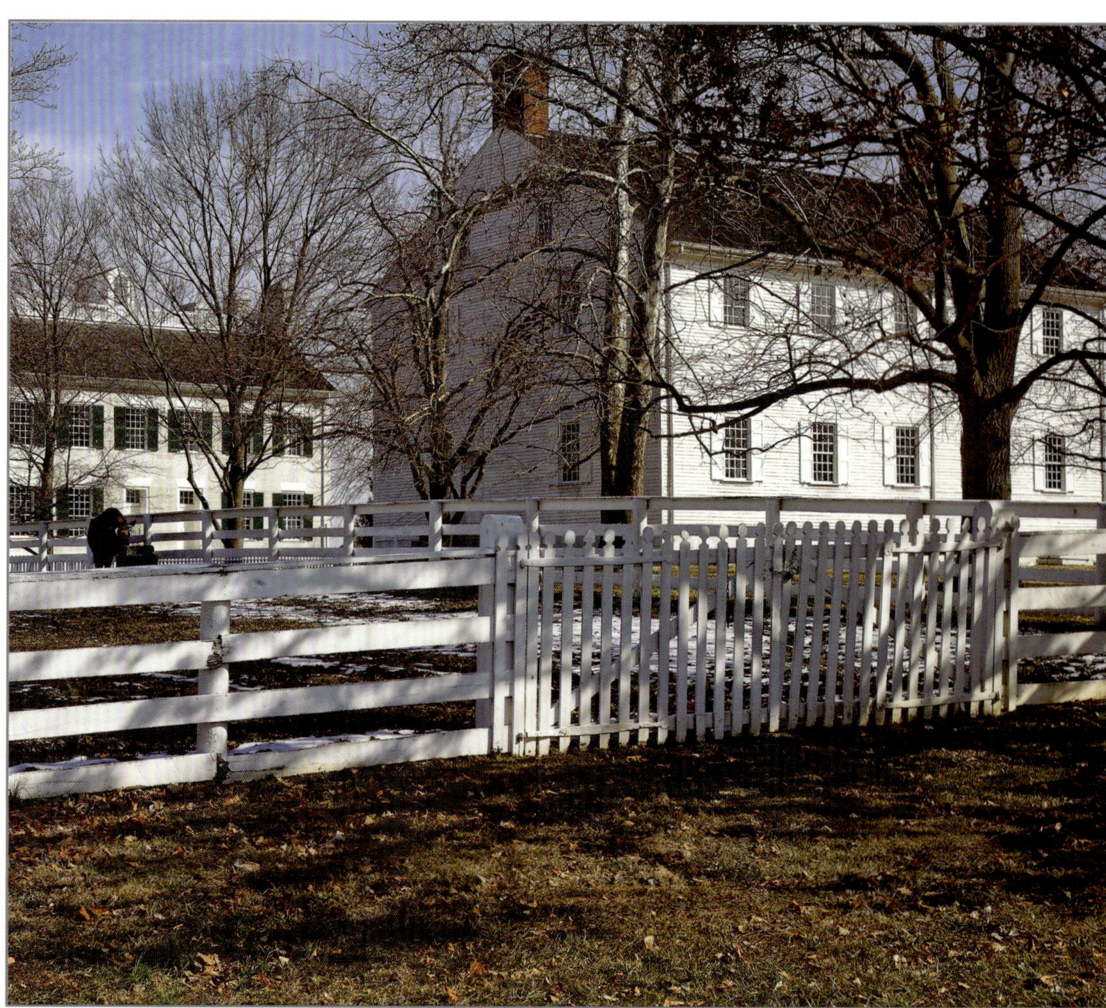

Right: A view of the rear of the Meeting House with the Centre Family Dwelling in the background.

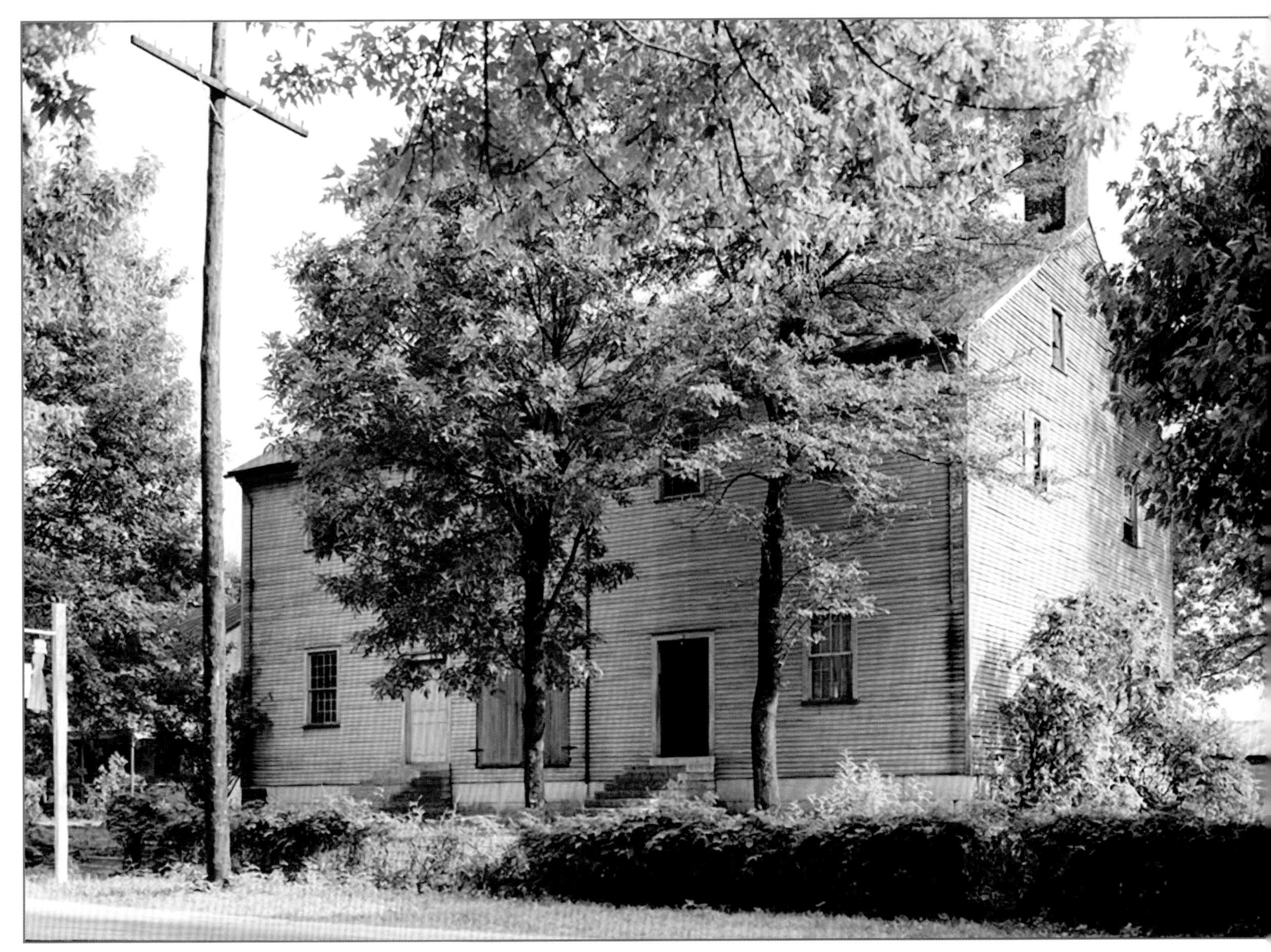

Following spread: Shaker Law mandated the Meeting House be centrally located in the Village with a free and open space to worship and large enough to hold all members. This was also the only structure allowed to be painted white. At 1:30 in the afternoon, members would gather for Sunday worship with male members entering and sitting on the east side with the women sitting on the west side. Visitors from the outside world would sit on benches along the outer walls. The 44 feet by 60 feet open span is made possible by a sophisticated inverted gravity truss system that carries the load of not only the main floor, but the two floors above it. Two feet thick foundation walls spaced every eight feet along with floor beams also help support the main floor. Construction began January 3, 1820, and completed October of that same year. The structure was dry fitted using mortise and tenon technology and the individual parts were numbered at the sawmill. It was then disassembled and reassembled on its present-day site.

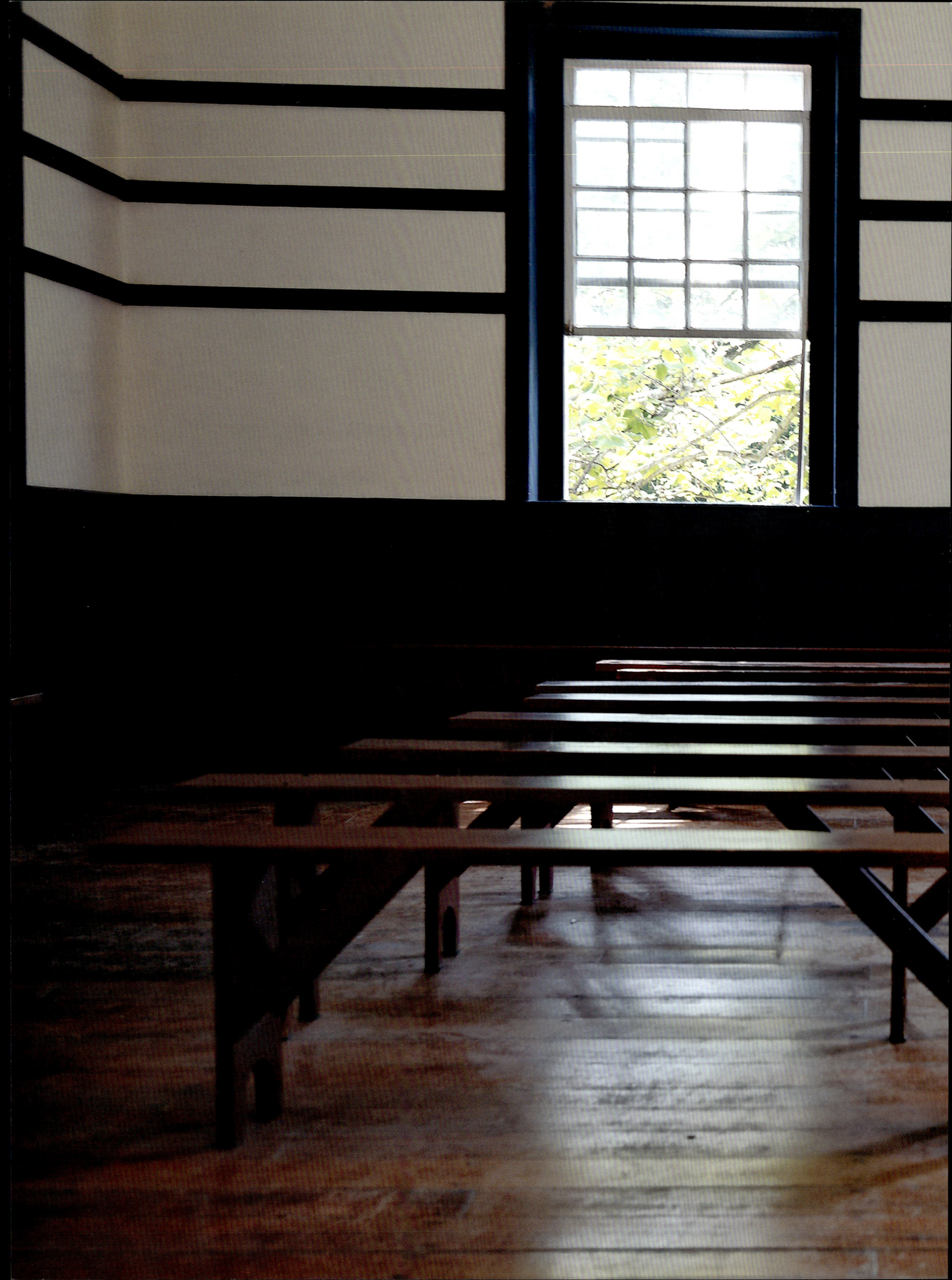

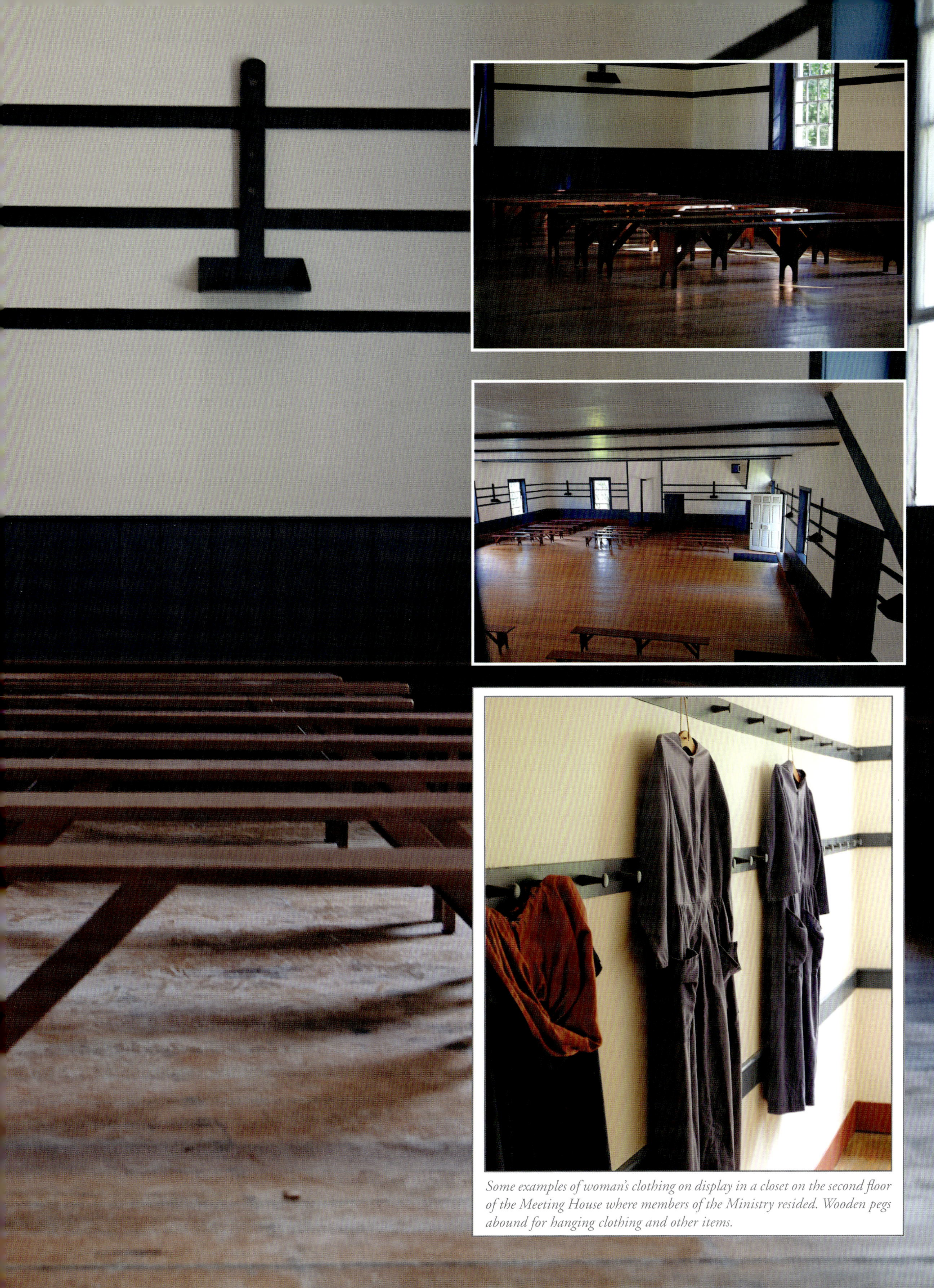

Some examples of woman's clothing on display in a closet on the second floor of the Meeting House where members of the Ministry resided. Wooden pegs abound for hanging clothing and other items.

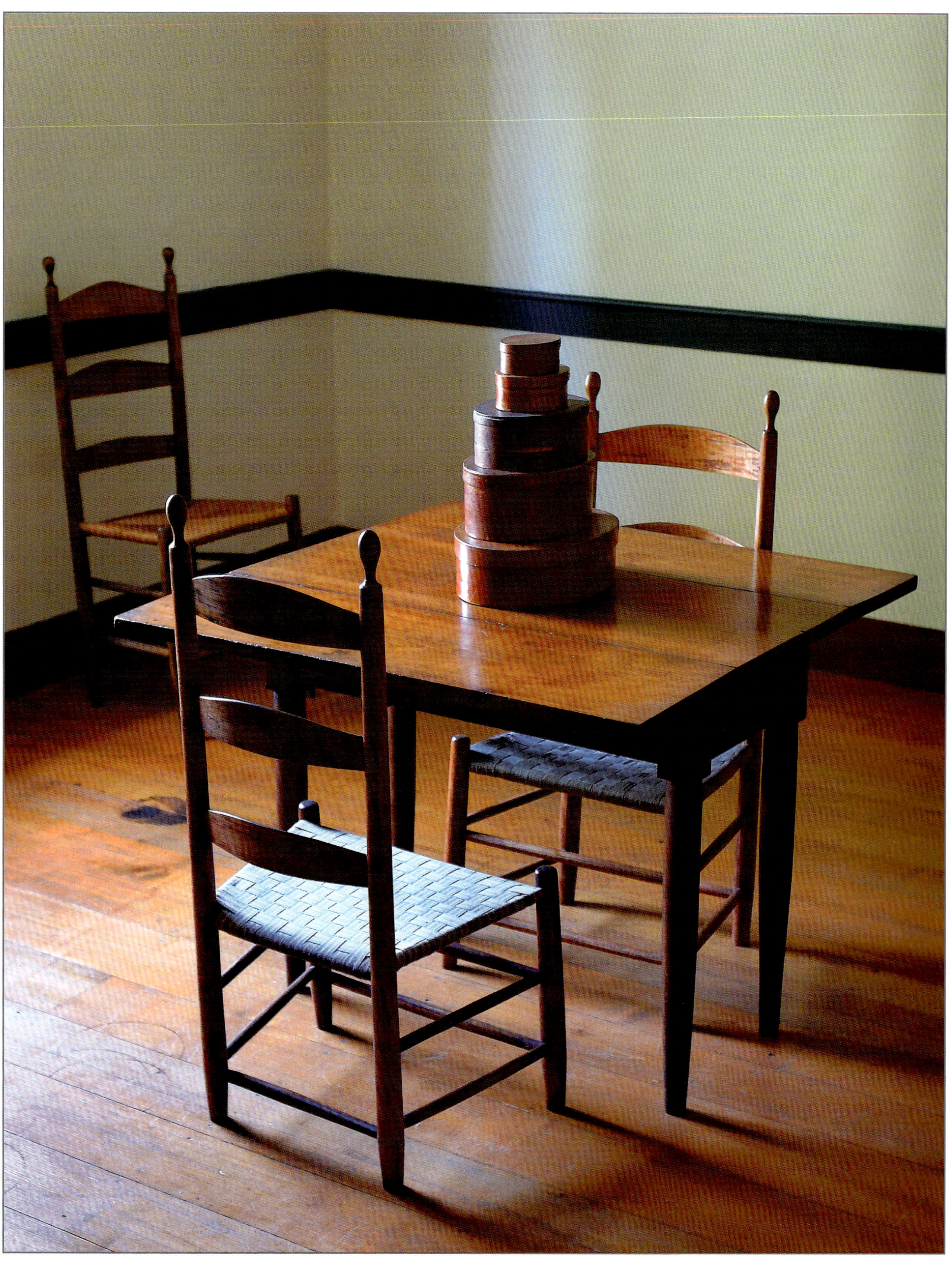

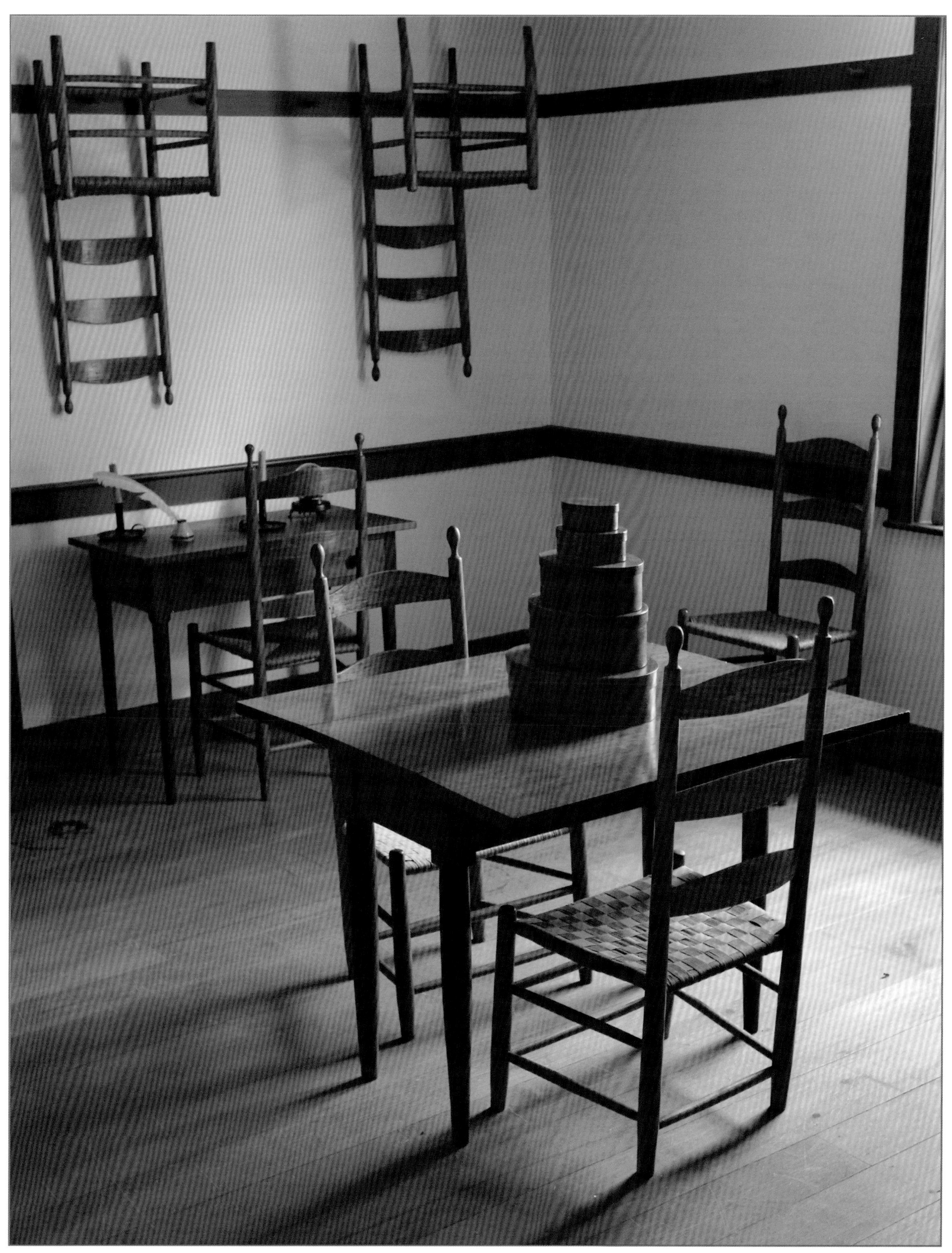

Located on the second floor were the Ministry's residences. They also included a central meeting room where they could meet to discuss matters of the Village or to entertain and meet with their counterparts from other communities. The furniture housed in this area is all original to Pleasant Hill and is part of the Dorothy Clay collection.

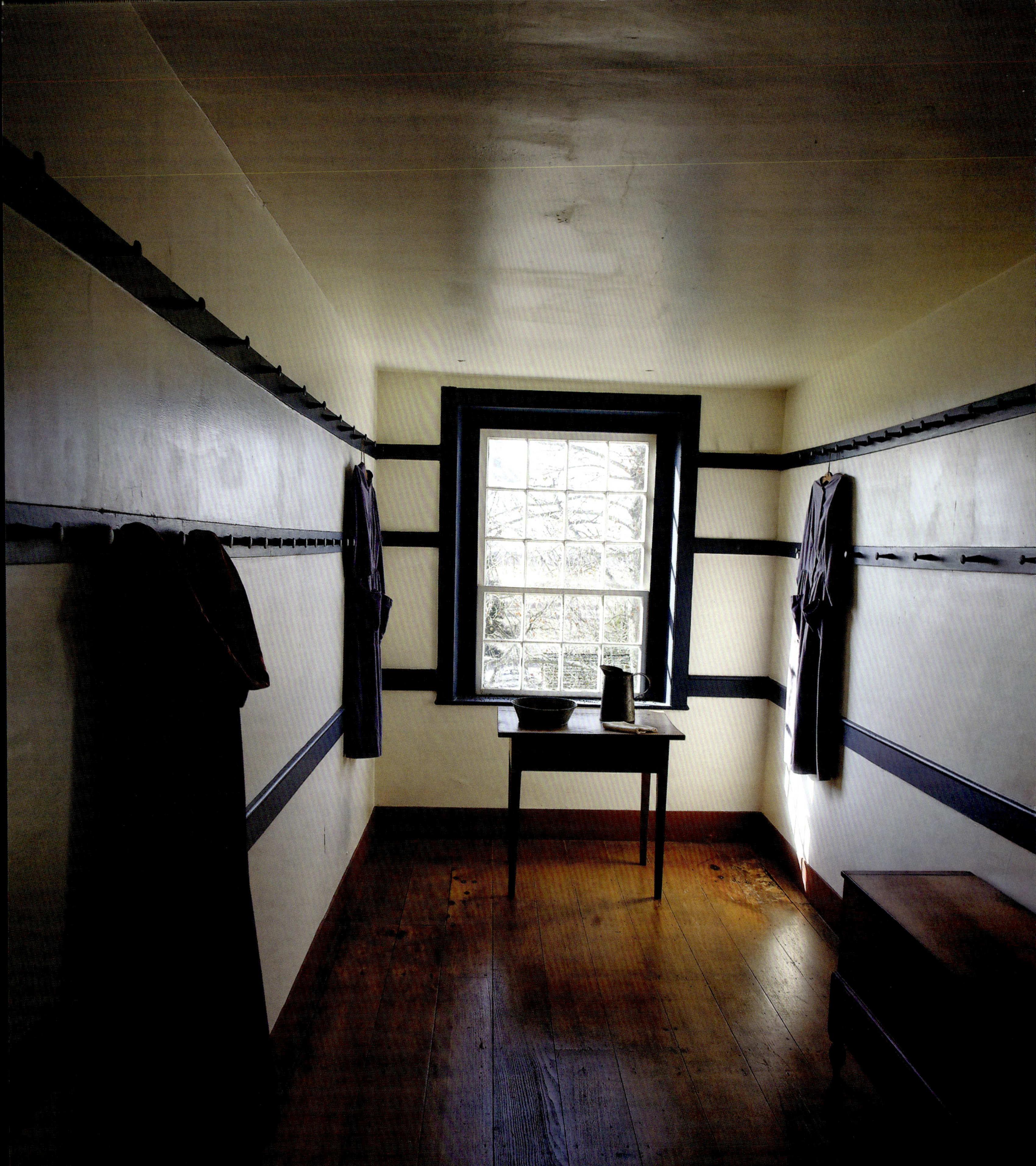

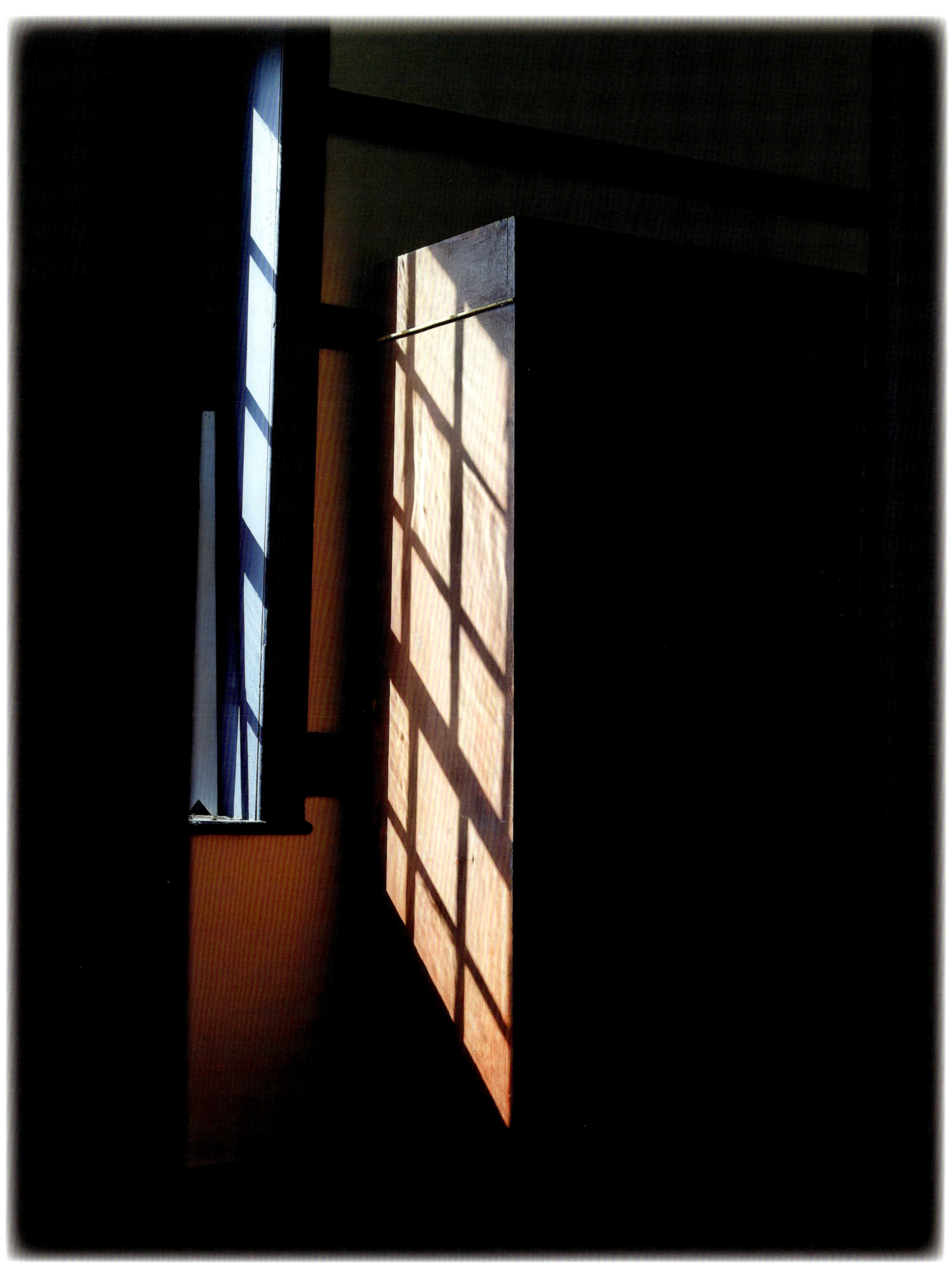

Another example of how light interacts with the architecture of Pleasant Hill. It has been said "if painters are the masters of light, the Shakers are the builders of it".

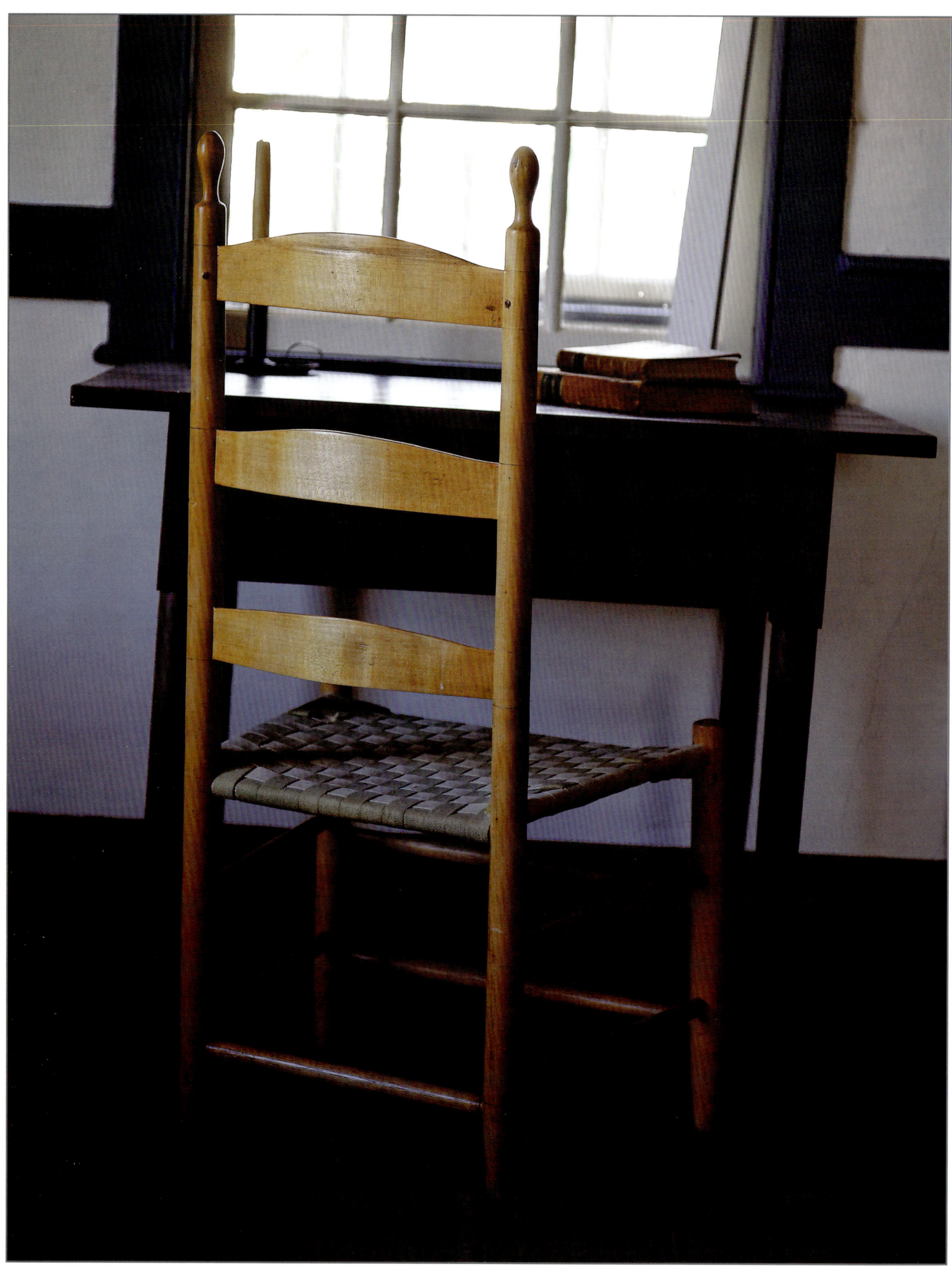

Another example of a Shaker desk located on the second floor of the Meeting House. Twin windows, separated by the stairway to the second floor, illustrate how the Shakers incorporated features into their buildings to take advantage of light and ventilation.

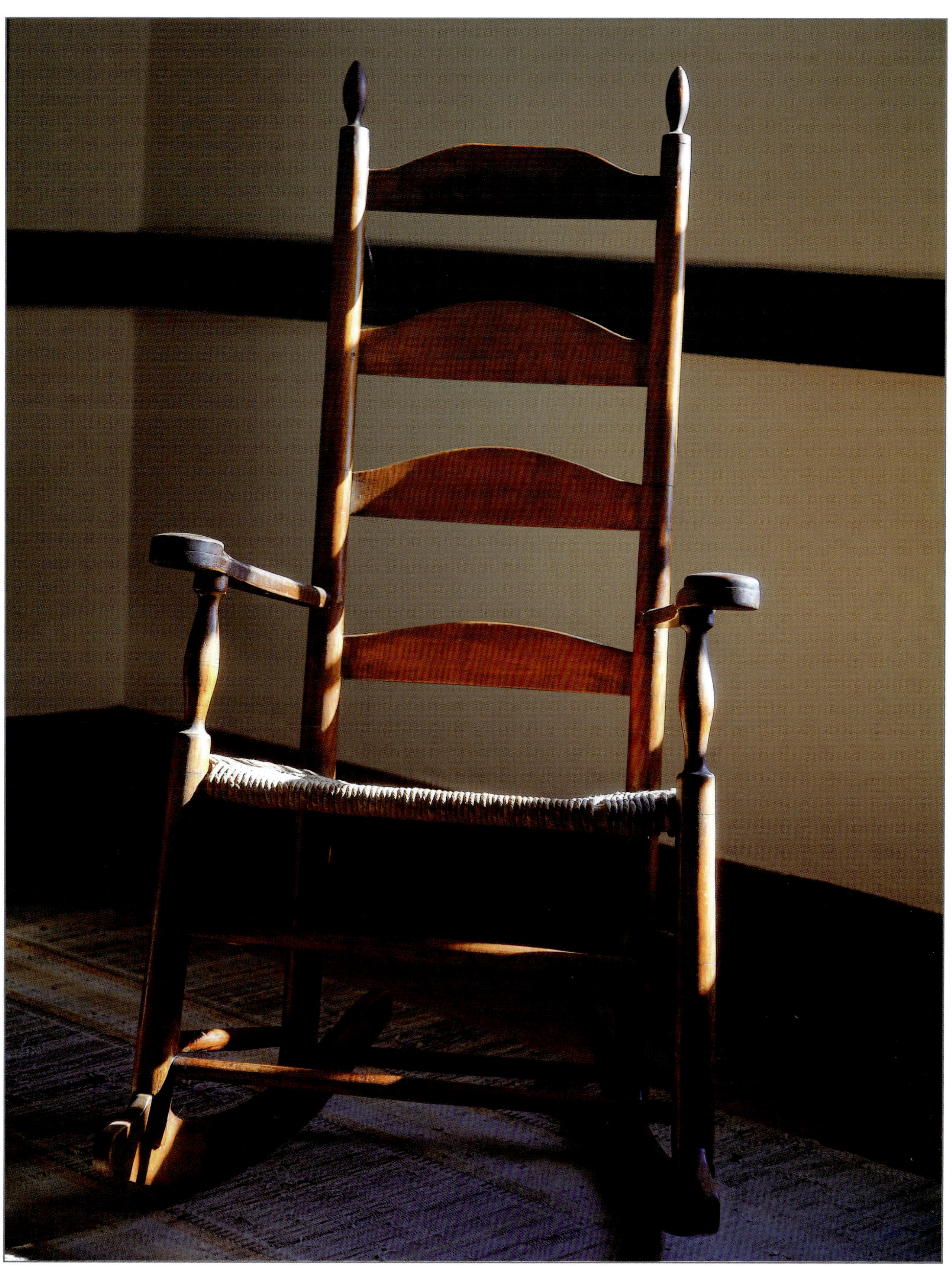

A classic Pleasant Hill Shaker rocker in one of the Ministry apartments on the second floor of the Meeting House.

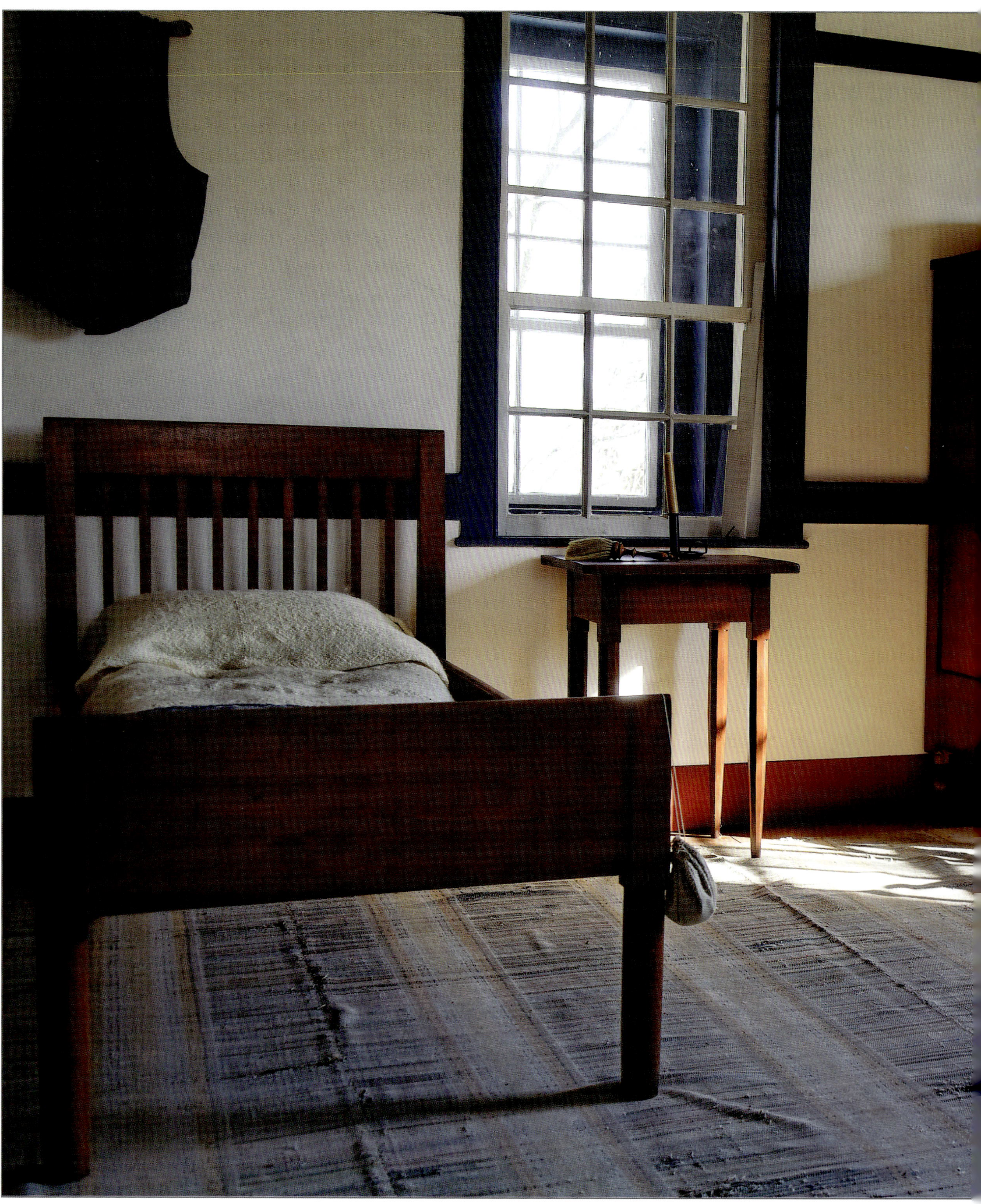

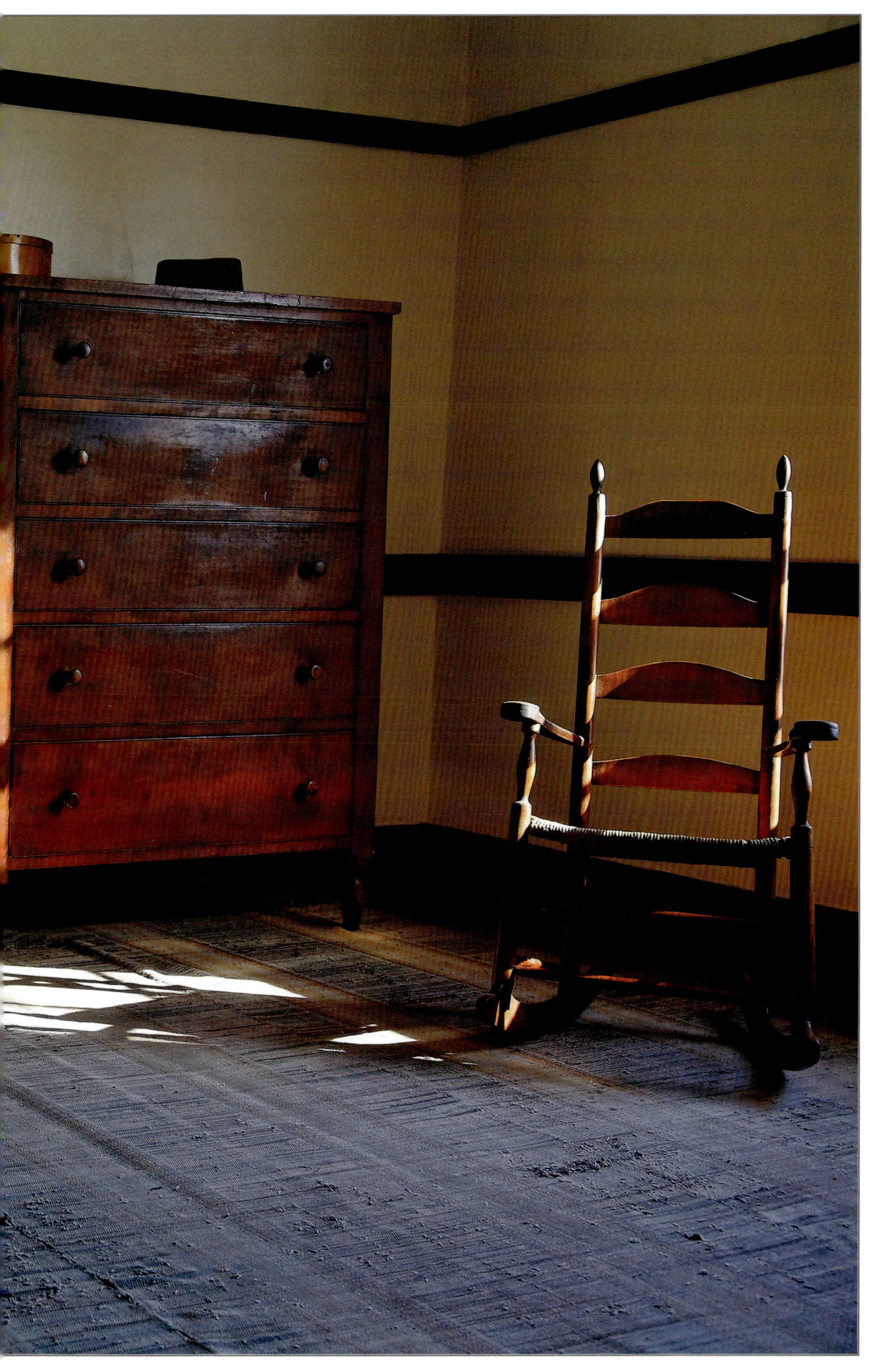

Simplistic beauty of Shaker furnishings providing both form and function. While the Shakers built their own furniture, the majority was for use in the community and not for sale to the outside world.

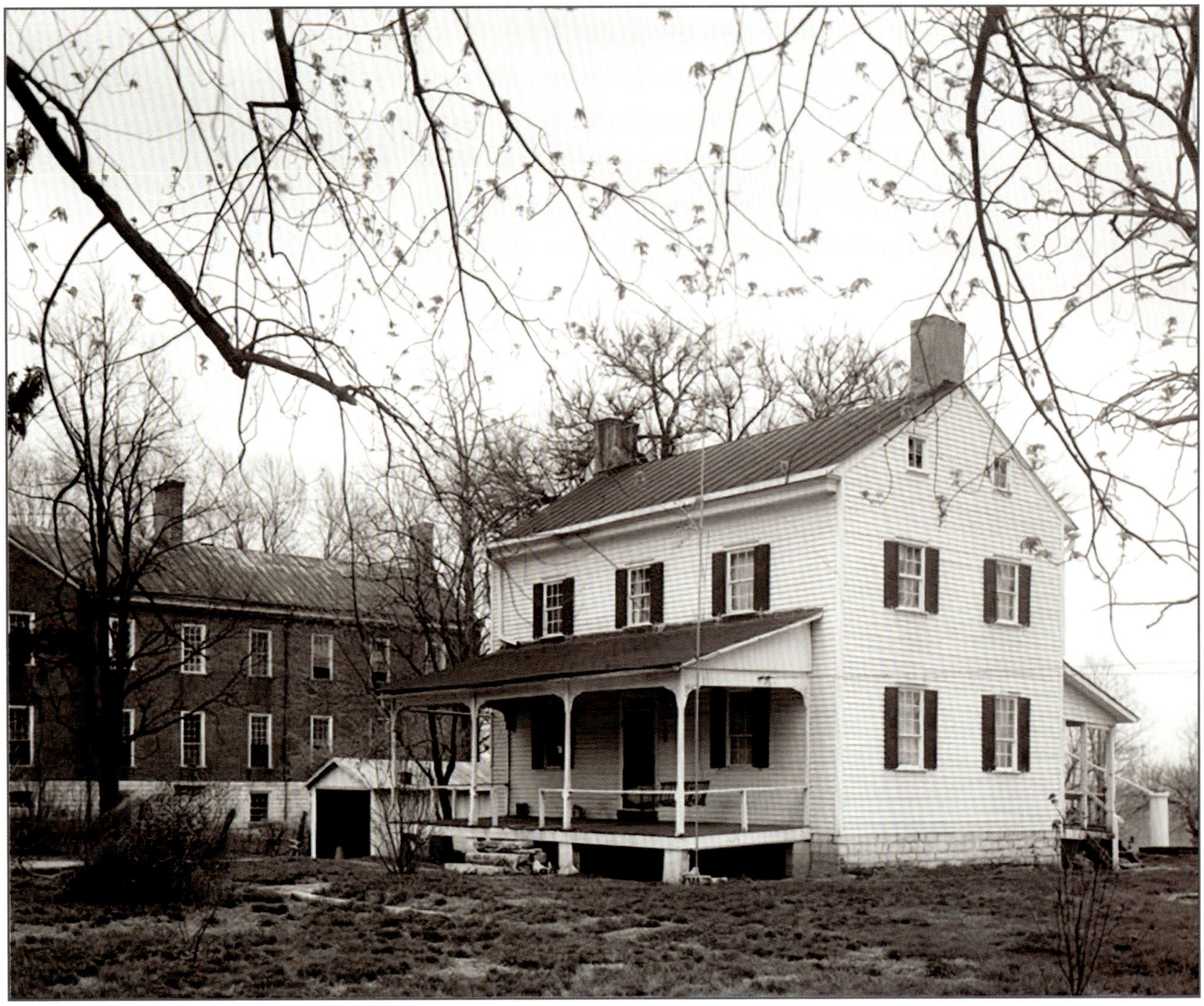

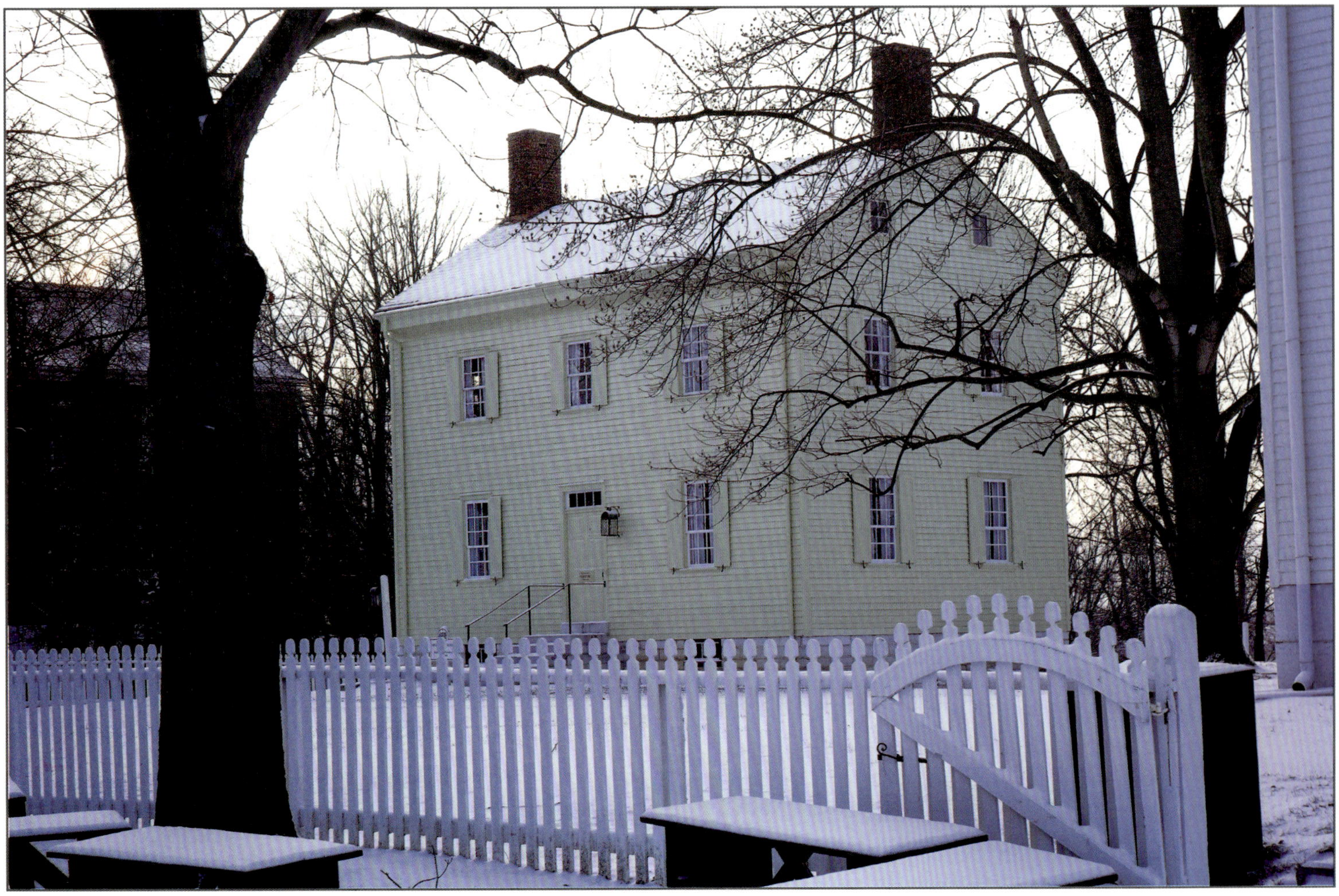

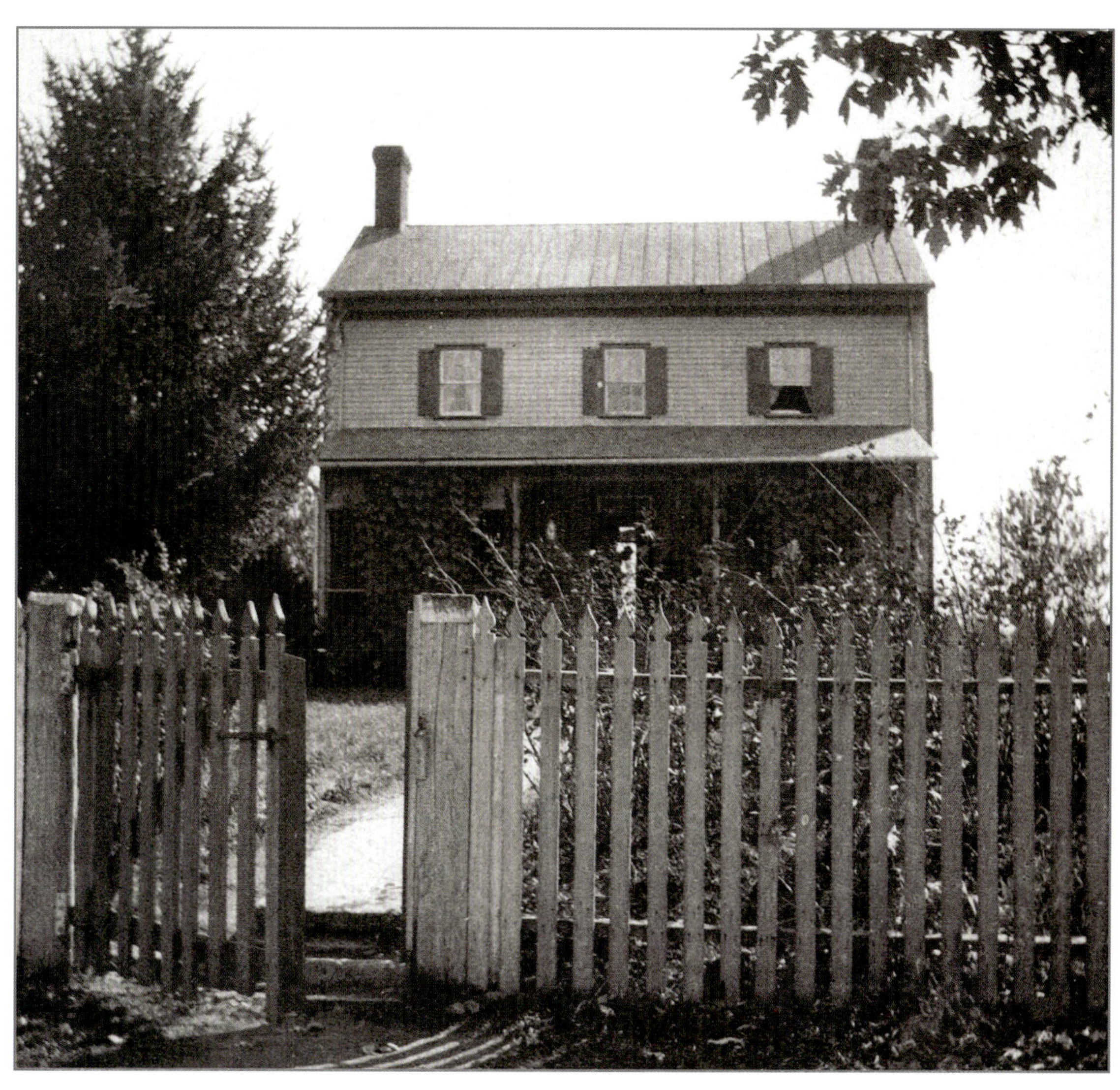

The Ministry's Workshop then and now. These photos from the 1940's show the addition of a front porch which was not original to the structure and was added post 1850's, the period to which the Village was restored.

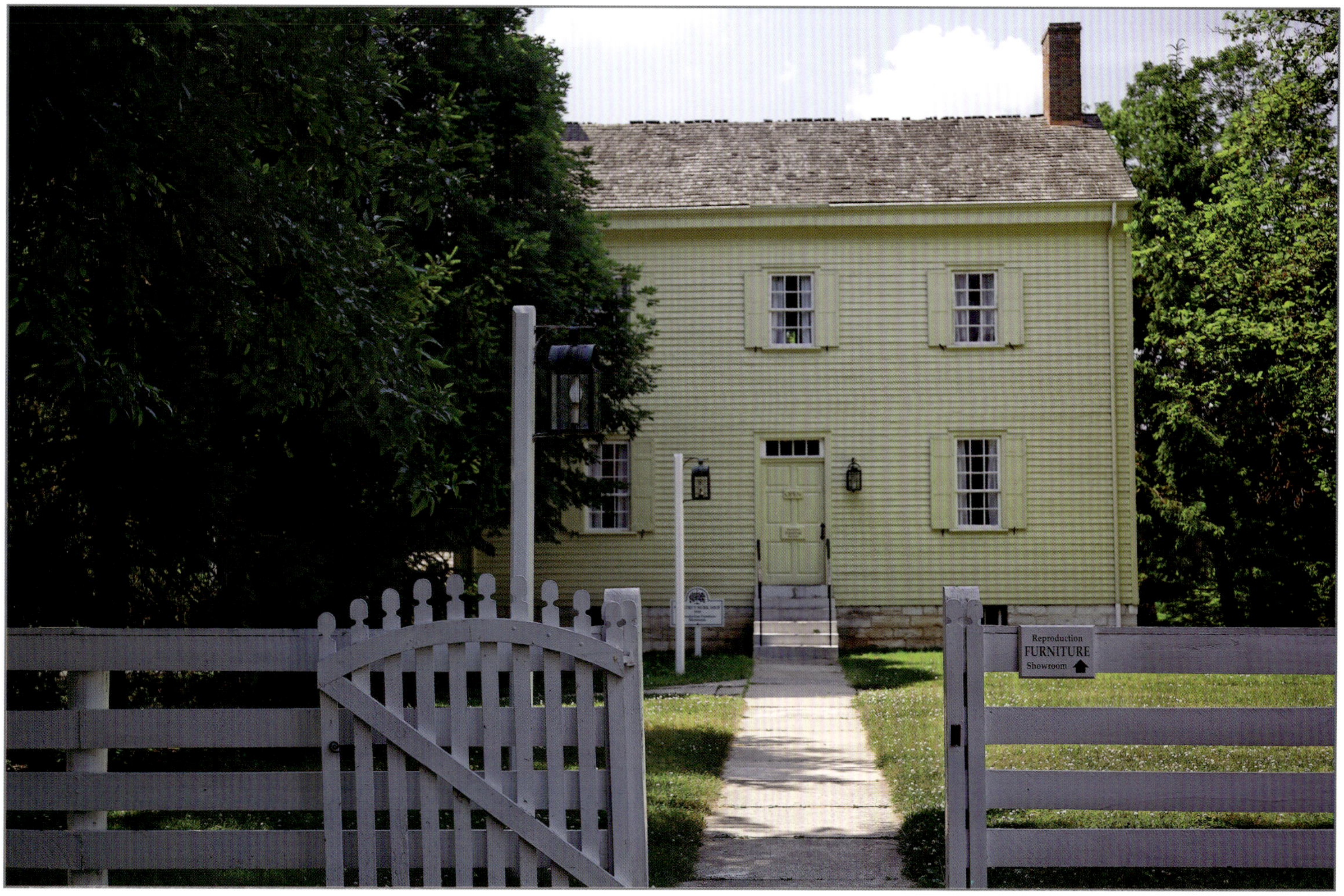

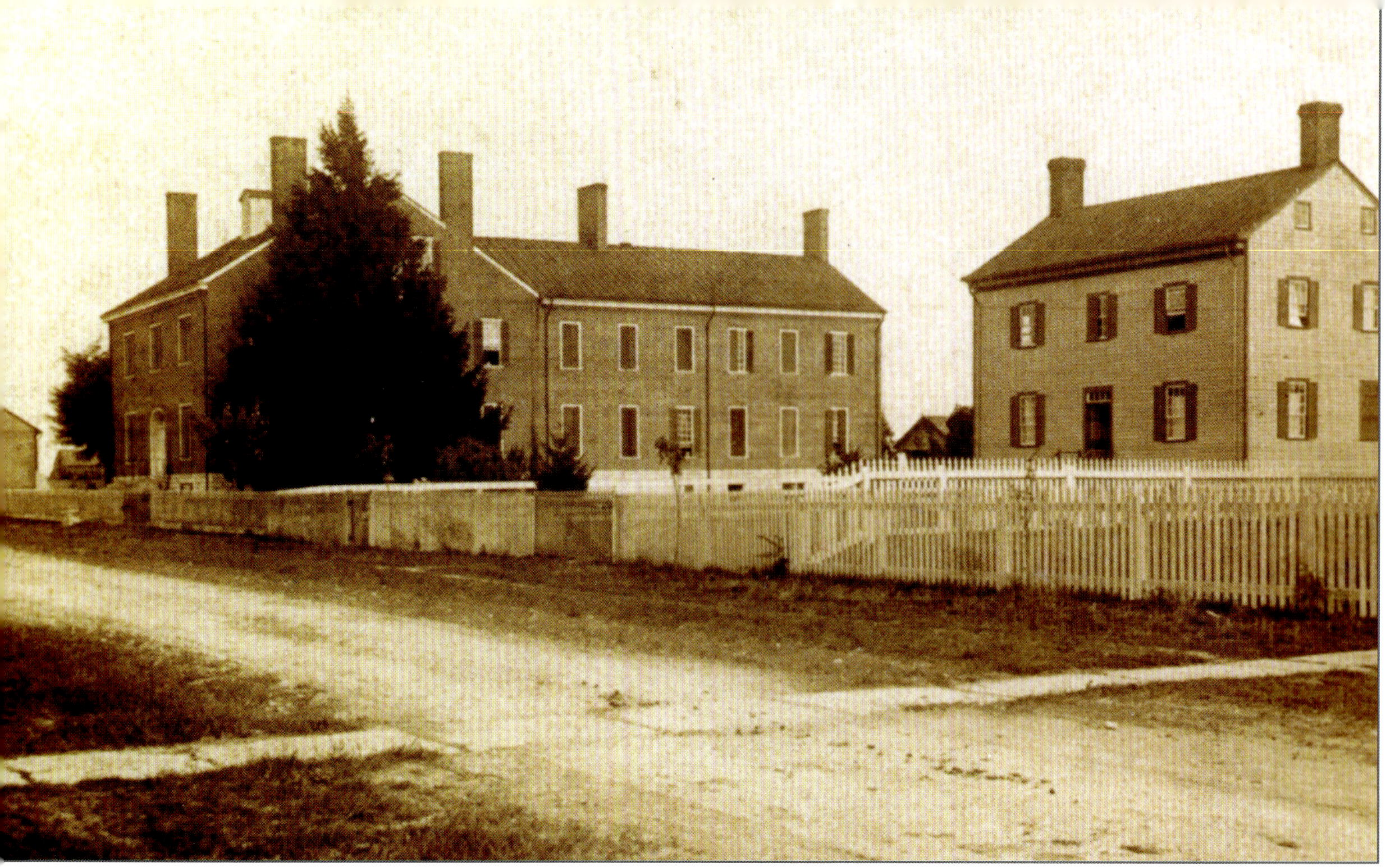

An archival photo showing both the Trustee's Building in the background and the Ministry's Workshop in the foreground. These structures, along with the Meeting House and Post Office were located on the South side of the Turnpike and open to the general public. Family Dwellings and support structures were located on the north side of the Turnpike and generally not open or available to the outside world.

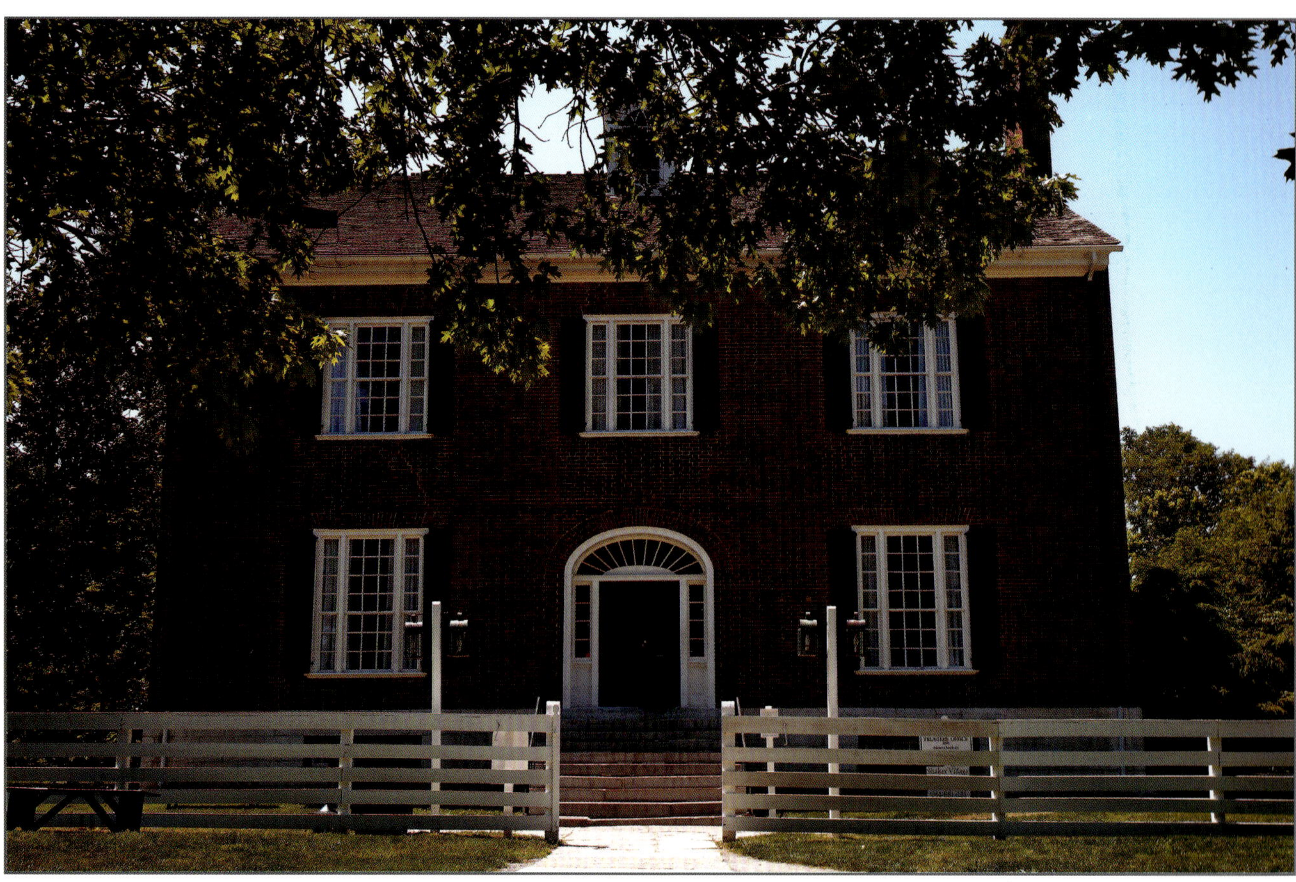

The Shakers referred to the Trustee's Building as "The World's Building". Trading Deacons and Trustees conducted business with the outside world here. Rooms and meals were available for people conducting business with the Shakers who, for whatever reason, may have needed overnight lodging.

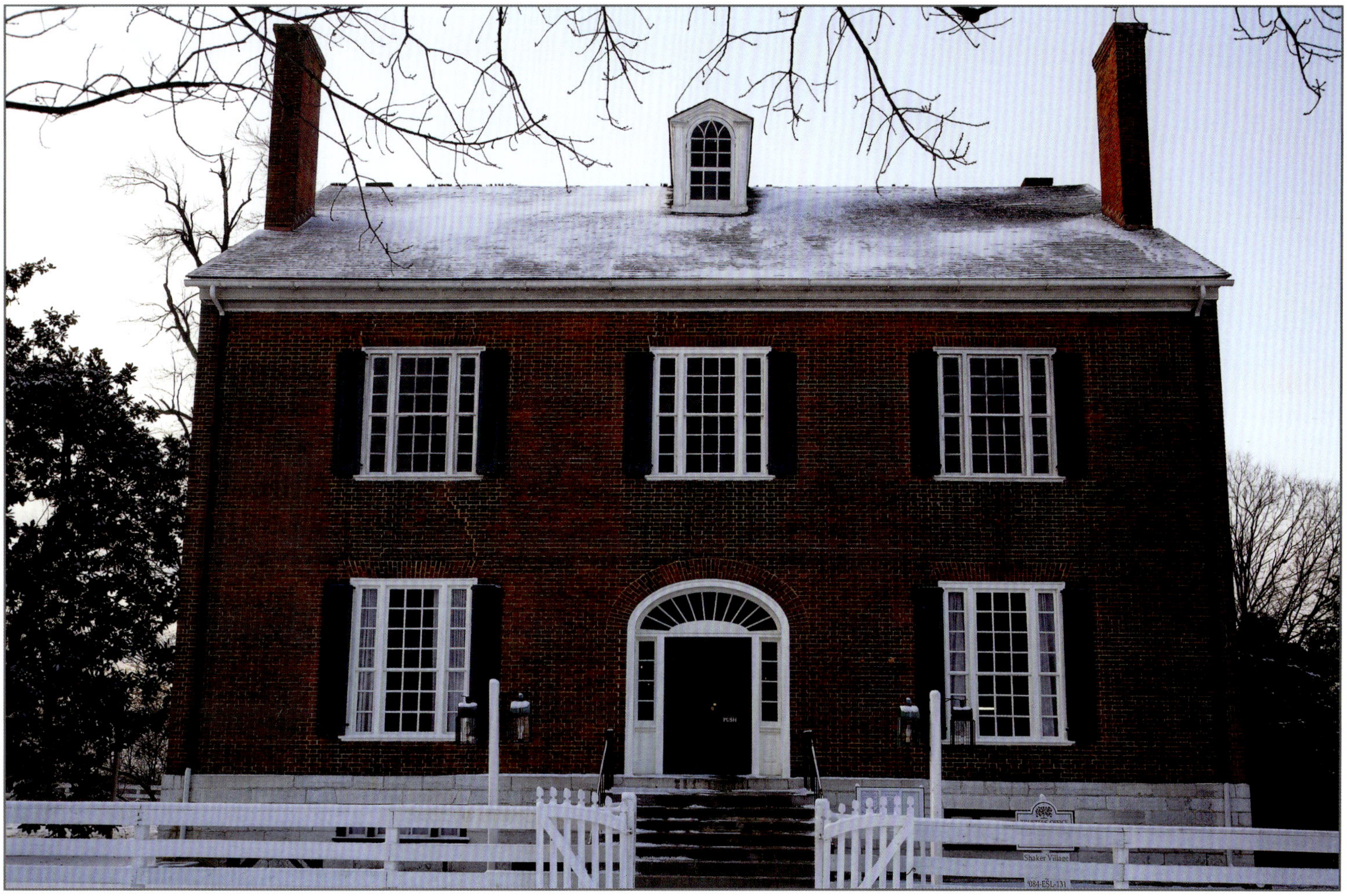

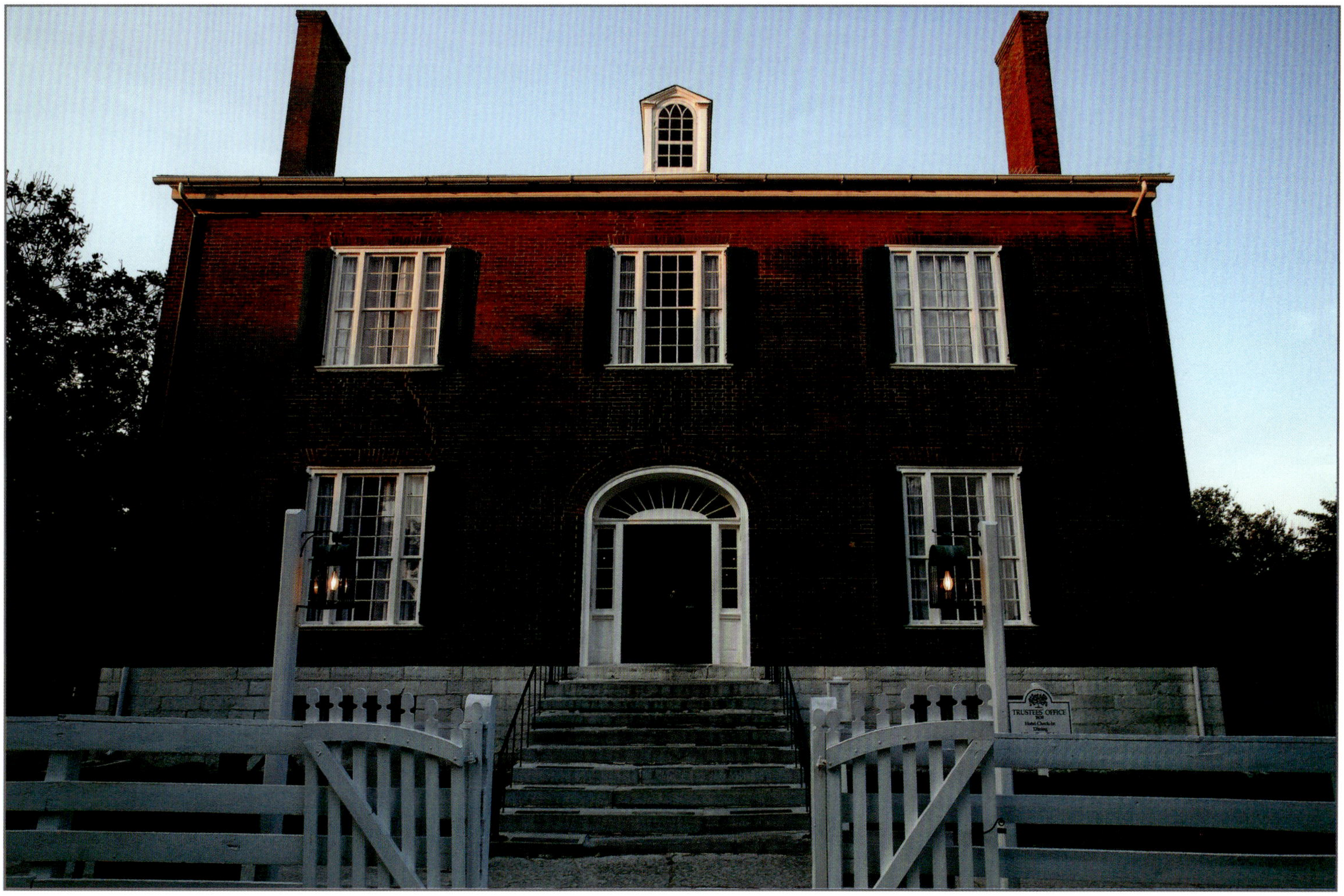

Exterior photos of the Trustee's Building in various seasons of the year and times of day.

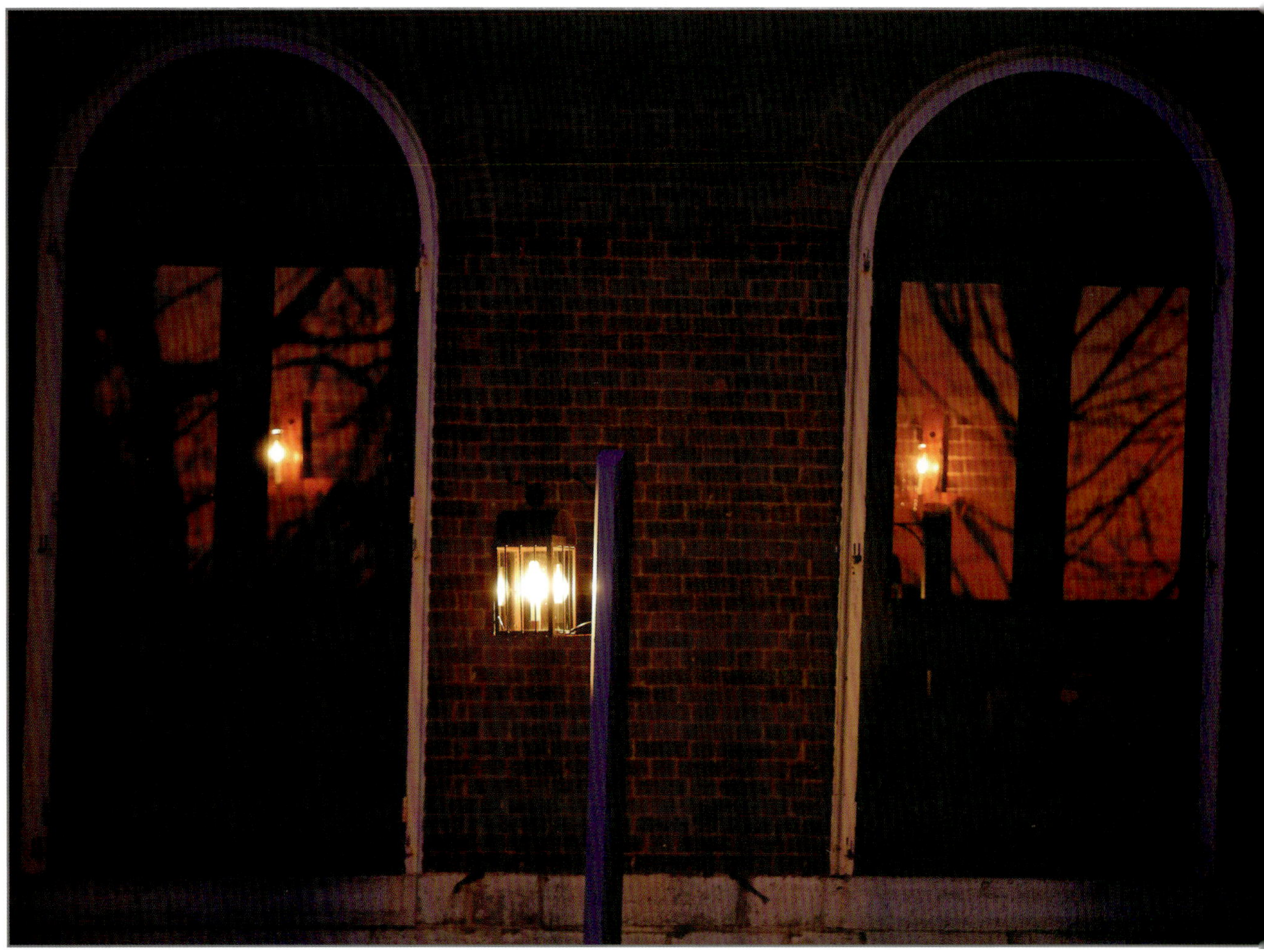

Windows in the Dining area of the Trustee's Building reflect the rising sun.

Below: A view from the front steps of the Trustee's Building.

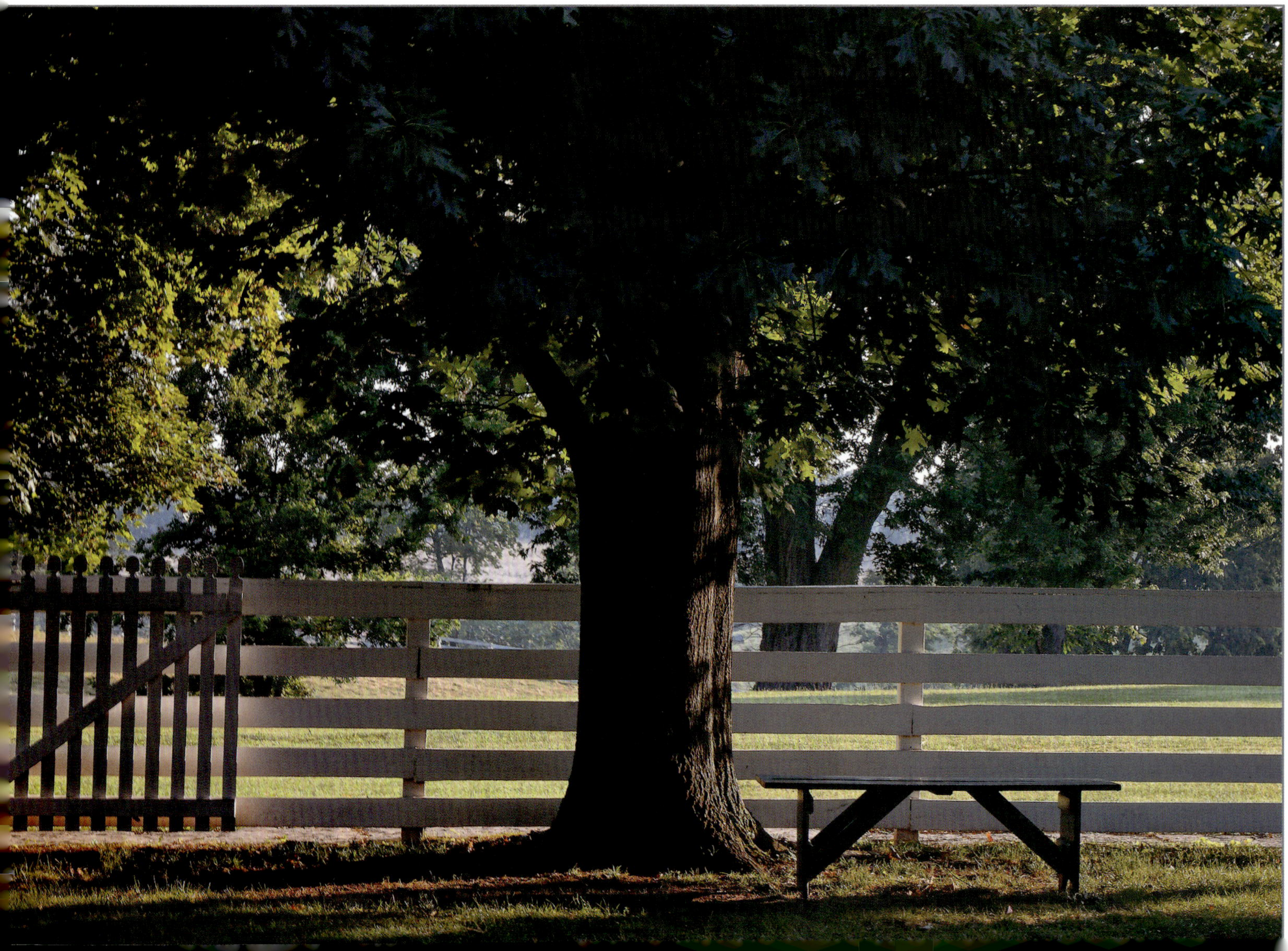

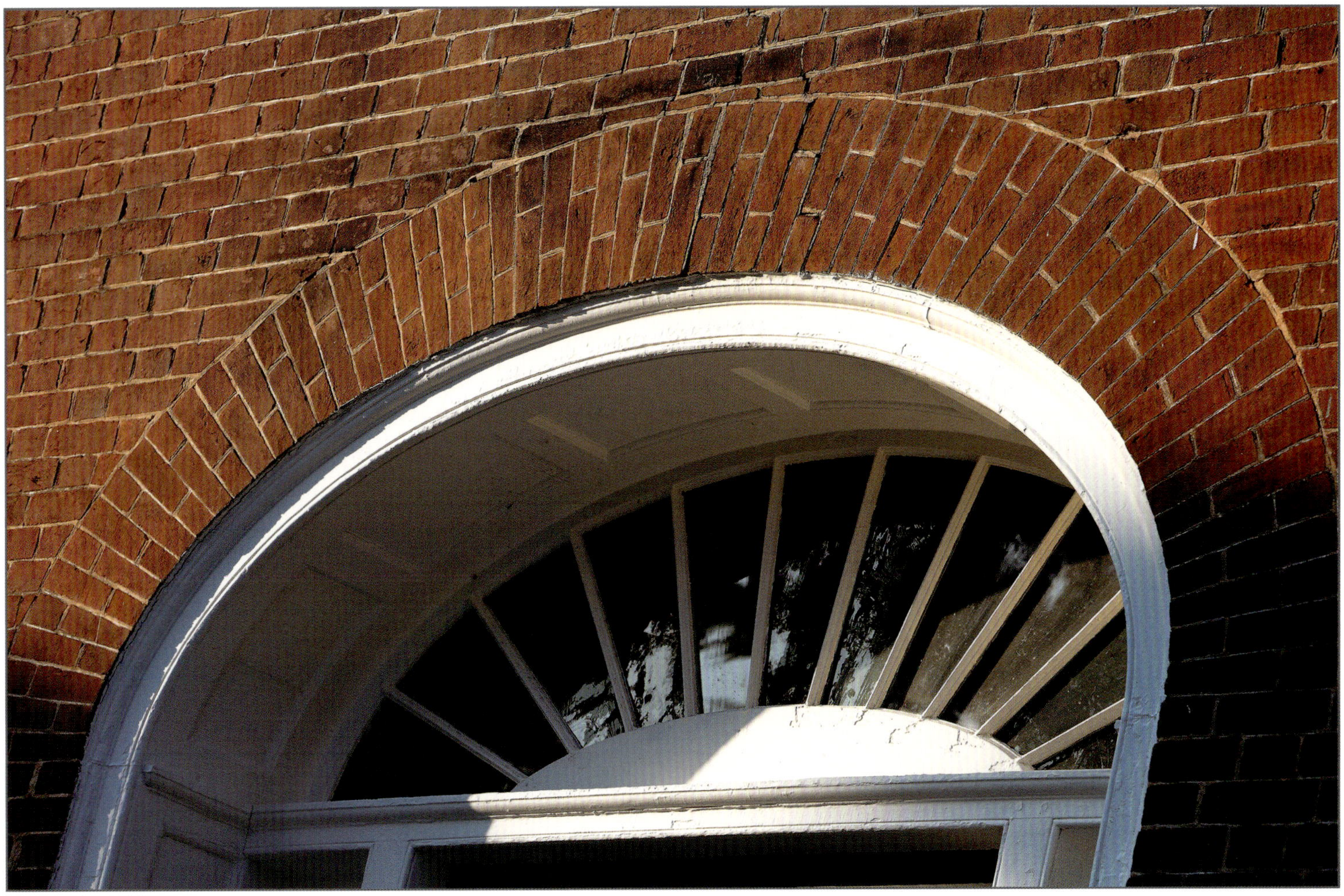

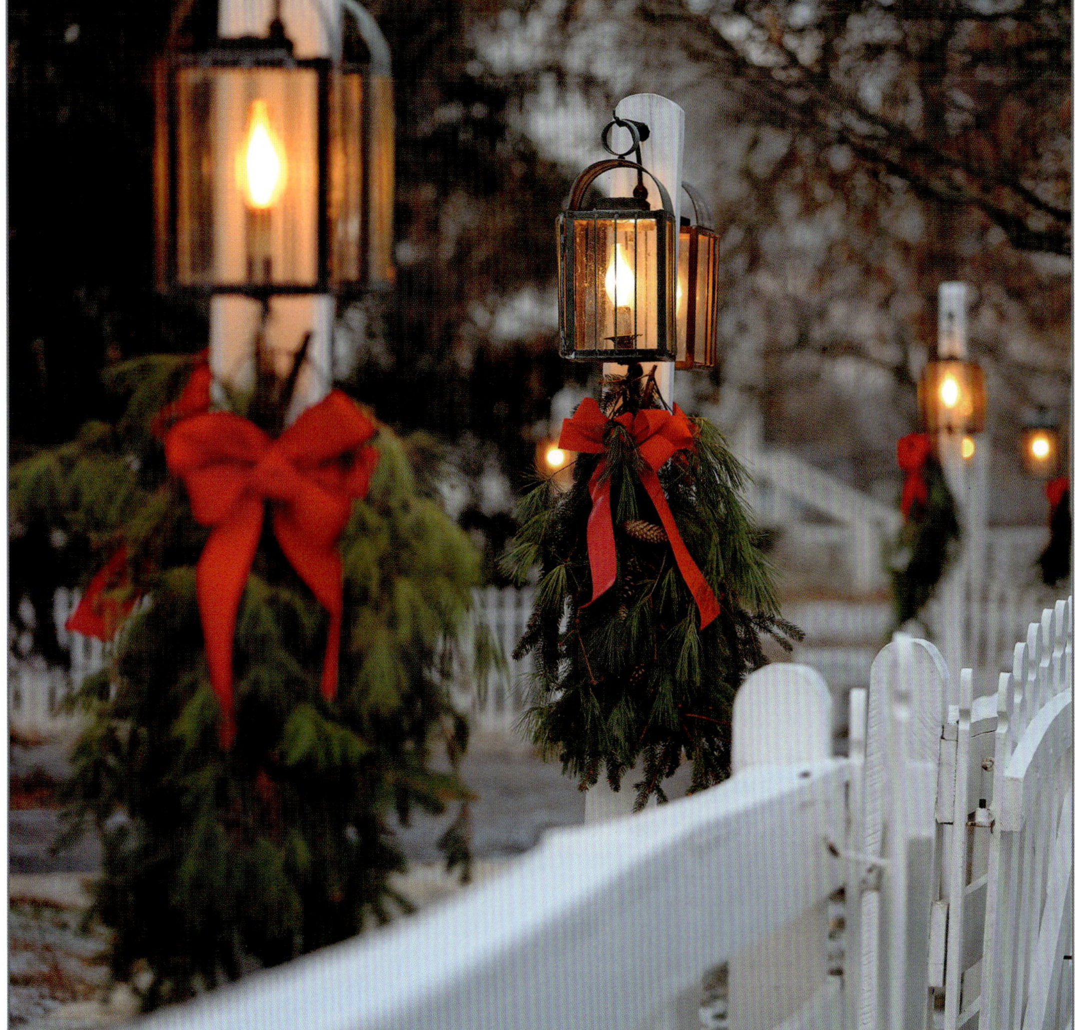

Above: The fanlight transom over the front door of the Trustee's Building is its trademark exterior feature.

Christmas wreaths and bows adorn the lamp posts outside the modern day Trustee's Building.

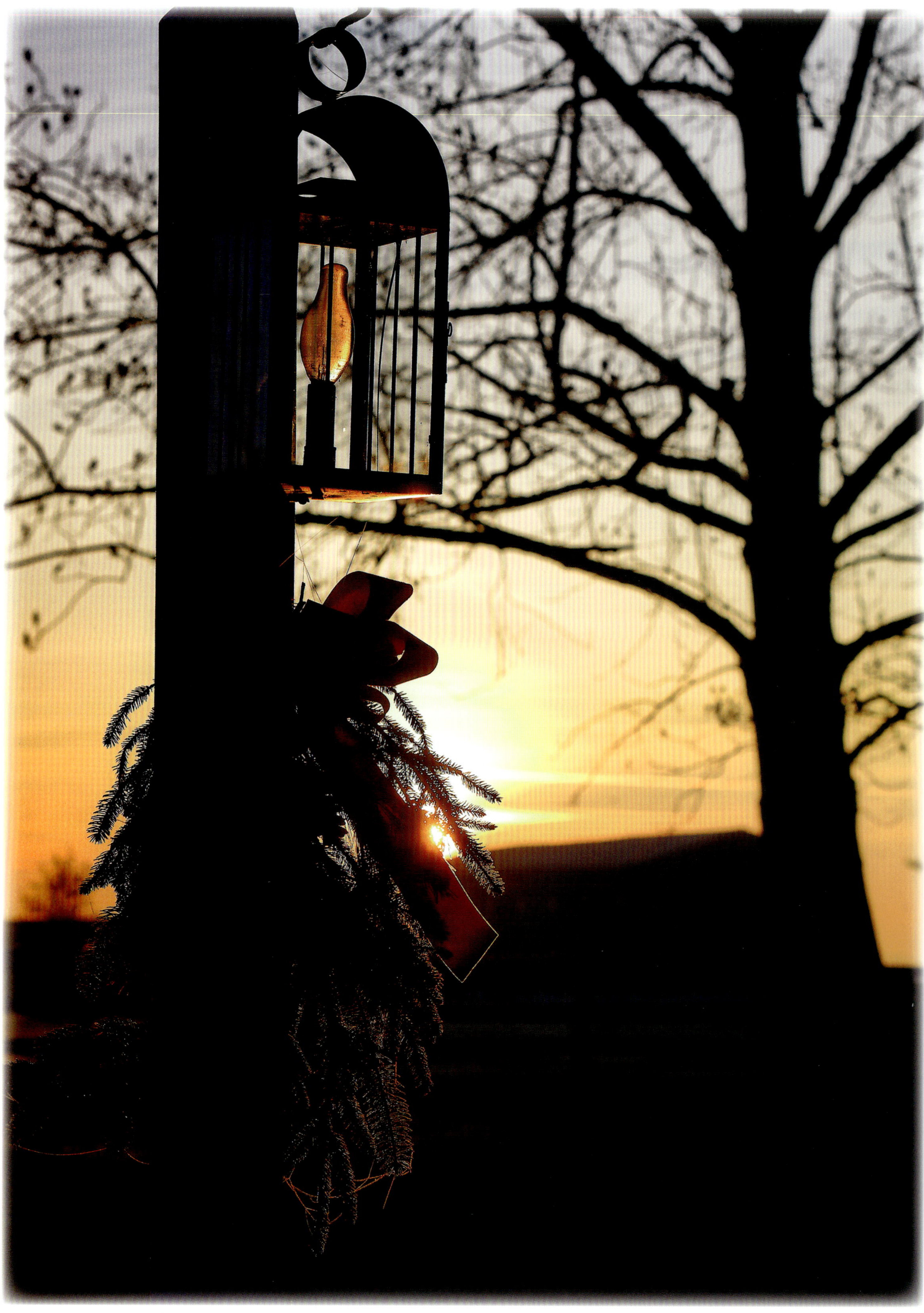

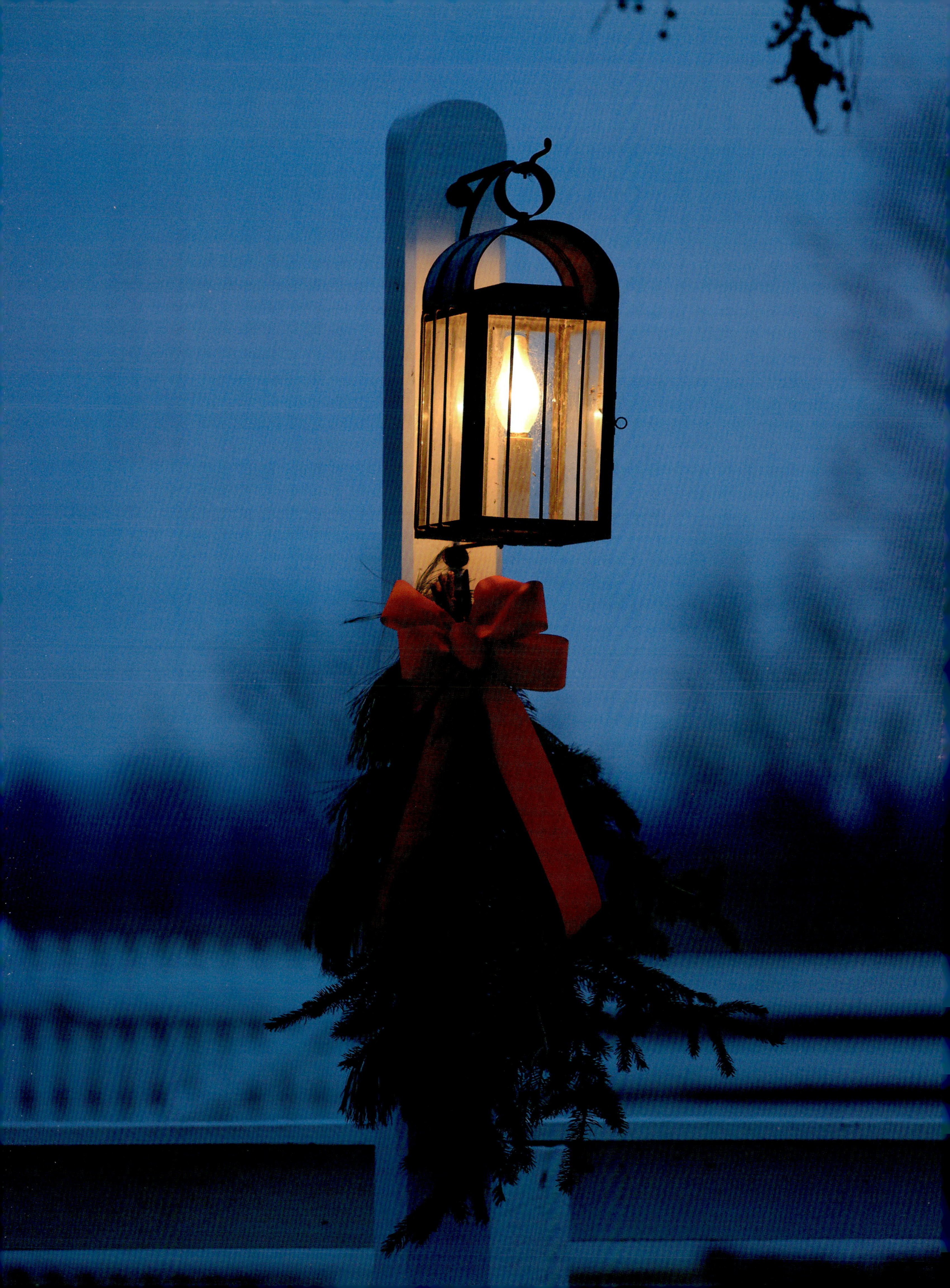

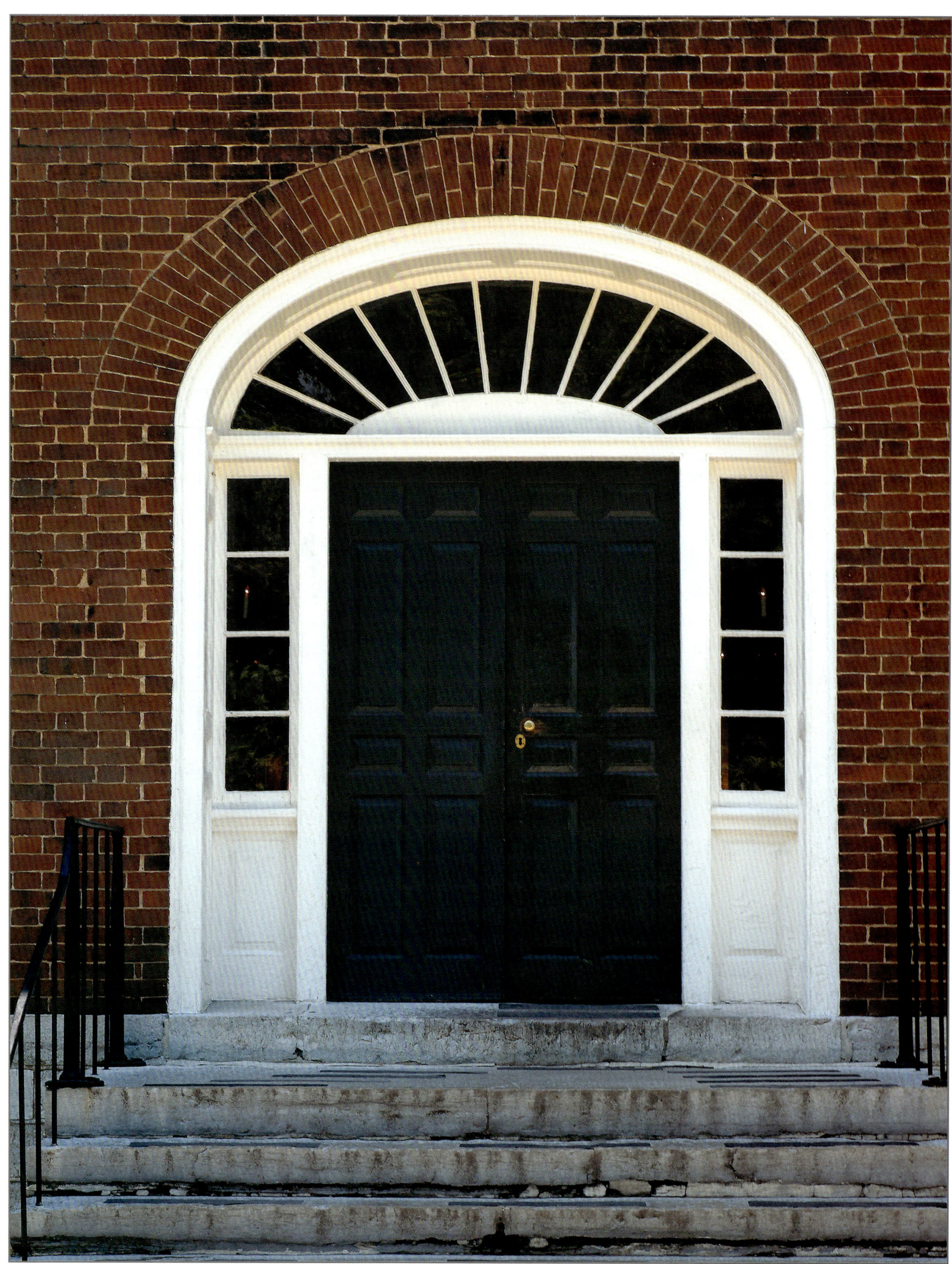

Another view of the Trustee's Building front door featuring the fanlight transom and sidelights.

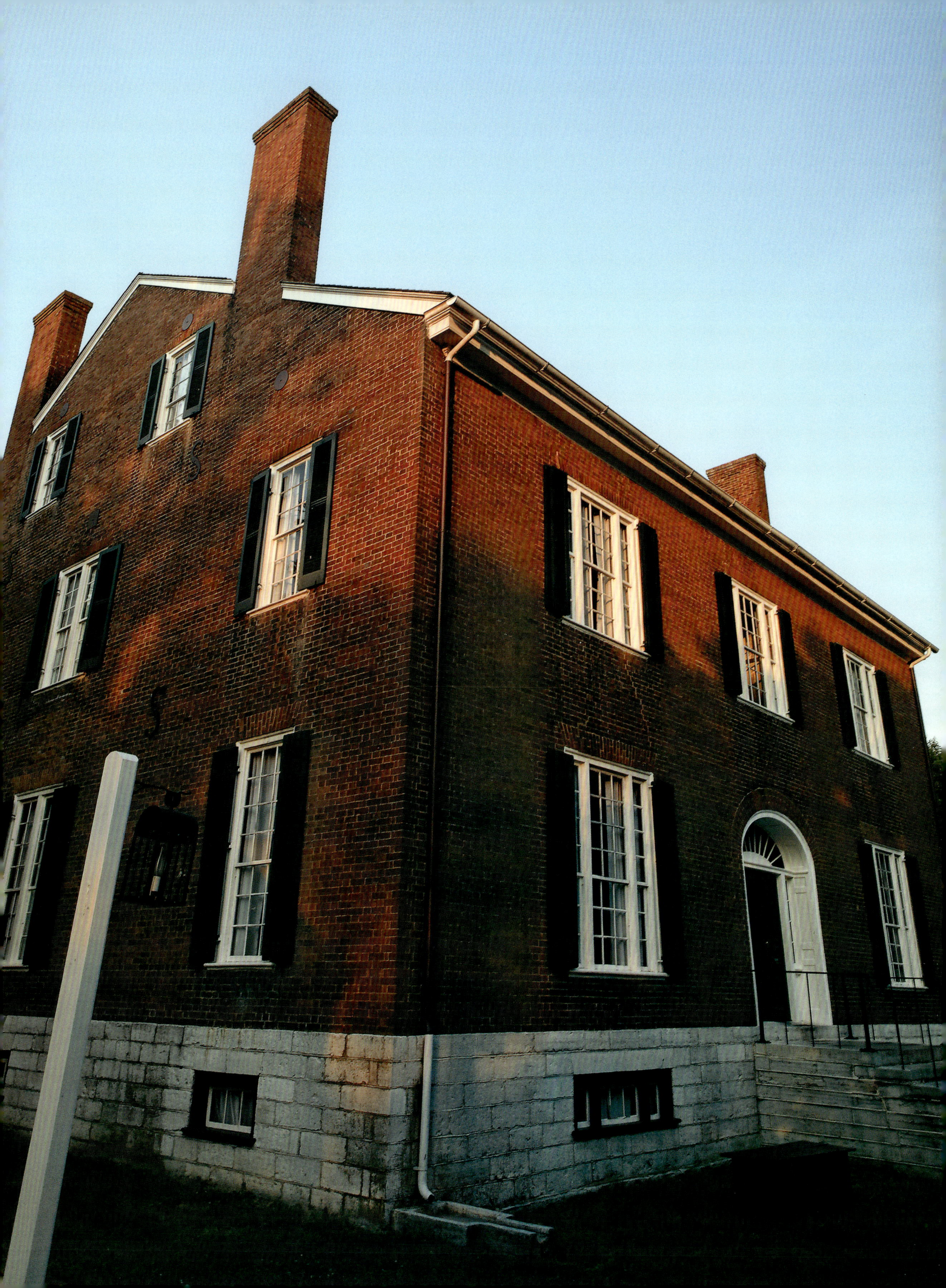

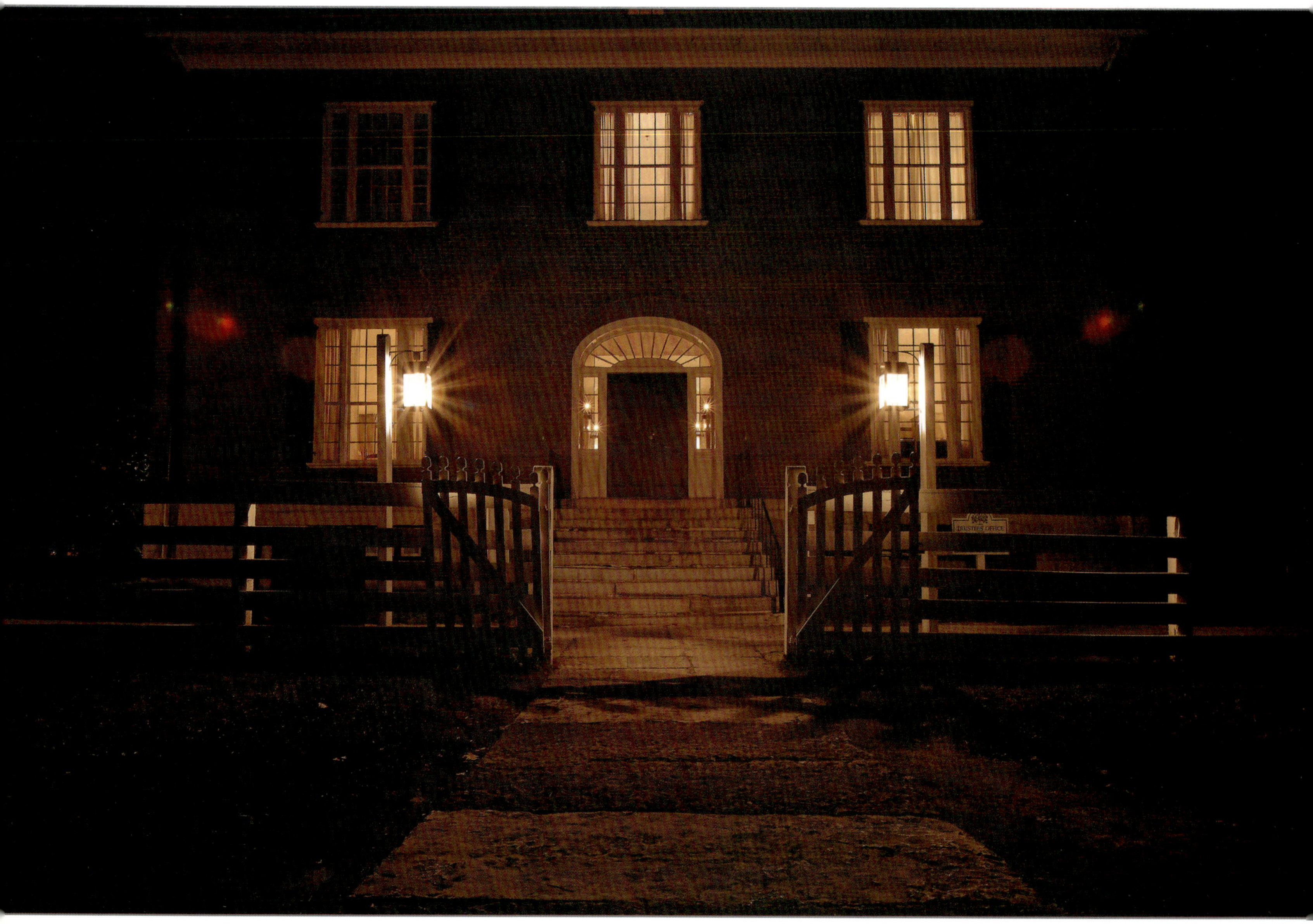

Night time photos of the Trustee's Building.

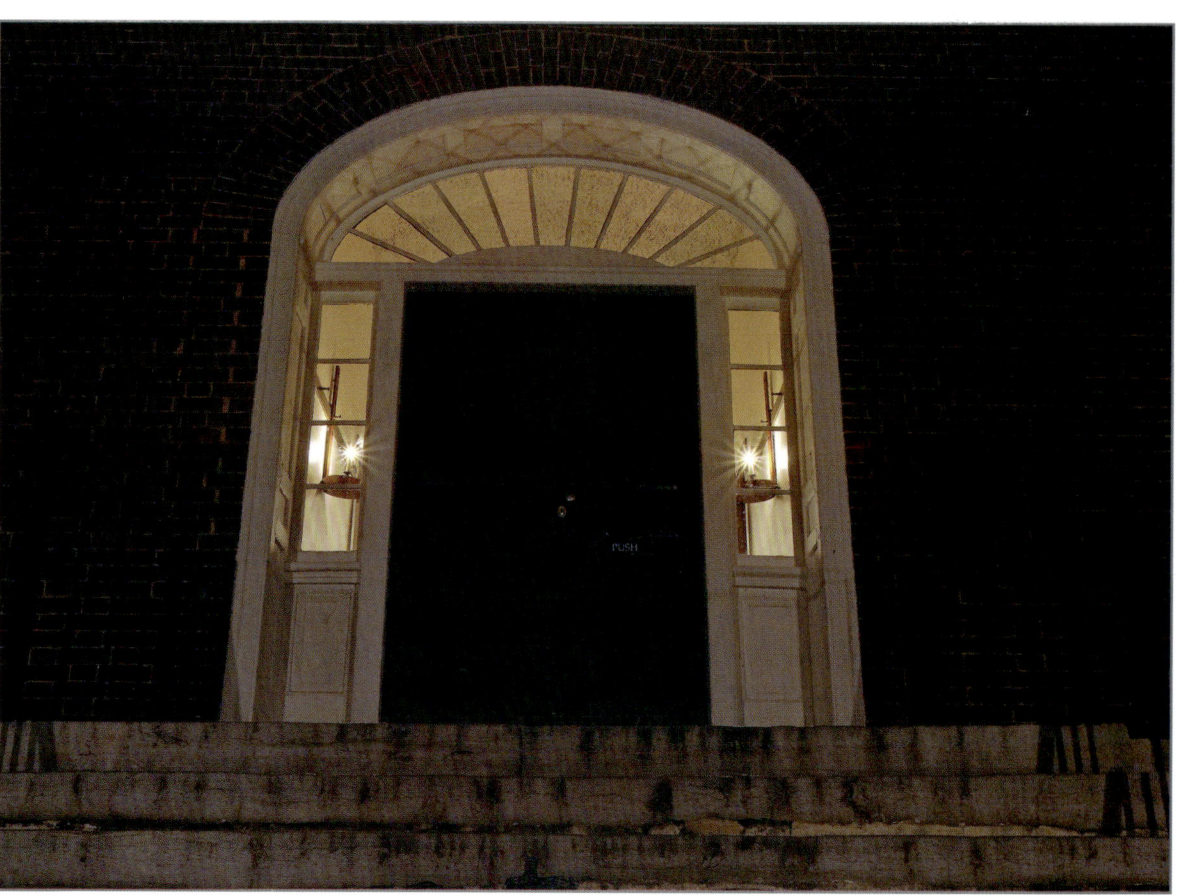

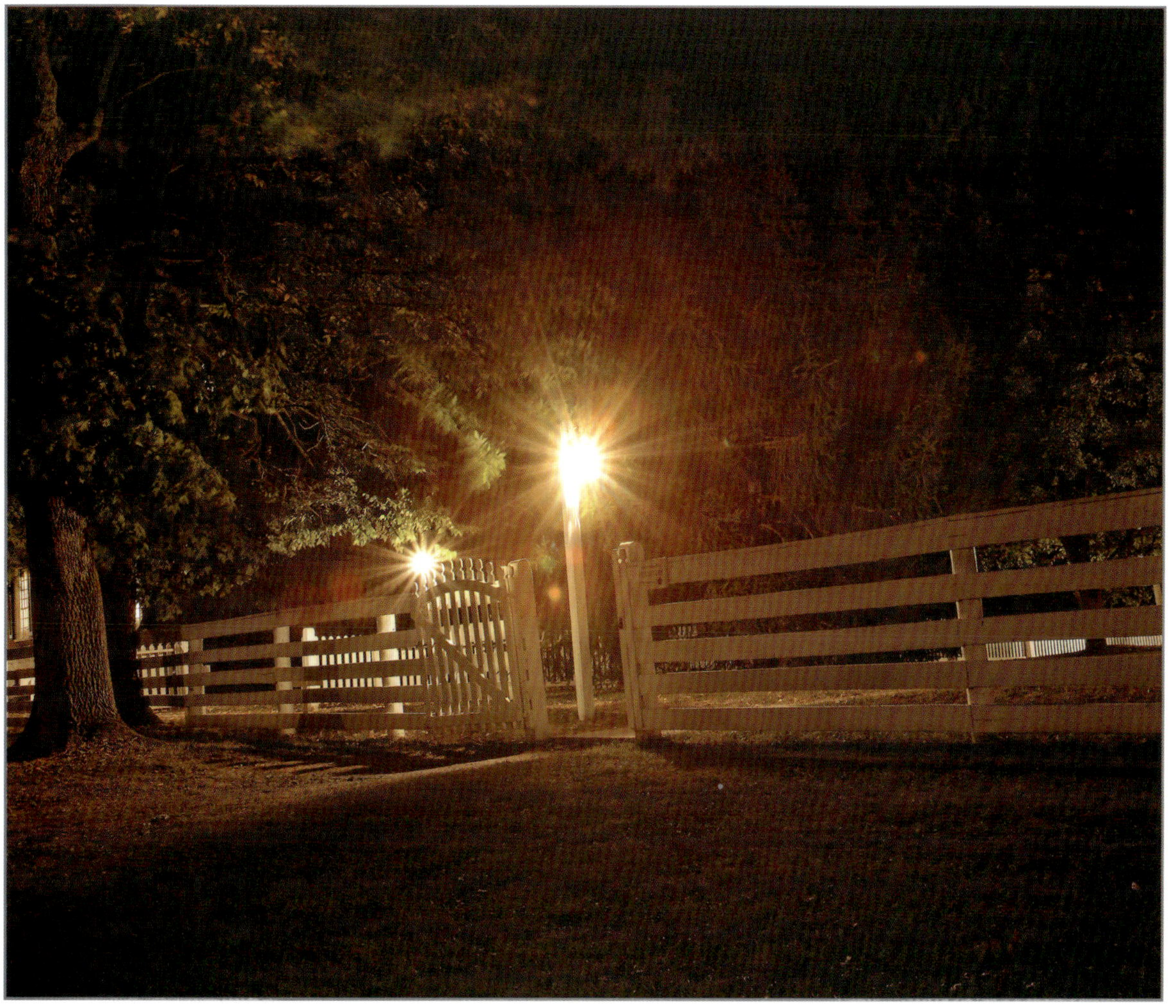

Night time photos of the main road as it appears today.

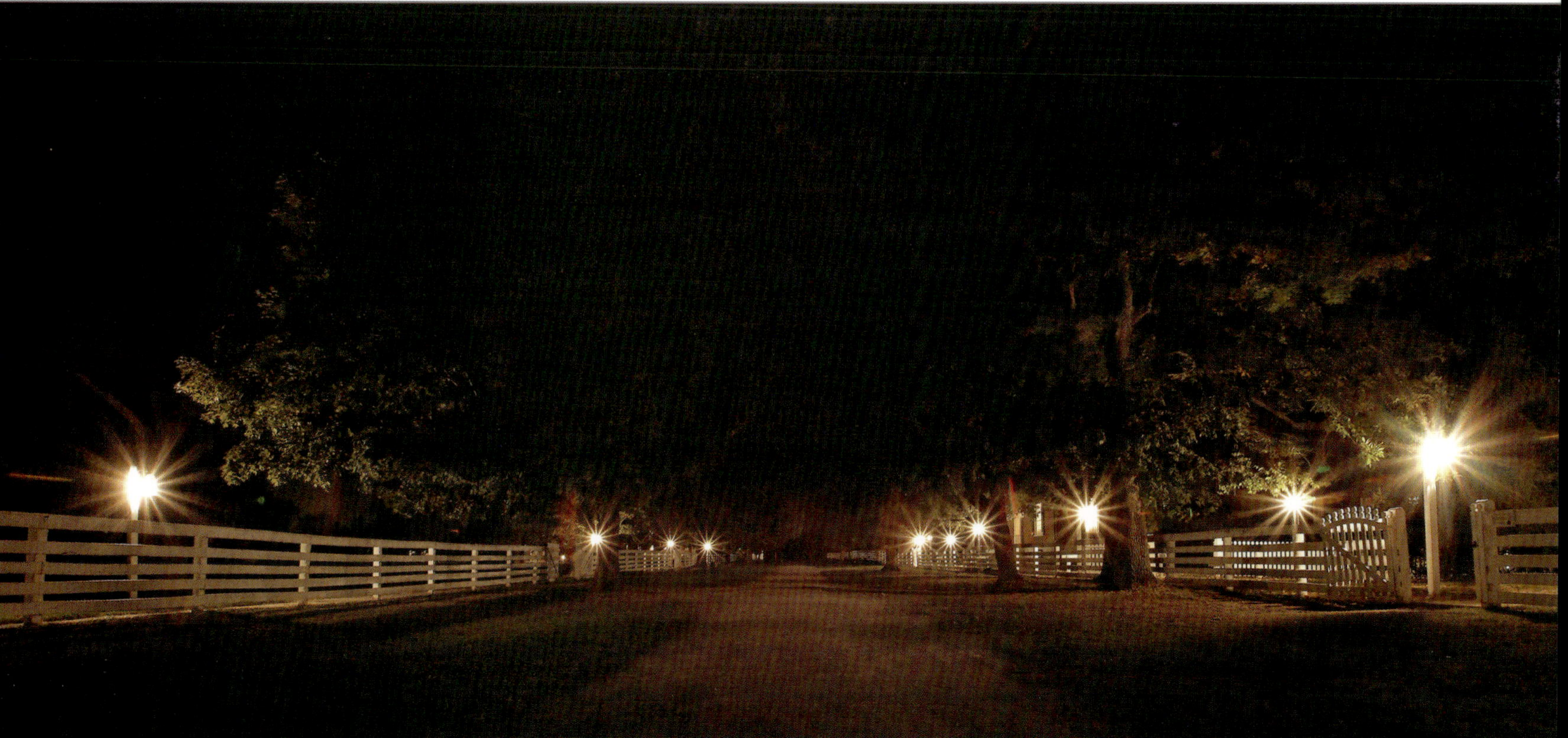

Roof access for the Trustee's Building provided both grace and functionality. The wooden "Shaker" shingles which can be seen in the photo were always in danger of catching fire by ambers from the numerous fireplaces in the structure.

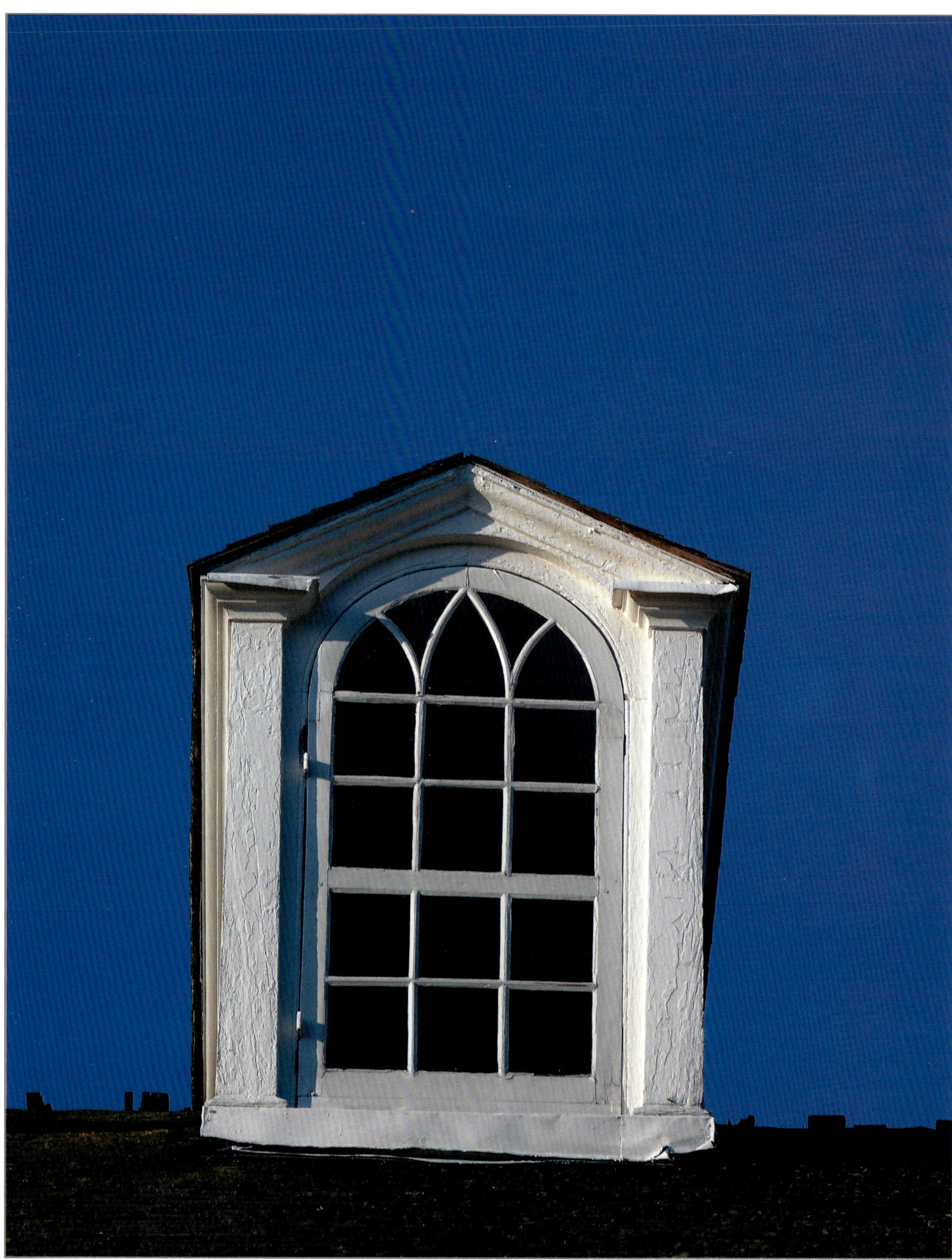

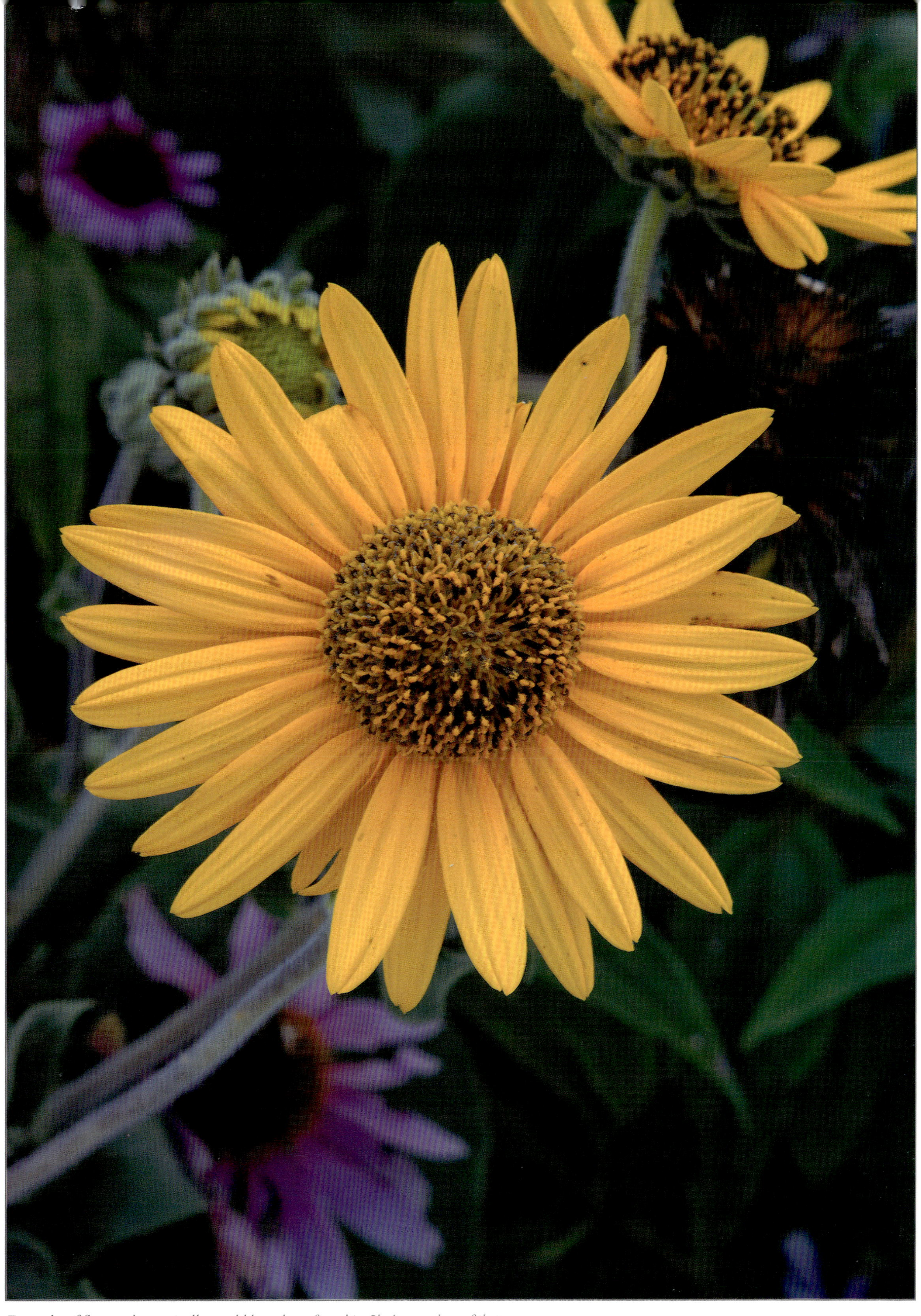

Examples of flowers that typically would have been found in Shaker gardens of that time. Every plant had a purpose and was not simply for decoration.

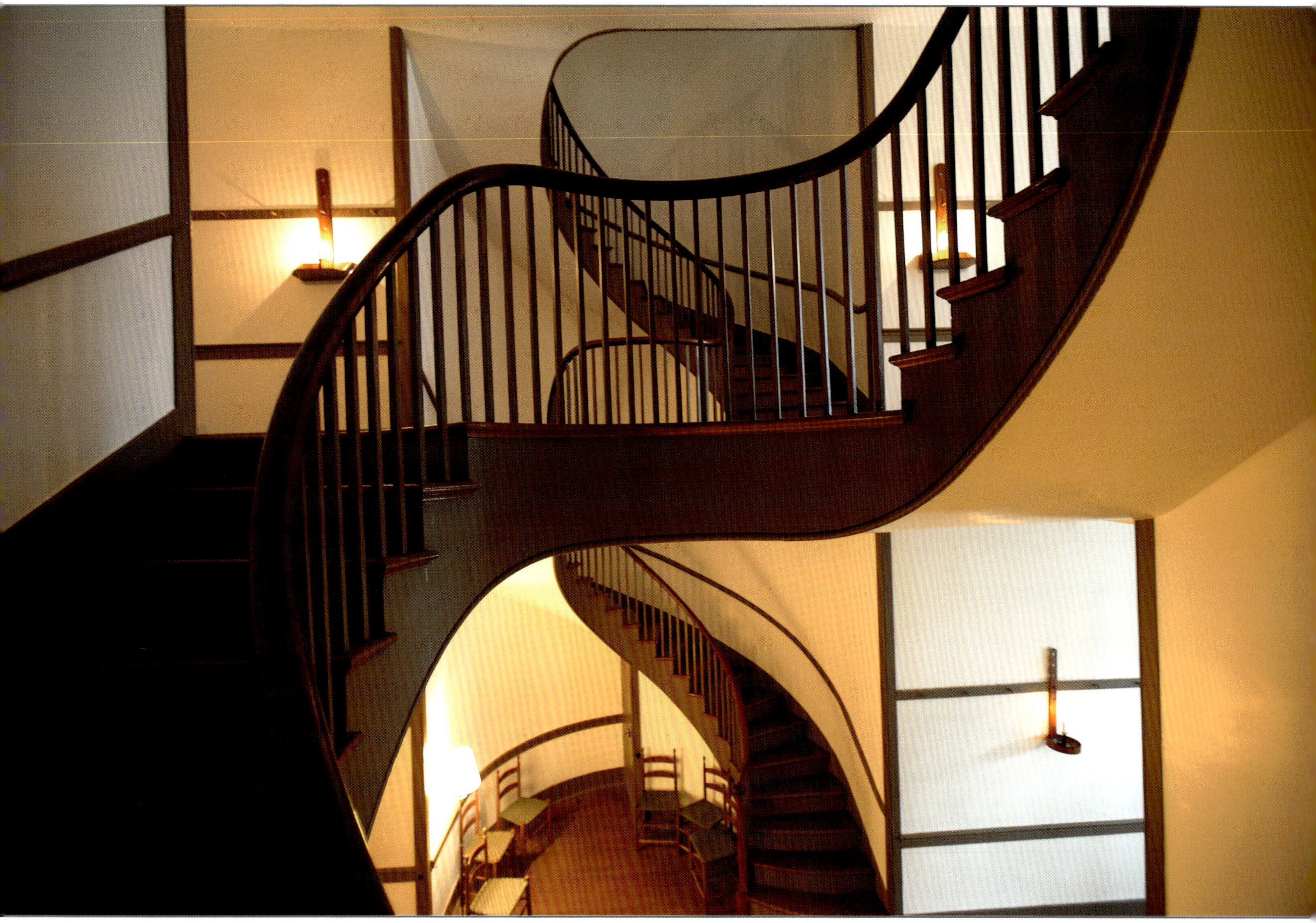

Micajah Burnett's crowning achievement in design was the twin cantilevered spiral staircases located in the Trustee's Building. Easily the most photographed feature of Pleasant Hill, one is amazed at the grace, beauty and workmanship of these stairs.

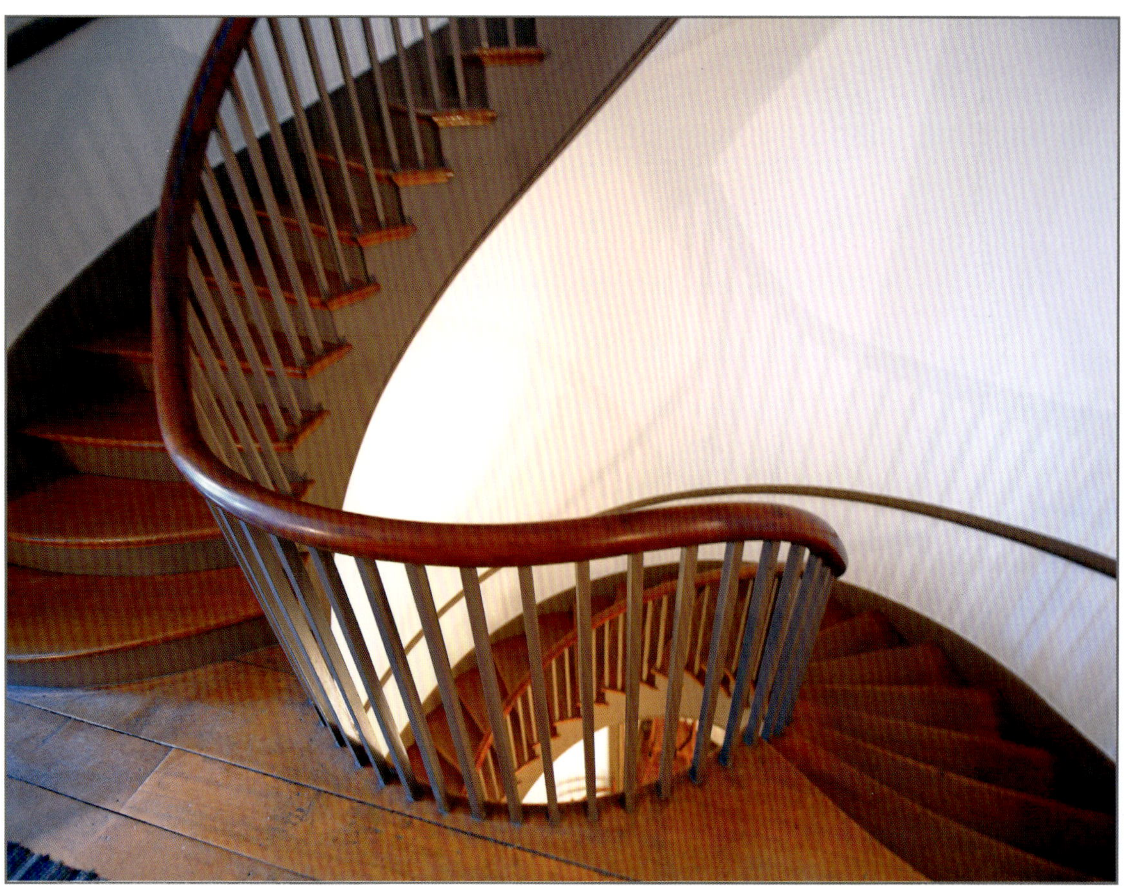

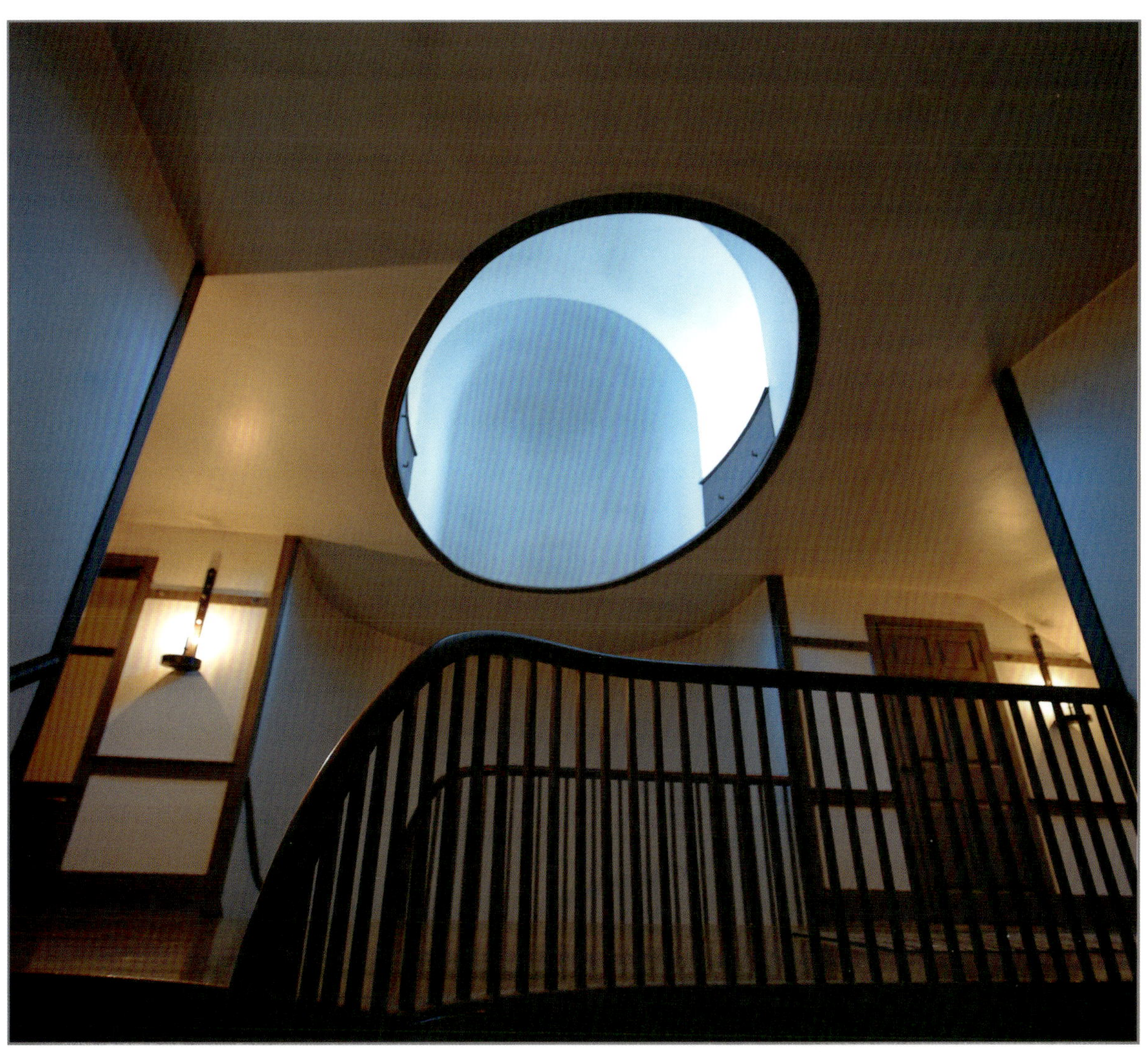

The skylight at the top of the spiral staircase providing both light and ventilation.

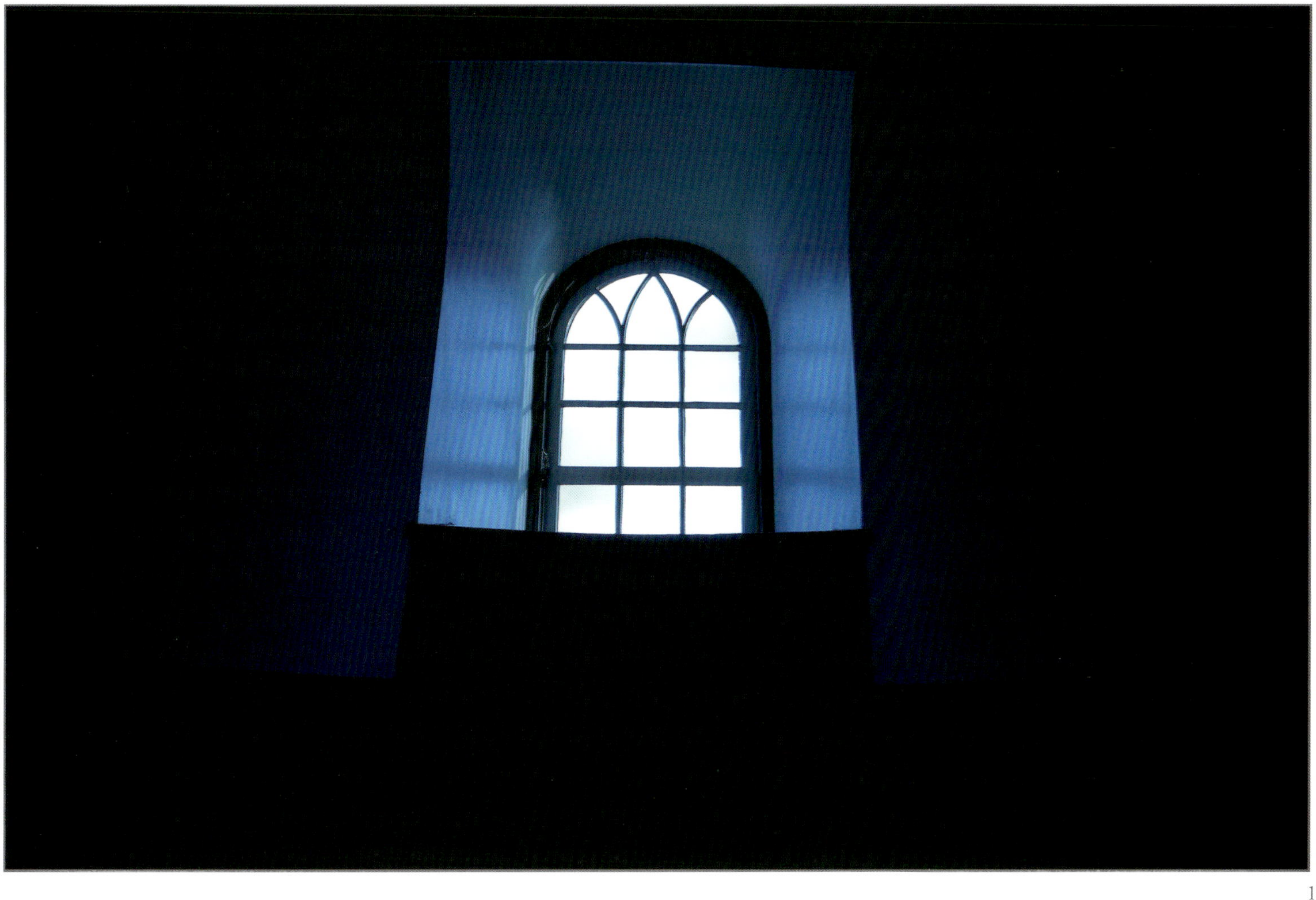

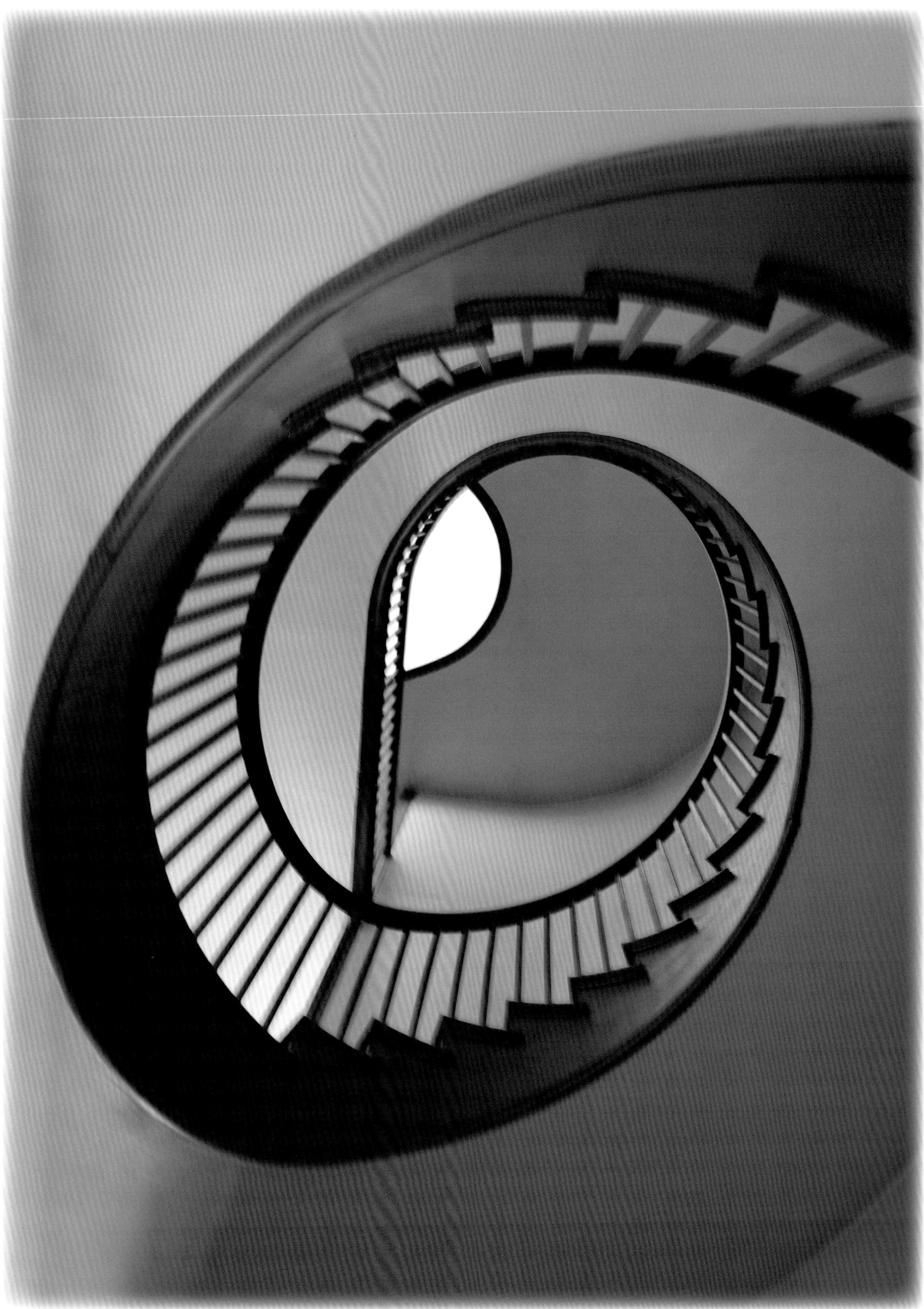

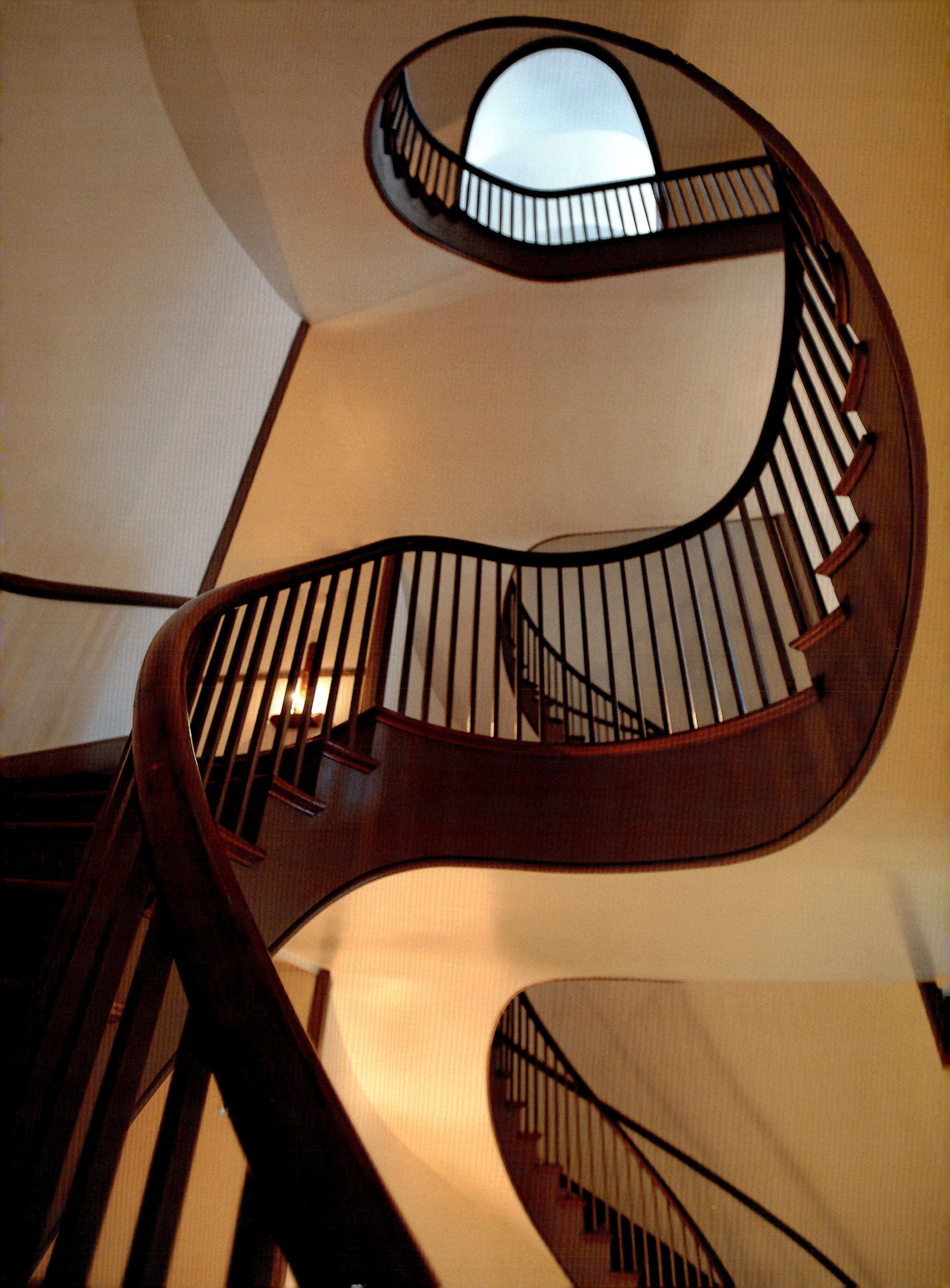

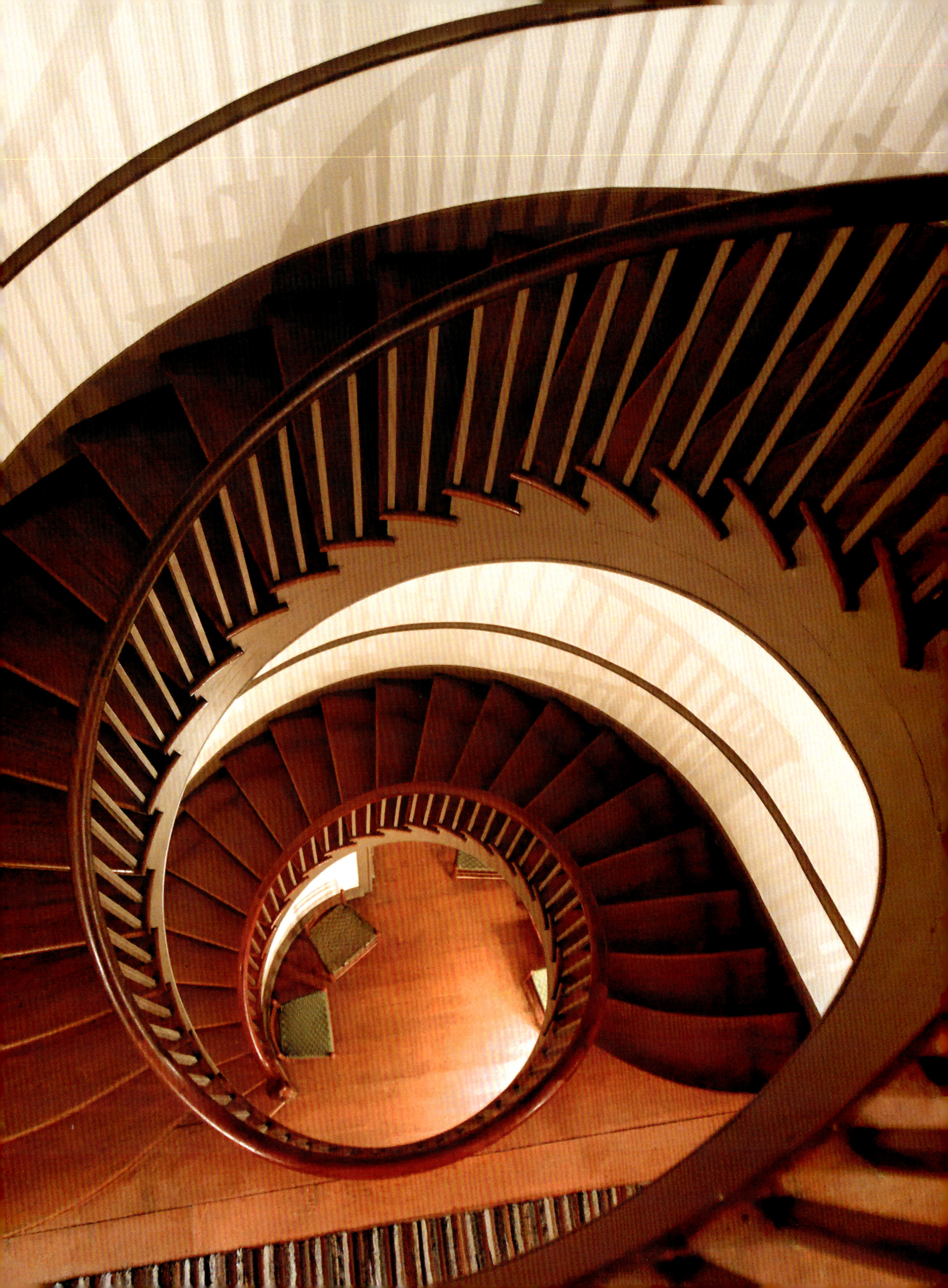

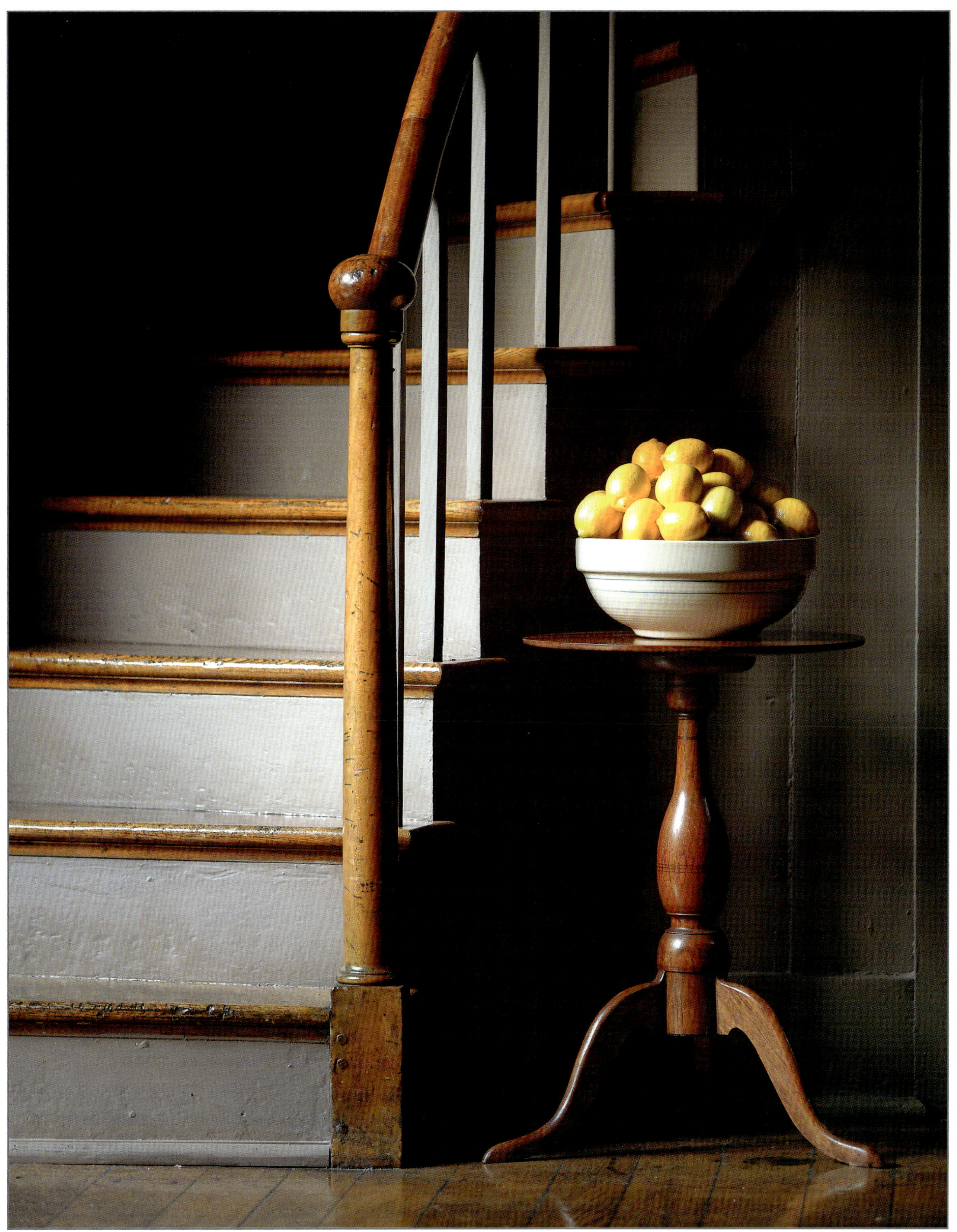

The Trustee's Building Dining Room's trademark bowl of lemons is another popular subject for photographers. Lemon pie is a popular desert at Shaker Village and uses the entire lemon in the recipe. Although not indigenous to Kentucky, lemons were brought back to the Village from trading trips to southern ports along with other citrus fruits and spices.

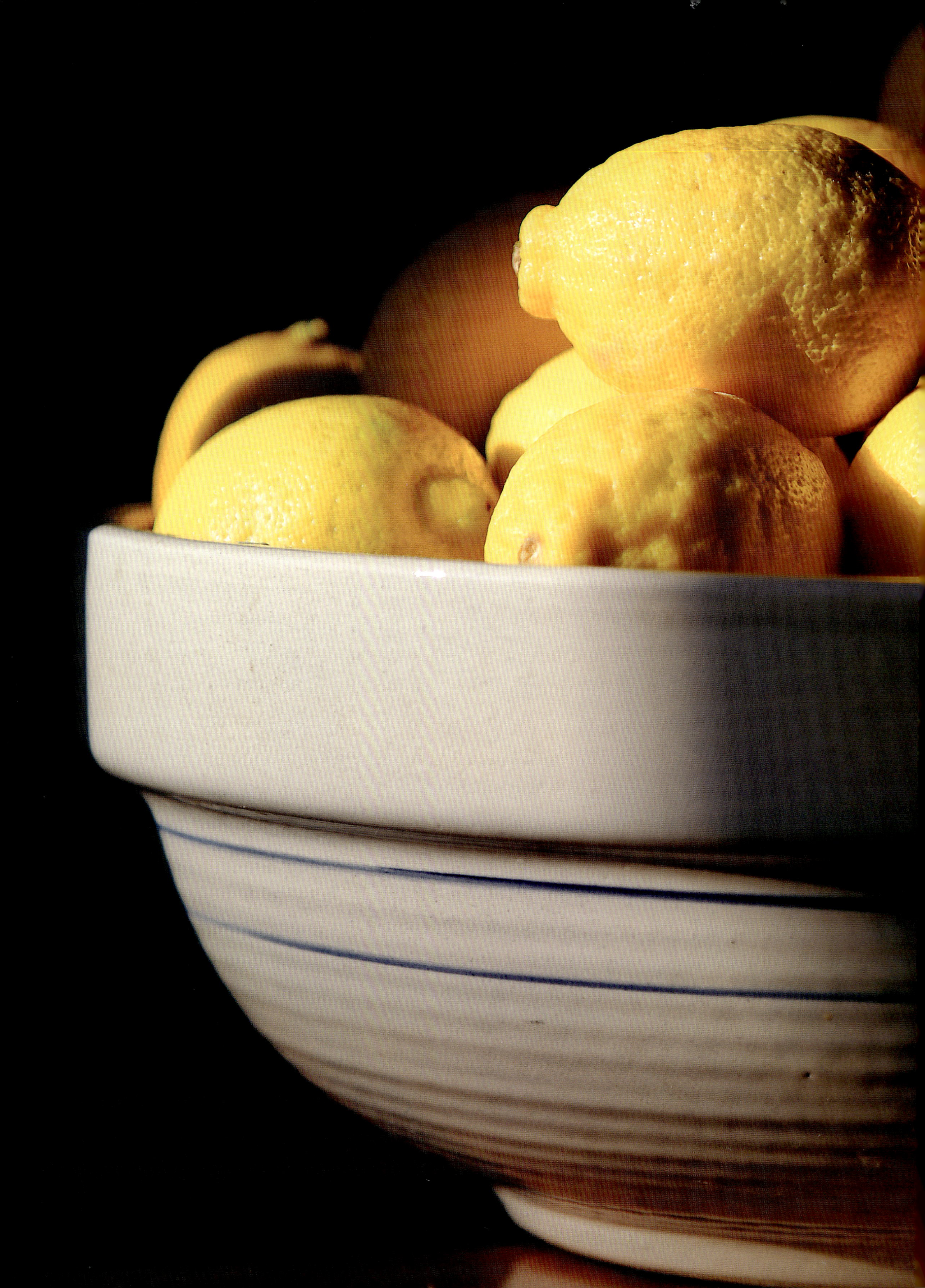

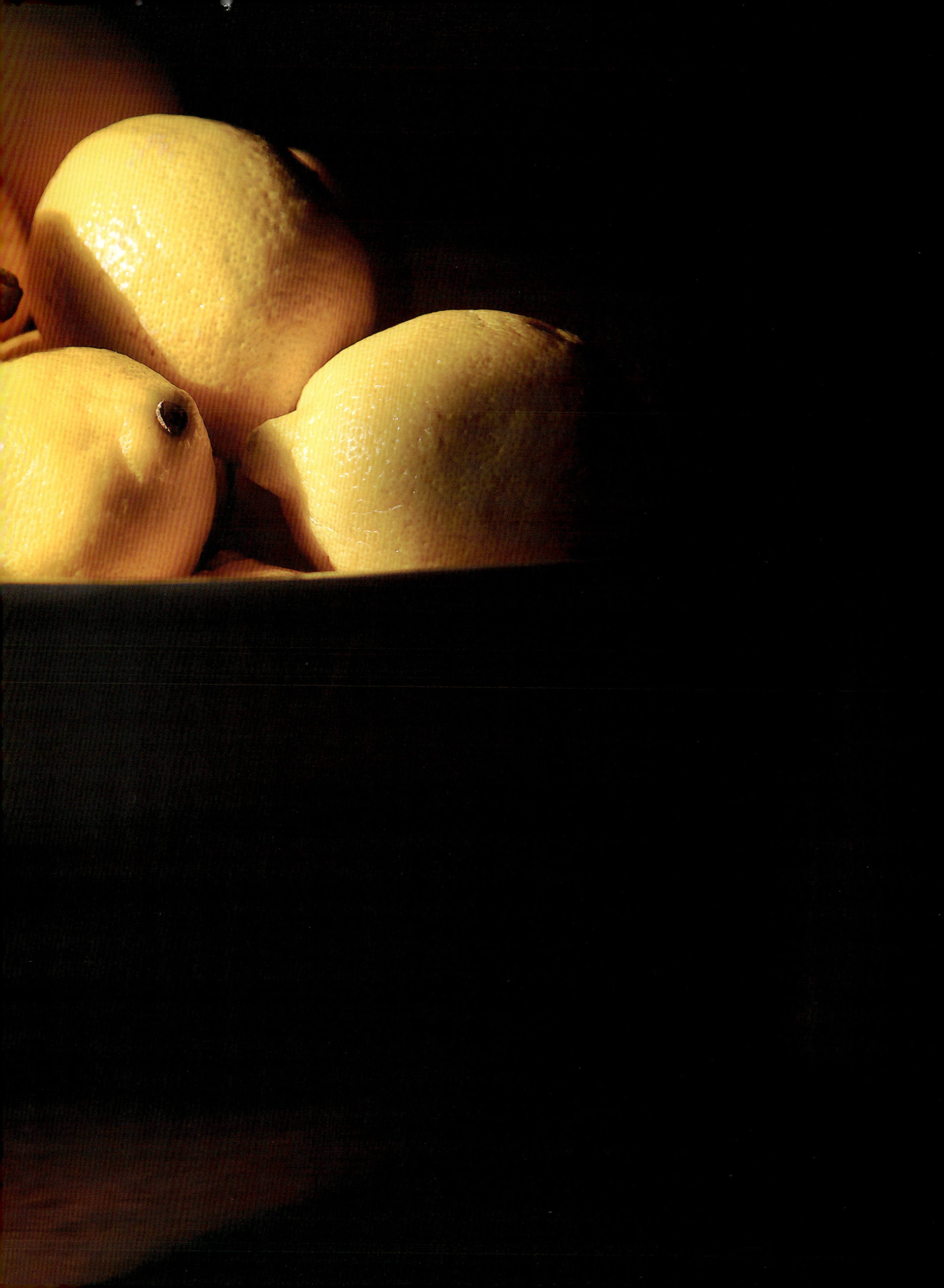

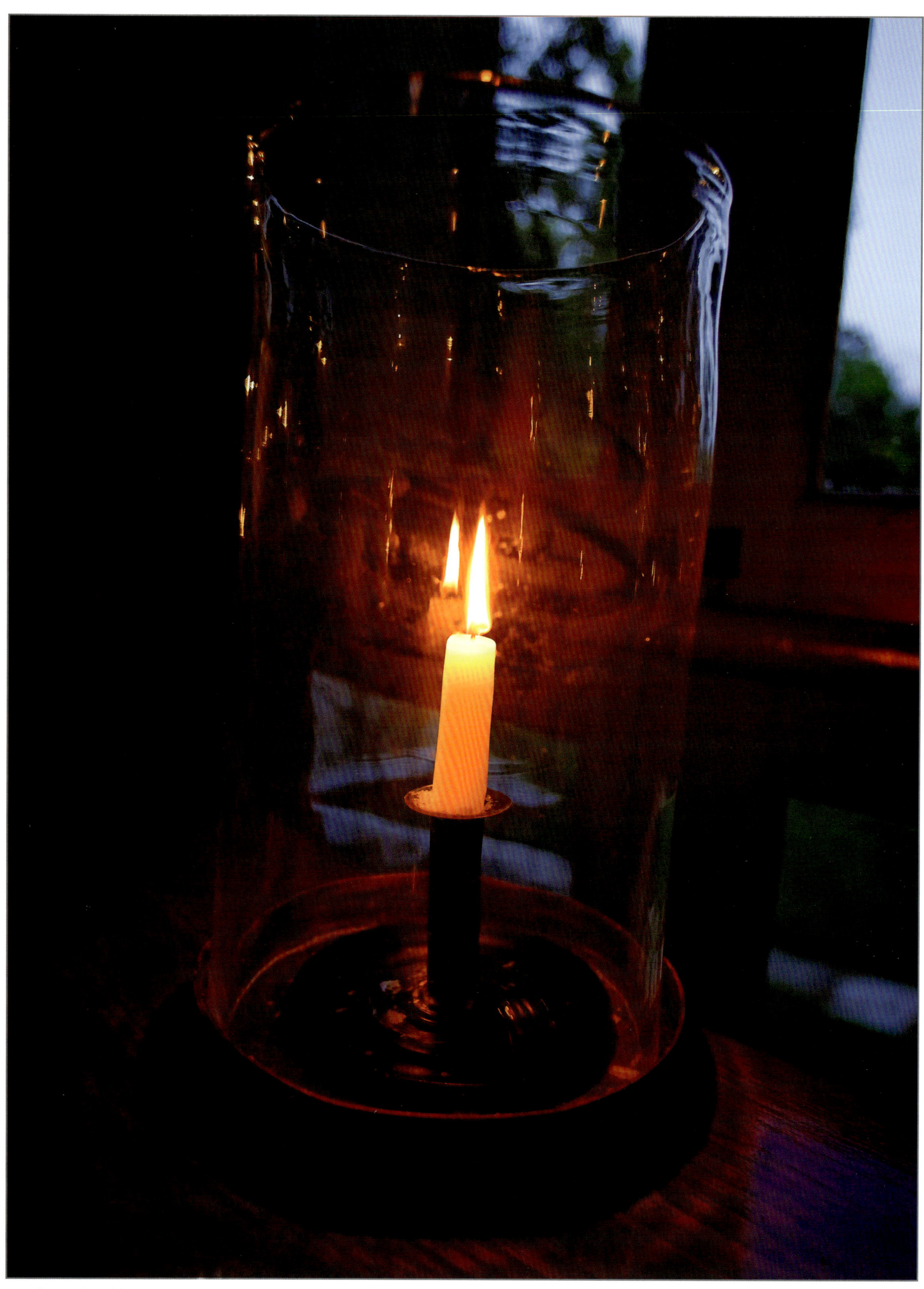

Candles on the tables add a warm glow to the atmosphere in the Dining Room.

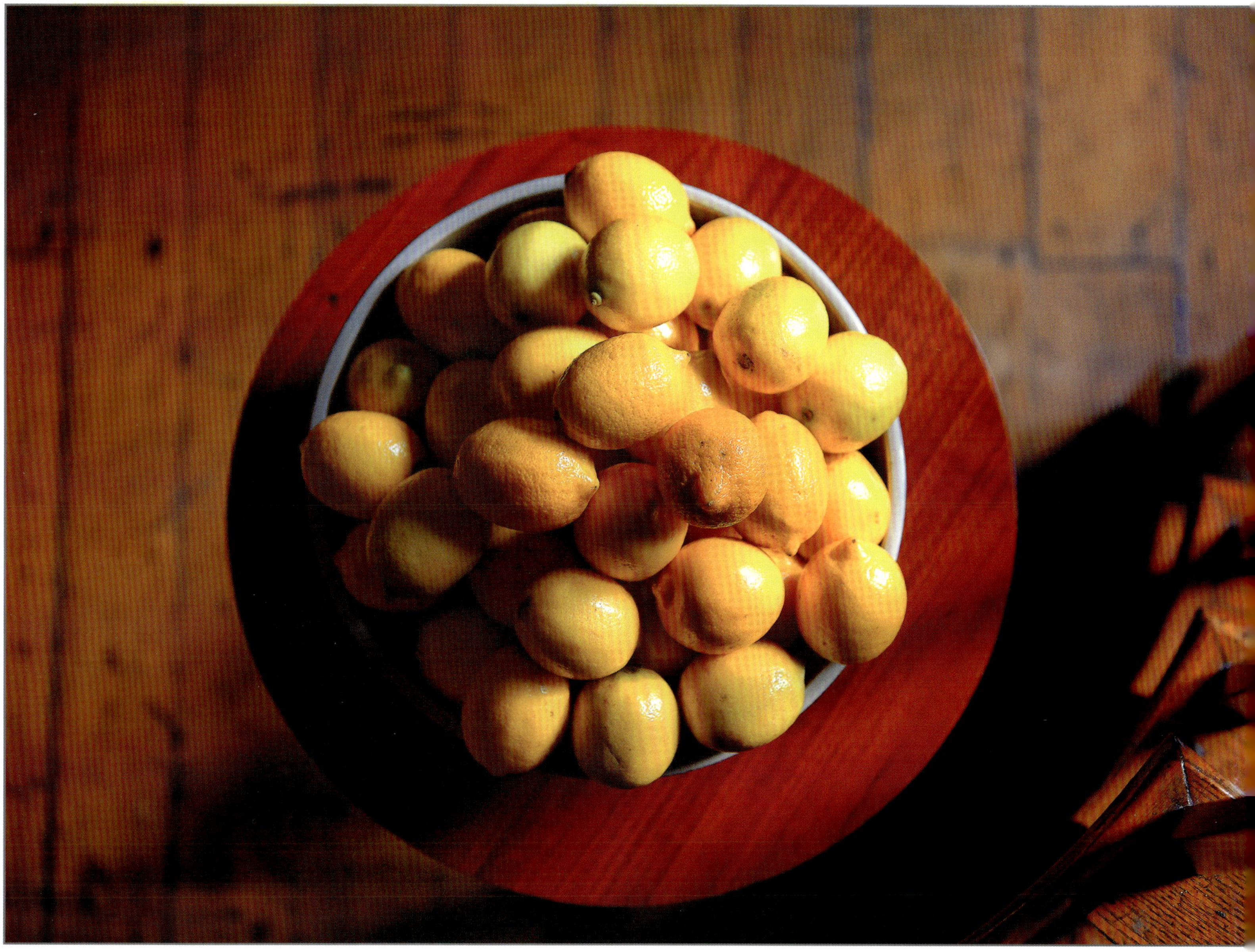

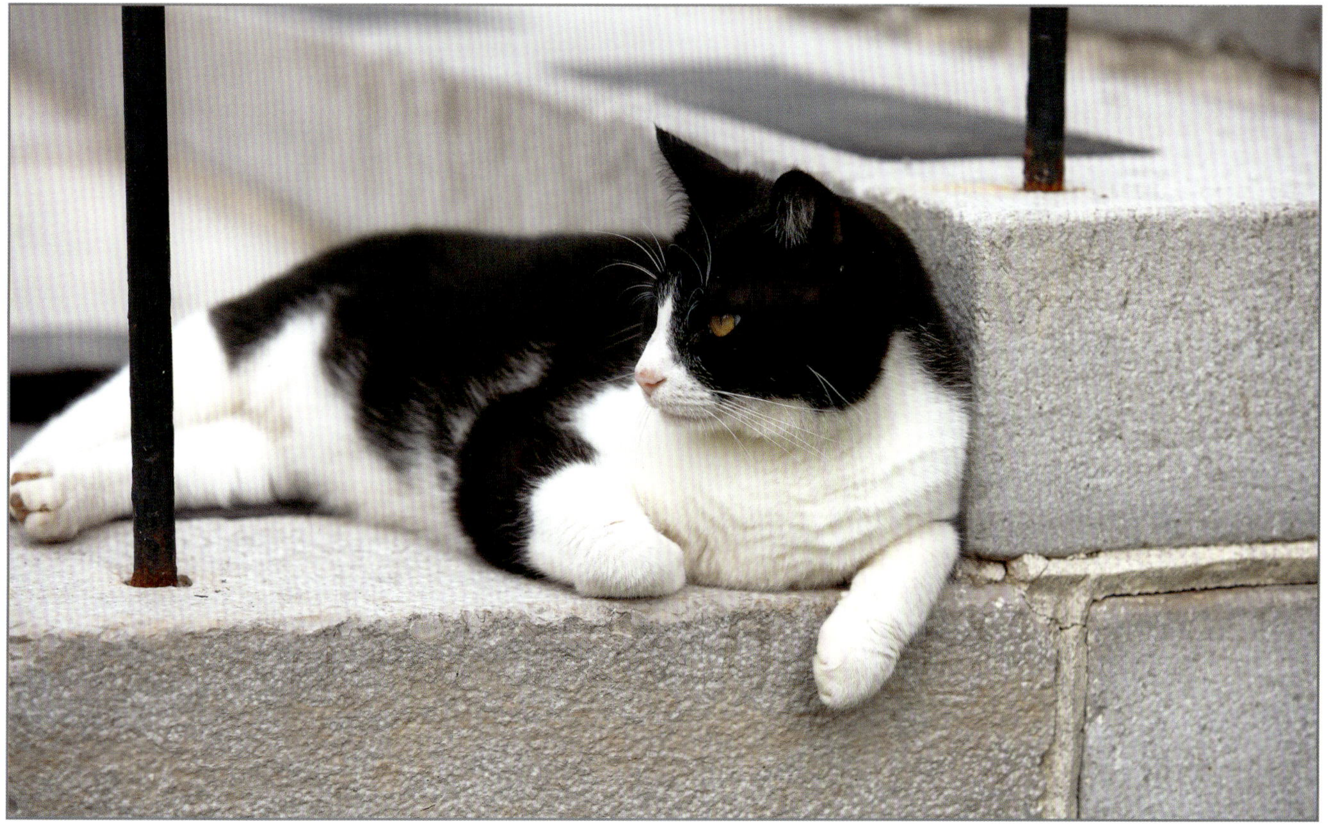

"Gabby", the Village's mascot, relaxes on the front steps of the Trustee's Building.

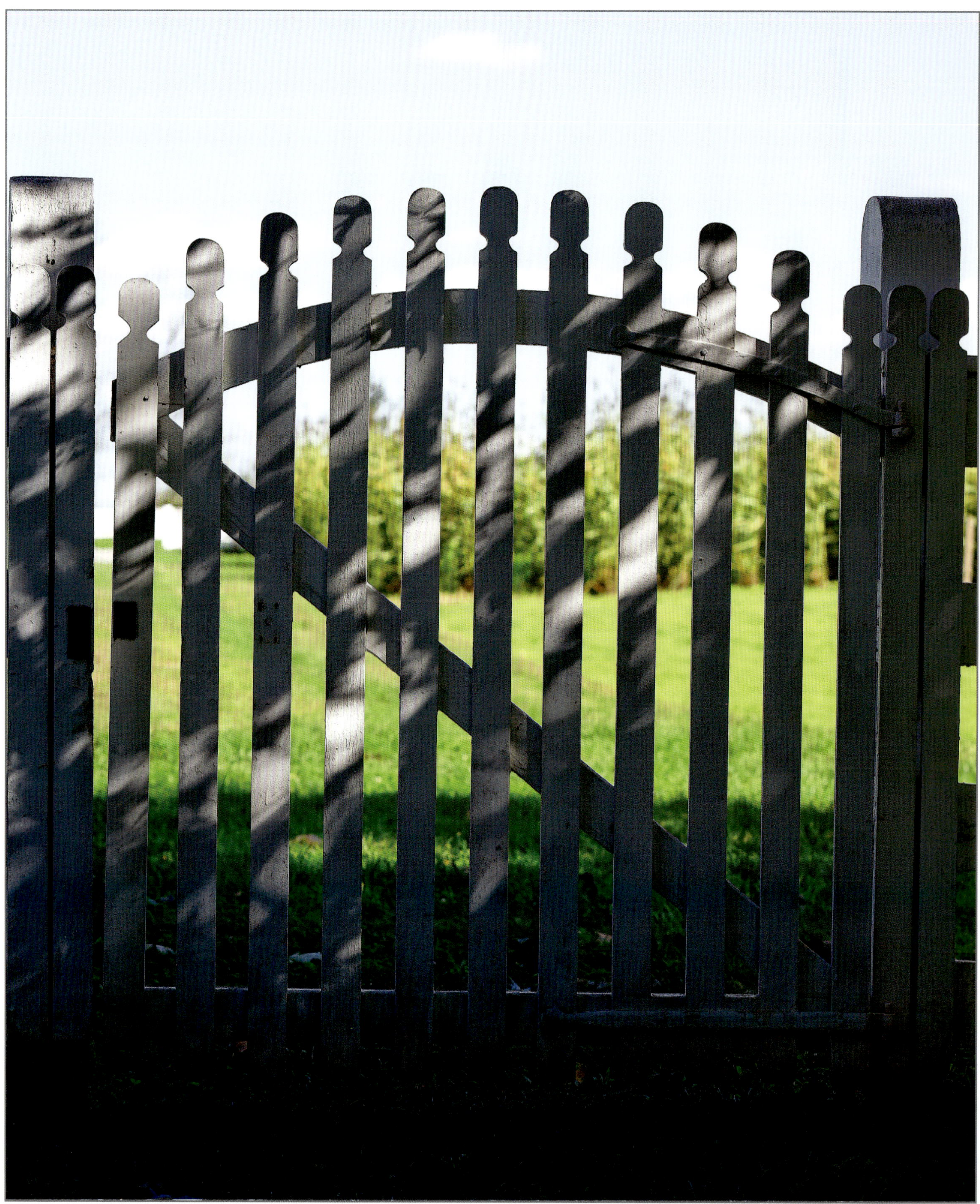

Another example of the decorative fencing that can be found at Pleasant Hill.

Opposite: Limestone sidewalks were laid from every building to every building including barns. Remnants of "sidewalks to nowhere" can be seen today where buildings formerly stood. While all the communities incorporated sidewalks, it was unusual for Kentucky and speaks to affluence of the Shakers at that time. Finding spiritual meaning in all things, the Shakers felt the sidewalks reflected the belief in the saying, "The path is straight and narrow to the Kingdom of God".

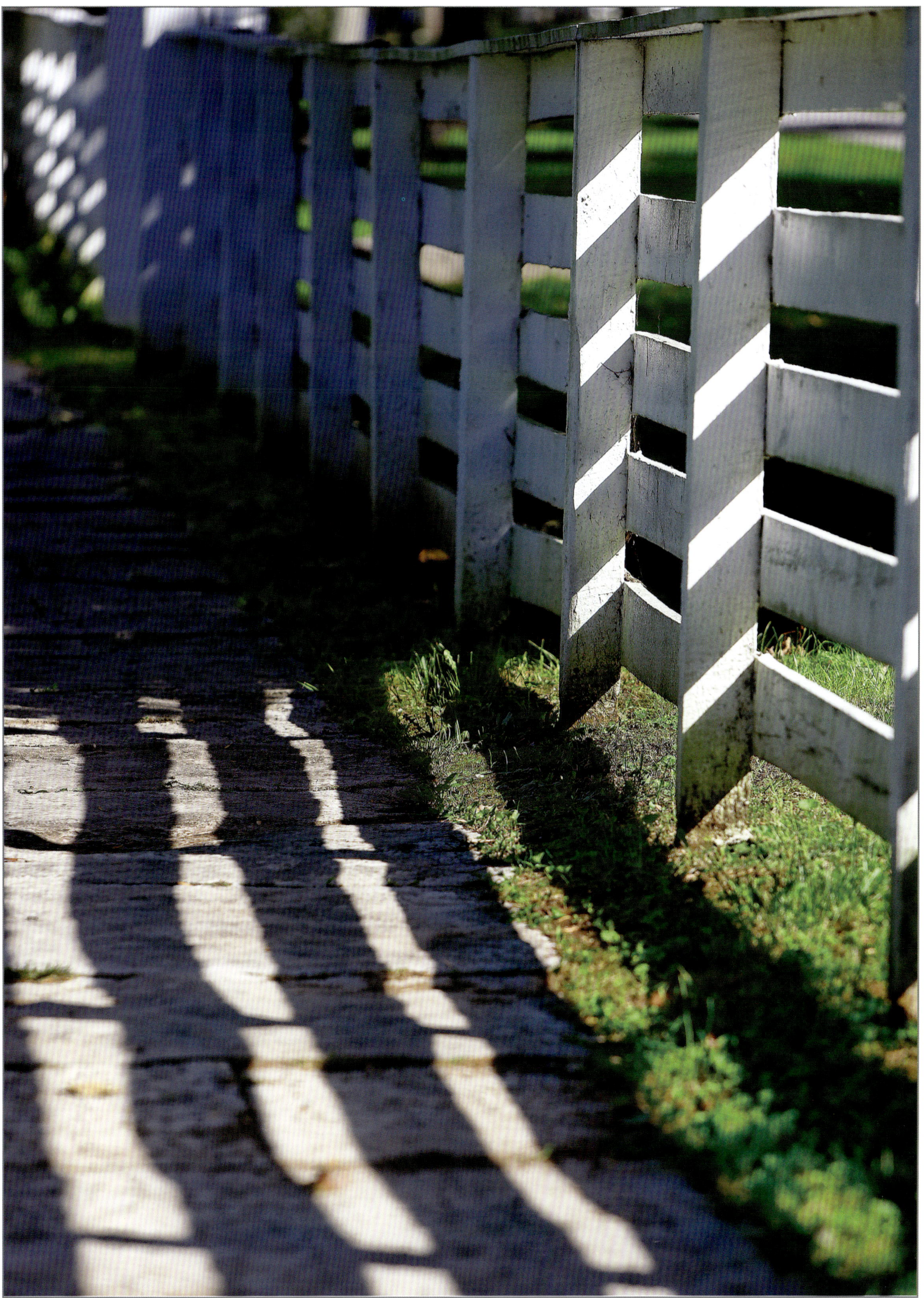

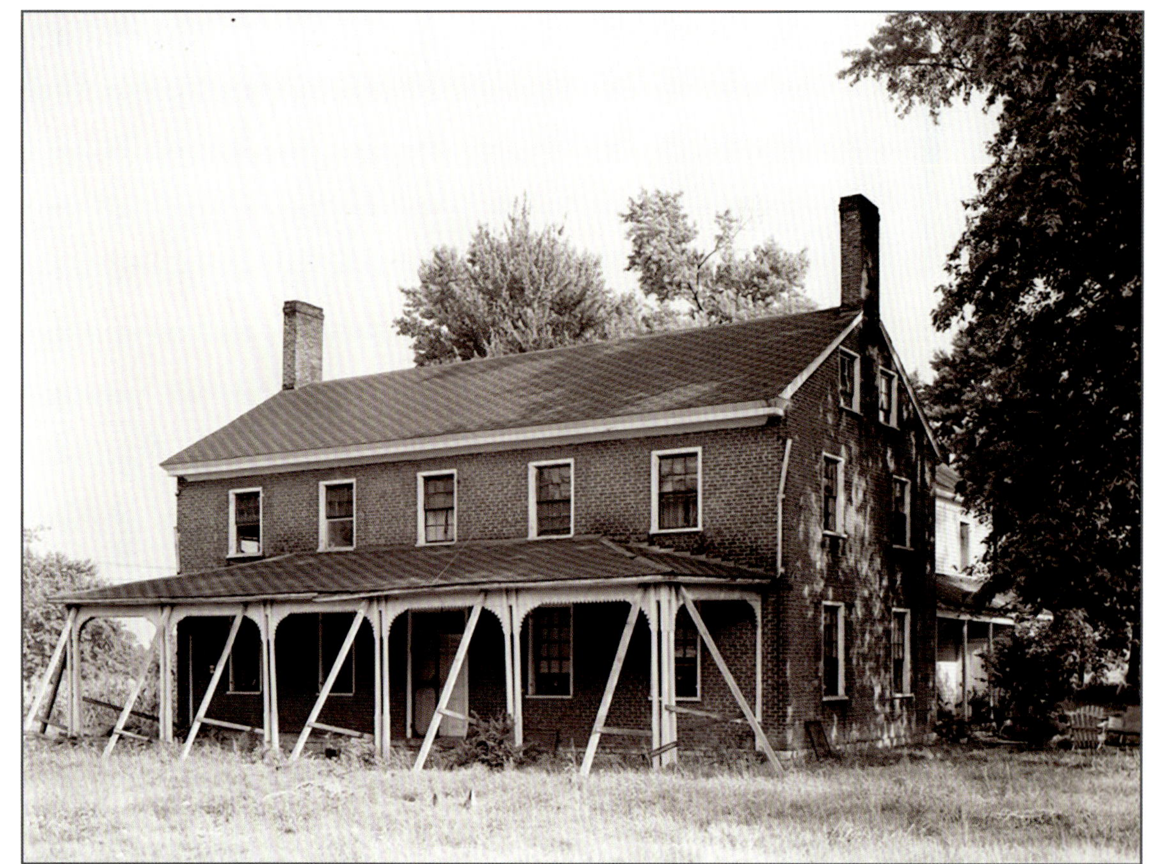

The East Family Brethren's Shop, a general work area for the men of the East Family, now showcases examples of broom making and carpentry. Several broom shops existed at the time to support the volume of the commercial venture. As hard times fell upon the Shakers in later years, the Trustee's Building was sold and operations moved to this structure.

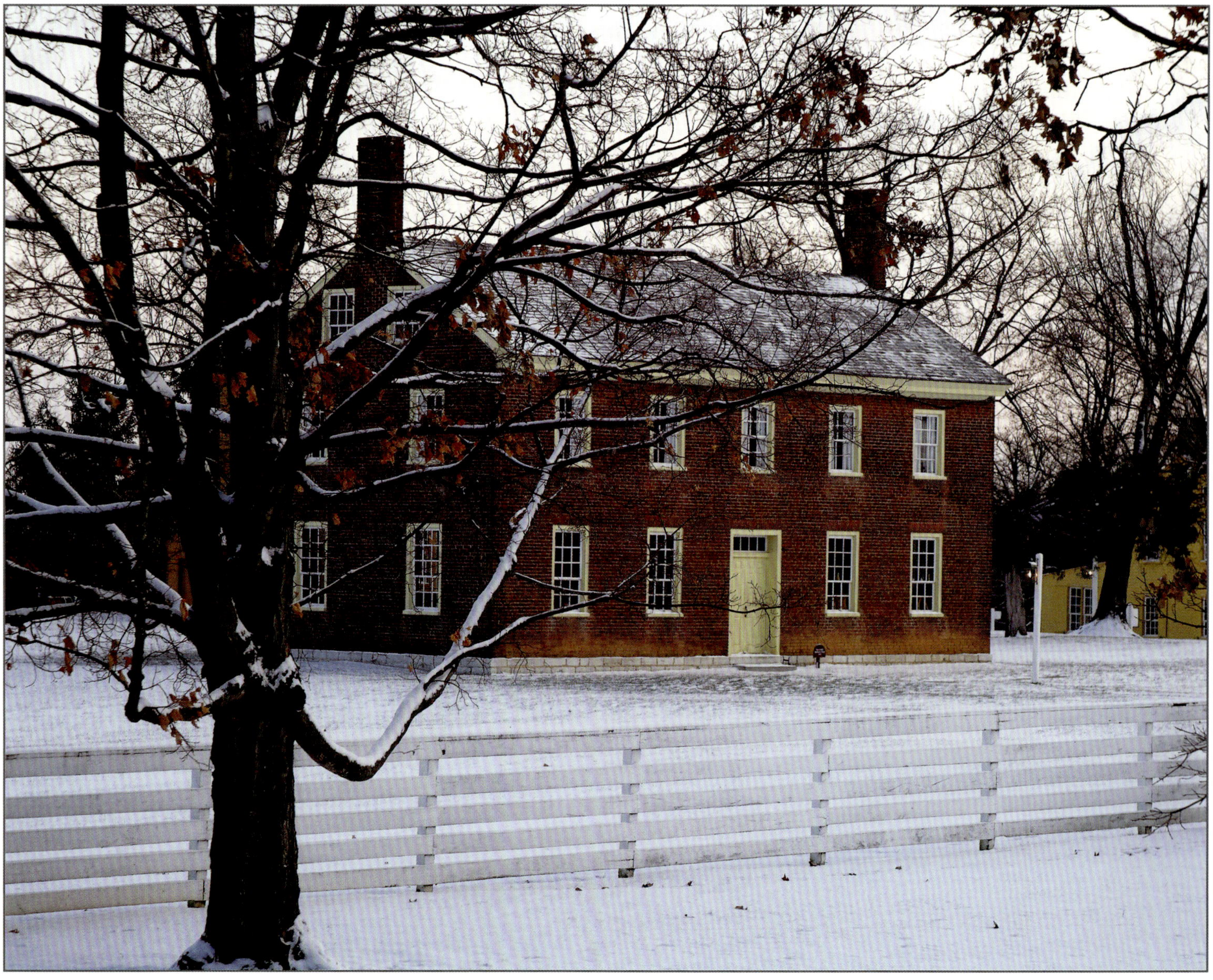

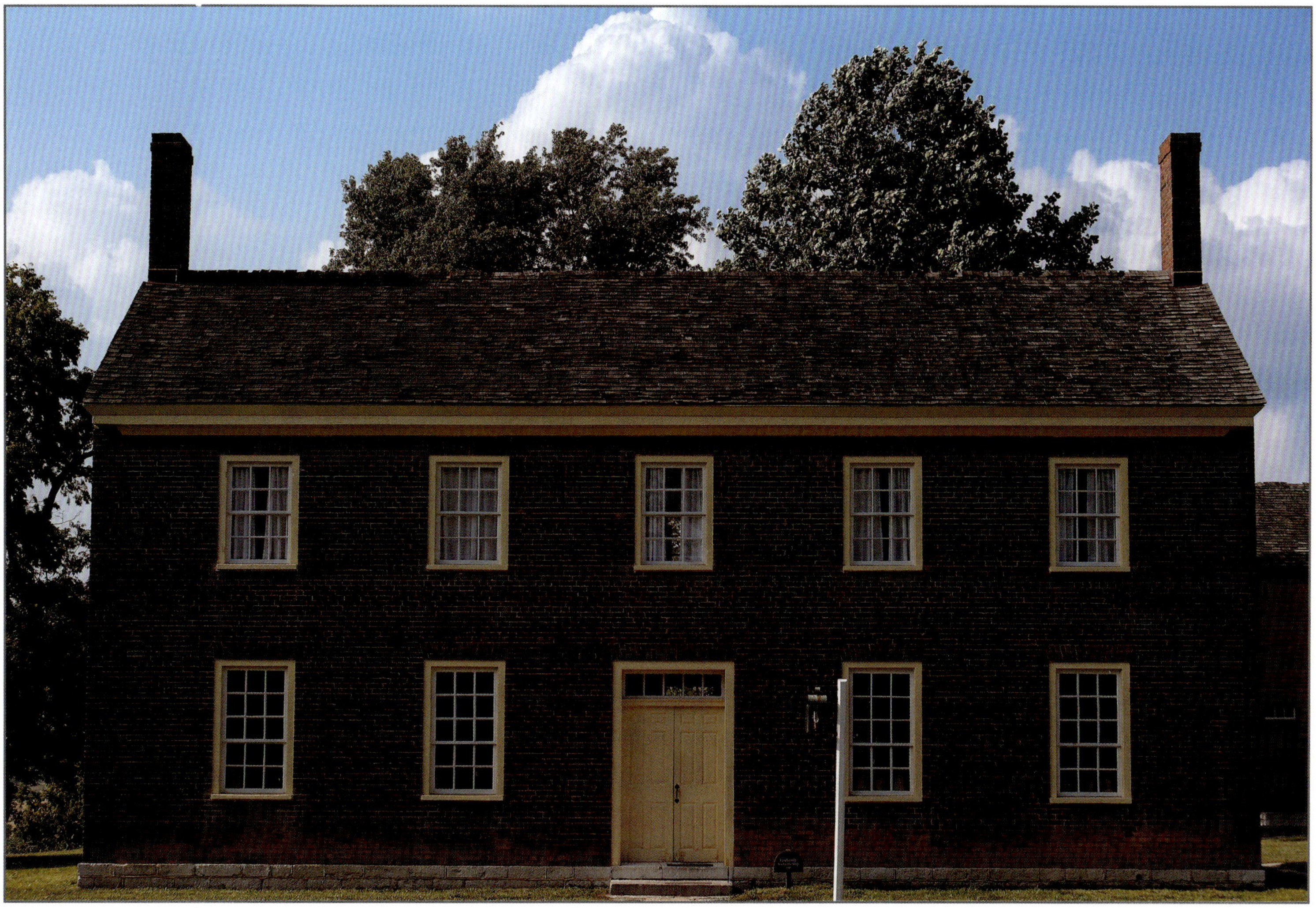

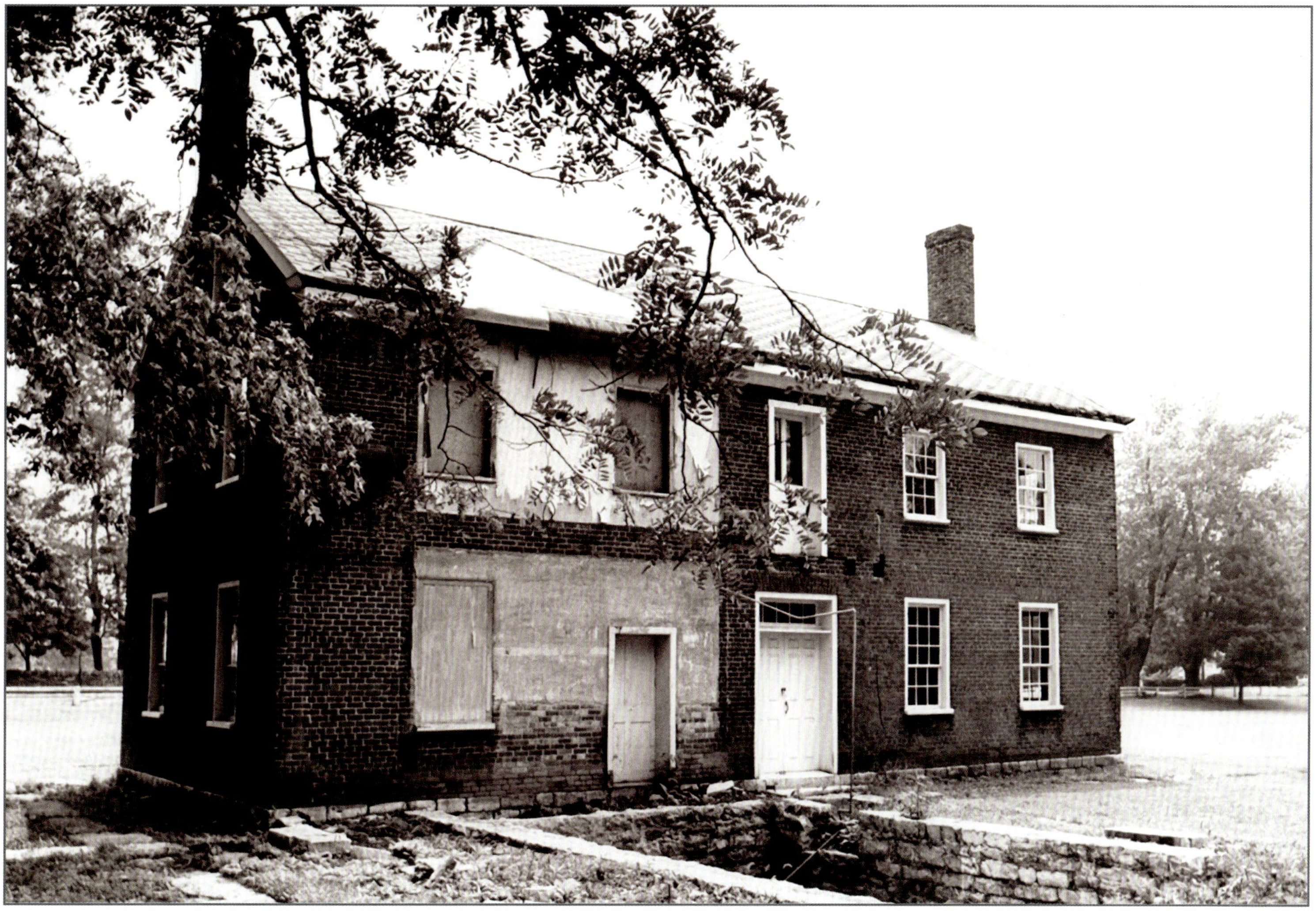

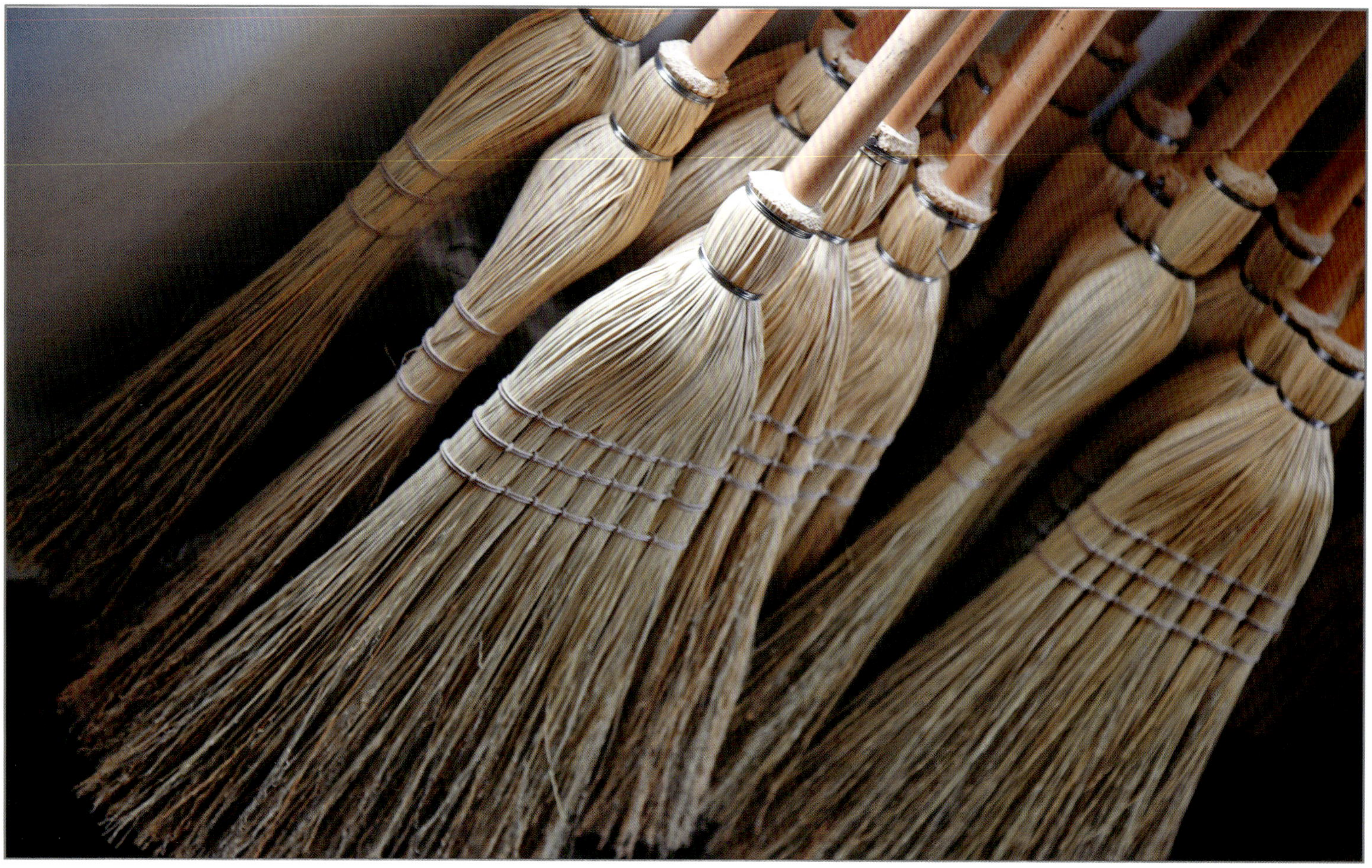

The flat broom was the direct result of a Shaker invention, the broom press. Before that, brooms were round and very inefficient in the Shaker's opinion.

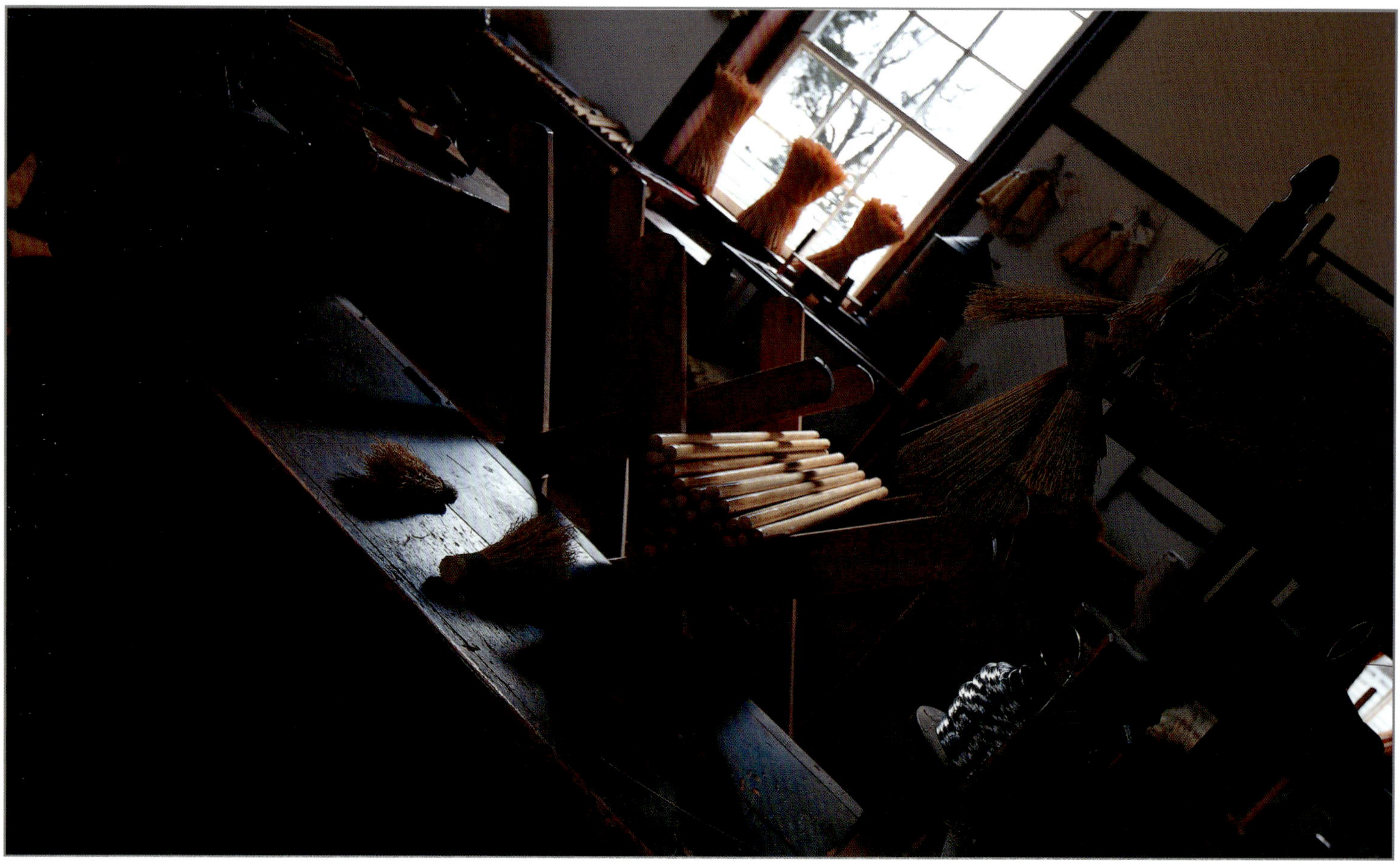

The Shakers grew their own corn straw for the brooms as well as turned the handles which were cut from trees on the property. They also grew their own hemp used to tie the brooms until the advent of wire.

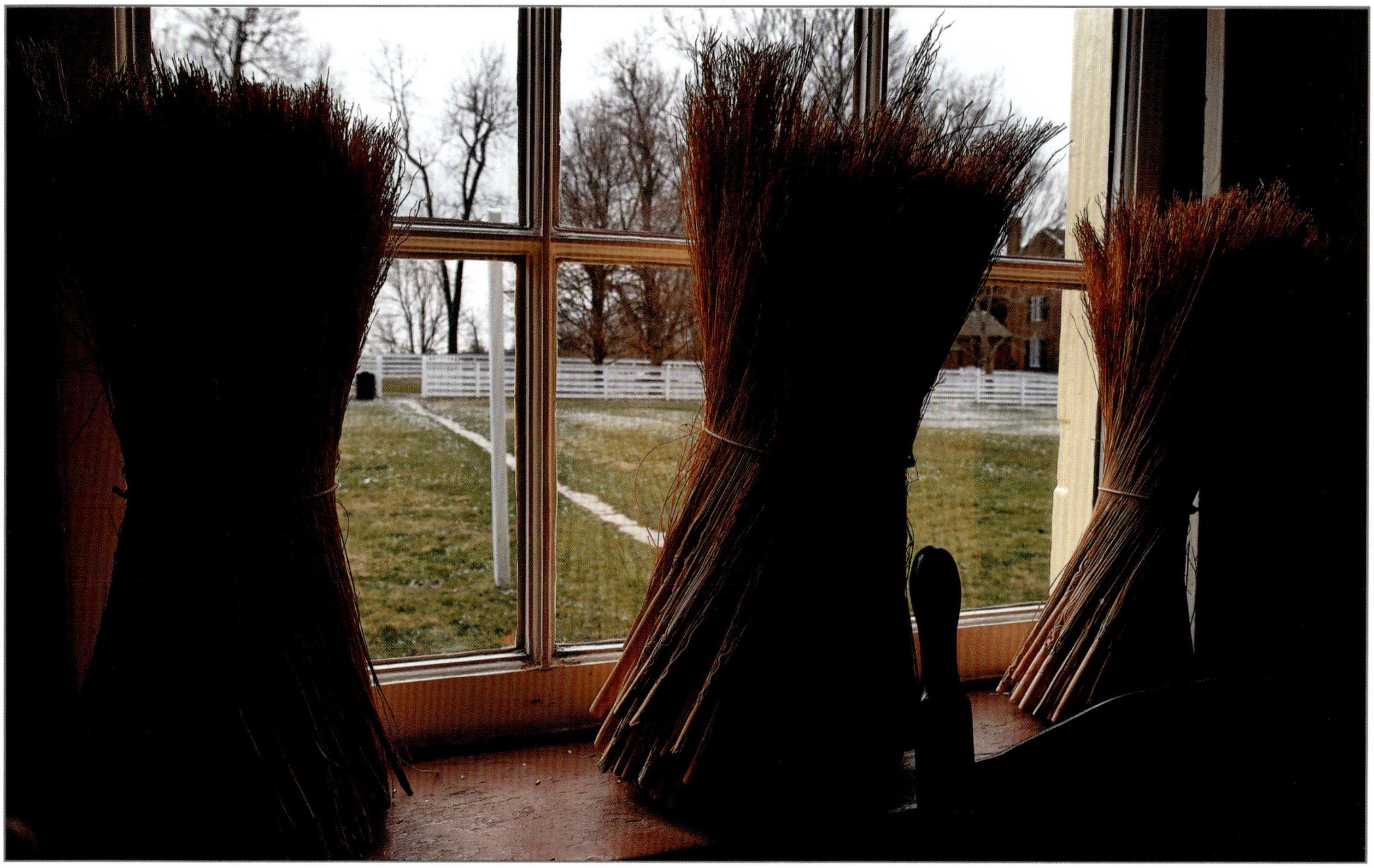

The bundles of straw in the East Family Brethren's Shop are another favorite subject for photographers visiting the Village.

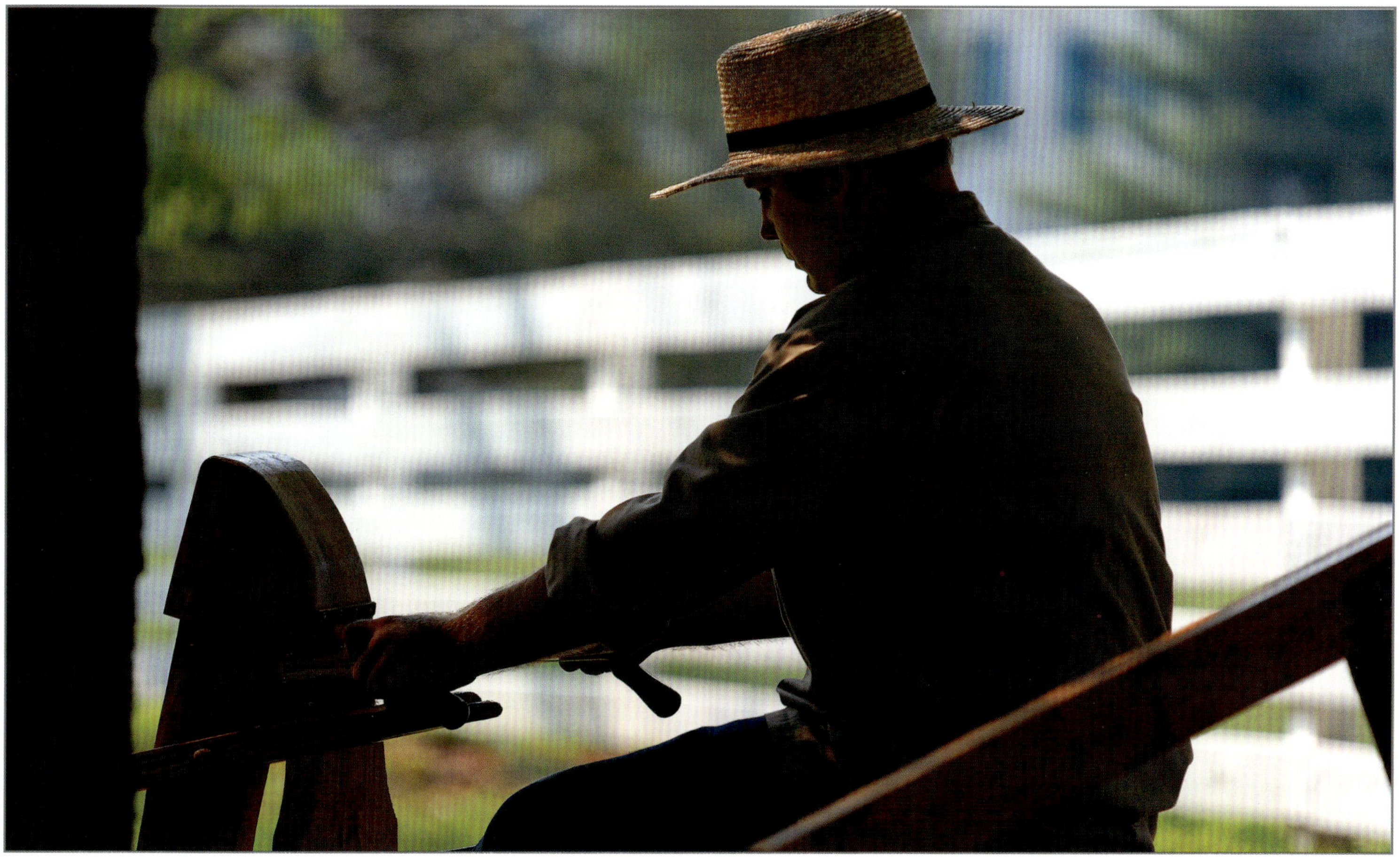

A costumed interpreter demonstrates the use of a shave horse.

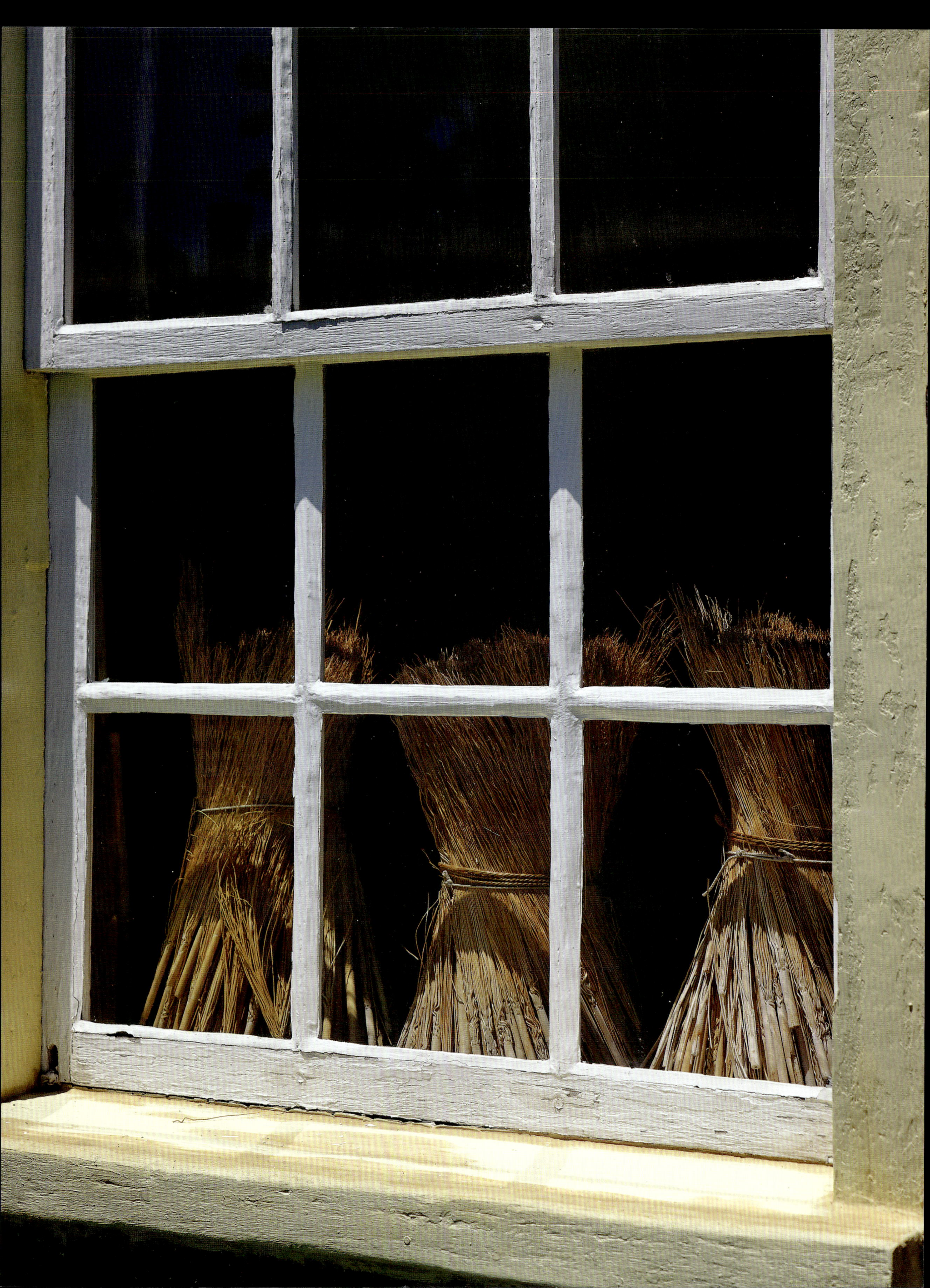

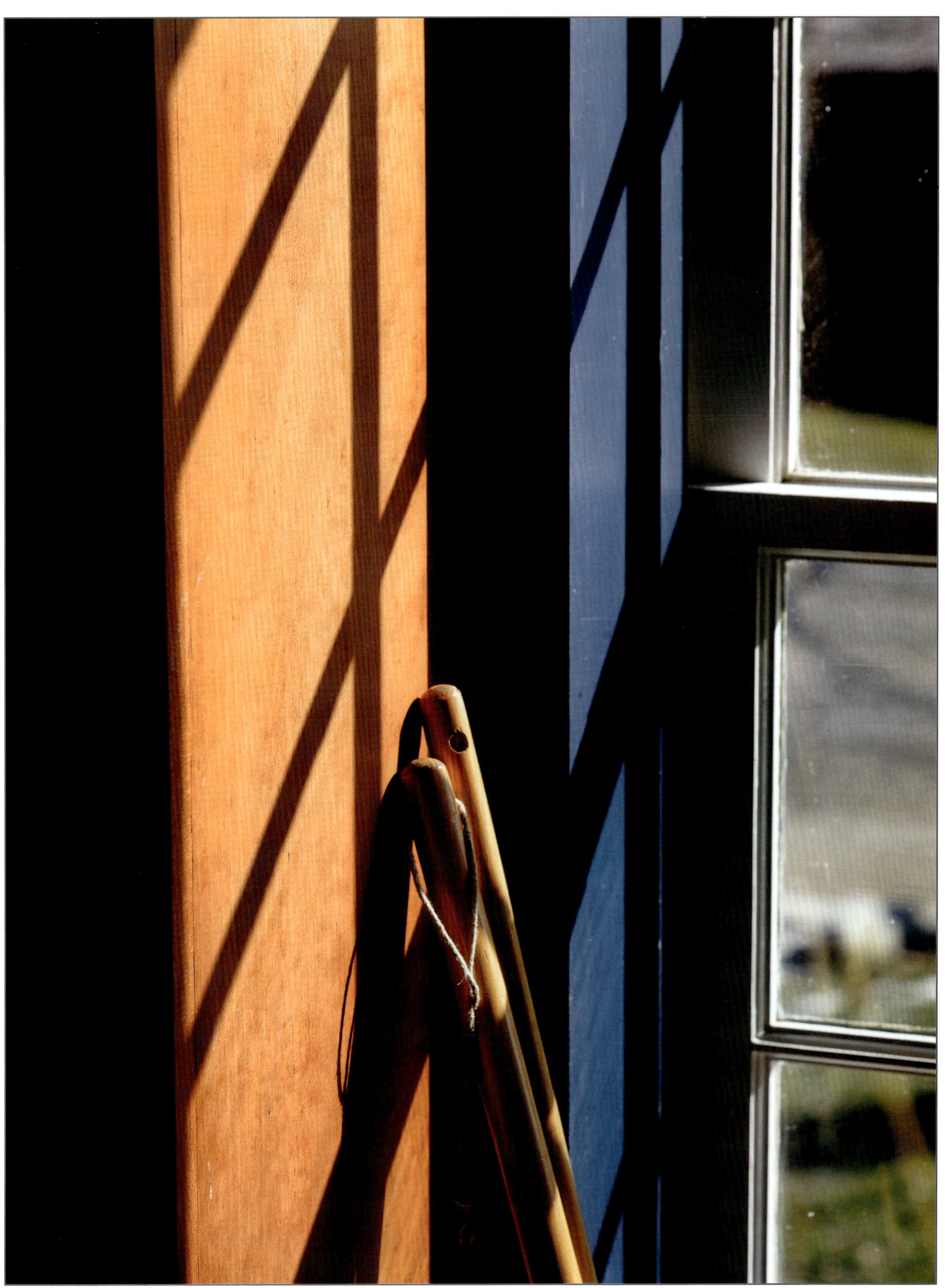

Work buildings like the East Family Brethren's Shop were also oriented and constructed to take advantage of the natural light.

The final quality control test for the Shaker's flat broom was if it could stand on its own. This one passed.

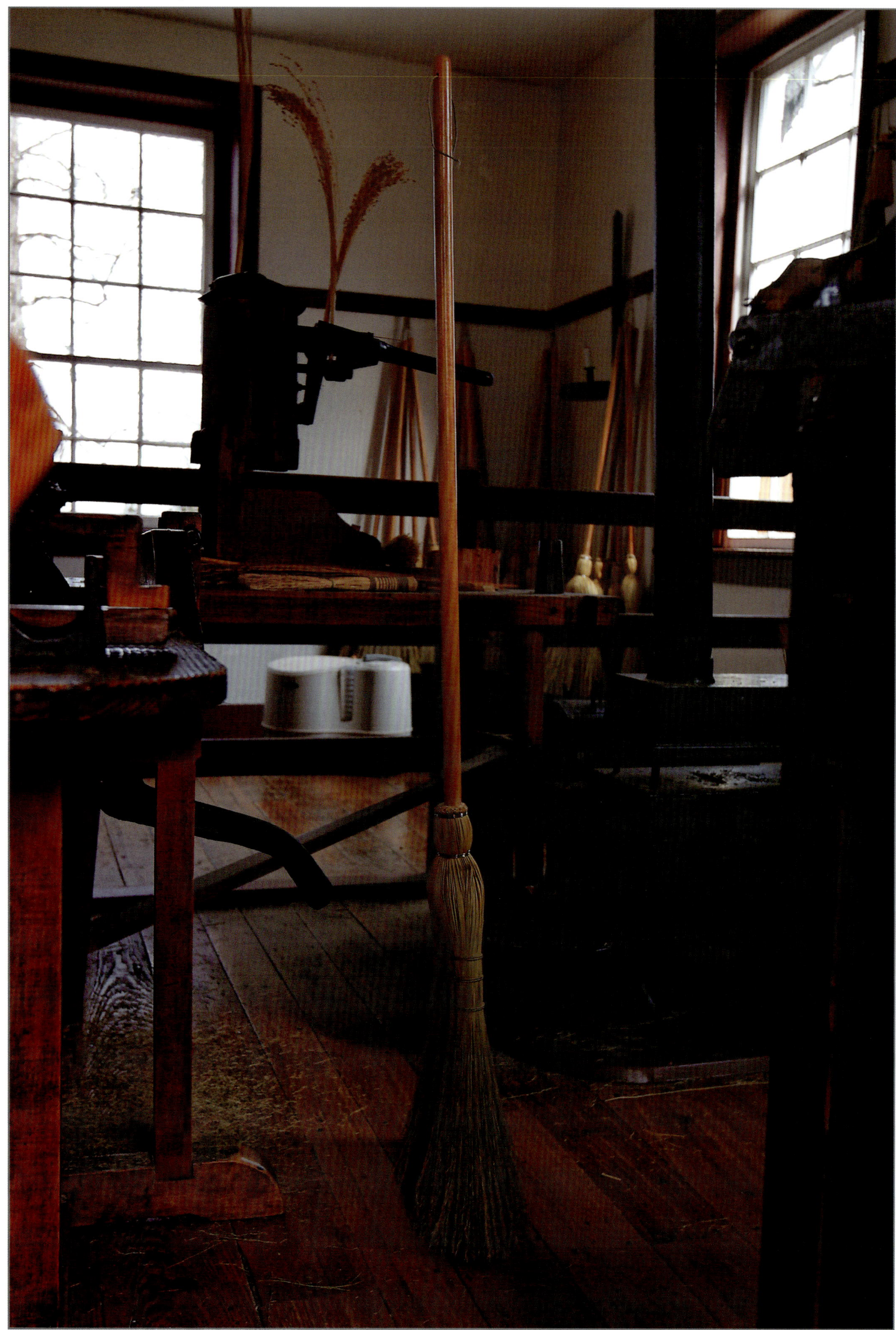

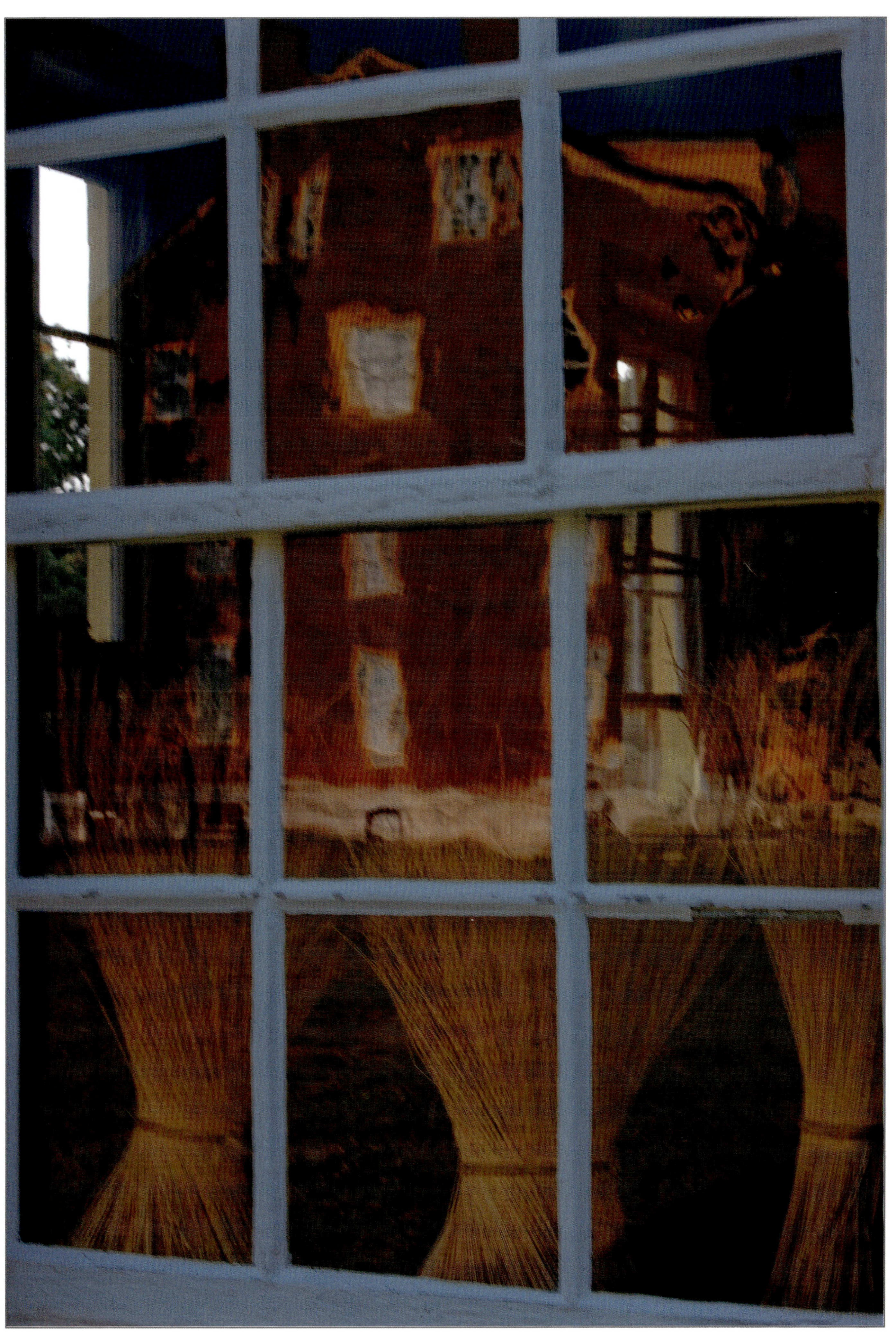

The East Family Dwelling is reflected in the glass of the Brethren's Shop.

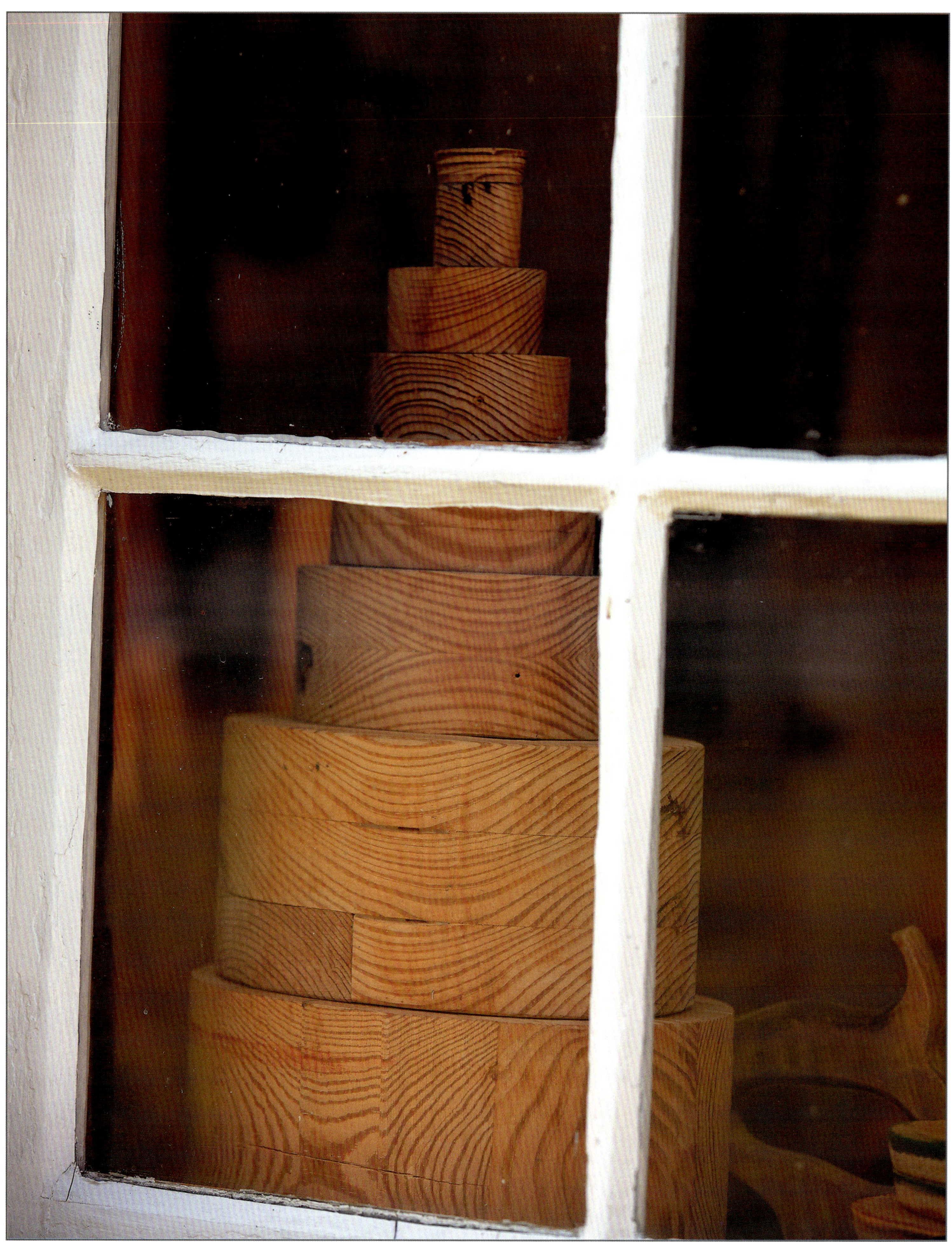

Oval wooden boxes were the storage device of the day in the 1800's. They served as storage for personal and other items as well as shipping containers for seeds. Manufacturing of the boxes was more for the Shakers' own use rather than a commercial venture at the time. Often referred to as Shaker boxes, there is a misnomer the Shakers invented them despite their existence for centuries. The Shakers did, however, improve upon the design and construction techniques to make the boxes stronger and more durable.

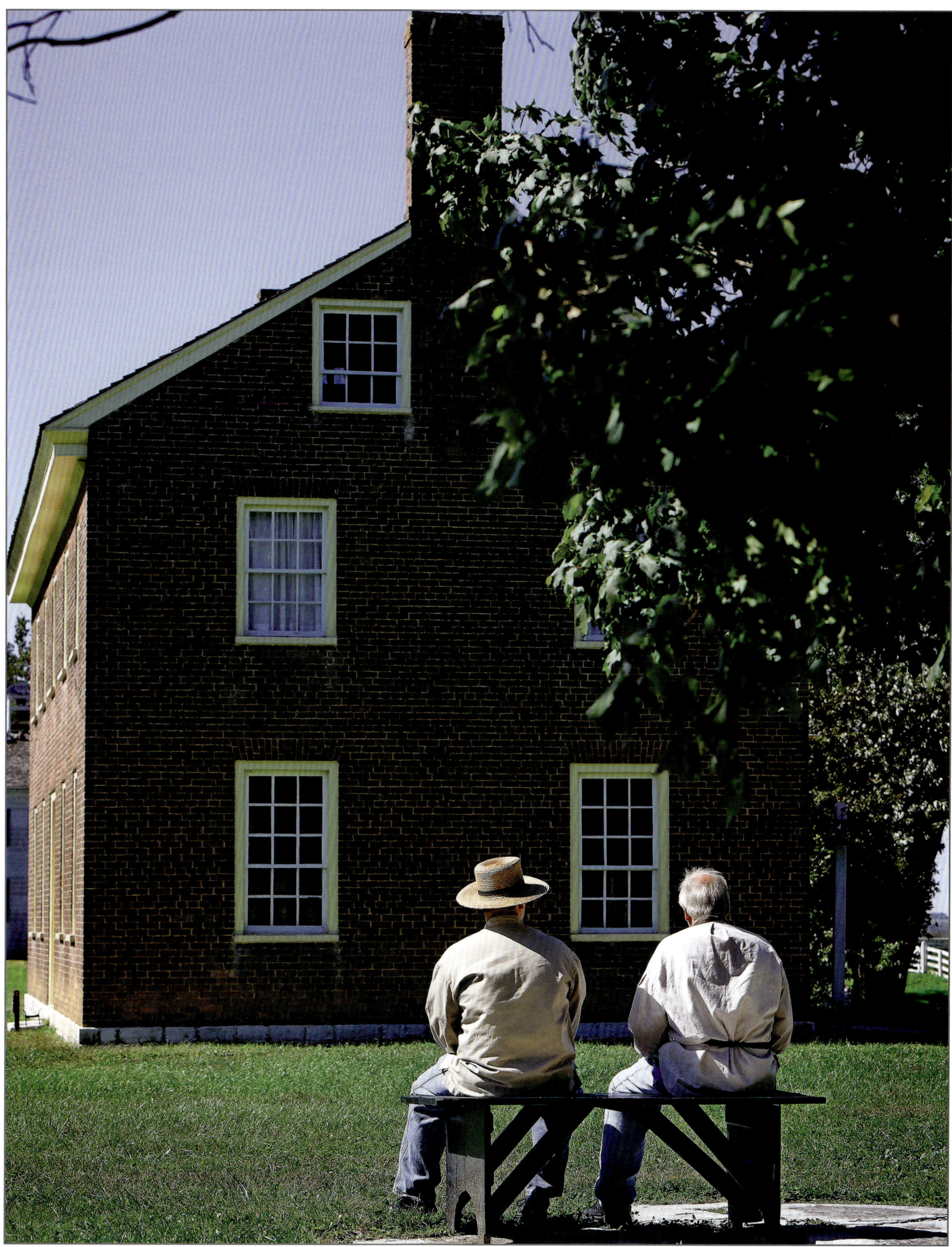

Costumed interpreters relax outside the East Family Brethren's Shop.

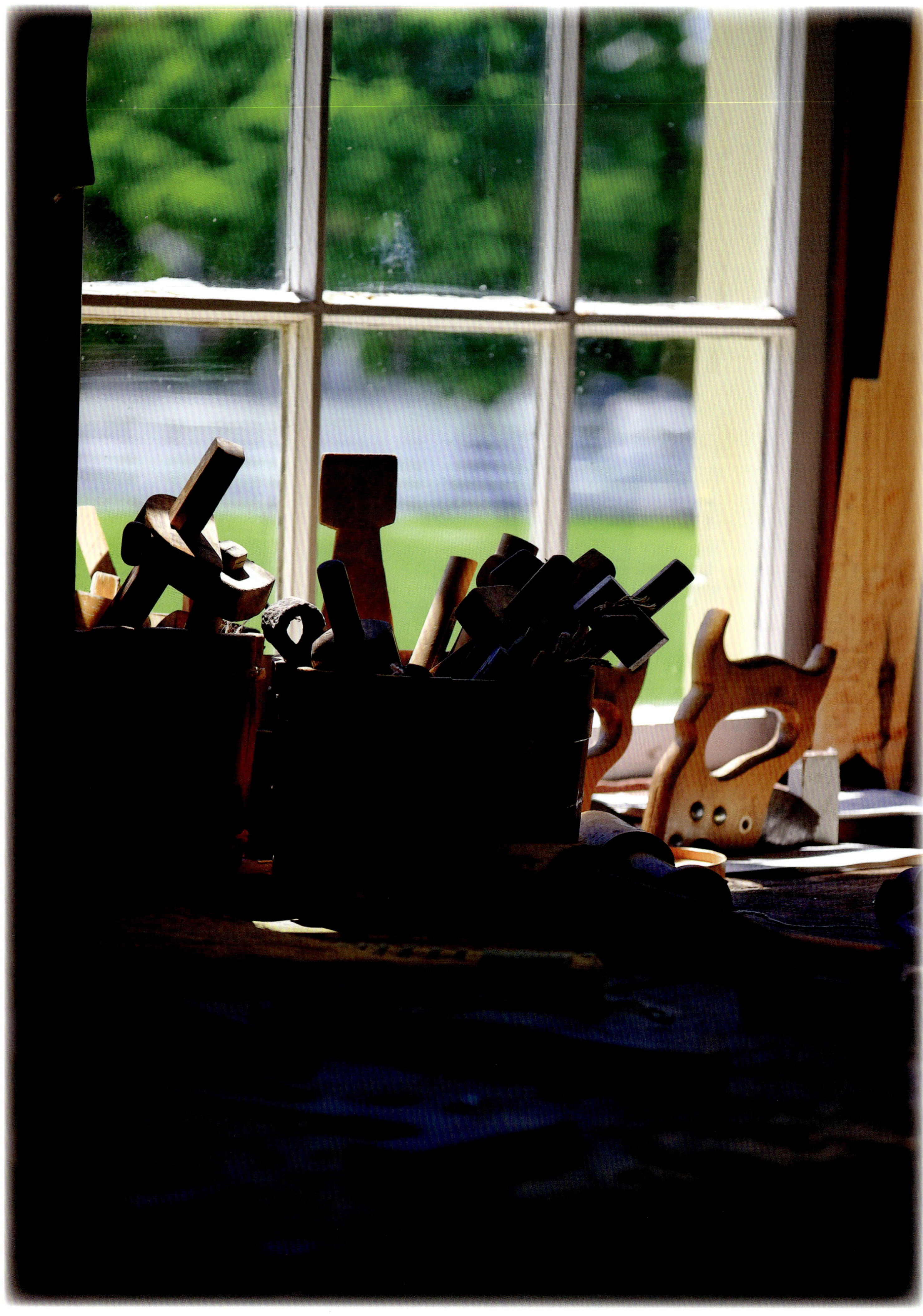

Tools of the carpentry trade commonly in use at the time are displayed in the East Family Brethren's Shop.

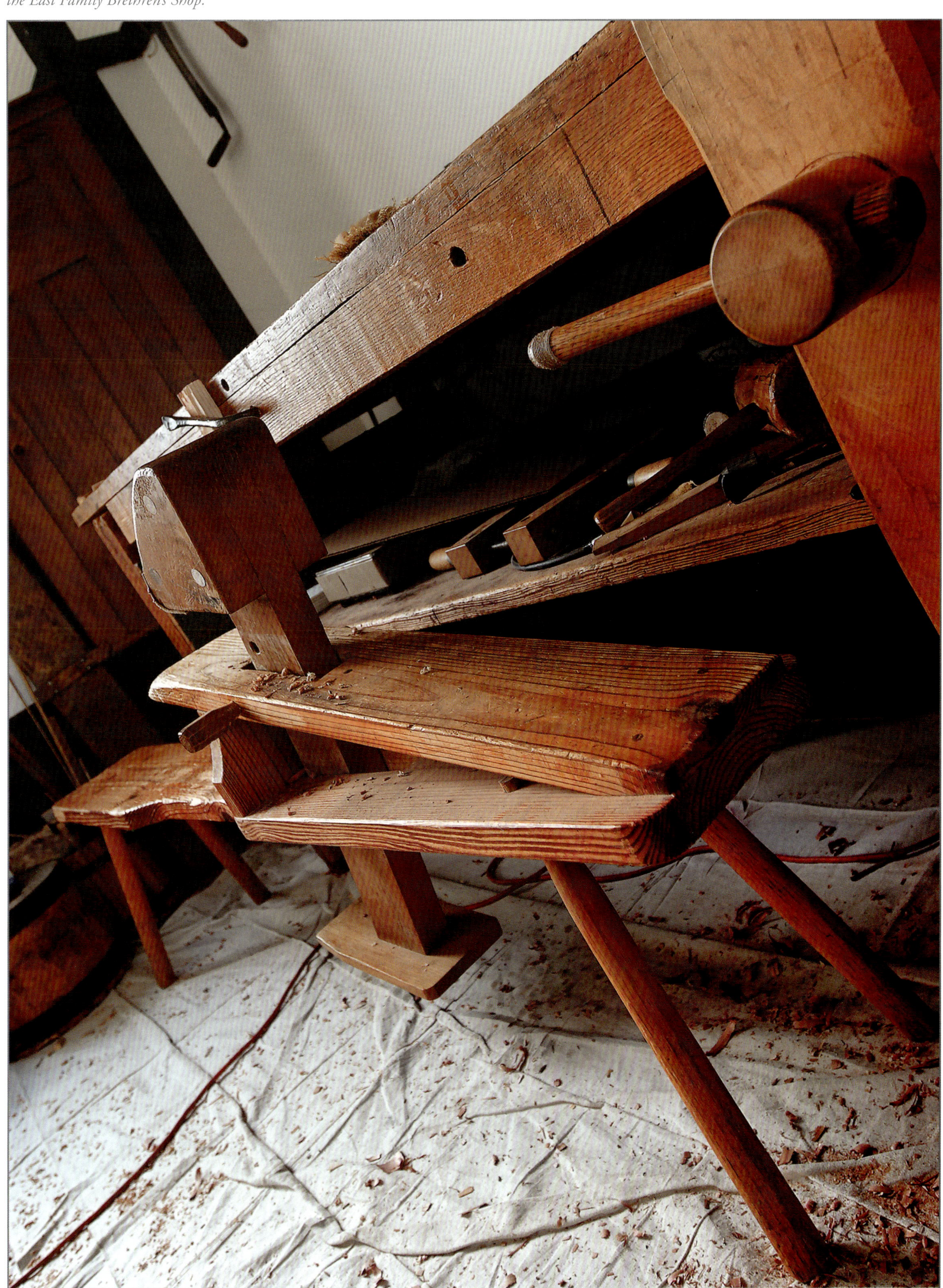

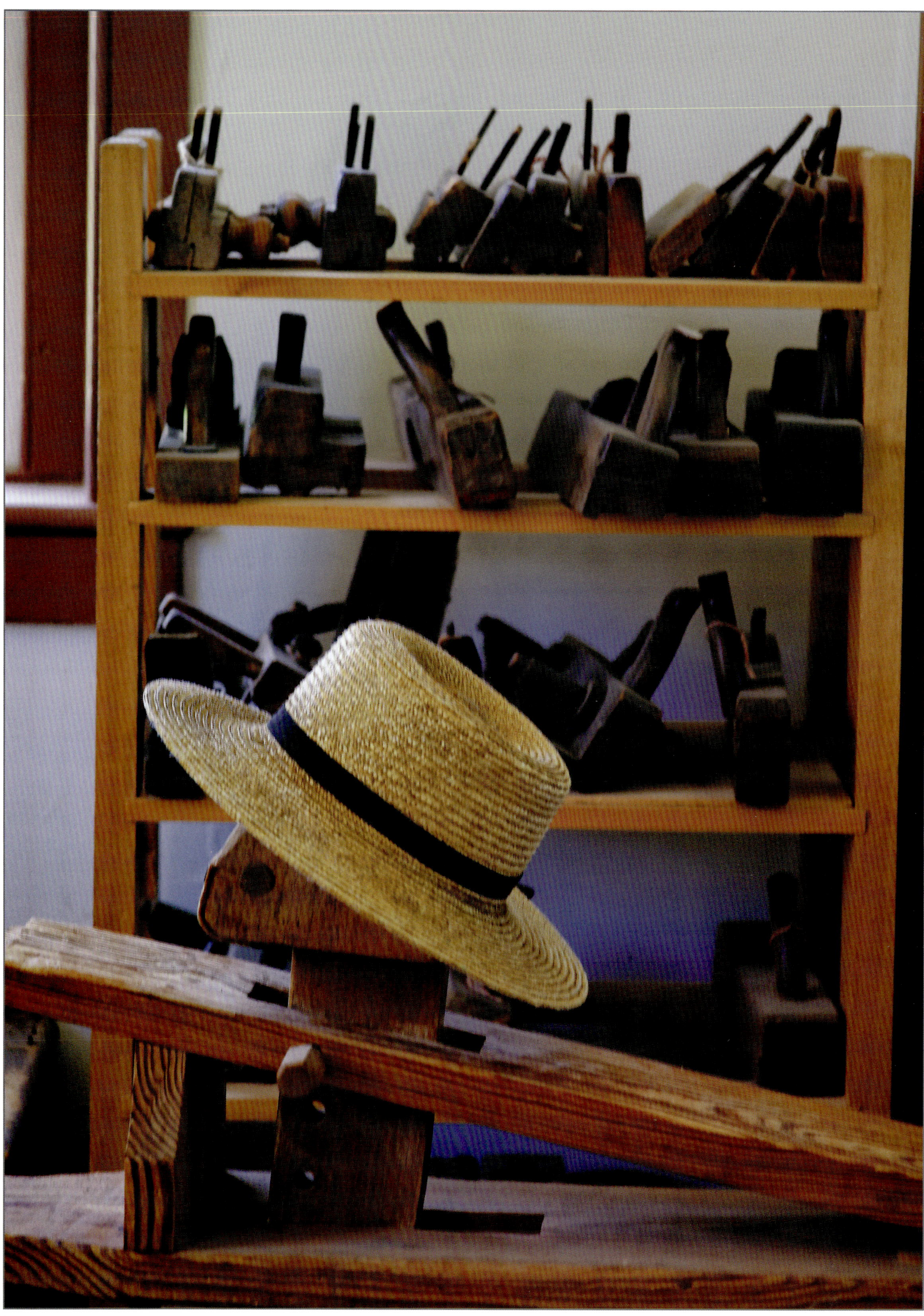

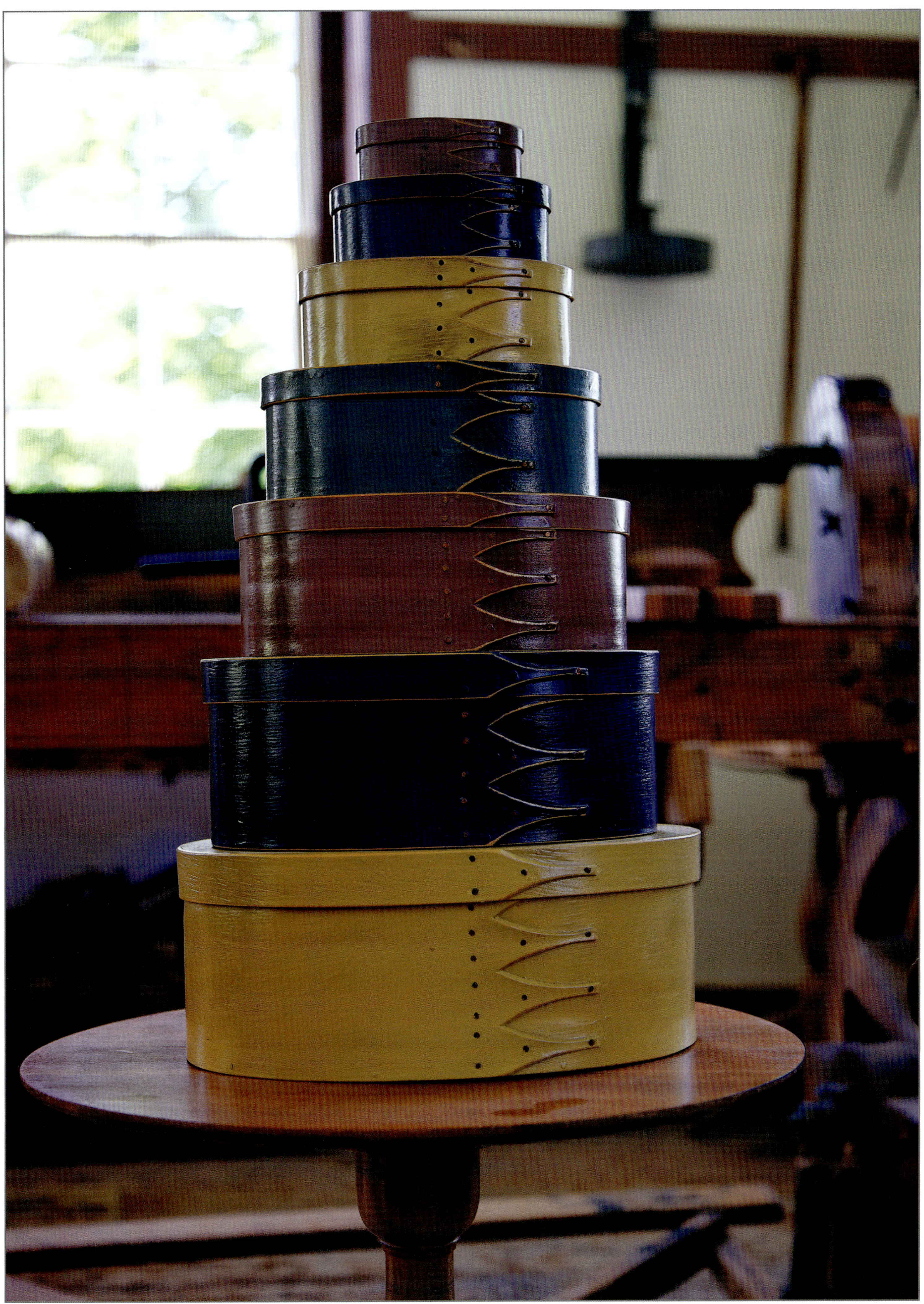

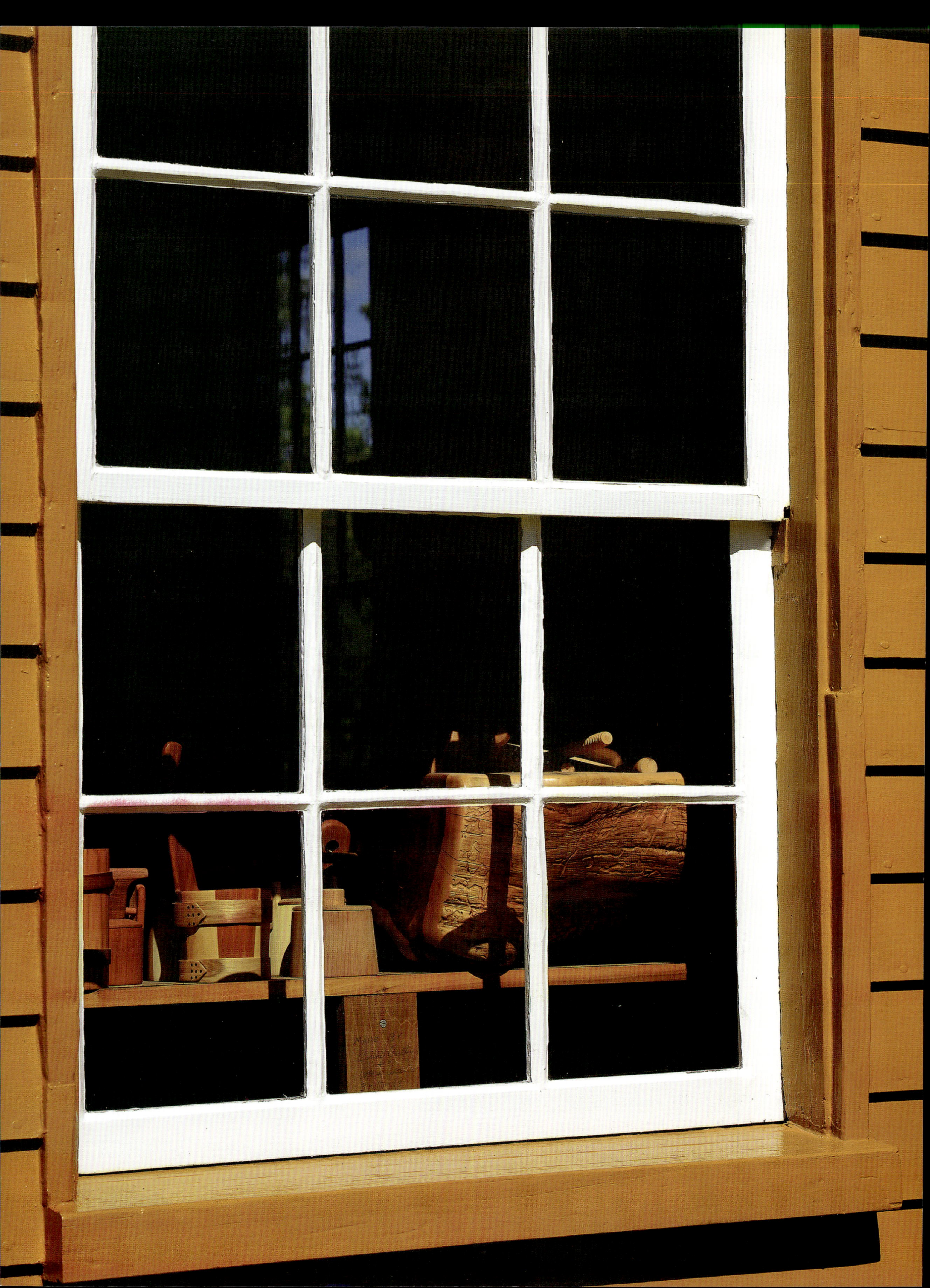
MADE BY

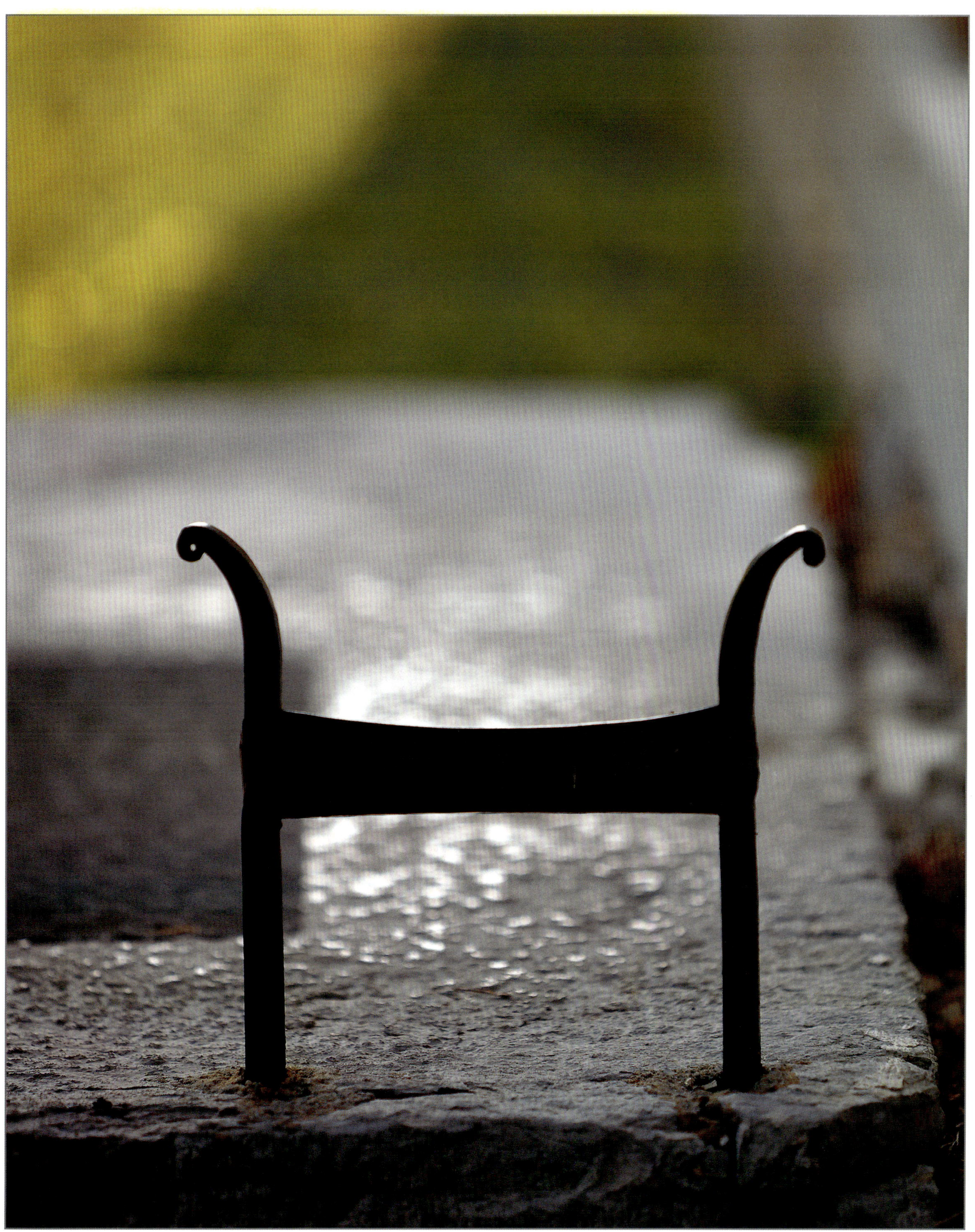

Opposite: A view through the window of the Cooper's Shop shows examples of the types of items that would have been made there.

Above: An example of a boot scraper outside the entrance to the East Family Brethren's Shop shows the importance the Shakers placed on cleanliness and order in both their daily and spiritual lives.

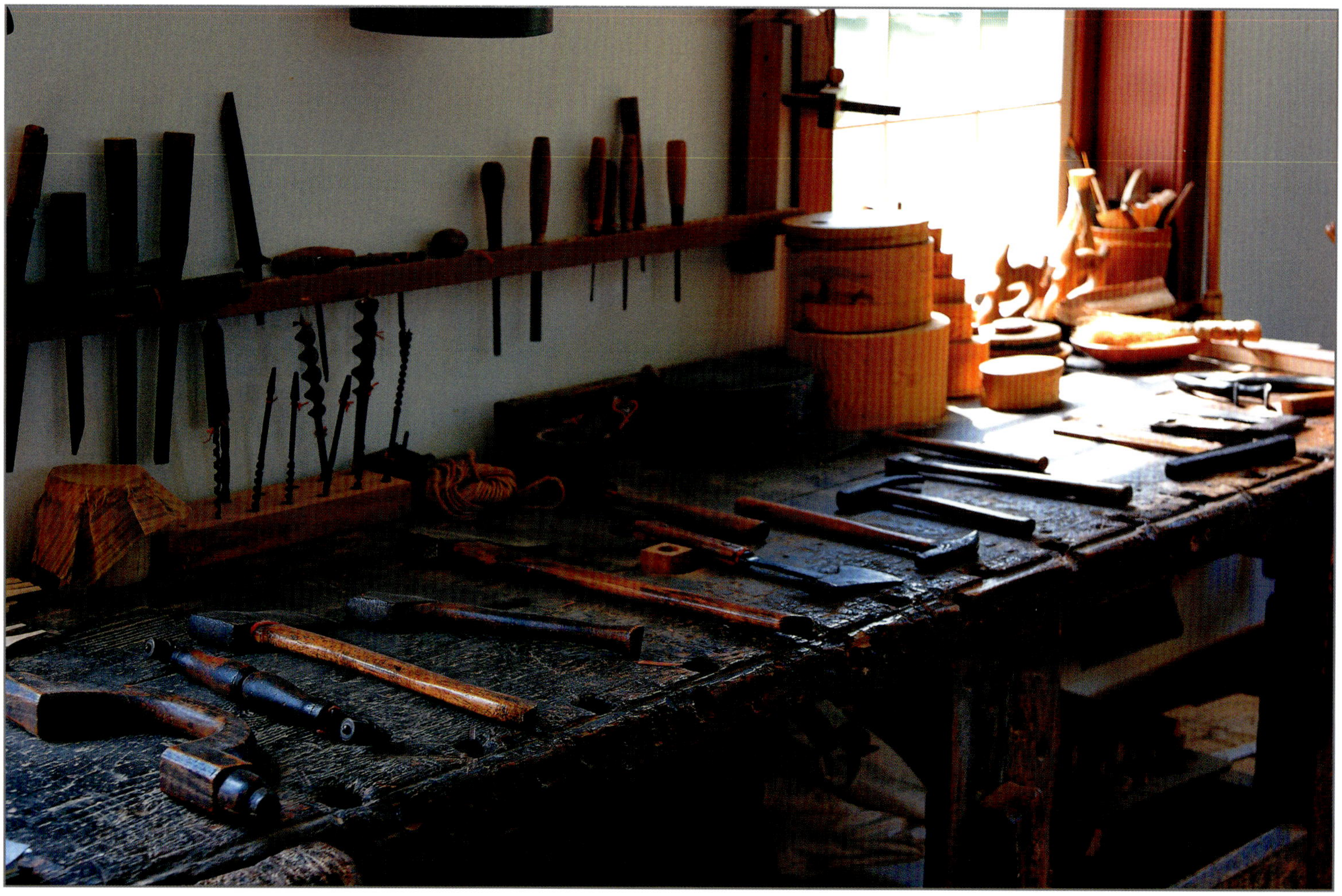

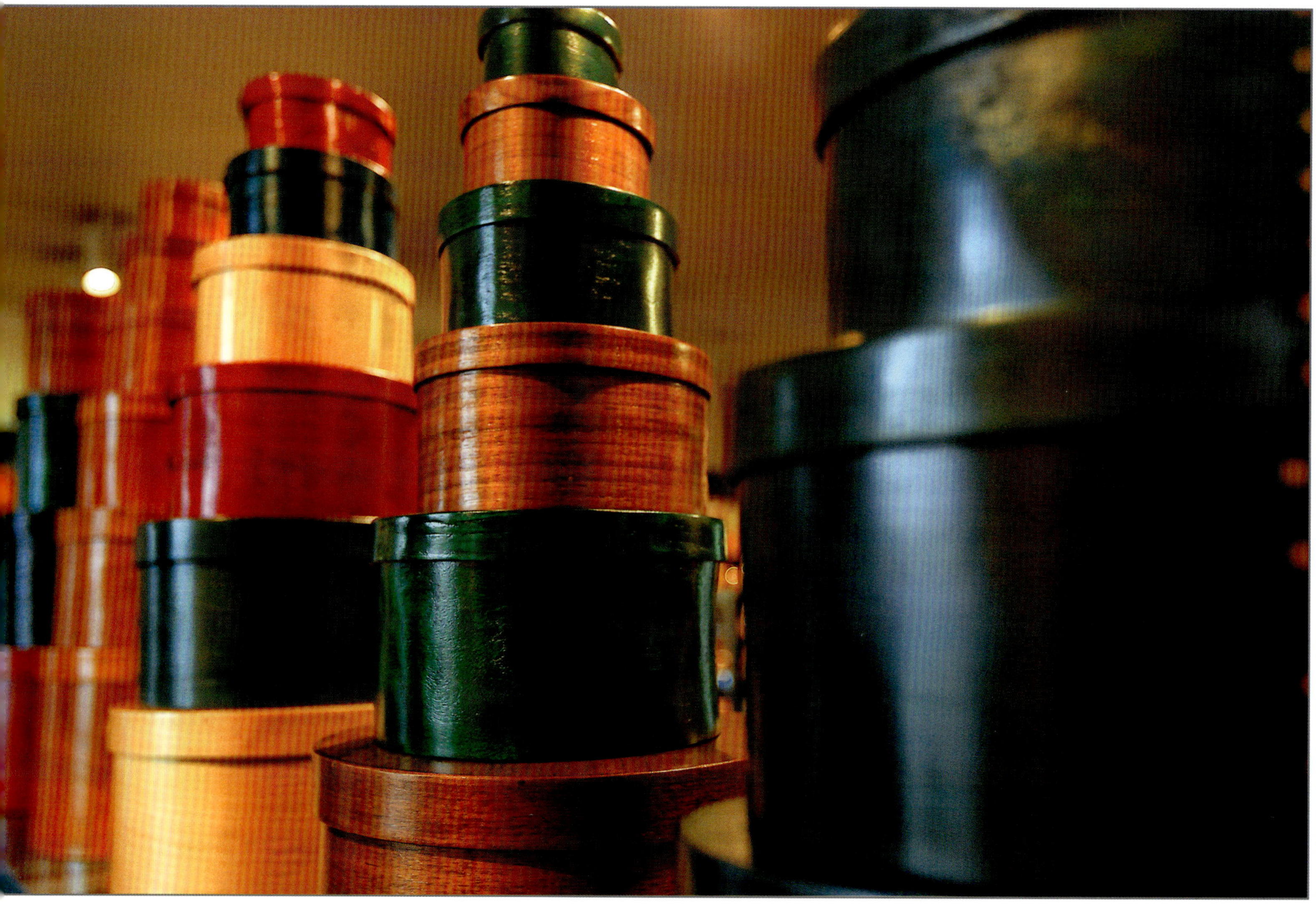

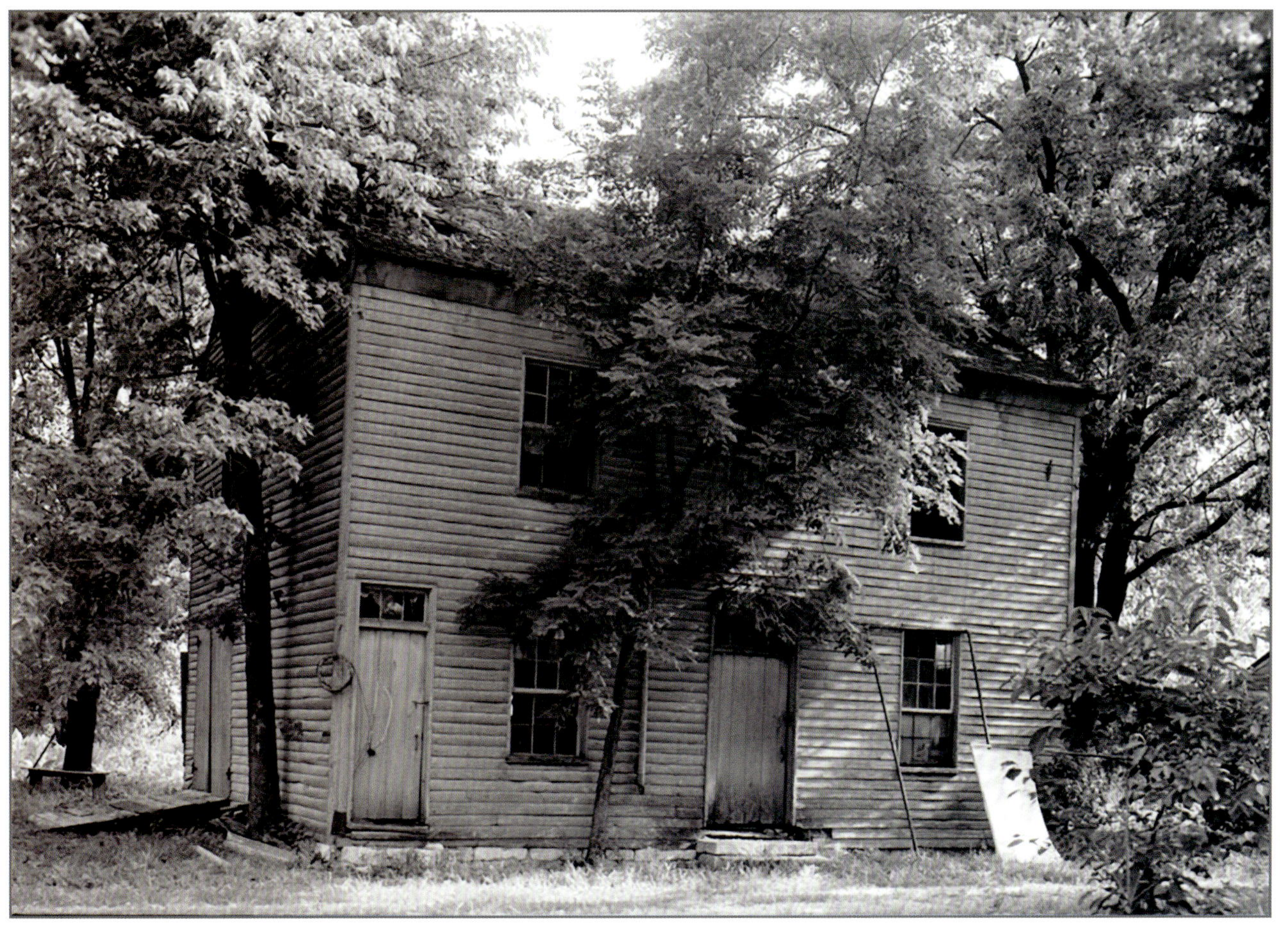

The Cooper's Shop before restoration. Sliding doors can be seen on the left side of the structure from the time it was used as a tractor shed.

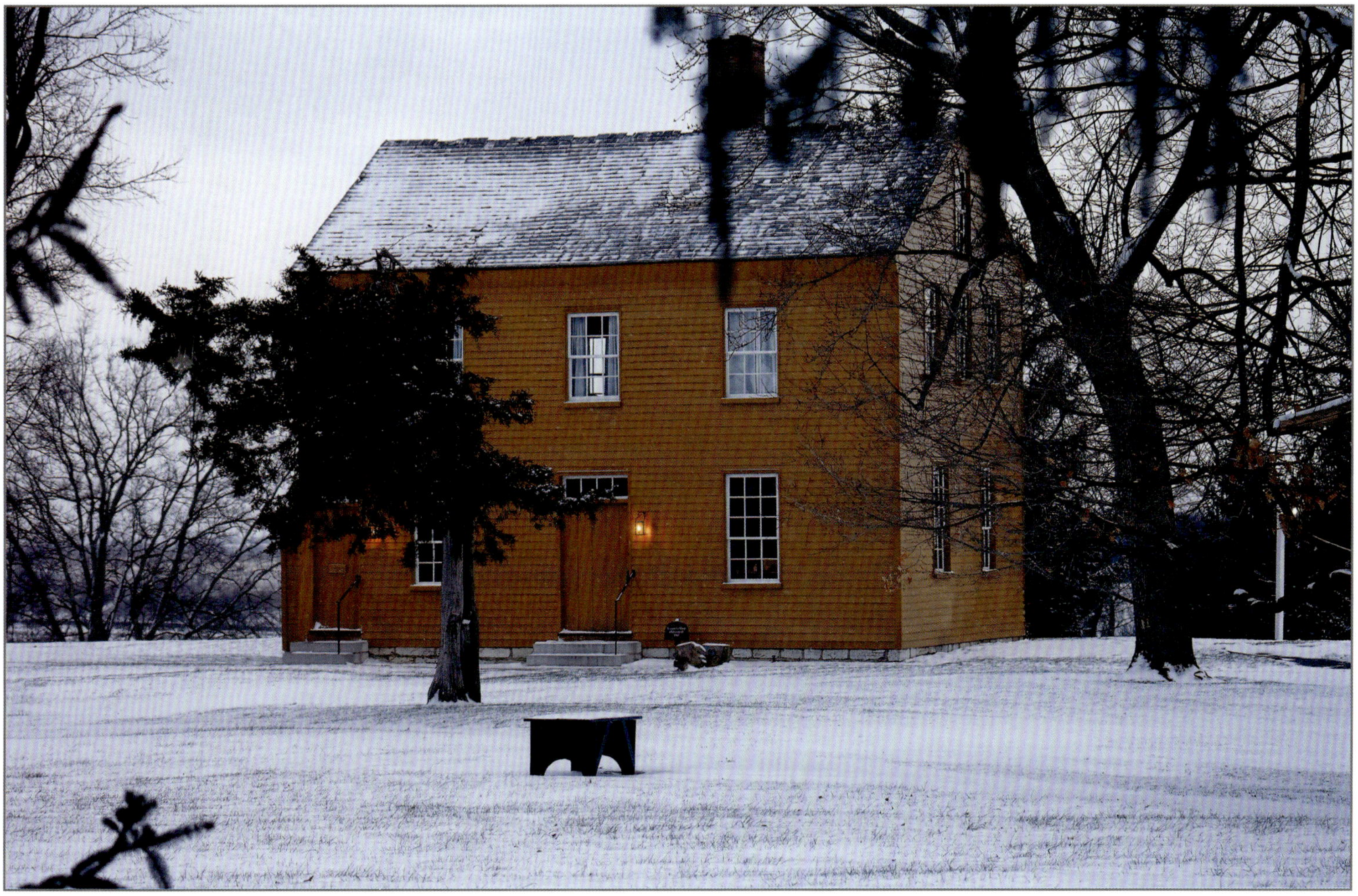

The Cooper's Shop in its restored condition today. Specialized trades such as coopers and blacksmiths were held by members throughout their time at the village. Other, less technical jobs were performed on a rotational basis by other members.

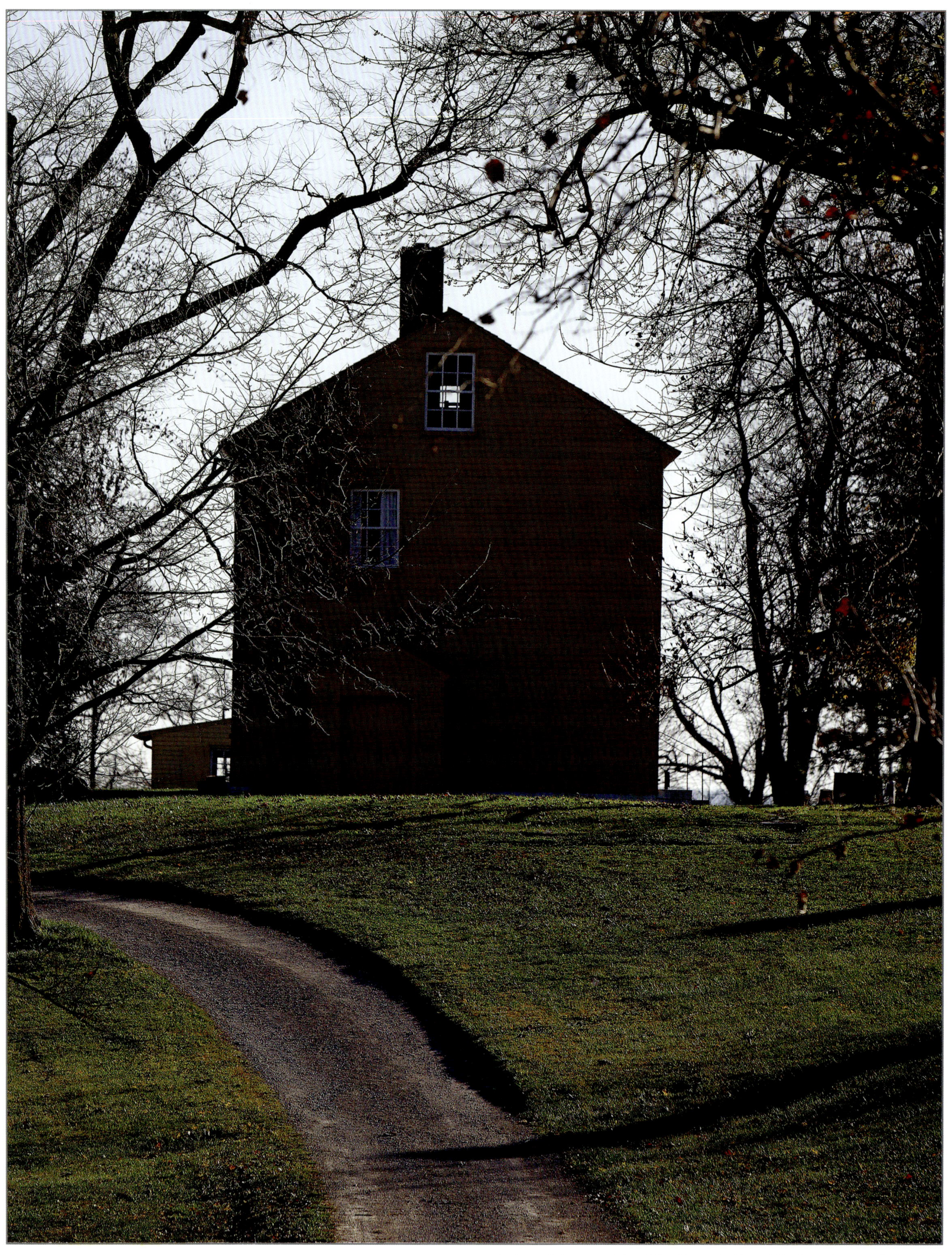

A view of the west side of the Cooper's Shop. The foundation of what was formerly one of the boys' dwellings is still visible next to it.

Opposite: The East Family Dwelling at sunrise.

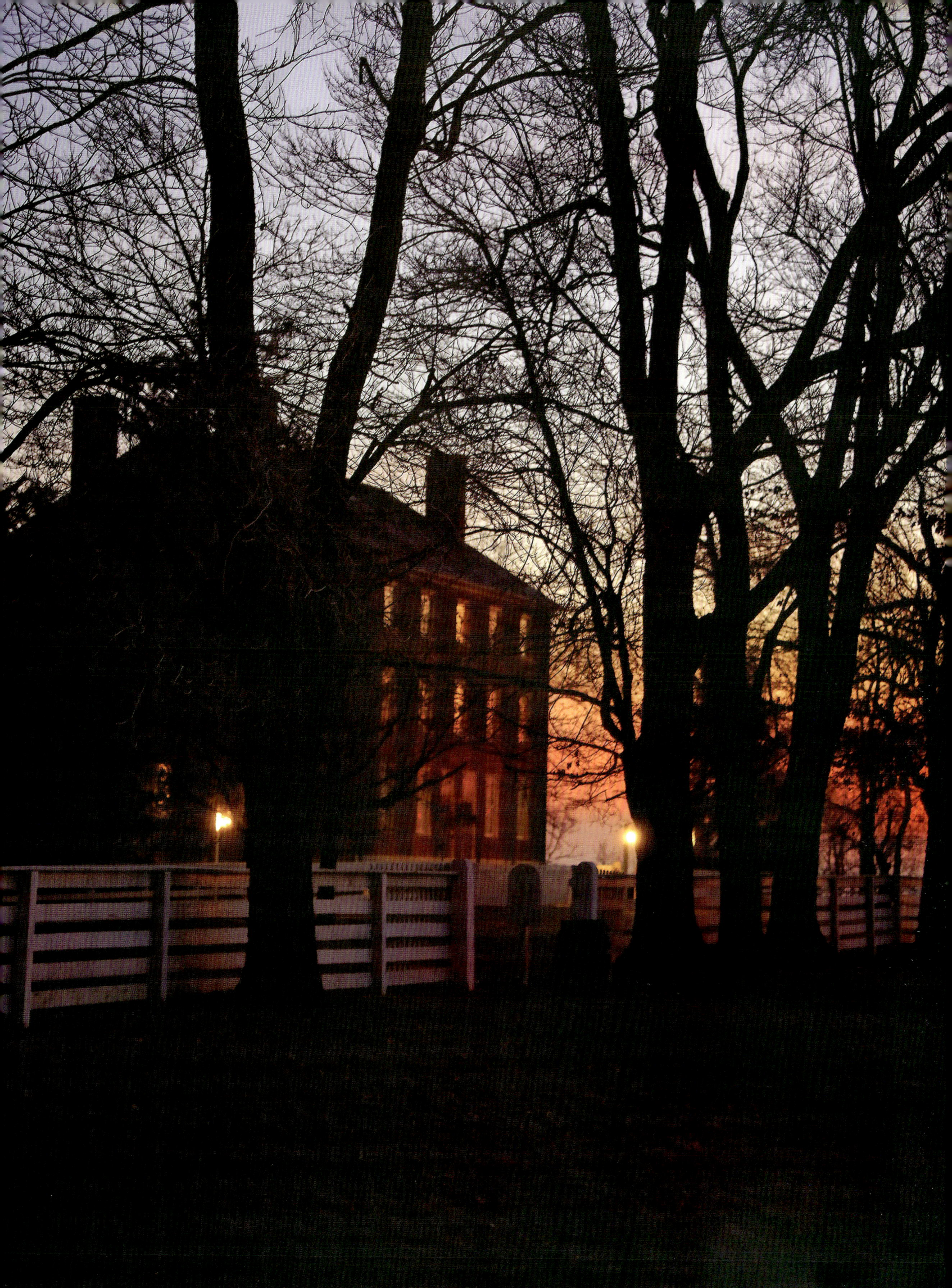

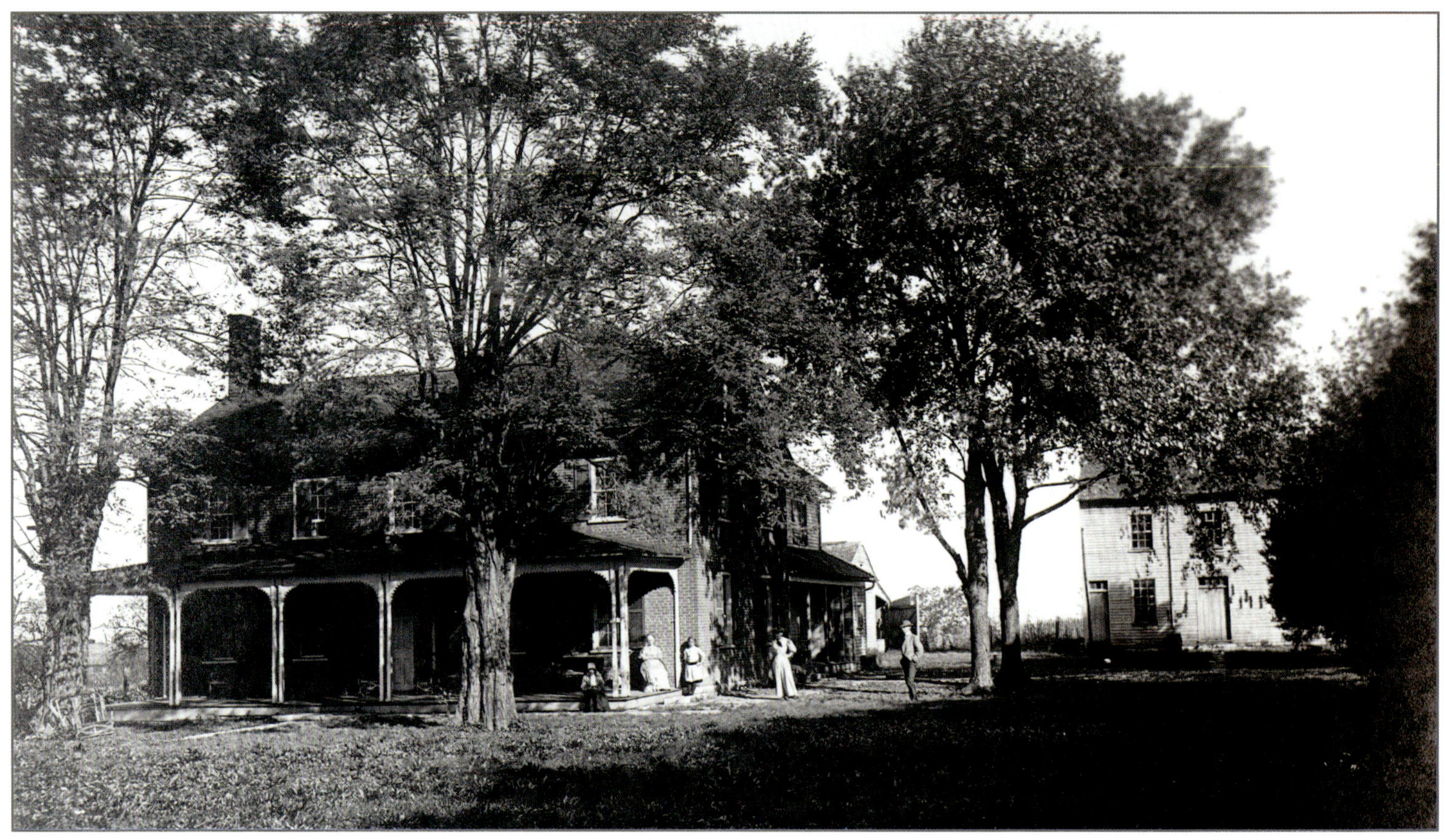

Archival photo of the East Family Brethren's Shop c. 1900. The porch was removed sometime before the restoration began and the ell at the rear of the building was removed during the restoration.

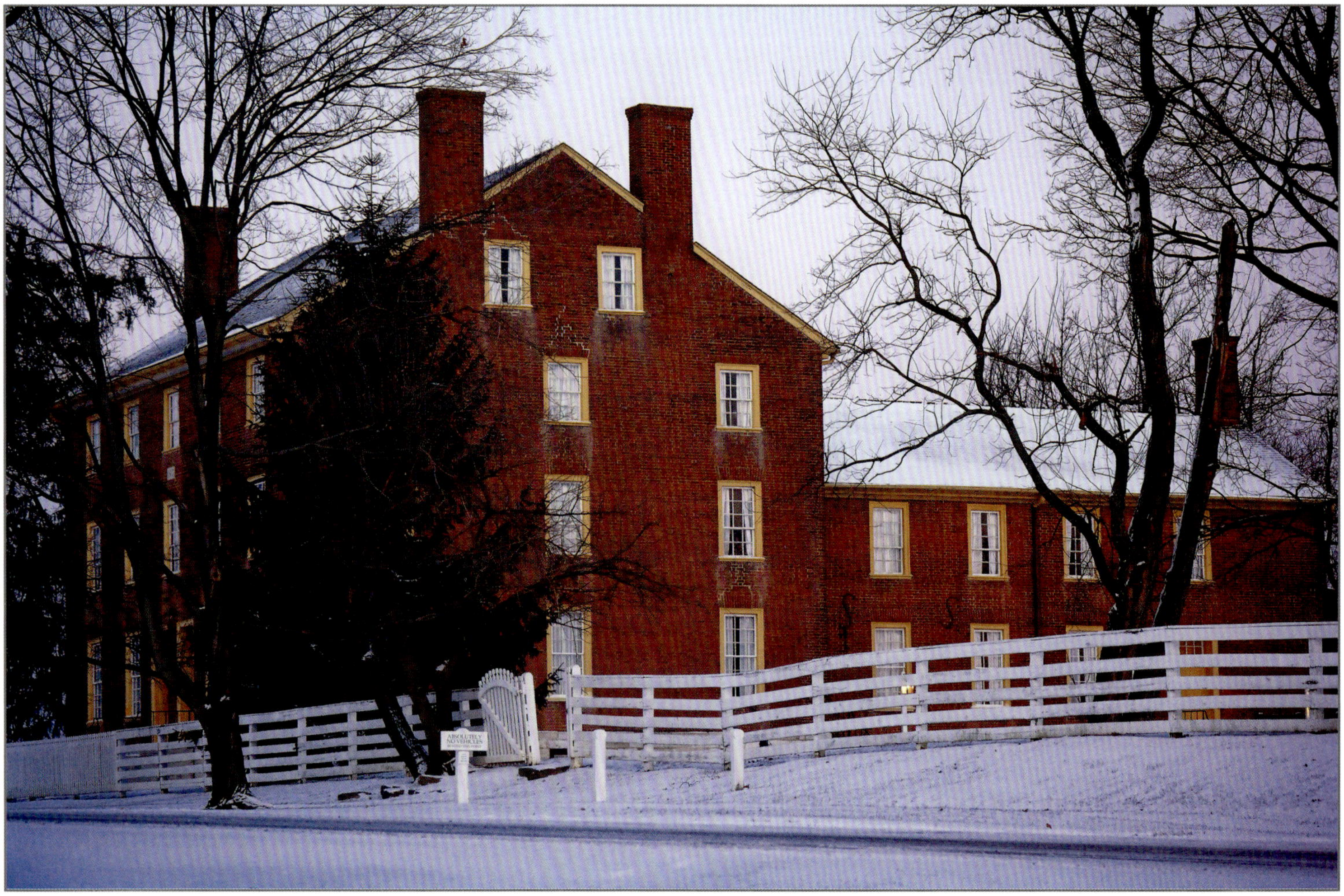

A view of the restored East Family Dwelling in the winter. The East Family Dwelling, also known as the Junior Order, was where new members who had signed the covenant began their lives as Shakers. As they matured spiritually, they would move to the Centre Family Dwelling and finally moved on to the West Family Dwelling where they would be cared for in their later years if the need arose.

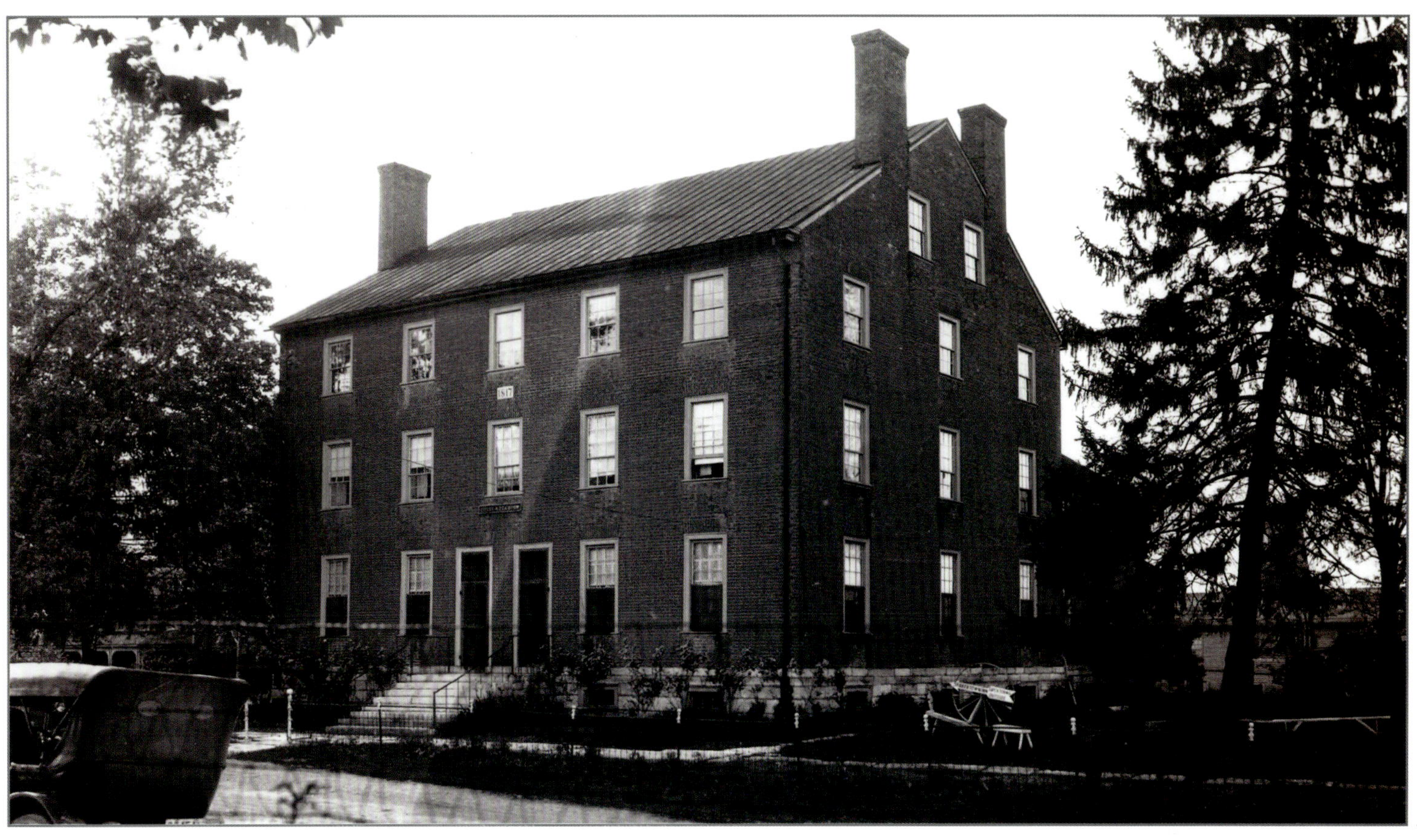

An archival photograph of the East Family Dwelling believed to be taken during its time as an inn.

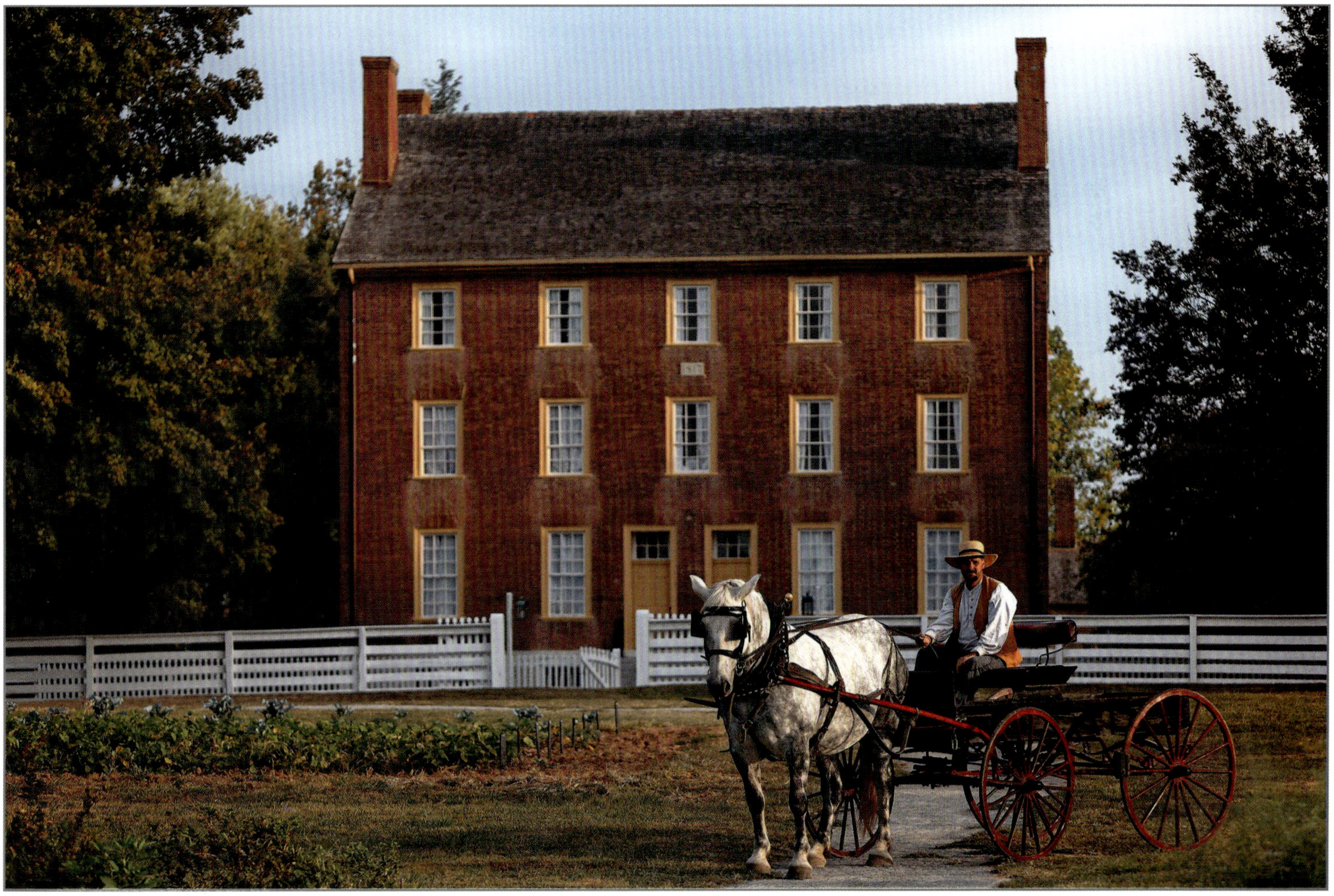

Views of the East Family Dwelling during various seasons of the year and times of day.

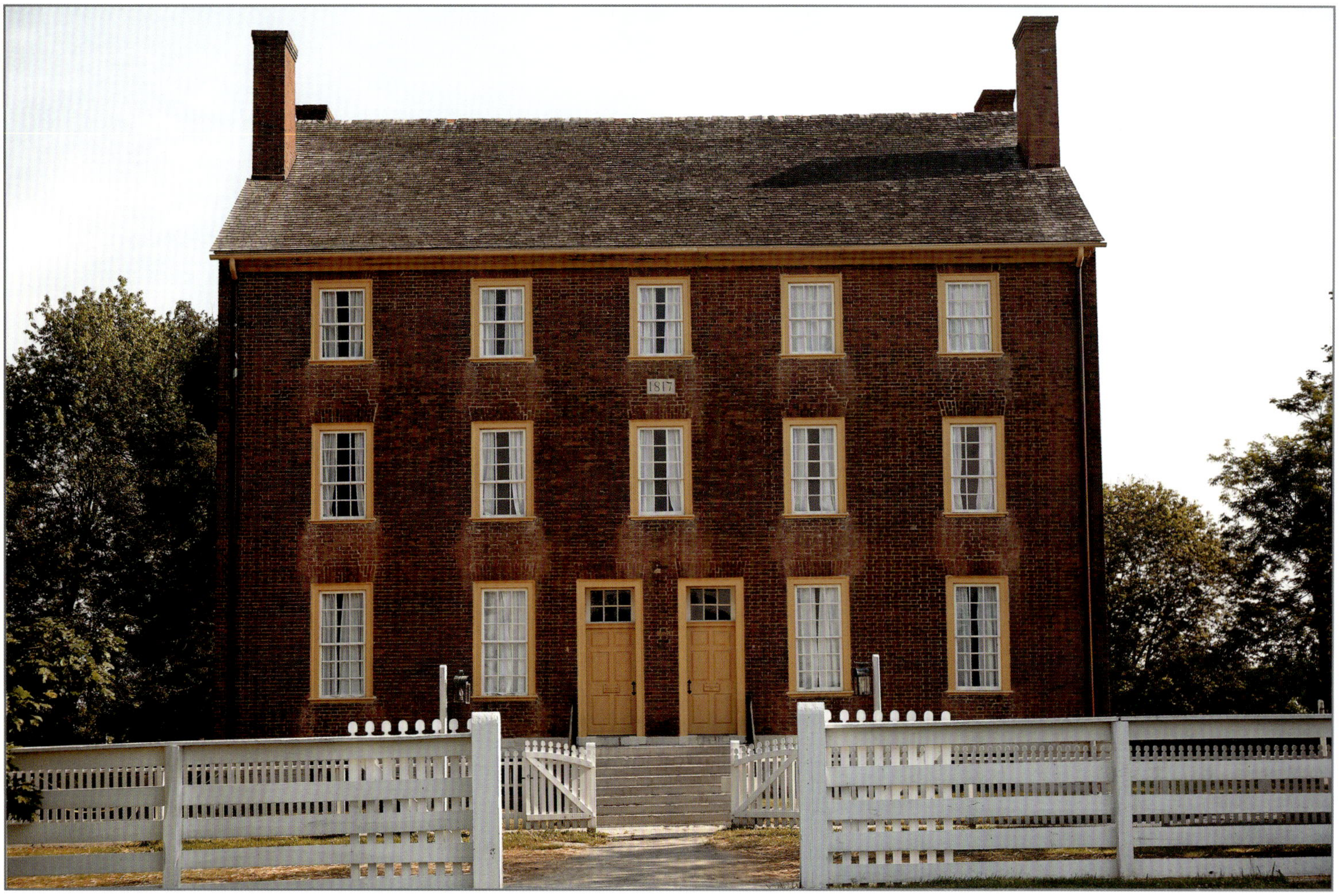

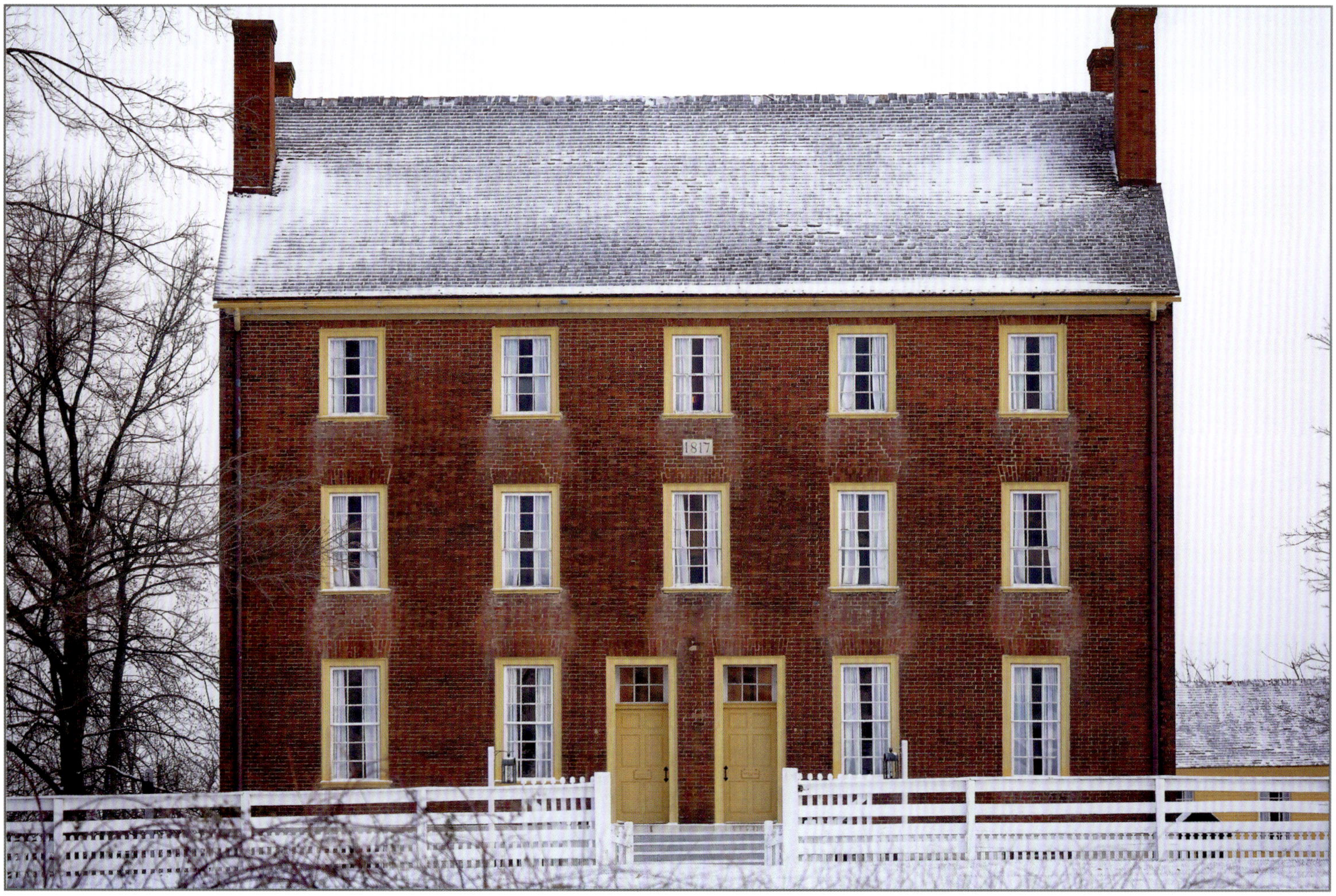

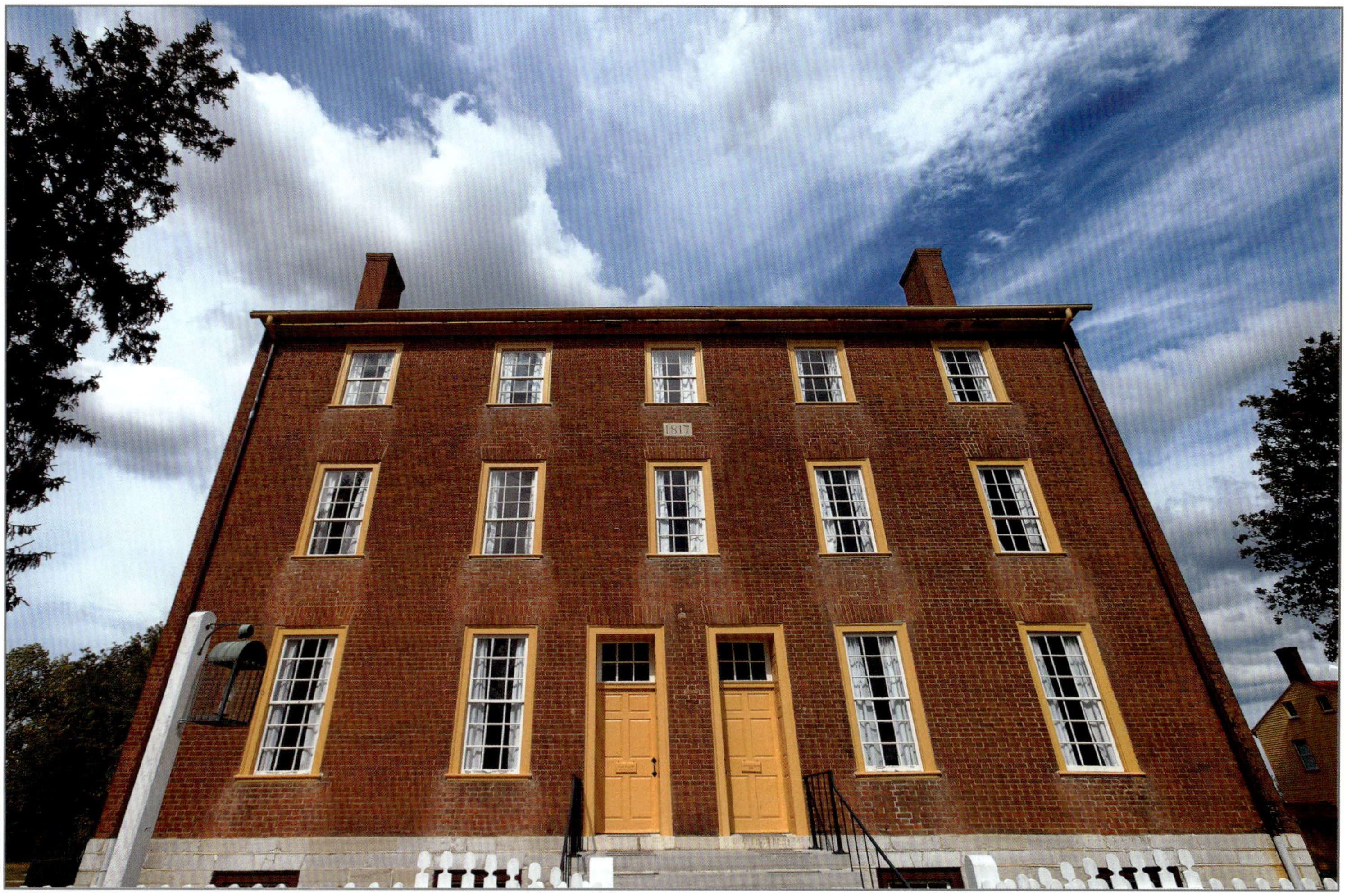

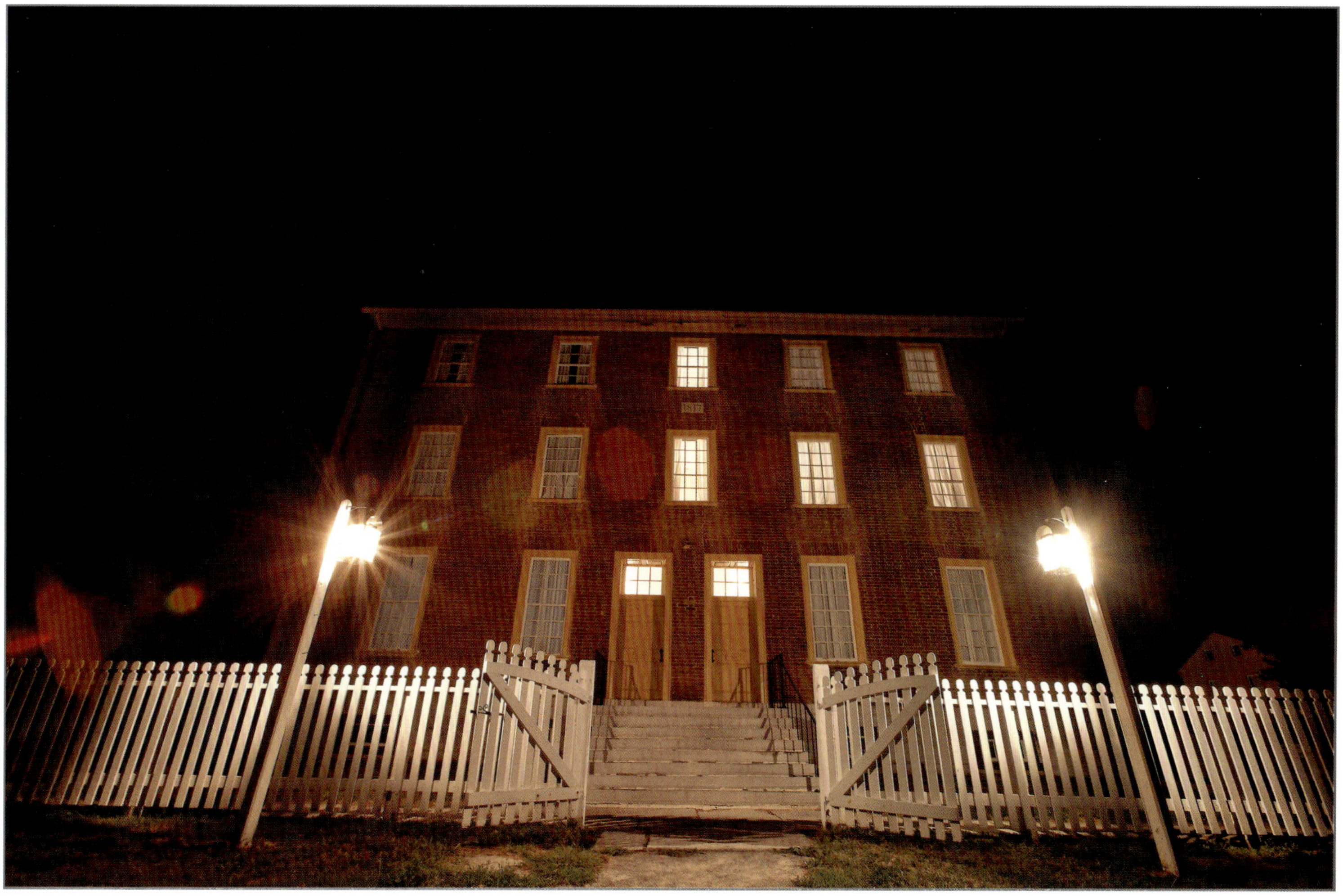

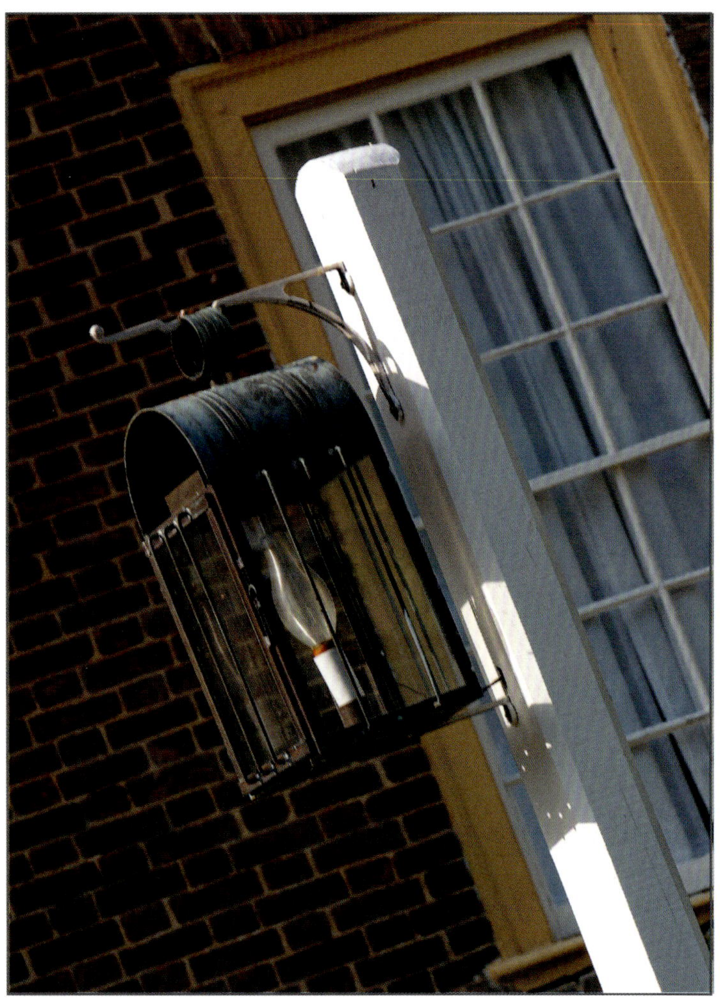

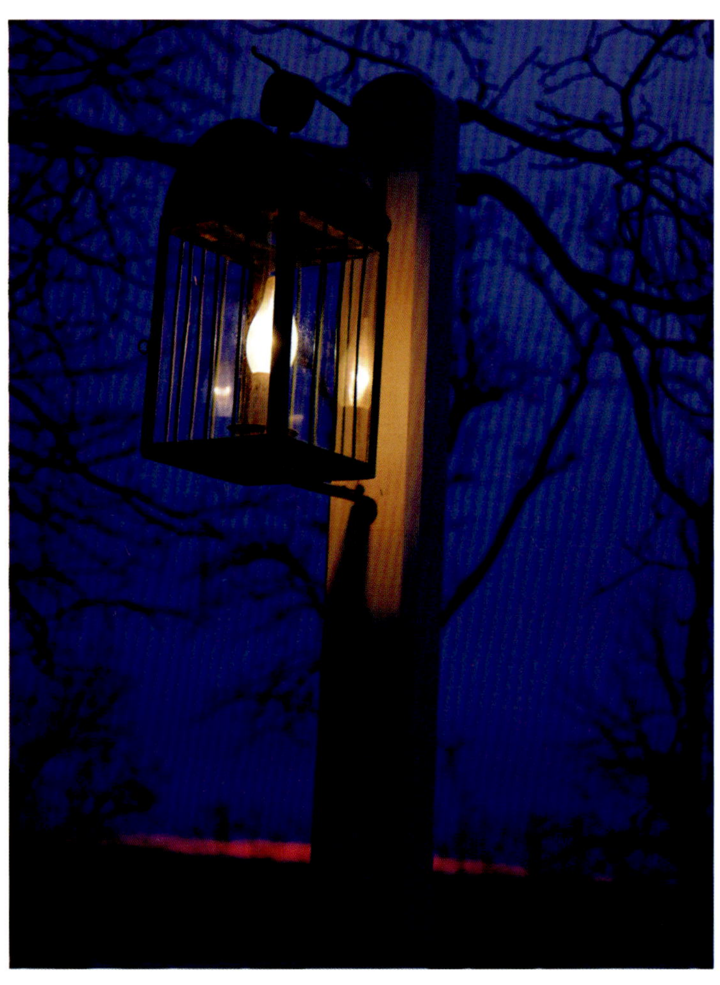

Lamp post outside the East Family Dwelling.

Right: The East Family Dwelling during restoration.

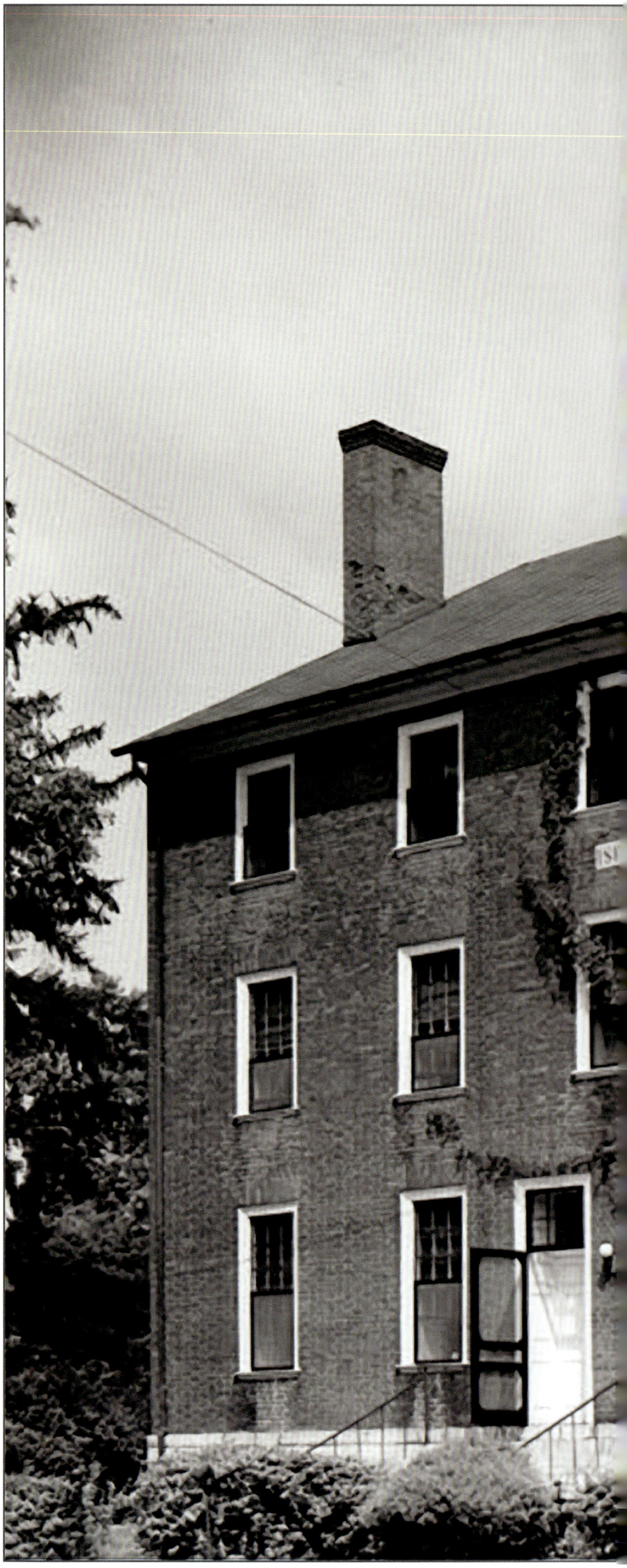

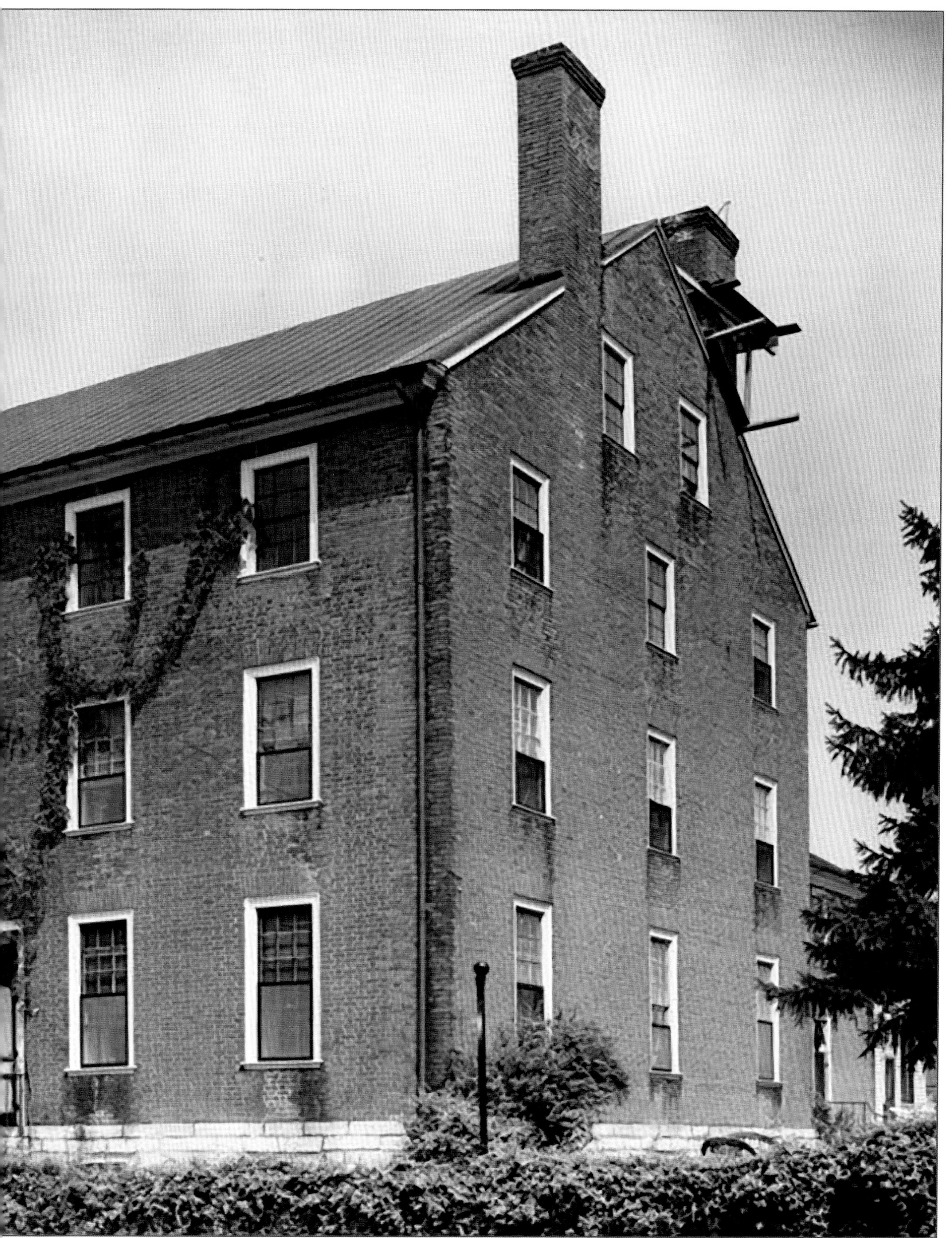

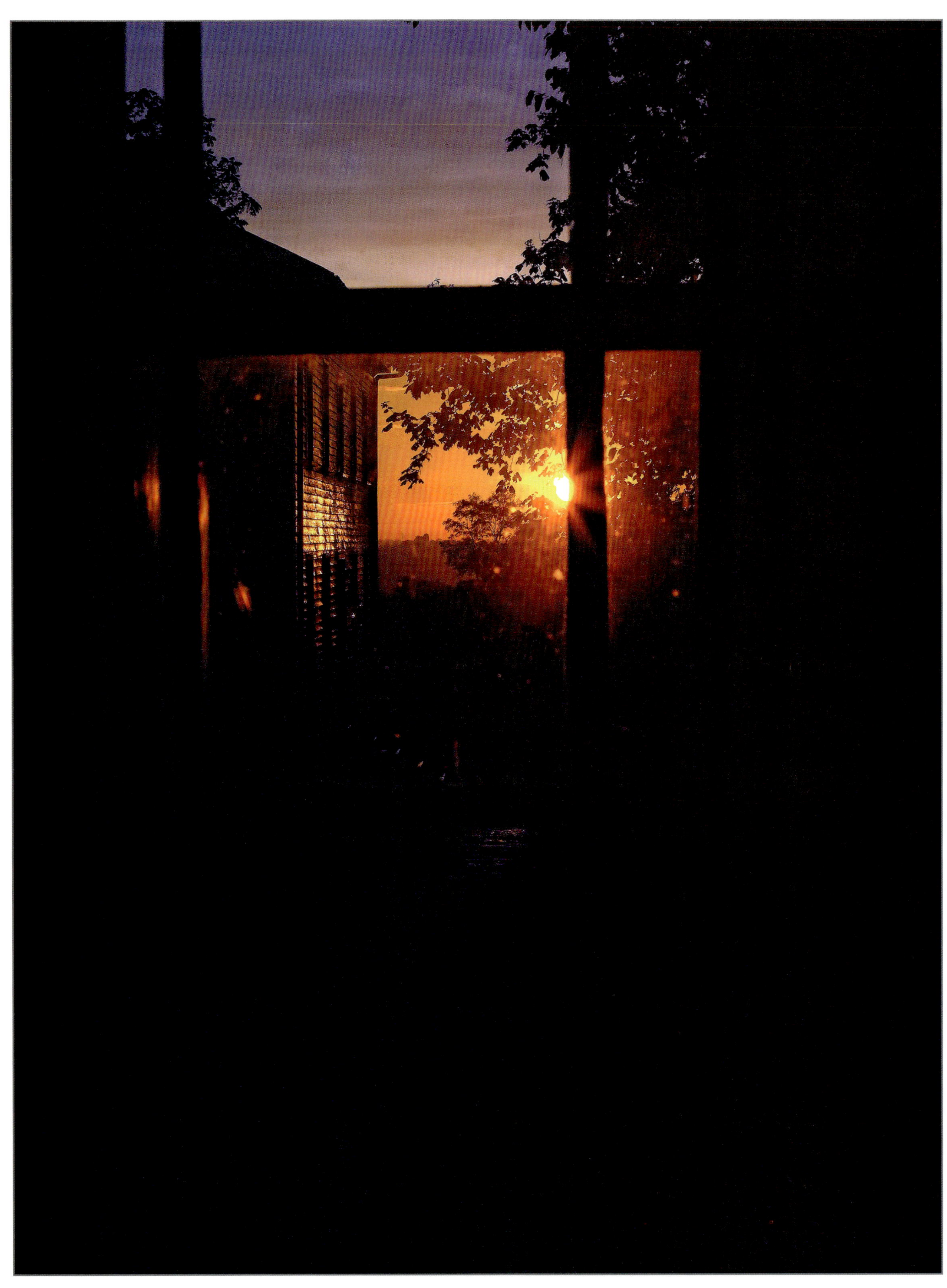

A view from inside the East Family Dwelling at sunrise looking towards the East Family Sister's Shop.

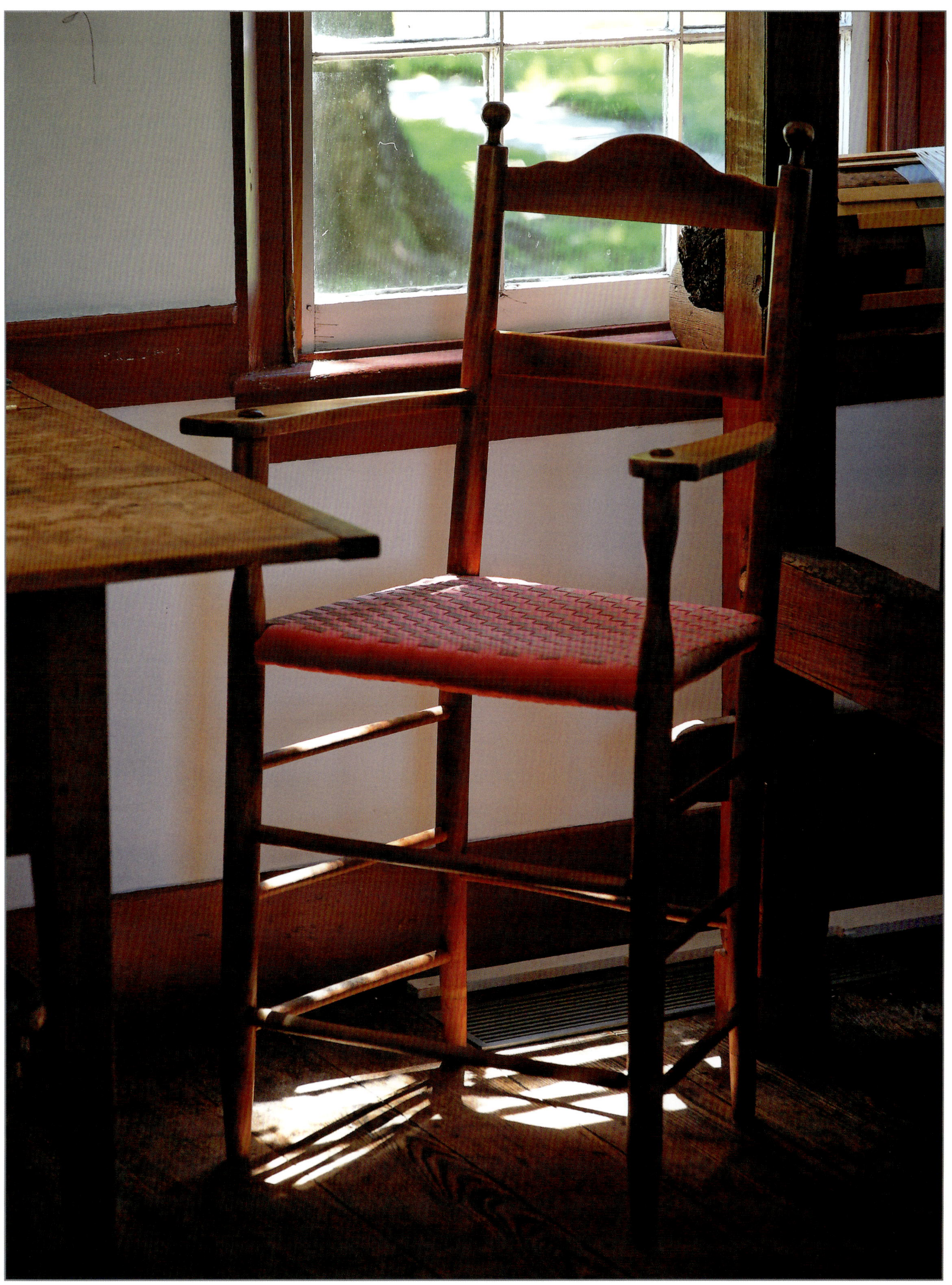

A weaver's chair on display in the East Family Sister's Shop.

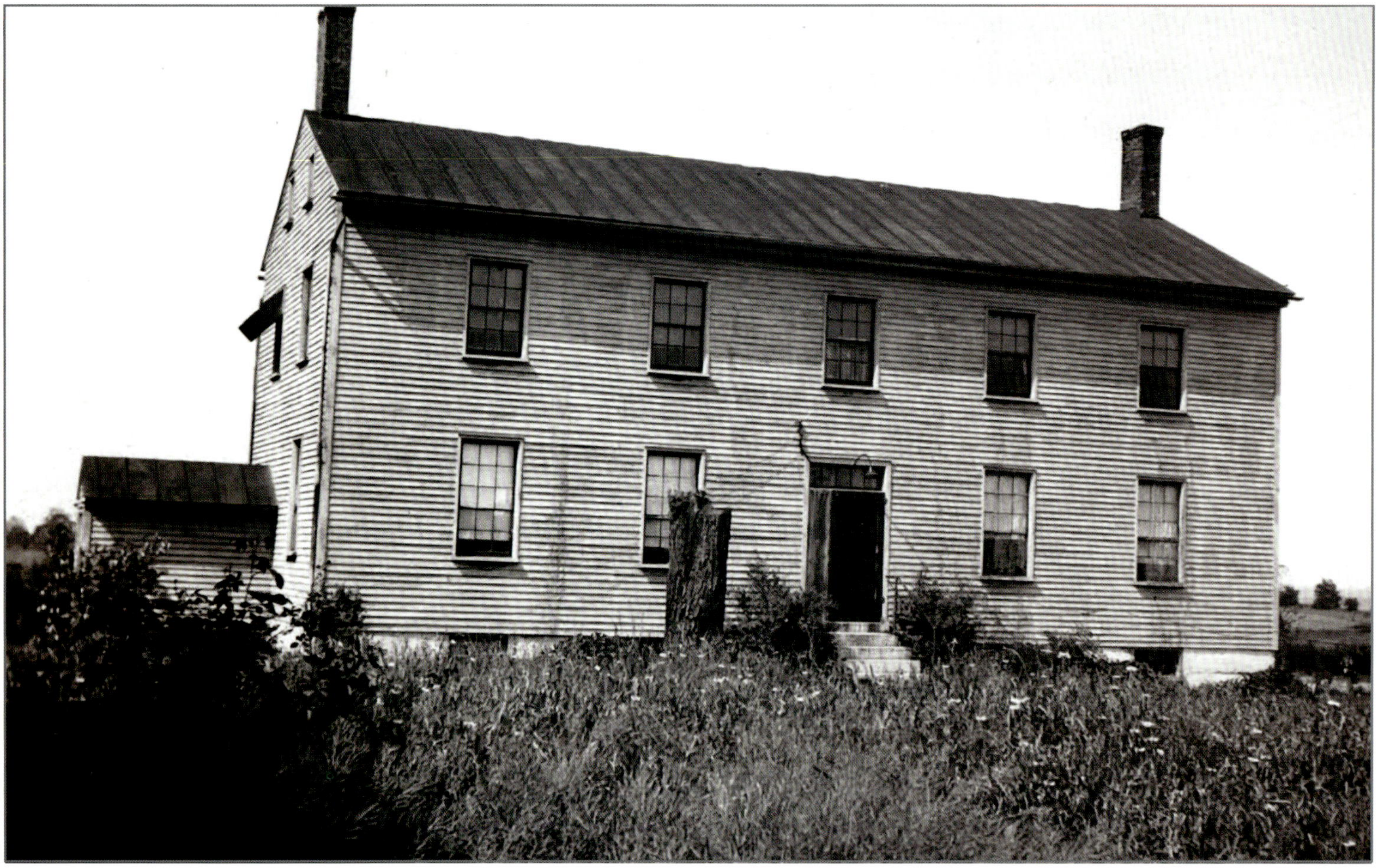

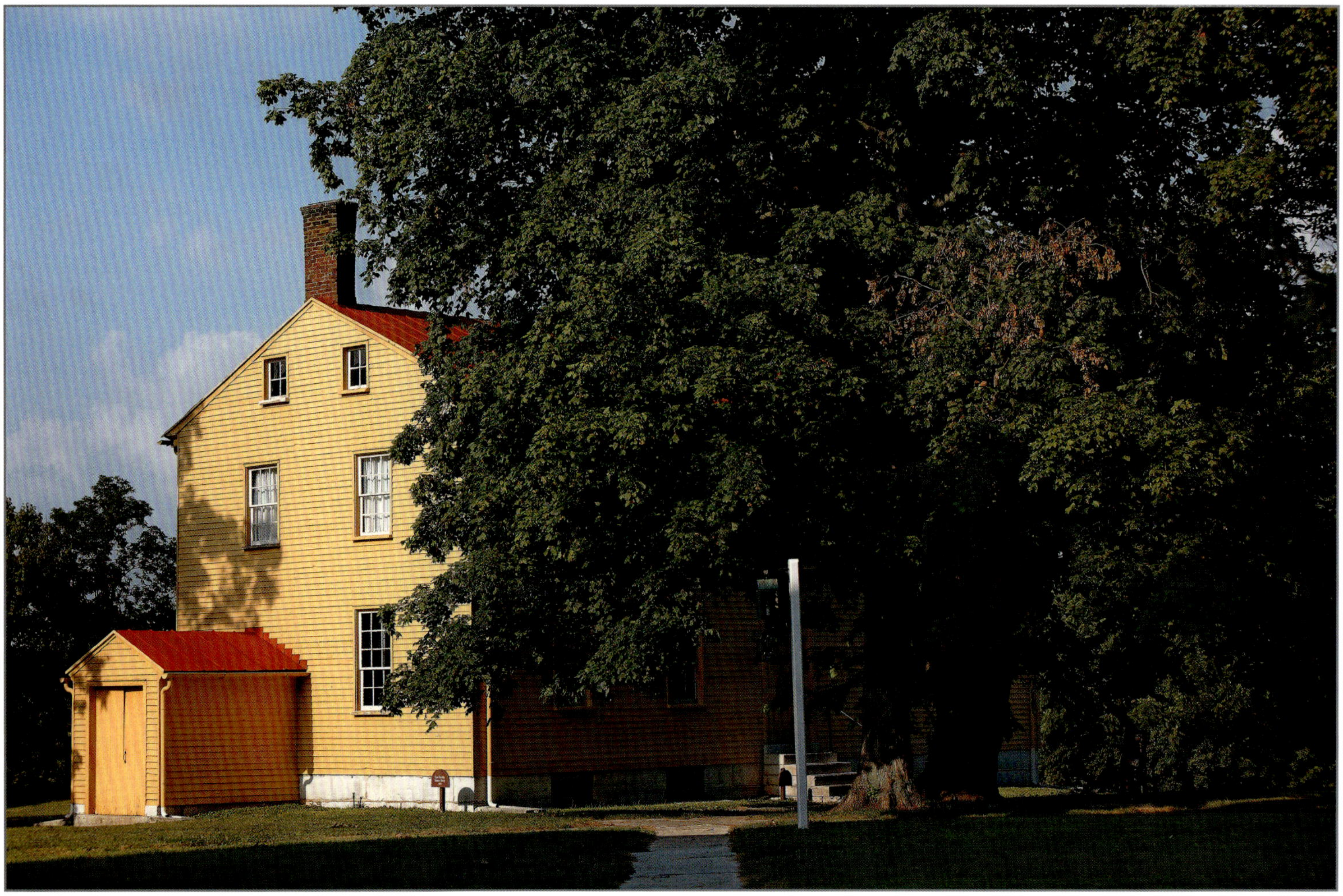

The East Family Sister's Shop then and now. For a number of years the top floor was used to raise silkworms. Silk scarves and other items were manufactured for sale to the outside world and given as gifts to members of other communities who visited the Village.

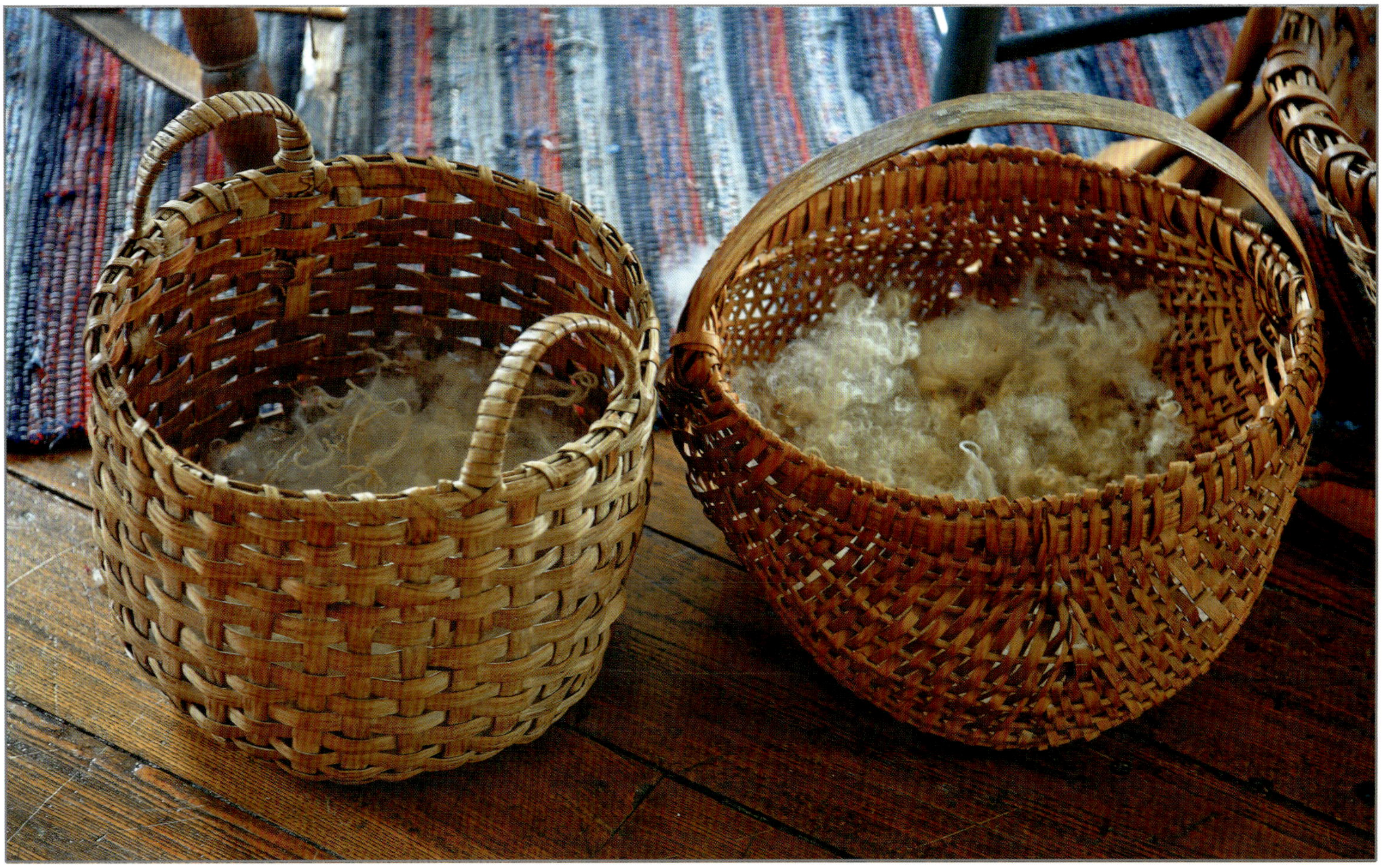

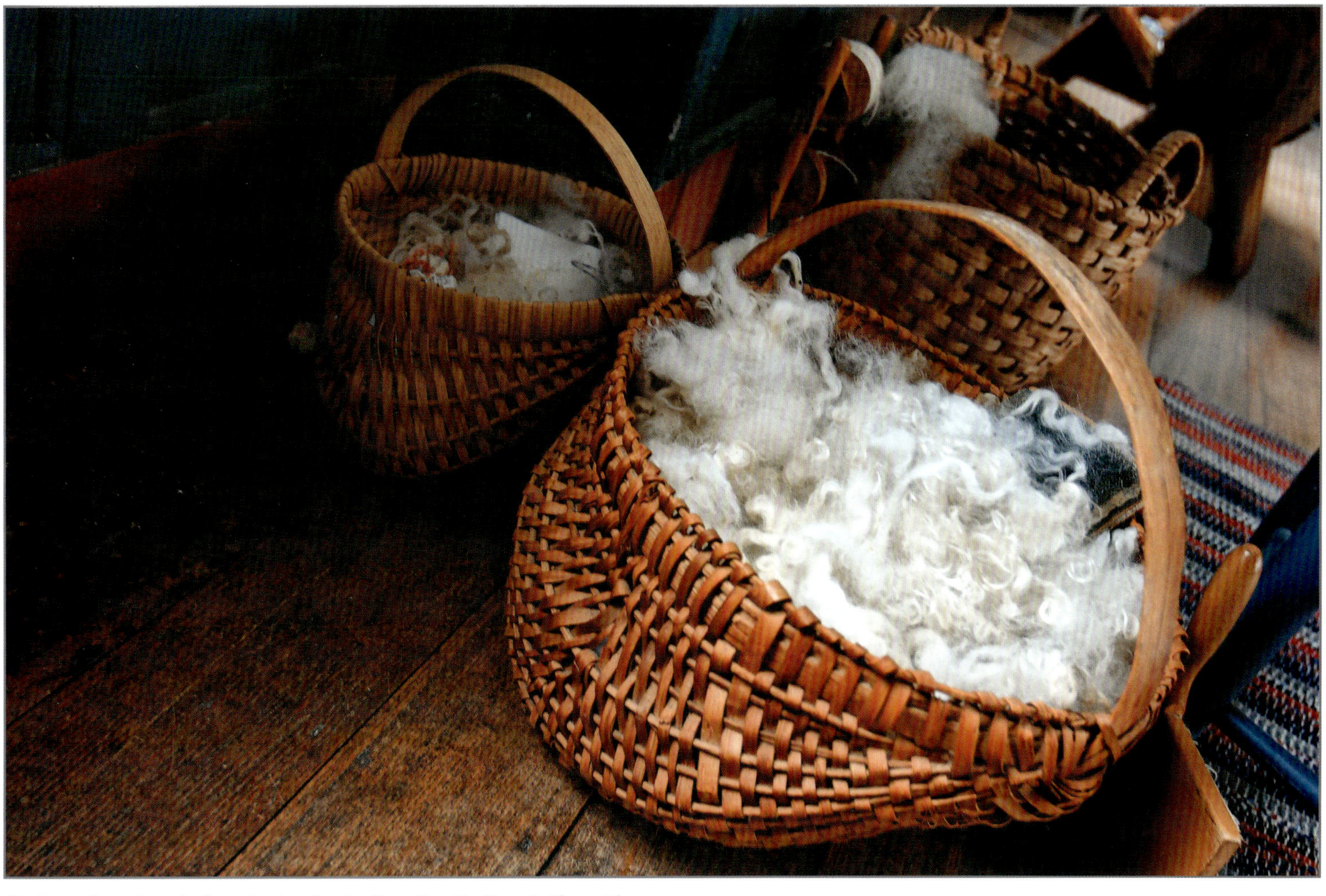

Baskets of wool ready for spinning in the East Family Sister's Shop. Flax was also grown onsite to be spun for linen and cotton was imported from the southern states.

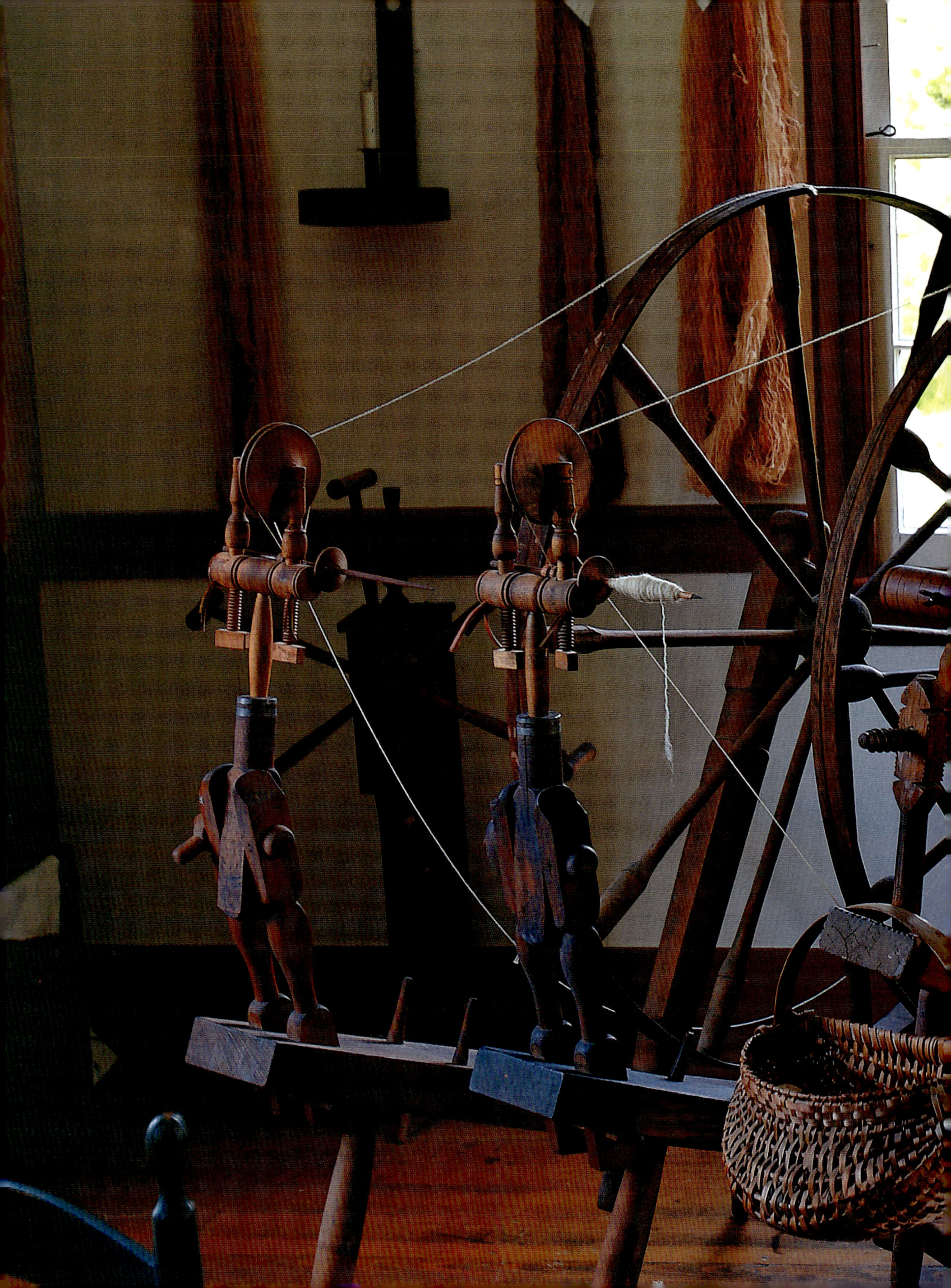

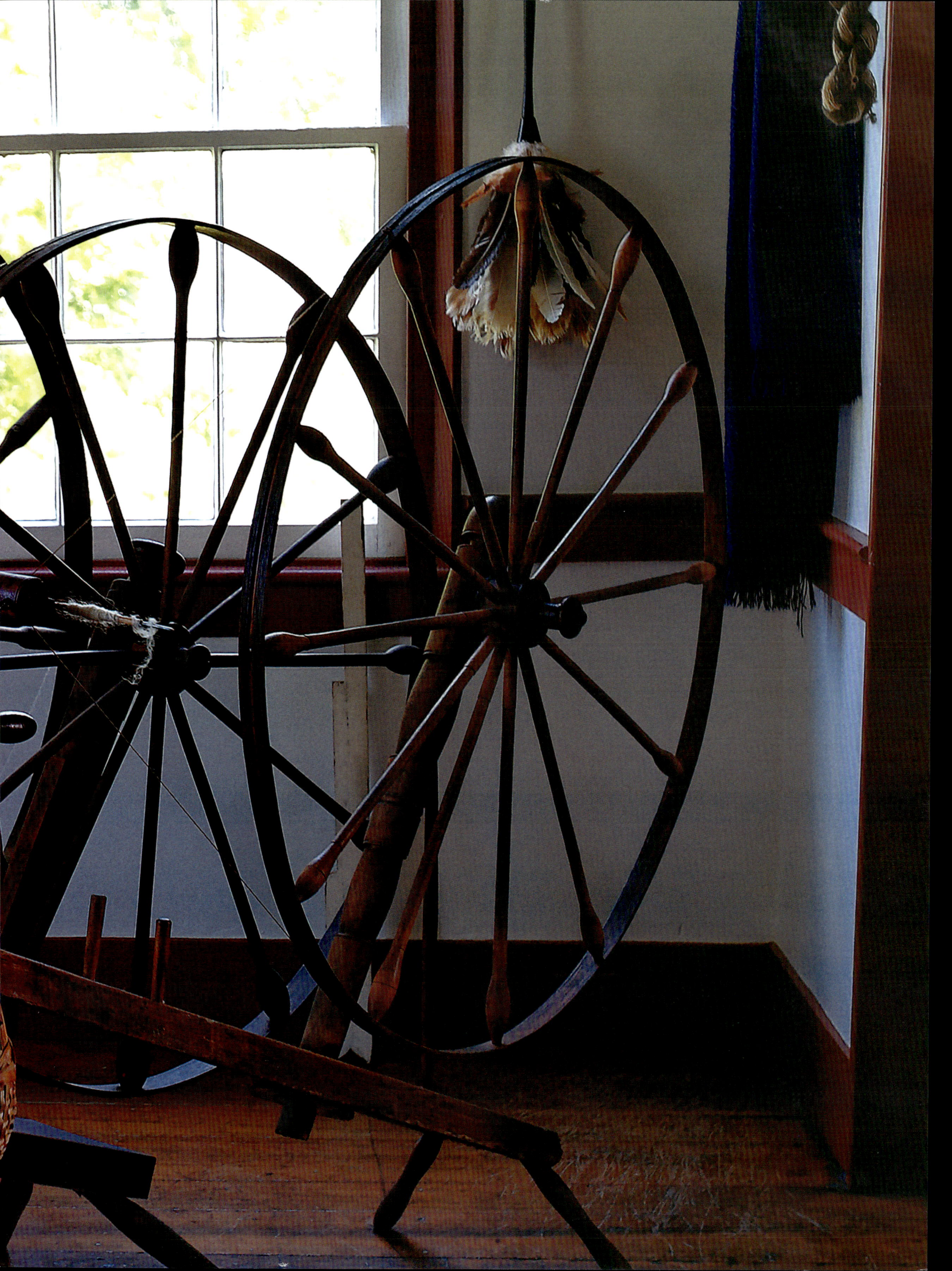

Previous spread: Examples of the "Walking Wheel" spinning wheels. For many years the Shakers spun their own yarn and made their own cloth. As the industrial revolution took hold and costs declined, the Shakers began to purchase cloth from the outside world. It was noted in journals many Shakers felt they would have to purchase enough cloth from the outside world to make two pairs of pants to their one pair because of the lesser quality. The Shakers embraced technology and purchased sewing machines from the outside world to make their work more efficient.

Below: A swift, also known as a weasel, was used to measure and keep track of how much yarn was to be used. After forty revolutions it would make a popping sound to let the person know the prescribed amount had been wound. Popular culture has it this is where the expression "Pop goes the weasel" came from.

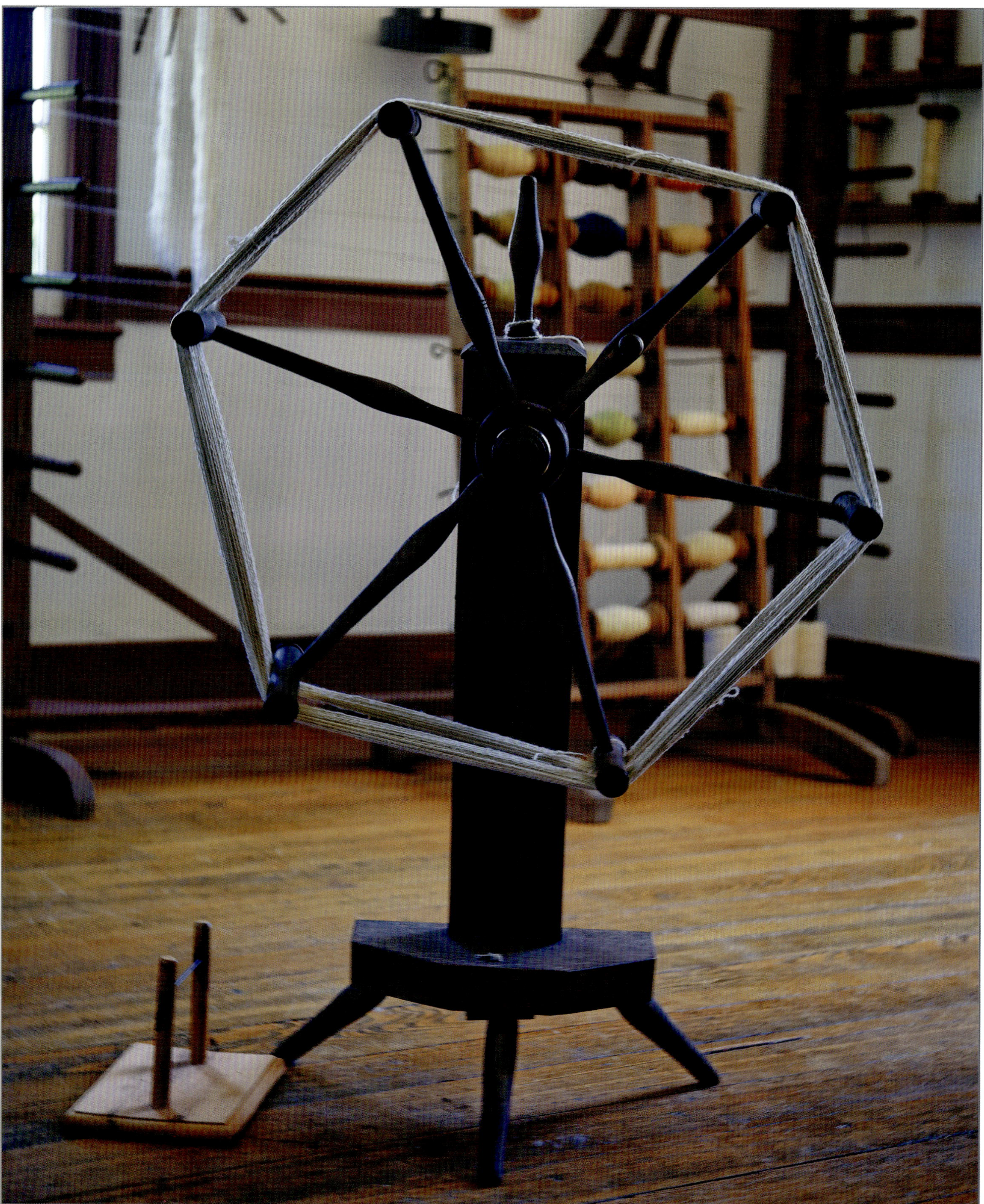

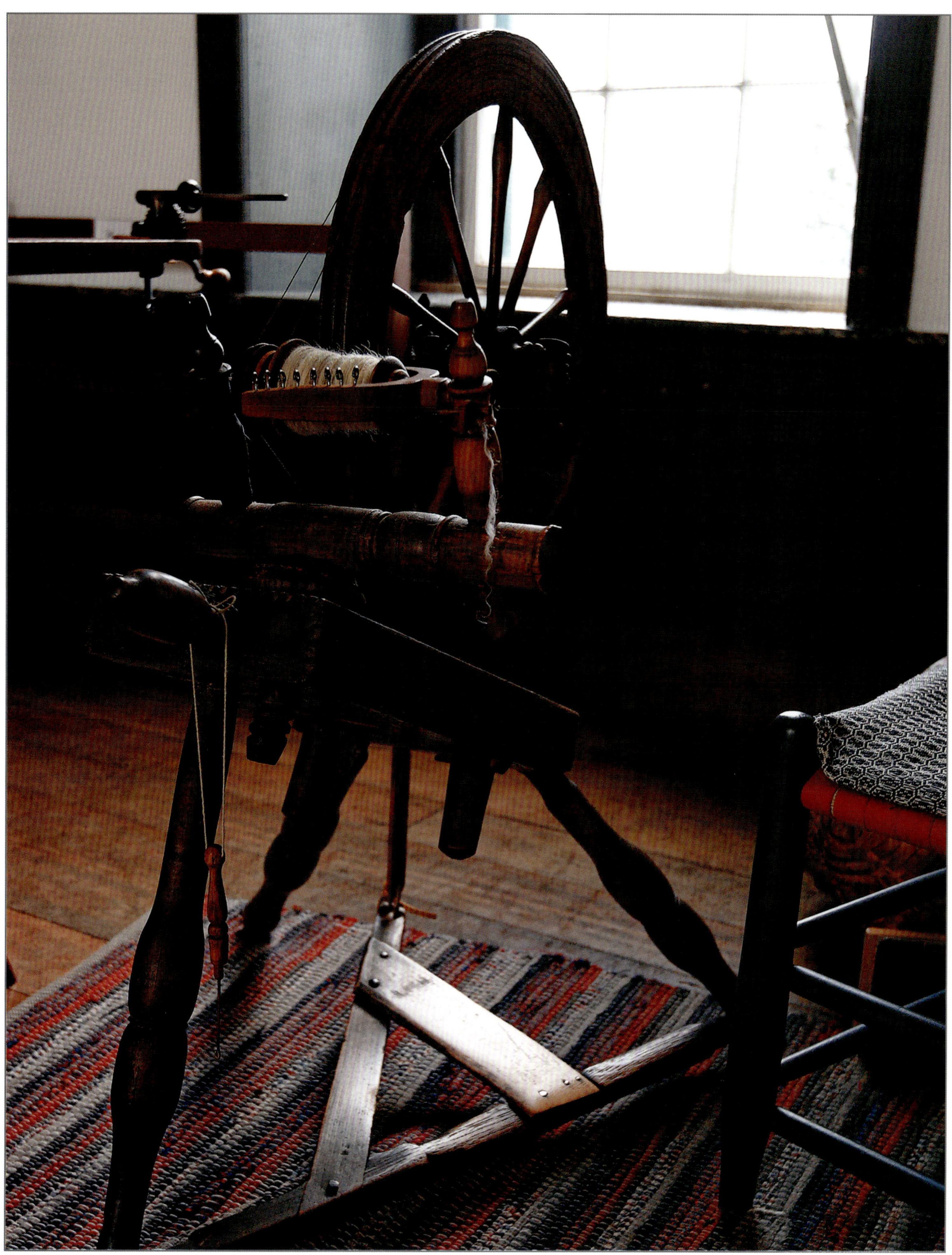

A Treadle Wheel, smaller than the Walking Wheel and generally used for spinning flax, could also be used for spinning other materials. The big advancement here was the smaller size allowing the operator to sit while using it.

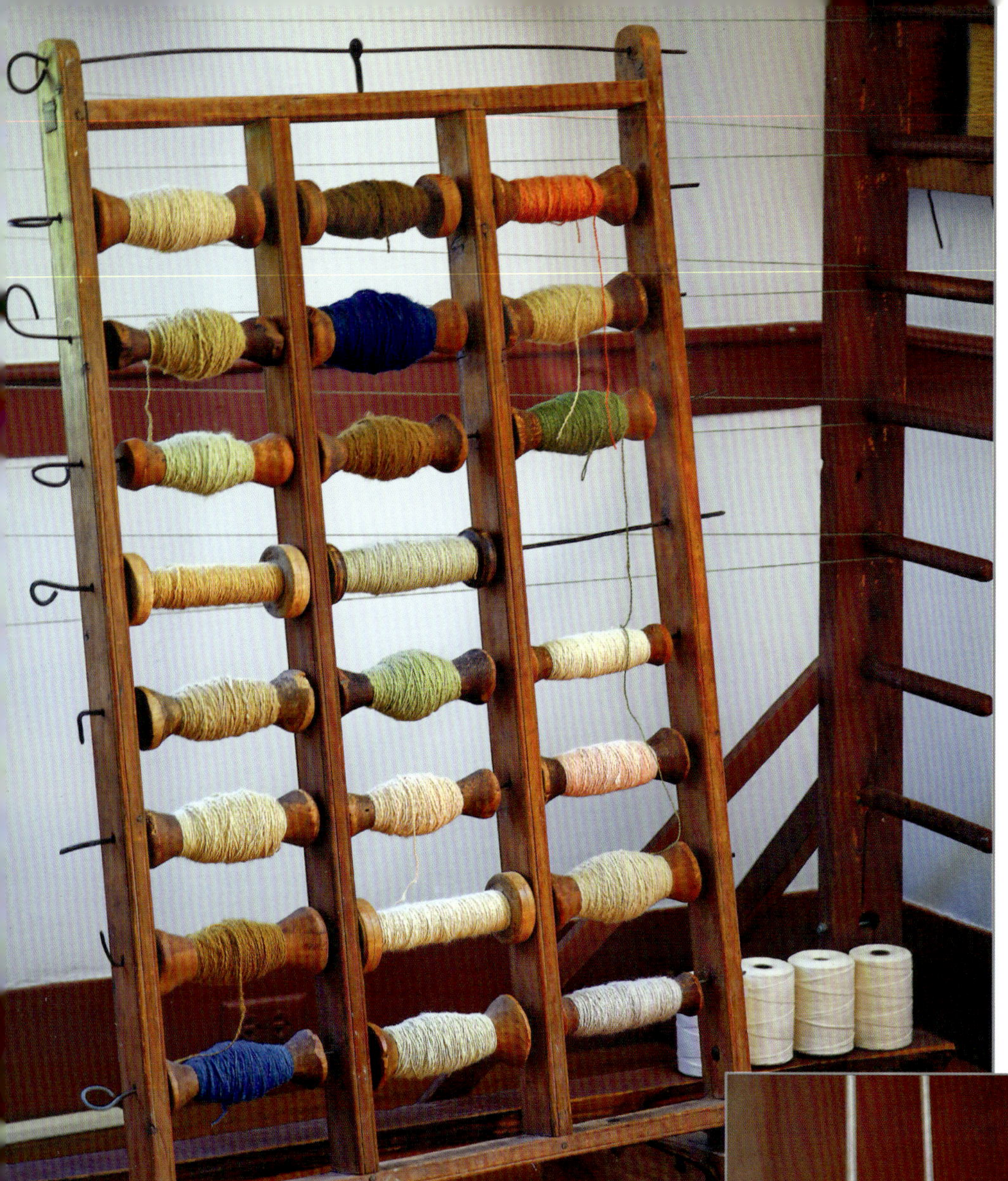

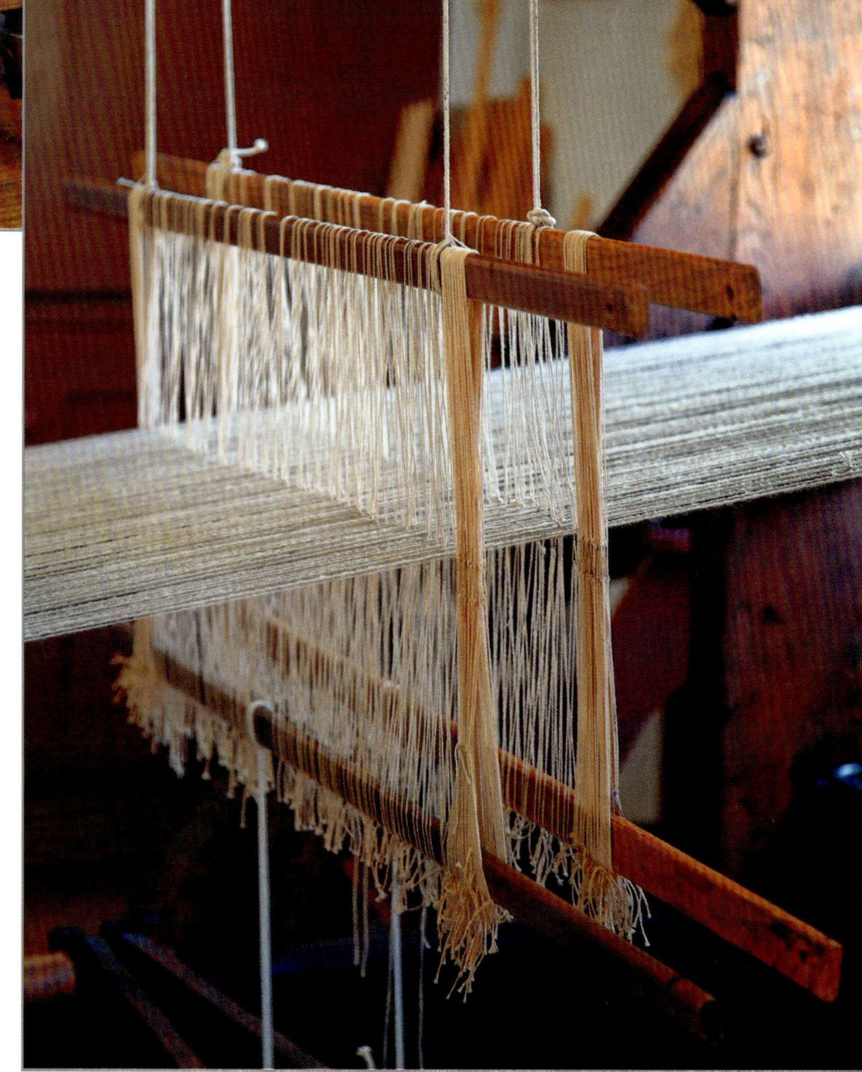

Above: Various colors of yarn racked and ready for weaving.

Right and opposite: The weft and waft of a loom in the East Family Sister's Shop. Setup for a particular pattern could take days to complete.

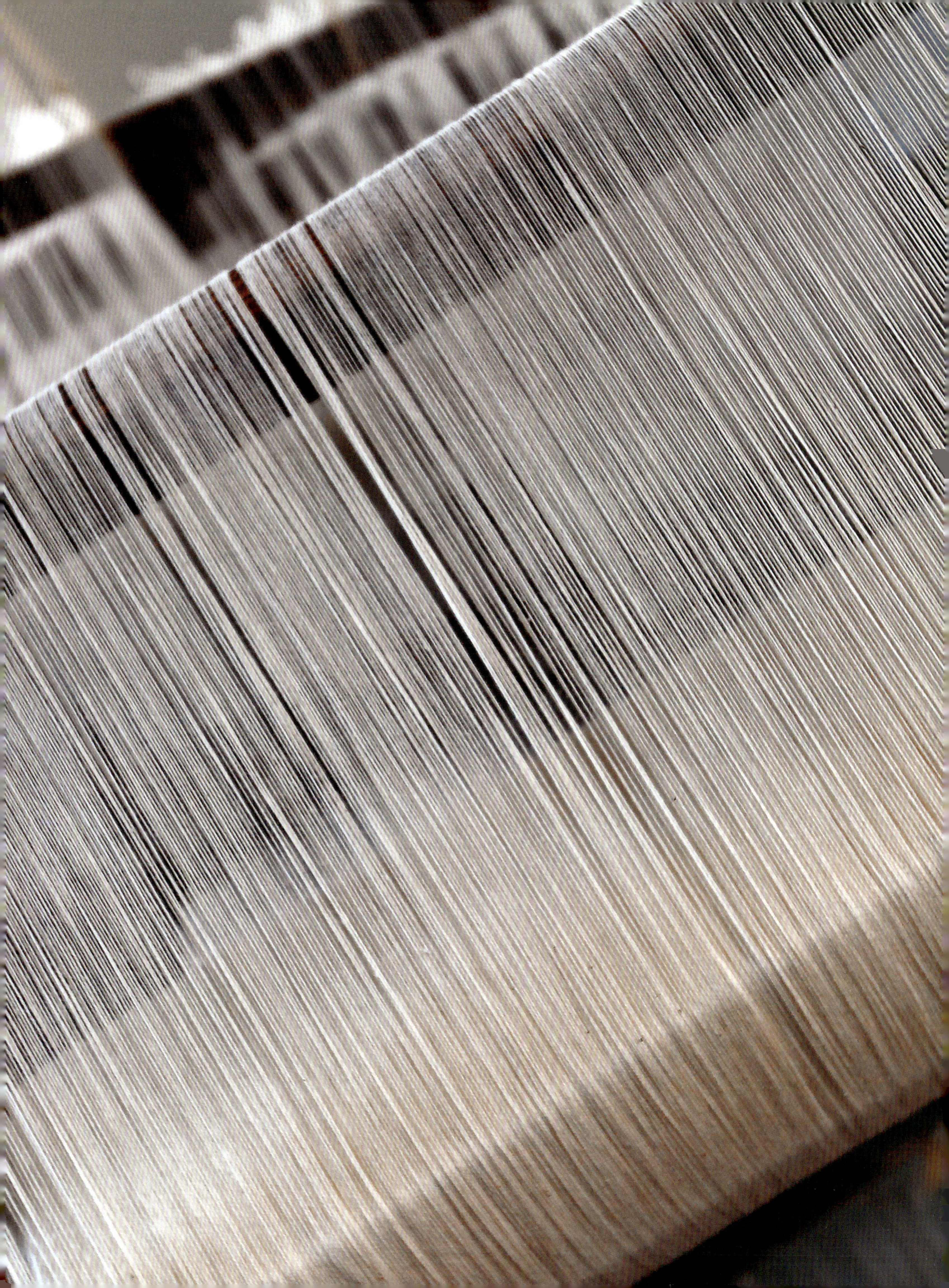

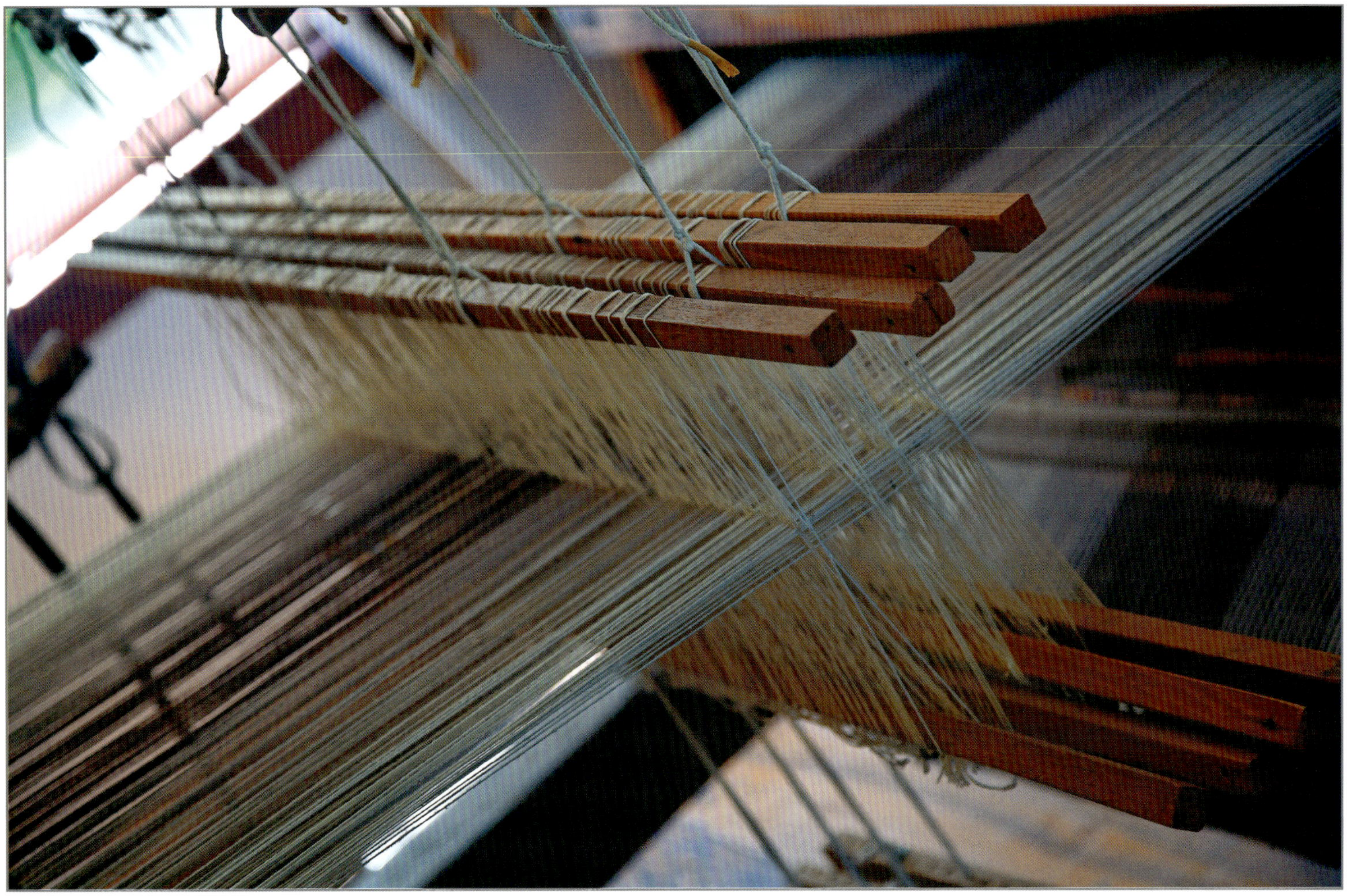

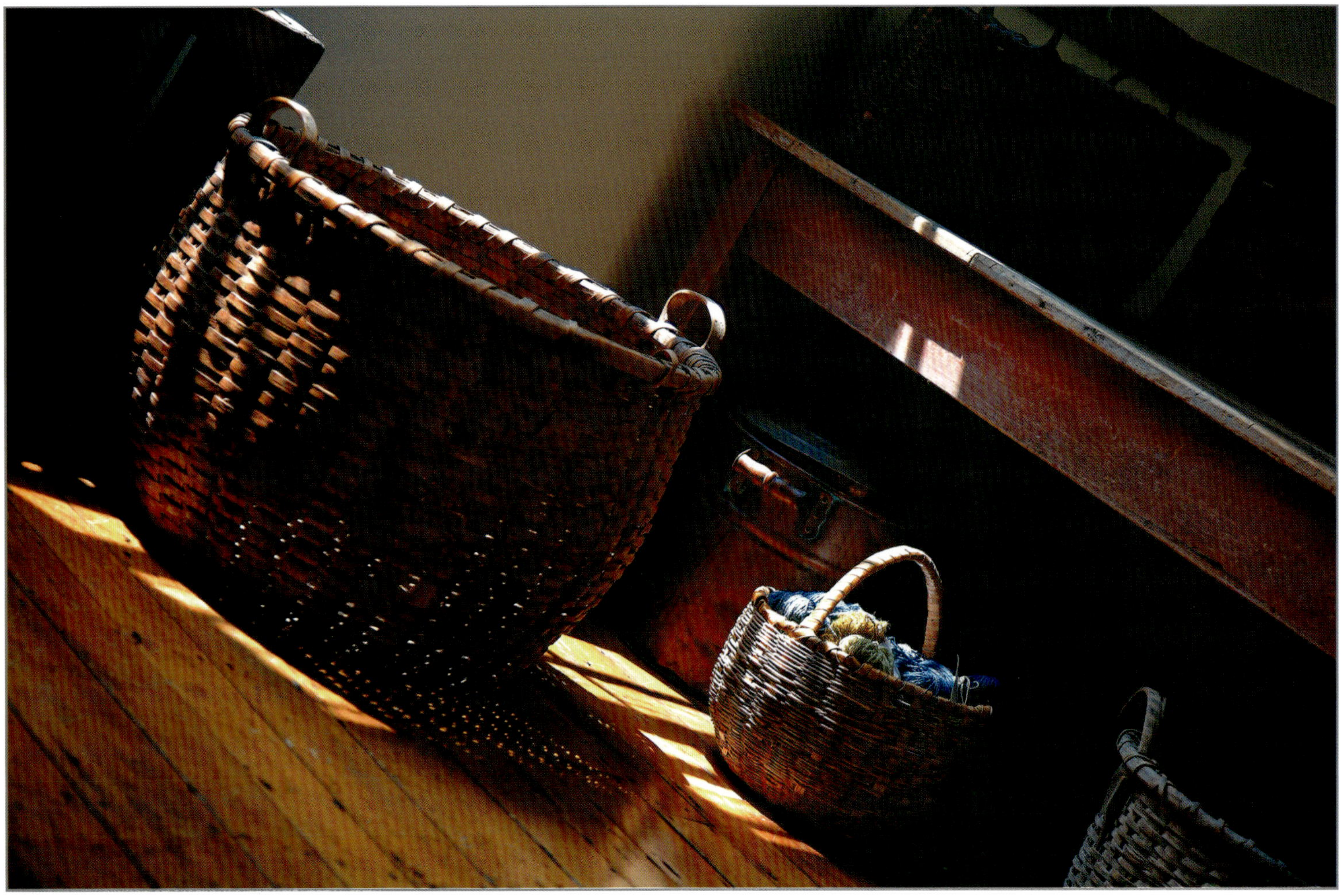

Baskets of various shapes and sizes are displayed in the section of the East Family Wash House where the dying process took place.

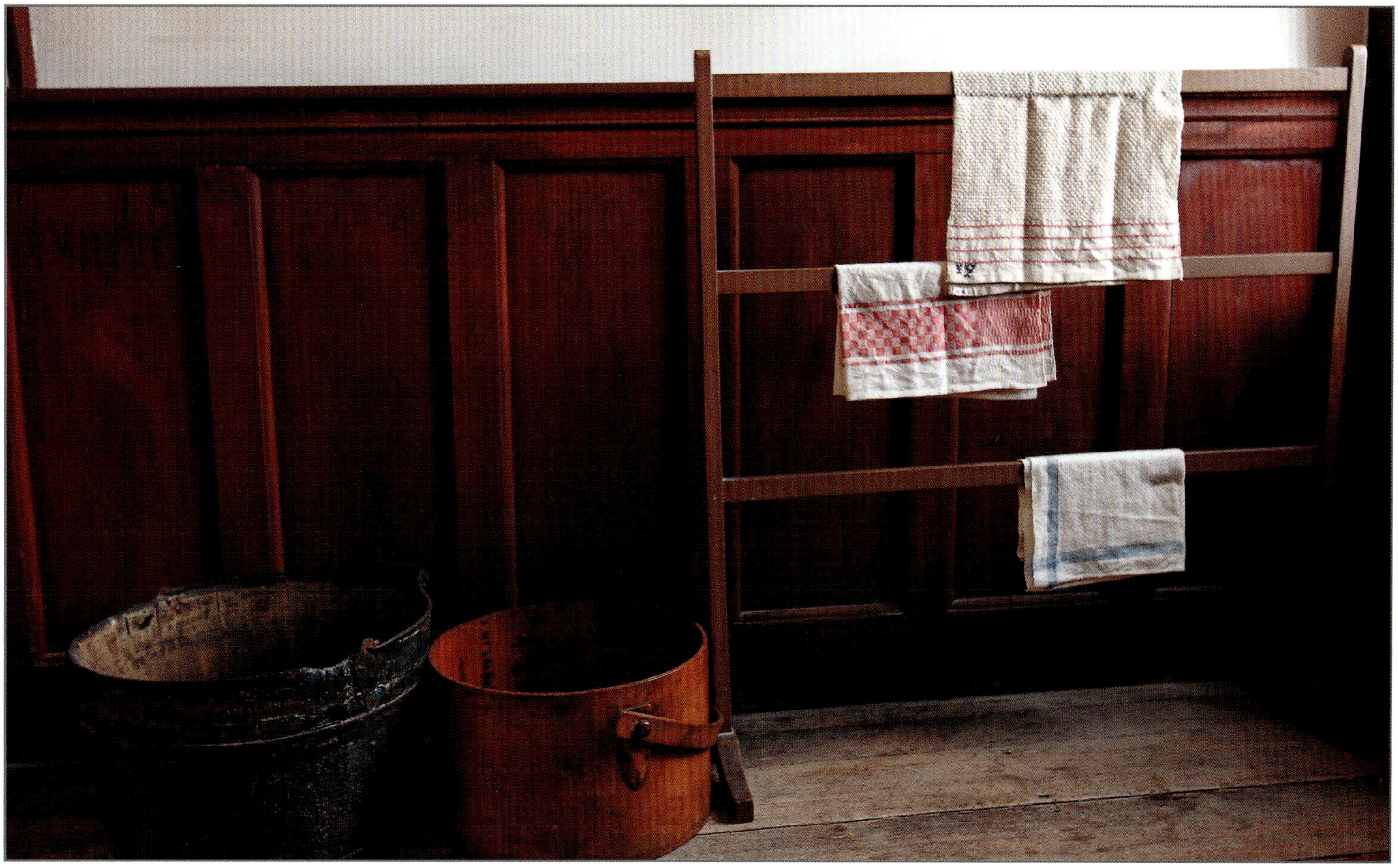

Cloths are on display in the wash area of the East Family Wash House. Member's items were identified by initials sewn into each item.

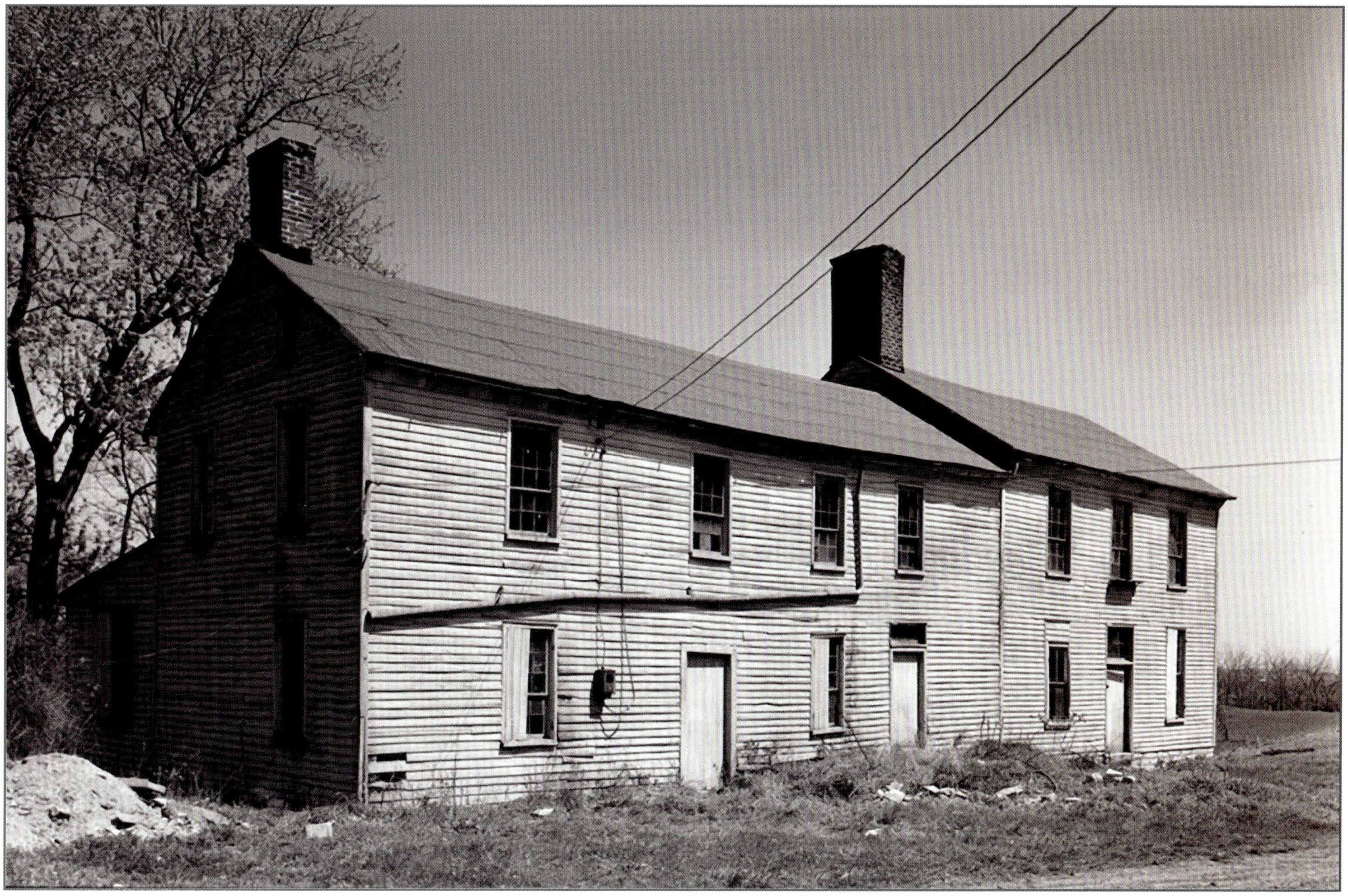

The East Family Wash House before restoration.

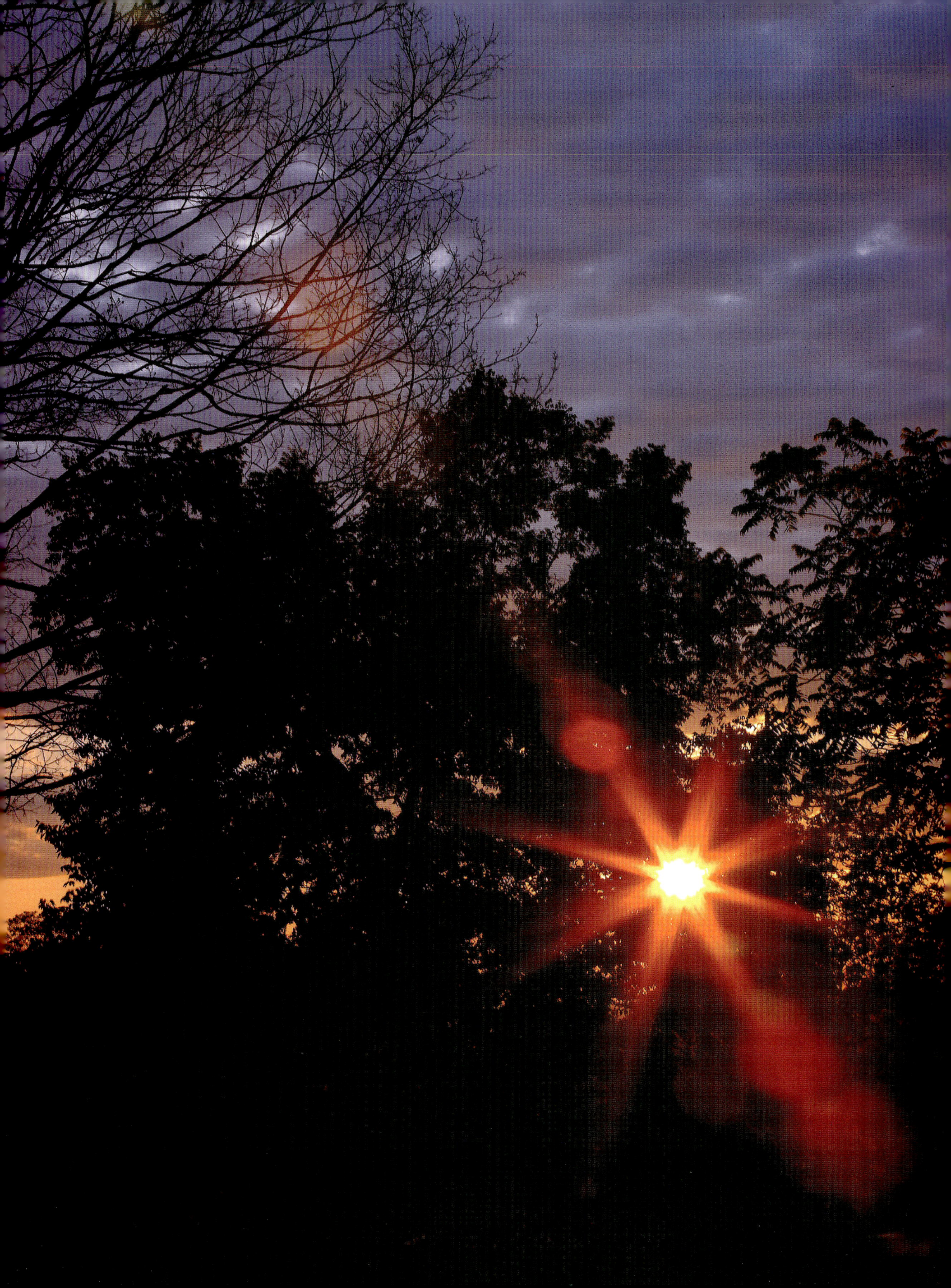

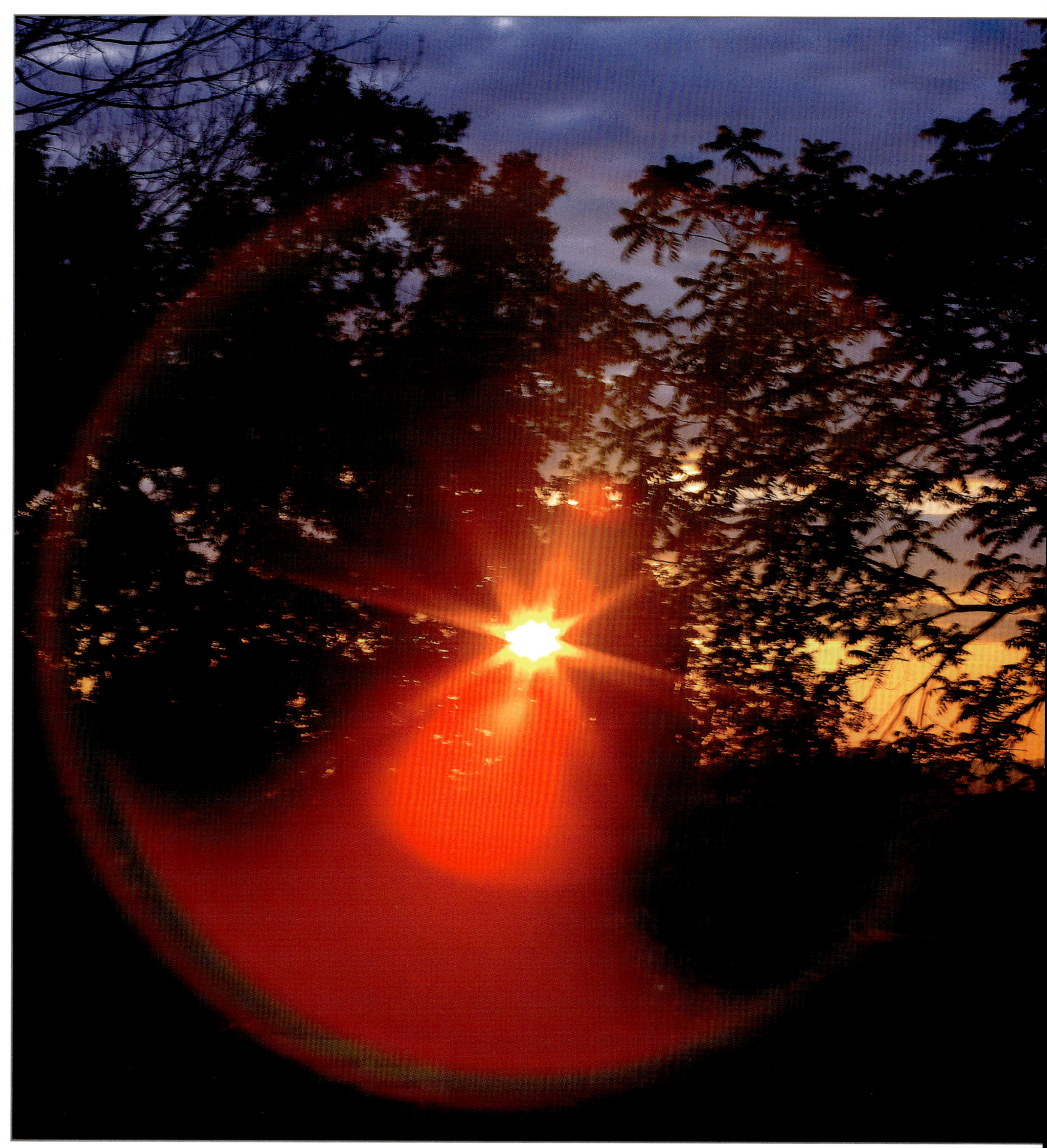

Sunrise through the trees on the east end of the Village.

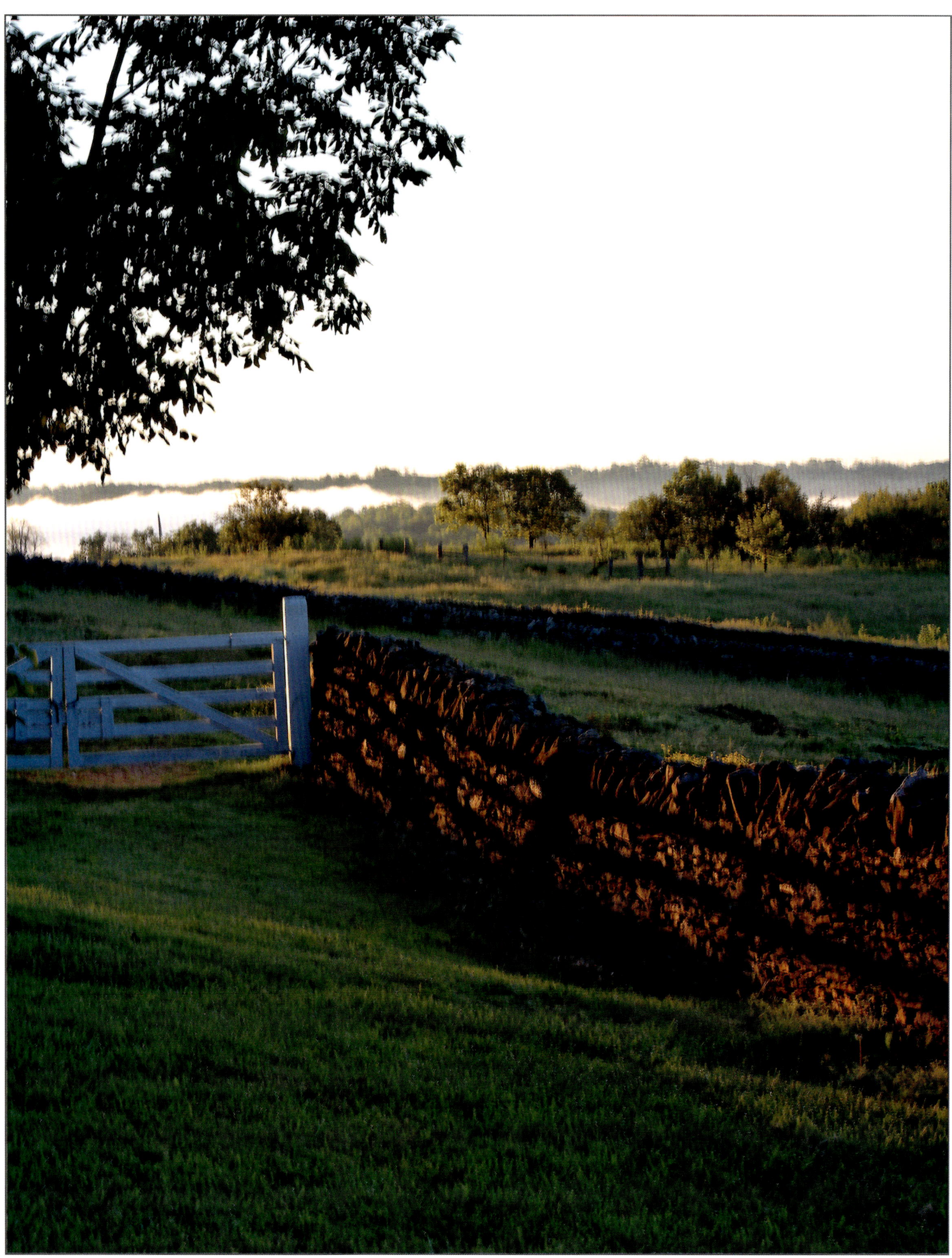

Dry stone fencing is another trademark of Pleasant Hill. The Shakers had up to forty miles of this fencing of which twenty miles exists today. Despite popular belief this was done with slave labor, the Shakers were not in favor of slavery and 1837 journal entries indicate these were constructed by an outside stone mason at a cost of $1,000 per mile at the time. The dry stone fencing at Pleasant Hill is the largest collection under private ownership outside of Great Britain. The international dry stone fencing competition is now held annually at Pleasant Hill.

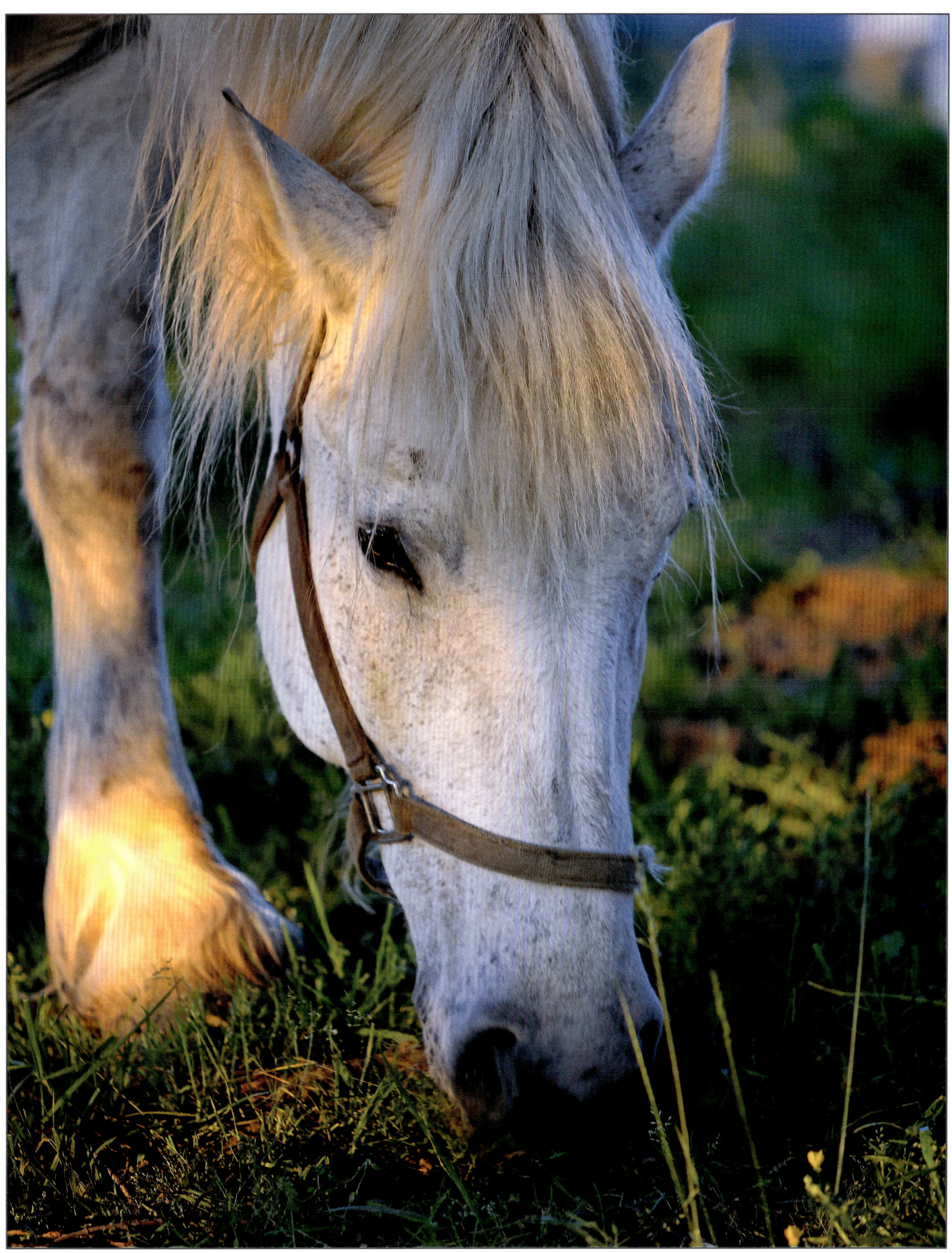

"Ivy", one of two percheron horses at Pleasant Hill, enjoys a morning graze. One of the missions of Pleasant Hill is the maintenance of historic breed stocks such as the percheron.

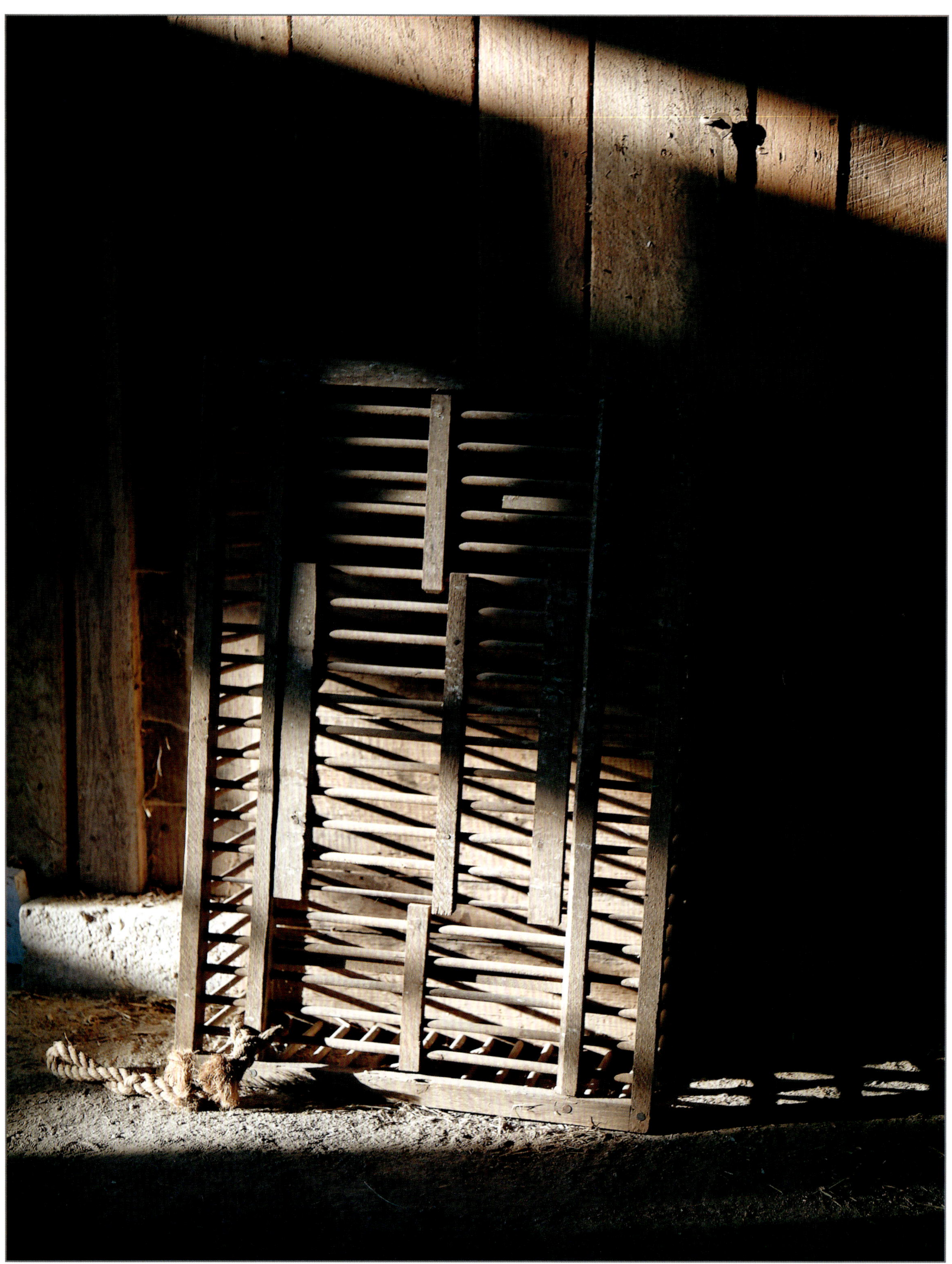

Items inside the barn located on the south side of the Turnpike. While not original to the Village, the structure serves as a shelter for historical breeds of animals and equipment found on the property.

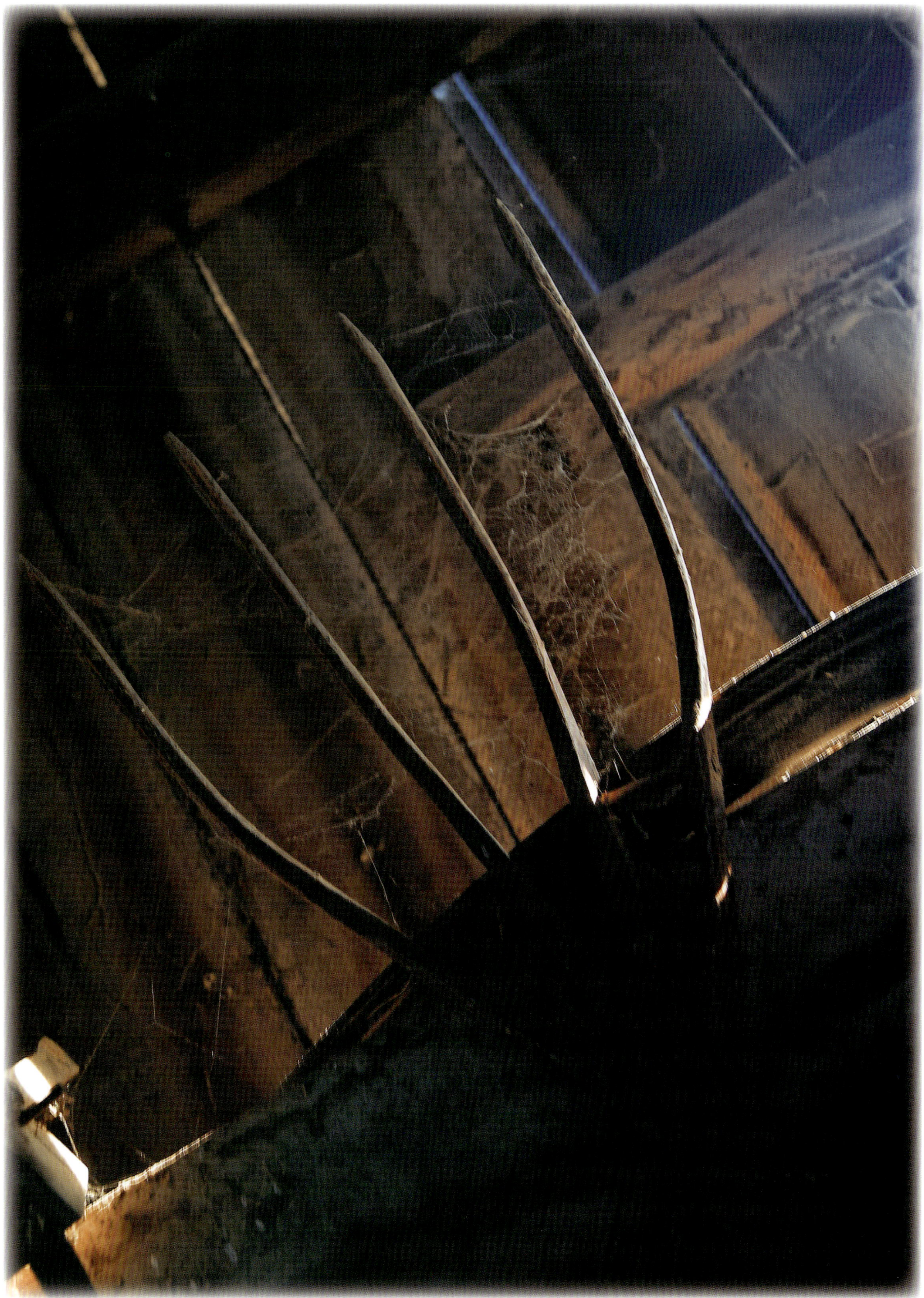

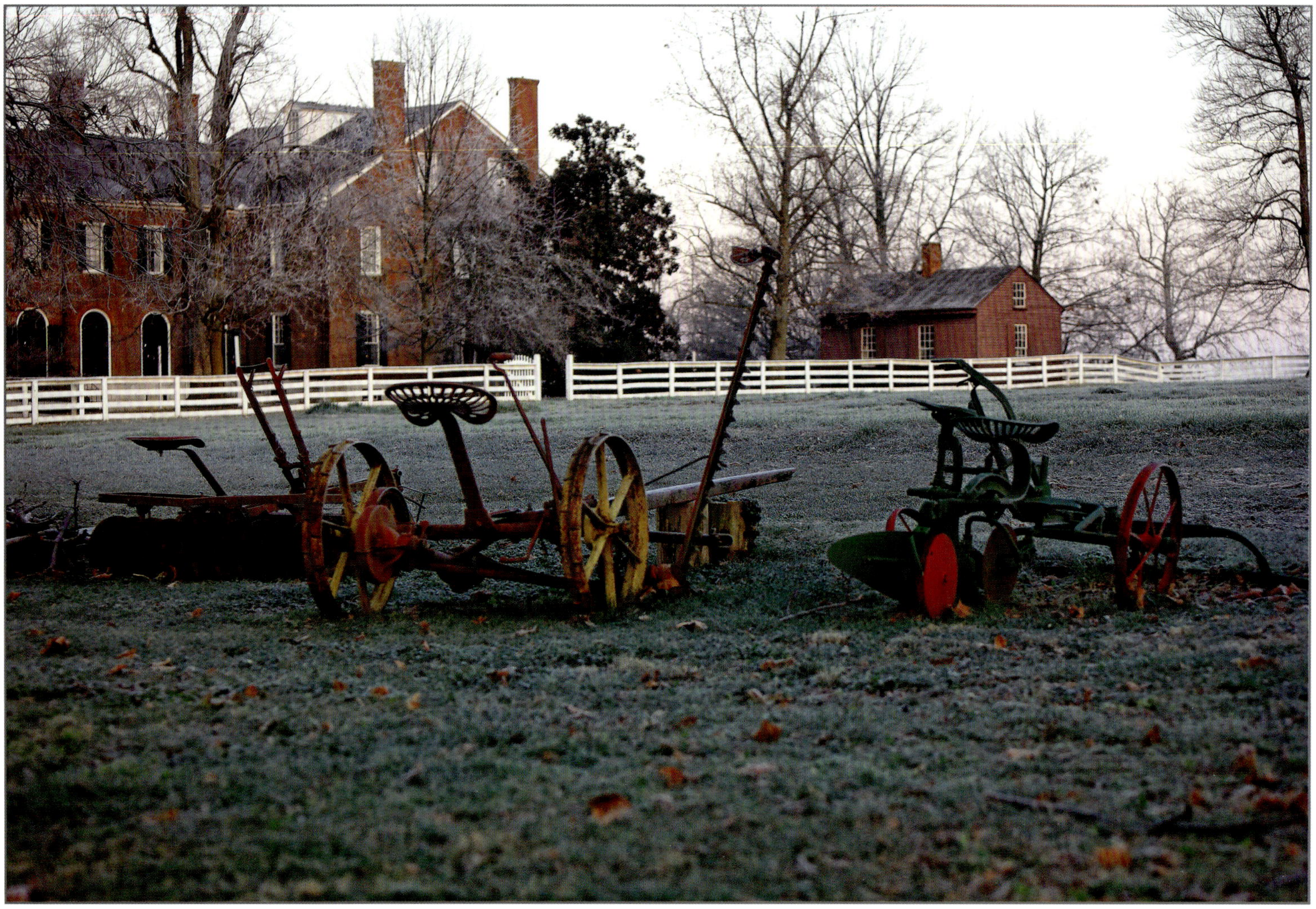

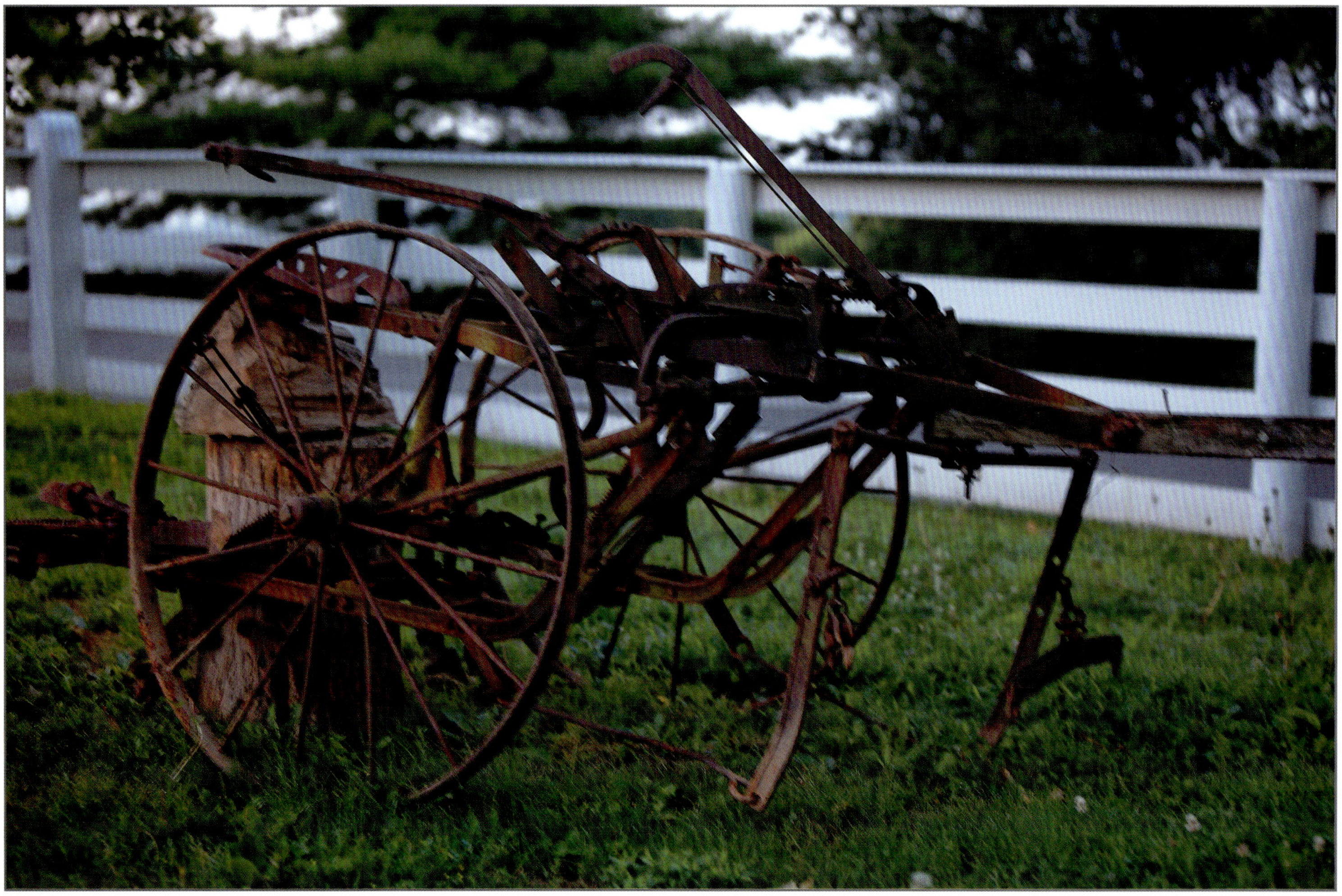

Examples of horse drawn plows and other equipment on display at the Village.

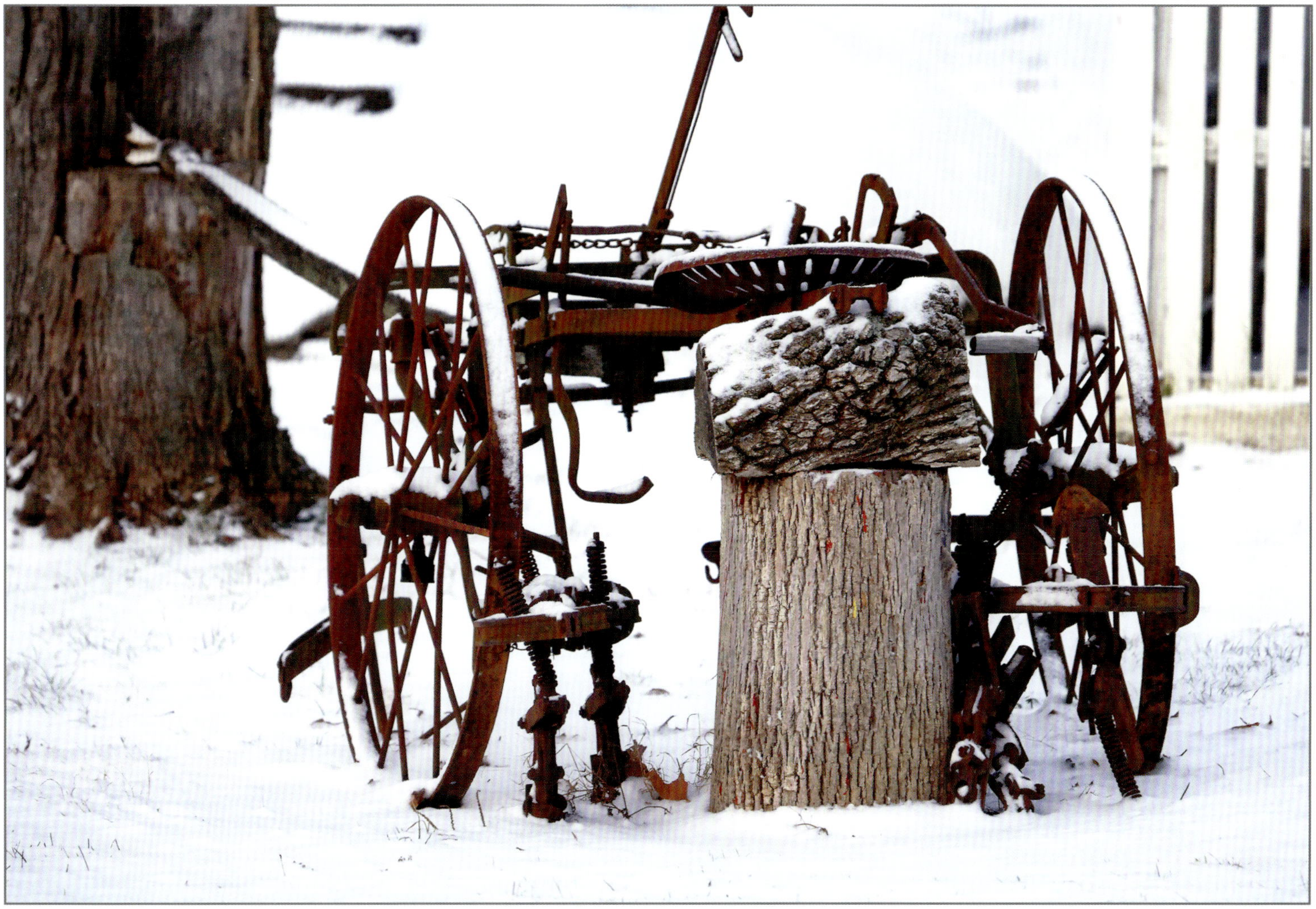

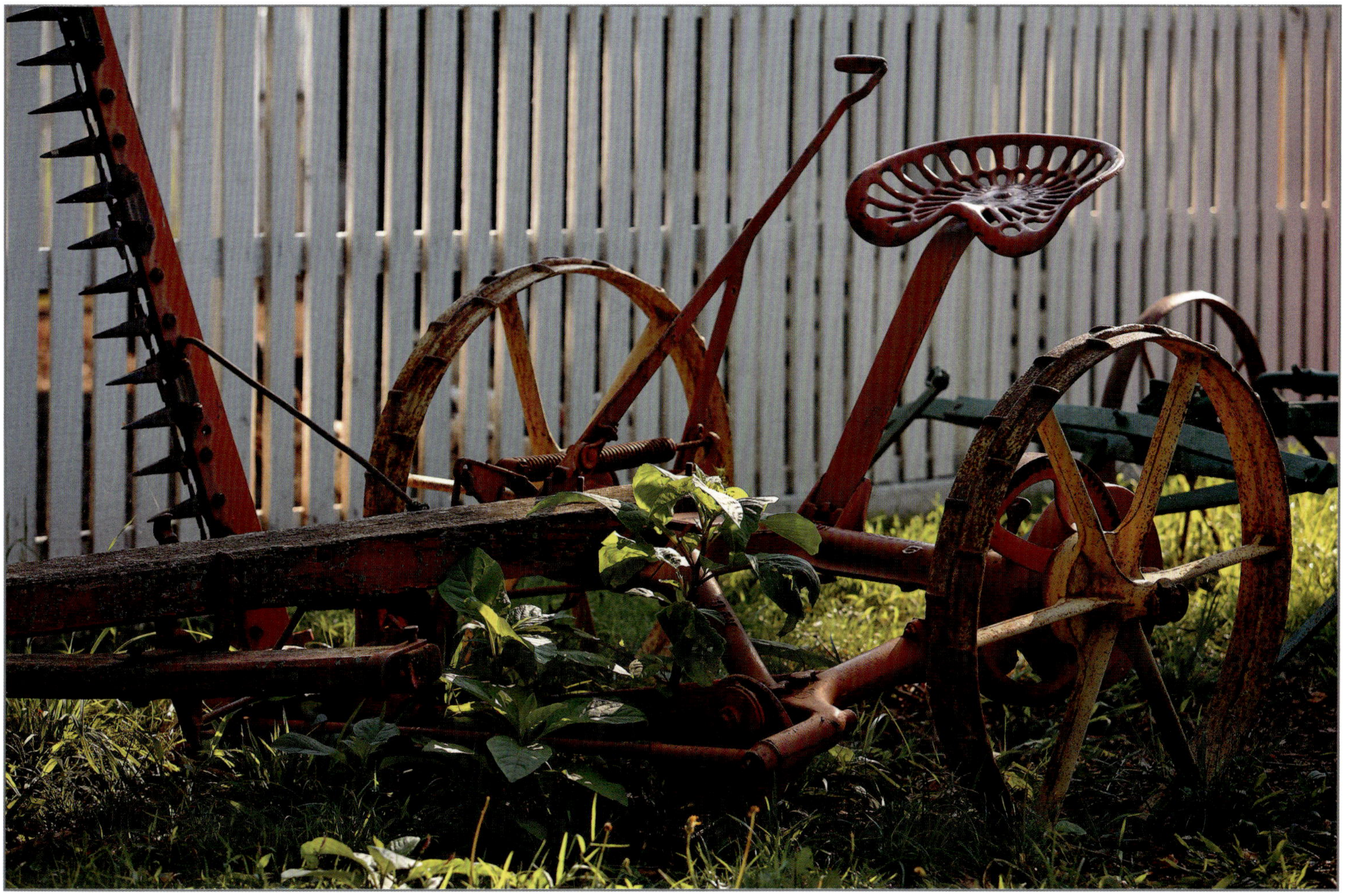

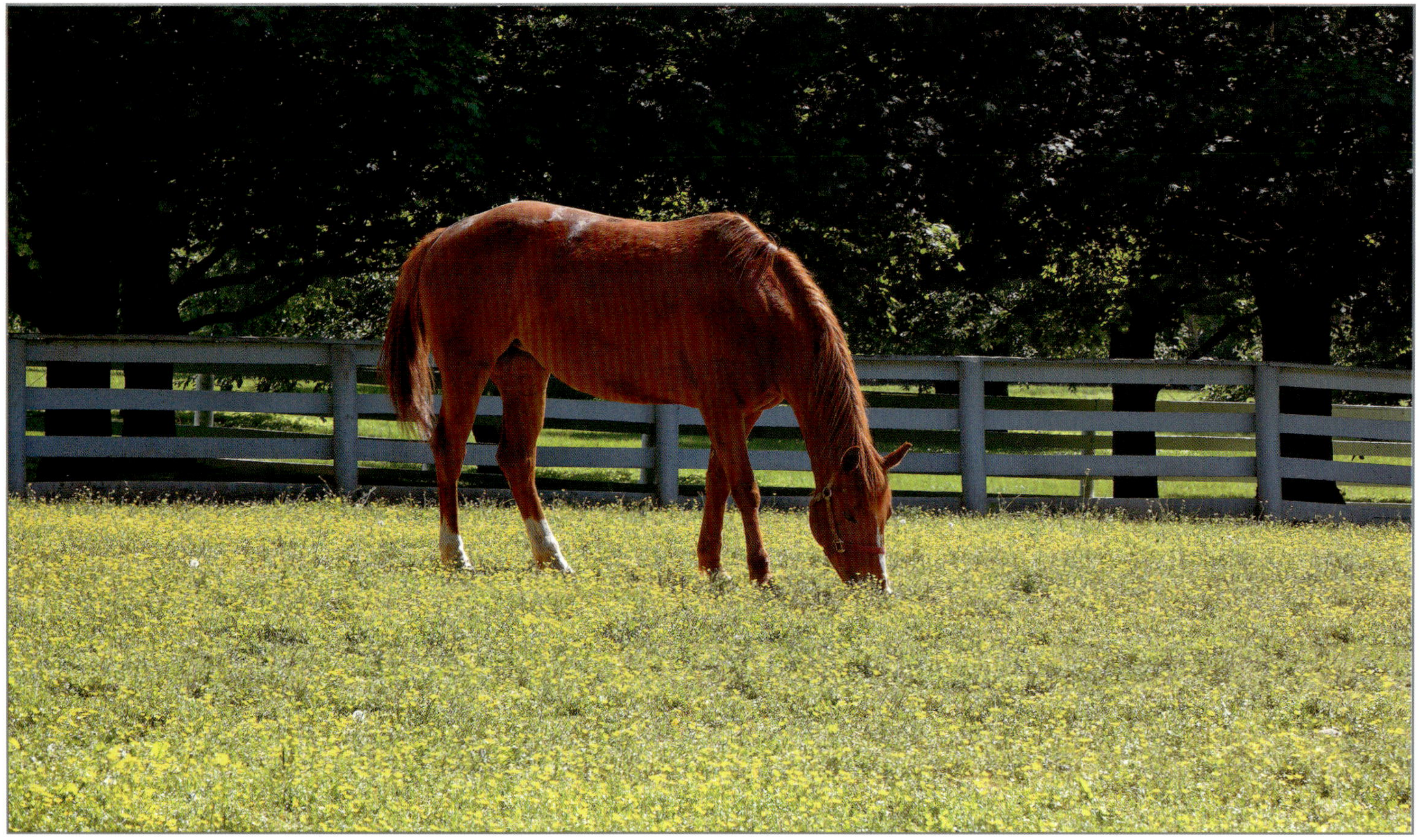

In addition to the draft horses used in the farming operations, the Shakers owned other types of horses for use as transportation.

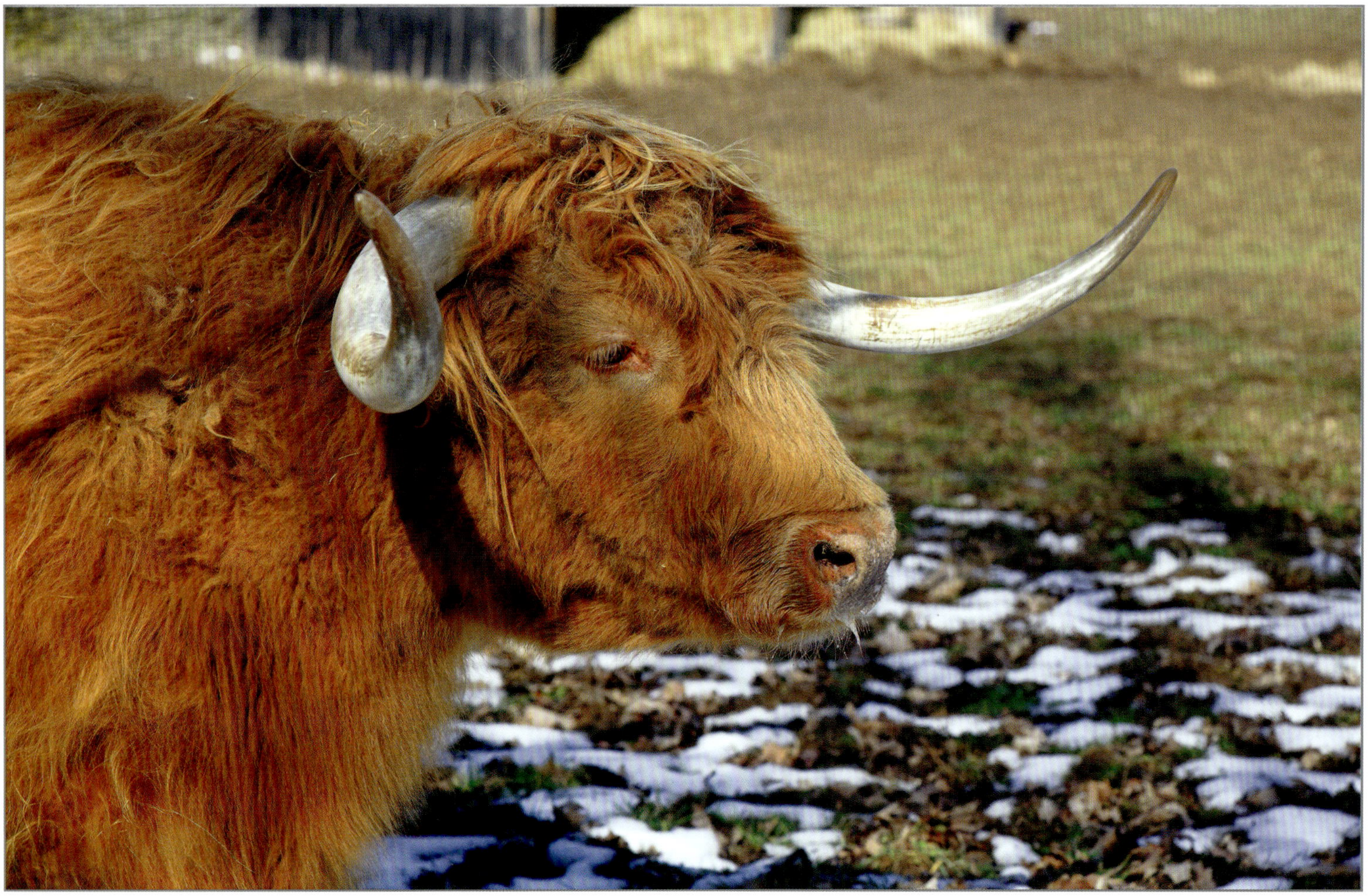

"McDuffy", a Scottish Highlander, is a recent addition to the Village. Although not originally raised at Pleasant Hill, the Scottish Highlander breed was raised for its beef at the Shaker community of Sabbathday Lake in Maine, a tradition that continues there to this day.

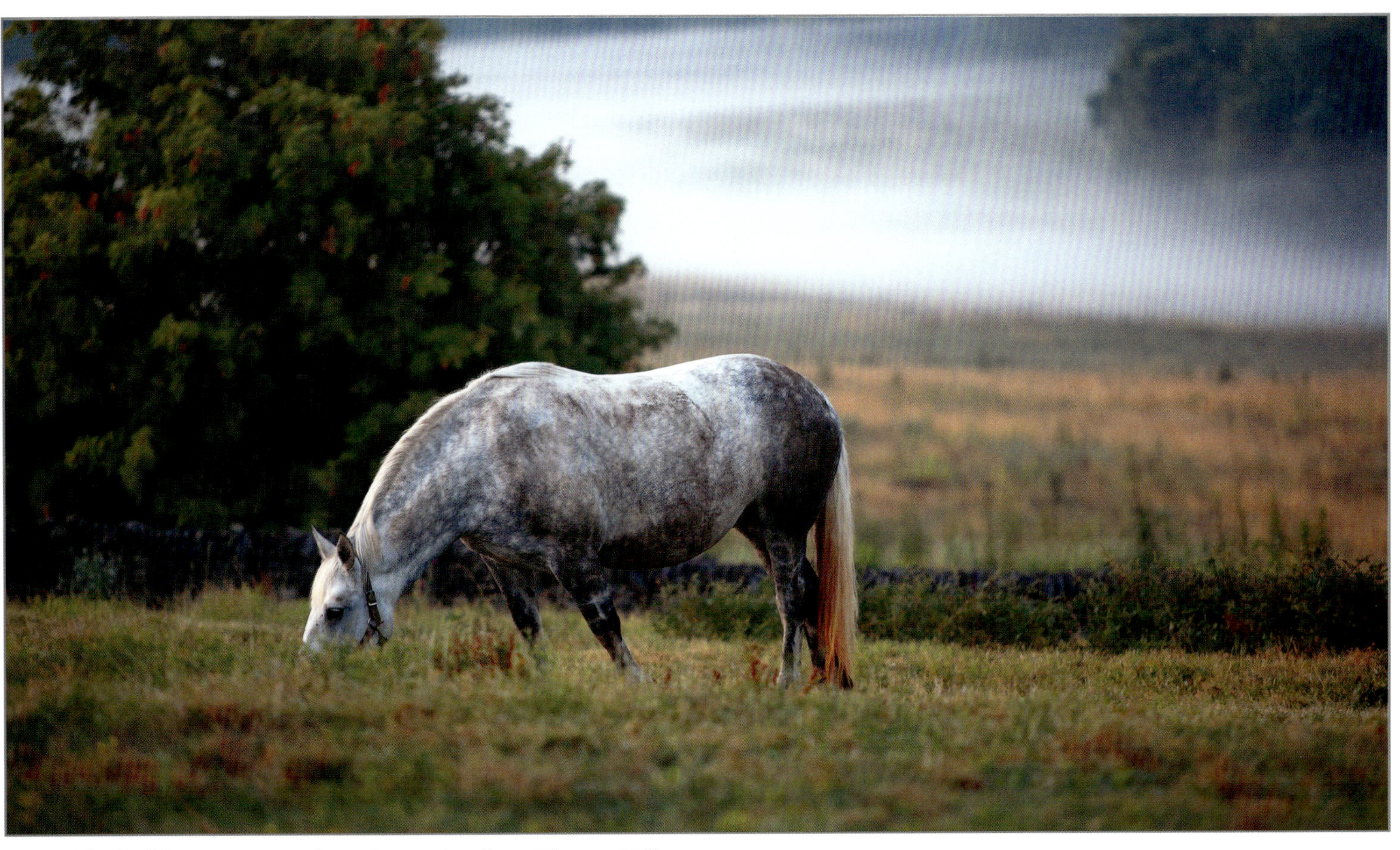

One of the draft horses grazes in the early morning fog at Pleasant Hill.

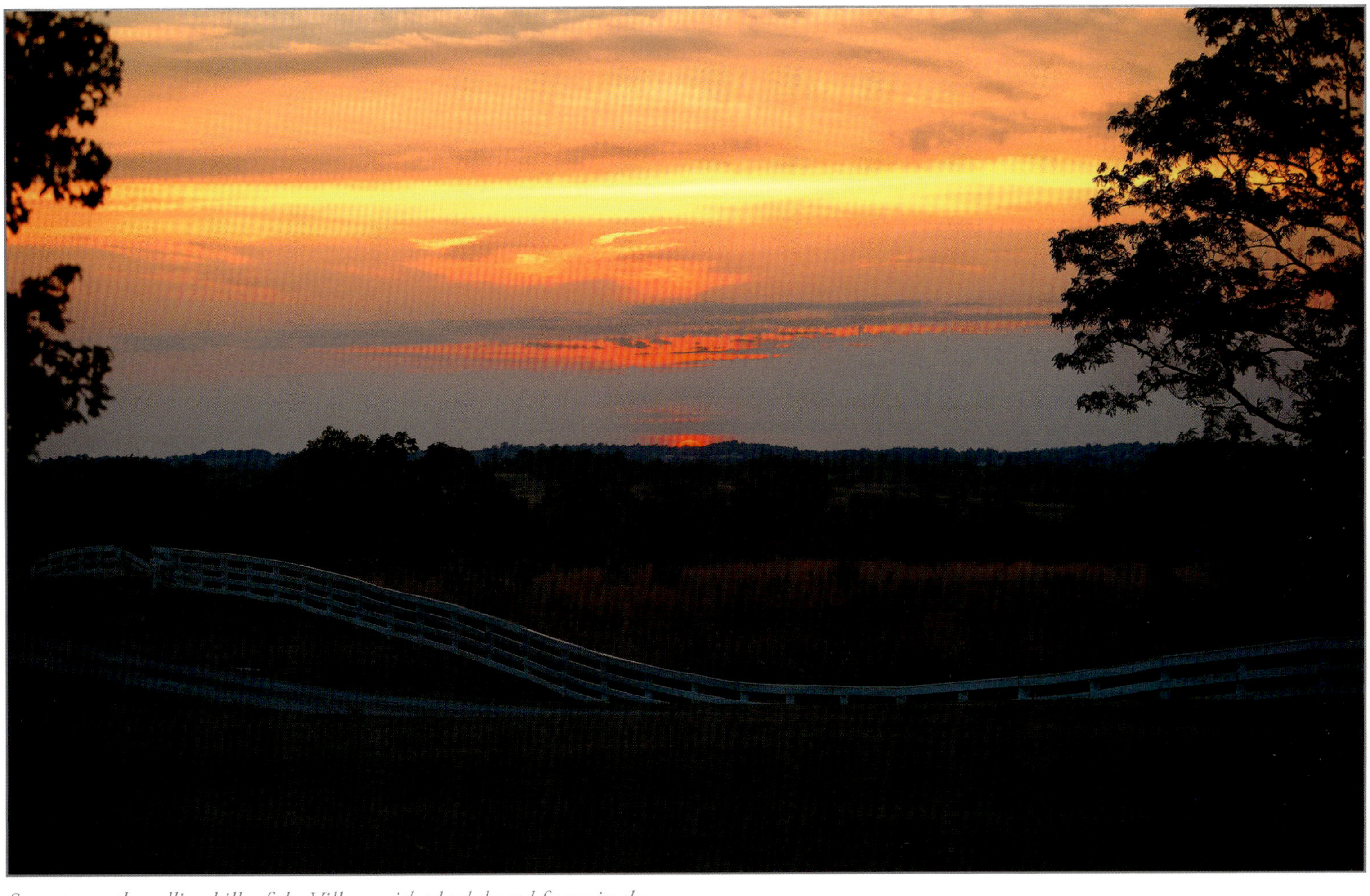

Sunset over the rolling hills of the Village with plank board fences in the foreground.

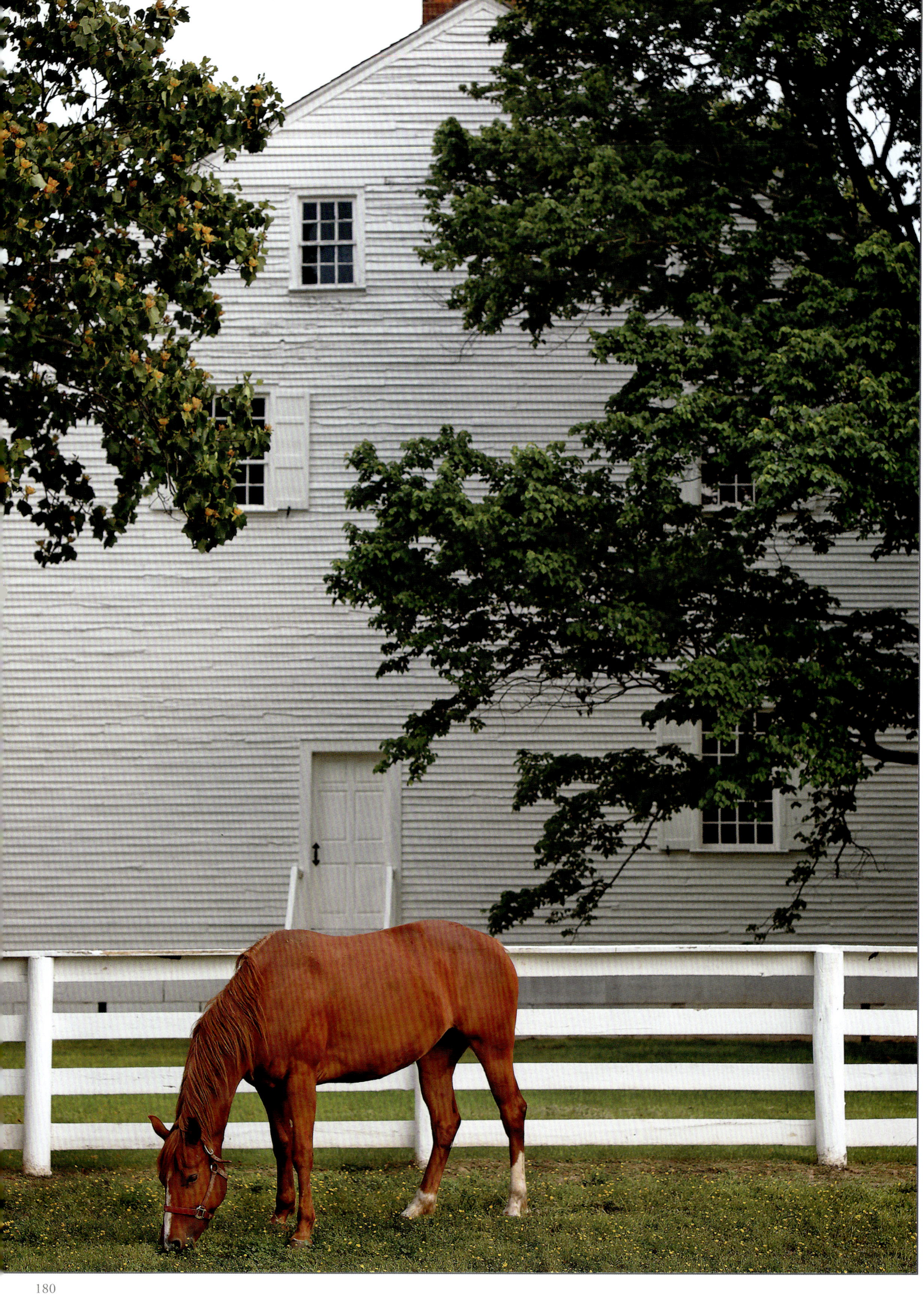

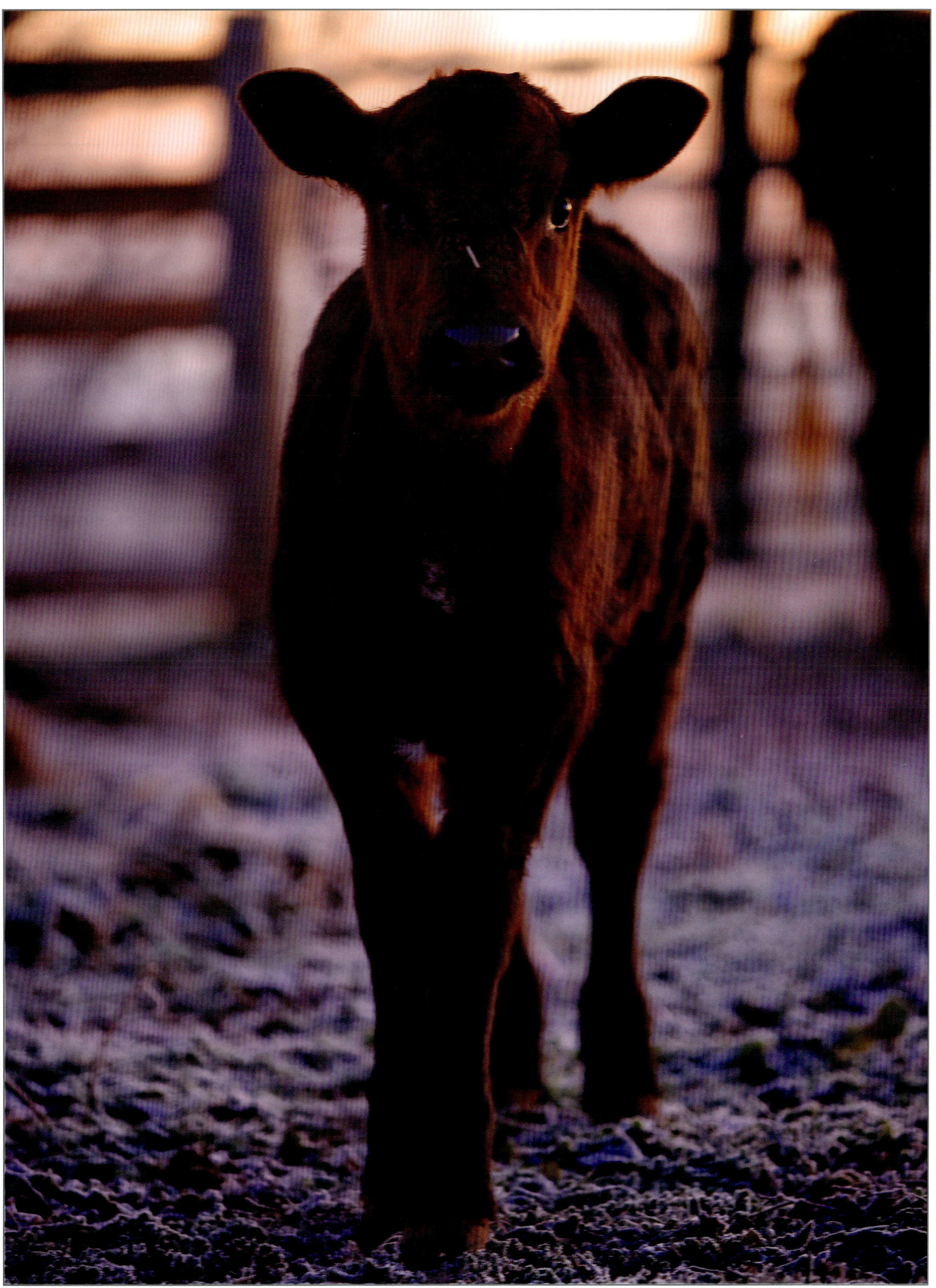

A curious calf strikes a pose in the early morning sunrise.

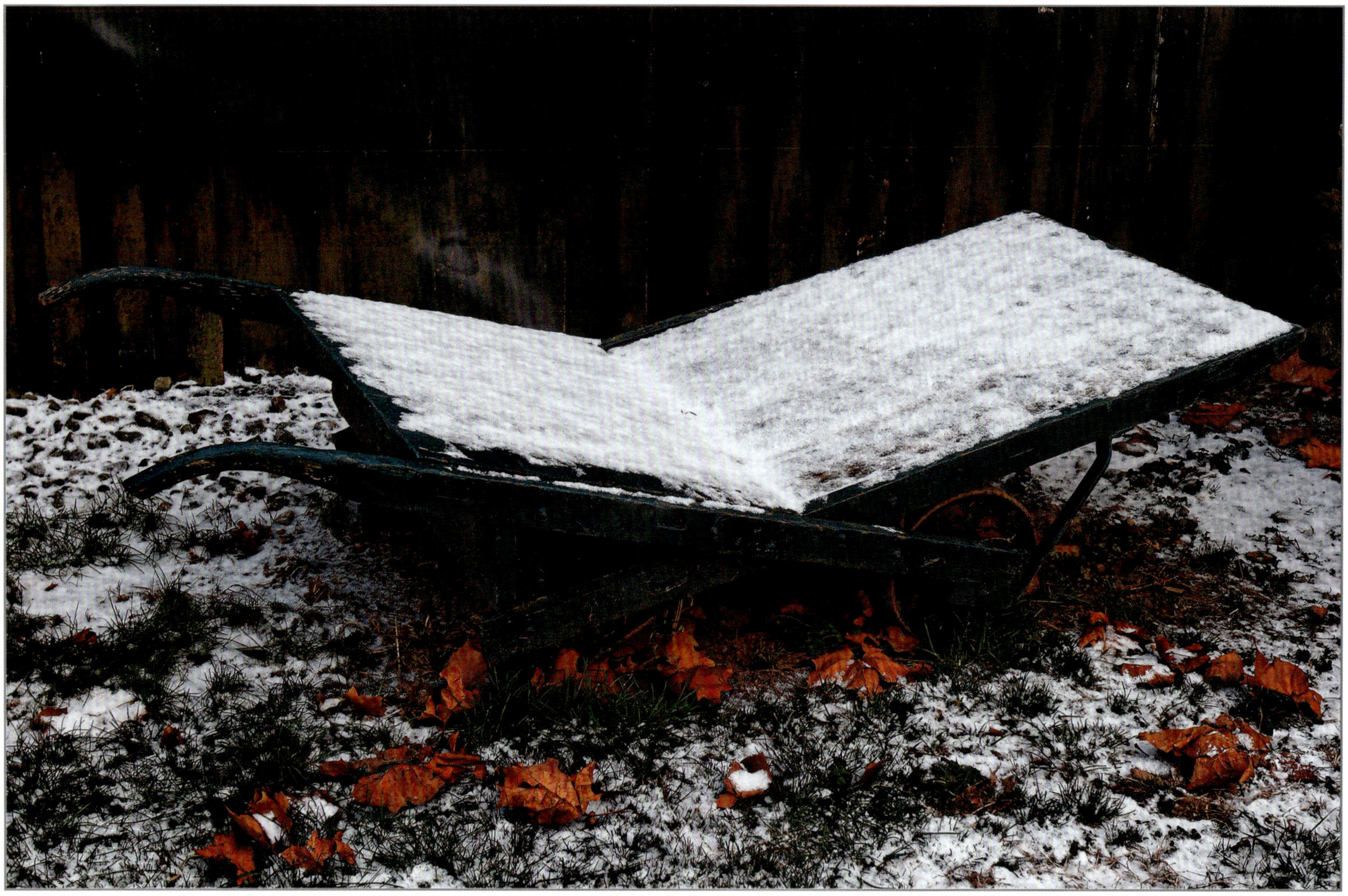

A steel-wheeled wheel barrel sits outside the barn on a winter's morning.

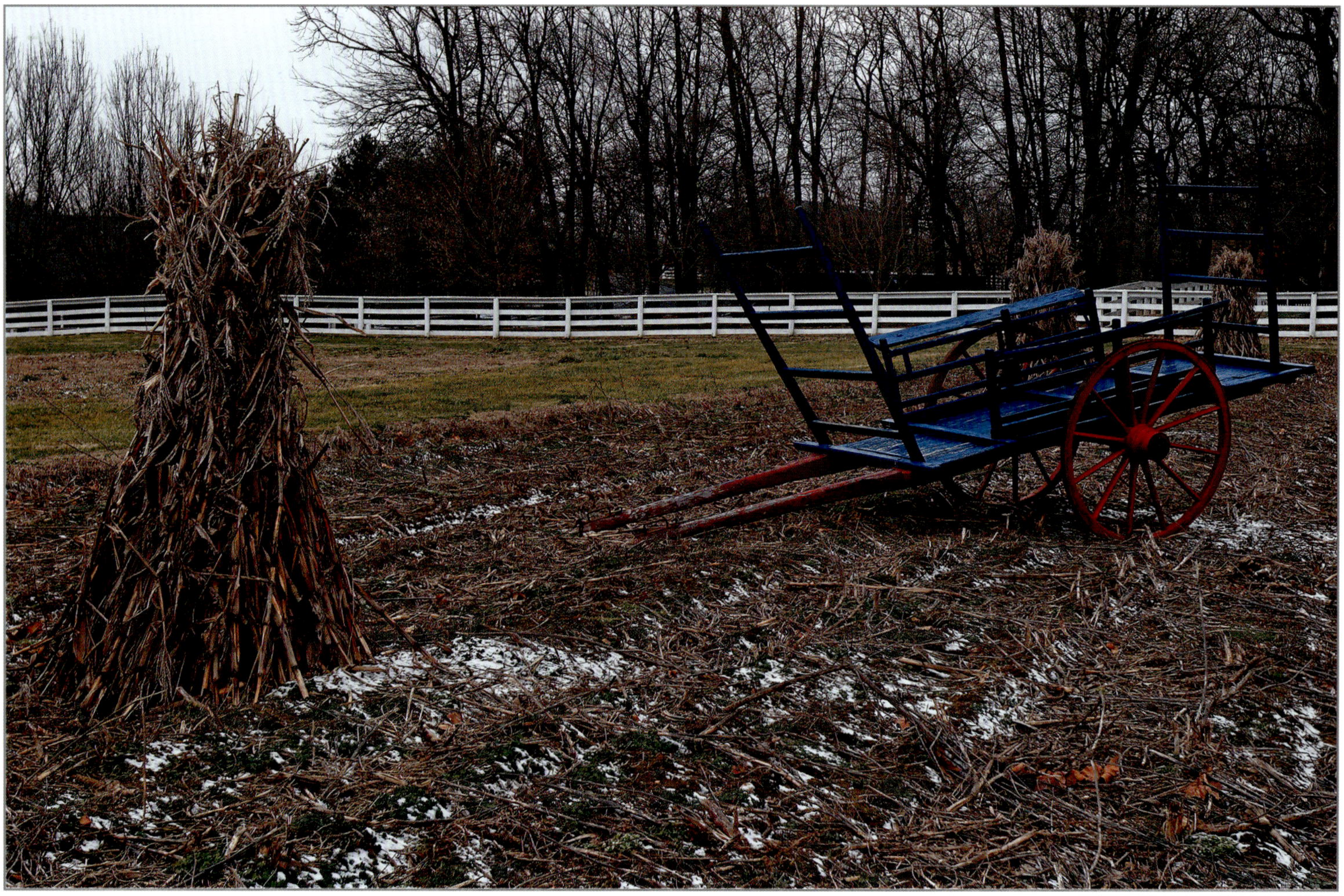

Fodder stalks were gathered after harvest and used as feed for the animals.

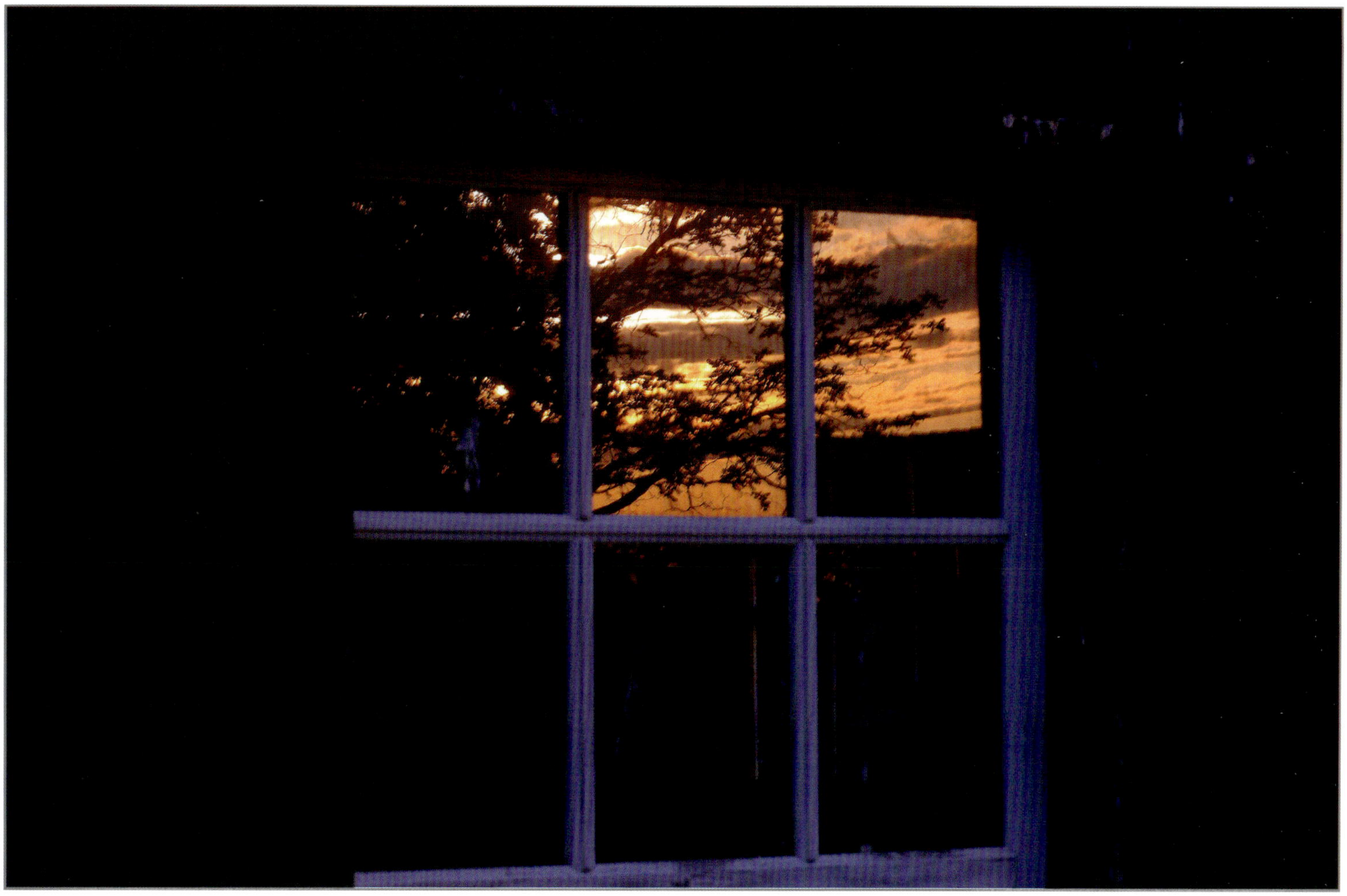

An early morning sunrise is reflected in the window of one of the outbuildings.

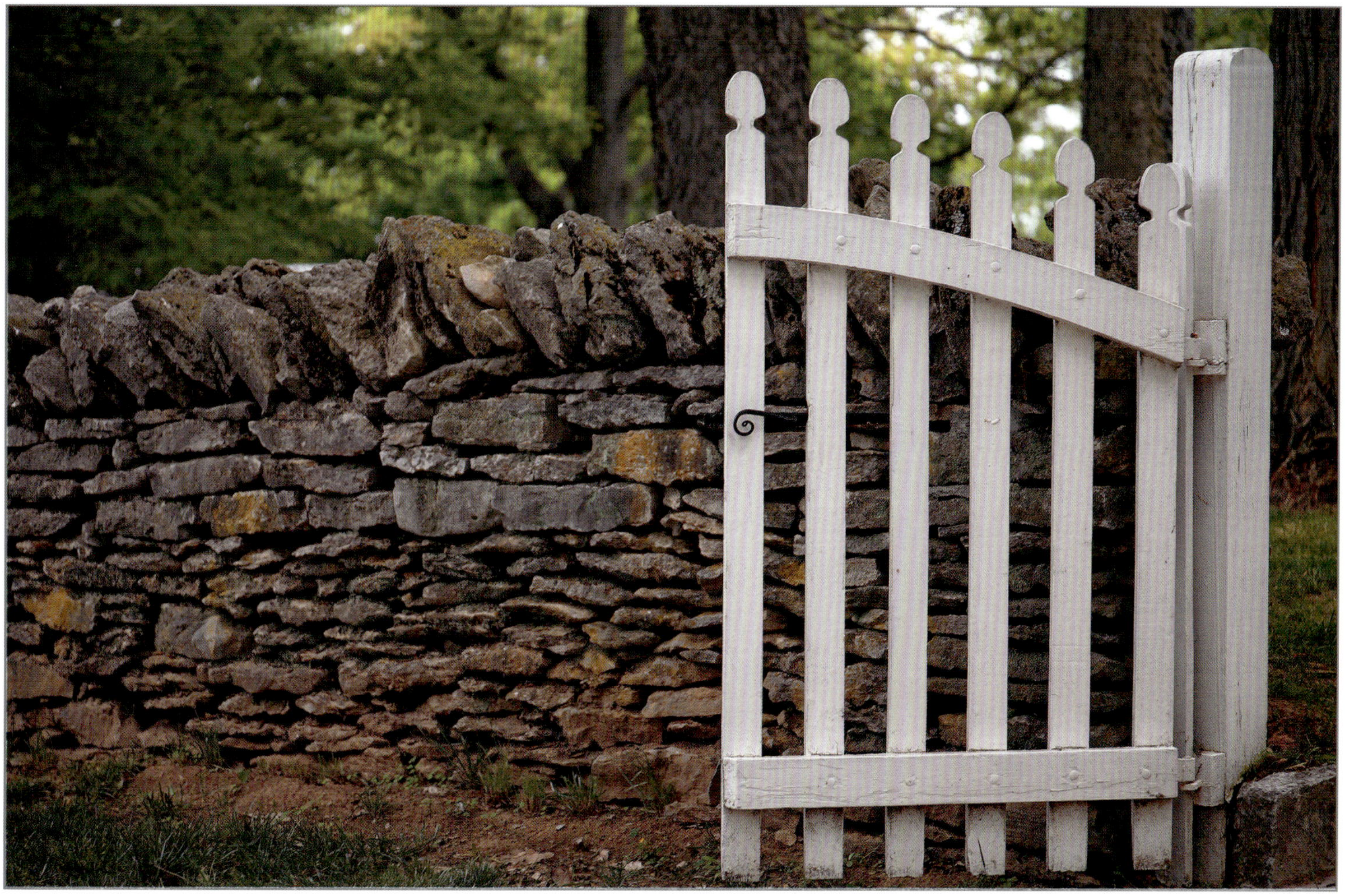

Another example of the dry stone fencing and decorative gates so common at the Village.

Remnants of building foundations at the North Lot Gathering Order.

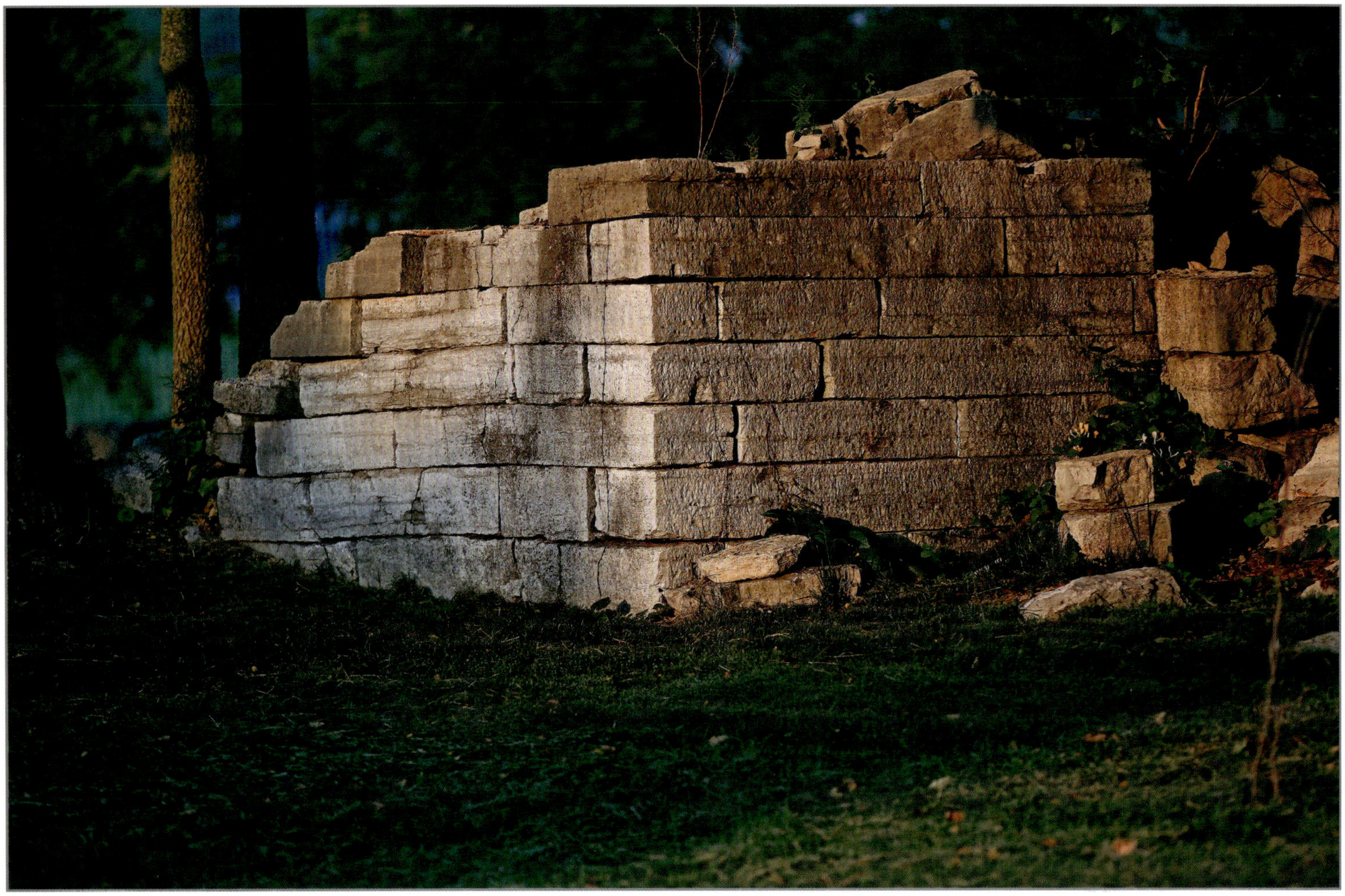

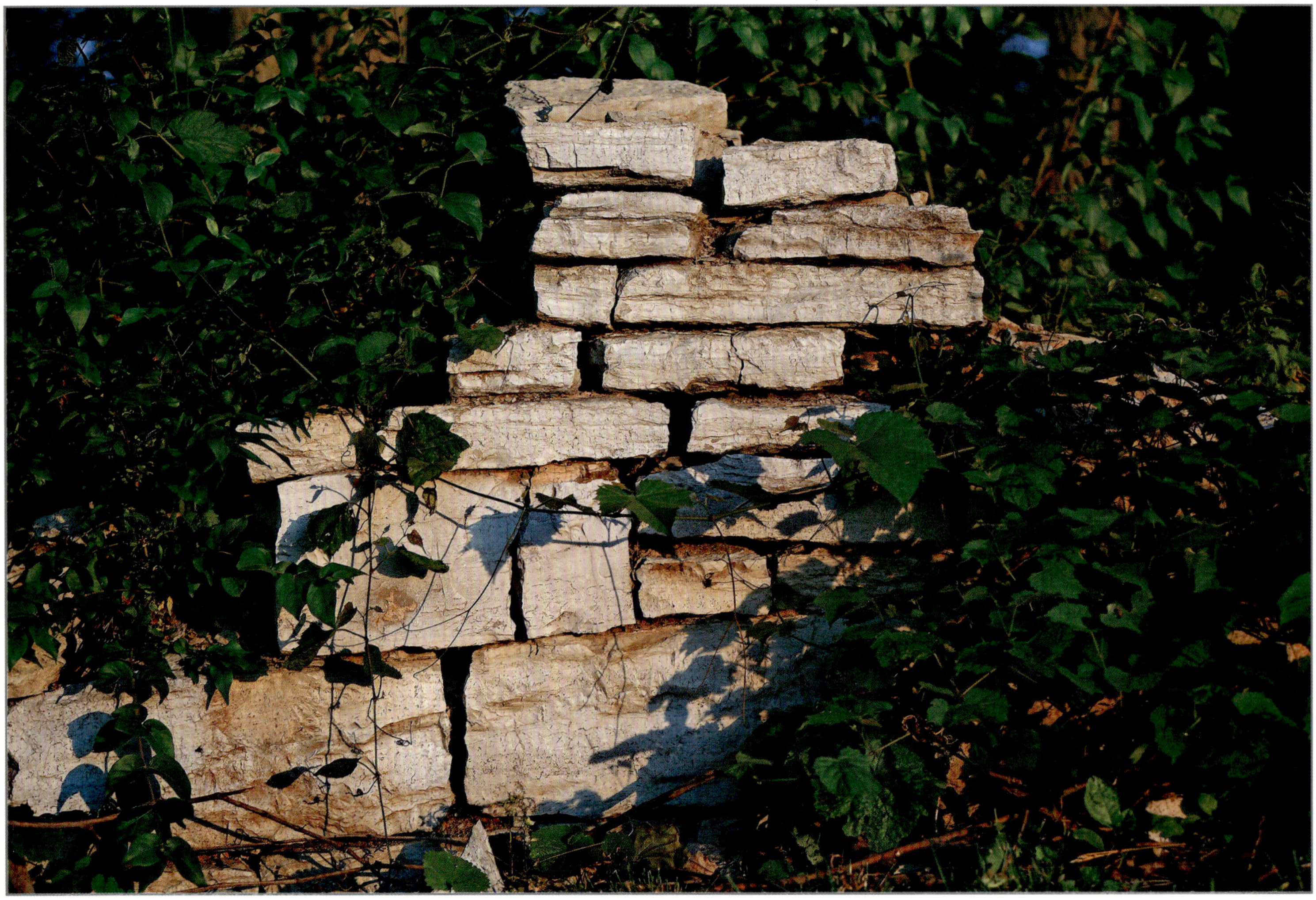

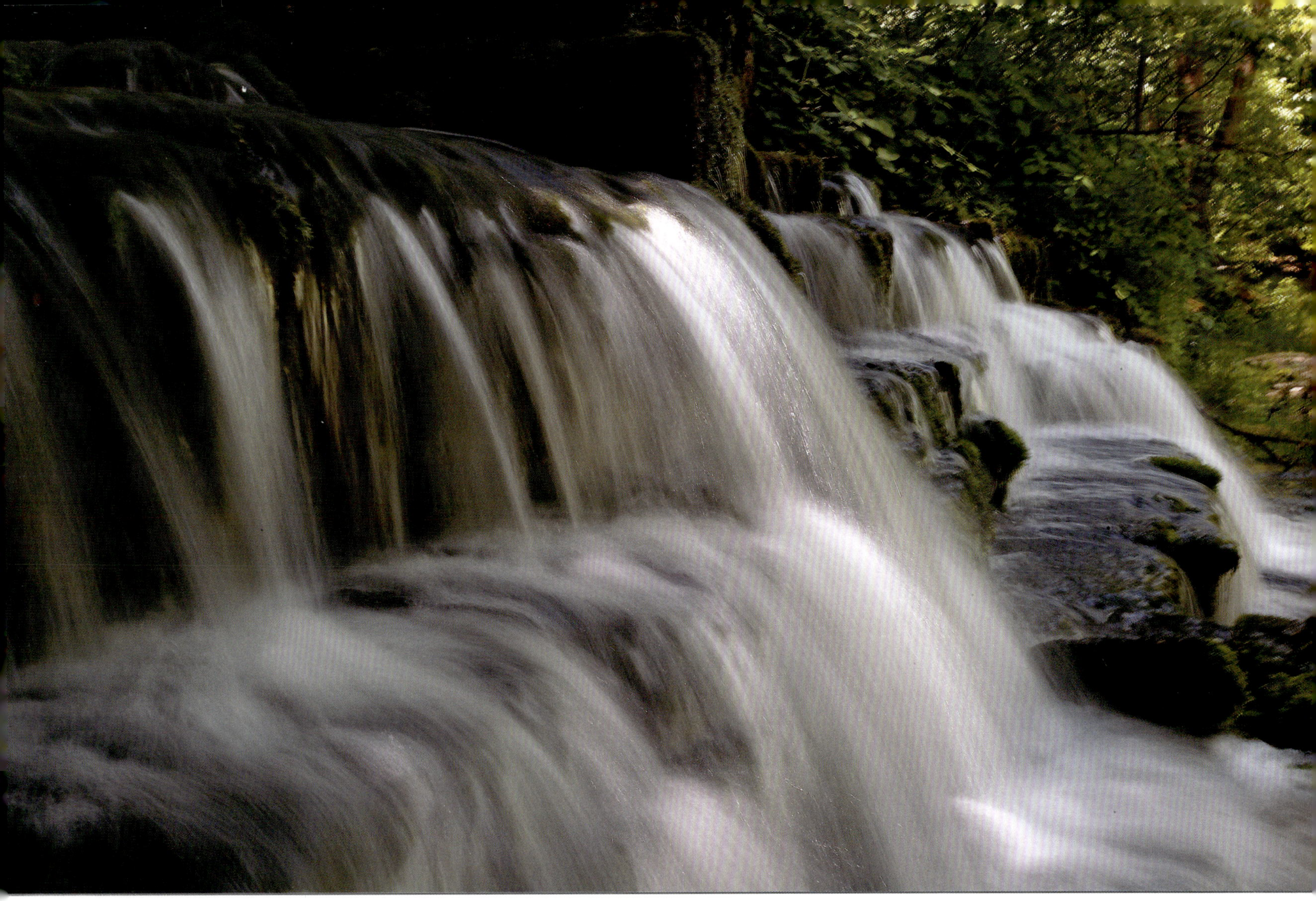

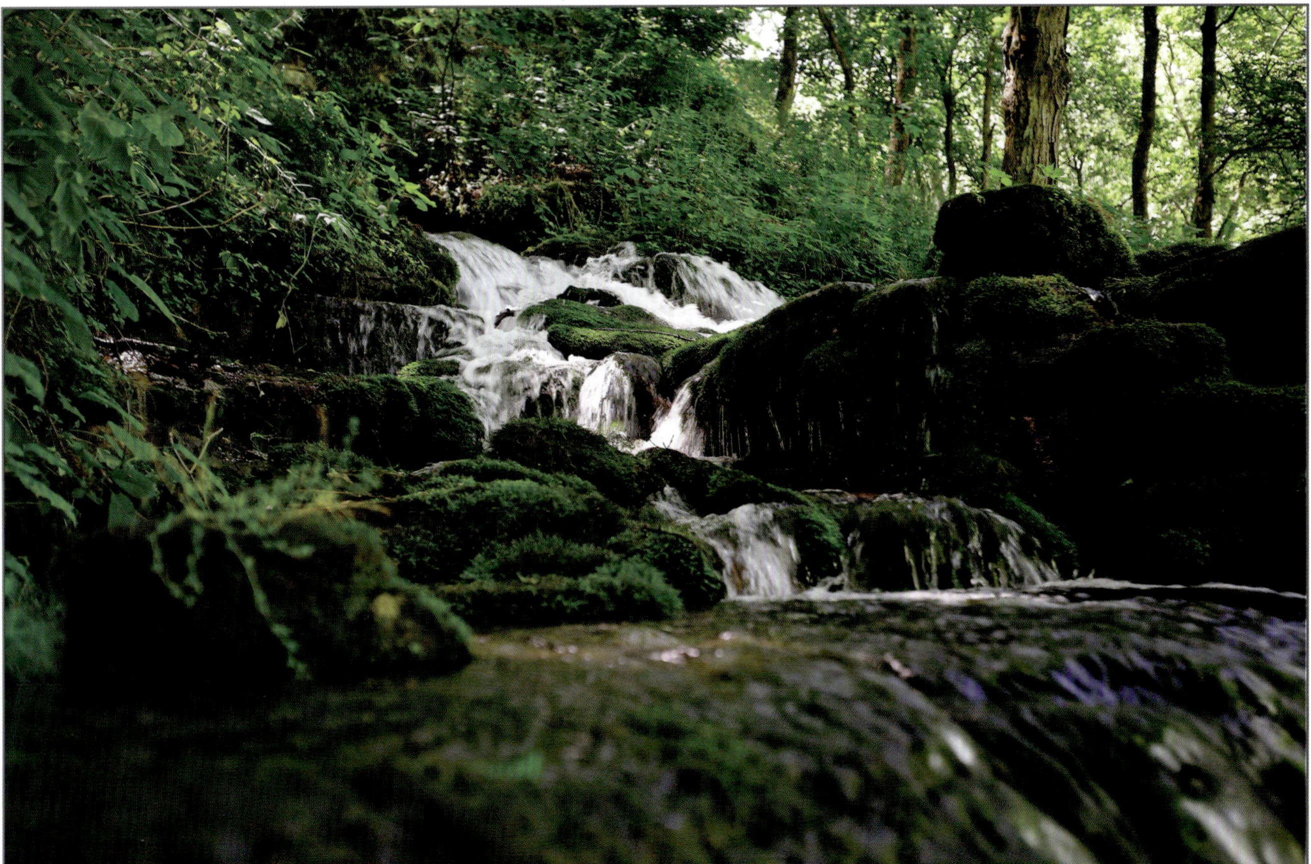

The Fulling Mill Falls, a spring fed waterfall that empties into Shawnee Creek, powered the fulling mill and grist mill once located there. After a piece of cloth had been woven, it was taken to the fulling mill where wooden hammers would pound it with fuller's earth in order to scour and cleanse it. The cloth was then hung on tenter frames to be stretched back to its original size.

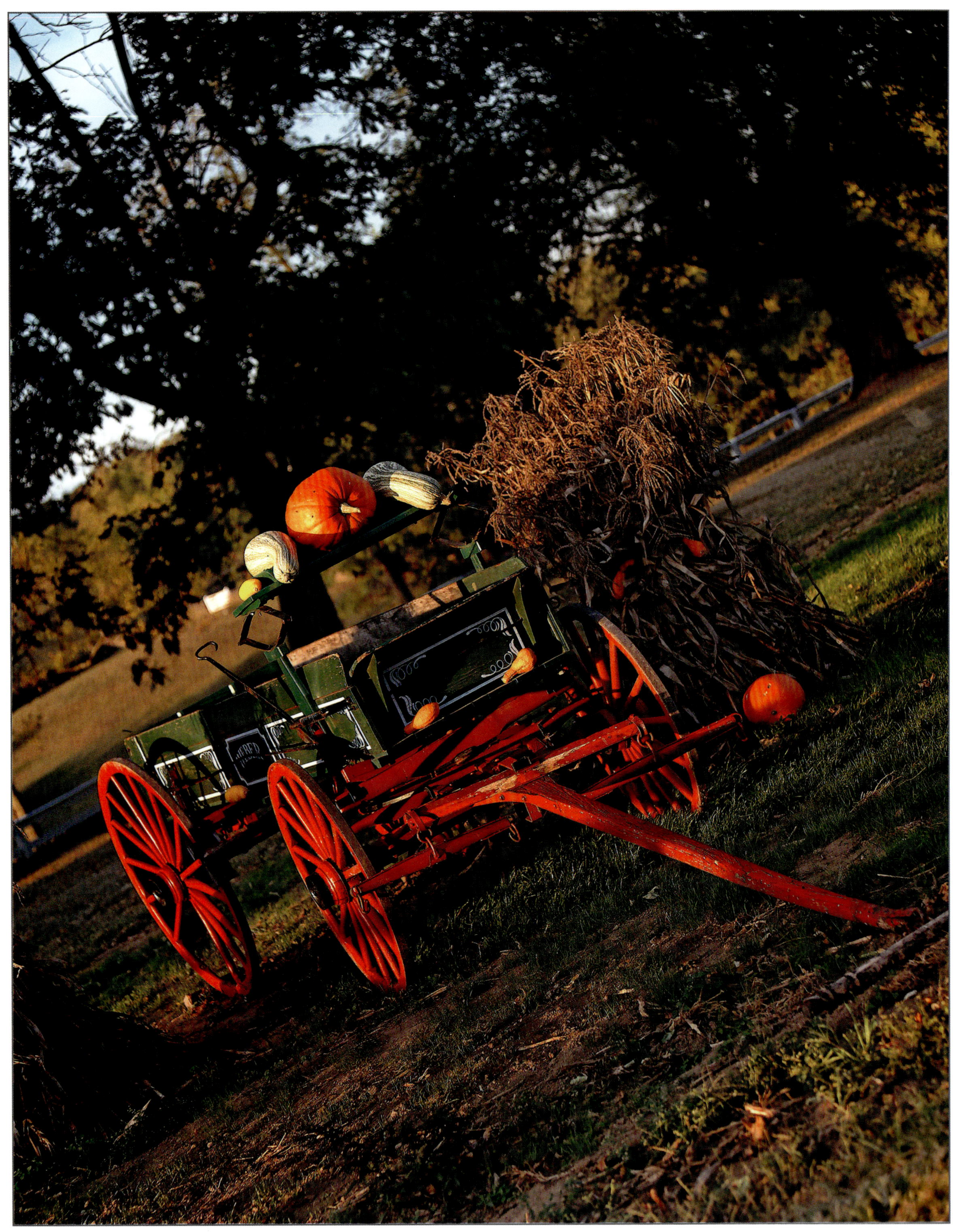

A period wagon with fruits of the harvest.

Opposite: Blacksmiths were another of the skilled trades at the Village. Shutter dogs and hinges for the buildings along with the tools that were used at the Village were made on-site.

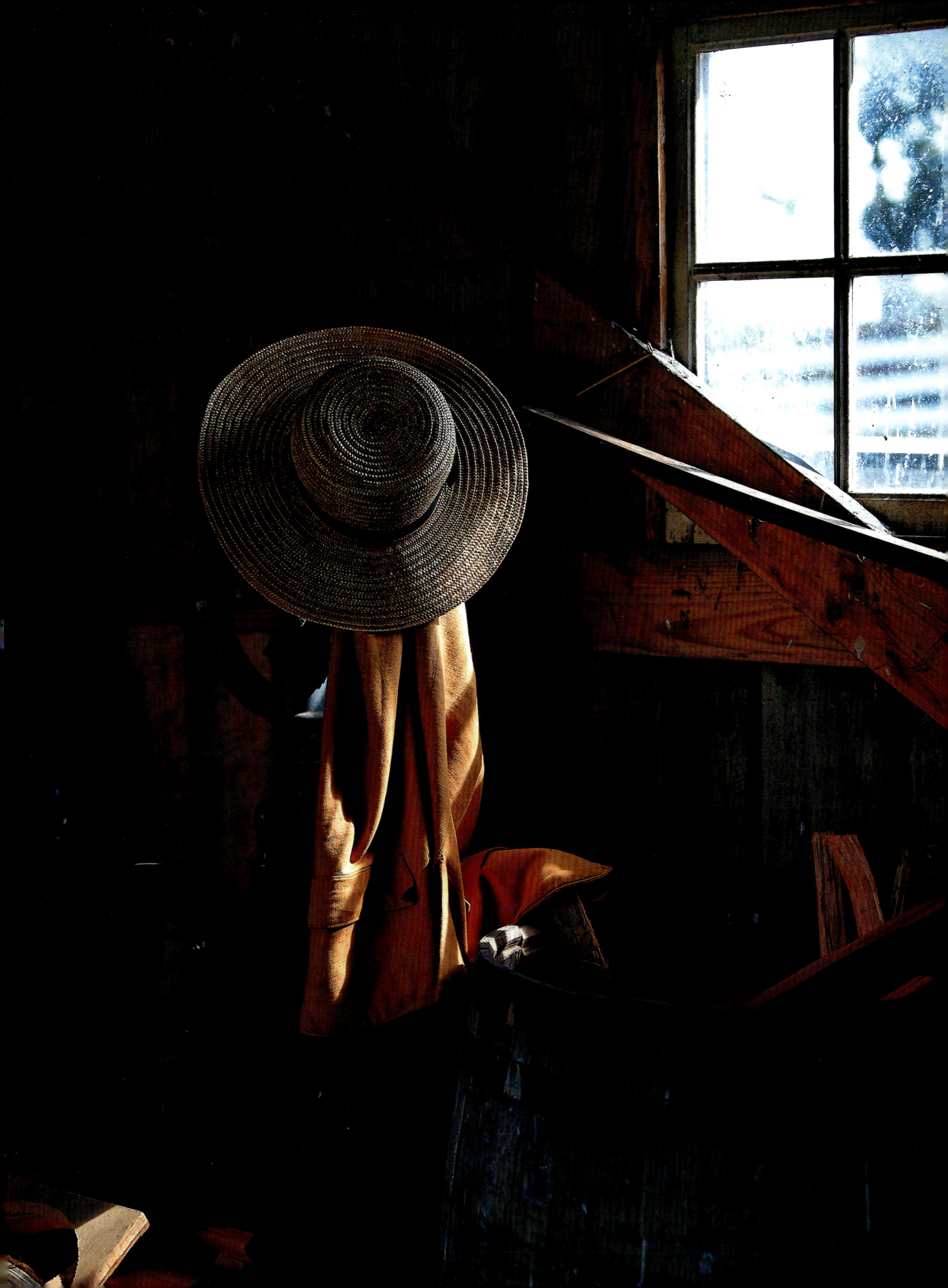

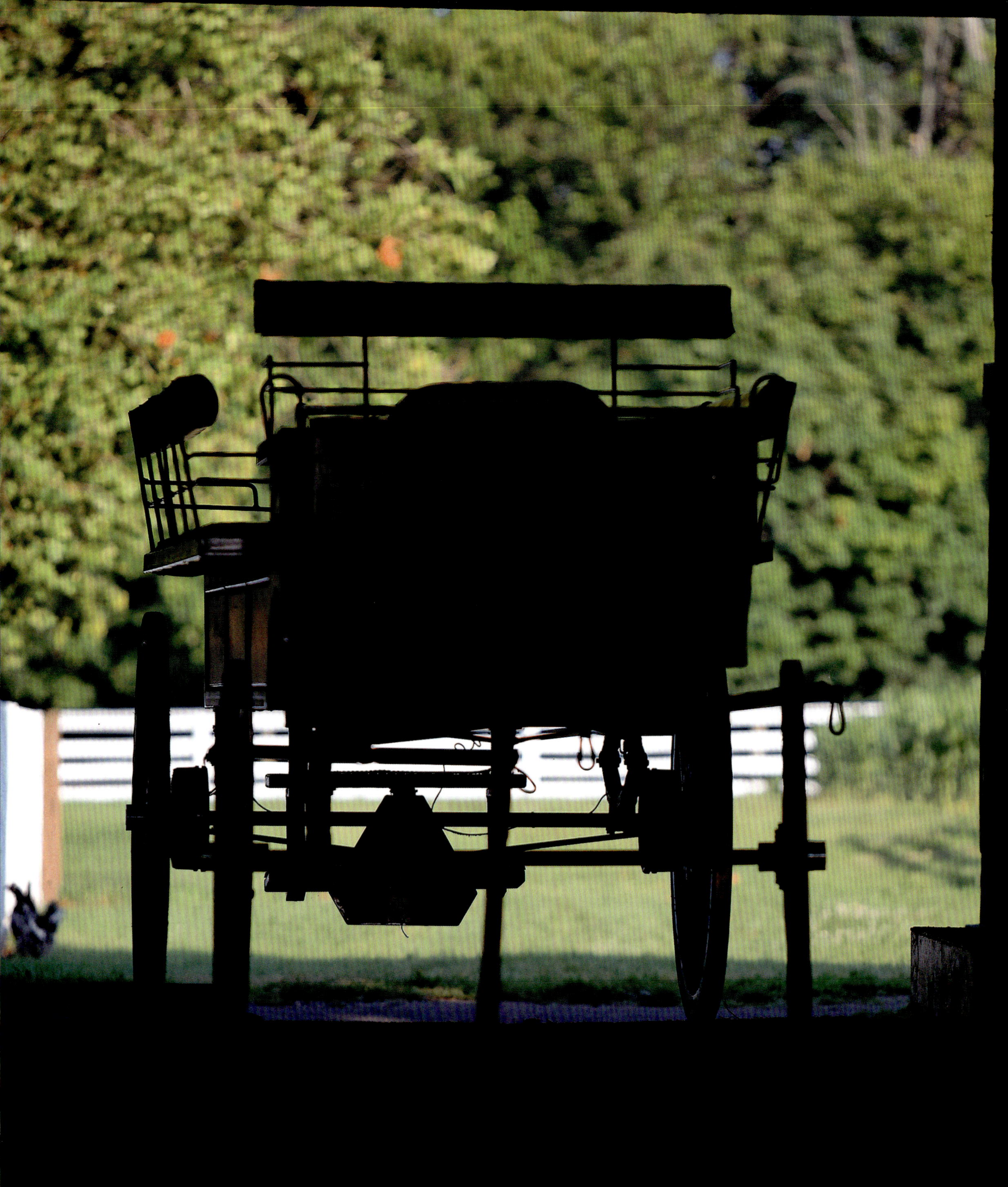

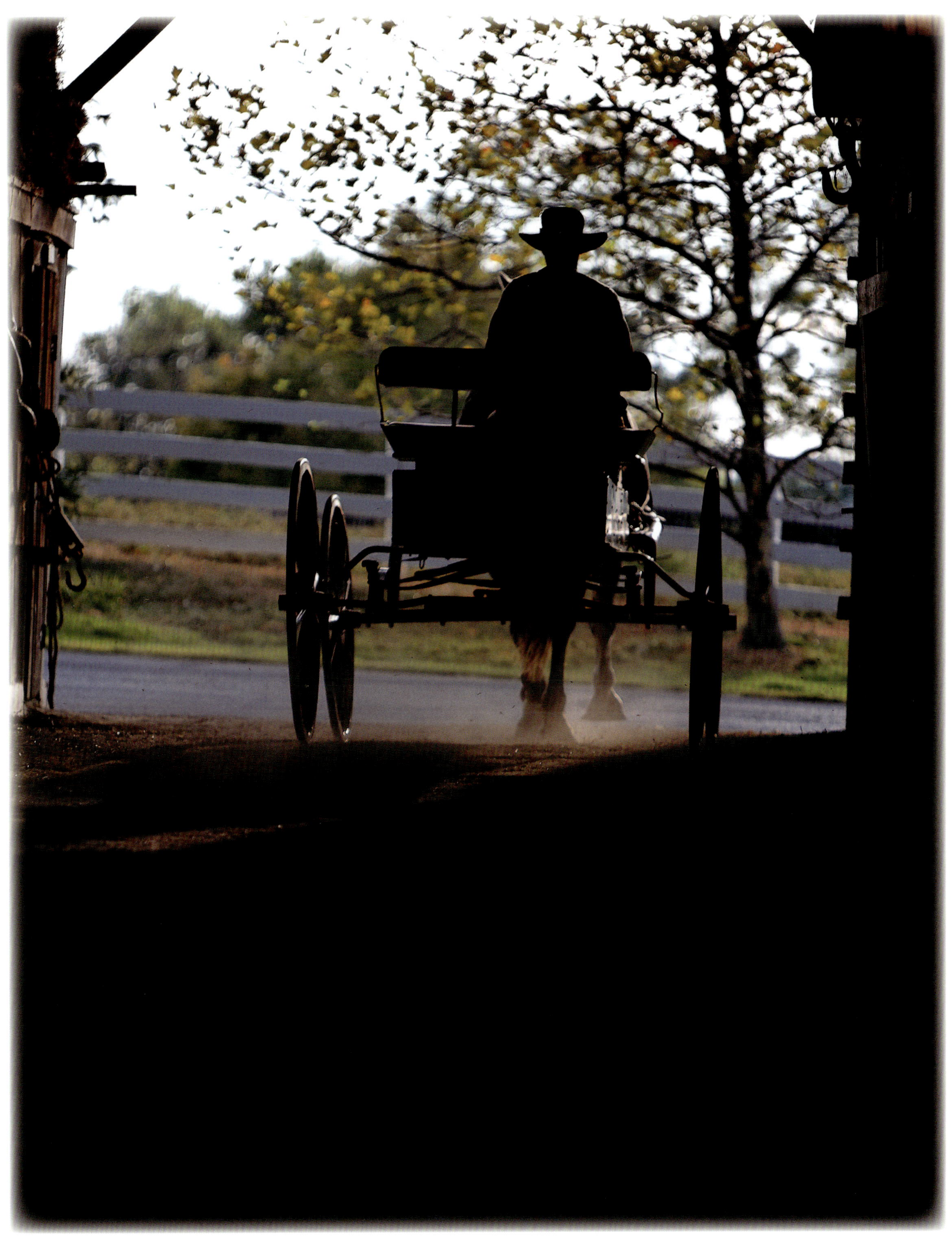

An example of a horse drawn wagon used at Pleasant Hill. The Shakers owned many pieces of "rolling stock" for both farm use and transportation. Centrally located on the Turnpike with easy access to rail and water routes, the Shakers traveled extensively. Some hold the belief the Shakers cloistered themselves in the Village once joining the order. Journal entries speak of the salesman, or "Trading Deacons" as they were called, traveling as far south as New Orleans to conduct business. Groups of Sisters, accompanied by at least one Brother, would travel to Lexington and other cities to shop. Visits to other Shaker communities were also very common.

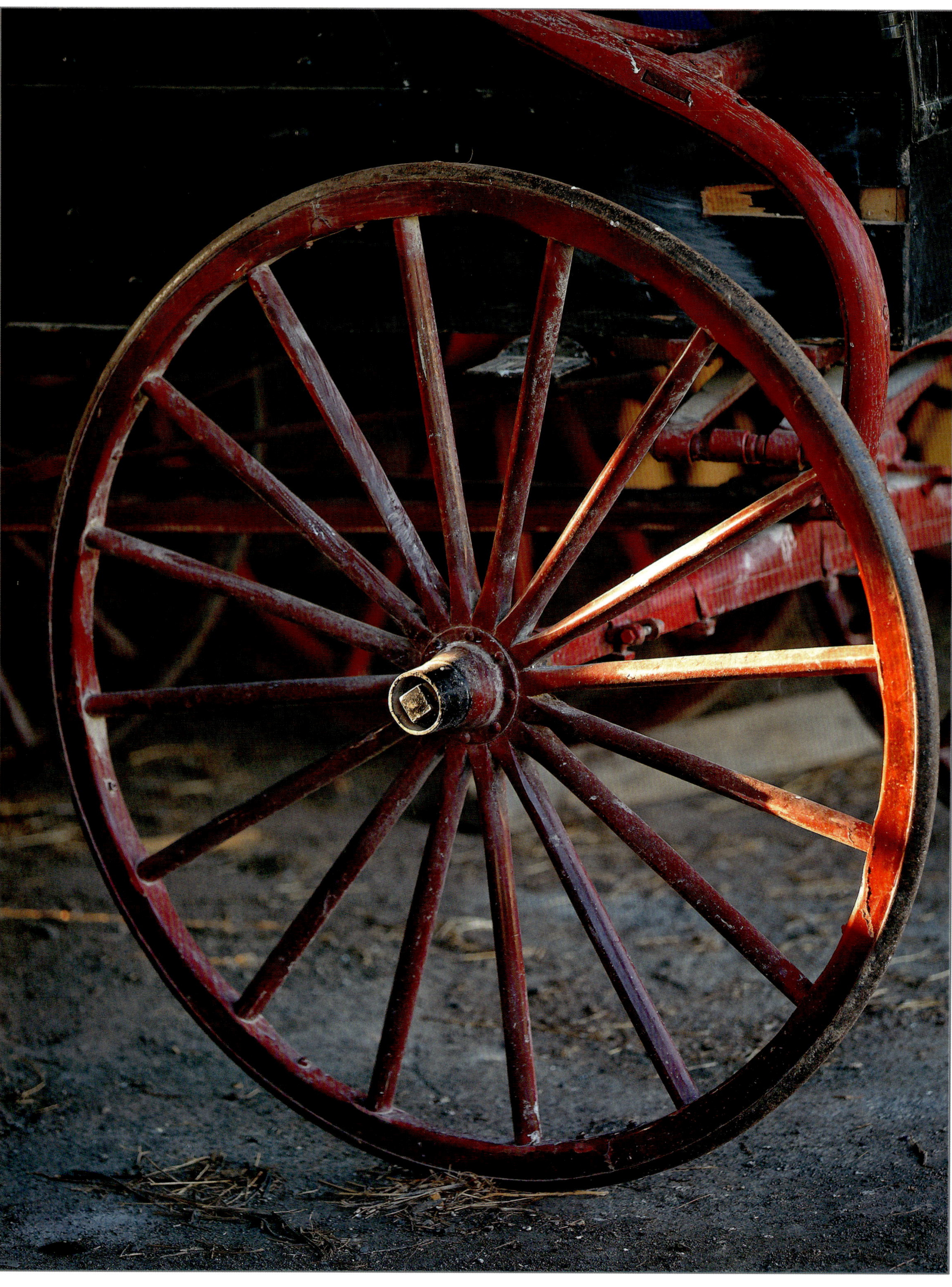

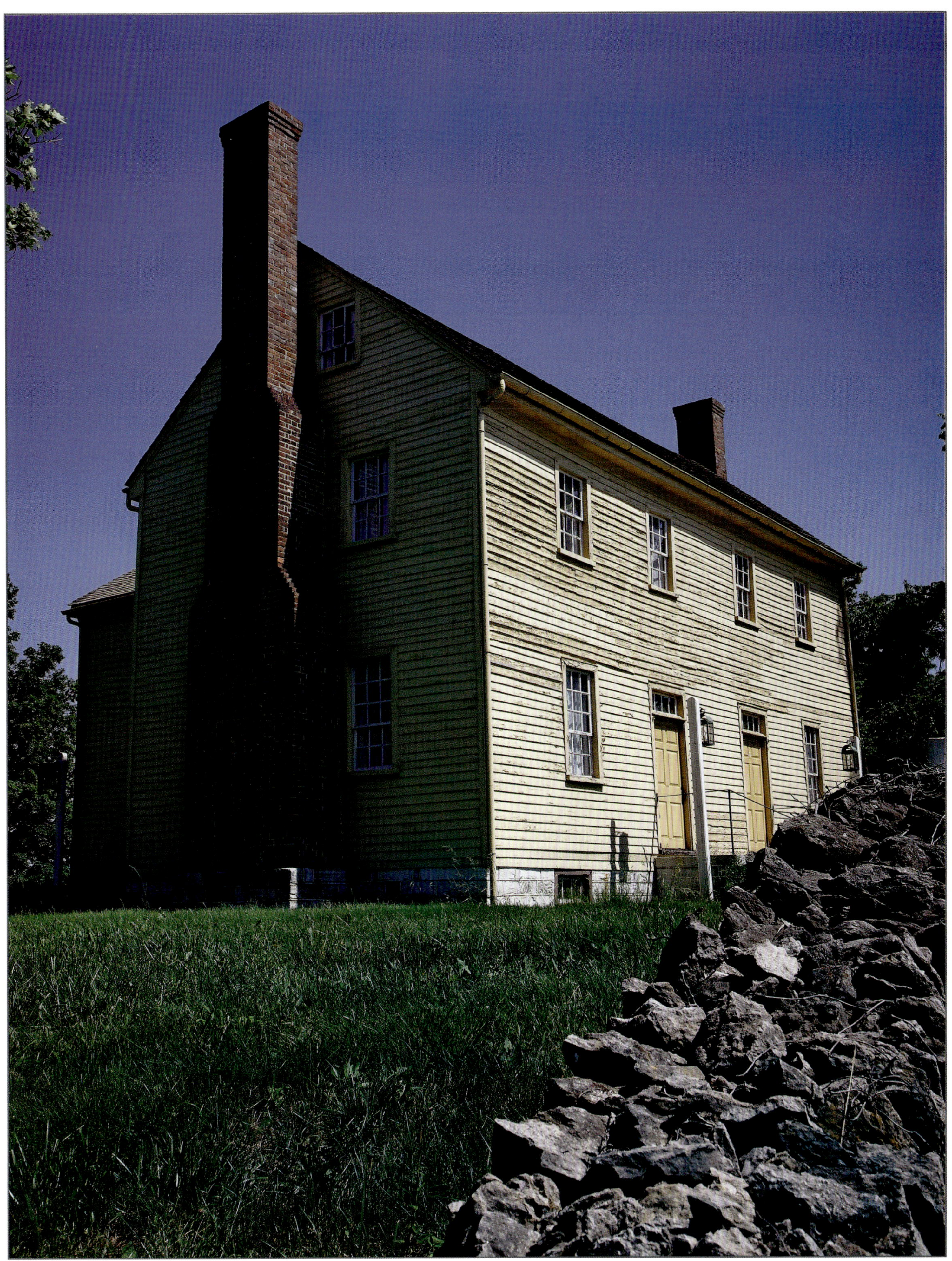

The North Lot Dwelling was one of two Gathering Orders at Pleasant Hill where new converts lived the life of a Shaker prior to signing the Covenant.

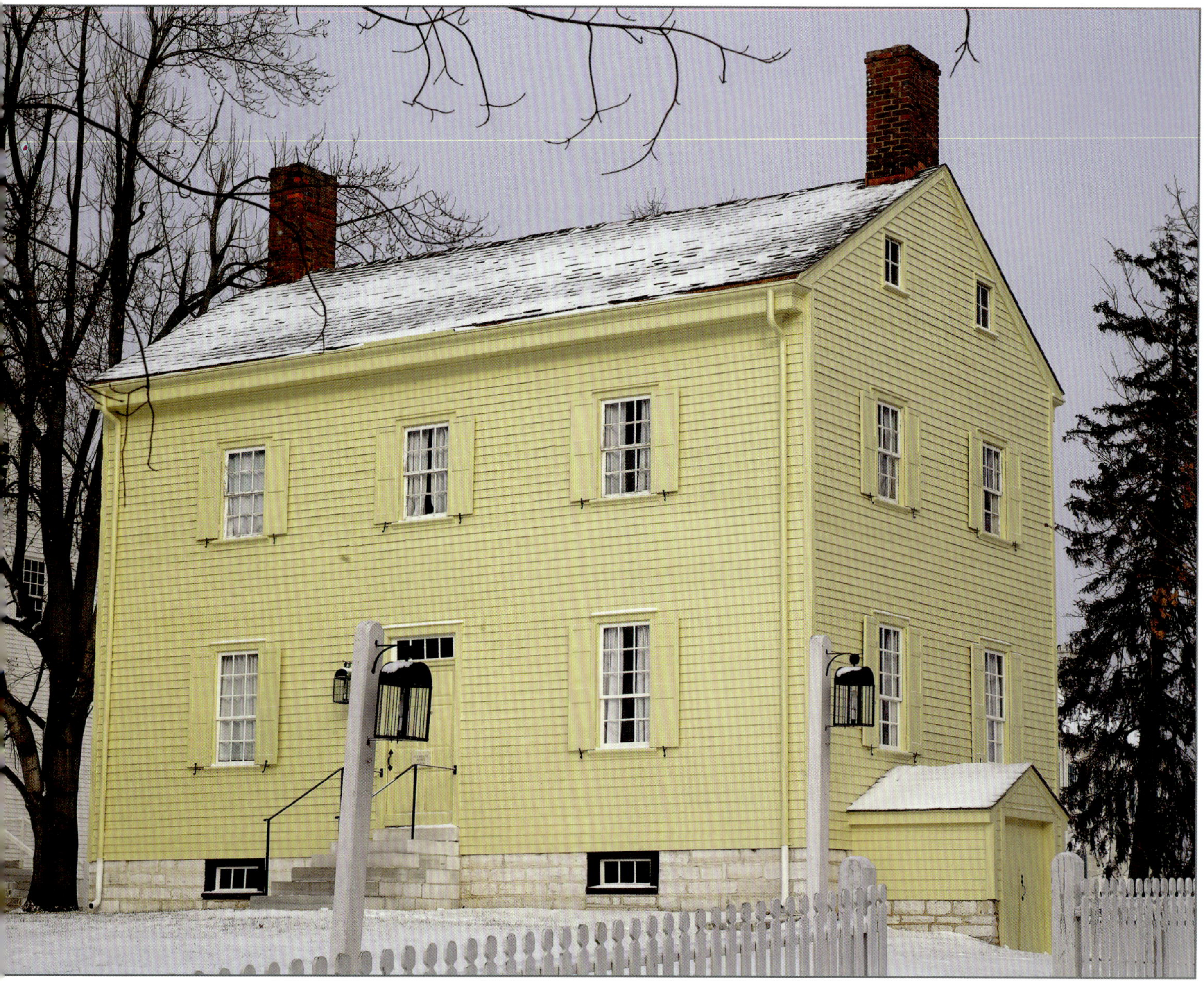

Above: A view of the rear of the Ministry's Workshop.

Right: Remnants of one of the mills on Shawnee Creek near the West Lot.

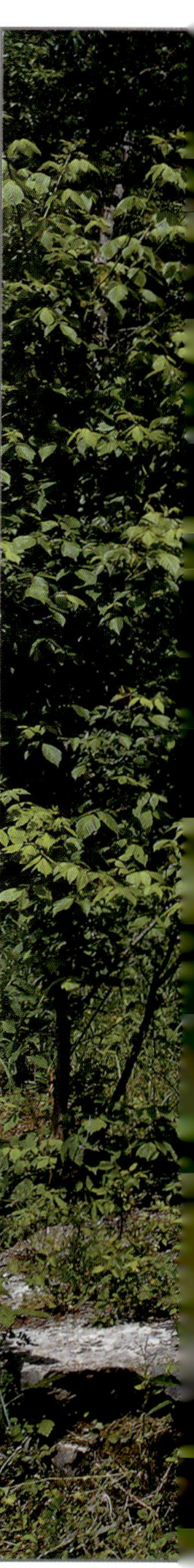

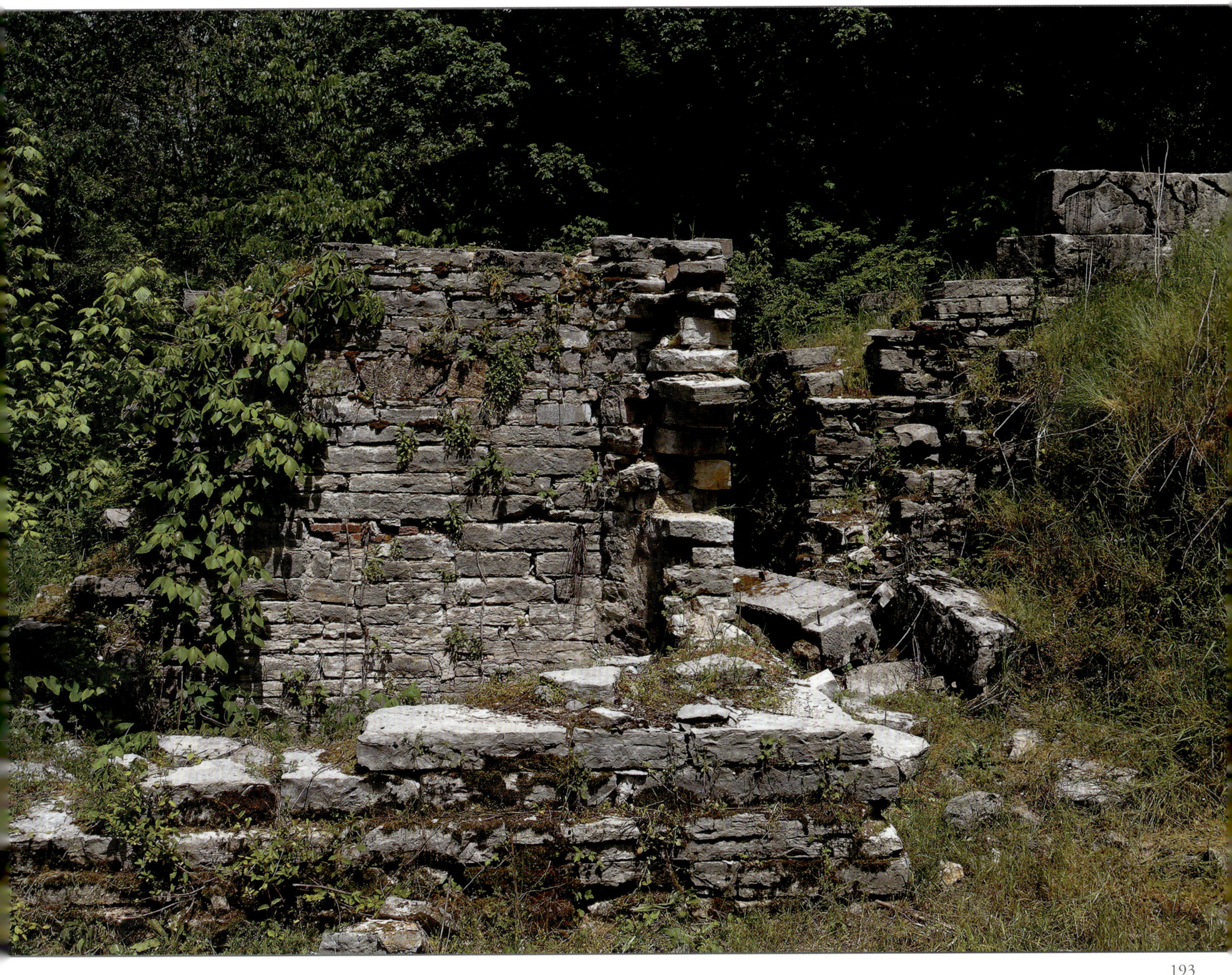

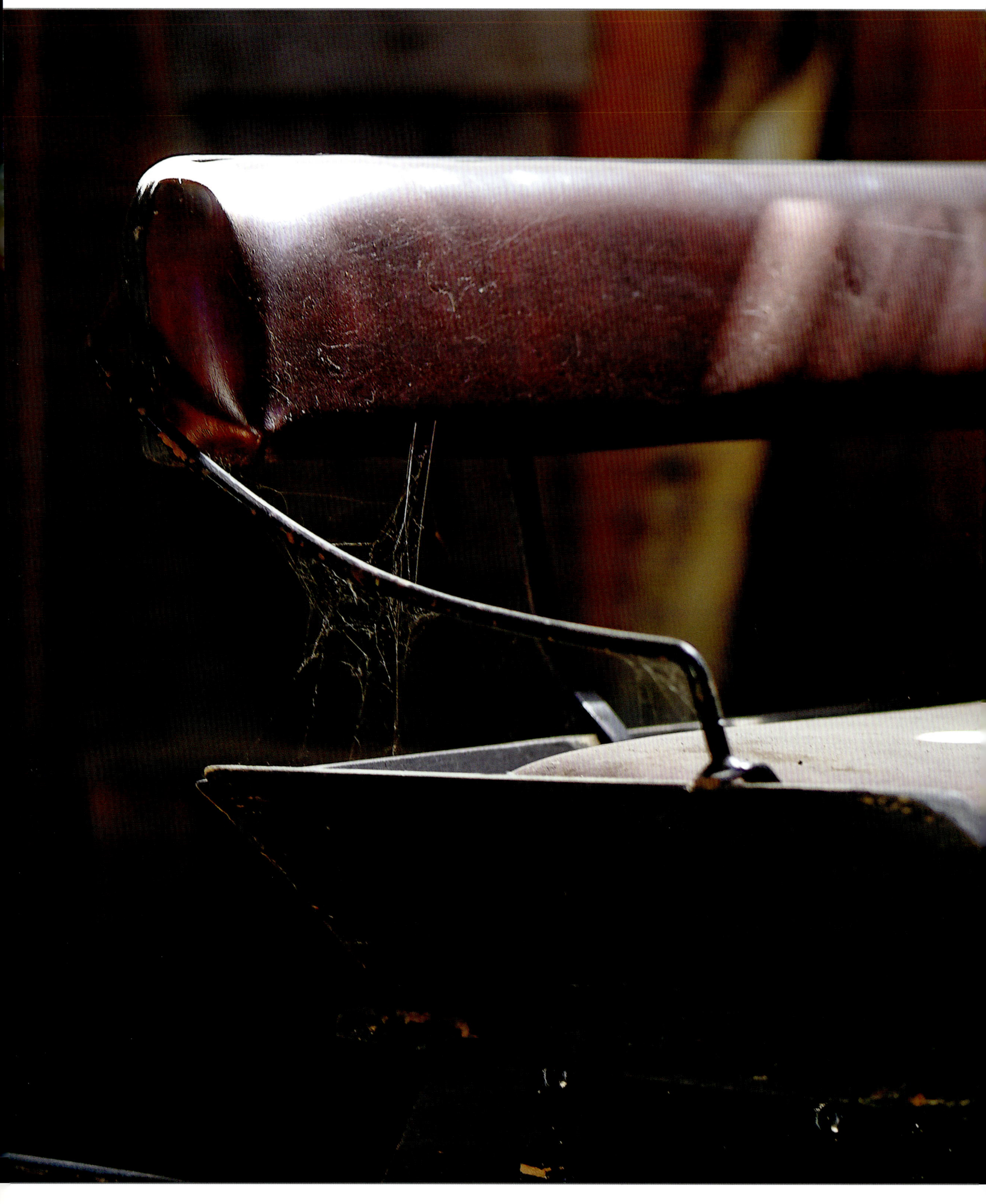

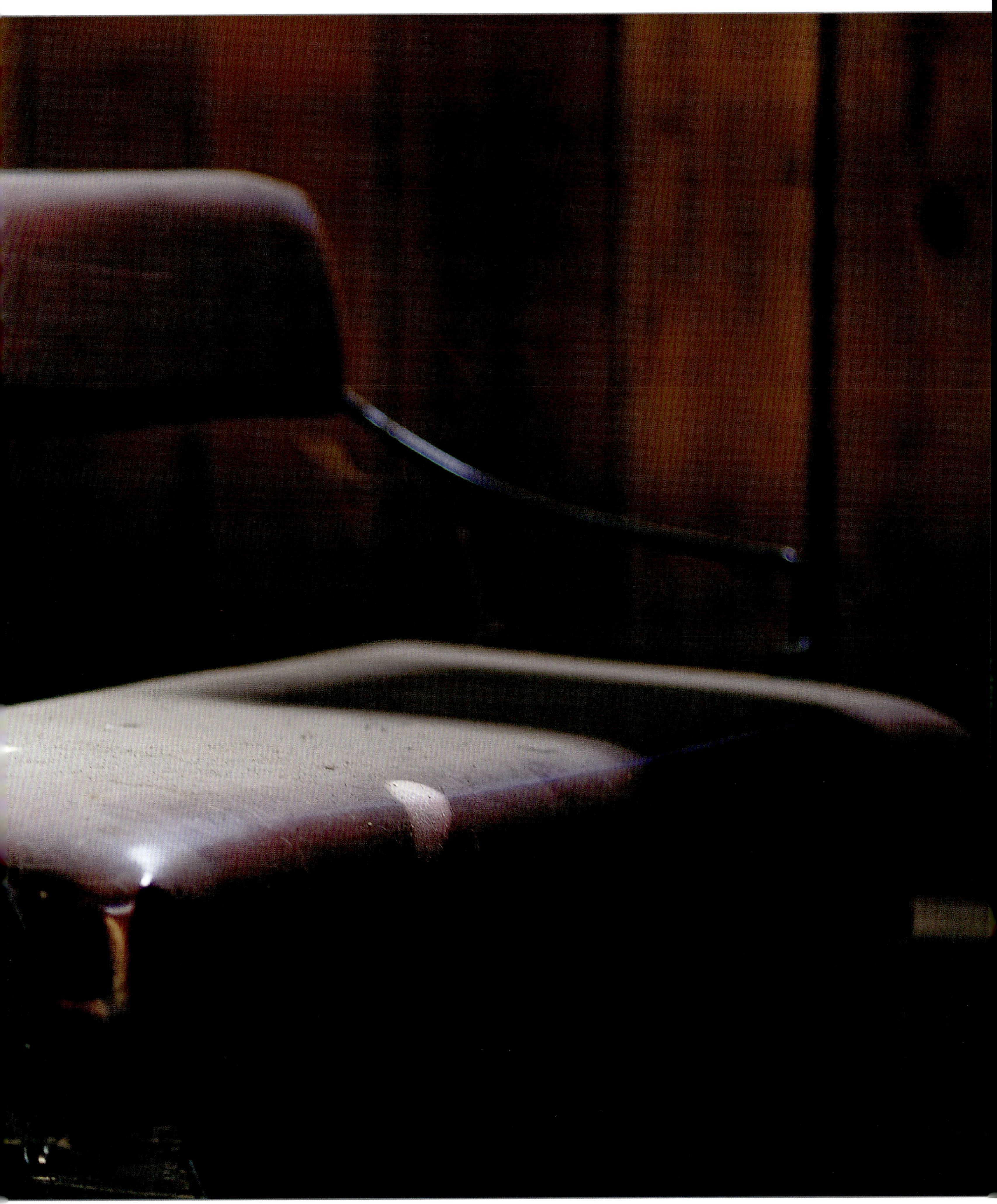

Following spread: A view of the present day grounds at night.

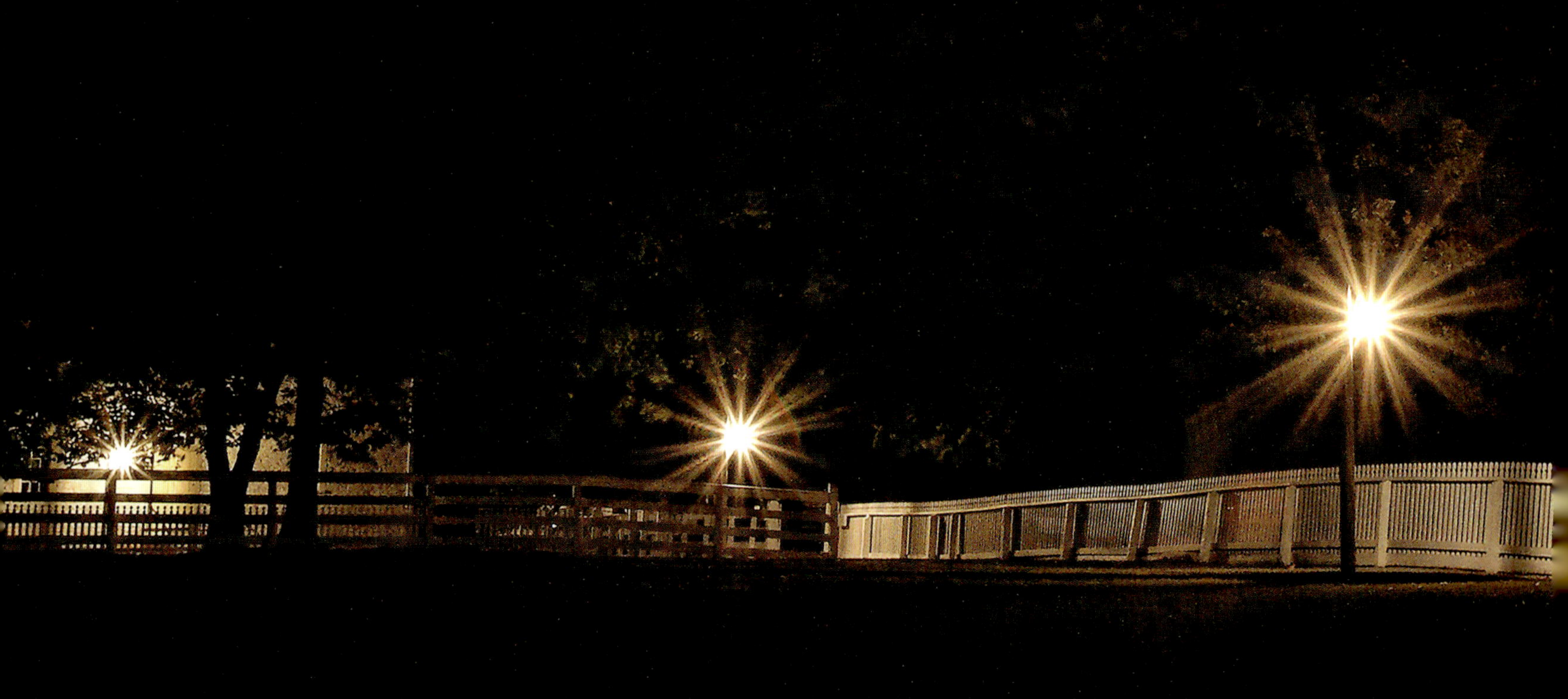

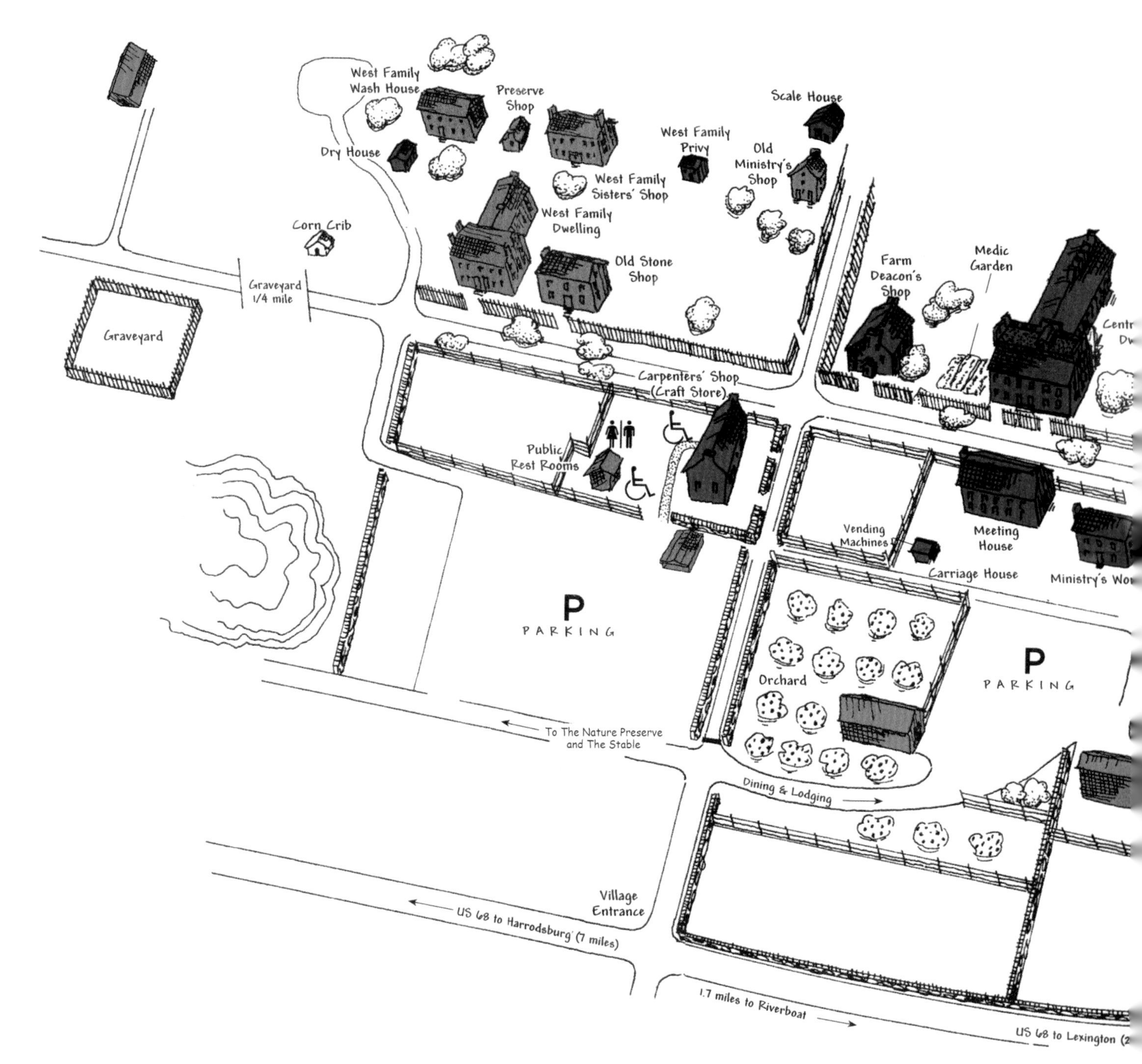
West Family
Wash House
Preserve
Shop
Scale House
West Family
Privy
Old
Ministry's
Shop
Dry House
West Family
Sisters' Shop
West Family
Dwelling
Corn Crib
Old Stone
Shop
Farm
Deacon's
Shop
Medic
Garden
Graveyard
1/4 mile
Graveyard
Carpenters' Shop
(Craft Store)
Public
Rest Rooms
Vending
Machines
Meeting
House
Carriage House
P
PARKING
Orchard
P
PARKING
To The Nature Preserve
and The Stable
Dining & Lodging
Village
Entrance
US 68 to Harrodsburg (7 miles)
1.7 miles to Riverboat

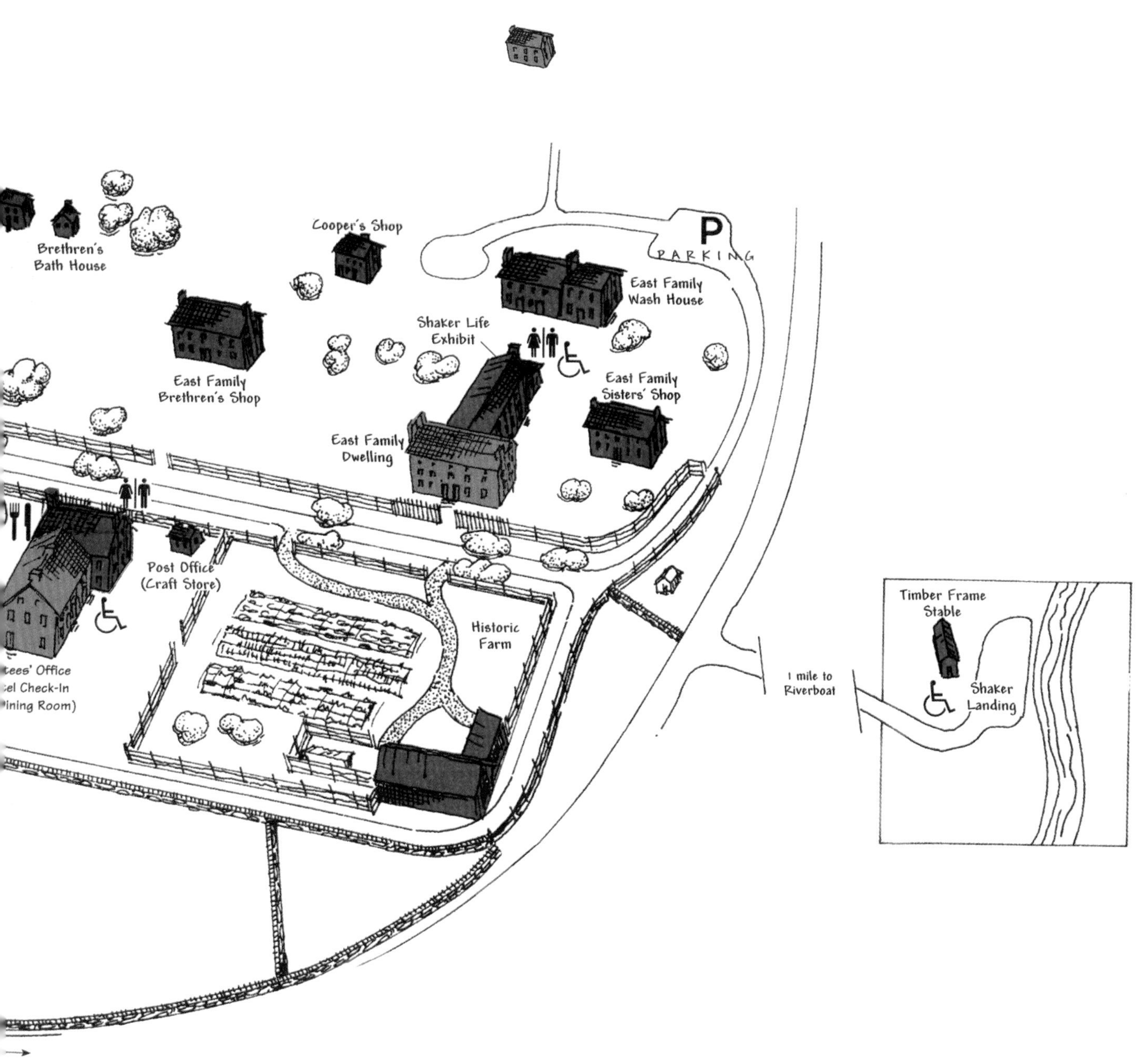
Brethren's
Bath House
Cooper's Shop
P
PARKING
East Family
Wash House
Shaker Life
Exhibit
East Family
Brethren's Shop
East Family
Sisters' Shop
East Family
Dwelling
Post Office
(Craft Store)
Historic
Farm
Timber Frame
Stable
1 mile to
Riverboat
Shaker
Landing

Index

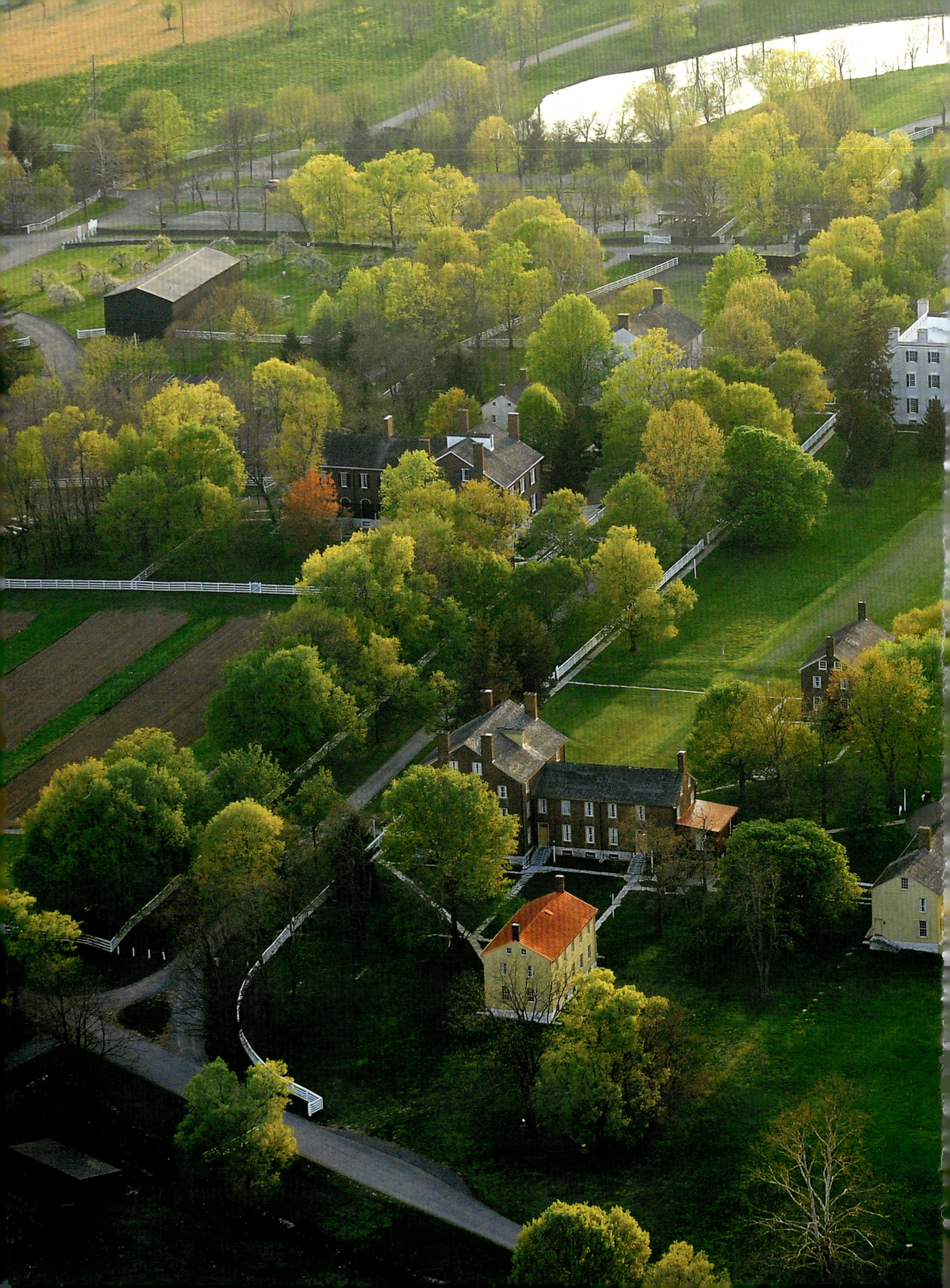

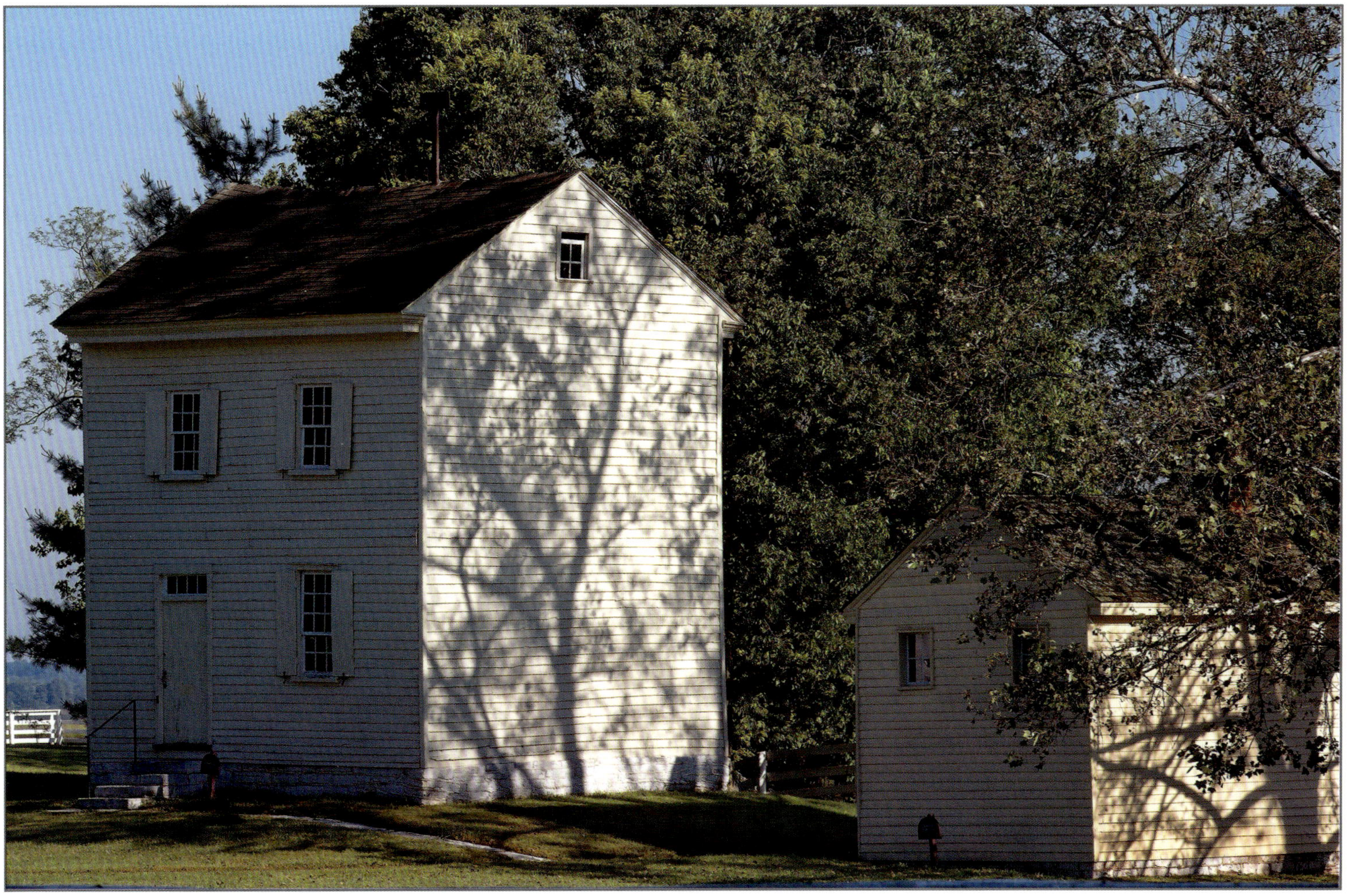

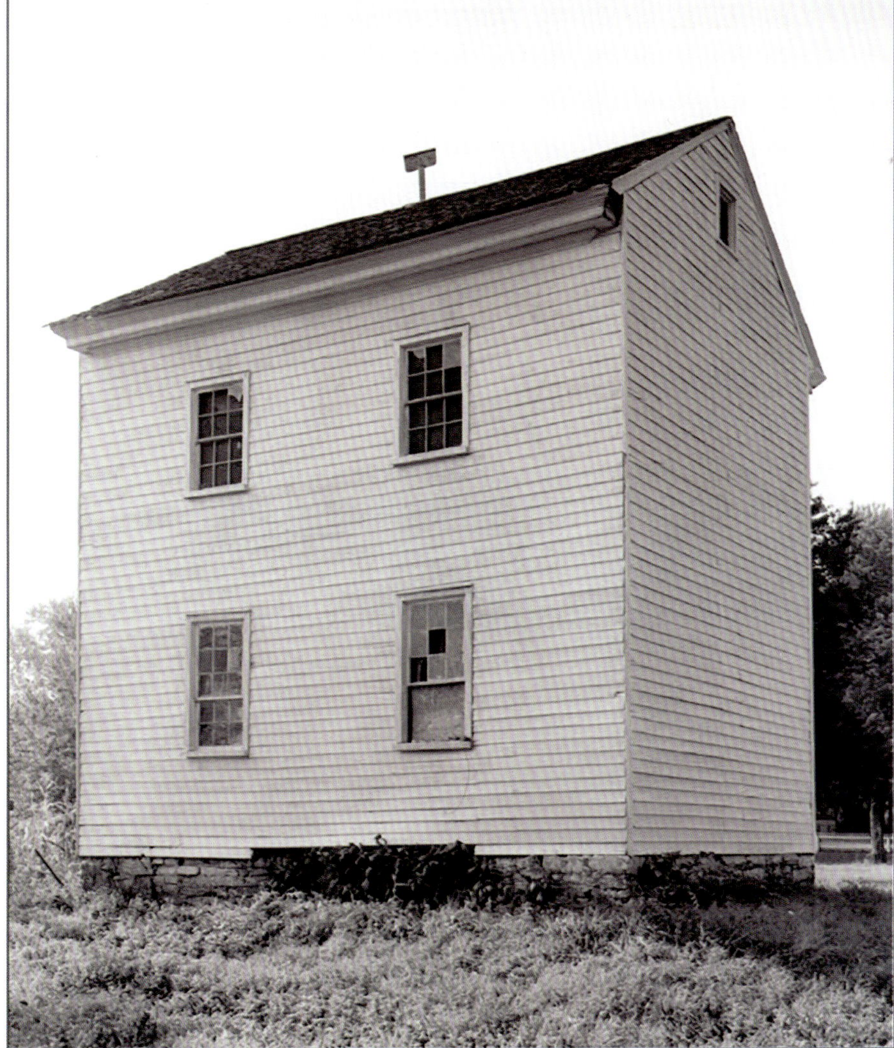

The rear of the Water House as it appeared in the 1940's.

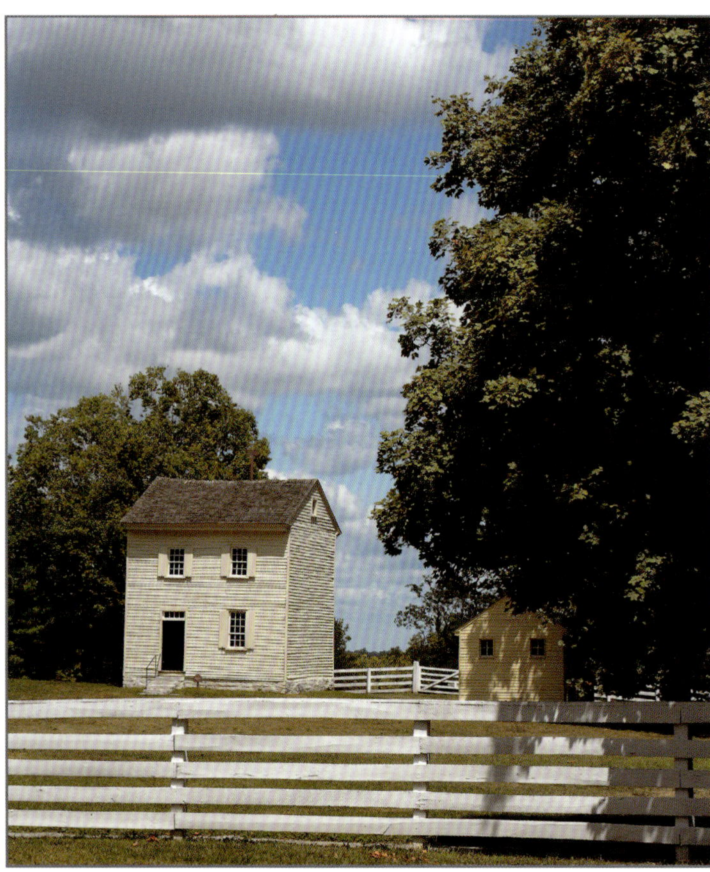

A view of the Water House and Wash House from the Trustee's Building. Notice the plank board fencing as opposed to the decorative fencing found in front of the dwellings.

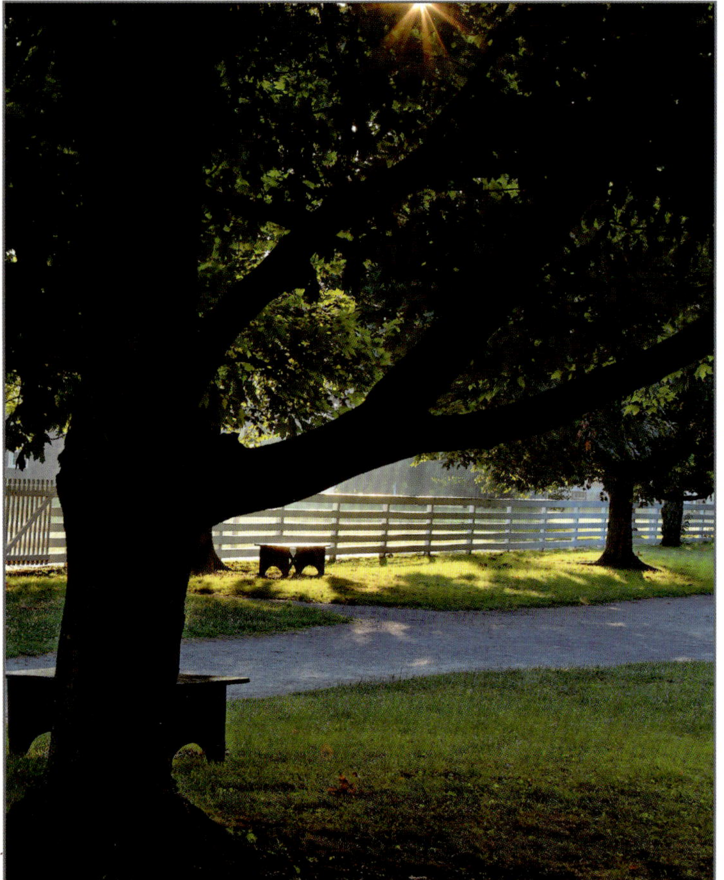

Sun peaks through the tress viewed from the Trustee's Building looking east.

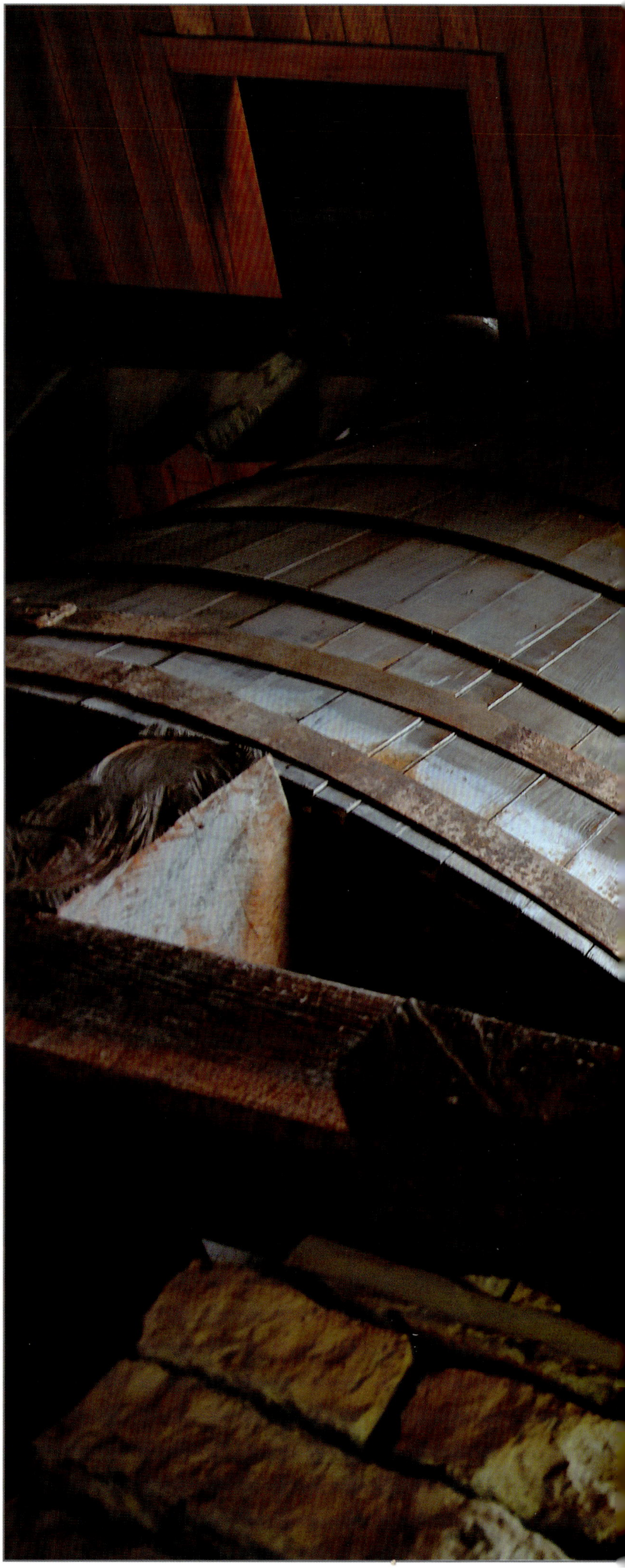

Right: The tank inside the Water House holds 4500 gallons of water which would have lasted about 24 hours. The wooden tank needed to be replaced about every ten years.